China

WORLD BIBLIOGRAPHICAL SERIES

General Editors:
Robert G. Neville (Executive Editor)
John J. Horton

Robert A. Myers
Ian Wallace

Hans H. Wellisch
Ralph Lee Woodward, Jr.

John J. Horton is Deputy Librarian of the University of Bradford and was formerly Chairman of its Academic Board of Studies in Social Sciences. He has maintained a longstanding interest in the discipline of area studies and its associated bibliographical problems, with special reference to European Studies. In particular he has published in the field of Icelandic and of Yugoslav studies, including the two relevant volumes in the World Bibliographical Series.

Robert A. Myers is Associate Professor of Anthropology in the Division of Social Sciences and Director of Study Abroad Programs at Alfred University, Alfred, New York. He has studied post-colonial island nations of the Caribbean and has spent two years in Nigeria on a Fulbright Lectureship. His interests include international public health, historical anthropology and developing societies. In addition to *Amerindians of the Lesser Antilles: a bibliography* (1981), *A Resource Guide to Dominica, 1493-1986* (1987) and numerous articles, he has compiled the World Bibliographical Series volumes on *Dominica* (1987), *Nigeria* (1989) and *Ghana* (1991).

Ian Wallace is Professor of German at the University of Bath. A graduate of Oxford in French and German, he also studied in Tübingen, Heidelberg and Lausanne before taking teaching posts at universities in the USA, Scotland and England. He specializes in contemporary German affairs, especially literature and culture, on which he has published numerous articles and books. In 1979 he founded the journal *GDR Monitor*, which he continues to edit under its new title *German Monitor*.

Hans H. Wellisch is Professor emeritus at the College of Library and Information Services, University of Maryland. He was President of the American Society of Indexers and was a member of the International Federation for Documentation. He is the author of numerous articles and several books on indexing and abstracting, and has published *The Conversion of Scripts and Indexing and Abstracting: an International Bibliography*, and *Indexing from A to Z*. He also contributes frequently to *Journal of the American Society for Information Science, The Indexer* and other professional journals.

Ralph Lee Woodward, Jr. is Professor of History at Tulane University, New Orleans. He is the author of *Central America, a Nation Divided*, 2nd ed. (1985), as well as several monographs and more than seventy scholarly articles on modern Latin America. He has also compiled volumes in the World Bibliographical Series on *Belize* (1980), *El Salvador* (1988), *Guatemala* (Rev. Ed.) (1992) and *Nicaragua* (Rev. Ed.) (1994). Dr. Woodward edited the Central American section of the *Research Guide to Central America and the Caribbean* (1985) and is currently associate editor of Scribner's *Encyclopedia of Latin American History*.

VOLUME 35

China

New Edition

Charles W. Hayford

Compiler

CLIO PRESS

OXFORD, ENGLAND · SANTA BARBARA, CALIFORNIA
DENVER, COLORADO

British Library Cataloguing in Publication Data

Hayford, Charles W.
China. New Ed. – (World bibliographical series; v. 35)
1. China – Bibliography
I. Title
016.9′51

ISBN 1-85109-235-8

ABC-CLIO Ltd.,
Old Clarendon Ironworks,
35A Great Clarendon Street,
Oxford OX2 6AT, England.

———————

ABC-CLIO Inc.,
130 Cremona Drive,
Santa Barbara,
CA 93116, USA.

Designed by Bernard Crossland.
Typeset by Columns Design Ltd., Reading, England.
Printed and bound in Great Britain by Bookcraft (Bath) Ltd., Midsomer Norton.

THE WORLD BIBLIOGRAPHICAL SERIES

This series, which is principally designed for the English speaker, will eventually cover every country (and many of the world's principal regions), each in a separate volume comprising annotated entries on works dealing with its history, geography, economy and politics; and with its people, their culture, customs, religion and social organization. Attention will also be paid to current living conditions – housing, education, newspapers, clothing, etc.– that are all too often ignored in standard bibliographies; and to those particular aspects relevant to individual countries. Each volume seeks to achieve, by use of careful selectivity and critical assessment of the literature, an expression of the country and an appreciation of its nature and national aspirations, to guide the reader towards an understanding of its importance. The keynote of the series is to provide, in a uniform format, an interpretation of each country that will express its culture, its place in the world, and the qualities and background that make it unique. The views expressed in individual volumes, however, are not necessarily those of the publisher.

VOLUMES IN THE SERIES

1 *Yugoslavia*, Rev. Ed., John J. Horton
2 *Lebanon*, Rev. Ed., C. H. Bleaney
3 *Lesotho*, Rev. Ed., Deborah Johnston
4 *Zimbabwe*, Rev. Ed., Deborah Potts
5 *Saudi Arabia*, Rev. Ed., Frank A. Clements
6 *Russia/USSR*, Second Ed., Lesley Pitman
7 *South Africa*, Rev. Ed., Geoffrey V. Davis
8 *Malawi*, Rev. Ed., Samuel Decalo
9 *Guatemala*, Rev. Ed., Ralph Lee Woodward, Jr.
10 *Pakistan*, David Taylor
11 *Uganda*, Rev. Ed., Balam Nyeko
12 *Malaysia*, Ian Brown and Rajeswary Ampalavanar
13 *France*, Rev. Ed., Frances Chambers
14 *Panama*, Eleanor DeSelms Langstaff
15 *Hungary*, Thomas Kabdebo
16 *USA*, Sheila R. Herstein and Naomi Robbins
17 *Greece*, Richard Clogg and Mary Jo Clogg
18 *New Zealand*, R. F. Grover
19 *Algeria*, Rev. Ed., Richard I. Lawless
20 *Sri Lanka*, Vijaya Samaraweera
21 *Belize*, Second Ed., Peggy Wright and Brian E. Coutts
23 *Luxembourg*, Carlo Hury and Jul Christophory
24 *Swaziland*, Rev. Ed., Balam Nyeko
25 *Kenya*, Rev. Ed., Dalvan Coger
26 *India*, Rev. Ed., Ian Derbyshire
27 *Turkey*, Merel Güçlü
28 *Cyprus*, Rev. Ed., P. M. Kitromilides and M. L. Evriviades
29 *Oman*, Rev. Ed., Frank A. Clements
30 *Italy*, Lucio Sponza and Diego Zancani
31 *Finland*, J. E. O. Screen
32 *Poland*, Rev. Ed., George Sanford and Adriana Gozdecka-Sanford
33 *Tunisia*, Allan M. Findlay, Anne M. Findlay and Richard I. Lawless
34 *Scotland*, Eric G. Grant
35 *China*, New Ed., Charles W. Hayford
36 *Qatar*, P. T. H. Unwin

Josephine Wishart Hayford
1915-96

Contents

Contents

Contents

Contents

Introduction

It is a truth universally acknowledged that China is a big country with a long history. Other aspects of China are more disputable, especially those which have to do with what are called 'Chinese characteristics'. The historian Wang Gungwu, in his essay 'The Chineseness of China', reminds us that 'China today is radically different from China in 1900, and almost every aspect of Chineseness underwent considerable change during the last 3,000 years' (*The Cambridge encyclopedia of China*, p. 11). China in the 1990s is changing as rapidly as at any time in history; prediction is therefore risky and careful study essential.

Even before there was any geographical or political unit known as 'China', there was debate over what were the boundaries and characteristics of civilization in the area. Outside China, there has also been a long tradition of debate about what was truly Chinese. In Japan, the founders of the early Japanese state turned to China for inspiration. Ennin, an 8th-century Japanese monk, was the first of many world travellers to leave an instructive record of what he saw. Among Westerners, curiosity and dispute over China go back at least to Marco Polo. His reports were taken to be fables at the time, but his image of China was influential for centuries; for example, Columbus took Marco Polo's accounts with him on his voyages. The European scholar Etienne Balazs observed that 'We do not speak of the discovery of China as we do of the discovery of America, because, although it was an event of probably equal importance, it did not happen suddenly but was a gradual process lasting several centuries' ('Significant aspects of Chinese society' in *Chinese civilization and bureaucracy*, p. 3). In the 20th century, foreign observers continue to interpret China in many ways. Some saw Mao's new China as the revolutionary hope for mankind while others saw it as the Red Menace. Given the variety of different 'Chinas' in the minds of Japanese, Westerners and Chinese over the centuries, perhaps we should speak of *inventing* a series of Chinas rather than *discovering* them.

Beginning in earliest times, there was no one place where 'Chinese' culture started nor one original set of ideas which could evolve into a unified and consistent tradition. The accumulation of archaeological evidence in recent decades shows that there was a diverse, competitive, inter-related set of cultures in what is now China. What we call the Shang (16th-11th centuries BCE) and Zhou (Chou; c. 1122-221 BCE) dynasties were among these overlapping local cultures which were based on settled grain agriculture and a family centred religion. The warriors of the contending states and philosophers of the One Hundred Schools of Thought in the Zhou dynasty debated both the moral basis of individual action and also the most rationally efficient way to build state political power. However, the ruthless political unification of the north and central regions by the Qin (Ch'in) dynasty in 221 BCE subordinated these rich regional cultures, such as the southern state of Chu (Ch'u), which grew in the lush mid-Yangzi region, and was more commercial and mystical that the totalitarian Qin. But the Qin, once it had hobbled regional sovereignty, did not hold its territory together for long.

The Han dynasty (202 BCE-220 CE) succeeded where the Qin had failed. Han emperors, aided by courtiers, kinsmen, eunuchs and aristocrats who eventually comprised a bureaucracy, worked out a flexible, eclectic pattern of imperial rule. The dynasty sponsored an imperial Confucianism which brought together and reinterpreted earlier Daoist, Legalist and Confucian ways of thought. This Han synthesis unified political, scientific, religious and moral concerns into one cosmological system with a common set of moral/scientific terms for all phenomena, from the course of the stars in the heavens and proper ritual behaviour for the emperor or the head of the family to the medical virtue of plants. The Han régime mixed force, persuasion and profit, and fostered an expansive, multi-cultural, multi-ethnic empire. So successful was this enterprise that down to the present day 'Han' is used to describe 'Chinese' people, while the characters so widely used in the writing systems of East Asia are called 'Han' characters (*Hanzi*, or, in Japanese, *Kanji*). During the period of so-called 'imperial China', which covered the centuries from the Han to the Qing dynasties, central control periodically disintegrated and was re-established by military force, but the dynastic pattern was remarkably tenacious. In fact, of the empires which dominated the early modern world, such as the Ottoman, Czarist Russian, Holy Roman, British and Mogul empires, only the contours of the Qing (Ch'ing) empire of the Manchus (1644-1911) are still discernable in today's political maps (and perhaps behaviour).

The perseverance of this imperial order was grounded in far more than political and military authority. To be sure, the realm was unified by often brutal force and regulated by often callous bureaucracy, but it was rooted in a village society and family system which provided spiritual nurture, economic structure and political stability. After the disintegration of the Han in the 3rd century CE, people of different classes and attitudes adapted Buddhism into Chinese forms; the sophistication of the new spirituality permanently changed the issues and options for all schools of thought. The Sui (581-618) and Tang (T'ang; 618-907) dynasties were far more successful than the attempts in Europe to reassemble the Roman Empire, and even more lasting than the revivals of the Empire in the Eastern Mediterranean. The Tang profited greatly from being the eastern terminus of the Silk Road, and hosted robust cultural and economic exchanges from all parts of Asia. This changing world was portrayed and discussed in poetry, fiction, history and art. Whereas leaders of greatness in all areas earned lasting fame, it was the common women and men who built the social foundation and provided the creative push; the balance of stability and change over the centuries of imperial China owed much to their collective, anonymous efforts.

The early imperial dynasties had been formed and ruled by militarized aristocrats and oligarchies. However, by the year 1,000 CE, shortly after the founding of the Song (Sung; 960-1279) dynasty, there unfolded an early 'modern China'. This new empire was held together by bureaucratic élites who were chosen through an examination system. They intertwined with powerful local landholding clans and effectively conducted factional, almost party-like, politics in a way which differed from earlier dynasties. National markets nurtured and were nurtured by a money economy, transportation networks and large cities, which in turn supported cultural transformation, such as printed books and self-consciously rational philosophy and science – to say nothing of teahouses and restaurants, lyric poetry, landscape painting and bound feet. The philosopher/statesmen of the period, most notably Zhu Xi (1130-1200), regenerated a more erudite Confucianism (while insisting they were simply returning to its roots) in order to compete with Buddhism and reinforce the family system. No realm in the 13th-century world matched the Song dynasty's wealth and sophistication. However, it was smaller in territory than the Tang or the Han, and found no way of dominating its militarily more powerful neighbours, whom it appeased, feared and looked down upon.

Rising from a base in Central Asia, the Mongols built on their own long political and military tradition, founded on the pastoral way of life, which was structurally different from that of grain based village societies; they eventually ruled the area of present-day China as a province of their continental empire. Genghis Khan and his followers devastated traditional cultures all around the rim of Asia, an experience from which many never recovered, but the Mongol imperial pacification and commercial policies encouraged long distance trade. After the fall of the Mongol Yuan (Yüan; 1276-1368) dynasty, the Ming dynasty (1368-1644) built a more systematically despotic imperial government on the Mongol model, while the domestic economy reached new heights. The lower Yangzi valley comprised both a fertile agricultural area and an urban complex of great wealth and cultural innovation. However, the Ming political system was too brittle and superficial, and their cultural vision too constricted, to deal with two major outside challenges, one from Central Asia, the other from the South Seas.

From early times, the maritime trade networks stretched from China, Korea and Japan to India and the Middle East and down the coast of Africa to Madagascar; there had also been cultural links across the Eurasian land mass, in the north by land, and in the south by sea. When the disintegration of the Mongol empire closed the safe routes which they had profitably maintained across the Silk Road, the lanes of ocean commerce prospered, and were quickly invaded by European pirates, missionaries, adventurers, conquerors and traders who sought to re-establish links with the East. By the end of the Ming, China was already part of this new and more intense world wide web, which also included North and South America; Chinese eagerly appropriated silver, maize, chilli peppers and tobacco, to mention only a few New World imports. This global system transformed all its component regions by magnificently rewarding commercial adaptation, institutional innovation and political conquest. However, the official Ming response to these dangers and opportunities was to shut the doors to outside trade and culture. After a series of successful exploratory voyages in the early 1400s led by the court eunuch Zheng He, the government withdrew support from further maritime exploration. Likewise, to the north, the Ming had no creative diplomatic or cultural policies to deal with the Manchus, a Central Asian people; the Great Wall symbolized the Ming closed-door, militaristic approach, which over-taxed the people to pay for a white elephant.

The Manchus took over China from the run-down and feckless Ming. The new leaders applied the lesson of their Mongol predecessors that it was essential to co-opt, rather than simply dominate, native Chinese élites. Their Qing (Ch'ing; 1644-1796) dynasty built on both Manchu and Chinese heritages. Rather than turn outward and embrace new global possibilities, however, the new Qing rulers conquered territory in Central Asia, which roughly doubled the land area of earlier dynasties and effectively established the geographical shape of modern China. The height of Qing prosperity in the 17th and 18th centuries saw stability and a doubling in the size of the population. Meanwhile, European empire builders took effective (and ruthless) advantage of oceanic opportunities, particularly by exploring the territory and products in North and South America – the legacy of Columbus thus became more powerful than that of Marco Polo. By the time they turned their attention to China in the imperialist expeditions and Opium Wars of the 19th century (fought in the name of Progress and Free Trade), the Qing order was also being challenged by internal rebels, who fought in the name of Christianity or local autonomy.

By the 20th century, the Manchus and the Qing régime had been transformed into symbols of backwardness and stagnation. In the early years of the century, the Empress Dowager Ci Xi attempted to bring about dynastic reform, but was successful only for a few years. After her death in 1908, Manchu reactionaries resisted political change while revolutionaries competed to create new ideas and institutions, speaking for the first time of 'China' as a nation rather than as a culture or a dynasty. The Republic of 1912 was therefore intended to create a 'New China'. The cosmopolitan Sun Yat-sen and his successor Chiang Kai-shek looked to a number of countries, including Japan, France, the Soviet Union, Germany and the United States, for help and inspiration in making their Nationalist Party (Guomindang) into an effective instrument of nation building. The intellectual youth behind the May Fourth Movement and New Culture period (1915-23) iconoclastically attacked all elements of China's past, which they now lumped together into one category labelled 'feudal', and looked to the West and Japan for a new culture to replace the old. However, the accomplishments of Chiang Kai-shek and the Nationalist Party, who established their government in 1928, were destroyed in the disastrous war with Japan, 1937-45. Meanwhile, the Chinese Communist Party, founded in 1921, embraced Marxism and mobilized many of the intellectual youth, before turning towards village China. Mao Zedong and his cohort of leaders developed the Party on a basis of village reform, military organization and anti-Japanese mobilization, convincing many Chinese that their Revolution was necessary to liberate China from the twin evils of Imperialism and Feudalism.

After the foundation of the People's Republic in 1949, the leaders of the Revolution enjoyed substantial support, and aligned China with the Soviet Union, as they debated which strategy would lead to a prosperous, stable and democratic nation. After a period of consolidation and a costly war in Korea, Mao Zedong promulgated a radical form of socialism which emphasized egalitarianism, mass mobilization, class struggle, autonomous economic development and the political dominance of the Communist Party. Under Mao's leadership, the Great Leap Forward of the late 1950s and the Great Proletarian Cultural Revolution of 1966-76 led to an internal struggle for power as well as fierce debate over ideological differences; these differences resulted in political repression, economic frustration and a devastating famine in the early 1960s. After Mao's death in 1976, Deng Xiaoping sponsored wide-ranging reforms which included markets as well as state planning, rehabilitated many Rightists who had been exiled or imprisoned, and promoted an Open Door policy of interchange with the outside world, while at the same time maintaining the exclusive leadership of the Communist Party, an allegiance to socialism, and the militant defence of China's unity and sovereignty. Deng's legacy of 'Socialism with Chinese characteristics', as underlined by the violent spring of 1989, aims to combine political firmness with economic growth, and to finally effectuate a 'Chinese way'.

The bibliography

This volume is a record of the description, debates and explanations of China over the centuries. It is a selective, annotated bibliography which covers all fields and disciplines. Subjects include scholarly and somewhat technical areas, such as geology or current economic analysis, but also range from fiction and poetry, painting and travel guides to instructions on how to cook a Chinese meal or brew a nice cup of tea. There are 1502 entries, which refer to more than 2,200 titles, primarily English-language books. China is too vast to be encompassed in one publication; accordingly, the World Bibliographical Series devotes more than one volume to the subject (as it also does in the case of the United States): *Hong Kong* (1990, no. 115), compiled by Ian Scott; *Macau* (1989, no. 105), compiled by Richard Louis Edmonds; *Taiwan* (1990, no. 113), compiled by Wei-chin Lee; and *Tibet* (1991, no. 128), edited by John Pinfold. I have excluded most individual government and commercial reports (except for yearbooks), highly technical works, theses and dissertations, pamphlets and unpublished documentary material. Unlike other volumes in the series, there was room to list only a few articles, chapters in volumes, and book reviews. Much to my regret, there was almost no room for works in other languages, although a few titles in French have been cited. However, there is a fair representation of European, Japanese and some Russian scholarship in translation, and I have tried especially hard to include both writings in English by Chinese and translations of Chinese works into English.

The target readership for the selection and the annotations is general readers: those who travel, teach, live or do business in China or wish to do so; advanced undergraduate and beginning graduate students; teachers at all levels; researchers who use English-language materials; and reference and collections librarians. The subject topics and divisions largely follow those of other volumes in the WBS series. Of particular interest in this volume are those sections which highlight China's distinctive characteristics, including: the life and thought of Sun Yat-sen; the life and thought of Mao Zedong; agriculture and rural political economy, covering village China both before and after 1949; science and technology, especially the magisterial volumes of Joseph Needham's *Science and Civilisation in China*; law, democracy and constitutions, including works on history and current debates; the 1989 crisis and its aftermath; food and cooking; medicine; and women, sex and gender studies. Entries are extensively indexed by author, title and subject, and many sections are followed by cross-references to other relevant titles.

A few words about the principles (and problems) of selection will help the reader. China has inspired a veritable mountain of writing. In the 1994-95 *Books in Print*, for example, there are fifty-four columns of titles which begin with the words 'China', 'China's' or 'Chinese'. We have room for only a small fraction of these books; in any case, to include larger numbers would overwhelm readers, rather than help them. Therefore, the goal is to seek balance and representation of topic and of approach, and to enable searches which will go beyond the items listed. The WBS series expects that publications be relatively accessible in North America, Great Britain and the English-speaking Commonwealth, although some out of print items will be found only in larger public libraries or university collections. The emphasis here is on publications from the 1980s and 1990s; however, there is a goodly representation of earlier works, especially of books which have been recently reprinted. Many sections cite classic works which retain the ability to inspire (or provoke), but works of antiquarian interest are not included. The cut-off date of publication was the end of 1995, but due to the vagaries of book distribution and an unwillingness to list unseen books, some 1995 publications could not be considered. A particular challenge to the bibliographer of China is the number of popular but not necessarily well researched books in fields such as religion and self-cultivation, revolution, medicine and the martial arts, not to mention quick weight loss and sex. Some of these works are stimulating, amusing or useful, but others reveal mostly their authors' inventiveness; they have not been included unless they contain substantial information on practices in China.

To select is to exclude, therefore many fine books do not appear here. I beg forbearance for my omissions, judgements, ignorance, mistakes and foibles. Readers are reminded that even (or especially) in our age of massive computer bibliographies, there is no substitute for a knowledgeable professional librarian or bookseller to help locate that most useful book, the one you discover for yourself!

Acknowledgements

Since 1991, when I began work on this project, many friends and colleagues have shared their thoughts, libraries or subject bibliographies with me, and some went over particular sections of this bibliography. I must first thank Frank J. Shulman, whose WBS volume, *Japan* (1989), was a model which I consulted almost daily. While serving as China/Inner Asia book review editor for the *Journal of Asian Studies*, I had access to a flow of new books from publishers, to the advice of reviewers, and to the prudence and erudition of David Buck, then the journal's editor. These colleagues are not be to blamed for mistakes in sections which they may not have seen or which were changed after they saw them. Chun-shu Chang was particularly assiduous and supportive, and Stanford University colleagues Albert Dien, Michel Oksenberg and Ramon Myers were enthusiastic, knowledgeable and helpful. The many others include: Wendy Abraham, Beatrice Bartlett, Richard Barrett, Ming K. Chan, Chow Wing-kai, Edward Farmer, Theodore Foss, Hill Gates, Dru Gladney, Ruth Hayhoe, Huang Shu-min, Chang-tai Hung, Dale R. Johnson, David Keightley, F. A. Kretschmer, Gregory B. Lee, Leo Ou-fan Lee, Lillian Li, Victor Mair, Melissa Macauley, Bernard Mosher, Andrew J. Nathan, Susan E. Nelson, Mary Backus Rankin, Thomas Rawski, John Regan, John Rohsenow, Morris Rossabi, Richard Smith, Nathan Sivin, Mark Swislocki, Bryan Van Norden, Arthur Waldron, Philip Williams and Dali Yang. Graduate students who gave careful and cheerful assistance include Rand Blackford, Nicole Butz and Edna Tow. During my teaching at Stanford, I occupied the office and used the book collection of James Ketelaar, who displayed (nearly) perfect forbearance. The office staffs of the Associated Colleges of the MidWest, and of the Northwestern and Stanford History Departments, especially Carmelita Rocha and Nan Bentley, were wonderfully supportive in both logistic and psychological ways. Of course, I owe a continuing debt of love and gratitude to my family, especially to my wife Elizabeth.

Like all scholarship, bibliography depends on libraries and on the librarians who build and maintain them. I am especially grateful to the Evanston Public Library and the Northwestern University Library, in which the initial work was done; to the library at the University of Illinois at Chicago; to the Regenstein Library of the University of Chicago; and at Stanford University, where I edited and finished the manuscript, to the Meyer Library, Green Memorial Library and the Harold L. Kahn Bunkō. Thanks also go to C. C. Cheng for the enlightened browsing policies at his Peking Book House and to Jeff Rice at Great Expectations, both in Evanston; to the Savvy Traveler and the Seminary Coop in Chicago; to Borders Books; and to the Stanford Bookstore in Palo Alto.

Finally, I owe a great debt of thanks to the editorial team at ABC-Clio, especially Julia Goddard and Robert Neville, for their much tried patience and good professional advice over the five years we have worked on this project.

Romanization and conventions

Chinese write their language with Chinese characters (*hanzi*), place their family names first, but follow no general conventions when using Western languages. Therefore, to reconcile Chinese practice, readers' convenience and bibliographical consistency presents problems which can be confronted but not overcome – at least, not until we all use Chinese!

The most daunting problem is that of romanization or transliteration, that is, representing the pronunciation of Chinese characters by writing them in the Roman alphabet. Pinyin, developed and altered a number of times from a system originated by Soviet scholars in the 1920s, is now official in the People's Republic and the most common romanization around the world. However, until recently, most writing about China in English (although not in other languages) used the Wade-Giles romanization, which was invented more than a century ago to transcribe all world languages, but used in the end only for Chinese. Neither pinyin nor Wade-Giles is used accurately in most publications. As if two duelling, inconstant romanization systems were not enough, geographical names are widely known in still a third system, one created by the Postal Service in the 19th century. Examples of Postal romanization include Peking, Nanking, Canton, Chungking and Hopei, which in pinyin would be Beijing, Nanjing, Guangzhou, Chongqing and Hebei, and in Wade-Giles would be Pei-ching, Nan-ching, Kuang-chou, Ch'ung-ch'ing and Ho-pei. Other linguistically more precise systems exist for the purpose of teaching or analysing the language, such as the system devised during the Second World War at Yale University, or *Gwoyeu Romatzyh* (GR) which spells each of the four tones differently. There are also venerable anomalies (kowtow, lychee, ketchup), while personal names are often idiosyncratic or based on pronunciation in other dialects. Some institutions have retained or revived historic romanizations, such as Peking University and Peking Union Medical College.

This volume used the most recent version of pinyin in the body of entries and in the subject index, but of necessity leaves titles and authors' names as they are found in the particular work (otherwise they could not be located in catalogues or reference works). This practice produces an inconsistency when one form of romanization appears in the title and another in the entry – irritating, but any other path would have been worse. There are cross-references from Wade-Giles to pinyin in the author and subject indexes for important names and terms. In many cases the pinyin and Wade-Giles are reasonably close (for instance, the common names 'Wang', 'Wu' and 'Li'), but in other cases they are not at all alike: how is one to know that 'Xi'an' (pinyin), 'Sian' (Postal romanization) and 'Hsi-an' (Wade-Giles) are in fact the same place? Therefore entries frequently supply Wade-Giles in parentheses, e.g. Bo Juyi (Po Chu-yi), Ci Xi (Tz'u Hsi), *guanxi* (*kuan-hsi*) and *ci* (*tz'u*); however, alternative romanizations usually only appear once in a section. Occasionally, when the pinyin is not apparent, I have supplied it in brackets. Birth and death dates are occasionally supplied.

The Asian practice of putting the family name first has generally been followed. However, when authors or public figures have chosen a form for use in English, we have respected their various particular choices, for example: Wing-tsit Chan, Chiang Kai-shek, Ambrose C. Y. King, Thomas H. C. Lee, T. V. Soong, Sun Yat-sen and Y. C. James Yen. In bibliographical descriptions, page numbers usually refer to the last page on which text occurs and do not include separately numbered introductory material.

Charles W. Hayford
Stanford, California / Evanston, Illinois
December 1996

The Country and Its People

1 **The heart of the dragon.**
Alasdair Clayre.   Boston, Massachusetts: Houghton Mifflin,
1985. 281p.

A companion to the television project *Heart of the dragon*, written by its producer and deploying its research and visual resources. The project presents rural and urban daily life in China in the early 1980s in the perspective of the country's vast scale and turbulent history. The book is richly illustrated with historical and contemporary art, scenery, landscapes of work, and quotidian vignettes. Chapter topics correspond to the film's episodes but are independently written: 'Remembering: Emperors and Rebels'; 'Believing: Heaven, Earth, and Man'; 'Marrying: Wives and Concubines'; 'Mediating: Caring and Control'; 'Eating: Frugality and Feasting'; 'Living: Labour and Harvest'; 'Working: Coal, Steam, and Steel'; 'Correcting: Crime and Punishment'; 'Understanding: The Body and the Universe'; 'Creating: Ink, Bamboo, and Rock'; and 'Trading: Into the Four Seas'. A book of readings was compiled to accompany the television series: *The Chinese: adapting the past, facing the future*, edited by Robert Dernberger et al. (Ann Arbor, Michigan: Center for Chinese Studies, University of Michigan, 1991. 2nd ed. 802p.).

2 **One day in China: May 21, 1936.**
Translated, edited, introduced by Sherman Cochran, Andrew C. K. Hsieh, Janis Cochran.   New Haven, Connecticut; London: Yale University Press, 1983. 290p. map.

An anthology of vignettes of daily life and concerns. In 1936, a national campaign solicited contributions from various local people to describe the great or small events of their lives on one day, 21 May. The translators group their selection from the resulting book, *Zhongguo di yi ri*, edited by Mao Dun and others (Shanghai, 1936), into four sections: '"Family" and Women', pieces by or about women in the family and at work; '"Heads" and Political Authority', providing glimpses (generally unfavourable) of leaders, or 'heads' (*zhang*) trying to control local society; '"Superstitions" (*mixin*) and Popular Religion', describing false doctrines,

1

wastefulness in popular religion (such as extravagant weddings and funerals), and the intrusion of Christianity; and '"Chinese Traitors" and the Enemy', on collaboration with and resistance to the Japanese occupation in North China.

3 East Asian civilizations: a dialogue in five stages.

William Theodore de Bary. New York; London: Columbia University Press, 1988. 160p. (The Edwin O. Reischauer Lectures, 1986).

These imaginative lectures set China in a wide context, dealing with East Asian civilizations (China, Korea and Japan) in four broad historical epochs. Four chapters deal with the 'dialogue' between the Confucian and competing traditions in the formative stage (11th to 2nd centuries BCE); the Buddhist Age (3rd to 10th centuries); the Neo-Confucian stage (11th to 19th centuries); and the modern period. Chapter five ponders the present and future role of Confucianism, and chapter six deals with new interactions between East and West.

4 Sources of Chinese tradition.

Compiled by William Theodore de Bary, Wing-tsit Chan, Burton Watson, with contributions by Yi-pao Mei, Leon Hurvitz, T'ung-tsu Ch'ü, John Meskill. New York: Columbia University Press, 1960. 976p. paperback edition with an added appendix, *Popular religion and secret societies*, 1963. 2 vols. (Introduction to Oriental Civilizations Series).

An extensive selection of 'source readings that tell us what the Chinese have thought about themselves, the universe they lived in, and the problems they faced living together'. The editors provide introductions to each chapter and comments on selections. There are companion volumes on India and Japan in the same series. Selections emphasize, but are not restricted to, philosophy and formal political writings, which are more fully represented in Chan's *Sourcebook in Chinese philosophy* (q.v.); religious texts are included (especially Buddhist), and some literature and essays, such as historical writing and early poetry. The later chapters – volume two of the paperback edition – form a survey of thought in the last two centuries, including basic essays by important thinkers and political leaders. A revised edition is being prepared.

5 China's quest for national identity.

Edited by Lowell Dittmer, Samuel S. Kim. Ithaca, New York: Cornell University Press, 1993. 305p.

Historians, political scientists, anthropologists, and students of literature explore the political and cultural meanings of 'Chineseness' in China's past and present. In the introductory chapter, 'In Search of a Theory of National Identity', the editors delineate theoretical writings on the relevance of identity to development, integration, international relations, and other worldwide issues. Eight further essays explore such topics as: national identity in pre-modern China; the late Qing-Republican crisis in identity; the construction of a unified national culture in late imperial China; the filial ideal and the transformation of an ethic; loss of identity among intellectuals in the Deng era; regional, national and global identities on the China coast; foreign policy and official national identity in China's role as a Third World state; and China's multiple identities in East Asia. The editors summarize and conclude in 'Whither China's Quest for National Identity?'

6   **Chinese civilization and society.**
Patricia Ebrey.   New York: Free Press, 1993. rev. ed. 429p. bibliog.
Ebrey brings together carefully chosen primary texts and documents, with helpful
commentary, in order to illustrate Chinese social and intellectual history. Intended as a
supplement to an undergraduate survey course, the book is also useful to the serious
general reader. The coverage complements that of de Bary et al., *Sources of Chinese
tradition* (q.v.), which emphasizes formal thought. Sections are arranged by dynasty,
but with an introductory table listing selections by topic. There are extensive
suggestions for further reading.

7   **Boundaries in China.**
Edited by John Hay.   London: Reaktion Books, 1994. 350p. bibliog.
(Critical Views Series).
Contains nine interdisciplinary essays, an interview, and an expatiating introduction
concerned not with 'boundaries' in an administrative sense, but with the human need
to set and test cultural limits, especially in the light of recent critical cultural theory.
Topics include boundary creation and control (body, space, time and bureaucracy) in
the Qin dynasty unification of the empire; death as the 'great boundary' and funerary
narrative in early China; boundaries in the poetic canon, in Yuan painting, and in the
dynastic transition from Ming to Qing; gender boundaries in Qing female education
and in Chinese opera; and discursive boundaries in William Hinton's *Fanshen* (q.v.)
and self-histories in present-day China.

8   **The tyranny of history: the roots of China's crisis.**
W. J. F. Jenner.   London: Allen Lane, Penguin Press, 1992. 255p.
A pessimistic, provocative polemic from a master of sinology. Jenner argues that in
spite of the incompetence and oppression of the Leninist state, China 'cannot manage
without an emperor, and cannot join the modern world with one'; he sees the empire
as bound together by cultural myths and an unwieldy system, 'new emperors', and
authoritarian bureaucrats, and feels that the only chance of partial mitigation is to free
regional cultures. In Henry Rosemont, Jr., *A Chinese mirror: moral reflections on
political economy and society* (La Salle, Illinois: Open Court, 1991. 130p.) a leading
scholar of Chinese philosophy analyses socialist humanist values in China and the
West following the events of Tiananmen in 1989, arguing that Confucian
communitarian thought is still a powerful source of inspiration.

9   **The burning forest: essays on Chinese culture and politics.**
Simon Leys.   New York: Holt/New Republic, 1985. 257p.
Contains scathing essays on contemporary Chinese sterility, the 'dupes' of Mao (such
as the writer Han Suyin, American China studies experts), and warm appreciations of
traditional China, including poetry and painting, the early missionary Matteo Ricci, a
paean to Father Huc's *Travels in Tartary and Tibet* which reveals much about Leys'
own allegiances. 'Simon Leys', the pen-name of Pierre Ryckmans, wrote several
earlier books of such essays: *Chinese shadows* (New York: Viking, 1977. 220p.),
translated from *Ombres Chinois* (Paris: Union Général d'Editions, 1974), which
became a sensation for its exposure of the systematic lies fed to foreign visitors, the
vapidity of Chinese daily life, and poisonous politics; and *Broken images* (London;
New York: St. Martin's, 1979. 156p.), with essays on the author Lu Xun, Chiang Kai-
shek, Mao Zedong, and Chinese museums.

3

10   **Evening chats in Beijing: probing China's predicament.**
Perry Link.   New York; London: W. W. Norton, 1992. 321p.

As the 1988-89 representative in Beijing for the Committee for Scholarly Communication with the People's Republic of China, Link was in contact with intellectuals and academic bureaucrats. Here he re-creates their debate and the turmoil in the months leading up to Spring 1989 and vividly describes their social and political world as both continuing and repudiating the tradition of Chinese intellectuals (*zhishifenzi*). Chapters describe the work-unit (*danwei*) system, corruption and repression; livelihood; history (the May Fourth movement, 'peasant consciousness', and the course of the intellectuals' relation with the revolution after 1949); identity, language and ideology; and the intellectuals' traditional but constantly evolving sense of responsibility for the world and worry over the nation, which partially explains their need to support a government they despise.

11   **The pride that was China.**
Michael Loewe.   London: Sidgewick & Jackson; New York:
St. Martin's, 1990. 296p. maps. bibliog. (Great Civilization Series).

A set of survey essays, each treating a topic from the imperial era (221 BCE-1911 CE) as a whole. This series describes dead civilizations – titles are all in the past tense, and none concern Western nations. Loewe's broad learning illuminates many topics, including: the natural setting; moments of dynastic change, dynastic succession and emperors of note; social distinctions; the spoken and written word; beliefs, hopes and fears; the organs of government; officials and their duties; crime and punishment; the creation and circulation of books; capital cities; tombs and their treasures; literature, scholarship and the arts; science, agriculture and commerce. There is a helpful section of further readings, arranged by chapter topics.

12   **China: ancient culture, modern land.**
Robert Murowchick, General Editor.   Norman, Oklahoma: University
of Oklahoma Press, 1994. 192p. maps. bibliog. (Cradles of
Civilization).

Fourteen specialists describe Chinese history and civilization in a beautifully produced survey aimed at the general reader, with photographs, maps and charts. The opening section presents the land and people from a geographer's standpoint. Chapters then portray epochs from prehistory to the Mongol invasions, with consideration of rituals, Chinese characters, philosophy and religion. The next section analyses historical themes of modern continuity and change: Ming and Qing society; China and the West; revolution, evolution and continuity; and the past, present and future. The bibliography lists books in English, arranged by chapter topic.

13   **Journey into China.**
National Geographic Society.   Washington, DC: National Geographic
Society, 1982. 518p. maps.

Portrays 'the geographical and human diversity of China as thoroughly and sensitively as possible'. The volume features the characteristic National Geographic combination of lush photographs of local personalities and scenery, a fair number of general maps, and informal essays. The essays were written by knowledgeable scholars or journalists, many of whom undertook special trips to do so. Topics include an historical summary, Peking, the Great Wall, the Yellow River Valley, the Silk Road, the Grand Canal, the Yangzi River, Tibet, and other regions of the country. Daily life in the early 1980s is the focus, rather than politics or ideology, but the work is suffused with China's unique history and culture.

14 **The heritage of China: contemporary perspectives on Chinese civilization.**
Edited by Paul S. Ropp. Berkeley, California; Oxford: University of California Press, 1990. 369p. maps. bibliog.

Ropp brings together thirteen thematic essays for students and readers with some general background. Subjects covered are: Western perceptions of China; early Chinese civilization; the evolution of government; laws and the rule of law in Chinese and Greek tradition; Confucian traditions and classics; Buddhist and Daoist traditions; science and medicine; women, marriage and the family; economic history in comparative perspective; late imperial social history in comparative perspective; Chinese art and its impact in the West; poetry in the Chinese tradition; and fiction. Each essay has notes for further reading, and there is a section of historical maps and a chronology. In *The legacy of China*, edited by Raymond Dawson (Oxford: Oxford University Press, 1964. Reprinted, Boston, Massachusetts: Cheng & Tsui, 1990. 392p.), substantial essays survey Western conceptions of China; literature; political structures; science and China's contribution to the world; poetry; and philosophical thought.

15 **Greater China: the next superpower?**
Edited by David Shambaugh. Oxford: Oxford University Press, 1995. 310p. bibliog. (Studies on Contemporary China).

These conference essays, first published in *China Quarterly*, no. 136 (December 1993), explore the implications of the cultural, economic and political 'China' which is no longer confined to national boundaries, but which, built on political and family networks, encompasses the People's Republic, Hong Kong, Taiwan and Southeast Asia. Topics include the economic and strategic consequences, the role of popular culture, and the implications for the future of political relations within the bloc.

16 **Chinese roundabout: essays in Chinese history and culture.**
Jonathan Spence. New York; London: Norton, 1992. 400p.

This publication contains essays and reviews from a master interpreter of Chinese affairs. The first block of writings concerns novels set in China, and Chinese and Westerners who crossed over into each other's cultures, including Mendes Pinto, Matteo Ricci, Sydney Gamble and André Malraux. The second block, 'The Confucian Impulse', includes 'The Seven Ages of K'ang-hsi', (K'ang-hsi, or Kangxi, was an emperor of the Qing dynasty, 1662-1722) and reviews of biographies. 'Sinews of Society' treats the food of the Qing dynasty, taxation, missionary medicine, and the impact of opium on China. 'After the Empire' provides reviews of books on the social history of the Republican period, Tiananmen, and the democratic 'spirits of opposition' in the poet Bei Dao and the physicist Fang Lizhi. The final block is made up of tributes to and reflections on Spence's mentors in sinology (Arthur Wright, Arthur Waley, John Fairbank and Fang Chao-ying).

17 **China in transformation.**
Edited by Tu Wei-ming. Cambridge, Massachusetts: Harvard
University Press, 1994. 253p.
Ten probing essays, first published in *Daedalus*, vol. 122, no. 2 (Spring 1993), explore
China's crisis of historical meaning and cultural identity in the early 1990s. Following
the débâcle of 1989, the development of 'Greater China' challenged the assumption
that agriculture defined the Chinese economy, authoritarianism defined the polity, and
family-centred hierarchy defined society. Essays consider the following topics: a
'failed Chinese modernity'; cultural identity and the politics of difference in South
China; law and legitimacy; cultural requisites for democracy, based on survey data;
the radicalization of China in the 20th century; the 'invention' of the peasant (rather
than the 'farmer') and the 'ideological re-definition' of China as 'feudal'; the narrative
reconstruction of reality during the Yan'an period (1937-45); and contending insights
from well-informed observers.

18 **The living tree: the changing meaning of being Chinese today.**
Edited by Tu Wei-ming. Stanford, California: Stanford University
Press, 1995. 295p.
This work has grown out of a conference published in *Daedalus*, vol. 120, no. 2
(Spring 1991). The editor argues in the chapter 'Cultural China: The Periphery as
Center', that creative initiatives now come from outside the political entity of China,
from worldwide cultural China. Eight essays meditate upon topics such as the 1830
novel, *Flowers in the mirror* (q.v.), whose 'inner world' shows 'considerable capacity
for self-awareness, self-criticism, and even self mockery'; *guanxi* ('personal ties' or
'connections') and network building; the peripheralization of traditional identity and
the problem of 'being Chinese' without the support of tradition; Chineseness outside
political China, especially in Southeast Asia and North America; 'The Construction of
Chinese and Non-Chinese Identities', which challenges the myth that the Han race
absorbed all comers, arguing that actually the Chinese have been 'constantly
amalgamating, restructuring, reinventing, and reinterpreting themselves'; and 'roots'
and the changing identity of Chinese in the United States.

19 **Yangtze: nature, history, and the river.**
Lyman P. Van Slyke. Reading, Massachusetts: Addison-Wesley,
1988. 211p. maps.
An engaging panorama of the Yangzi river, inspired by the work of the French
historian Fernand Braudel. Part One, 'Natural Time', describes the land, climate and
the geological formation of the region, including the famous Three Gorges. Part two,
'Social Time', deals with historic population migration and settlement; the Grand
Canal and its economic functions; merchants, commerce and products on the river,
including useful descriptions of important products; and junks and junkmen. The
chapter entitled 'History, Symbolism, and Imagery' discusses historical topics such as
the poet Qu Yuan, legends from the period of Three Kingdoms (220-65 CE), and the
Taiping rebels; Westerners on the river; and the controversy over building dams at
Gezhouba and the Three Gorges. John Hersey, *A single pebble* (New York: Knopf,
1956. 181p.) is a poignant novel of a young American engineer's journey up the
Yangzi river; he hopes to dam the river and to change China, but is himself
transformed.

20 **The Chineseness of China: selected essays.**
Wang Gungwu.   Hong Kong; New York: Oxford University Press,
1991. 354p. maps. bibliog.
A compilation of the essays and addresses of a wide-ranging and resourceful scholar.
The title essay, reprinted from *Cambridge encyclopedia of China* (q.v.), considers the
changes in the idea and territory of China over the centuries. Other essays gracefully
consider topics such as Chinese history, Overseas Chinese, and the present condition
and future prospects of China.

21 **China: a country study.**
Edited by Robert Worden et al.   Washington, DC: US Government
Printing Office, 1988. 4th ed. 590p. maps. bibliog. (Area Handbook
Series).
A comprehensive handbook. The chapter length essays, accompanied by many black-
and-white photographs, copious maps and statistical tables, provide background
information for the general reader on all aspects of present-day China. Topics covered
include the historical setting, the physical environment and population, the economic
context, trade and transport, science and technology, politics, foreign relations,
security and defence. The bibliography lists many books and articles from the 1980s
by chapter topic.

22 **Body, subject, and power in China.**
Edited by Angela Zito, Tani E. Barlow.   Chicago; London: University
of Chicago Press, 1994. 307p.
A major collection of essays in critical cultural theory which explore the way the body
is socially constructed in art, medicine, ritual, fiction, politics and language. The
editors' introduction cogently argues that traditional 'common sense truth' must be
replaced by innovative analysis of discourse, subjectivity and constructed difference.
The lead essay interprets the invisibility of the body in Chinese art, in particular the
absence of the nude. Following essays examine: body surfaces in the 18th century as
the medium in which virtue becomes real; the reasons why Chinese medical science
did not always focus on the body; contemporary medical practice; the politicized body
in the People's Republic; the 'kowtow' (*ketou*) in tribute rituals of foreign emissaries
to Beijing; Ming-Qing 'beauty-scholar' romance novels; the novels of Xiao Hong; and
the category 'women' (*funü*) as a modern invention. See also Mark Elvin's chapter
'Tales of *Shen* and *Xin*: Body-person and Heart-mind in China During the Last 150
Years', in part four of *Fragments for a history of the human body*, edited by Michel
Feher (New York: Zone Books, 1989).

Cultural atlas of China.
See item no. 1433.

The Cambridge encyclopedia of China.
See item no. 1439.

Contemporary atlas of China.
See item no. 1450.

Geography and Geology

General

23 **The geography of contemporary China: the impact of Deng Xiaoping's decade.**
Edited by Terry Cannon, Alan Jenkins.   London; New York: Routledge, 1990. 316p. maps. bibliog.

Geographers from Britain, Germany and Hong Kong present overview essays for students and general readers. An introduction outlines political developments from 1949 to 1989. Subsequent chapter topics include: spatial inequality and regional policy; historical perspectives on the current geography of China; understanding and transforming the physical environment; demographic patterns and policies; old problems and new solutions in rural China; industry, energy and transport; processes, policies and patterns in urbanization; the impact of foreign investment and trade on the spatial structures of the economy; the environmental impact; and geographical perspectives on defining and defending the state. Throughout are tables, maps, suggestions for further reading, and ten 'case-studies', short descriptions of selected topics, such as 'loess' (a deposit of wind-blown dust), 'from collective farm to family farm management', and 'the oil industry'.

24 **Key economic areas in Chinese history: as revealed in the development of public works for water-control.**
Chi Ch'ao-ting.   London: Allen & Unwin, 1936. Reprinted, New York: Paragon, 1963. 168p. maps.

A classic work in historical geography, and among the first to apply Marxist concepts to show the effects of dynastic water control systems for irrigation, transport by river and canal, and flood management, on regional development. It is still useful for its insights into the relationship between environment, imperial bureaucratic programmes, and economic regionalism.

25   China's regional development.
David Goodman.   London; New York: Routledge, 1989. 204p. maps.
A symposium which scrutinizes the geographically varying impact of reform policies
of the 1980s. The introduction and opening articles describe background political
perspectives and economic and financial policies. Topics include: the impact of
foreign trade on regionalization; energy, communication and transport sectors of the
economy; Special Economic Zones (SEZs); national minorities and the internal
frontier; and studies of particular provinces – Shandong as an 'atypical' coastal
province, and Shaanxi as 'China's powerhouse'. There are a dozen maps. *China's
spatial economy: recent developments and reforms*, edited by G. J. R. Linge,
D. K. Forbes (Hong Kong: Oxford University Press, 1990. 225p.) has short chapters
on rural versus urban bias, freight and passenger patterns and transport development,
especially railroads, seaports, migration, Shanghai, Tianjin, and issues and prospects.

26   The history of cartography.
Edited by J. B. Harley, David Woodward.   Chicago; London:
University of Chicago Press, 1987. 2 vols. maps. bibliog.
Volume two, book two, *Cartography in the traditional East and Southeast Asian
societies* (1994. 970p.), includes essays on China as part of a magisterial series of
scholarly volumes on the history and significance of cartography from all times and
cultures. Previous scholars assumed that modern European mathematical cartography,
deemed detailed, scientific and objective, was superior to 'pre-modern' and non-
Western traditions. These volumes argue, however, that map-making must be
appreciated in aesthetic, intellectual and cultural contexts, and that the displacement of
rich, earlier traditions by sterile modern cartography is not pure progress. Maps in
imperial China are described and analysed as political, aesthetic and religious objects,
sometimes being compared to calligraphy or landscape painting, sometimes to
governmental inventories, and sometimes to literati encyclopaedias.

27   Chinese landscapes: the village as place.
Edited by Ronald G. Knapp.   Honolulu: University of Hawaii Press,
1992. 313p. maps.
Provides eighteen descriptions of villages as geographic and physical structures,
written by anthropologists, geographers, historians, a sociologist, and a veterinary
ecologist. The studies cover: the rural New Territories of Hong Kong; commercially
developing Taiwan; arid inner Asia; the rice-growing Yangzi valley, Sichuan and
Canton; and the original heartland of dry grain North China. Introductory essays
provide an overview of topics covered in the individual essays, such as village design,
layout, physical setting and ecology, settlement patterns, *fengshui* (geomancy), and the
principles by which all these changed over time. There are numerous diagrams and
photographs, and the authors write clearly for a non-technical audience. Roughly half
the essays concern villages where tradition is strong, while half look at villages in
transition, whether changed by revolutionary principles (such as Dazhai village in
Shanxi) or by commercial development.

28   The changing geography of China.
Frank Leeming.   Oxford; Cambridge, Massachusetts: Blackwell,
1993. 199p. maps. bibliog. (IBG Studies in Geography).
A clear, balanced and brief text for students, focusing on the present but providing
historical background, with many figures, tables, maps and charts. Leeming first

9

sketches the 'many faces' of China, then devotes chapters to resources and physical environment; historic foundations; political background since 1949; the countryside; the industrial system and state economy; urban China; and regional change. There is a brief 'Guide to Further Reading'. Older but still basically sound introductions include the fuller work of Keith Buchanan, *The transformation of the Chinese earth* (London: Bell; New York: Praeger, 1970. 336p.) which emphasizes the interaction of social, economic and political forces; and T. R. Tregear's, *China: a geographical survey* (London: Hodder & Stoughton; New York: Wiley, 1980. 372p.) which recasts the material from his *An economic geography of China* (New York: Elsevier, 1970. 208p.).

29 China: the geography of development and modernization.

Christopher Pannell, Laurence Ma.   London: Edward Arnold; Washington, DC: Halstead Press, 1983. 342p. maps.

A comprehensive introduction, in which Pannell and Ma survey the following topics: historical and political geography; population; agriculture; planning, transport and trade; selected industries; urban development; and a geographic appraisal of China's modernization. There are separate chapters on Taiwan, Hong Kong and Macao, as well as numerous maps and charts.

30 China: people and places in the land of one billion.

Christopher J. Smith.   Boulder, Colorado; San Francisco; Oxford: Westview Press, 1991. 355p. maps. bibliog.

An innovative survey of China, its people, and concepts of modern geography, which synthesizes scholarship but retains the personal feeling found in journalistic and travel accounts. Smith first provides a 'cognitive map' of the book which charts the back-and-forth relationships between culture, politics and environment. The book presents standard concepts (e.g. geography, culture and politics; spatial organization of production, distribution and consumption; the city; population and the role of the state), but also deals with the 'geography of everyday life' (women's place in the new China; the delivery of urban services; food and housing; crime and punishment; and human rights). There are many excerpts, references, maps, tables and pictures. A select bibliography lists English-language articles and books by topic.

31 China: area, administration, and nation building.

Joseph B. R. Whitney.   Chicago: University of Chicago, Department of Geography, 1970. 330p. (Department of Geography Research Paper, no. 123).

This pioneering historical and theoretical analysis of administrative geography focuses on how central governments since the 13th century laid the cultural, geographical and economic basis for a political, territorial nation-state, with a final section assessing the situation under Mao. Chapters discuss: theoretical models; traditional administrative structure and modern change; stability and change in the hierarchy of administrative areas; and the size of administrative areas, which considers the effects of revenue collection, administrative costs, and geographical distribution of county capitals. There are numerous tables and maps.

32   **The geology of China.**
Yang Zunyi, Cheng Yuqi, Wang Hungzhen.   Oxford: Clarendon Press,
1986. 303p.

In this work, prominent Chinese specialists survey Chinese geology, including topics
such as stratigraphy, magmatic and metamorphic rock, and geotechnic development.
There are illustrations and twenty plates.

33   **Physical geography of China.**
Zhao Songqiao.   Beijing: Science Press; New York; Winchester,
England: John Wiley, 1986. 209p. maps.

A comprehensive and well illustrated text which emphasizes detailed description
rather than analysis. The first section presents a detailed but selective presentation of
topics such as climatology, geomorphology, surface and groundwater. The second part
provides regional case-studies.

Inner Asian frontiers of China.
See item no. 169.

The pattern of the Chinese past.
See item no. 891.

The agriculture of China.
See item no. 980.

Cultural atlas of China.
See item no. 1433.

Maps and atlases

34   **An historical atlas of China.**
Albert Herrmann, edited by Norton Ginsberg, prefatory essay by Paul
Wheatley.   Chicago: Aldine; Edinburgh: Edinburgh University Press,
1966. new ed. 88p.

Redrafts *Historical and commercial atlas of China*, by Albert Herrmann (Cambridge,
Massachusetts: Harvard-Yenching Institute, 1935 [Harvard-Yenching Monographs,
no. 1]) and adds a set of modern maps showing population, language, land use, etc., as
of the 1960s. The historical maps show the extent of Chinese control in various
dynasties, and include historical renderings of general Asia, Central Asia, and
Southern Asia, as well as city plans of historic capitals. Wheatley's essay discusses
Herrmann's strengths and lacunae, and illuminates many problems of historical
cartography. The index of names uses Wade-Giles, but includes a number of foreign
renderings of Chinese places.

35 **China: a provincial atlas.**
Chiao-min Hsieh, Jean Chine Hsieh.   New York: Macmillan, 1995.
303p. bibliog.

A handsomely produced volume aimed at the general public. Part one includes general maps on population distribution, nationalities, soil, agriculture, transport, minerals, tourism, etc. Part two provides landform maps for each province and several major cities, with accompanying texts summarizing history, major features, and basic information. Still useful is Hsieh Chiao-min's work, edited by Christopher Salter, *Atlas of China* (New York: McGraw-Hill, 1973. 282p.), especially the historical, economic and landform maps. *Atlas of the People's Republic of China* (Beijing: Foreign Languages Press, China Cartographic Publishing House, 1989. 113p. maps) is a standard official atlas, based on the Chinese edition of 1983. Fifty-one topographic and administrative colour maps, with a brief gazetteer, incorporate further data from the mid-1980s.

36 **The national economic atlas of China.**
Compiled and edited by Institute of Geography, Chinese Academy of Sciences and State Planning Committee, State Information Center, Institute of Statistics, State Statistical Bureau; supported by State Planning Committee, Chinese Academy of Sciences, State Statistical Bureau, and National Bureau of Surveying and Mapping.   Hong Kong: Oxford University Press, 1994. 314p.

A lavish volume, with data and views taken from official Chinese sources; it was compiled in order to 'portray, systematically and completely, on maps, the state of social and economic development in China'. It comprises 265 multi-colour maps divided into ten groups: resources, including weather, minerals, forests, tourist resources, water and fish; population; agriculture; industry; large and medium size enterprises; major industrial products and important equipment; network of communications and carrying capacity; building, urban construction and environmental protection; commerce, foreign trade, banking and tourism; and regional distribution in education, science and technology, health care and sports. Data is as recent as 1990. The work also includes four handbooks of descriptive notes to maps bound separately in pockets.

37 **The Times atlas of China.**
The Times of London.   London: Times Newspapers; New York: Times Books, 1974. 144p.

A comprehensive atlas. The 'History' section provides sixteen maps showing the geographical extent and administrative divisions of the major dynasties. The 'Modern China' section is comprised of thirteen maps, taken from *Atlas of China* (Washington, DC: Central Intelligence Agency, 1971), and indicating minority peoples, climate, agriculture, roads and waterways, railways, minerals and energy, industry and trade, administrative divisions and frontiers. The concluding and most extensive section, 'Physical Maps', shows the regions, followed by a maps of each province and plans of thirty-one cities. The editors have 'unhesitatingly' adhered to the Wade-Giles system of romanization, but the twenty-seven page index gives pinyin as well.

The population atlas of China.
See item no. 422.

Tourism and Travel Guides

Tourism

38 **Tourism in China: geographic, political, and economic perspectives.**
Edited by Alan A. Lew, Lawrence Yu.   Boulder, Colorado;
San Francisco; Oxford: Westview Press, 1995. 256p.

Brings together fourteen scholarly essays on the evolution, organization, and social, cultural, and environmental impact of international and domestic tourism in China since 1978. Part one discusses the evolution of the tourism industry and government tourist policies. Part two analyses national tourist organizations, the hotel sector as a marker of economic development and social change, and hospitality education in China. Part three focuses on domestic tourism, the Chinese landscape as a tourist attraction, and overseas Chinese tourism. Part four concerns 'Outer China', (Xinjiang, Guizhou) and a comparison of state production and artisan production in Yunnan. Part five is entitled 'Conclusions and Future Prospects'.

Travel guides

39 **Insight guide: China.**
Singapore: APA Publications; Boston, Massachusetts: Houghton
Mifflin, 1995. 3rd ed. 406p. maps.

An urbane evocation of the contemporary life and sights of China, with background essays on history and culture. The 'Travel Tips' provide a perfectly adequate listing of major hotels, restaurants, tourist sites, etc.; however, the distinguishing feature of the series is the stunning photography, making this an excellent choice for the armchair traveller. As is true of most guides in this section, the maps are not detailed enough for on the ground use, but cheap street and transport maps are available in most Chinese cities.

40 The silk road.
Judy Bonavia. Lincolnwood, Illinois: Passport Books, 1989. 320p. maps.

A general guide to the areas of China west of Xi'an, including Xi'an itself, Gansu province, Lanzhou and Kashgar. A section is devoted to the oasis town of Dunhuang and the Mogao caves, famous for the Buddhist wall paintings. There are many photographs, excerpts from literary writings, some practical travel advice, and a section entitled 'Suggested Reading'.

41 China – a travel survival kit.
Michael Buckley, Alan Samalgaski, Robert Storey, Chris Taylor, Clem Lindenmayer. Hawthorn, Australia: Lonely Planet, 1994. 4th ed. 1,059p. maps. (Lonely Planet Survival Travel Kit Series).

Contains detailed practical information for the adventurous independent traveller, as well as copious, sometimes breezy background on culture and history. The tone is realistic, emphasizing candid evaluations from the experienced authors rather than received wisdom. Most guides tacitly assume that the reader is at home or in a tour group, and not in acute need of the location of bus stops (with Chinese characters), bike rentals, cheap food and hotels, detailed city maps, addresses of police stations, hitchhiking protocol, and the etiquette for responsible tourism; the 'Lonely Planet' series supplies all this and more, maintaining that it is 'rough' but rewarding to meet people in a country where one cannot pre-book a city-to-city itinerary on the train and where the germ theory of disease has not taken root.

42 Imperial China.
Charis Chan. London: Viking, 1991; London; New York: Penguin Books, 1992. 164p. maps.

A description of China's buildings and architecture for the tourist and general reader, amply illustrated with photographs, plans and maps. Chan starts with a chapter outlining the cosmic background and structural principles of Chinese architecture in general, including explanations of building terms. Subsequent chapters describe the architecture of the Beijing palaces, tombs, temples and parks built by the emperors of the Ming and Qing dynasties, including the Forbidden City, the Summer Palace, and other imperial structures in or near Beijing.

43 China.
Charis Chan. Lincolnwood, Illinois: Passport Books, 1994. rev. ed. 306p. maps.

A well-rounded general introduction to China and China touring, with excellent photographs, brief background sketches of major topics in history and culture, descriptions of major cities and tourist attractions, and a reasonable amount of specific information on hotels and restaurants. An attractive feature of the Passport series is the inclusion of 'literary excerpts', describing famous or relevant events or

14

characteristics. In addition to those listed separately in this section, other volumes of this series include: *Fuzhou*, by Caroline Courtauld (1988. 144p.), featuring Fuzhou, Quanzhou and Xiamen; *Hangzhou and Zhejiang province*, by Simon Holledge, Lynn Pan (1987. 143p.), which includes Hangzhou, Shaoxing and Ningbo; and *Yunnan*, by Patrick R. Booze (1987. 208p.), including Kunming, the Stone Forest, Dali and Xishuangbanna.

44 Handbook for China.
Carl Crow, with an introduction by H. J. Lethbridge. Hong Kong; Oxford; New York: Oxford University Press, 1984. 390p. maps.

A reprint of the fifth edition of Crow's *Handbook for China (including Hong Kong)* (Hong Kong; Shanghai; Singapore: Kelly & Walsh, 1933). Lethbridge's introduction points out that a wave of new-style tourists came to the 'Far' East after the First World War; Carl Crow (1883-1945), the genial American journalist and public relations agent, used his Shanghai experience to provide the travel details and cultural background for them. Still piquant – but only occasionally still relevant – are Crow's descriptions of shopping, servants, hunting and fishing, pidgin English and stamp collecting.

45 China: a literary companion.
A. C. Grayling, Susan Whitfield. London: Murray, 1994. 289p. map.

Although not strictly a tourist guide, this compilation of excerpts from missionaries, travellers, exiles, literary tourists, and poets would fit nicely into a traveller's bag. Short selections are grouped into topical chapters, such as places (Beijing, Shanghai, and famous rivers), mutual perceptions, the poet in the landscape, literature and literati, and 'Communist' China. *The traveller's reading guide*, edited by Maggy Simony (New York: Facts On File, 1993. rev. ed. 510p.) includes a selective list of novels, popular history, and travel writing relating to China, most accompanied by the editor's brief comments.

46 Magnificent China: a guide to its cultural treasures.
Petra Haring-Kuan, Yuchien Kuan. San Francisco: China Books and Periodicals, 1989. 450p. maps.

A comprehensive travel guide and portable encyclopaedia. It opens with travel information and selected essays on history and culture (the section on architecture is especially good). Detailed descriptions of each of the cities and major sites open to foreign tourists at the time of writing form the meat of the volume. In the case of the major attractions, these are historical and practical essays of great value, complete with maps and street plans from the German edition.

47 Xi'an.
Simon Holledge. Lincolnwood, Illinois: Passport Books, 1993. 149p. maps.

A volume in the 'Passport Books' series. Xi'an is a city most famous for the so-called 'Underground Army' of terracotta soldiers, but is also worthwhile for sites ranging from prehistory to recent history. The book sketches the background for Banpo Museum, built *in situ* over the site on one of the most significant neolithic village excavations. It also describes the following: the Terracotta Army Museum and nearby (as yet unopened) tomb of Qin Shi Huangdi; the Han dynasty imperial tomb at Maoling; Tang dynasty tombs and the Huaqing Hot Springs, also site of the 'Xi'an Incident', in which Chiang Kai-shek was kidnapped; and the Edgar Snow Memorial Museum.

48 **The China guidebook.**
Fredric M. Kaplan, Julian Sobin, Arne J. de Keijzer.   Boston,
Massachusetts; New York: Houghton Mifflin, 1993. 13th ed. 800p.
maps. (Eurasia Travel Guides).

A comprehensive guide and practical reference book, which is frequently updated. Part one, 'China at a Glance', has briefings on history, geography, economy and the Democracy Movement. Part two, 'Planning a Trip to China', details China's travel policies, travel options (group tour or independent travel), costs and when to go. Part three, 'Getting to China', gives practical information on travel and packing. Part four, 'Travelling in China', includes tips on getting along in China, customs, money, health, domestic travel, hotels, mail, food, recreation and shopping. Part five sketches 'Doing Business with China'. Part six provides six expert essays on schools, health care facilities (including acupuncture), religion, arts and handicrafts, archaeological sites, and travel for Overseas Chinese. Part seven gives travel particulars for cities and sites from Anshan to Zhuhai. Part eight contains an annotated reading list, a Chinese language guide, and a list of tour operators.

49 **Shanghai.**
Lynn Pan, May Holdsworth, Jill Hunt, revised by Don Cohn.
Lincolnwood, Illinois: Passport Books, 1992. 144p. maps.

A volume in the Passport series, giving both general background and tourist information on facts, sights and excursions in and from Shanghai. Other works on Shanghai include Pan's *In search of old Shanghai* (Hong Kong: Joint Publishing, 1982. 143p. maps), a fascinating piece of practical detective work, which describes the present location and condition of sites of historical events. An evocative guide from the 1930s is *All about Shanghai and environs*, with a new introduction by H. J. Lethbridge (1935. Reprinted, Hong Kong: Oxford University Press, 1983. 225p. maps).

50 **China's food: a traveller's guide to the best restaurants, dumpling stalls, teahouses, and markets in China.**
Nina Simonds.   New York: HarperCollins, 1991. 428p. bibliog. maps.

A knowledgeable survey of food and eating in the People's Republic, arranged as a practical guidebook. After an introduction giving tips on etiquette, beverages (tea, wine, beer), and ordering a meal, chapters describe twenty-seven cities, with background on each city, restaurants (with addresses and telephones numbers), street food, and detailed descriptions of regional cuisine. Sections are devoted to Northern, Eastern, Sichuanese, and Guangdong cooking. The bibliography comprises a list of books on food, history and cooking.

51 **In search of old Nanjing.**
Barry Till, Paula Swart.   Hong Kong: Joint Publishing Company,
1982. 241p. maps.

Like Pan's *In search of old Shanghai* (q.v.), this is a combination guidebook and history, giving the background of events by describing the locations and surviving buildings in which they took place. *Nanjing, Wuxi, Suzhou, and Jiangsu province*, by Caroline Courtauld, May Holdsworth (Lincolnwood, Illinois: Passport Books, 1988. 160p.) is a brief tourist guide in a well-regarded series.

52 Beijing.
Edited by Dieter Vogel. Hong Kong: APA Perspectives, 1989. 305p. maps. (Insight Guides).

A beautifully produced guide from the Insight Guide series, noted for its elegant background essays for the armchair traveller and photography which combines beauty with insight into daily life. The section 'Travel Tips' gives brief details on hotels, restaurants and schedules. *Beijing* (Lincolnwood, Illinois: Guidebook Company, Passport Books, 1995. 208p. maps) is a useful guide, strong on current travel information and details. *Beijingwalks*, by Don Cohn, Zhang Jingqing (New York: Holt, 1992. 271p. maps. bibliog. [Henry Holt Walks Series]) lays out six practical walking tours of historic districts, with maps, illustrations, and excellent historical background. *Biking Beijing*, by Diana B. Kingsbury (San Francisco: China Books, 1994. 213p. maps) provides information on how to rent a bicycle, where to ride it, tips on what you will see, and some hotel, restaurant and general tourist information.

53 Blue guide: China.
Frances Wood. London: A & C Black; New York: Norton, 1992. 571p.

The most detailed and historically oriented of the major guides, with standard practical travel information, in a thick but portable format. For most travellers interested in cultural background it will be preferable to the rather outdated, more expensive, but still beloved Nagel's *China* (Geneva: Nagel, 1982. 1,503p. maps). Nagel's still has the densest information – in what other guide is there a multi-page disquisition on the imperial sewer system? Wood, a seasoned China hand and scholar, supplies circumstantial descriptions of historical sites and sights, often recounting events from both ancient and recent history. There are maps and plans for most cities, but no photographs.

Travellers' Accounts

54 **Land without ghosts: Chinese impressions of America from the mid-nineteenth century to the present.**
Edited by R. David Arkush, Leo Ou-fan Lee, foreword by John K. Fairbank. Berkeley, California; Los Angeles; Oxford: University of California Press, 1989. 309p.

An anthology of travel writings on America which reveal as much about changing Chinese concerns as they do about America. Thirty-six pieces and a number of cartoons, divided into six sections, cover periods from the 1840s to the 1980s, each with a substantial introduction. The perception of America changes from exotic to menacing in the 19th century, and from model to flawed to familiar in the 20th century. High points include Liang Qichao's 'The Power and the Threat of America'; the anthropologist Fei Xiaotong's complaint about the 'shallowness of cultural tradition in America' as a 'land without ghosts'; a 1930s description of a young white Communist organizing Blacks in Alabama; and a revealing satiric cartoon sequence of American life during the Second World War. Liu Zongren's, *Two year in the melting pot* (San Francisco: China Books, 1984. 205p.) is a deftly written memoir of a Chinese journalist's sojourn in the United States and becoming aware of cultural differences and how to accept them.

55 **Two visits to the tea countries of China and the British plantations in the Himalaya.**
Robert Fortune. London: Murray, 1853. 3rd ed. 2 vols.

After the Opium Wars, the British East India Company commissioned Robert Fortune to travel in China – strictly forbidden by the Qing government – to gather seeds and specimens; he obtained 20,000 tea bushes, and the Company proceeded to break China's tea monopoly by introducing production in India and Ceylon. *Two visits* is typical of Fortune's accounts of his four expeditions; they were widely read for their level, detailed descriptions of Anhui, Fujian and the lower Yangzi valley and their circumstantial accounts of plants, farming (including opium, cotton, indigo and tea), and local life.

56   **The Yangtze valley and beyond.**
Isabella Bird.   London: Murray, 1899. Reprinted, with an introduction
by Pat Barr, London: Virago, 1985; Boston, Massachusetts: Beacon,
1987. 547p. map.

Mrs Bird travelled the world with a sharp eye, an appetite for new places, and a
camera; in Victorian England and America her many books were attentively read for
their descriptions and quoted for their opinions. In China she travelled from Shanghai
up the Yangzi valley to Hankow, then through the gorges to Sichuan. She describes
with great gusto (and reveals late Victorian attitudes toward) the rigours of travel, the
natural scenery, the life and activities of the people, missions and Christianity, opium,
and the role of foreigners. Many of her original photographs are included.

57   **On the road in twelfth century China: the travel diaries of Fan
Chengda (1126-1193).**
James M. Hargett.   Weisbaden, Germany: Franz Steiner-Verlag, 1989.
343p. map. bibliog. (Müncher Ostasiatische Studien, no. 52).

Introduces, explicates and translates two travel diaries of Fan Chengda, which
describe a wide expanse of China at a time when the country was split into the Jin
dynasty territory around present-day Beijing and the surviving Southern Song court in
Hangzhou. *South China in the twelfth century: a translation of Lu Yü's travel diaries,
July 3 – December 6, 1170* (Hong Kong: Chinese University Press, 1981. 232p.),
translated and edited by Chun-shu Chang, Joan Smythe, presents the elegant travel
journals of Lu Yu (1125-1210). Burton Watson includes excerpts from Lu's diary of a
trip to Sichuan in *The Old Man Who Does as He Pleases: selections from the poetry
and prose of Lu Yu* (New York; London: Columbia University Press, 1973. 121p.).

58   **Travels in Tartary, Thibet, and China, 1844-1846.**
Evariste Huc, Joseph Gabet, translated by William Hazlitt, edited with
an introduction by Paul Pelliot.   London: George Routledge & Sons,
1928. 2 vols. (The Broadway Travellers). Reprinted in one volume,
New York: Dover, 1987.

Abbé Huc and Joseph Gabet, Lazarist missionaries, travelled from Peking across
'Tartary' – the lands occupied by the Mongols – to Lhasa, only to be dramatically
expelled by the Chinese minister. Their *Souvenirs d'un voyage dans la Tartarie et le
Thibet* (Paris, 1850; New York, 1851) was appreciated for its dialogues, scenic
descriptions, and observations on Chinese characteristics. Pelliot concludes that Huc
'had a somewhat ardent imagination', and rearranged (though probably did not
completely fabricate) what he saw for artistic effect. Evariste Huc's work, *A journey
through the Chinese Empire* (New York: Harper & Brothers, 1855. 2 vols.) recounts
subsequent travels through China proper, with vignettes of daily life. See Simon Leys
'The Peregrinations and Perplexities of Père Huc', in *The burning forest* (q.v.).

59 **High Tartary.**
Owen Lattimore. Boston, Massachusetts: Little, Brown, 1930. 386p.
Reprinted, with a new introduction by the author, New York: AMS
Press, 1975. Reprinted, with an introduction by Orville Schell, New
York; Tokyo, London: Kodansha, 1995.

Provides colourful, informative accounts of travels in Central Asia and what is now
Xinjiang, then known as Chinese Turkestan. A companion volume is Lattimore's *The
desert road to Turkestan* (Boston, Massachusets: Little, Brown, 1929. Reprinted, with
an introduction by the author, New York: AMS, 1975. Reprinted, with a new
introduction by David Lattimore, New York; Tokyô, London: Kodansha International,
1995. 387p.). Eleanor Holgate Lattimore's work, *Turkestan Reunion* (New York: John
Day, 1934. Reprinted, with an introduction by Owen Lattimore, New York: AMS
Press, 1975. Reprinted, New York; Tokyo, London: Kodansha, 1995. 323p.) is a
complementary account of the journey. Many themes of Lattimore's later scholarship
emerge: the pastoral way of life, the influence of geography and climate, and the
interaction of Chinese and Inner Asian culture.

60 **The early arrival of dreams: a year in China.**
Rosemary Mahoney. New York: Fawcett Columbine, published by
Ballantine Books, 1990. 208p.

Uses the form of a number of books from the 1980s: the teacher or student discovers
Chinese society as seen through a year in one of its darkest corners, a provincial foreign
languages department, in this case Hangzhou. China is seen as baffling, infuriating,
repellant, and fascinating. Mahoney's Chinese characters have the intensity of a
mediaeval miniature, incised with short taut strokes of saturated color, while the incidents,
character revelation, and development of the narrator are those of a crafty novelist.
Mahoney discovers that to love China is to weep; this is not a heartwarming book but a
deeper, more difficult, and perhaps more lasting one. A comic novel built on a similar
experience is *Teaching Little Fang* by Mark Swallow (London: Macmillan, 1990. 256p.).

61 **A photographer in old Peking.**
Hedda Morrison, foreword by Wang Gungwu. Hong Kong; Oxford;
New York: Oxford University Press, 1985. 266p. bibliog. maps.

Morrison went to Beijing to run a photographic studio in 1933, and left only in 1946.
Her photographs and accompanying memoirs of the old city are grouped thematically:
walls, palaces and parks, including the Forbidden City; temples and *pailou* (memorial
arches); street life, shops and markets, including opium smokers and acrobats; food
and entertainment, including Beijing duck and opera; arts and crafts; and suburban
areas such as the Western Hills. Her volume, *Travels of a photographer in China,
1933-1946* (Hong Kong; New York: Oxford University Press, 1987. 246p.), similarly
covers her travels, mainly in North China, including the villages of Ding Xian.

62 **The great Chinese travellers.**
Edited and introduced by Jeannette Mirsky. New York: Random
House, 1964. Paperback edition, Chicago: University of Chicago Press,
1974. 309p.

An anthology of writings from the most famous Chinese travellers available in
translation: Emperor Mu (travelled 1001-945 BCE); Zhang Qian (Chang Ch'ien;

c. 123 BCE), the Han dynasty general and Ambassador to Bactria; Xuan Zang (Hsuan-tsang; 645 CE), whose travels for the Tang emperor to gain the Buddhist sutras were the basis for the novel *Journey to the West*; the Daoist Chang Qun (Ch'ang Ch'un; 1220), who visited the imperial Mongol court; Rabban Sauma (1250) who travelled in Europe; a 13th-century visitor to Cambodia; the famous early 15th-century naval expeditions of Zheng He (Cheng Ho); an 18th-century seaman; and excerpts from 19th-century scholars, students and ambassadors.

63 Chinese encounters.

Inge Morath, Arthur Miller.   New York: Farrar, Straus, Giroux, 1979. 255p.

The memoir, with beautiful photographs, of a 1978 trip, which bears witness to the 'collapse of an orthodoxy' following Mao's death in 1976. Miller interviews many prominent writers and intellectuals and makes astute, compassionate observations about their recovery from the Maoist version of socialism; he notes the dishonesty and defensiveness 'of political systems trying to feign success, not only to foreigners, but fundamentally to themselves'. See also Miller's *Salesman in Beijing* (q.v.).

64 Two kinds of time.

Graham Peck.   Boston, Massachusetts: Houghton Mifflin, 1950. 725p. maps.

This has long been an underground classic, neglected because at the time of publication the American public wanted to hear nothing troublesome or complicated about China. Peck came to China just after the 1937 outbreak of the war with Japan; his work and travels took him through China until the eve of the 1949 Revolution. The book is a superbly written mixture of comic adventure, travel description, battle reporting, and caustic social analysis of old China from oppressed village to privileged leadership, and is especially sharp on the confrontation of the Nationalist régime with idealistic Americans. Peck's line drawings of daily life and war are witty and acidly observed. A paperback edition contains parts one and two (Boston, Massachusetts: Houghton Mifflin, 1968. 353p.), covering up to 1941.

65 Marco Polo: the description of the world.

Marco Polo, edited, translated by A. C. Moule, Paul Pelliot.   London: Routledge, 1938; New York: AMS Press, 1976. 2 vols. maps. bibliog.

Polo (1254?-1324?) walked across Asia, became an official in the Mongol empire, toured Kublai Khan's China, and returned through South Asia. His oral tales, transcribed by a cellmate and then circulated in over 100 manuscripts, were based on fact, though often garbled, puffed up, or based on hearsay. Moule and Pelliot's is the standard scholarly edition, with useful notes and textual criticism, continued in A. C. Moule, *Quinsai with other notes on Marco Polo* (Cambridge, England: Cambridge University Press, 1957) and Paul Pelliot, *Notes on Marco Polo* (Paris: Adrien-Maisonneuve, 1959-73. 3 vols.). Still useful is *The book of Ser Marco Polo, the Venetian, concerning the kingdoms and marvels of the East*, translated and edited by Sir Henry Yule (London: 3rd ed. revised by Henri Cordier, 1903. Reprinted, New York: Dover Books, 1993. 2 vols.). Reading editions include Ronald Latham, *Travels of Marco Polo* (Harmondsworth, England: Penguin Books, 1967. 380p.). Leonardo Olschki, *Marco Polo's Asia: an introduction to his 'Description of the World' called 'Il Milione'* (Berkeley, California; Los Angeles: University of California Press, 1960.

459p. maps) consolidates diverse scholarship in urbane essays. A popular but generally careful biography is *Marco Polo: Venetian adventurer*, by Henry Hart (Norman, Oklahoma: University of Oklahoma Press, 1976. 306p.).

66 Ennin's travels in Tang China.
Edwin O. Reischauer. New York: Ronald Press, 1955. 341p.

Ennin, a learned, inquisitive 8th-century Japanese monk, was dispatched to China to study Buddhist scriptures and bring them back to Japan. He preceded Marco Polo by centuries, and was far better informed than the illiterate Venetian. This detailed and vivid depiction of Tang China provides the background needed to understand Ennin's diary, which Reischauer translated in *Ennin's Diary: the record of a pilgrim to China in search of the law* (New York: Ronald Press, 1955. 454p.). Ennin records details of daily life, travel, food, customs, festivals, scenic attractions, and Buddhist practice; he reveals a land of order and prosperity, even though the late Tang period is generally considered to be a time of relative disintegration.

67 Voyager from Xanadu: Rabban Sauma and the first journey from China to the west.
Morris Rossabi. Tokyo; New York; London: Kodansha International, 1992. 219p.

A fascinating account of the cross-Asian pilgrimage of a Nestorian Christian monk starting in 1275-78. The Mongol court in Peking supplied Rabban Sauma with introductions to the Mongol court of Persia; from there he travelled on to Trebizond, Constantinople, Naples, Rome and Paris. Rossabi supplies the general reader with concise background on the worlds of Islam, Judaism, Christianity and Mongol rule, which Rabban Sauma saw and attempted to bring into a dialogue. A roughly contemporaneous travel account is *The mission of Friar William of Rubruck: his journey to the court of the Great Khan Möngke 1253-1255* by Friar William of Rubruck, with translation, introduction, notes, and appendices by Peter Jackson with David Morgan (London: Hakluyt Society, 1990. 312p. [Hakluyt Society Second Series, no. 173]). Jonathan Spence's *A question of Hu* (New York: Knopf, 1988. 187p.) is the story of a Chinese man brought to Paris in the 1720s and placed in an asylum where he goes mad of neglect and isolation.

68 Iron and silk.
Mark Salzman. New York: Random House, 1986. 211p.

Recounts the experiences of a young American, who went from Yale to teach English in Changsha in 1982. His position as a teacher gives him a vantage point on student and school life; his knowledge of the martial arts and study with a traditional teacher give entry into a more traditional China. Salzman writes bright, sharp stories of discovery, which he made into a movie of the same title. Part of the work's charm and significance is that the author does not dwell on national politics, but depicts incidents and individuals, both happy and unhappy.

69 From Heaven Lake: travels through Sinkiang and Tibet.
Vikrim Seth. London: Chatto & Windus, 1983; New York: Vintage Books, 1987. 178p.

A sharp-eyed, acid-penned journey to the West. Seth, then a Stanford PhD student, studied economics at Nanjing University. In the summer of 1981 he hitchhiked home to India via the oases of Xinjiang in Western China, through the Himalayas, across the basin and plateau of Qinghai, and from Tibet to Nepal. He recounts not only his adventures and the assortment of people he met on this unusual itinerary, but also the beauty of the land and the swiftness of change. He treats his China experiences in a volume of verse and translations, *The humble administrator's garden* (Manchester, England: Carcenet Press, 1985. 62p.).

70 **Inscribed landscapes: travel writings from imperial China.**
Translated with annotations and an introduction by Richard E. Strassberg. Berkeley, California; Los Angeles; Oxford: University of California Press, 1994. 580p. maps.

Contains fifty selections from Chinese travel writings, with maps, portraits, paintings and drawings. The Tang dynasty developed the genres of lyric travel account (*youji*) and personal travel diary (*riji*). Strassberg's extensive introduction, 'The Rise of Chinese Travel Writing', first broadly characterizes travel writing in the West as giving religious and cultural significance to odysseys, quests, pilgrimages, crusades, exiles, explorations and exotic journeys. By contrast, Chinese writings, while equally diverse in form, were primarily domestic, scorned profit, and were little interested in foreign countries or the 'Other'; they expressed lyricism, spirituality and locality in quite different ways. These selections demonstrate Chinese traditional attitudes toward nature, history, the individual, society and writing itself.

71 **Flowers on an iron tree: five cities of China.**
Ross Terrill. Boston, Massachusetts; Toronto: Little, Brown, 1975. 423p. maps. bibliog.

Terrill, as an Australian scholar living in the United States, was allowed travel in China during the 1960s and 1970s not available to Americans. Here he combines travel impressions with library research to open a window on China in the 1970s with relaxed but informative essays on: Shanghai; Dairen (Dalian), in Manchuria; Guangdong; Hangzhou; Wuhan; and Beijing. For each he sketches the history, local characteristics, and present living conditions, though little of the Cultural Revolution disorder appears.

72 **Thomson's China: travels and adventures of a nineteenth century photographer.**
John Thomson, with an introduction and new illustration selection by Judith Balmer. Hong Kong; Oxford; New York: Oxford University Press, 1993. 226p. (Oxford in Asia Hardback Reprints).

Reprints eight chapters of travel description, some photographs, and an appendix from *The straits of Malacca, Indo-China and China, or ten years' travels, adventures and residence abroad* (London: Sampson Low, Marston, Low, and Searle, 1875). Thomson's preface proclaims that 'at last the light of civilization seems indeed to have dawned in the distant East', and describes his travels in China during the 1860s and 1870s to prove it. Thomson (1837-1921) resolutely describes and summarily evaluates Chinese sights, from Canton to Peking, as well as many of the Chinese he encountered. Li Hongzhang is 'the picture of a military leader, tall, resolute, and calm, a man of iron will, the finest specimen of his race', whereas the Great Wall is 'simply a gigantic useless stone fence'. A separate volume reprints the sections of the original which deal with Malacca and Indo-China. For the photographs, see Thomson's *China and its people in early photographs* (New York: Dover Publications, 1982. 272p.), which was reprinted from *Illustrations of China and its people* (London: Sampson Low, Marston, Low, and Searle, 1873-74. 4 vols.).

73 Behind the wall: a journey through China.
Colin Thubron.   London: Heineman, 1987; New York: Atlantic Monthly Press, 1988. 307p.

Thubron studied Mandarin, swotted up on China's culture and history, and travelled by himself through many parts of newly opened China in the early 1980s. He talked with many types of Chinese, from university students to bath attendants, and vividly recreates his observations, vacillations and discoveries. Thubron's openness contrasts with the testy *Riding the iron rooster: by train through China* by Paul Theroux (New York: Putnam's, 1988. 480p.), which continues the author's world rail travails; Theroux talked with many varieties of Chinese on his train tour, and sketches a claustrophobic, spiritually impoverished country. A rosier, more humourous series of adventures of a young American is Bill Holm's *Coming home crazy: an alphabet of China essays* (Minneapolis: Milkwood Editions, 1990. 251p.), while David Kellogg's work, edited by Dorothy Stein, *In search of China* (London: Hilary Shipman, 1989; Honolulu: University of Hawaii Press, 1991. 422p. maps), includes realistic views of low cost trekking though China and sharply critical views of traditional Tibetan culture.

74 Imperial China: photographs, 1850-1912.
Historical texts by Clark Worswick, Jonathan Spence.   New York: Penwick, distributed by Crown Publishers, 1978. 151p.

A compilation of photographs of common people, dignitaries, and scenic spots, with essays on historic background and on photography in imperial China. An index lists commercial and amateur photographers of China, 1846-1912. *The face of China: as seen by photographers and travellers, 1860-1912*, preface by L. Carrington Goodrich, historical commentary by Nigel Cameron (Millerton, New York: Aperture Books, 1978. 158p.) covers much the same ground with a well arranged selection of photographs and excerpts from travel writings, and with brief notes on the pioneer photographers. The photographers include John Thomson, Ernest Henry Wilson and John Henry Hinton.

Barbarians and mandarins: thirteen centuries of western travelers in `China.
See item no. 314.

An Australian in China, being the narrative of a quiet journey across China to British India.
See item no. 322.

Pilgrims and sacred sites in China.
See item no. 543.

Learning from Mt. Hua: a Chinese physician's illustrated travel record and painting theory.
See item no. 1286.

Flora and Fauna

75 **The birds of China.**
Rodolphe Meyer De Schauensee, scientific editing by Eleanor
D. Brown, colour plates by John Henry Dick, John A. Gwynne, Jr.,
H. Wayne Trimm.   Washington, DC: Smithsonian Institution Press,
1984. 602p. bibliog.
A descriptive catalogue, rather than a field guide, to all of the 88 families and 1,195
species of birds occurring in China. A short account of each is followed by species
accounts; these describe the adult male (plus female and immatures, if different) with
characteristics most likely to be seen in China, subspecies, and general ranges in and
outside China. De Schauensee's introduction describes the geography of China and the
recent history of ornithology in the country (mainly Western). Almost half the species
are illustrated in black-and-white drawings or in the section of thirty-seven colour
plates. The volume includes a bibliography of ornithological writings from the 19th
century to the present, a 'Variant Names List', a 'Checklist of the Birds of China', and
indexes to Latin and English names.

76 **The giant panda.**
George B. Schaller, Hu Jinchu, Pan Wenshi, Zhu Jing.   Chicago;
London: University of Chicago Press, 1985. 298p. maps.
The authors provide a detailed scientific description of the giant panda from the first
years of an international project to develop a comprehensive conservation plan
sponsored by the Chinese government and the World Wildlife Foundation. Since
pandas have the intestines of a carnivore, they faced a major evolutionary problem
when human settlement drove them into areas where they were forced to subsist
almost exclusively on bamboo. In the 1970s the periodic flowering and dormancy of
the panda's bamboo caused the starvation of a large percentage of the population.
Schaller devotes chapters to physical characteristics; the panda in history; the
climate, environment and pandas of the Wolong Natural Reserve in Western Sichuan;
food and feeding strategy; movement and activity patterns; population dynamics and
social behaviour; and whether the panda is a bear or a raccoon. Keith and Liz

Laidler's work, *Pandas: giant of the bamboo forest* (London: BBC Books, 1992. 208p.) is an illustrated synthesis of recent scholarship on the species.

77   **The last panda.**
      George B. Schaller.   Chicago; London: University of Chicago Press, 1993. 291p.

Schaller, a gifted natural history writer, frankly describes his own participation in the scientific panda project of the 1980s, the contours of 'panda politics', and, at more length, the beauties and dangers of the panda's natural environment. Also treated are red pandas, golden monkeys and takins. The existence of the panda is endangered by their evolutionary unfitness, the encroachment on their habitat by land hungry villagers, and poaching. Schaller also reports on bureaucratic ineptitude, the pressures of international economics, the greed generated by profitable 'rent-a-panda' programmes, and the mixed possibilities of success for the conservation programme. A section entitled 'Suggested Reading' lists accessible works.

78   **Living treasures: an odyssey through China's extraordinary nature reserves.**
      Tang Xiyang.   New York: Bantam Books; Beijing: New World Press, 1987. 174p. map.

Surveys China's designated nature reserves and their plants and animals, with many colour photographs. Tang, although a journalist, rather than a naturalist or zoologist, was appointed editor of an official nature magazine in Beijing; he toured 'panda land' and others of China's more than three hundred nature reserves in order to inform and arouse Chinese readers. This book, with hundreds of beautiful photographs, recounts his encounters with pandas, crested ibises, Siberian cranes, Yangzi alligators, and such, as well as endangered medicinal herbs and plants. One chapter surveys China's nature reserves, and the book ends with sections of plates illustrating rare plants and animals under Chinese government protection.

79   **China: mother of gardens.**
      Ernest Henry Wilson.   1929. Reprinted, New York: B. Blom, 1971. 408p.

An 'amended and thoroughly revised' version of *A naturalist in Western China, with vasculum, camera, and gun* (London: Methuen, 1913. Reprinted, London: Cadogan Books, 1986. 2 vols. map). This is a classic travel book in the imperial scientific tradition, described on the title page of the 1913 version as 'being some account of eleven years' travel, exploration, and observation in the more remote parts of the Flowery Kingdom'. 'Chinese Wilson', director of Boston's Arnold Arboretum, introduced many plants and trees from China to North America. He made three expeditions from 1903-11 through Western Hubei, Sichuan and the marches of Tibet. The book describes and evaluates flora, fauna, habitats and 'natives'. E. H. M. Cox, *Plant hunting in China: a history of botanical exploration in China and the Tibetan marches* (London: Collins, 1945. 230p. Reprinted, Hong Kong: Oxford University Press, 1986) chronicles the adventures of Wilson and his peers.

80   **The natural history of China.**
       Zhao Ji, General Editor, with Zheng Guangmei, Wang Huadong, Xu
       Jialin.   New York: McGraw-Hill, 1989. 223p. maps.
A general introduction to the geography, plants, animals and birds of China, with
more than 250 colour photographs. Chapters cover 'The Geography of China'; forests;
rivers, lakes and sea coasts; mountains; grasslands; deserts; and conservation and
nature protection. For each of these habitats, there are descriptions and pictures of the
flora and fauna, as well as a consideration of how humans have changed the
ecosystems. Appendices list the typical animals of each major natural region, with
Latin names.

**Two visits to the tea countries of China and the British plantations in the
Himalaya.**
See item no. 55.

The golden peaches of Samarkand: a study of T'ang exotics.
See item no. 145.

Prehistory and Archaeology

81 **The shape of the turtle: myth, art, and cosmos in early China.**
Sarah Allen.   Albany, New York: State University of New York Press,
1991. 230p.

A stimulating application of Claude Lévi-Strauss' anthropological theories of
transformations, ancient cosmology and political thought, especially the succession
and foundation myths of the early Chinese dynasties (Xia, Shang and Zhou). Allen
sees a binary opposition between the sage-king and subordinate figures which is
reflected in art and ritual.

82 **The archeology of ancient China.**
Chang Kwang-chih.   New Haven, Connecticut; London: Yale
University Press, 1986. 4th ed. 450p. maps. bibliog.

The most comprehensive and balanced survey; an expanded, revised edition is in
process. The work covers prehistory and the formation process of Chinese civilization
to roughly 1,000 BCE. This 1986 edition presents a great deal of information clearly,
with more than 300 charts, city plans, diagrams, photographs and maps. The most
important conclusion to emerge is that early Chinese civilization was not
homogeneous or centred in one heartland, but rather evolved out of several regional
cultures. *China's buried kingdoms*, by the Editors of Time-Life Books (Alexandria,
Virginia: Time-Life Books, 1993. 168p. maps. bibliog.) is a handsomely illustrated
survey from the Zhou to Han dynasties, focusing on archaeology and daily life, with a
chapter on the 'underground army' of Qin Shi Huangdi. *The cradle of the east: an
inquiry into the indigenous origins of techniques and ideas of neolithic and early
historic China, 5000-1000 B. C.*, by Ping-ti Ho (Hong Kong: Chinese University
Press; Chicago: University of Chicago Press, 1976. 440p.) is a pioneering and
controversial survey synthesis. In it Ho examines pottery, metallurgy, early Chinese
characters, and the origins of agriculture, to show independent development, not
Western dispersal, even claiming that the 'yellow earth' of China was responsible for
much of the brilliance of early Chinese civilization – loess is more.

83 **Art, myth, and ritual: the path to political authority in ancient China.**
K. C. Chang.   Cambridge, Massachusetts: Harvard University Press, 1983. 142p. maps.

Contains lectures by an archaeologist which interpret the proposal that 'art and myth in ancient China were inextricably related to politics'. Chang (Chang Kwang-chih) argues that civilization developed in the Xia (Hsia), Shang and Zhou dynasties as a manifestation of the accumulated wealth of a politically constructed minority. They built political command by constructing and manipulating military power, beliefs in kinship hierarchy, the moral authority of the ruler, exclusive access to the gods and ancestors (as through rituals, art and the use of writing), and access to wealth itself. Chang opens with a discussion of the literary and archaeological sources, then analyses topics such as towns, clans, shamanism, art, writing and the rise of political authority.

84 **Shang civilization.**
K. C. Chang.   New Haven, Connecticut; London: Yale University Press, 1980. 417p.

A multifaceted presentation of the Shang, China's first so-called dynasty, based on archaeological and literary sources. Chang is the leading scholar on China's prehistory; this and the volumes listed above synthesize a broad range of work by colleagues and students. *Studies of Shang archeology: selected papers from the International Conference on Shang Civilization*, edited by K. C. Chang (New Haven, Connecticut; London: Yale University Press, 1986. 325p.) contains eleven scholarly papers, nine of which are translated from Chinese; a number describe the famous Tomb Five of Fu Hao.

85 **The great bronze age of China: an exhibition from the People's Republic of China.**
Edited by Wen Fong.   New York: Metropolitan Museum of Art, Knopf, 1980. 386p. maps.

A basic work on prehistory, with 121 colour plates and 130 black-and-white illustrations. The 1980 exhibition of eighty-five bronzes from China's first three dynasties (the Xia, Shang and Zhou – roughly the 21st to 3rd centuries BCE) was the first 'blockbuster' to come from China after American diplomatic recognition in 1978; the inclusion of eight terracotta figures and horses from Qin Shi Huangdi's 'underground army' established it as a major cultural event. This catalogue of the exhibition includes introductory essays by scholars in the People's Republic and North America, in which they lucidly summarize the state of knowledge (and reveal some of the scholarly debates). Essays cover methods and approaches to bronze age arts, including a technical discussion of bronze casting; the bronze age: a modern synthesis; and burial customs. Brief chapter essays introduce each chronological section of the catalogue. The plates and illustrations are dramatically colourful.

86 **Sources of Shang history: the oracle-bone inscriptions of bronze age China.**
David Keightley.   Berkeley, California; Los Angeles; London: University of California Press, 1968. 281p.

A handbook for the study of the oracle bone texts, their social background, the language in which they were written, their problems, and how to read them.

Edward L. Shaughnessey's *Sources of Western Zhou history: inscribed bronze vessels* (Berkeley, California; Los Angeles; Oxford: University of California Press, 1992. 357p.) describes the vessels and how to read their inscriptions as historical sources. The explanations in both volumes are technical but accessible to a diligent amateur.

87 The origins of Chinese civilization.
Edited by David Keightley. Berkeley, California; Los Angeles; London: University of California Press, 1983. 617p. (Studies on China).

Seventeen technical but mostly clear chapters summarize and debate present knowledge about, and approaches to, the 'complex of cultural traits we now refer to as Chinese civilization'. Part one, 'Environment and Agriculture', contains chapters on climate, geology, evolution of the environment, the domestication of plants, and the origins of cereal grains and food legumes. In part two, 'Cultures and Peoples', seven chapters discuss: local cultures and their interaction; Soviet views on the origins of Chinese civilization; debates on the indigenous origins of metallurgy and bronze; and the origins of the Chinese people. Part three discusses the origin of Chinese characters and the structure of archaic Chinese. Part four, 'Tribe and State', comprises four studies of the Chinese and their neighbours and the debates on state formation. There are ample references, tables, illustrations, twelve maps and a glossary/index.

88 Anyang.
Li Chi. Seattle, Washington; London: University of Washington Press, 1977. 304p.

Dr Li, one of China's first Western trained archaeologists, was the chief archaeologist on the epoch-making excavations, carried out in the 1930s, of the Shang dynasty capital, Anyang, in Henan province. He led the team which unearthed quantities of 'oracle bones', the tortoise shells on which ancient diviners read and wrote their prophecies. Li's book first provides the history of the study of these 'dragon bones', which amounts to a short history of the introduction of scientific archaeology in China. Li then describes the excavations and the discoveries to which they led. *The birth of China: a survey of the formative period of Chinese civilization* by Herlee Glessner Creel (London: Cape, 1937; New York: Ungar, 1954. 402p.) is based on Chinese literary sources and on talks with Chinese archaeologists in the 1930s; Creel provides a then up-to-date and still readable survey of Shang and Zhou politics and society, including many charming anecdotes. The development of scientific archaeology amid civil war and foreign invasion in the 1920s and 1930s is vividly described in Jia Lanpo, Huang Weiwen, *Story of Peking Man: from archaeology to history* (Beijing: Foreign Languages Press; Hong Kong; New York: Oxford University Press, 1990. 270p.).

89 Out of China's earth: archeological discoveries in the People's Republic of China.
Qian Hao, Chen Heyi, Ru Suichu. New York: Harry N. Abrams; Beijing: China Pictorial, 1981. 206p.

A dramatically illustrated presentation of the most impressive post-1949 archaeological findings. The descriptions by authors Qian, Chen and Ru evoke the grandeur of the excavations and provide accounts of their social context, but do not discuss the range of Chinese and Western interpretations about them. Chapters concern: the Yin (Shang dynasty) ruins and the Tomb of Fu Hao; 'Music,

Craftsmanship, and Tragedy in the Tomb of Marquis Yi'; the 'terra cotta army' of the Qin dynasty; the Han tombs of an aristocratic family in Mawangdui, Changsha, in Hunan; royal family tombs at Mancheng, with jade burial suits; 'horse and swallow', the famous flying horse; the culture of the Huns excavated in Inner Asia; the excavations at the Tang dynasty capital, Xi'an; and silk paintings and figurines from the Silk Road.

90 **China in antiquity.**
Henri Maspéro, translated by F. A. Kierman, introduction by D. C. Twitchett. Amherst, Massachusetts: University of Massachusetts Press, 1978. 527p.

A readable, lightly annotated translation of the classic and influential *La Chine antique* (Paris: Boccard, 1927. rev. ed. 1965). Maspéro's presentation of the Shang and Zhou periods down to the Qin unification is still remarkable for its scholarly but almost poetic vision of a religious, social and political whole. The research draws on written texts, rather than archaeology, and is in the French anthropological tradition which tended to seek myth and universal patterns which organize 'primitive' societies. Twitchett's introduction appraises the work and suggests readings to supplement it.

The pivot of the four quarters: a preliminary enquiry into the origins and character of the ancient Chinese city.
See item no. 439.

Ancient Chinese bronzes from the Arthur M. Sackler Collections.
See item no. 1298.

Suspended music: chime-bells in the culture of bronze age China.
See item no. 1327.

History

Historiography

91 Historians of China and Japan.
Edited by W. G. Beasley, E. B. Pulleyblank.   Oxford: Oxford
University Press, 1961. 351p.

Contains essays on the development of historical writing as a genre in traditional
China and Japan. The nineteen essays on China cover the early chronicles through
official history under the Han and Tang to history as a guide to bureaucratic practice
under the Qing. An earlier sketch is Charles S. Gardner, *Chinese traditional
historiography* (Cambridge, Massachusetts: Harvard University Press, 1938. 2nd
printing with additions and corrections by L. S. Yang, 1961). A sophisticated special
study is Denis Twitchett, *The writing of official history under the T'ang* (Cambridge,
England: Cambridge University Press, 1992. 290p.). T. H. Barrett, *Singular
listlessness: a short history of Chinese books and British scholars* (London:
Wellsweep, 1989. 125p.) provides an urbane essay on book collecting and China
studies in Great Britain from the 17th century to the present. *Essays on the sources for
Chinese history*, edited by Donald Leslie, Colin Mackerras, Wang Gungwu (Canberra:
Australian National University Press, 1973. 378p.) contains twenty-six essays on the
nature, location and use of primary sources for all periods of Chinese history; these
sources range from archaeology for the ancient period to newspapers for the modern.

**92 Discovering history in China: American historical writing on the
recent Chinese past.**
Paul A. Cohen.   New York; London: Columbia University Press, 1984.
237p. bibliog. (Studies of the East Asian Institute).

An influential critique of post-Second World War American studies of modern China.
Chapter one considers Fairbank and Teng's *China's response to the West* (q.v.) and
Levenson's *Confucian China and its modern fate* (q.v.) and their once widely accepted
theory that the defining Chinese movements and ideas were reactive to and derivative
from the West. Chapter two, 'Moving Beyond "Tradition and Modernity"', critiques

the tendency to see the two as polar opposites; in fact, Cohen holds, China could modernize without Westernizing or destroying tradition. Chapter two, 'Imperialism: Reality or Myth?', discusses recent critiques of imperialism. Chapter four, 'Toward a China-centered History of China', argues for a new balance. William T. Rowe, 'Approaches to modern Chinese history', in *Reliving the past: the worlds of social history*, edited by Olivier Zunz (Chapel Hill, North Carolina: University of North Carolina Press, 1985, p. 236-96) critically reviews Chinese, Japanese and Western historiography on feudalism, the agrarian régime (including the Asiatic mode of production), the local community, state and society, and commerce and capitalism.

93 **Revolution and history: the origins of Marxist historiography in China, 1919-1937.**
Arif Dirlik.   Berkeley, California; Los Angeles; London: University of California Press, 1978. 299p. bibliog.

A sophisticated intellectual history and philosophical analysis. Dirlik analyses the problems of assimilating China into schemes of world history and the debates among the first generation of Chinese Marxist historians. He finds that the development of creative socialist insights on class, ideology and materialism gave way to a party-dominated, simple definition of traditional China as 'feudal'.

94 **Rescuing history from the nation: questioning narratives of modern China.**
Prasenjit Duara.   Chicago; London: University of Chicago Press, 1995. 275p.

A historiographical analysis and critique both of modern Chinese nationalists (Sun Yat-sen, Kang Youwei and Liang Qichao), and of the nation-centred histories written by Western scholars. Duara questions the claim that the nation-state in both India and China is the exclusive vessel of reason and progress and disparages the 'linear' histories which ignore alternatives. Chapters look at: the way in which historians have treated these alternatives and how they must be differently seen; popular religion, including local temples; the role of secret brotherhoods and popular racism in the Republican Revolution; the genealogy of *fengjian* ('feudalism'), or decentralized power, in creating a space for civil society, especially in the countryside; and federalism and centralism in modern China. A final chapter compares critics of modernity in China and India.

95 **History in Communist China.**
Edited by Albert Feuerwerker.   Cambridge, Massachusetts: M. I. T. Press, 1968. 382p. bibliog.

Brings together seventeen essays analysing scholarship done by Chinese Marxist historians on various periods and topics, including the 'roots of capitalism' debate. Feuerwerker's introduction is a critical study of how Marxist precepts have been forced on history in China. James Harrison, *The Communists and Chinese peasant rebellions: a study in the rewriting of history* (New York: Atheneum, 1969. 363p. [Studies of the East Asian Institute]) analyses the application of Marxist class theory, and sketches the major rebellions. Dorothea A. L. Martin, *The making of Sino-marxist world view: perceptions and interpretations of world history in the People's Republic of China* (Armonk, New York; London: M. E. Sharpe, 1991. 156p. ([Studies on Contemporary China]) examines the treatment of world history in textbooks.

96 **Politics and sinology: the case of Naitō Kōnan (1866-1934).**
Joshua A. Fogel. Cambridge, Massachusetts; London: Council on East
Asian Studies, distributed by Harvard University Press, 1984. 420p.
(Harvard East Asian Monographs, no. 114).

The intellectual biography of an important figure in Japanese sinology and opinion
leader. Naitō's historiography saw 'modernity' in China as beginning with the
transition from the 9th to 11th centuries, a now widely accepted periodization. Fogel
sketches the context of mid-Meiji Japan, 1890s ideas on the reform of China and the
importance of the Qing dynasty in Chinese history, as well as Naitō's response to
Republicanism in China. Tam Yue-him's 'An Intellectual's Response to Western
Intrusion: Naitō Kōnan's View of Republican China', in *The Chinese and the
Japanese* (q.v.) is a pithy, insightful essay. Stefan Tanaka, *Japan's orient: rendering
pasts into history* (Berkeley, California; Los Angeles; London: University of
California Press, 1993. 305p.) focuses on Shiratori Kurakichi (1865-1925), a
developer of Sinology at Tokyo University, on the Research Bureau of the South
Manchurian Railway, and on the task of creating an understanding of history with
China and Japan, and not Europe, at the centre.

97 **Curious land: Jesuit accommodation and the origins of Sinology.**
David Mungello. Weisbaden, Germany: Steiner, 1985. (Studia
Leibnitia, Supplementa, no. 25). Reprinted, Honolulu: University of
Hawaii Press, 1989. 405p.

Discusses the 17th-century Jesuits in China and their impact in Europe. Matteo Ricci
and his followers developed a synthesis of Confucianism and Christianity; their
scholarly studies of Chinese history, language, and philosophy reflect flexibility and
empathy. Mungello first reviews the state of knowledge in 17th-century Europe, then
recounts the development of Ricci's policy of accommodation and its amplification in
the works of his followers (especially Martino Martini). Their translations of
Confucian classics, analysed here in detail, introduced Chinese philosophy to the west
and their reports on current events (such as the Manchu invasion) created a lasting
image. European 'proto-Sinologists' built on Jesuit material for speculations which
were sometimes philosophically profound, as in the case of Leibniz, and sometimes
bizarre, for instance the claim that Chinese was the original universal language.

98 **Soviet studies of premodern China: assessments of recent
scholarship.**
Edited by Gilbert Rozman. Ann Arbor, Michigan: Center for Chinese
Studies, University of Michigan. 247p. bibliog. (Michigan Monographs
in Chinese Studies, no. 50).

American and European scholars describe and briefly assess Soviet work on Chinese
history and literature down to the late Qing dynasty. Rozman's introduction and
background notes discuss the history and structure of Soviet China studies, and are
followed by individual chapters devoted to archaeology and early history, successive
dynasties, and periods of literature.

99   **American studies of contemporary China.**
Edited by David Shambaugh.   Washington, DC: Woodrow Wilson
Center Press; Armonk, New York: M. E. Sharpe, 1993. 369p. bibliog.
(Studies on Contemporary China).

A major history and critique of scholarship on post-1949 China, with extensive
references to recent books and articles. Part one covers 'The Evolution of
Contemporary China Studies in the United States'. In part two, 'Disciplinary
Surveys', five essays describe leading practitioners, important books and articles, and
present state of controversies in the study of Chinese society, the humanities, Chinese
economy, politics and security studies. In part three, 'The China Studies Community',
essays characterize the nature and structure of specialists in academia, government,
private sector (businesses, law firms, banks and travel), and journalism, including
'why journalists make mistakes'. In part four, 'Infrastructure', essays describe:
language training facilities and theories; library resources; scholarly exchange; and the
changing structure of finance.

100   **Oriental despotism: a comparative study of total power.**
Karl August Wittfogel.   New Haven, Connecticut: Yale University
Press, 1957. 556p. bibliog.

Karl Marx was vague as to whether societies in Asia were somehow feudal or whether
they showed an Asiatic mode of production lacking social conflict or true historic
change. Wittfogel, trained in 1920s German Marxist social theory, attempted several
times to express a break-away Marxist understanding before this version, which
centred on hydraulic control and did not primarily concern China; his theory was
widely read but little condoned among Sinologists. See, for instance: Frederick
W. Mote, 'The growth of Chinese despotism: a critique of Wittfogel's theory of
Oriental despotism as applied to China', (*Oriens Extremus*, vol. 8, no. 1 [August
1961], p. 1-14), which concisely describes Ming and Qing imperial authority. Timothy
Brook, *The Asiatic mode of production in China* (Armonk, New York: M. E. Sharpe,
1989. 204p.) introduces articles by PRC historians and theorists. Fu Zhengyuan,
Autocratic tradition and Chinese politics (Cambridge, England: Cambridge University
Press, 1993. 401p.) argues that the tradition and nature of government in China is
autocratic, and provides Ming, Qing and contemporary examples.

Ssu-ma Ch'ien: grand historian of China.
See item no. 129.

**Asian frontier nationalism: Owen Lattimore and the American policy
debate.**
See item no. 169.

The life and thought of Chang Hsueh-ch'eng, 1738-1801.
See item no. 202.

The Mozartian historian: essays on the work of Joseph R. Levenson.
See item no. 242.

**Ku Chieh-kang and China's new history: nationalism and the quest for
alternative traditions.**
See item no. 245.

John Fairbank and the American understanding of modern China.
See item no. 400.

Japanese studies of modern China since 1953: a bibliographical guide to historical and social science research on the nineteenth and twentieth centuries.
See item no. 1490.

Understanding Communist China: Communist China studies in the United States and the Republic of China, 1949-1978.
See item no. 1491.

Surveys and topical studies

101 **China in world history.**
S. A. M. (Samuel Adrian Miles) Adshead. New York: St. Martin's Press, 1995. 2nd ed. 433p. bibliog.
An innovative history of China's relations with other major centres of civilization in Western Eurasia, Africa and America, and with what Adshead calls an 'emerging world civilization or super-civilization'. Each of six chapters analyses a period of Chinese history, compares it with contemporaneous civilizations, explores the avenues of communication (embassies, commerce, missions, pilgrimages, espionage, hearsay and rumour), then considers what travelled along those avenues (people, trade goods, techniques, ideas, values, pathologies, institutions and myths). Finally, Adshead speculates as to how these interchanges contributed to world institutions – ecological, political, cultural and technological – amounting to an emerging world system, an integrating entity to which modern national revolutions were actually opposed. Notes and a bibliography list relevant books and articles in Western languages. The second edition adds an epilogue on events since 1988.

102 **An outline history of China – from ancient times to 1919.**
Bai Shouyi. Beijing: Foreign Languages Press, 1982. 565p. (China Knowledge Series).
A standard and virtually official general narrative history of China, translated from *Zhongguo tongshi gangyao* (Shanghai: Peoples Publishing House, 1980). There is an emphasis on economic structures and political leaders, and many famous incidents are recounted. Chapters describe: antiquity, myth and legend; the slave state in the Shang and Zhou dynasties; the transition from slavery to feudalism; the growth of feudal society in the Qin to Yuan dynasties; and the twilight of feudalism in the Ming-Qing period. The final chapter describes late Qing semi-colonial, semi-feudal society, and the old democratic (bourgeois) revolution. The index gives Chinese characters for the English terms used.

103   **Chinese civilization and bureaucracy: variations on a theme.**
Etienne Balazs, translated by H. M. Wright, edited by Arthur F.
Wright.   New Haven, Connecticut; London: Yale University Press,
1964. 309p.

Contains sixteen key essays by an Hungarian sinologist who taught in Paris until his
death in 1963. As a victim of fascism, Balazs was sensitive both to Confucian glory
and to the tyranny of the imperial bureaucratic state; China was Europe's 'mirror
image', in which capitalism began, but was smothered by an autocratic bureaucracy
and permanent scholar-official class. Part one, 'Institutions', includes the influential
essays 'Significant Aspects of Chinese Society' and 'China as a Permanently
Bureaucratic Society', as well as studies of Chinese feudalism, the birth of capitalism,
fairs, Chinese towns, Marco Polo, and studies of landownership from the 4th to the
14th centuries. Part two, 'History', includes 'History as a Guide to Bureaucratic
Practice' and 'Tradition and Revolution in China'. Part three comprises studies of the
social and cultural crisis after the Han dynasty, running from poetry to economic
policy.

104   **China's cultural legacy and communism.**
Edited by Ralph C. Croizier.   New York; Washington, DC; London:
Praeger, 1970. 313p.

Provides essays and excerpts (many translated from Chinese), with introductions,
annotations and suggestions for further reading. The editor builds on Joseph
Levenson's insight that Chinese Communism was never sure when to bury China's
cultural legacy, when to mummify it in museums, and when to glorify it. The Party
was born during the anti-traditional New Culture Movement of the 1920s, but the
People's Republic initially claimed legitimacy from tradition, which Mao's Cultural
Revolution of the 1960s abominated. These essays explore this historical dilemma in
relation to museums, monuments, history and archaeology, philosophy and religion,
literature, language, architecture, science, performing and visual arts, and cuisine.

105   **A history of China.**
Wolfram Eberhard.   Berkeley, California; London: University of
California Press, 1977. 4th ed. 338p.

A vigorous survey, first published in 1950 and frequently revised. Eberhard stresses
material civilization, social formation, and technology, and is especially useful on the
role of non-Han peoples.

106   **China: a new history.**
John King Fairbank.   Cambridge, Massachusetts: Harvard University
Press, 1992. 519p. 24 maps. bibliog.

A sweeping personal interpretation. The introduction considers approaches to China's
history, geography, the village basis of family and culture, and Inner Asia's long
relation with China. Part one, 'The Rise and Decline of Imperial Autocracy', deals
with: prehistory to the first unification under the Qin and Han dynasties; reunification
in the Buddhist age under the Tang; the height of empire under the Northern and
Southern Song; the rise of non-Chinese rule and the Mongols; and governmental and
economic success under the Ming and Qing. Part two, 'Late Imperial China, 1600-
1911', covers the 'paradox of growth without development' and frontier unrest in
Inner Asia, the new maritime order and the European challenge, early modernization,

and the decline of morale. Part three, 'The Republic of China, 1912-1949', describes quests for a Chinese civil society and Nationalist and Communist competition. Part four recounts the rise and fall of Mao's revolutionary approach and Deng Xiaoping's reforms. Social and cultural themes discussed include: sexism and the subordination of women; the role of intellectuals; the role of technology; and authoritarian government and independent society. The lightly annotated 'Suggested Reading' (p. 435-90) supplements that offered in *United States and China* (q.v.).

107 **United States and China.**
John King Fairbank.   Cambridge, Massachusetts: Harvard University Press, 1981. 4th ed. 606p. maps. bibliog. (American Foreign Policy Library).

Long the most widely recommended basic introduction, this work is outdated but still useful. The 1948 edition is still readable as a committed but scholarly interpretation of China in revolution. The historical sections of the 1981 edition are basically reliable, and its 'Suggested Reading' (p. 481-580) is a well selected, prudently annotated bibliography of English-language scholarly books. Fairbank's *The great Chinese revolution, 1800-1985* (New York: Harpers, 1986. 396p.) synthesizes insights from the modern volumes of *Cambridge history of China* which Fairbank edited or co-edited; although the organization is generally chronological, this is not a survey, but a series of essays, often presenting fresh turns and novel observations.

108 **China's struggle to modernize.**
Michael Gasster.   New York: Knopf, 1983. 2nd ed. 211p. maps. bibliog.

An incisive, brief, interpretive history of China from the 1890s to the 1980s, focusing on intellectual debates and political battles. The central theme, developed in sophisticated detail, is the working out of 'Chinese-type modernization'. A bibliography lists basic sources and monographs. Other useful narrative texts include Edwin E. Moise, *Modern China: a history* (London; New York: Longman, 1994. 2nd ed. 250p. maps [Present and the Past]) and Ranbir Vohra, *China's path to modernization: a historical review from 1800 to the present* (Englewood Cliffs, New Jersey: Prentice-Hall, 1992. 2nd ed. 308p. maps. bibliog.).

109 **A history of Chinese civilization.**
Jacques Gernet, translated by J. R. Foster.   Cambridge, England: Cambridge University Press, 1982. 772p. 28 maps. bibliog.

The fullest of the one-volume surveys, this work slightly revises *Le monde chinois* (Paris: Librairie Armand Colin, 1972); a new edition is announced. Parts one and two describe the 'archaic monarchy' and the rise, evolution and decline of the Qin-Han centralized state. Part three shows post-Han 'barbarians' and remnant aristocrats vying for political control and adapting Buddhism, whose place in 'medieval civilization' Gernet explores in detail. Parts four ('From Middle Ages to Modern Times') and five deal with the transition from a Tang 'aristocratic' to a Song 'mandarin' empire, with a consequent opening to the world and a 'Chinese Renaissance'. Parts six and seven describe the sinicized Inner Asian empires and the Mongol occupation of China, leading to the Ming 'reign of autocrats and eunuchs'. The 'beginnings of modern China' come in urban revival, large-scale business, craft industry, technical progress, and mercantile society, with complementary developments in Neo-Confucian thought and practical knowledge. Parts eight and nine chronicle the 'authoritarian paternalism' of the Qing, 'enlightened despots', prosperity, and intellectual continuity, coupled with a 'deterioration of the political and social climate'. Part ten, 'China Crucified', sketches the disintegration of the traditional economy and society, and the 20th-century revolutions. The People's Republic receives fewer than twenty pages. There is a fifty-five page chronological table.

110   **Rebellions and revolutions: China from the 1800s to the 1980s.**
      Jack Gray.   Oxford University Press, 1990. 456p. maps. bibliog.
      (The Short Oxford History of the Modern World).
A comprehensive text dealing with modern history in terms of two major themes: the causes of the collapse of the Chinese Empire; and the prolonged failure of China to respond to the challenge of the West compared with the success of Japan. The narrative is densely political, but pays close attention also to economic questions such as the land system and agricultural development. The work includes an epilogue, 'The Road to Tiananmen', and there are extensive recommendations for further reading and a chronology.

111   **The rise of modern China.**
      Immanuel C. Y. Hsu.   Oxford University Press, 1995. 5th ed. 1,017p.
      maps. bibliogs.
A well-produced standard history of China, covering the period 1600 to the present, and designed for undergraduates and the general reader. Hsu, an eminent diplomatic historian, writes a detailed political narrative of the period, and provides many illustrations, maps and charts. Extensive chapter bibliographies list books and articles in English and Chinese.

112   **China: a macro-history.**
      Ray Huang.   Armonk, New York; London: M. E. Sharpe, 1988.
      277p. maps.
An original and energetic overview of Chinese history. Huang combines the 'macro' – big picture – with well chosen sketches of historical figures and problems. The emphasis is on political and economic developments, rather than cultural achievements. Another such strong interpretation is John Schrecker, *The Chinese Revolution in historical perspective* (New York; Westport, Connecticut; London: Greenwood, 1991. 240p. [Contributions to the Study of World History, no. 19]), which reinterprets Chinese history as a conflict of *junxian*, or centralized forms of government and controlled economy starting with the Qin dynasty, and *fengjian*, or decentralized local government and market economy. Schrecker then describes the Chinese Revolution from 1800 to the present.in terms of this conflict.

113   **China's imperial past: an introduction to Chinese history and
      culture.**
      Charles O. Hucker.   Stanford, California: Stanford University Press,
      1975. 474p. maps. bibliogs.
A clear and balanced introduction for the general reader and student, covering all aspects of Chinese history and civilization to 1850. A short version is Hucker, *China to 1850* (Stanford, California: Stanford University Press, 1978. 162p.). Conrad

Schirokauer, *A brief history of Chinese civilization* (San Diego, California: Harcourt Brace Jovanovich, 1991. 415p. maps. bibliog.) is a text which surveys prehistory to the present, with coverage of literature, thought and art. W. Scott Morton, *China: its history and culture* (New York: Lippincott & Crowell, 1995. 2nd ed. 323p.) provides a straightforward narrative. More expansive is Charles P. Fitzgerald, *China: a short cultural history* (New York: Praeger, 1961. 3rd ed. 624p. maps), which emphasizes political history and personality, but which also considers art, literature and cultural atmosphere.

114 Perspectives on modern China: four anniversaries.

Edited by Kenneth Lieberthal, Joyce Kallgren, Roderick MacFarquhar, Jr., Frederic Wakeman. Armonk, New York; London: M. E. Sharpe, 1991. 448p. (Studies on Modern China).

Sixteen original scholarly essays mark the coinciding 1989 anniversaries of the Opium War (1839), May Fourth (1919), the People's Republic (1949-79), and the Deng decade (1979-89). Scholars of each of these periods relate its significance in economics, society and culture, politics, and interaction with the outside world, with many thoughtful comparisons.

115 Chinese history in economic perspective.

Edited by Thomas Rawski, Lillian M. Li. Berkeley, California; Oxford: University of California Press, 1992. 362p. bibliog.

Brings together ten papers from a 1990 conference. A substantial introduction argues that Confucians, Marxists and Western historians study economic phenomena, but few use a 'true economic approach or perspective'; such economic perspectives include: 'choice', 'rationality', 'self-interest', 'opportunity cost', 'equilibrium', 'exit', and 'entry' of labour and resources to and from the market. One group of papers uses market theory and archival material to show that foreign trade had deep penetration and effect despite its small percentage of the economy. Another group deploys the concept of entry/exit to indirectly analyse the impact of the railroad on the overall economy; the 'traditional' river or junk trade actually grew. Papers on farm economics estimate whether the rural economy was developing adequately. An ingenious analysis of the changing willingness to store grain from month to month is used to calculate local interest rates. Other essays examine the surprisingly high economic competence of the Qing state, infanticide and family planning, land and income distribution, and women's work.

116 China: tradition and transformation.

Edwin O. Reischauer, John K. Fairbank. Boston, Massachusetts; London: Houghton Mifflin, 1989. rev. ed. 551p. maps.

Drawn from decades of experience supervising dissertation research at Harvard University and teaching the undergraduate survey known as 'rice paddies', this handsomely produced survey text, originally published in the 1960s, offers interpretations which were long accepted as standard. The coverage is both political and cultural, accompanied by excellent maps and illustrations of artistic developments. The material is reworked from John K. Fairbank, Edwin O. Reischauer, Albert M. Craig, *East Asia: tradition and transformation* (Boston, Massachusetts; London: Houghton Mifflin, 1989. rev. ed. 1,027p.), which surveys China, Japan, Korea and Vietnam from the earliest times to the present.

117 **The modernization of China.**
Edited by Gilbert Rozman. New York: Free Press; London: Collier
Macmillan, 1981. 551p. maps. bibliog.
A team of scholars appraise and analyse China's history from the 18th century to the
People's Republic, using theories of modernization developed at Princeton by Cyril
Black and his colleagues. Part one, 'The Legacy of the Past', analyses the
international context; political structure; economic structure and growth; social
integration; and knowledge and education. Part two, 'The Transformation', covers the
same analytical topics for the 20th century. Concluding chapters summarize the
argument, appraise the People's Republic as a modernizing society, and present
China's modernization in historical perspective. The bibliography lists works cited in
the text.

118 **China's cultural heritage: the Qing dynasty, 1644-1912.**
Richard J. Smith. Boulder, Colorado; San Francisco: Westview Press,
1994. 2nd ed. 386p. maps. bibliog.
Explores China's culture as inherited and developed in the last imperial dynasty,
encompassing institutions, material culture, and customs, as well as social action.
Chapters cover: the Qing inheritance (geography, historical background); political
order (imperial rule, administrative integration); social and economic institutions
(social classes, socioeconomic organization); language and symbolic reference;
thought (Confucian moral order, Daoist flight and fancy); religion (official sacrifices,
Buddhism and religious Daoism, popular religion); art; literature; and social life (life-
cycle ritual, amusements). The book closes with the chapter, 'Tradition and
Modernity, 1860-1993'. There are many illustrations and tables, together with an
extensive list of books and articles (including works in Chinese of special interest).

119 **The search for modern China.**
Jonathan Spence. New York; London: Norton, 1990. 876p. maps.
bibliog.
A rich, enormously detailed record of the past four hundred years of China's history,
from the decline of the Ming dynasty in the 1600s to the tumult of 1989. Spence
presents many particular insights and cameo histories of individuals in his sweeping
narrative, but abstains from textbook summations or focus on scholarly controversies.
His main theme is how China's history illuminates its present and the ongoing
frustration of the rulers, reformers, revolutionaries and critics who tried to unify and
modernize China. The 'Further Readings' section suggests English-language books,
arranged by topic.

120 **The gate of heavenly peace: the Chinese and their revolution,
1895-1980.**
Jonathan D. Spence. New York: Viking, 1981. 465p. maps. bibliog.
A compelling series of interlocking biographical essays drawing on the research of
many scholars. Spence portrays three successive generations of writers, those led by
Kang Youwei, Lu Xun, and the fierce feminist Ding Ling, who all bade 'farewell to
the beautiful things' in order to follow revolution and build China. Spence portrays
them, their followers (including Liang Qichao, Qu Qiubai, Xu Zhimo, Shen Congwen,
Wen Yiduo and Lao She), and their writings, and sketches the political leaders who
competed to lead revolution.

Chinese civilization and society.
See item no. 6.

The pride that was China.
See item no. 11.

China: ancient culture, modern land.
See item no. 12.

The heritage of China: contemporary perspectives on Chinese civilization.
See item no. 14.

The Chinese civil service: career open to talent?
See item no. 693.

Chinese eunuchs: the structure of intimate politics.
See item no. 694.

China and the West: society and culture, 1815-1937.
See item no. 803.

The pattern of the Chinese past.
See item no. 891.

Ancient China to 221 BCE (Zhou, Qin)

121 **The *tso chuan*: selections from China's oldest narrative history.**
Translated by Burton Watson.   New York: Columbia University
Press, 1989. 232p. (Translations from the Oriental Classics).
Zuozhuan – 'the commentary of Mr. Zuo' – is a chronicle of intrigue, battles, omens
and scandals during the period 722-468 BCE, originally found in the form of a
commentary on the *Spring and Autumn Annals*. It was influential partly because
Confucius was said to have edited the work to show moral judgment in history, and
partly because of its tersely poetic and dramatic stories. Watson recounts the history
and significance of the text in his introduction, then chooses thirty-seven narratives
considered to be most interesting to modern readers, accompanied by brief
explanatory notes.

122 **The first emperor of China: the story behind the terracotta army
of Mount Li.**
Arthur Cotterell.   London: Macmillan; Harmondsworth, England:
Penguin, 1981. 208p. maps. bibliog.
A popular illustrated study of Qin Shi Huangdi (Ch'in Shih-huang Ti; 259-210 BCE),
the rise of the Qin state, and a generally reliable account of the famous terracotta
'underground army' guarding his tomb. R. W. L. Guisso, *The first emperor of China*
(New York: Carol Publishing Group, 1989. 216p. maps), is a handsome visual and

text presentation, which grew from a Canadian National Film Board project. An intense historical novel of Qin court intrigue is Jean Levi, translated by Barbara Bray, *The Chinese emperor* (San Diego, California; New York; London: Harcourt, Brace, Jovanovich, 1987. 341p.), originally *Le grand empereur et ses automates* (Paris: Éditions Albin Michel, 1985). Sinological studies include: Derk Bodde, *China's first unifier: a study of the Ch'in dynasty as seen in the life of Li Ssu, 280?-208 B. C.* (Leiden, the Netherlands: E. J. Brill, 1938. Reprinted, with a new preface, Hong Kong: Hong Kong University Press, 1967. 270p.); and Derk Bodde, *Statesman, patriot, and general in ancient China: three 'Shih-chi' biographies of the Ch'in dynasty* (New Haven, Connecticut: American Oriental Society, 1940. Reprinted, New York: Kraus, 1967. 75p.). In *The politics of historiography: the First Emperor of China*, edited by Li Yu-Ning (White Plains, New York: International Arts and Sciences Press, 1975. 357p.), there are translations of relevant sections of Sima Qian's *Shiji* as well as historical debates from the People's Republic.

123 **Ancient China in transition: an analysis of social mobility, 722-222 B.C.**
Cho-yun Hsu.   Stanford, California: Stanford University Press, 1965. 240p. maps. bibliog.

A lucid, key history of Chinese societies in the Chunqiu (Spring and Autumn) and Zhanguo (Warring States) periods, showing how a stratified society ruled by local aristocratic feudal families was eventually unified under an imperial bureaucratic government which fostered considerable social mobility. Chapter one, 'Problems and Background', discusses sources (mainly literary), the theories of Max Weber, and the structure of ancient society (peasants, merchants and artisans, servants and slaves, nobility). The body of the book traces in clear detail the changes wrought by the interaction of armies and warfare, new cities and states, commercial and technological development (especially bronze and iron), and philosophical ideas.

124 **Western Chou civilization.**
Hsu Cho-yun, Katheryn M. Linduff.   New Haven, Connecticut; London: Yale University Press, 1988. 421p. maps. (Early Chinese Civilization Series).

A broad, integrated study, aimed at scholars and serious general readers, of the rise and spread of Zhou civilization (8th-11th centuries BCE) and its position in the history of China. Introductory chapters treat the North China world and the Zhou 'nation' before it conquered and replaced the Shang. Six chapters then explain the success of the Zhou conquest, which early thinkers attributed to the 'Mandate of Heaven', but which Hsu and Linduff associate with the development of humane and rational thought; political history; and institutional structure, paying attention to economic and military organization. Two chapters cover art and daily life. The emphasis is on literary sources, but recent archaeological discoveries are also acknowledged.

125 **New perspectives on Chu culture during the Eastern Zhou period.**
Thomas Lawton.   Princeton, New Jersey: Princeton University Press, 1991. 211p. bibliog.

The state of Chu flourished in the area of present-day Hunan from the 8th century until it was taken over by Qin in 249 BCE. It was one of the early regional cultures now understood to make up the complex of ancient China. Four scholarly conference papers assess new archaeological evidence and reinterpret known written records to debate whether Chu was derivative or distinctive. Essays include two on the styles of Chu bronzes, which grew out of Shang and Zhou dynasty styles but differed from them; a detailed discussion of a recently unearthed double coffin; and an examination of the nature of Chu court music in the Eastern Zhou period. There are numerous black-and-white photographs. A transcript represents the interplay of views among other scholars at the conference.

126 **Sanctioned violence in early China.**

Mark Edward Lewis. Albany, New York: State University of New York Press, 1990. 374p. bibliog.

Examines underlying changes which occurred in the three centuries leading up to unification in 221 BCE; the 'sanctioned violence' of the title includes warfare, hunting, sacrifice, punishments and vendettas. Lewis shows that changes in their forms, uses and social distribution reflect new institutions and new ways in which people interacted. During this period, authority changed from customary, communal, kin-based, and ritual to the absolute reign of a single, cosmically charged ruler who deployed dependents and servants, rather than vassals or kin; the unit of political society evolved from city-based kin group to a territorial state; and ideology changed from individual and family honour to service of a state hierarchy representing the earthly rule of Heaven.

127 **Eastern Zhou and Qin civilizations.**

Li Xueqin, translated by K. C. Chang. New Haven, Connecticut; London: Yale University Press, 1985. 527p. maps. bibliog. (Early Chinese Civilizations Series).

A discussion of the life and material culture of the Late Zhou and Qin dynasties, which synthesizes new archaeological work carried out by one of the leaders of the field in China. The Eastern (Later) Zhou (770-221 BCE) and Qin (221-206 BCE) periods were pivotal and chaotic; Li outlines problems and controversies, providing the reader with a feel for the richness and significance of the material. Part one surveys the most important discoveries in the states of North, East, South and Southwest China. Qin, in present-day Shaanxi province, is accorded two chapters. Part two devotes chapters to particular topics, such as bronze vessels, tools, mirrors, iron, precious metals, lacquer, silk, coins and seals.

128 **Ancient Sichuan and the unification of China.**

Steven F. Sage. Albany, New York: State University of New York Press, 1992. 320p. bibliog. (SUNY Series in Chinese Local Studies).

In the first millennium BCE, while the states of the North China plain were warring and amalgamating, the states of Shu and Ba in Sichuan were also developing, making the area a key to the rivalry between the Qin and Chu states. Sage's lively study uses new archaeological and textual evidence to describe this rise from peripheral obscurity to a central role by the time of Qin conquest; the Qin push to unification was greatly strengthened by their extension of military bureaucracy and the development of waterworks (Dujiangyan).

129   **Records of the Grand Historian: Qin dynasty.**
      Sima Qian, translated by Burton Watson.   Hong Kong; New York:
      Renditions-Columbia University Press, 1993. 221p.

Known as the 'father of Chinese history', Sima Qian (Ssu-ma Ch'ien; ca. 145-ca. 86
BCE) compiled the *Shiji*, or *Records of the Grand Historian*, in an attempt to record
all history; Sima's fascination with character, ideas and incident has been compared to
Shakespeare's. Stephen W. Durrant, *The cloudy mirror: tension and conflict in the
writings of Sima Qian* (Albany, New York: State University of New York Press, 1995.
226p. bibliog. [SUNY Series in Chinese Philosophy and Culture]) is a fresh critical
study, in which the author argues that Sima's inspiration and influence were as much
literary as historical. Watson's translations are aimed at general readers, as is his life-
and-times biography, *Ssu-ma Ch'ien: grand historian of China* (New York; London:
Columbia University Press, 1958. 276p.). Watson further translates *Records of the
Grand Historian: Han dynasty* (Hong Kong; New York: Renditions-Columbia
University Press, 1993. rev. ed. 2 vols.). Other introductory selections are: *Records of
the grand historian: chapters from the* Shih chi *of Ssu-ma Ch'ien*, translated by
Burton Watson (New York; London: Columbia University Press, 1969. 356p.); and
Historical records, translated and edited by Raymond Dawson (Oxford: Oxford
University Press, 1994. 176p. [World's Classics]). An annotated, complete translation
in seven volumes is under way: *The grand scribe's records*, edited by William
Nienhauser (Bloomington, Indiana: Indiana University Press, vols. I, II, 1995).

130   **The Ch'in and Han empires, 221 B.C.-A.D. 220.**
      Edited by Denis Twitchett, Michael Loewe.   Cambridge, England;
      London; New York; New Rochelle, New York; Melbourne;
      Sydney: Cambridge University Press, 1986. 981p. maps. bibliog.
      (The Cambridge History of China, vol. 1).

Provides comprehensive standard accounts of political history, institutions, law and
thought. The editors' introduction discusses written and archaeological sources,
historical scholarship, and the general characteristics of early empires. Five chapters
of political history then relate the history of the Qin dynasty, and the rise, rule and fall
of the Han dynasty. Further chapters comprise short monographs on the topics of: Han
foreign relations; the structure and practice of government; institutions; Qin and Han
law; economic and social history; religious and intellectual background; the concept
of sovereignty; the development of Confucian, Legalist and Daoist thought; and the
philosophy of religion from Han to Sui (3rd to 7th centuries), especially Buddhism
and popular Daoism.

The origins of statecraft in China.
See item no. 687.

Early Chinese literature.
See item no. 1110.

Ancient Chinese bronzes from the Arthur M. Sackler Collections.
See item no. 1298.

Han dynasty and Period of Disunion (202 BCE-6th century CE)

131 **Han social structure.**
Ch'ü T'ung-tsu, edited by Jack L. Dull. Seattle, Washington;
London: University of Washington Press, 1972. 550p. bibliog.
(Han Dynasty China).

Contains documents dealing with the society of the Han dynasty. Part one comprises descriptive chapters on 'Kinship', 'Marriage', 'Position of Women' (as wives, sorceresses, etc.), 'Social Classes', and 'Powerful Families'. Ch'ü comments in particular on the role of the consort families (families of emperors' wives), the rise of the scholar as official, and 'guests' (or retainers, sometimes viewed as slaves). Part two presents between seventy-one and eighty-eight documents apiece for the topics of kinship and marriage, social classes, and powerful families. These documents provide the reader with copious and sometimes colourful details with which to understand the social structure of this formative dynasty. There is an extensive index of names and topics.

132 **Hsün Yüeh (A. D. 148-209); the life and reflections of an early medieval Confucian.**
Chen Chi-yun. Cambridge, England: Cambridge University Press, 1975. 242p. bibliog.

A biography and intellectual history. Xun Yue was a scholar-official whose mixture of Confucianism and Daoism reflected the spirit of the times. The analysis is further developed in Ch'en Ch'i-yun, *Hsün Yüeh and the mind of late Han China: a translation of the 'Shen-chien' with introduction and annotations* (Princeton, New Jersey: Princeton University Press, 1980. 225p.).

133 **State and society in early medieval China.**
Edited by Albert Dien. Hong Kong: Hong Kong University Press, 1990; Stanford, California: Stanford University Press, 1991. 414p. bibliog.

Dien brings together eleven scholarly essays on the neglected period from the late Han to Tang dynasties. Topics include: the sale of office in the later Han, with a discussion of whether the phenomenon represented corruption or official punishment; the *shi* or scholar-officials as the Later Han upper class; conflicts between mediaeval genteel families (*shi*) and local power holders; the problem of tenant farmers and bound retainers; aristocratic families in the Eastern Jin and Southern dynasties; Buddhist adaptation; and élite political conflicts. A concluding chapter speculates on the nature of dynastic power over time, space and structure.

134 **Medieval Chinese society and the local 'community'.**
Tanigiwa Michio, translated by Joshua Fogel. Berkeley, California: University of California Press, 1985. 141p.

Presents imperial China from the 1st to 10th centuries as a society founded on a broad base of independent family farms (the 'local community') under the direction of a centralized, autocratic, but superficial state. The section of Tanigiwa's work translated here was the summary introduction for a collection of specialized essays. The translator explains that Tanigiwa was important in postwar Japanese historiography as he moved away from the rigid universal Marxist scheme of stages, in which slave society gave way to 'feudalism' in the period from the Han to the Tang dynasties.

135 **In the shadow of the Han: literati thought and society at the beginning of the Southern dynasties.**
Charles Holcombe. Honolulu: University of Hawaii Press, 1994. 238p. map. bibliog.

After the fall of the Western Jin dynasty in 318, exiles set up the Eastern Jin court in the south, near present-day Nanjing. Confucian scholars were forced to re-imagine their communities in this new, disunited land and rethink their traditions of political legitimation. This is one of the few sophisticated English-language histories of the 'period of disunion' which concluded with reunification under the Sui in 589. Holcombe draws on modern social theory to describe court and literati debates, the changing society and economy, and whether these 'literati' formed a class. He also draws comparisons with the contemporary problems of the successors to the Roman Empire and explores the question of whether there was a universal 'middle ages' and feudalism.

136 **Crisis and conflict in Han China, 104 BC to AD 9.**
Michael Loewe. London: Allen & Unwin, 1974. 340p. maps.

A narrative of nine political turning points in the mature years of the dynasty, culminating with the reform interregnum of Wang Mang. Loewe analyses a political change in which 'Reformists', who called for a return to the Confucian Golden Age of the Zhou dynasty, gradually replaced pragmatic 'Modernists', who derived their tradition from Qin dynasty soldiers and bureaucrats whose policies of Legalism led to the unification of the Empire in 221 BCE.

137 **Divination, mythology, and monarchy in Han China.**
Michael Loewe. Cambridge, England: Cambridge University Press, 1994. 353p. maps. (University of Cambridge Oriental Publications, no. 48).

This publication comprises thirteen previously published articles, with updated notes and a consolidated bibliography. A new introduction, 'The History of the Early Empires', provides an incisive discussion of modern historiography on the period, summarizes recent developments in all aspects of the field, and describes a judicious selection of books and articles. Topics of the articles are grouped around three themes: mythology as an organizing principle in Han life and politics; the prevalence of divination in public and private life; and the change in the public legitimation of the dynasty, from its initial claim to be the heir by conquest to the Qin, to a claim to moral right to rule expressed in Confucian terms.

138   **Courtier and commoner in ancient China: selections from the 'History of the Former Han'.**
Pan Ku, translated by Burton Watson.   New York; London: Columbia University Press, 1974. 282p. (Translations from the Oriental Classics).

Contains selections for the general reader of biographies from *Hanshu*, one of China's great histories, by Ban Gu (32-92 CE). A fuller selection is provided in Homer Dubs, *History of the former Han dynasty* (Baltimore, Maryland: Waverly Press, 1938-55. 3 vols.).

139   **Food and money in ancient China.**
Pan Ku, translated, edited by Nancy Lee Swann.   Princeton, New Jersey: Princeton University Press, 1950. Reprinted, New York: Octagon Books, 1974. 482p. bibliog.

An annotated translation, with a substantial introduction, of the sections dealing with economics, food and commerce (*shihuozhi*) from Sima Qian's *Shiji* and from the official history of the Han dynasty, *Hanshu*, written by Ban Gu. Another Han document, *Yantie lun*, describes the lively debate between Confucians and Legalists at the Han court in the 2nd century BCE over the practicality and morality of government role in the economy; it is translated in Esson M. Gale, *Discourses on salt and iron: a debate on state control of commerce and industry in ancient China* (Leiden, the Netherlands: E. J. Brill, 1931. Reprinted, Taipei: Ch'eng-Wen, 1967; New York: Paragon Book Gallery, 1967. 110p.).

140   **The Han dynasty.**
Michelle Pirazzoli-t'Serstevens, translated by Janet Seligman.   New York: Rizzoli, 1982. 240p.

A handsomely illustrated general history of the Han, drawing on archaeological and written records to present the general reader with accounts of politics, life and art. *Han civilization*, by Wang Zhongshu, translated by K. C. Chang (New Haven, Connecticut; London: Yale University Press, 1982. 261p.), is a thoroughly illustrated summary of post-1949 archaeological discoveries. *Everyday life in early imperial China during the Han period, 202 BC-AD 220*, by Michael Loewe (London: Dorset Press; New York: Putnam's, 1968. 208p. map) is an account aimed at general readers, which focuses on material culture and the life of the common people. Chapters cover geography, government, army, society, religion, urban and rural life, commerce and industry.

Chinese ideas of life and death: faith, myth, and reason in the Han period (202 BC-AD 220).
See item no. 507.

The bureaucracy of Han times.
See item no. 684.

Trade and expansion in Han China.
See item no. 801.

Poetry and politics: the life and works of Juan Chi (210-263).
See item no. 1197.

Sui and Tang dynasties (589-907)

141 Han Yü and the T'ang search for unity.
Charles Hartman. Princeton, New Jersey: Princeton University Press, 1986. 459p. bibliog.
A biography and assessment of the ideas of Han Yü (768-824), who presaged the Neo-Confucian revival in the Song dynasty; he turned back to 'pure' Confucianism, and, along with Liu Zongyuan (773-819), advocated a return to the *guwen* prose style of the Han dynasty. The opening chapter of Hartman's book describes Han's political career and his era. The following chapters present Han's political vision, his proposals to reunify the Tang under an effective emperor, and the intellectual atmosphere of the time, which was heavily influenced by Buddhism. Han's major writings are discussed in detail. Chapter four, 'The Unity of Style', argues that his *guwen* style was rooted in his political and intellectual vision, rather than aesthetics.

142 The medieval Chinese oligarchy.
David Johnson. Boulder, Colorado: Westview Press, 1977. 281p. bibliog.
Studies the structure of the élite families (*shidafu*) that dominated the government, the sources of their power to remain in the élite, and the reasons for their eventual erosion over the course of the Tang dynasty. Johnson argues that the *shidafu* were an oligarchy, not a feudal aristocracy as in Europe; families indeed sustained their position over time, but through control of access to government office, rather than through legal heredity or juridical legitimacy.

143 State and scholars in T'ang China.
David McMullen. Cambridge, England: Cambridge University Press, 1988. 423p. bibliog.
A rounded study of scholars, education, schools and Confucian learning under the Tang, which discusses the cult of Confucius, the classics and their commentaries, state ritual, and attitudes towards literary scholarship. McMullen finds that the state and political élites sponsored most of this activity, as private or local élite scholarship emerged only during the Song dynasty. Buddhist learning and scholars are not covered.

144 The background of the rebellion of An Lushan.
Edwin Pulleyblank. London: Oxford University Press, 1955.
Reprinted, Westport, Connecticut: Greenwood, 1982. 264p. bibliog.
The mid-8th-century rebellion of military governor An Lushan forced the emperor Xuanzong to flee the capital with his paramour, Yang Guifei, who had adopted An Lushan; on route to Sichuan, the emperor's guard forced her to commit suicide, one of China's romantic tragedies. More prosaically, the rebellion exposed and hastened dynastic breakdown, allowed foreign invasions, and forced political and fiscal reorganization, making way for the eventual change from an aristocratic to a bureaucratic empire. Pulleyblank's ground-breaking study discusses the background of An Lushan and the dictatorship of Li Linfu, meticulously analyses the economic, political and military structure of the mid-Tang period, and sketches the long-term results of the rebellion.

145 **The golden peaches of Samarkand: a study of T'ang exotics.**
Edward H. Schafer. Berkeley, California; Los Angeles; London:
University of California Press, 1963. 399p. maps. bibliog.

A classic of sinology and an engrossing history. Schafer explores the cultural and economic circulation of people, goods, plants, animals, sacred objects and books, both within the Tang multi-cultural empire and from abroad, especially Central Asia and India. Chapters describe the 'glory of Tang', then go on to recount Tang reports and fantasies on all manner of exotic objects, from jewels and fruits through sandalwood and slaves to Buddhist relics and zithers. The emphasis is literary, with many exacting and readable translations of poetry included. Equally fine is Schafer's *The vermillion bird: T'ang images of the South* (Berkeley, California; Los Angeles; University of California Press, 1967. 380p.), which explores 'senses, sensibilities, and imaginations' with respect to the then colonial frontiers and peoples of Nam Viet, in the tropical south, that is, roughly present-day Guangdong and Vietnam.

146 **Financial administration under the T'ang dynasty.**
Denis Twitchett. Cambridge, England: Cambridge University Press,
1970. 2nd ed. 386p. maps. bibliog. (University of Cambridge Oriental
Publications, no. 8).

A technical analysis of government tax and spending policies, which is used to help understand the nature of Tang dynasty power and how it changed. Topics include land tenure, taxation, state monopolies, money and credit, the canal system, and financial administration. The 1970 edition adds a postscript which reviews developments in the field since the 1959 edition.

147 **Sui and T'ang China, 589-906, Part 1.**
Edited by Denis Twitchett. Cambridge, England; New York; Port
Chester, New York; Melbourne; Sydney: Cambridge University Press,
1979. 850p. maps. bibliog. (The Cambridge History of China, vol. 3).

Contains definitive narrative accounts of political and military history. The editor's introduction discusses the establishment of national unity, institutional, economic and social change, and also deals with Sui and Tang China and the wider world, and the problem of sources. Nine monographic chapters then cover the Sui (581-617) and the Tang dynasties, among them the reign of Gaozu (Li Yuan; r. 618-26), Taizong (Li Shimin; r. 626-49); Gaozong (r. 649-83); Empress Wu and her Zhou dynasty (Wu Zetian; r. 690-705); Xuanzong (r. 712-56); and the decline and end of the Tang period. Another volume was planned to cover other aspects of the period.

148 **The Sui dynasty.**
Arthur F. Wright. New York: Knopf, 1978. 237p. maps.

A magisterial and readable history of the short but pivotal Sui dynasty (581-617) which reunited the empire, but, like the Qin, could not stabilize dynastic control. Wright describes how the Yang family blended southern culture (including Buddhism) and northern military politics to restore imperial cultural hegemony and pave the way for the Li family to establish the more long-lived Tang dynasty.

149   **Mirror to the Son of Heaven: Wei Cheng at the court of T'ang T'ai-tsung.**
      Howard Wechsler.   New Haven, Connecticut; London: Yale
      University Press, 1974. 259p. map. bibliog.
Wei Zheng (580-643) was an aristocratic general and Tang court official whose life
spanned the founding reigns of Gaozu and Taizong. Wechsler uses this official career to
illuminate the personalities and policies of these emperors and explore how they built
and fought with the bureaucracy which renewed the empire on the model of the Han.

150   **Offerings of jade and silk: ritual and symbol in the legitimation of the T'ang dynasty.**
      Howard J. Wechsler.   New Haven, Connecticut; London: Yale
      University Press, 1985. 313p. bibliog.
Wechsler uses anthropological and religious approaches to provide a lively history of
political rituals and symbols of the early Tang emperors. The work covers portents,
accession ceremonies, ancestral cults, imperial tombs, the Mingtang (an imperial
temple building), imperial tours of inspection and the calendar. These symbols and
rituals, Wechsler finds, were not fixed or inherited, but were consciously debated
between contending schools of thought and selected by the emperors to demonstrate a
new political openness rather than the Han dynasty emphasis on a closed ruling
family. New conceptions of power derived from Buddhism and Daoism, from an
unprecedented expansion of empire, and from a need for additional sources of
legitimation to support the widened ambition of the government to control society.

151   **Perspectives on the T'ang.**
      Edited by Arthur F. Wright, Denis Twitchett.   New Haven,
      Connecticut; London: Yale University Press, 1973. 458p.
Contains twelve broad essays, as well as a substantial introduction which sets the
study of the Tang in four perspectives – history, thought and religion, institutions, and
poetry. Part one, 'Institutions and Politics', includes essays on: the composition of the
Tang ruling élite; governmental factionalism; and the middle Yangzi in Tang politics.
Part two, 'Thought and Religion', contains essays on: Tang Taizong and Buddhism;
the imperial patronage of Buddhism; and historical and literary theory in the 8th
century. Part three, 'Literature', comprises essays on: the contemplation of the past in
Tang poetry; the poet Li Bo; and allusion and Tang poetry.

Ennin's travels in Tang China.
See item no. 66.

The writing of official history under the T'ang.
See item no. 91.

Son of heaven: founder of the T'ang dynasty.
See item no. 347.

The Empress Wu.
See item no. 348.

Religion and society in T'ang and Sung China.
See item no. 502.

Buddhism under the T'ang.
See item no. 582.

The Nan-chao kingdom and T'ang China's southwestern frontier.
See item no. 801.

The T'ang code.
See item no. 870.

Northern and Southern Song dynasties (960-1368)

152 **Court and family in Sung China, 960-1279: bureaucratic success and kinship fortunes for the Shih of Ming-chou.**
Richard Davis. Durham, North Carolina: Duke University Press, 1986. 353p. bibliog.

Relates the history of the Song dynasty through the rise and fall of one family, named Shi. From their arrival in Mingzhou, near present-day Ningbo, they set about rising socially and achieved great success by educating their sons to pass the exams for government office. They became favourites of the emperors, but fell disastrously out of favour at the end of dynasty. Davis also studies the wives and concubines who worked for family success.

153 **Daily life in China on the eve of the Mongol invasion, 1250-1276.**
Jacques Gernet, translated by Hope M. Wright. London: Allen & Unwin; New York: Macmillan, 1962; Stanford, California: Stanford University Press, 1970. 254p. maps. (Daily Life Series).

An engaging portrait of Chinese society at its apogee in the Southern Song. Hangzhou unexpectedly became the capital of the dynasty when horse-riding invaders drove the emperor out of the north; it became a self-confident centre of urban culture and commerce, soon to be conquered by the Mongols and admired by Marco Polo. Gernet uses 13th-century guidebooks, paintings, fiction, recipe books and poetry to give a full social portrait of a bustling commercial society. Chapter topics include housing, clothing, cooking; the life cycle (birth, education, marriage and the position of women, illness and death); the seasons and the universe; and leisure. It was published first as *La vie quotidienne en Chine à la veille de l'invasion Mongole, 1250-1276* (Paris: Hachette, 1959).

154 **Statesmen and gentlemen: the élite of Fu-chou, Chiang-hsi, in Northern and Southern Sung.**
Robert P. Hymes. Cambridge, England; New York: Cambridge University Press, 1986. 379p. bibliog.

Studies gentry families in Fuzhou, a county of Song dynasty Jiangxi province. Hymes finds that the group maintained itself over several generations, with few new entrants;

that they came in the Southern Song to exert a control over local society relatively independent of the central government; that officials from the area came to pursue local interests rather than national policies; and that these officials did not form a separate national élite, but were integrated into a local élite by marriage, school ties and cultural interests.

155 **Ordering the world: approaches to state and society in Sung dynasty China.**
Edited by Robert P. Hymes, Conrad Schirokauer.   Berkeley, California; London: University of California Press, 1993. 437p. bibliog. (Studies on China).

Reproduces ten scholarly articles which were presented at a 1986 conference. These scholars feel that earlier views of the struggle between reformers and conservatives should be modified; that the 13th-century 'Neo-Confucian' shift away from government policies, identified with Zhu Xi (statesman and historian), should not be seen as an abandonment of world improvement identified with Wang Anshi (statesman), but rather as a new set of means using local and voluntary forms of social action. Topics of articles include: Su Xun's pragmatic statecraft; state power and economic activism during Wang Anshi's 'new policies', 1068-85; the political visions of Sima Guang and Wang Anshi; Zhu Xi's sense of history; Zhu Xi's community granary in theory and practice; charitable estates as an aspect of statecraft; Southern Song views of famine relief; the historian Li Xinquan and the dilemmas of statecraft; Wei Liaoweng's thwarted statecraft; and Chen Dexiu and statecraft.

156 **Change in Sung China: innovation or renovation?**
Edited with an introduction by James T. C. Liu, Peter Golas. Lexington, Massachusetts: D. C. Heath, 1969. 100p. (Problems in Asian Civilizations).

A study anthology, which asks whether the technological advances and economic development of the Song period were merely 'change within tradition' or constituted modernization in the sense of genuine developmental change. The editors' introduction sets out the problem and main historiographical views. The body of the book presents excerpts from Chinese, Japanese and Western historians. There are chapters on: general assessments, including a summary of the influential hypothesis of the Japanese scholar, Naitō Kōnan, who saw Song China as early modern; the developing economy, including early-ripening rice, iron and coal industries, change in the countryside, and capitalism; centralized government; and the Neo-Confucian vision of philosophy and society. There is a section of suggestions for additional reading.

157 **China turning inward: intellectual-political changes in the early twelfth century.**
James T. C. Liu.   Cambridge, Massachusetts: Harvard University Press, 1988. 209p.

Analyses the political conflicts and summarizes the intellectual changes which occurred during the reign of Gaozong (r. 1127-62) of the Southern Song. Liu sees a developing defensiveness towards Buddhism and 'barbarians' and a withdrawal of Confucian thinkers from activism; he feels that this change prepared the way for the eventual dominance of Zhu Xi's orthodox Neo-Confucianism in later dynasties.

158 **Reform in Sung China: Wang An-shih (1021-1086) and his new policies.**

James T. C. Liu.   Cambridge, Massachusetts: Harvard University Press, 1959. 140p. bibliog. (Harvard East Asian Series, no. 3).

A political biography of Wang Anshi, a powerful Prime Minister, essayist and poet who proposed to save the Song dynasty by radical fiscal reform, agricultural reorganization, and bureaucratic restructuring. Opponents charged that the unintended consequences of these reforms would be disastrous. *Wang An-shih, practical reformer?*, edited with an introduction by John Meskill (Boston, Massachusetts: D. C. Heath, 1963. 99p. [Problems in Asian Civilization]) is a study anthology aimed at college students preparing research essays. The introduction describes Wang's career and the scholarly debate over it. The body of the book provides edited excerpts from Wang's 'Ten Thousand Word Memorial' and 'Current Extravagance', the judgements of his contemporaries and later Chinese, modern reappraisals, and suggestions for additional reading.

159 **An introduction to the civil service of Sung China: with emphasis on its personnel administration.**

Winston W. Lo.   Honolulu: University of Hawaii Press, 1987. 297p. bibliog.

Outlines and briefly analyses the formal structures and operation of the central government bureaucracy, both civilian and military. Topics include recruitment, personnel supervision and the allocation of jobs. E[dward] A. Kracke, Jr., *Civil service in early Sung China, 960-1067* (Cambridge, Massachusetts: Harvard University Press, 1953. Reprinted, 1968. 262p. [Harvard-Yenching Institute Monograph Series, no. 8]) is a classic study of the earlier period.

160 **Commerce and society in Sung China.**

Shiba Yoshinobu, translated by Mark Elvin.   Ann Arbor, Michigan: University of Michigan, Center for Chinese Studies, 1970. 228p. (Michigan Abstracts of Chinese and Japanese Works on Chinese History, no. 2).

A leading Japanese historian provides a wide-ranging study of the Song economy drawing on official histories, poems and belles-lettres. Chapters consider: the development of communications and transport (shipping, management, investment); the formation of a nation-wide market, especially in rice and handicrafts; cities and markets; the development of commercial organization (brokers, lodges for merchants, wholesalers); characteristics of commercial capital; and commerce and society (expansion of consumption, increase of non-farming occupations in the countryside, and the commercial spirit). The work is a slightly abridged translation of *Sōdai shōgyō-shi kenkyū* (Tokyo: Kazama shōbō, 1968).

161 **The country of streams and grottoes: expansion and settlement, and the civilizing of the Sichuan frontier in Song times.**

Richard van Glahn.   Cambridge, Massachusetts: Council on East Asian Studies, Harvard University, Harvard University Press, 1987. 305p. bibliog. (East Asian Monographs, no. 123).

An imaginative exploration of the social, economic, political and military processes through which the frontier pushed out or absorbed non-Han peoples; Chinese-style agriculture and industry (including salt mining) were the base for political and social expansion. Paul Smith, *Taxing heaven's storehouse: horses, bureaucrats, and the destruction of the Sichuan tea industry, 1074-1224* (Cambridge, Massachusetts: Harvard University Council on East Asian Studies, Harvard University Press, 1991. 489p. [Harvard-Yenching Institute Monograph Series, no. 32]) gives vivid details on the political economy. Wang Anshi's ambitious plans included a government monopoly on tea, by this time a basic consumer commodity; this monograph analyses the reform attempt, its frustration, and its lingering influence. Hugh R. Clark, *Community, trade, and networks: southern Fujian province from the third to the thirteenth century* (Cambridge, England: Cambridge University Press, 1991. 266p.) analyses commercialization, trade, demography, urbanization and agriculture on the south-east coast in the pre-modern era.

On the road in twelfth century China: the travel diaries of Fan Chengda (1126-1193).
See item no. 57.

South China in the twelfth century: a translation of Lu Yü's travel diaries.
See annotation to item no. 57.

Central Asia and non-Han dynasties to 1800

162 **The perilous frontier: nomadic empires and China.**
Thomas J. Barfield.   Cambridge, Massachusetts; Oxford: Basil Blackwell, 1989. 325p. map. bibliog. (Studies in Social Discontinuity).
Barfield applies anthropological models of tribal and state development to explain how small and poor nomadic societies constructed large empires and sometimes dominated China. He argues that Xiongnu, Turkic and Mongol nomadic leaders were not mindless barbarians, but rather canny strategists, aware of their situation and able to build on pastoral military traditions. The emphasis here is on Central Asian politics, with Chinese material included to show the problems faced by nomad strategists.

163 **Western and Central Asians in China under the Mongols: their transformation into Chinese.**
Ch'en Yüan, translated, annotated by Ch'ien Hsing-hai, L. Carrington Goodrich.   Los Angeles: Monumenta Serica Institute, 1966. 328p. bibliog. (Monumenta Serica Monograph, no. 15); Nettetal, Germany: Steyler Verlag, 1989. paperback ed. 328p.
In the late 13th and early 14th centuries, the Mongols added China to an empire encompassing dozens of peoples, the Western Region (*Xiyu*) of China being an especially rich ethnic mix. Chen sketches the lives of 132 individuals in that region in

order to provide a rich portrait of the social and cultural interaction of Confucianism, Daoism, Buddhism, Islam and Christianity. The adoption of Chinese customs is assumed to constitute the 'transformation' into 'Chinese', not an addition to or union with other identities. The translation is based on a collection of Chen's studies published in Beiping (Beijing) in 1935; the translators' annotations refer to later scholarship.

164 **Legitimation in imperial China: discussions under the Jurchen Chin dynasty (1115-1234).**
Chan Hok-lam. Seattle, Washington; London: University of Washington Press, 1984. 267p. bibliog. (Publications on Asia of the Henry M. Jackson School of International Studies, no. 38).
In the early 12th century, Jurchen (also called Jurched) peoples defeated the Liao dynasty and drove the Song court to the south. They were of Tungusic stock, not Han Chinese, so their Jin (Golden) dynasty required special arguments to establish its legitimacy. Part one of this broad ranging study explores the issue of legitimacy in global political theory and Chinese history. Part two opens with a valuable chapter describing the historical setting of the dynasty, then examines the discussions and debates over legitimate succession. Part three discusses sources.

165 **Conquerors and Confucians: aspects of political change in late Yüan China.**
John Dardess. New York; London: Columbia University Press, 1973. 240p. bibliog. (Studies in Oriental Culture).
Discusses the way in which the momentum of Chinese politics transformed Mongol conquerors into Confucian rulers and returned China to virtual autonomy under foreign rule. Dardess examines the records of the Mongol rulers to show how their initial impulse to root out all resistance was transformed into an accommodation with Chinese expectations. The inability of the Mongol emperor to control debate between reformers and conservatives led ultimately to dynastic decline.

166 **Alien regimes and border states, 907-1368.**
Edited by Herbert Franke, Denis Twitchett. New York: Cambridge University Press, 1994. 864p. maps. bibliog. (Cambridge History of China, vol. 6).
The editors provide nine authoritative essays on non-Han dynasties in what is now Chinese territory: the Khitan (Qidan) Liao dynasty (907-1125); the Tangut (Xi Xia; Hsi Hsia) dynasty (999-1127); the Jurchen (Jin) dynasty (1115-1234); and the Mongol (Yuan) dynasty (1260-1368). Essays treat not only themes of conquest and sinification, but cultural and social history; government, society and the impact on Chinese social structure; changes in legal codes; and the reign of Khubilai Khan. The bibliography and essays on sources will prove essential for scholars. For earlier periods and realms beyond China, see *Cambridge history of early Inner Asia*, edited by Denis Sinor (Cambridge, England; New York: Cambridge University Press, 1990. 518p.), which covers the period down to the Mongols. Herbert Franke, *China under Mongol rule* (Aldershot, England; Brookfield, Vermont: Ashgate Publishing, 1994. 324p.) reprints thirteen specialist articles on history writing, Mongol rulers, cultural history and biography.

167 **Peace, war, and trade along the Great Wall: nomadic-Chinese interaction through two millennia.**
Sechin Jagchid, Van Jay Symons. Bloomington, Indiana: Indiana University Press, 1989. 266p. bibliog.

Western scholars once followed Chinese precedent in seeing a hard border between Chinese and pastoral societies, one marked by a series of fortifications misleadingly referred to as the 'Great Wall'. This book, using recent work which builds on Owen Lattimore's, recognizes the border region as a zone of cultural interaction, economic interdependence, and political mixing. The Mongols established the Yüan dynasty and inspired Manchu institutions; the Qing was based on the political and military heritage of the steppe, while operating in a Chinese cultural milieu.

168 **China under Mongol rule.**
Edited by John D. Langlois, Jr. Princeton, New Jersey: Princeton University Press, 1981. 487p. bibliog.

Contains twelve essays on aspects of the Yuan which constitute a multi-faceted history. A substantial introduction by the editor examines the establishment of the dynasty by Khubilai Khan and the record of his successors, with a consideration of ways in which to appraise them. Sections then deal with: institutions (the imperial government, writing official history, education); thought; Mongols and Tibetans in China; and art and literature (painting, 'Northern' drama). Elizabeth Endicott-West, *Mongolian rule in China: local administration under the Yüan Dynasty* (Cambridge, Massachusetts: Harvard University Council on East Asian Studies, 1989. 217p.) is a scholarly study of local government, but also includes a general assessment of the relations between Yuan government and society.

169 **Inner Asian frontiers of China.**
Owen Lattimore. London: Oxford University Press, 1940. 585p. maps. various reprints.

Lattimore, raised in China speaking Chinese, became one of the most important historians of Central Asia. He explained how the nomadic way of life interacted with settled farming peoples to produce a zone of distinctive frontier political, social and economic patterns around the rim of Asia from China to the Middle East. The essays in this 1940 volume present various aspects of Lattimore's theories of geography and politics. James Cotton, *Asian frontier nationalism: Owen Lattimore and the American policy debate* (Manchester, England: Manchester University Press, 1989. 181p. [Studies on East Asia]) evaluates Lattimore's *oeuvre*, showing that a romantic allegiance to Mongol nationalism, rather than Marxism, animated his views. Lattimore's *Studies in frontier history: collected papers, 1928-1958* (London: Oxford University Press, 1962. 565p.) includes scholarly and popular essays and a staggering bibliography of his published work.

170 **Traders and raiders on China's northern frontiers.**
Edited by Jenny F. So, Emma C. Bunker. Seattle, Washington; London: University of Washington Press, Arthur M. Sackler Gallery, Smithsonian Institution. 1995. 203p. maps. bibliog.

A handsomely illustrated exhibition catalogue, with introductory essays on the people, the land, the economy, and trade and contact from the 2nd millennium BC to the Qing era. This provides an excellent introduction to Sino-Central Asian relations from the point of view of material objects. *Empires beyond the Great Wall: the heritage of Genghis Khan*, edited by Adam Kessler (Los Angeles: Natural History Museum, 1994. 175p. maps) also catalogues an exhibition of gold, bronze, ceramic, wood and textile objects from ten People's Republic museums. There are attractive photographs of exhibits and plentiful maps, but scholars have found inaccuracies in the historical chapters; the title is misleading, as the empires concerned mostly preceded Genghis (a.k.a. Chinghis), and the Manchus' Qing dynasty is not included. Chapters cover: origins; the Eastern Hu and Xiongnu; the Xianbei and Wuhuan; the Qidan and their Liao dynasty; and the Mongol era and the Yuan.

171 **China under Jurchen rule: essays on Chin intellectual and cultural history.**
Edited by Hoyt Tillman, Stephen H. West. Albany, New York: State University of New York Press, 1995. 385p. bibliog. (SUNY Series in Chinese Philosophy and Culture).

This clearly presented scholarly symposium challenges the Sino-centric view that the Jurched Jin dynasty was simply a 'foreign' political conquest leading to the cultural absorption of the tribal conquerors. The editors argue that the Jin polyethnic state involved interaction as well as control, and that Jurched rule needs to be understood as part of an enduring tension between the North and the South. After a helpful introductory overview of Jin history and institutions, essays examine the following topics: public schools; innovations in Confucianism, Daoism and Buddhism (previously neglected in Jin history because of Zhu Xi's importance in the contemporary Southern Song); painting; literature; the emergence of the *zhugongdiao*, or 'all keys and modes' form of drama; and poetry.

172 **History of Chinese society: Liao (907-1125).**
Karl Wittfogel, Feng Chia-sheng. Philadelphia: American Philosophical Society/American Council of Learned Societies, 1949. 752p. bibliog. (History of Chinese Society).

The Liao dynasty was founded in 907 by Khitan (Qidan) peoples – their name spread westward as 'Khitai' and reached Europe as 'Cathay', by which China was long known. The dynasty ruled in north China before succumbing to the Mongols in 1125, but its experience and precedents persisted. This volume was the first of a planned but never consummated dynasty-by-dynasty series, the 'History of Chinese Society'. The general introduction presents stimulating theoretical perspectives. Succeeding chapters translate extensive materials for a comprehensive description and analysis of politics, society, economics and culture. Jing-shen Tao, *Two Sons of Heaven: studies in Sung-Liao relations* (Tucson, Arizona: University of Arizona Press, 1988. 173p.) examines military, political and cultural relations.

Khubilai Khan: his life and times.
See item no. 352.

Yüan thought: Chinese thought and religion under the Mongols.
See item no. 496.

China among equals: the Middle Kingdom and its neighbors 10th-14th centuries.
See item no. 798.

China and Inner Asia from 1368 to the present day.
See item no. 799.

Chinese legal tradition under the Mongols.
See item no. 870.

Chinese art under the Mongols: the Yüan dynasty (1279-1368).
See item no. 1253.

Chinese theater in the days of Kublai Khan.
See item no. 1334.

Ming dynasty (1368-1644)

173 **Praying for power: Buddhism and the formation of gentry society in late-Ming China.**
Timothy Brook. Cambridge, Massachusetts; London: Council on East Asian Studies, Harvard University, distributed by Harvard University Press, 1993. 403p. bibliog. (Harvard-Yenching Institute Monographs, no. 38).
A social portrait of three lower Yangzi counties near Ningbo. Brook argues that local gentry families patronized Buddhist monasteries and religious activities to express and promote their identity as a 'hegemonic élite'; by resisting the dominance of government authority they expanded a private sphere, which some see as a budding civil society. Earlier scholars such as Ho Ping-ti and Chang Chung-li disagreed as to whether the 'gentry' was an examination-based official élite dependent on the central government, or primarily local power holders; Brook sees an interaction in which local élites used and were used by the imperial power.

174 **The glory and fall of the Ming dynasty.**
Albert Chan. Norman, Oklahoma: University of Oklahoma Press, 1982. 428p. map. bibliog.
An overall historical account whose distinctive strength is its wealth of details and references. The first section, 'The Ming Empire in Ascendancy', devotes chapters to government, army, people, culture and religion, and economics. 'The Ming Empire in Decline' comprises chapters on the same topics, with additional chapters on the final years, which describe rebels and bandits, and the fall of Beijing in 1644. The conclusion assesses the greatness and weakness of the Ming dynasty.

175 **Confucianism and autocracy: professional élites in the founding of the Ming.**
John W. Dardess. Berkeley, California; London: University of California Press, 1982. 358p. bibliog.
Dardess first applies sociological theory by analysing Confucians in 14th-century China as professionals: they had a set course of training, ordered and generalized

knowledge, a distinct social status differing from that of laymen, and a public service ideal of world salvation. He then shows that in 1368 the first Ming emperor drew on these Confucians when he designed a centralized government to implement innovative reform. The ensuing 'theory and practice of despotism' set an enduring pattern of interaction between Confucians and emperors. On the one hand, the ruler was the architect of autocratic control; on the other, he aspired to be a teacher and promote the 'psycho-behavioral reform of mankind' through schools, moral example and economics. The ambivalent Confucian response combined conformity and dissent, again in an enduring pattern.

176   Early Ming China: a political history 1355-1435.

Edward L. Dreyer.   Stanford, California: Stanford University Press, 1982. 315p. maps. bibliog.

A broad political history. The opening chapter, 'The Early Ming in Chinese History', sympathetically explains the political problems that faced the Ming emperors in their efforts to re-constitute an ideal Chinese polity. Issues included military organization and institutions; reinvigorating the examination system and Confucian administration; and (more important in retrospect than to Ming officials) foreign trade and diplomatic relations. Chapter two, 'The Rise of the Ming Empire, 1352-1368', focuses on Zhu Yuanzhang, who became the Hungwu emperor (r. 1368-98), one of the most famous despots in Chinese history. The next five chapters analyse the reigns of the first five Ming emperors, 1368-1435. A final chapter, 'Ming History: The Roads Not Taken', downplays any sense of determinism.

177   Early Ming government: the evolution of dual capitals.

Edward L. Farmer.   Cambridge, Massachusetts: Harvard University Press, 1976. 271p. bibliog. (Harvard East Asian Monographs, no. 66).

An insightful and original examination of the bases of early Ming power. Farmer organizes his analysis around the evolving decision of Zhu Yuanzhang (Ming Taizu) to shift from the 'southern capital' (Nanjing) to the 'northern capital' (Beijing). Official arguments for this change, and a scrutiny of its results, afford an unusual historical penetration into defence and logistical thought processes and political organization.

178   The chosen one: succession and adoption in the court of Ming Shizong.

Carney T. Fischer.   Sydney: Allen & Unwin, 1990. 230p. bibliog.

Choosing a successor was a crucial issue in the imperial system; the 'ritual' governing succession was not formalistic show but the stuff of politics. Fischer's first section summarizes succession practices from the Han to the Song. The 1521 succession of the Shizong Emperor was problematic because the previous emperor died without an heir; the son of his uncle succeeded, and was required by ritual to be posthumously adopted in order to maintain the imperial family line – not an issue in non-Han dynasties but at the heart of the Confucian ritual regulation of family, society and morality for the ethnically Chinese Ming. The court debated the ritual regulations governing private family structure and dynastic legitimacy. A final section draws out the implications for understanding Chinese politics.

179 **The care-taker emperor.**
Ph. de Heer.   Leiden, the Netherlands: E. J. Brill, 1986. 226p. (Sinica Leidensia, no. 17).

A sound monograph which tells a good story. In 1449, the Mongols captured the emperor (Zhengtong) in battle; his younger brother took the throne, but when the former Emperor was returned, he was locked away, and the new emperor ruled until deposed seven years later. De Heer dramatically recounts this crisis as a way of exposing the structure and conflicts of Ming imperial rule, arguing that the emperor's main roles were as religious and moral leader, head of the ruling clan, warrior and highest political authority.

180 **1587: a year of no significance: the Ming dynasty in decline.**
Ray Huang.   New Haven, Connecticut; London: Yale University Press, 1981. 396p.

Describes the late imperial predicament in a dramatic 'snapshot' of one year, with detailed portraits of the Wanli emperor; his chief Minister Zhang Juzheng; the 'upright official' Hai Rui [Hai Jui]; the unorthodox philosopher Li Zhi; and others. Huang implies that political gridlock doomed any chances of modern transformation even before Europeans came to dominate world politics and economy. Technical but clear is Huang's *Taxation and governmental finance in sixteenth-century Ming China* (Cambridge, England: Cambridge University Press, 1974. 385p.).

181 **When China ruled the seas: the treasure fleet of the dragon throne, 1403-1433.**
Louise Levathes.   New York; London; Toronto; Sydney; Tokyo; Singapore: Simon & Schuster, 1994. 252p. bibliog.

A sprightly account of China's naval feats, traditions of geographical exploration, and relations with foreigners, aimed at the general reader but grounded in scholarly sources. Between 1405 and 1433, the Moslem court eunuch Zheng He [Cheng Ho] mounted seven voyages with fleets of as many as 100 ships, which reached the coast of Africa, preceding and dwarfing the expeditions of Columbus. Levathes first recounts Chinese legends of exotic overseas realms and enthusiastically speculates about Chinese travels to the Americas, then relates the political background for the Ming voyages. Court politics led to the expeditions, but Confucian fundamentalist opposition to eunuchs and foreign exploration eventually led to the scuttling of further excursions. The most thorough scholarly treatment is still *Ma Huan: Ying-hai Shenglan, 'The Overall Survey Of the Ocean's Shores'*, translated and edited by J. V. G. Mills (Cambridge, England; New York: Cambridge University Press, 1970 [Hakluyt Society Extra Series, no. 42]), which presents the journals of Zheng He's interpreter, with a sixty-five-page introduction and copious annotations.

182 **The Ming dynasty, 1368-1644, Part I.**
Edited by Frederick W. Mote, Denis Twitchett.   Cambridge, England; New York; Port Chester, New York; Melbourne; Sydney: Cambridge University Press, 1988. 406p. maps. bibliog. (Cambridge History of China, vol. 7).

A standard, detailed, reign-by-reign political history. The introduction provides a vigorous overview of the period, the problems of studying it, and its place in Chinese history as the only ethnically Chinese dynasty to rule all of China between the fall of the Tang dynasty and 1911. Chapters then analyse: the rise of the Ming, 1330-167; military origins; the reigns of the sixteen emperors; the Southern Ming; and historical writing during the Ming. Another volume is planned to cover social, intellectual, economic, and other matters.

183 **The peasant rebellions of the late Ming dynasty.**
James Bunyan Parsons. Tucson, Arizona: University of Arizona
Press for the Association for Asian Studies, 1970. 378p. (Association
for Asian Studies Monographs, no. 26).

Describes in detail the rebellions and local uprisings which accompanied the decline of the dynasty in the early 17th century, particularly those led by Zhang Xianzhong, who set up a government in Sichuan, and Li Zicheng, who took Beijing and the throne in 1644, bringing about the alliance between Chinese and Manchu forces which established the Qing dynasty.

184 **The Southern Ming, 1644-1662.**
Lynn A. Struve. New Haven, Connecticut: Yale University Press,
1984. 297p. bibliog.

Chronicles and analyses the loyalist remnants of the Ming court in the south, which lasted for eighteen years after the fall of Beijing in 1644. Jerry Dennerline, *The Chia-ting loyalists: Confucian leadership and social change in seventeenth century China* (New Haven, Connecticut; London: Yale University Press, 1981. 389p.) dramatizes the conflicts which local élites faced in deciding whether loyalty was owed to the deposed Ming or the regnant Qing.

185 **Disorder under heaven: collective violence in the Ming dynasty.**
James W. Tong. Stanford, California: Stanford University Press,
1991. 326p. bibliog.

In order to test statistically social science theories of collective violence in traditional societies, Tong examines more than six hundred cases of rebellion or banditry in the Ming, as recorded in local histories and government reports. He develops numerous tables, charts and graphs to correlate these actions with size of harvests, disasters, famine relief, evaluation of officials, geography, and such. He vividly describes many instances of 'predatory banditry', finding that the incidence of this increased as administrative control decayed, and was higher in the south. After reviewing contending theoretical approaches based on Marxist class analysis or Durkheimian social anomie, Tong argues that the 'rational choice' model fits the data more consistently; violence was the result of the individual calculation of need, opportunity and probable benefit.

186 **The Great Wall of China: from history to myth.**
Arthur Waldron. Cambridge, England; New York: Cambridge
University Press, 1990. 296p. maps. bibliog.

Explores the history of military walls and their cultural significance. The introduction, 'What is the Great Wall of China?', demonstrates that there was not a continuous wall existing from the Qin dynasty (nor is it the only man-made object visible from outer space!). Part one summarizes the origins and strategic value of early Chinese walls. Part two, 'The Making of the Great Wall', studies early Ming dynasty defence strategy against steppe invaders; impending failure led to frantic debate between bureaucratic and military factions. Wall building sapped dynasty finances; according to Waldron, the fall of the Ming resulted more from lifeless foreign strategy, factional bickering, and cultural defensiveness than from military weakness. Part three considers the place of the Great Wall in foreign policy and its development into a symbol of nationalism and patriotic resistance in the 20th century.

The poet Kao Ch'i (1336-1374).
See item no. 351.

The censorial system of Ming China.
See item no. 689.

Chinese government in Ming times.
See item no. 690.

Late imperial society and economy

187 **Crisis and transformation in seventeenth century China: society, culture, and modernity in Li Yü's world.**
Chang Chun-shu, Shelley Hsueh-lun Chang.   Ann Arbor, Michigan: University of Michigan Press, 1991. 452p. bibliog.

A multi-faceted study of state, society, economy and culture in the Ming-Qing dynastic transition, roughly 1630-1700. The focus is on the life and work of the versatile and enterprising scholar-writer-publisher Li Yü (1611-80). The Changs take Li as characteristic of a 17th-century China that 'accentuated progress, business, science, and technology'. Chapters cover: Li's response to sociopolitical change and the making of a professional writer; state and society in Li's plays; the individual and society in Li's fiction; and Li's world in historical perspective.

188 **Superfluous things: material culture and social status in early modern China.**
Craig Clunas.   London: Basil Blackwell; Urbana, Illinois; Chicago: University of Illinois Press, 1991. 219p.

An innovative analysis of the late Ming dynasty 'world of goods' as a discourse of material culture using a symbolic language – 'a way of sending and receiving messages about society and about an individual's place within it'. In this nascent consumer culture, members of the élite made consumption choices about clothes, furniture, books and art; these choices were more social than aesthetic. Clunas deploys and challenges theories developed for the European birth of a consumer society, which China prefigured and paralleled. Chapters explore the books, themes and terms of Ming connoisseurship literature, and then examine luxury objects as commodities (an appendix gives selected prices for works of art and antiques, 1520-1620). The final chapter examines consumption and class. The conclusion carefully speculates on the common 'invention of taste' in China and Europe; consumption in China, however, was restricted geographically and socially.

189 **Chinese local élites and patterns of dominance.**
Edited by Joseph W. Esherick, Mary Backus Rankin. Berkeley,
California: University of California Press, 1990. 469p. bibliog.
(Studies on China, no. 11).
Contains eleven scholarly essays, with an analytical introduction and concluding
remarks by the editors, from a cutting edge 1987 conference of social historians,
anthropologists and political scientists. Elites in Ming, Qing and Republican China
were far from being the uniform national gentry class sometimes assumed; they
included scholars, merchants, militarists, village leaders, landlords and clan patriarchs.
They deployed cultural symbols in addition to economic, political and military force,
producing shifting relations with the central state. Topics covered here include:
Zhejiang gentry; Sichuan salt merchants; Guizhou militarists; and Jiangsu, North
China and Guangdong local politics. James Cole, *Shaohsing: competition and
cooperation in nineteenth century China* (Tucson, Arizona: University of Arizona
Press, 1986. 315p. [Monographs of the Association for Asian Studies, no. 44]) studies
the strategies of competition and cooperation of Shaoxing, a city in Zhejiang famous
for its merchants and scholars (Lu Xun was a Shaoxing native).

190 **State and society in China: Japanese perspectives on Ming-Qing
social and economic history.**
Edited by Linda Grove, Christian Daniels. Tokyo: Tokyo University
Press; New York: Columbia University Press, 1984. 507p.
The editors bring together articles from the 1950-60s, representing dominant
approaches and insights by major Japanese scholars, many of whom take advantage of
Marxist insights. Essays include studies of handcraft industries and the 'roots of
capitalism', land tenure, popular uprisings, the social nature of the village and foreign
trade.

191 **Rural China: imperial control in the nineteenth century.**
Kung-chuan Hsiao. Seattle, Washington; London: University of
Washington Press, 1960. 783p. bibliog. (Far Eastern and Russian
Institute Publications on Asia).
A encyclopaedic monument of erudition, combing and collecting sources on the
rationale, methods and effects of the system of control over rural China as exercised
by the Qing government during the 19th century, especially at the lowest
administrative or sub-administrative level. Part one describes villages, markets and
towns, and their administrative divisions, the *baojia* and *lijia* (government-ordered
self-governing local units). Part two describes the instruments of rural control: police;
tax collection; famine relief; and ideological control. Part three, 'The Effects of
Control', describes the responses of villagers in organizing local institutions as well as
feuds and riots.

192 **The ladder of success in imperial China: aspects of social mobility,
1368-1911.**
Ho Ping-ti. New York; London: Columbia University Press, 1962.
386p. bibliog. (Studies of the East Asian Institute).
Examines the relations between the examination system, social mobility and local
élites. Ho assembles statistical material from local publications to show substantial

social mobility, and also builds portraits of families and local élites, such as the Yangzhou salt merchants. He thus disputes *The Chinese gentry: studies on their role in nineteenth-century Chinese society*, by Chang Chung-li, introduction by Franz Michael (Seattle, Washington; London: University of Washington Press, 1955. 250p.), in which Chang analyses how many candidates took the government exams, in what regions and how many passed. He also estimates the size of the gentry before and after 1850, when the government inflated the numbers of examination graduates to gain support. He divides the educated gentry into 'upper' and 'lower' strata, and then describes the 'examination life' of the gentry, that is, how they prepared for the exams, the role of corruption, and the eventual collapse of the examination system.

193 Local merchants and the Chinese bureaucracy, 1750-1950.
Susan Mann. Stanford, California: Stanford University Press, 1987. 278p.

The survival of traditional states into modern times depended on their ability to mobilize new tax revenues for welfare, defence and investment. Mann's key study examines this exploitative relation between bureaucrats and merchants – taxation without representation but not without recourse – from the apogee of Qing power to imperial decay, with an epilogue on commercial taxation in the People's Republic. The introduction examines state-building and market taxes in pre-socialist China in comparison with other agrarian empires. Succeeding chapters examine the merchants' 'liturgical' function, that is, how they as private citizens performed public duties, and the 18th-century interplay of state regulation, local markets and liturgical leadership. Two chapters then analyse the innovative 19th-century *lijin* [likin] taxes, which levied commerce at unprecedented but low rates. Two final chapters examine tax farming, tax brokerage and state-building in the late Qing and early Republic.

194 Japan, China, and the modern world economy: toward a reinterpretation of East Asian development, ca. 1600 to ca. 1800.
Frances V. Moulder. Cambridge, England; New York; Melbourne: Cambridge University Press, 1977. 255p. bibliog.

An initial use of Immanuel Wallerstein's world-systems approach; the book is not widely accepted by China specialists, but remains a clear presentation of a major theoretical perspective. Moulder's central concern is why China and Japan, faced with a presumably equal global challenge, had such different responses. The introduction first discusses how China and Japan are considered in contending theories of development and underdevelopment. Moulder puts weight not on internal factors or traditional values, but on China's higher level of incorporation into the world economy; the resulting dislocation of the state weakened its power to control the regions, mobilize their resources, and finance modern enterprises.

195 National polity and local power: the transformation of late imperial China.
Min Tu-ki, edited by Philip A. Kuhn, Timothy Brook, translated by Choe Hei-ji. Cambridge, Massachusetts: Council on East Asian Studies and Harvard-Yenching Institute, 1990. 309p. bibliog. (Harvard-Yenching Institute Monographs Series, no. 27).

These scholarly articles by an influential Korean historian discuss late Qing politics and social change. Topics include: the nature of Qing rule; the function of lower educated élites; the *ti* vs. *yong* (principle vs. utility) formula; 'feudalism' *(fengjian)* as an issue in Chinese history; provincial assemblies; and disputes between central government and local élites over railroads in Zhejiang.

196 **The fall of imperial China.**
Frederic Wakeman, Jr.   New York: Free Press; London: Collier Macmillan, 1975. 276p. bibliog. (Transformation of Modern China Series).
An analytical survey covering the years from the 17th-century rise of the Manchus to the end of the Qing mandate in 1911. Wakeman does not try to seek 'prerequisites to modernization', as do historians who see in this period the roots of capitalism, but he does 'try to isolate the inner sources of social change in China before the heyday of European imperialism' which shaped China's possibilities for modernization. The first three chapters analyse a society of peasants, gentry and merchants, while the next eight chapters deal with early and high Qing, the western invasion, rebellion, the illusion of restoration and self-strengthening, and the fall of the dynasty.

The Chinese city between two worlds.
See item no. 429.

Cities of Jiangnan in late imperial China.
See item no. 432.

Shanghai: from market town to treaty port, 1074-1858.
See item no. 433.

Hankow: commerce and society in a Chinese city, 1796-1889.
See item no. 435.

Family, field, and ancestors: constancy and change in China's social history, 1550-1949.
See item no. 601.

Popular culture in late imperial China.
See item no. 1244.

Late imperial intellectual life

197 **Man and nature in the philosophical thought of Wang Fu-chih.**
Alison H. Black.   Seattle, Washington; London: University of Washington Press, 1989. 375p.
Explores the early Qing thought of Wang Fuzhi (1619-92) in an attempt to understand Neo-Confucian conceptions of the nature of the universe, man's place in it, and how things are conceived to change – 'how far is the world that man inhabits a given, and how far is it the product of his own mind, imagination, and labors?' Black sketches the problems of cross-cultural interpretations, Wang Fuzhi's reconstruction of Song

dynasty philosophy, and the contrast between Western concepts of 'creation' versus the Chinese typical assumption of the universe as 'expressionism'. *Procès ou création: une introduction à la pensée des lettrés chinois: essai de problématique interculturelle*, by François Jullien (Paris: Éditions du Seuil, 1989. 313p.) presents the terms and concepts of Wang's essay concerning 'process' and 'creation' as a key into his thought.

198   **The rise of Confucian ritualism in late imperial China: ethics, classics, and lineage discourse.**
Wing-kai Chow.   Stanford, California: Stanford University Press, 1994. 344p. bibliog.

Surveys and re-assesses the response of scholar-élites to social and economic changes from the late Ming dynasty to the middle of the 1800s. Chow argues in a detailed examination of particular texts and scholars that they created new forms of Confucianism based on 'ritualism' and 'purism'. Confucian Classics were studied to fortify the construction of family lineages; ritualism helped to reconstitute society under gentry control. 18th-century 'evidential scholarship' used philology to clarify the classics and purify thought, reacting against Ming dynasty Daoist and Buddhist syncretism. These new forms were the basis of Confucianism as it was on the eve of the direct confrontation with the West.

199   **From philosophy to philology: intellectual and social aspects of change in late imperial China.**
Benjamin A. Elman.   Cambridge, Massachusetts; London: Council on East Asian Studies, Harvard University, distributed by Harvard University Press, 1984. 368p. (Harvard East Asian Monographs, no. 110).

A key cultural history with many ramifications. An examination of social, economic and intellectual transactions in the lower Yangzi valley in the 18th century undermines claims that China changed only in response to the West. Elman shows that there was an 'unravelling' of Ming Neo-Confucianism. Literati such as Dai Zhen, Zhang Xuecheng and many others blamed the Ming collapse on speculative Song Neo-Confucianism (*lixue*) and produced a 'revolution in discourse' as they professionalized their roles. The following re-evaluation of tradition drew on their publishing and library activities and their 'evidential research' (*kaozhengxue*) in critical philology, mathematics, epigraphy, phonology and archaeology. Elman extends this approach in *Classicism, politics, and kinship: the Ch'ang-chou school of New Text Confucianism* (Berkeley, California; London: University of California Press, 1990. 409p.).

200   **Waiting for the dawn: a plan for the prince: Huang Tsung-hsi's** *Ming-i tai-fang lu.*
Huang Tsung-hsi, translated and edited, with an introduction, by William Theodore de Bary.   New York; London: Columbia University Press, 1993. 340p. (Translations from the Asian Classics).

Early in the period of Manchu rule, Huang Zongxi (1610-95) composed what de Bary's substantial introduction calls 'the most enduring and influential critique of Chinese despotism through the ages'; later reformers drew much inspiration from it.

Huang's 'liberal Confucian vision' advocated the rule of law, schools as centres of public opinion, and reliance on literati scholar-officials (*shi*). The *Plan* consists of twenty-one essays, on such topics as the prince, ministers, law, schools, the selection of scholar-officials, the military, finance and eunuchs. Huang Tsung-hsi, translated by Julia Ching, *The records of Ming scholars* (Honolulu: University of Hawaii Press, 1987. 376p.) presents a substantial selection from Huang's *Mingru xuean*, a biographical history of Ming Confucianism.

201 **Orthodoxy in late imperial China.**
Edited by Kwang-ching Liu. Berkeley, California; London: University of California Press, 1990. 364p. bibliog. (Studies on China, no. 10).

A wide-ranging and ground-breaking scholarly symposium. The introduction argues that disproportionate attention has been paid to minority impulses of rebellion and reform, neglecting the dominant orthodoxies; moreover, this dominant 'socioethics' encompassed the spiritual and religious, and extended to cosmology, ritual and symbolic representation which united political élites and popular masses. Essays explore these core beliefs in ruler, family, hierarchy, legal and ritual codes, judicial practice, education and individual thinkers.

202 **The life and thought of Chang Hsueh-ch'eng, 1738-1801.**
David Nivison. Stanford, California: Stanford University Press, 1966. 336p. bibliog.

An intellectual biography of Zhang Xuecheng, best known for his ideas on the writing of history based on detailed research rather than moral deduction; Zhang saw himself as an independent, almost professional, intellectual. *Tai Chen's 'Inquiry into goodness': a translation of the 'Yuan shan', with an introductory essay*, translated by Chung-ying Cheng (Honolulu: East-West Center Press, 1971. 176p.) loosely translates an important treatise by Dai Zhen (1723-77), another key figure in the breakaway from abstract philosophy to evidential studies; Dai is carefully investigated in Elman's *From philosophy to philology* (q.v.).

203 **Bitter gourd: Fang Yi-chih and the impetus for intellectual change.**
Willard Peterson. New Haven, Connecticut; London: Yale University Press, 1979. 228p.

A rich intellectual biography of Fang Yizhi (1611-71), one of a constellation of literati who spanned the Ming-Qing dynastic transition. Other thinkers who reworked Confucian thought in this period are also well studied: Joanna Handlin, *Action in late Ming thought: the reorientation of Lü K'un and other scholar officials* (Berkeley, California; Los Angeles; London: University of California Press, 1983. 256p.), on Lu Kun (1536-1618), who wrote educational works for women and illiterates; Edward T. Ch'ien, *Chiao Hung and the restructuring of Neo-Confucianism in the late Ming* (New York; London: Columbia University Press, 1986. 367p.), on Jiao Hong (1540?-1620) and his reshuffling of Buddhism and Daoism; and Willard J. Peterson, 'The Life of Ku Yen-wu (1613-1682)' (*Harvard Journal of Asiatic Studies*, no. 28-29 [1968-69], p. 114-56, p. 201-47), on Gu Yanwu, a Ming loyalist who developed critical history, geography and philology; he criticized the centralized imperial administration (*zhunxian*) and favoured regional local government (*fengjian*).

Early and high Qing dynasty (1664-1796)

204 **Monarchs and ministers: the Grand Council in mid-Ch'ing China, 1723-1820.**
Beatrice S. Bartlett. Berkeley, California: University of California Press, 1990. 417p. bibliog.

Questions the common view of Chinese government as an absolute monarchy in which the emperor dominated the bureaucracy and the country by charisma and fear. Bartlett studies the flow of documents in specific cases to describe the mid-dynasty transformation of the Grand Council, a key bureaucratic institution and battleground between the emperor and his ministers. Her study suggests that high ministers allowed the emperor the appearance and illusion of control, but actually ran affairs most of the time – ministerial administration rather than imperial autocracy.

205 **The emperor's four treasuries: scholars and the state in the late Ch'ien-lung era.**
R. Kent Guy. Cambridge, Massachusetts: Council on East Asian Studies, Harvard University, distributed by Harvard University Press, 1987. 289p. bibliog. (East Asian Monographs, no. 129).

A fresh and detailed view of the 'literary inquisitions' of the Qianlong Emperor, long viewed as simply mad despotism. The Emperor set out in the 1770s to edify and distract literati by hiring them to edit a vast encyclopaedia; the enterprise expanded to encompass editing and publishing all major Chinese works in the *Siku quanshu* (Complete library of the four treasuries). Assembling writings from private households for this project developed into an inquisition, which indeed turned paranoid. The inquisition terrorized thousands of scholars and ended up suppressing writings deemed seditious, military or frontier works, works honouring the Ming or criticizing previous foreign rule, or, in the end, even those which contained characters for the names of emperors.

206 **Soulstealers: the Chinese sorcery scare of 1768.**
Philip A. Kuhn. Cambridge, Massachusetts; London: Harvard University Press, 1990. 299p. bibliog.

'In the year 1768, on the eve of China's tragic modern age, there ran through her society a premonitory shiver: a vision of sorcerers roaming the land, stealing souls'. So begins Kuhn's story into which he weaves a picture of an economic gilded age and an analysis of the politics of an impacted society, in which common people have only 'fantasies of power', the autocrat cannot understand society or control bureaucracy, and bureaucracy can only dither and obstruct. Malicious accusation was a chance for power in a society where ordinary people had little. The Qianlong Emperor feared anti-Manchu sedition and ordered an inquisition. The persecution of scapegoats represented the 'moral nemesis' of a zero-sum society impacted by overpopulation, a worsening ratio of resources per capita, and declining social mobility. Transformation was eventually to be sought outside the imperial system, in rebellion and revolution.

207 **Pirates of the South China Coast, 1790-1810.**
Dian H. Murray. Stanford, California: Stanford University Press, 1987. 243p. bibliog.

China's military decline and administrative degeneracy were shown even before the Opium War by an inability to deal with the 'water world' off the coast of Guangdong. The court was preoccupied with internal problems, such as the White Lotus Rebellion and sectarian uprisings; imperial officials were therefore unprepared to deal with the new situation created when the successful 1790s Tay-son rebellion in Vietnam recruited Cantonese pirates to its navy. The resulting naval force developed a culture which resembled pirate cultures elsewhere, including male homosexuality and women leaders. The Qing did not defeat these rebels, but rather bought off their leaders with a policy of 'pardon and pacification'.

208 **Chinese society in the eighteenth century.**
Susan Naquin, Evelyn S. Rawski. New Haven, Connecticut; London: Yale University Press, 1987. 270p. bibliog.

A balanced overview aimed at upper level undergraduates or scholars working in other fields, written as a chapter for an as yet unpublished volume of the *Cambridge history of China*. The first part presents government policies, social relations and cultural life. The second part looks at diversity among ten 'regional societies' and long-term changes in the economy and society. The authors emphasize that the 18th century was both self-contained and also the introduction to later problems of overpopulation, monetary deflation, economic deterioration, administrative decline and rural discontent.

209 **Voices from the Ming-Qing cataclysm: China in tiger's jaws.**
Edited, translated by Lynn A. Struve. New Haven, Connecticut; London: Yale University Press, 1993. 303p. bibliog.

The Manchu invasion of China in the 1640s was not only a military encounter but also a cultural crisis which challenged the Confucian way of life. Struve presents and annotates agonized eye-witness accounts of Ming loyalists and Qing collaborators, European missionaries, artists, merchants, maidservants and eunuchs to present a vivid and personal history of this epochal transition. Included is the *Yangzhou shiri ji* (Account of ten days in Yangzhou), whose graphic description of Manchu atrocities became a revolutionary pamphlet in the late Qing period.

210 **The great enterprise: the Manchu reconstruction of imperial order in seventeenth century China.**
Frederic Wakeman, Jr. Berkeley, California; London: University of California Press, 1985. 2 vols. maps.

The fall of the Ming and the quick accession of the Qing in 1644 was the 'most dramatic succession in all of Chinese history'. Wakeman recounts the personalities and events involved on an epic scale, but also analyses the more long-term processes: 17th-century commerce, which tied China to the New World through vast and wavering flows of silver; the social disintegration of the Ming order, partly caused by fiscal problems, partly by administrative decay; and the political consolidation of Manchu rule, which began generations before 1644 and took until the 1680s to complete. Both turncoat Han Chinese and ambitious Manchus had to compromise; they built a '*Pax Manchurica*' which was politically more successful and effective than Ming rule, but which remained morally uneasy about collaboration.

211 **Bureaucracy and famine in eighteenth century China.**
Pierre-Étienne Will, translated by Elborg Forster.   Stanford,
California: Stanford University Press, 1990. 364p.

A richly documented account of effective bureaucratic response to 1740s drought and famine in North China, with wide-ranging insights into the nature of government-society interactions. Will contrasts this success with 19th-century famine relief, which was based on coordinating the effects of the private gentry. This work was revised from *Bureaucratie et famine en Chine au dix-huitième siècle* (Paris; New York: Mouton, École des Hautes Études, 1980).

212 **The magistrate's tael: rationalizing fiscal reform in eighteenth century Ch'ing China.**
Madeleine Zelin.   Berkeley, California; London: University of
California Press, 1984. 385p. maps. bibliog.

Puts forward the revisionist argument that the early Qing dynasty, especially under the Yongzheng emperor (r. 1723-35), creatively worked to develop rational and efficient bureaucratic rule, but that this momentum was lost later in the century. Zelin focuses on 1720s efforts to create an efficient, fair and responsive tax base for legitimate provincial needs; various regions are shown to have had different fiscal natures and varying success. Canny local bureaucratic resistance doomed reform efforts, leaving the dynasty to face later challenges with ramshackle finances.

Emperor of China: self-portrait of K'ang-hsi.
See item no. 355.

Local government in China under the Ch'ing.
See item no. 686.

To achieve wealth and security: the Qing imperial state and the economy, 1644-1911.
See item no. 894.

Nourish the people: the state civilian granary system in China, 1650-1850.
See item no. 896.

The elegant brush: Chinese painting under the Qianlong Emperor, 1735-1795.
See item no. 1271.

Invasion, imperialism and rebellion (1796-1911)

213 **China and Christianity: the missionary movement and the growth of Chinese anti-foreignism, 1860-1870.**
Paul A. Cohen.   Cambridge, Massachusetts: Harvard University Press, 1963. 392p. (Harvard East Asian Series, no. 11).

A provocative study of Protestant and Catholic missionaries in China following the Opium Wars, which discusses their expansive activities, local gentry resistance, and the futile efforts of Qing diplomats to mediate between imperialism and anti-foreignism. Part one traces the anti-Christian tradition back to the late Ming and early Qing periods. Part two analyses the following topics: China, Christianity and the international pressure brought by France and Britain in the 1860s; gentry and official opposition to Christianity, which became synonymous with anti-foreignism; missionary abuses of power; the 1870 Tientsin Massacre, which ended an era of compromise; and the hardening of a xenophobia which became a strand in 20th-century nationalism. Cohen puts these issues into an even broader perspective, with many references, in 'Christian missions and their impact to 1900', in *Late Ch'ing China*, part I, p. 543-91 (q.v.).

214 **The origins of the Boxer uprising.**
Joseph W. Esherick.   Berkeley, California; London: University of California Press, 1987. 451p. bibliog.

A key study of the anti-foreign, anti-Christian movement which in 1900 killed thousands of Chinese Christians and some missionaries, then besieged the foreign legations in Beijing. Esherick blends sociology, anthropology and history to argue that in the late 19th century North China villagers organized mass nationalist resistance in response to imperialist bullying (and native Christians), imported goods and gods, missionary arrogance, state fiscal crisis and natural disasters. Their 'uprising' (not 'rebellion', since the Qing court initially supported it) did not spring, as was earlier thought, from the remnants of the White Lotus Society (a secret society responsible for a rebellion at the turn of the 19th century) though activists did use the vocabulary of spirit possession, village drama, invulnerability rituals and martial arts. *Recent Chinese studies of the Boxer movement*, edited by David Buck (Armonk, New York; London: M. E. Sharpe, 1987. 223p.) brings together nine 1980 conference papers; the analytic introduction professes doubt that the Boxers were proto-nationalists. For coverage of the missionary experience, see Nat Brandt, *Massacre in Shansi* (Syracuse, New York: Syracuse University Press, 1994. 336p.) and Eva Jane Price, *China journal 1889-1900: an American missionary family during the Boxer Rebellion* (New York: Scribners, 1989. 289p.).

215 **The opium war, 1840-1842: barbarians in the Celestial Empire in the early part of the nineteenth century and the way by which they forced the gates ajar.**
Peter Ward Fay.   Chapel Hill, North Carolina: University of North Carolina Press, 1975. 406p. bibliog.

An attractively written narrative history of the wars and diplomacy which forced the Qing dynasty to accept Western trade and diplomacy. Fay treats the opium trade in

India, activities of missionaries, the Canton crisis, the conduct of the war, and treaty settlements. *Commissioner Lin and the Opium War* by Hsin-pao Chang (Cambridge, Massachusetts: Harvard University Press, 1964. 319p.) describes the career of Lin Zexu (1785-1850), who was responsible for the suppression of the opium trade in Canton, the rise of the opium trade as a problem for the court, and Lin's diplomacy. Chang blames Lin's failure on a general lack of understanding of the new global challenge. For a different explanation, see *The inner opium war* by Polachek (q.v.). Frederic Wakeman, Jr., *Strangers at the gate: social disorder in South China, 1839-1861* (Berkeley, California; Oxford: University of California Press, 1966. 276p) assesses the effects on Guangdong society and how local anti-foreignism made new demands on the central government. Arthur Waley, *The Opium War through Chinese eyes* (London: Allen & Unwin, 1958. Reprinted, Stanford, California: Stanford University Press, 1968. 258p.) translates Commissioner Lin's writings and diaries, including an ode of apology to the Gods of the Sea for polluting their kingdom with confiscated opium.

216   **The commercial revolution in nineteenth century China: the rise of Sino-Western mercantile capitalism.**
Yen-p'ing Hao.   Berkeley, California: University of California Press, 1986. 394p. bibliog.

Traces the evolution of commerce from the Canton system and the opium trade of the 1830s to the 1880s, dealing with changes in money supply, forms and use of credit, agricultural commercialization, transport, and the formation of new types of entrepreneurship. Hao argues that the 19th-century commercial revolution allowed China to develop economically by appropriating and adapting foreign practices; he rejects arguments from the 'dependency' and 'world economy' schools of thought that foreign trade was equivalent to imperialism which could only injure China. By seeing this period as revolutionary, he also downplays earlier commercial development in China, a feeling not shared by scholars working in earlier periods.

217   **The Taiping revolutionary movement.**
Jen Yu-wen, with the editorial assistance of Adrienne Suddard.   New Haven, Connecticut; London: Yale University Press, 1973. 616p. bibliog.

The fullest narrative in English of the Taiping Rebellion or *Taiping Tianguo* (Heavenly Kingdom of Great Peace), in which self-professed converts to Christianity formed effective armies and egalitarian social organizations to almost overthrow the dynasty in the 1850s. The author emphasizes their revolutionary aspirations and accomplishments. Mr Jen (a.k.a. Chien Yu-wen or Jian Youwen) was trained in China, Oberlin College, University of Chicago, and Union Theological Seminary, but spent the early part of his active life in Chinese politics and the army; he retraced many of the Taiping army campaigns, and published voluminous writings in Chinese, drawing on both research and personal investigation. This book summarizes those writings and presents many detailed human judgements.

218 **Rebellion and its enemies in late imperial China: militarization and social structure, 1796-1864.**
Philip A. Kuhn.   Cambridge, Massachusetts: Harvard University
Press, 1980. 254p. paperback, with new preface. bibliog. (Harvard East
Asian Series, no. 49).

A key study of social organization over three generations of rebellion. The book begins with a consideration of the traditional 'a-military' culture of Confucian élites, then goes on to consider whether 'modern' history began when militarized local leadership changed the nature of their mediation between the Manchu state and society. Chapters discuss: Qing policy towards local militia from the 1796 White Lotus Rebellion to the Taiping rebellion; the structure of local militarization and the evolving relationship with state bureaucracy; the militarization of the orthodox élite as motives changed from local control to imperial defence; and the socio-strategic problems posed by the Taiping rebellion and the breakdown of the traditional state. Together with articles in *Late Ch'ing China*, part I (q.v.), this work forms a sophisticated analysis of 19th-century rebellions.

219 **The Taiping rebellion: history and documents.**
Franz Michael.   Seattle, Washington; London: University of
Washington Press, 1965-71. 3 vols. (Far Eastern and Russian Institute
Publications on Asia, no. 14).

Volume one provides a brief narrative of the rebellion (1850-64) and its suppression. Volumes two and three translate and annotate all surviving Taiping documents. Rudolph Wagner, *Reenacting the heavenly vision: the role of religion in the Taiping Rebellion* (Berkeley, California: University of California Press, 1982. 134p. [China Research Monographs, no. 25]) uses fresh insights from comparative religion to review the teachings of the Taipings. A classic foreign view based on eye-witness evidence is Thomas Taylor Meadows, *The Chinese and their rebellions* (London: 1856. Reprinted, Stanford, California: Academic Reprints, 1953; Shannon, Ireland: Irish University Press; New York: Barnes & Noble, 1972. 656p. maps).

220 **Millenarian rebellion in China: the Eight Trigrams uprising of 1813.**
Susan Naquin.   New Haven, Connecticut; London: Yale University
Press, 1976. 384p. bibliog.

Describes a botched 1813 rebellion which led to the arrest of leaders who had planned to lead 100,000 rebels to take over the Forbidden City and depose the dynasty: more than 20,000 members of the Eight Trigrams sect were killed during the subsequent suppression. Using over 400 of their depositions, preserved in recently opened government archives, Naquin vividly recreates the social and religious world and daily lives of these sectarian rebels. Part one traces the sectarian organization and its popular Buddhist ideology which went back to at least the Yuan dynasty and which used Eight Trigram terminology drawn from the *Ijing* (Book of changes). Parts two and three depict the consolidation and mobilization periods, when White Lotus leaders, believing the millennium to be near, turned inherited ideology into rebel uprisings; however an initially bumbling government response eventually overwhelmed the rebels. Appendices include details of sample confessions, donations to the Eight Trigram sects, and the cost of living in the 1810s.

221 **'Secret societies' reconsidered: perspectives on the social history of modern South China and Southeast Asia.**
Edited by David Ownby, Mary Somers Heidhues. Armonk, New York; London: M. E. Sharpe, 1993. 259p. bibliog.

Six essays explore 18th- and 19th-century sworn brotherhoods, societies and associations whose rituals and political agendas facilitated local cooperation and protected members against a jealous state. They were called 'secret' not because they were necessarily clandestine or rebellious but because they were private, that is, not government sponsored or approved. The substantial introduction assesses and lists earlier Chinese and Western writings and the theoretical literature; the work of Jean Chesneaux, a French scholar of the 1960s and 1970s, is praised as pioneering but criticized for romanticizing local groups as forerunners of popular revolution. One of the societies is analysed in Dian H. Murray, in collaboration with Qin Baoqi, *The origins of the Tiandihui (Heaven and Earth Society): the Chinese Triads in legend and history* (Stanford, California: Stanford University Press, 1993. 351p.).

222 **Rebels and revolutionaries in North China, 1845-1945.**
Elizabeth J. Perry. Stanford, California: Stanford University Press, 1980. 324p. bibliog.

A sophisticated social science analysis. Perry originally set out to supplement social science explanations of the Chinese revolution (peasant nationalism, land reform, Communist organizational strategy). She examined a case-study region, Huaibei, where the Nian Rebels of the mid-19th century and the Red Spears of the early 20th century had created a tradition of rebellion. Perry found that in fact modern revolutionaries had difficulty mobilizing these groups, who theoretically should have welcomed them; 'rebels' in the 19th century had not set out to overthrow the government but grew out of the ecological need to form village self-defence organizations, promoted and led by rural élites. Earlier interpretations include *Popular movements and secret societies in China, 1840-1950,* a symposium edited by Jean Chesneaux (Stanford, California: Stanford University Press, 1972. 328p.), and *Peasant revolts in China 1840-1949* by Jean Chesneaux, translated by Charles Curwen (London: Thames & Hudson; New York: W. W. Norton, 1973. 180p. maps), which interpret rebels as revolutionary material waiting only for Chinese Communist Party organization.

223 **The inner opium war.**
James M. Polachek. Cambridge, Massachusetts: Council on East Asian Studies, Harvard University, 1992. 400p. bibliog. (East Asian Monograph, no. 151).

An important revisionist study of the men, cliques and political debates in the 1840s and 1850s (the Opium War itself is not a central subject). Polachek finds that the Confucian statecraft (*jingshi*) tradition was creative and resilient; however, the political system so valued consensus and was so buffeted by continual crisis that innovation was difficult for structural, rather than cultural reasons. Three opening chapters analyse early 19th-century political and literary factions, which often expressed their views and affected opinion through poetry; four chapters then trace political manoeuvring during the period 1835-50. Commissioner Lin Zexu's actions at Canton (forcefully repossessing great quantities of European-owned opium and destroying it) are seen as motivated more by domestic political concerns than by foreign policy analysis; his faction used war issues to promote itself, and propagated a myth of 'victory' over the British at Canton which misled later generations.

Foreign investment and economic development in China, 1840-1937.
See item no. 892.

The dragon and the iron horse: the economics of railroads in China, 1876-1937.
See item no. 893.

Late Qing dynasty (1860-1911)

224 **Li Hung-chang and China's early modernization.**
Edited by Samuel C. Chu, Kwang-ching Liu. Armonk, New York; London: M. E. Sharpe, 1994. 308p. bibliog.
Li Hongzhang (1823-1901) was a central political figure of his time, long blamed for a presumed late Qing failure to modernize; these thirteen scrupulous essays, some previously published in English or Chinese, afford a more rounded judgement. The introduction and conclusion summarize the book's findings, and describe historical sources and earlier studies. Sections include: 'The Rise of Li Hung-chang'; 'Li in the Role of National Official'; 'Li as a Diplomat', which analyses relations with Japan, Korea and the Liuqiu (Ryukyu) islands; and 'Li as a Modernizer', on Li's difficult pioneering experience with the Jiangnan (Kiangnan) Arsenal, the China Merchants Steam Navigation Company, and the Beiyang (Peiyang) Navy. Some articles appeared in *Chinese Studies in History*, vol. 24, no. 1-2 (Fall-Winter 1990-91), vol. 24, no. 4 (Summer 1991), and vol. 25, no. 1 (Fall 1991).

225 **Reform in nineteenth century China.**
Edited by Paul Cohen, John Schrecker. Cambridge, Massachusetts: East Asian Research Center, Harvard University Press, 1976. 396p. bibliogs. (East Asian Monographs, no. 72).
Brings together thirty-one papers and discussions from a workshop at which scholars from North America, China, Japan and Korea exchanged ideas and developed hypotheses on late Qing reform movements and ideas; they generally show how reform developed from indigenous traditions, rather than from inspiration from the West. Topics discussed fall into nine major areas: political reforms in Chinese history; economic aspects; social contexts; intellectual contexts; local and provincial reforms; women; sovereignty and self-strengthening; new coastal and treaty port reformers; and the reform movement of 1898.

226 **Orphan warriors: three Manchu generations and the end of the Qing world.**
Pamela Kyle Crossley.   Princeton, New Jersey: Princeton University Press, 1990. 305p. bibliog.

Accounts of the Manchu dynasty have tended to slight the Manchus, as historians accepted the myth that China absorbs all conquerors. Crossley first demonstrates how Manchu ethnic identity was consciously constructed by early Qing emperors, and then absorbingly chronicles its decline through the lives of a Manchu clan during the period 1840s-1920s. The grandfather, Guancheng, was a publisher, local magistrate and soldier who lived through the devastation of the Opium Wars. His son, Fengrui, saw the family fortunes tumble as the Taipings attacked Manchu 'devils' and ravaged the ancestral estate; he rebuilt the family printing business but retreated psychologically into literary fantasy. His son, Jinliang, joined the Manchu reformists of the 1860s, survived anti-Qing nationalism, served the warlord Zhang Zuolin after 1911, and tried to restore the deposed Emperor Puyi.

227 **Late Ch'ing China, 1800-1911, Part 1.**
Edited by John K. Fairbank.   Cambridge, England; London; New York; Melbourne: Cambridge University Press, 1978. 713p. maps. bibliog. (Cambridge History of China, vol. 10).

Provides comprehensive surveys of politics and foreign relations. The introduction sketches the 'Old Order' (society, government, foreign relations). Substantial chapters then treat: Qing Inner Asia in 1800; dynastic decline and the roots of rebellion; Canton trade and the Opium War; the treaty system and treaty ports; the Taiping rebellion; Sino-Russian relations, 1800-62; the Qing order in Mongolia, Xinjiang and Tibet; the 1860-72 Qing (Tongzhi) restoration; the Self-Strengthening Movement (1861-95) and the pursuit of Western technology; and Christian missions and their impact. As in the following volume, the extensive bibliography comments on and lists sources and secondary works in many languages.

228 **Late Ch'ing 1800-1911, Part 2.**
Edited by John K. Fairbank, Kwang-ching Liu.   Cambridge, England; London; New York; Melbourne: Cambridge University Press, 1980. 734p. maps. bibliog. (Cambridge History of China, vol. 11).

Continues the preceding volume. Chapters are devoted to: economic trends, 1870-1911; foreign relations, 1866-1905 (acceleration of imperialism, the Japanese expansion into Korea, the Boxer Uprising, the 1905 Russo-Japanese War); changing Chinese views of Western relations, 1840-95; the military challenge (post-Taiping armies, the Muslim revolts, the 1885 Sino-French War, and the Sino-Japanese War); intellectual change and the reform movement, 1890-98 (western impact, Kang Youwei [a radical reformer], the débâcle of the 1898 One Hundred Days Reforms); Japan and the Revolution of 1911; late Qing political and institutional reforms, 1901-11; government, merchants and industry; the republican revolutionary movement (revolutionary parties of Sun Yat-sen and Liang Qichao, the fall of the Qing 1908-12, the birth of the Republic); and currents of social change (the privileged classes, the common people, the growth of a sub-proletariat).

229 **A mosaic of the hundred days: personalities, politics, and ideas of 1898.**
Luke S. K. Kwong.   Cambridge, Massachusetts; London: Council on East Asian Studies, Harvard University, distributed by Harvard University Press, 1984. 356p. bibliog. (Harvard East Asian Monographs, no. 112).

A revisionist study which maintains that the retrospective accounts of Kang Youwei and Liang Qichao overemphasized their roles in the One Hundred Days Reform, an ill-fated movement which sought to persuade the emperor to adopt a constitutional form of monarchy and establish a parliament. Kwong finds: that Liang and Kang were not intimates of the Guangxu Emperor and did not dominate the reform 'movement'; that reforms were limited and futile; and that later reform ideas should not be read back into this period. Chapter one and an epilogue assay the historiographic problems. Chapters sketch the crisis of the dynasty, the role of the Empress Dowager, the hapless Emperor, and the rise of Kang Youwei. Chapters then reconstruct the ideological rivalries and political manoeuvring of the summer of 1898 and the outcomes of the attempted coup.

230 **Shen Pao-chen and China's modernization in the nineteenth century.**
David Pong.   Cambridge, England; New York; Port Chester, New York; Melbourne; Sydney: Cambridge University Press, 1994. 395p. bibliog.

Shen Baozhen (1820-79) was one of the galaxy of able officials who renovated the old order with a strategy of 'self-strengthening' after the mid-century rebellions. Mary Wright's *Last stand of Chinese conservatism* (q.v.) surmises that these efforts failed because Confucian cultural and political stability was incompatible with modernization. However, Pong is among those scholars who respectfully disagree, and his introduction cogently rehearses the issues and earlier scholarship. Shen rose during the Taiping rebellion, became governor of Jiangxi, but resigned to run the Fuzhou (Foochow) Navy Yard from 1866 to 1875. Frustration of the reform programme was not due to cultural rejection or lack of potential for change; Shen as a Confucian embraced science and technology, and China has recently actualized potential for transformation. Rather, reforms were frustrated by the Court's withdrawal of support for local reform, and by its inability to mobilize itself fiscally for modern investment.

231 **China, 1898-1912: the Xinzheng revolution and Japan.**
Douglas R. Reynolds.   Cambridge, Massachusetts: Council on East Asian Studies, Harvard University, distributed by Harvard University Press, 1993. 308p. bibliog. (Harvard East Asian Monographs, no. 160).

Argues that the years before 1911 were, contrary to the histories sympathetic to frustrated radical reformers, a 'Golden Decade'. The government produced rapid and effective political and economic programmes by emulating and adapting those carried out earlier in Japan. Reynolds calls these *Xinzheng* (new systems) reforms a 'revolution' more important than that of 1911. Topics covered include: the 'intellectual revolution' created by Chinese students studying in Japan, who ranged from future warlords to Lu Xun; Japanese teachers, advisers and Buddhist missionaries in China, who had deep influence because Chinese local leaders welcomed their ideas; the creation of modern Chinese terminology by taking terms from Japanese to use in textbooks, new magazines and encyclopaedias; educational reform and military modernization; new police and prison systems; and legal, judicial and constitutional reforms.

232 **Mercenaries and mandarins: the Ever-Victorious Army in nineteenth century China.**
Richard J. Smith.   Millwood, New York: KTO Press, 1978. 271p.
(KTO Studies in American History).

Supporters of the Qing dynasty hired the American military adventurer, F. T. Ward, to raise and lead foreign soldiers against the Taiping rebels of the 1850s; their initial victories earned them the imperial title 'Ever-Victorious Army'. Smith gives a balanced assessment of the real but scarcely decisive contributions of Ward, of Charles ('Chinese') Gordon, who took over after Ward was killed in 1862, and of the impact of the Western armaments they used. Steven Leibo, *Transferring technology to China: Prosper Giquel and the Self-strengthening movement* (Berkeley, California: Center for Chinese Studies, Institute of East Asian Studies, 1985. 175p. [China Research Monographs, no. 28]) shows further Manchu use of foreigners. *The devil soldier: the story of Frederick Townsend Ward*, by Caleb Carr (New York: Random House, 1991. 366p. maps. bibliog.) is a romanticized account of this Yankee filibuster.

233 **The last stand of Chinese conservatism: the T'ung-chih restoration, 1862-1874.**
Mary C. Wright.   Stanford, California: Stanford University Press, 1957. 1962, 2nd printing with additional notes. 429p. bibliog.

A basic pioneer study. After the near success of the Taiping rebellion, the 1861 accession of the Tongzhi ('Union for Order') Emperor was the occasion for a Restoration, a successful Sino-Manchu renewal of Confucian rule. Based on a mastery of published official documents, Wright describes the military and social suppression of rebellion, the rehabilitation of the economy, the Self-Strengthening Movement, and the modernization of foreign relations. Her conclusion, now debated, is that the eventual 'dismal failure' of the Restoration was not the result of Manchu stupidity, imperialist aggression, historical accident, or the rule of foreign Manchus; rather, 'requirements of modernization' ran counter to 'the constituent elements of the Confucian system itself'. A brief last chapter views the Nationalist traditionalism of the 1930s as a 'distorted echo' of the 1860s.

The arms of Kiangnan: modernization in the Chinese ordinance industry, 1860-1895.
See annotation to item no. 853.

China's struggle for naval development, 1839-1895.
See item no. 853.

Intellectual transition (1890-1949)

234 Wang Kuo-wei: an intellectual biography.

Joey Bonner. Cambridge, Massachusetts: Harvard University Press, 1986. 314p. bibliog.

Wang Guowei (1877-1927) was considered by his contemporaries to be China's greatest modern scholar of the classics; the foundation for later scholarship was his skeptical and creative editing of classical texts and organization of oracle bone texts newly discovered at Anyang. Bonner's study of his life and thought shows that Wang learned much in the years 1898-1907 from Japan's initial appropriation of Western scholarship, especially that of Naitō Kōnan, and that he saw the role of the scholar-intellectual as central in revitalizing China. His suicide in 1927 was a *cause célèbre*.

235 Liang Ch'i-ch'ao and intellectual transition in China, 1890-1907.

Hao Chang. Cambridge, Massachusetts: Harvard University Press, 1971. 342p. bibliog. (Harvard East Asian Series, no. 61).

Liang Qichao (1873-1929) was an important influence in the appropriation of Western learning into Chinese thought; as a political activist, journalist and teacher-philosopher he left a lasting imprint (not least on Mao Zedong). Chang first sketches the intellectual setting and the influence of Kang Youwei, then shows that Liang's 'metamorphoses of the mind' grew out of impulses formed in Qing thought before the coming of the West. Chang substantially revises Joseph R. Levenson, *Liang Ch'i-ch'ao and the mind of modern China* (Cambridge, Massachusetts: Harvard University Press, 1953. rev. ed., 1959. 256p.), which saw Liang as emotionally torn between tradition and modernity, *ti* and *yong*. Philip C. Huang, *Liang Ch'i-ch'ao and modern Chinese liberalism* (Seattle, Washington; London: University of Washington Press, 1972. 231p.) is especially good on Liang's political activities and Japanese borrowings, and includes a useful 'comment on the literature'. Hao Chang, *Chinese intellectuals in crisis: search for meaning and order (1890-1911)* (Berkeley, California; London: University of California Press, 1987. 223p.) discusses Kang Youwei (1858-1927), Tan Sitong (1864-98), Zhang Binglin (1869-1936); and Liu Shipei (1884-1919).

236 The May Fourth Movement: intellectual revolution in modern China.

Chow Tse-tsung. Cambridge, Massachusetts: Harvard University Press, 1960. 486p. (Harvard East Asian Studies, no. 6).

A basic study of the New Culture Movement, 1915-23, during which young intellectuals rejected the Confucian tradition and promoted ideas of science and democracy. Chow first sketches the economic, political and social background. Part one then chronicles the forces that precipitated the movement; literacy and intellectual activities; the May Fourth 1919 student demonstrations in Beijing against Japanese imperialism; the ensuing national support from merchants, industrialists and workers; intellectual controversies over democracy, capitalism, socialism and westernization; and the split between radical political activism and cultural liberalism. Part two, 'Analysis of Main Intellectual Currents', describes the Literary Revolution and New Thought movements, which promoted vernacular writing and cosmopolitan philosophies, then considers interpretations and evaluations. Lin Yusheng, foreword by Benjamin I. Schwartz, *The crisis of Chinese consciousness: radical antitraditionalism in the May Fourth era* (Madison, Wisconsin: University of Wisconsin Press, 1979. 201p. bibliog.) is a philosophical study of the 'cultural iconoclasm' of Hu Shi, Chen Duxiu, Lu Xun and other New Culture thinkers.

237 **Between tradition and modernity: Wang T'ao and reform in late Ch'ing China.**
Paul A. Cohen. Cambridge, Massachusetts: Harvard University Press, 1974. 357p. bibliog. (Harvard East Asian Series, no. 77).

Relates the life and times of one of the first Chinese to achieve a full Western education and develop a career in treaty port China as one of the first professional journalists. Wang Tao (1828-97) helped James Legge translate the Confucian classics, was a pioneering newspaper entrepreneur and developed a reform programme for China which blazed a path for later thinkers. Cohen's final section develops an influential dichotomy between 'littoral' – coastal and treaty port – China and 'inland' China; he shows how a growing cultural gap between the two areas affected twelve representative thinkers and politicians.

238 **Anarchism in the Chinese revolution.**
Arif Dirlik. Berkeley, California: University of California Press, 1991. 326p. bibliog.

Argues persuasively that Chinese social radicalism was not invented in the New Culture period (1915-23) nor by Marxists, as historians supposed and Maoists insisted, but in the earlier years of the century by Chinese who adapted the anarchism of Kropotkin, Bakunin, Proudhon and Tolstoy. In the early years of the century anarchism defeated socialism in the contest for the allegiance of young intellectuals, and introduced many concepts of radical culture into the revolutionary discourse. In the 1920s, anarchism lost out organizationally to the Nationalist Party and the emerging Communists who mobilized the appeal of nationalism.

239 **The discourse of race in modern China.**
Frank Dikötter. London: C. Hurst; Stanford University Press, 1992. 251p. bibliog.

An examination of the change from traditional to modern ideas of race. Whereas earlier scholars maintained that traditional China had a concept of cultural virtue, not racism, Dikötter finds that ideas of physical superiority over surrounding peoples did exist. From the Tang dynasty, when Africans were brought to China, some associated 'coal-black' skin with slavery. Chinese racism defended psychologically against Buddhism, Central Asians, and Europeans (at first disdained for their half-baked, 'ash-white' skins). In the late 19th and early 20th century, Chinese thinkers, including Kang Youwei and Liang Qichao, adapted European 'scientific' racism and social Darwinism; some advocated the absorption of the yellow and black races into the white. In the Republican period, racial discourse in textbooks, periodicals and popular writings advocated the new 'science' of eugenics; eventually the discourse shifted to 'nation', leaving 'race' behind.

240 **Hu Shih and the Chinese renaissance: liberalism in the Chinese revolution, 1917-1937.**
Jerome B. Grieder.   Cambridge, Massachusetts: Harvard University
Press, 1970. 420p. bibliog. (Harvard East Asian Series, no. 46).

A lucid intellectual biography set against the background of the social, political and intellectual problems of the 1920s and 1930s. Hu Shi (1891-1962), a philosopher and cultural activist who later served as Ambassador to the United States, took his undergraduate degree at Cornell and PhD at Columbia University with John Dewey; upon his return to China, he used his Chinese learning and Dewey's pragmatism to present a programme of cultural revitalization – 'renaissance'. Grieder finds Hu broadly liberal in his view of the political primacy of the individual, the rule of law, the rationality of the political process, but open to the charge of élitism.. Chou Min-chih, *Hu Shih and intellectual choice in modern China* (Ann Arbor, Michigan: University of Michigan Press, 1984. 304p. bibliog.) is a thematically organized presentation of Hu's thought on subjects such as American society, Christianity, cosmopolitanism, Chinese culture and classical thought.

241 **Intellectuals and the state in modern China: a narrative history.**
Jerome B. Grieder.   New York: Free Press; London: Collier
Macmillan, 1981. 395p. bibliog. (Transformation of Modern
China Series).

Grieder provides a thoughtful account of how key intellectuals developed political thought and organized themselves for political change in the period up to 1949. After chapters on the Confucian 'inheritance' and its internal critics, the work discusses the following: the 19th-century rebels and reformers (Taipings, Kang Youwei); 1911 intellectuals (especially Yan Fu, Sun Yat-sen, Liang Qichao and Zhang Binglin); and New Culture figures (especially Cai Yuanpei, Li Dazhao, Hu Shi and Chen Duxiu). The last chapters analyse the political ideology of the emerging revolution (Mao Zedong) and its relation to China's crisis and earlier thought. Y. C. Wang, *Chinese intellectuals and the West: 1872-1949* (Chapel Hill, North Carolina: University of North Carolina Press, 1966. 557p.) is a richly detailed series of studies on the thought and influence of intellectuals who studied in Europe, Japan and North America, and includes many tables and statistics.

242 **Confucian China and its modern fate.**
Joseph Levenson.   Berkeley, California; Los Angeles; London:
University of California Press, 1958, 1964, 1965. 3 vols. Reprinted in
one volume with original pagination, Berkeley, California: University
of California Press; London: Routledge & Kegan Paul, 1968.

A formative intellectual and cultural history. Volume one, *The problem of intellectual continuity*, introduces the argument that Confucians, like all peoples confronted with the West, were torn between an allegiance to tradition and an attraction to cosmopolitan rationality; modern Chinese history saw successive attempts to reconcile native values with universal truths. Volumes two, *The problem of monarchical decay*, and three, *The problem of historical significance*, further develop the problem of provincialism and cosmopolitan modernity, *ti* and *yong*, traditionalism versus iconoclasm. Levenson's essayistic style wields metaphor, epigram, pun and paradox rather than linear narrative. After his death by drowning in 1969, *The Mozartian historian: essays on the work of Joseph R. Levenson*, edited by Maurice Meisner,

Rhoads Murphey (Berkeley, California: University of California Press, 1976. 203p. bibliog.) commemorated Levenson and critiqued his themes and methods, especially the relevance of his own Jewish religious commitment. His work is also discussed in Cohen, *Discovering history in China* (q.v.).

243   **Li Ta-chao and the origins of Chinese Marxism.**
Maurice Meisner.   Cambridge, Massachusetts: Harvard University Press, 1967. 326p. (Harvard East Asian Series, no. 27).
A pioneering scholarly study which argues convincingly that Li Dazhao (1888-1927) made the adaptation (or 'sinification') of Marxism on which Mao's revolution was built. Earlier Marxism was an urban, élitist philosophy; Li's essays and teachings, which Meisner lucidly explains, developed Populism, Nationalism and Revolution to form a philosophy relevant to China's villages. Meisner first sketches Li's early years and education, including his years at Waseda University in Tokyo. Following chapters show Li as a leader in the New Culture Movement and at Peking University, where he formed the study group (briefly including Mao Zedong) which led to his re-examination of Marxism and co-founding of the Party. Meisner then carefully explains the theoretical problems and Li's innovations. After several years of leading the northern section of the Party, Li was arrested from the grounds of the Russian embassy in Beijing and garrotted.

244   **China and Charles Darwin.**
James Reeves Pusey.   Cambridge, Massachusetts: Council on East Asian Studies, Harvard University, 1983. 354p. bibliog. (Harvard East Asian Monograph, no. 100).
Illuminates late 19th- and early 20th-century thought, which was pervaded by social Darwinism. Chinese thinkers reinterpreted (or misunderstood) the concept of struggle, which Darwin barely mentioned; they saw conscious competition among groups such as race or nation, not individual adaptation. Chapters discuss individual thinkers such as Kang Youwei, Liang Qichao, Yan Fu, Sun Yat-sen, the anarchists Wu Zhihui, Li Shizeng and Zhang Binglin; and a final chapter discusses New Culture thinkers Chen Duxiu and Hu Shi, and implications for the nature of their radical successors, who had little to add to the earlier obsession with national and racial survival.

245   **Ku Chieh-kang and China's new history: nationalism and the quest for alternative traditions.**
Laurence A. Schneider.   Berkeley, California; London: University of California Press, 1971. 337p. bibliog.
Explores the life and writings of an iconoclastic and revisionist student of the Confucian historical canon from the 1920s to the 1940s. Gu Jiegang (1893-?) subjected Confucian dogma to skeptical and rigorous textual and political criticism but neither rejected the past nor embraced Westernization; rather, he scoured China's alternative traditions for an 'acceptable past' as the basis for a new history and a new relation with the masses which only a morally committed intellectual could broker. These alternative traditions were: popular culture and folklore; the proto-scientific scholarship within the Confucian mainstream; Inner Asian peoples; and the ancient rivals of Confucius, such as the philosopher Mozi (c470-c391 BCE).

246 **The Chinese enlightenment: intellectuals and the legacy of the May Fourth Movement of 1919.**
Vera Schwarcz. Berkeley, California; Los Angeles; London: University of California Press, 1986. 393p. bibliog.

A social and intellectual account of a generation's travails, conveyed through personal histories. The May 1919 student demonstrations crystallized a generation of intellectuals who launched a never fulfilled quest for 'enlightenment' – emancipation from a feudal past of autocracy, bureaucracy and dogmatism. Schwarcz discusses the following topics: this generation's 1910s formation; social and intellectual agendas of the New Culture movement; debates and rivalries, 1925-27; struggles for a new enlightenment, 1928-38; and redefinitions of the May Fourth legacy after 1949, especially in the Democracy Movements of the early 1980s. In Schwarcz's *Time for telling truth is running out: conversations with Zhang Shenfu* (New Haven, Connecticut; London: Yale University Press, 1992. 256p.), one of this generation tells his story of the Communist Party's early organization and frustration of enlightenment ideals.

247 **In search of wealth and power: Yen Fu and the West.**
Benjamin I. Schwartz. Cambridge, Massachusetts: Belknap Press of Harvard University Press, 1964. 298p. bibliog.

A key study in the history of thought. Yan Fu (1853-1921) translated Darwin, Adam Smith, J. S. Mill and Montesquieu to in effect create basic European political thought for the pivotal generation of Chinese thinkers 1898 and 1911. Schwartz explores the reasons why Yan selected certain works and how he chose (or coined) Chinese terms to express them; translation was not passive transmission but active appropriation and interpretation. Yen looked to European thought not for individual freedom and democracy, but for political tools to build *fu qiang* (wealth and power) for a new Chinese nation.

248 **Anarchism and Chinese political culture.**
Peter Zarrow. New York: Columbia University Press, 1990. 338p. bibliog.

Zarrow sets out to demonstrate that early 20th-century anarchists stood at the forefront of the radical intelligentsia; their basic concepts were rooted in Confucian political discourse of late imperial China, and came to represent a yearning for political, economic, social and cultural freedom in the move from imperial Confucianism to Marxism. The history of the Chinese revolution is thus not simply the history of Chinese Marxism. Chapter one discusses background and antecedents in traditional thought; chapters two and three describe rival anarchist groups in Paris and Tokyo. Chapters four to seven explore the main themes of anarchist philosophy: utopianism; revolutionary theory; feminism; and the relation between culture and nation. Chapters eight to ten describe the role of anarchism in political events in the 1910s and 1920s, and chapter ten offers conclusions.

The gate of heavenly peace: the Chinese and their revolutions 1895-1980.
See item no. 120.

The last Confucian: Liang Shuming and the Chinese dilemma of modernity.
See item no. 361.

Fei Xiaotong and sociology in revolutionary China.
See item no. 362.

Chen Duxiu, founder of the Chinese Communist party.
See item no. 370.

A modern China and a new world: K'ang Yu-wei, reformer, and utopian, 1858-1927.
See item no. 372.

Search for modern nationalism: Zhang Binglin and revolutionary China, 1869-1936.
See item no. 384.

Buddhism in late Ch'ing political thought.
See item no. 583.

Sex, culture, and modernity in China: medical science and the construction of sexual identities in the early Republican period.
See item no. 641.

Traditional medicine in modern China: science, nationalism, and the tensions of cultural change.
See item no. 677.

Art and revolution in modern China: the Lingnan (Cantonese) school of painting, 1906-1951.
See item no. 1293.

Primitive passions: visuality, sexuality, ethnography, and contemporary Chinese cinema.
See item no. 1344.

Political and social change (1900-49)

249 **The golden age of the Chinese bourgeoisie, 1911-1937.**
Marie-Claire Bergère, translated by Janet Lloyd. New York:
Cambridge University Press, 1990. 356p. maps. bibliog.

A rich social and political history, slightly revised from *L'âge d'or de la bourgeoisie Chinoise* (Paris: Flammarion, 1986). The first section characterizes and describes the bourgeoisie as the 'urban élite connected with business', in distinction from Marxist definitions which include all manner of modern social groups. The picture is most detailed for Shanghai, where Bergère shows life-styles and even maps providing the location of banks, factories, shops and organizations in 1919. The second part of the book examines the relation of the bourgeoisie to the state after the 1911 Revolution; Bergère argues that the bourgeoisie initially had substantial autonomy, probably the greatest of any social group in Chinese history, but suffered a gradual subordination to Chiang Kai-shek and the Nationalists by the 1930s.

250 **Bandits in Republican China.**
Phil Billingsley. Stanford, California: Stanford University Press,
1988. 375p. bibliog.
In the 1930s, 'bandits' (*tufei*), conservatively estimated at twenty million, were feared
by foreigners and romanticized as Robin Hood social bandits. Billingsley
demonstrates that bandit gangs actually played far more diverse and difficult roles:
they did indeed respond to political corruption and state negligence, but more
commonly robbed, murdered and raped their neighbours than their well-armed
oppressors, with whom successful bandits judiciously cooperated. Chapters analyse:
the recruitment, organization, daily lives, and impact of bandits; the bandit king Bai
Lang (known as 'White Wolf'); the social anatomy of Henan, where bandits reigned;
and the 1923 Lincheng Incident, which created diplomatic repercussions because
foreigners were kidnapped. Diana Lary, *Warlord soldiers: Chinese common soldiers,
1911-1937* (Cambridge, England: Cambridge University Press, 1985. 177p.) describes
this group's lives and work.

251 **Culture, power, and the state: rural North China, 1900-1942.**
Prasenjit Duara. Stanford, California: Stanford University Press,
1988. 326p. bibliog.
An influential analysis of the changing relationship between state and society in the
early 20th century. Duara holds that in late imperial China there had been a 'cultural
nexus of power' which wove together government, gentry and village. This nexus
gained self-reinforcing authority from religious institutions (such as the temple),
social organizations (such as the lineage), and economic networks (such as irrigation
cooperatives and markets). Taxes, bureaucracy and police intrusion burgeoned with
the state's new ambition to control local society and reform local culture by stamping
out 'superstition', but produced only 'state involution', bureaucratic growth without
structural change. Traditional village leaders, feeling powerless and discredited,
withdrew and were replaced by entrepreneurial 'local bullies'. With local élites and
the state now lacking legitimacy, a space opened for revolutionary organization.

252 **Republican China, 1912-1949, Part 1.**
Edited by John K. Fairbank. Cambridge, England; London;
New York; New Rochelle, New York; Melbourne; Sydney: Cambridge
University Press, 1983. 1,002p. maps. bibliog. (Cambridge History of
China, vol. 12).
A comprehensive scholarly work, covering the Republican period from the fall of the
Manchus to the accession of Mao. Fairbank's introduction, 'Maritime and Continental
in China's History', reinterprets the historic tension between inland North China and
South China's commercial tradition, which was taken up by coastal treaty ports.
Topical chapters authoritatively discuss: economic trends, 1912-49; the foreign
presence in China (foreign network, diplomats, missionaries, economic interests); the
era of Yuan Shikai, 1912-16; the Peking government, 1916-28; the warlord era;
intellectual change, 1895-1920; May Fourth and the New Culture movement; literary
trends; the Chinese Communist movement to 1927; the Nationalist movement
(Guomindang Revolution, 1923-28); and the Chinese bourgeoisie, 1911-37.

253 **Republican China, 1912-1949, Part 2.**
Edited by John K. Fairbank.   Cambridge, England; London; New
York; New Rochelle, New York; Melbourne; Sydney: Cambridge
University Press, 1986. 1,092p. maps. bibliog. (Cambridge History
of China, vol. 13).

Continues the work cited in entry no. 252. The introduction reviews evolving
perspectives on modern China's history. Chapters then cover: international relations,
1911-31 (fall of the Qing; Japan in Manchuria; Twenty-One Demands [made by
Japan]; Japan, Moscow and Washington in the 1920s); the Nanjing decade, 1927-37;
the Communist movement, 1927-37; the agrarian system, which summarizes the
important contention that the farm sector grew until the depression and political
instability of the 1930s; peasant movements; the development of local government;
the academic and professional community, 1912-49; literary trends, 1927-49; Japanese
aggression and China's international position, 1931-49; Nationalist China, 1937-45;
the Communist movement, 1937-45; the Nationalist-Communist conflict, 1945-49;
and Mao Zedong's thought to 1949. Each volume includes a substantial
bibliographical essay and an extensive listing of works in many languages.

254 **To the people: James Yen and village China.**
Charles W. Hayford.   New York; London: Columbia University Press,
1990. 304p. bibliog. (U.S. and Pacific Asia: Studies in Social,
Economic, and Political Interaction).

Explores the ambiguous relationship between intellectuals and the countryside and the
attempts to construct a Chinese form of liberalism. Y. C. James Yen (Yan Yangchu;
1890-1990), who graduated from Yale in 1918, taught literacy to the Chinese Labor
Corps in France, then returned to China to found the Mass Education Movement in
1923. The Ting Hsien [Dingxian] Experiment in Rural Reconstruction from 1926-37
organized People's Schools, economic cooperatives, agricultural improvement,
medicine, culture (including literature and village plays), and politics. In 1948, Yen
secured American support for the Joint Commission on Rural Reconstruction. Hayford
also examines 'Chinese pastoral' – the representation of the village in literature,
sociology and popular culture, and argues that China had 'farmers', rather than
'peasants'.

255 **Chinese women in a century of revolution, 1850-1950.**
Ono Kazuko, edited by Joshua A. Fogel, translated by Kathryn
Bernhardt, Timothy Brook, Joshua A. Fogel, Jonathan Lipman, Susan
Mann, Laurel Rhodes.   Stanford, California: Stanford University
Press, 1989. 255p.

The translators' introduction briefly describes women's history in the West and notes
that the book is more a history of women in the Chinese revolution than a modern
history of Chinese women. Chapters include: 'Women Who Took to Battle Dress';
'Between Footbinding and Nationhood';'The Red Lanterns and the Boxer Rebellion';
'Women in the 1911 Revolution'; 'Casting Off the Shackles of the Family'; 'The Rise
of Women Workers'; 'The Transformation of Rural Women'; and 'The Impact of the
Marriage Law of 1950'. The work was originally published in Japanese as *Chūgoku
jōsei-shi* (Tokyo: Heibonsha, 1978).

256 **The making of a hinterland: state, society, and economy in inland north China, 1853-1937.**
Kenneth Pomeranz. Berkeley, California; Oxford: University of California Press, 1993. 336p. maps. bibliog.

Highlights social and ecological change in poor, inland North China to test whether the Qing political system was losing the capacity to govern because of imperialism. Pomeranz finds mixed results. State administration did indeed develop more efficient ways to extract and focus resources; however, foreign pressure now forced the defence of coastal China, to the detriment of the hinterlands. The Grand Canal had traditionally enriched this region but when public works were neglected by cash starved governments, flooding and deforestation increased. Economic imperialism, sometimes seen as invariably destructive, also had geographically varying effects: new markets benefitted this hinterland, but local militarism prevented political and economic integration. Jerome Chen, *The highlanders of China: a history, 1895-1937* (Armonk, New York; London: M. E. Sharpe, 1992. 302p.) also studies the hinterland of western Hubei, eastern Sichuan and western Hunan.

257 **Chinese elites and political change: Zhejiang province in the early twentieth century.**
R. Keith Schoppa. Cambridge, Massachusetts: Harvard University Press, 1982. 280p. maps. bibliog. (Harvard East Asian Series, no. 96).

Studies the geography, politics and ideas of élites in Zhejiang, an important lower Yangzi valley province before 1937. Schoppa elucidates how first the Manchus, then the early Republic political system dealt with the problem of building local foundations for a nation. Sections include: 'The Context of Elite Activity'; 'The Sociopolitical Ecology of the Four Zhejiangs'; and 'Locality, Province, and Nation in Early Twentieth Century Politics'. Schoppa's *Blood road: the mystery of Shen Dingyi in revolutionary China* (Berkeley, California; Los Angeles; London: University of California Press, 1995. 322p. maps. bibliog.) is a fast paced story of a revolutionary disciple of Sun Yat-sen's who was assassinated in 1928. Shen was a revolutionary from a landlord family, a journalist and educator, poet, and a member of both the Communist and Nationalist parties; through his story, Schoppa provides an insight into local revolution and national change.

258 **China in disintegration: the Republican era in Chinese history, 1912-1949.**
James E. Sheridan. New York: Free Press; London: Collier Macmillan, 1975. 338p. bibliog. (Transformation of Modern China Series).

A survey of the period between the fall of the Manchus and the establishment of the People's Republic which takes the successive attempts to build political integration as the central theme. The description of the warlords and their depredations is especially valuable. Edward Dreyer, *China at war, 1901-1949* (London; New York: Longman, 1995. 422p. maps. bibliog. [Modern War in Perspective]) draws current scholarship together into a detailed military history. In addition to an analytical narrative of campaigns and battles of the warlords, the Sino-Japanese War 1937-45, and the military confrontations between the Nationalists and the Communists to 1949, Dreyer considers institutional modernization, organizational structure, and the role of the army in politics.

259 **Rickshaw Beijing: city people and politics in the 1920s.**
David Strand. Berkeley, California; Oxford: University of California
Press, 1989. 364p. bibliog.
An innovative social history of Beijing in the 1920s. The rickshaw, introduced from
Japan, provided a new livelihood for working-class Chinese, but also led to labour
conflicts and disruptive competition with new streetcars. The strife drew in the Beijing
Chamber of Commerce, which represented reforming private merchants, and the
municipal police department, representing the 'more intrusive, regulatory, and tutelary
state'. Traditional groups, such as guilds, volunteer fire fighters and militia corps,
charities, labour gangs, and 'noblesse oblige' élites continued to operate. New
political styles emerged both in face-to-face situations, such as teahouses, and in mass
demonstrations in new 'public space'. Strand argues that the May Fourth 1919
demonstrations and the almost Luddite riots against the new streetcars in 1929 showed
the emergence of a 'public sphere' based on mass political participation in new rituals
and greater state ambition to control and guide local society. The work includes many
period photographs.

260 **Student protests in twentieth century China: the view from
Shanghai.**
Jeffrey N. Wasserstrom. Stanford, California: Stanford University
Press, 1991. 428p. bibliog.
A social history of Shanghai students and their influence in the Chinese revolution.
The introduction discusses theories of political culture as developed by historians of
the French Revolution. Part one, 'The Warlord Era, 1911-1927', dramatizes the issues,
tactics, organization and mobilization in student demonstrations of 4 May 1919 and 30
May 1925. Part two, 'The Nationalist Period, 1927-1949', looks at the anti-Japanese
movements of 1931 and the anti-government struggles of the 1940s, with an epilogue,
'The May 4th Tradition in the 1980s'. Thematic chapters draw on social science and
linguistic theories concerning symbolic processes (such as public ceremonies, rituals,
revolutionary festivals and political theatre) by which students transmuted common
emotion (culture) into organized action (politics). John Israel, Donald W. Klein,
Rebels and bureaucrats: China's December 9ers (Berkeley, California; London:
University of California Press, 1976. 303p.) looks at seminal student anti-Japanese
demonstrations in 1935.

**Urban change in China: politics and development in Tsinan, Shantung,
1890-1949.**
See item no. 427.

**Native place, city, and nation: regional networks and identities in
Shanghai, 1853-1937.**
See item no. 430.

**Reform the people: changing attitudes towards popular education in
early 20th century China.**
See item no. 1038.

Schoolhouse politicians: locality and state during the Chinese Republic.
See item no. 1041.

The alienated academy: culture and politics in Republican China, 1919-1937.
See item no. 1045.

Going to the people: Chinese intellectuals and folk literature. 1918-1937.
See item no. 1243.

The 1911 revolution and the early Republic

261 **Reform and revolution in China: the 1911 Revolution in Hunan and Hubei.**
Joseph Esherick. Berkeley, California; Oxford: University of California Press, 1976. 324p. bibliog. (Michigan Studies on China).

An examination of the social and political origins of the Republican revolution in two key mid-China provinces from 1898. Esherick downplays national intellectual reformers and the influence of Sun Yat-sen to trace the development of an urban reform élite; these men built local power as the basis for a new Chinese nation, but at the expense of the central government. Their Western-inspired reforms in schools, local administration, and industrialization were costly, élitist and culturally alien, which split the urban reform élites from the rural masses. The book finishes with a narrative analysis of 1911-12 in the provinces and the establishment of a socially reactionary new régime.

262 **Backward toward revolution: the Chinese Revolutionary Party.**
Edward Friedman. Berkeley, California; Oxford: University of California Press, 1974. 237p. bibliog.

Explores the ideas and organizational innovations in Sun Yat-sen's Chinese Revolutionary Party (the forerunner of the Nationalist Party). Sun's halting attempts to understand and make political use of rural proletarians, including the social bandit, 'White Wolf', was a turning point in bringing reformist intellectuals together with more radical rural organizations.

263 **The Chinese Revolution of 1911: new perspectives.**
Edited by Hsueh Chun-tu. Hong Kong: Joint Publishing, 1986. 234p.

A group of essays by scholars in the People's Republic, first published in *Chinese Studies in History*, vol. 16, no. 3-4 (1983). Like *China's Republican Revolution*, edited by Shinkichi Etō, Harold Schiffrin (Tokyo: University of Tokyo Press, distributed in North America by Columbia University Press, 1994. 279p.), it contains detailed studies of localities and personalities. *The Revolution of 1911: turning point in modern Chinese history*, edited by Dong Caishi, written by Lu Bowei, Wang Guoping (Beijing: Foreign Languages Press, 1991. 544p. maps. bibliog.) presents mainstream interpretations in a straightforward narrative. Winston Hsieh, *The historiography of the 1911 Revolution* (Stanford, California: Hoover Institution Press, 1975. 165p.) discusses the canons and scholarship of successive schools of interpretation: the orthodox Nationalist school; the Neo-orthodox school in the People's Republic; and recent historiography in Taiwan.

264 **Russia and the roots of the Chinese revolution, 1896-1911.**
Don C. Price. Cambridge, Massachusetts: Harvard University Press, 1974. 303p. bibliog. (Harvard East Asian Series, no. 79).

Chinese nationalists at the turn of the century looked to Russia for examples and lessons; Peter the Great was a model of an enlightened despot and the anarchists were models for anti-authoritarians. Price describes the periodicals initiated by the new intellectuals, and finds much that does not fit into earlier studies which focused principally on Sun Yat-sen's followers. The wide-ranging discussions held between nationalists, anarchists, socialists and monarchists showed that the Chinese were open to a panoply of foreign ideas, including the idea of revolution.

265 **Elite activism and political transformation in China: Zhejiang province, 1865-1911.**
Mary Backus Rankin. Stanford, California: Stanford University Press, 1986. 427p. bibliog.

Provides both a detailed description of the political and intellectual developments in a key province leading up to the 1911 Revolution, and a revisionist argument about its causes. Rankin argues that expanded commercialization and growing global interaction led to the growth of a successful public sphere. Zhejiang élites created and participated in non-government organizations, in areas such as education, welfare, famine relief, publishing and reform. They implicitly criticized Manchu government inertia and resisted centralization. This reformist, activist élite formed well before the belated Qing post-1900 reforms, absorbed new roles and occupations, and transcended urban-rural or provincial-local divisions. In this view, Rankin differs from those who see the Revolution as caused by the fragmentation of the gentry, the emergence of detached urban élites, and class polarization produced by imperialism.

266 **China's Republican Revolution: the case of Kwangtung, 1895-1913.**
Edward J. M. Rhoads. Cambridge, Massachusetts: Harvard University Press, 1975. 366p. maps. bibliog. (Harvard East Asian Monographs, no. 81).

Rhoads discusses the intellectual, economic and social development of the 1911 Revolution in Guangdong, the development of urban mass nationalism, the downfall of the Qing, and the establishment of a new provincial government. For a parallel history of Zhejiang province, see Mary Backus Rankin, *Early Chinese revolutionaries: radical intellectuals in Shanghai and Chekiang, 1902-1911* (Cambridge, Massachusetts: Harvard University Press, 1971. 340p. map. bibliog. [Harvard East Asian Monographs, no. 50]), which argues that intellectuals, among them the famous woman revolutionary Qiu Jin, were at the centre of a modernization movement that led to the events of 1911.

267 **The revolutionary army: a Chinese nationalist tract of 1903.**
Tsou Jung, introduction and translation with notes by John Lust.
The Hague, Paris: Mouton & Co., 1968. 151 + 84p.

The most famous (and scurrilous) attack on the Manchu race and government. Zou Rong (1885-1905), an educated youth from Sichuan, rhetorically caught the new arguments of revolution, race, nationalism and republicanism; his pamphlet was widely read as part of the turn from monarchy and reform to republicanism and revolution. Lust prints both the original Chinese text and an annotated English translation, with an extensive biographical introduction.

268 **China in revolution: the first phase, 1900-1913.**
Edited, with an introduction by Mary C. Wright.   New Haven,
Connecticut; London: Yale University Press, 1968. 503p.

A significant symposium volume. Wright's introduction, 'The Rising Tide of Change', which her untimely death prevented her from continuing, summarized recent work on the Revolution. She argues that there was in the 20th century 'one single revolution' whose salient features were rooted in this early 20th-century experience. Individual essays cover: 'Reform and Revolution in China's Political Modernization'; the triumph of anarchism over Marxism, 1906-07; the Constitutionalists; political provincialism; the role of the bourgeoisie and the gentry; military power in the genesis of the revolution; Yuan Shikai; and Sun Yat-sen.

269 **The presidency of Yuan Shih-k'ai: liberalism and dictatorship in early republican China.**
Ernest P. Young.   Ann Arbor, Michigan: University of Michigan
Press, 1977. 347p. bibliog. (Michigan Studies on China).

A key study of Yuan Shikai (1859-1916), a powerful general and official of the Qing dynasty who took power after the 1911 Revolution as President of the Republic. Earlier histories blamed Yuan's villainy for the disintegration of the Republic, but Young evaluates the deeper causes. Centralizers such as Yuan argued that China needed a strong state to stave off imperialism and reform the nation; however local élites held that national power had to be built from the bottom up. Chapters describe: China in the early 20th century; the birth of the Republic; Yuan's presidential team; the liberal Republic and Yuan's confrontation with it; establishing the dictatorship; Yuan's programmes, including foreign policy and the response to Japan's Twenty-One Demands; domestic reforms, such as a new school system; the monarchical attempt; and the presidency in history. For Yuan's successful reform rule as provincial governor, see Stephen R. MacKinnon, *Power and politics in late imperial China: Yuan Shi-kai in Beijing and Tianjin, 1901-1908* (Berkeley, California; Oxford: University of California Press, 1980. 260p.).

270 **From war to nationalism: China's turning point, 1924-1925.**
Arthur Waldron.   Cambridge, England: Cambridge University Press,
1995. 366p. maps. bibliog.

Combines a military history of the Jiangsu-Zhejiang and the Zhili-Fengtian Wars with a reassessment of the political, social and intellectual transformations which they precipitated. Waldron argues that First World War technology and tactics transformed warfare in China, raising stakes, costs and impacts. The 1924 wars devastated the comparatively stable system which had replaced the Qing; they also destroyed political confidence, and (even more than the more often cited New Culture and May Thirtieth movements) cleared the way for radical revolution and nationalism. Final sections describe the set of new words (including 'warlord'), attitudes, cultural forms (including cartoons), and institutions which were forged in the aftermath of these wars, and make general theoretical comparisons with nationalism and revolution in other countries.

Yuan Shih-k'ai.
See item no. 365.

The warlords and regional governments (1911-49)

271 **Warlords and Muslims in Chinese Central Asia: a political history of Republican Sinkiang, 1911-1949.**
Andrew D. W. Forbes. Cambridge, England: Cambridge University Press, 1986. 376p. bibliog.

A political history of an ethnically diverse region of Central Asia. Xinjiang, China's largest province, was conquered by the Manchus in the 17th century, but was not controlled by a Chinese government until 1949 (if then). Forbes uses British consular intelligence, travellers' reports, and scholarship in Chinese, Western and local languages, in order to throw light on Russian or Chinese influences and on the power struggles and personal rivalries among Muslim groups in Uigurstan (Turfan), Altishar (Tarim Basin), and Zhungaria. For a key episode in the struggle for autonomy see Linda Benson, *The Ili rebellion: the Moslem challenge to Chinese authority in Xinjiang, 1944-1949* (Armonk, New York: M. E. Sharpe, 1990. 265p.).

272 **Warlord: Yen Hsi-shan in Shansi province, 1911-1949.**
Donald G. Gillin. Princeton, New Jersey: Princeton University Press, 1967. 334p. maps. bibliog.

Yan Xishan (1883-1960), the warlord of Shanxi province, continued the late Qing conservative tradition of using Western technology to protect Chinese values. He established a cohesive regional government in Shanxi province which fostered industry and transport, reorganized schools, and extended administrative control, only to be ravaged by the Japanese invasion. Studies of other regional militarists who belie the term 'warlord' include: on Zhang Zuolin, Gavan McCormack, *Chang Tso-lin in Northeast China, 1911-1928: China, Japan, and the Manchurian idea* (Stanford, California: Stanford University Press, 1977. 334p.); on Feng Yuxiang, James Sheridan, *Chinese warlord: the career of Feng Yu-hsiang* (Stanford, California: Stanford University Press, 1966. 386p.); on Wu Peifu, Odoric Y. K. Wou, *Militarism in modern China: the career of Wu P'ei-fu* (Folkestone, England: Dawson, Australian National University Press, 1978. 349p.); and on Liu Xiang, Robert Kapp, *Szechwan and the Chinese Republic: provincial militarism and central power, 1911-1938* (New Haven, Connecticut; London: Yale University Press, 1973. 198p.).

273 **The Kwangsi way in Kuomintang China, 1931-1939.**
Eugene William Levich.   Armonk, New York; London: M. E. Sharpe,
1993. 363p. maps. bibliog. (Studies on Modern China).
Argues that Li Zongren (Li Tsung-jen; 1891-1970) and Bai Chongxi (1893-1966)
organized an anti-Communist, anti-Japanese 'model province' in Guangxi, based on
Confucian values and the legacy of Sun Yat-sen. Sections study 'Origins and
Ideology', 'Political Administration', and Economic Administration'. Levich views
the Guangxi Clique's development programmes and anti-imperialism as supporting
the nation rather than dividing it. Diana Lary, *Region and nation: the Kwangsi clique
in Chinese politics, 1925-1937* (Cambridge, England: Cambridge University Press,
1974. 276p. maps. bibliog.) sees the regional power of the clique as being in
competition with the nation.

274 **The power of the gun: the emergence of modern Chinese
warlordism.**
Edward A. McCord.   Berkeley, California; Oxford: University of
California Press, 1993. 436p. bibliog.
Disputes earlier views of the period 1860s-1920s as the fragmentation of Qing
military rule directly into local warlordism. McCord studies the central provinces of
Hunan and Hubei, using comparative theories of the military and the state to discern
several stages involving both central decline and local construction of power: armies
were drawn into politics by ambitious local politicos, then took advantage of their
authorized positions to build new political machines. Other key studies include: Ch'i
Hsi-sheng, *Warlord politics in China, 1916-1928* (Stanford, California: Stanford
University Press, 1976. 282p.), which traces the emergence of the concept; Anthony
B. Chan, *Arming the Chinese: the western armaments trade in warlord China, 1920-
1928* (Vancouver, Canada: University of British Columbia Press, 1982. 180p.), which
shows that the arms trade flooded the country with modern weapons but did not bring
imperialist control, as competition freed warlords from dependent relationships with
particular countries; and Edmund S. K. Fung, *The military dimension of the Chinese
Revolution: the New Army and its role in the Revolution of 1911* (Vancouver, Canada:
University of British Columbia Press, 1980. 349p.).

275 **The urban origins of rural revolution: élites and masses in Hunan
province, China, 1911-1927.**
Angus W. McDonald, Jr.   Berkeley, California; Oxford: University of
California Press, 1978. 369p. maps. bibliog.
McDonald provides a social, economic and political history of Hunan, the site of Mao's
failed but instructive Autumn Harvest Uprisings of 1927. Chapters analyse: 'Power'
(military governments after 1911); 'Wealth' (land, commerce and new industries); and
'Prestige' (schools, education reform, New Culture, the mass education movement and
the foundation of the Communist and Nationalist parties). Radicals emerged from the
urban élite student movements, rather than from villages or factories; civilian élites
turned to new professional soldiers to protect them. Chapters narrate and examine the
labour and peasant movements before 1926, leading to the Northern Expedition (a
military campaign intended to unify China, mounted in 1926) and the Great Revolution
of 1925-27. The epilogue argues that Mao's 'Report on the Hunan Peasant Movement'
constituted an important turning point; the subsequent military and organizational
success was based on party workers leaving the city to enter the village.

The Nationalist era (1927-49)

276 **The Shanghai capitalists and the Nationalist government, 1927-1937.**
Parks Coble.   Cambridge, Massachusetts: Council on East Asian
Studies, Harvard University, distributed by Harvard University Press,
1980. 2nd ed., 1986. 357p. bibliog. (Harvard East Asian Monographs,
no. 134).

Analyses the efforts of the Nationalist Party and the Nanking government (1928-37) to
control and exploit Shanghai capitalists through appeals to patriotism, confiscatory
taxes and physical intimidation. Coble argues that Chiang Kai-shek's government
therefore did not represent the bourgeoisie, as charged by critics at the time and by
later scholars; capitalists and entrepreneurs were excluded from decision making,
while the government was not effective in promoting business. The Nationalists did
not 'represent' the interests of any class, but primarily those of a strong state. The
preface to the second edition reviews recent scholarship, including Joseph Fewsmith,
*Party, State, and local élites in Republican China: merchant organizations and
politics in Shanghai, 1890-1930* (Honolulu: University of Hawaii Press, 1984. 275p.),
which characterizes the Nanking régime as 'authoritarian-corporatist'.

277 **The abortive revolution: China under Nationalist rule, 1927-1937.**
Lloyd Eastman.   Cambridge, Massachusetts: Harvard University
Press, 1974. Paperback ed., with an added preface and appendix,
'Formation of the Blue Shirts', 1990. 398p. bibliog. (Harvard East
Asian Monographs, no. 153).

A discussion of the politics of the 'Nanking Decade'. The book's main theme is that
Chiang Kai-shek and the Nationalists 'quickly lost revolutionary momentum and
became a military dictatorship primarily concerned with maintaining itself in power';
that the central government was weak in relation to the provinces; and that the régime
did not rest on a class basis of rural landlords and urban capitalists. Chapters deal with
the Blue Shirts (an anti-Communist gendarmerie), fascism, and factional rivalry with
the CC clique; the 1934 Fujian rebellion (in which rebels from the Cantonese 19th
Route Army made a pact with the Communists, instead of fighting them); Nanking
and the economy; social traits and political behaviour in Guomindang China; and
'Democracy and Dictatorship: Competing Models of Government'. So Wai-chor, *The
Kuomintang left in the National Revolution, 1924-1931* (Hong Kong: Oxford
University Press, 1991. 290p.) explains the failure of the left by Wang Jingwei's 'de-
radicalized' ideology and compromise with regional militarists.

278 **Seeds of destruction: Nationalist China in war and revolution,
1937-1949.**
Lloyd Eastman.   Stanford, California: Stanford University Press,
1984. 311p. bibliog.

A political history of Chiang Kai-shek's Nationalist party and government during and
after the Sino-Japanese war, which addresses the question 'who lost China?' Eastman
analyses the following topics: Chiang Kai-shek's weak but dictatorial attempts to gain
control of Yunnan and Sichuan provinces; peasants, taxes and Nationalist rule; politics

within the régime and the Youth Corps; the Nationalist Army during the War of Resistance and against the Communists; Jiang Jingguo (Chiang Ching-kuo, 1910-88), Chiang's eldest son, and the gold yüan monetary reform of 1948, which led to ruinous inflation; and Chiang Kai-shek's 1948 indictment of the Nationalist Party as 'decrepit and degenerate'. The conclusion, 'Of Storms and Revolutions', considers the various factors in the collapse of Nationalist China.

279 **The Nationalist era in China, 1927-1949.**
Lloyd E. Eastman, Jerome Ch'en, Suzanne Pepper, Lyman P. Van Slyke. Cambridge, England; New York; Port Chester, New York; Melbourne; Sydney: Cambridge University Press, 1991. 406p.
Chapters of this work cover political history as reprinted from *Republican China, 1912-1949. Pt 2* (q.v.): 'Nationalist Government During the Nanking Decade, 1927-1937'; 'The Communist Movement, 1927-1937'; 'Nationalist China During the Sino-Japanese War, 1937-1945'; 'The Chinese Communist Movement During the Sino-Japanese War, 1937-1945'; and 'The KMT-CCP Conflict, 1945-1949'.

280 **Passivity, resistance, and collaboration: intellectual choices in occupied Shanghai, 1937-1945.**
Fu Poshek. Stanford, California: Stanford University Press, 1993. 261p. bibliog.
Examines writers and intellectuals in Japanese-occupied Shanghai and sees their dilemmas in terms of three possible strategies – passivity and withdrawal, defiance and resistance, or collaboration. Fu shows that the later condemnation or idealization of these choices was too simple; strategies were complex and individuals had difficult reasons for making them, including conscious echoes of earlier occupations of China in the Yüan and Qing dynasties.

281 **Shanghai, 1927-1937: municipal power, locality, and modernization.**
Christian Henriot. Berkeley, California; Oxford: University of California Press, 1993. 288p. bibliog.
This work argues, in contrast to widespread assumptions, that the city government of Shanghai functioned remarkably well in the decade before the war with Japan. Henriot analyses the complex relationships between provincial and national governments, national and local Nationalist Party, business élites, and 'traditional' organizations such as guilds, networks of personal ties and native place associations, all of which were involved in a certain amount of effective organization.

282 **China's bitter victory: the war with Japan.**
Edited by James C. Hsiung, Steven Levine. Armonk, New York; London: M. E. Sharpe, 1992. 333p. bibliog.
A key symposium in which Chinese, Japanese and American scholars contribute essays describing the conduct of the war with Japan, and its economic, political and cultural consequences. A substantial introduction sets the individual essays in context and evaluates the scholarly issues. Dick Wilson, *When tigers fight: the story of the Sino-Japanese war* (London: Hutchison, 1982; New York: Penguin, 1983. 269p.)

provides a straightforward narrative of the war. Ch'i Hsi-sheng, *Nationalist China at war: military defeat and nationalist collapse, 1937-1945* (Ann Arbor, Michigan: University of Michigan Press, 1982. 309p.) looks at the interaction of political manoeuvring and military strategy.

283 **War and popular culture: resistance in modern China, 1937-1945.**
Chang-tai Hung.   Berkeley, California; London: University of California Press, 1994. 432p. bibliog.

Relates how 'resistance intellectuals' created a new popular culture to mobilize the masses against Japan. Hung first describes the rise of modern urban popular culture in the treaty ports and Shanghai. Chapters two to five describe their wartime metamorphoses: spoken drama (as opposed to traditional opera forms) produced street plays; the National Salvation Cartoon Propaganda Corps and Feng Zikai produced satirical popular cartoons; newspapers produced new language and new roles, including the war correspondent; and popular forms, such as drum singing, were used as propaganda. Chapter six describes the crucial process of ruralizing the urban forms in the Communist areas, including the village drama movement, border region newspapers, new language, and an emerging border region culture. Chapter seven, 'A New Political Culture', argues that the newly ruralized popular culture was basic to the socialist revolution.

284 **Roads not taken: the struggle of opposition parties in twentieth century China.**
Edited by Roger B. Jeans.   Boulder, Colorado: Westview Press, 1992. 385p. bibliog.

These sixteen articles on minor or opposition parties, with a general introduction, fill the gap left by histories which concentrate on the Nationalists and the Communists. The articles explore cultural difficulties and personal rivalries to explain why the mostly liberal rivals never developed a mass base or military power. Some articles present thinkers who worked individually in the 1920s and 1930s but became leaders of the 'third road' Democratic League in the 1940s: Zhang Junmai (Carson Chang; 1887-1963), a philosopher who promoted constitutionalism; and Huang Yanpei (1878-1965) who promoted vocational education. Other articles sketch smaller political parties or organizations: the anti-Japanese National Salvation Association, founded in 1936; the minor parties of 1945-50; and the post-1989 Overseas Democracy Movement.

285 **The Northern Expedition: China's national revolution of 1926-28.**
Donald A. Jordan.   Honolulu: University of Hawaii Press, 1976. 341p. maps. bibliog.

A narrative analysis of the Great Revolution – Chiang Kai-shek's military campaign to unify China and the radical political campaign to revolutionize it. This radical nationalist movement is described and analysed in *The May Thirtieth movement: events and themes* by Richard W. Rigby (Canberra: Australian National University Press, 1980. 271p.), which provides a full treatment of popular response when British police killed student demonstrators in Shanghai, 30 May 1925; left-wing Guomindang (Nationalists) and Communists responded quickly, and developed an anti-imperialist and anti-feudal programme and organizations. Jessie Gregory Lutz, *Chinese politics and Christian missions: the anti-Christian movements of 1920-28* (Notre Dame,

Indiana: Cross Cultural Publications, 1988) studies the Guomindang and Communist use of student anti-Christian organizations. C. Martin Wilbur, *The Nationalist Revolution in China, 1923-1928* (Cambridge, England: Cambridge University Press, 1984. 232p.) reprints his magisterial synthetic chapters from *Republican China*, Pt. I (q.v.).

286 Civil war in China: the political struggle, 1945-1949.

Suzanne Pepper. Berkeley, California; Los Angeles; London: University of California Press, 1978. 472p.

A political history which focuses on the polices and practices which the Communist and Nationalist parties deployed towards various social groups, leading to a military conflict which decided the outcome. Part one, 'The Last Years of Kuomintang Rule', emphasizes Chiang Kai-shek's strategic military blunders, economic mismanagement, systematic alienation of intellectuals and students, rather than international factors such as the presence, or lack, of support from America or Russia. Part two, 'The Communist Alternative', discusses: the intelligentsia's critique of the CCP, showing that there was no initial acceptance; the return to land reform, downplayed in the wartime United Front; the return to the cities, as the CCP sought urban allies; the takeover from the Nationalists as the People's Liberation Army marched south; and the politics of the Civil War, which summarizes how each major group was wooed.

287 Policing Shanghai 1927-1937.

Frederic E. Wakeman, Jr. Berkeley, California; London: University of California Press, 1995. 507p. bibliog.

A panoramic social history of the Nationalist government's attempt to control Shanghai by establishing a Chinese police force, an ambition vitiated by poor administration and corruption. Wakeman's portrait is broad, for the police force dealt with public health, housing, traffic, commercial licensing, entertainment, labour unions, kidnapping, censorship, indigence, narcotics, prostitution, and racketeering problems, while simultaneously pursuing a programme of recovering national sovereignty over the concessions and controlling popular disorder and unrest within the Chinese sectors of the city through secret police activity. However, Wakeman also notes the connections and continuities between this effort to bureaucratize society and the preceding late Qing reforms and the later Communist programmes, the 'lamentable durability of governmentalized autocracy'.

288 Thunder out of China.

Theodore H. White, Annalee Jacoby. New York: William Sloane, 1946. 331p. Reissued, with a new preface, 1961. Reprinted, Jersey City, New Jersey: Da Capo Press, 1980.

A classic best seller which reports on wartime China and American policy by *Time* magazine correspondents, describing the pre-1949 history of modern China in a vivid journalistic style. Opening chapters, many based on first-hand observation, focus on the plight of the peasant and the outbreak of war with Japan. Succeeding chapters describe wartime Chungking, Chiang Kai-shek's political problems, the personality and programme of General Joseph Stilwell (Chiang Kai-shek's American chief-of-staff), and the disagreement between Chiang and Stilwell. The Chinese Communists are described as a powerful, popular, but not democratic force for revolutionary change.

289   **Missionaries of revolution: Soviet advisers and Nationalist China, 1920-1927.**
C. Martin Wilbur, Julie Lien-ying Howe.   Cambridge, Massachusetts: Harvard University Press, 1988. 904p.

In April 1927 Beijing police raided the Soviet Embassy and seized files documenting Soviet involvement with Sun Yat-sen's Nationalist Party, the Chinese Communist Party, and their relations with the Soviets. Wilbur and Howe's *Documents on Communism, Nationalism, and Soviet advisers in China* (New York: Columbia University Press, 1956) authenticated and annotated fifty of these documents. This volume reprints those and adds some thirty new documents. An introductory monograph brings together information on the Soviet advisers led by Michael Borodin, their finances, their motives, their experience in China, and their fates in later years, all in the light of the interrelation between the USSR, the Comintern, the Nationalists and the CCP.

Li Ta-chao and the origins of Chinese Marxism.
See item no. 243.

Chen Duxiu, founder of the Chinese Communist party.
See item no. 370.

Sisters and strangers: women in the Shanghai cotton mills, 1919-1949.
See item no. 1011.

The Communist Revolution and its origins (1921-49)

290   **China shakes the world.**
Jack Belden.   New York: Harpers, 1949. 524p. Reprinted, with an introduction by Owen Lattimore, New York; London: Monthly Review Press, 1970; Beijing: Foreign Languages Press, 1989.

A classic of reporting on the last stages of the Communist revolution in North China; the analysis is deeper than Snow's *Red star over China* (q.v.), but its publication was less well timed. Belden's *Still time to die* (Philadelphia: Blakiston, 1944. 322p.) and *Retreat with Stilwell* (New York: Knopf, 1943. 368p.) were powerful accounts of the Japanese invasions of North China and Burma. He returned to China in 1946 to report on the village revolution ignited by Japanese invasion and the Border Region Government's attempt to build political legitimacy. Belden was skeptical of Mao and the CCP's attempt to co-opt this 'people's war'. There are memorable action portraits of 'Field Mouse', a local guerrilla commander, and 'Gold Flower', a revolutionary woman.

291 **Origins of the Chinese revolution, 1915-1949.**
Lucien Bianco, translated by Muriel Bell. Stanford, California:
Stanford University Press; London: Oxford University Press, 1971.
223p. maps. bibliog.

A lucid interpretive summation of views from the 1950s and 1960s, originally published as *Les origines de la révolution Chinoise 1915-1949* (Paris: Editions Gallimard, 1967). Chapters cover 'The End of a World', 'Intellectual Origins', 'Early Years of the Communist Party', 'Social Causes of the Chinese Revolution', 'Reform or Revolution?' and 'The Red Army Triumphs'. Bianco revisits some of the topics in his chapter, 'Peasant Movements', in *Republican China, 1912-1949 Pt 2* (q.v.). A useful narrative, though outdated in some respects by access to new sources, is James Pinckney Harrison, *The long march to power: a history of the Chinese Communist Party, 1921-1972* (New York; Washington, DC: Praeger, 1972. 647p. maps. bibliog.).

292 **Making revolution: the Communist movement in Eastern and Central China, 1937-1945.**
Chen Yung-fa. Berkeley, California; London: University of
California Press, 1986. 690p. maps.

A detailed chronicle of the Chinese Communist Party anti-Japanese base areas in Anhui and Jiangsu provinces under the New Fourth Army during the war. Chen considers organizational factors, the process of state formation, and the rivalries of power politics, but eschews overall theory; rather, he shows cadres addressing (but not always solving) political and military problems on the local level. The guerrilla bases left behind by the Long March are likewise documented in Gregor Benton, *Mountain fires: the Red Army's three year war in South China, 1934-1938* (Berkeley, California; London: University of California Press, 1992. 639p.). *Moral economy and the Chinese Revolution* by Chen Yung-fa, Gregor Benton (Amsterdam: Universiteit van Amsterdam, Anthropologisch-Sociologisch Centrum, 1986. 112p.) critiques the moral economy school of theory, particularly as presented by Ralph Thaxton in *China turned rightside up: revolutionary legitimacy in the peasant world* (New Haven, Connecticut: Yale University Press, 1983. 286p. maps. bibliog.).

293 **P'eng P'ai and the Hai-Lu-Feng Soviet.**
Fernando Galbiati. Stanford, California: Stanford University Press,
1985. 484p. maps. bibliog.

A detailed study of the early 1920s peasant movement led by Peng Pai (1896-1929) in Haifeng and Lufeng counties, in East Guangdong. Galbiati portrays the social history of the area; Peng's development from the scion of a local gentry family into the organizer of the Peasant Union and leader of the southern radical wing of the revolution, 1925-27; the fleeting Hai-Lu-Feng Soviet; and the counter-revolution, ending for Peng with his execution in 1929. Kamal Sheel, *Peasant society and Marxist intellectuals in China: Fang Zhimin and the origin of a revolutionary movement in Xinjiang region* (Princeton, New Jersey: Princeton University Press, 1989. 265p. bibliog.) also presents the ecological, economic and political history of the Xinjiang region of Fujian province since the Ming dynasty, and then uses the analysis of the moral economy school to show how the leader Fang Zhimin, like Peng Pai and Mao, interacted with local peasants to produce a distinctive revolution.

294   **The tragedy of the Chinese revolution.**
Harold R. Isaacs.   Stanford, California: Stanford University Press,
1961. 2nd rev. ed. 392p.
A classic, dramatic account, filled with a wealth of personal detail and source material, of the founding and early years of the Chinese Communist Party, the Northern Expedition and the 'Great Revolution' of 1925-27, and the subsequent 'Russian-made debacle'. Isaacs arrived in Shanghai shortly after the events discussed, and as an activist reporter knew many of the participants; he makes an impassioned argument that Stalin's policies suppressed mass initiative; as a result, Stalinists spitefully accused Isaacs of Trotskyism. The first edition was published in 1938, substantially revised in 1951, and reissued with minor changes and a new preface in 1961. Isaacs' *Re-encounters in China: notes of journey in a time capsule* (Armonk, New York; London: M. E. Sharpe, 1985. 192p.) describes his 1980 return, life and revolution in 1930s Shanghai, his meetings with old revolutionary friends such as Soong Qingling (the widow of Sun Yat-sen), and their sad fate in Mao's China.

295   **The found generation: Chinese Communists in Europe during the twenties.**
Marilyn A. Levine.   Seattle, Washington; London: University of
Washington Press, 1993. 287p. bibliog. (Jackson School Publications
in International Studies).
More than 1,600 young Chinese men and women travelled to France and Germany during and just after the First World War; unlike the American 'lost generation', they were optimistic, politically committed, and determined to transform their world. Levine describes the rise in China of the Work-Study Movement, which sent students to study and work in French factories, and the Chinese Labor Corps. She explores the individual experiences of prominent students (Wang Guangqi, Li Shizeng, Cai Hesen, Zhao Shiyan and Zhou Enlai) and shows how factory experience, exposure to Marxism, and political conflict led radicals to form the ECCO (European Chinese Communist Organizations). On their return to China, many ECCO activists became influential politicians, including Zhou Enlai, Deng Xiaoping, Li Lisan and Zhu De.

296   **The Long March: the untold story.**
Harrison Salisbury.   New York: Harper & Row, 1985. 420p.
The Long March, which has gone down in CCP history as a great turning point, was a 6,000 mile epic journey undertaken by 100,000 CCP soldiers in 1934 when the Nationalist armies had dislodged them from their Soviet bases. Mao led the March and eventually arrived in north Shaanxi with only 8,000 people. Salisbury, long a New York *Times* correspondent covering the Communist world, obtained Chinese government support to retrace the route of Mao's epochal 1934-35 Long March and to interview survivors and Chinese Party historians. His lively narrative, whose dedication is to the 'heroic men and women of China's Long March', provides a more complete account of political rivalries than earlier narratives. However, Salisbury does not critically evaluate sources or sift archival material to revise interpretations, as does Benjamin Yang, *From revolution to politics: Chinese Communists on the Long March* (Boulder, Colorado: Westview Press, 1990. 338p.).

297 **China in revolution: the Yenan way revisited.**
Mark Selden. Armonk, New York; London: M. E. Sharpe, 1995.
294p. maps. bibliog.

An expanded edition of Selden's *The Yenan way in revolutionary China* (Cambridge, Massachusetts: Harvard University Press, 1971. 311p. maps. [Harvard East Asian Series, no. 62]). This pivotal study argues that the 1937-45 experience in Yan'an – Mao's headquarters in Shaanxi province – generated a characteristic vision which endured through the Cultural Revolution. Selden describes the area's history and ecological predicament, failed attempts at land revolution, and the 1936 arrival of Long March survivors. The 1942 military and political crisis led to a rectification (*zhengfeng*) campaign to implement the 'mass line' ('from the people, to the people'); the campaign enforced party discipline, established interaction with the masses, and created new institutions and responses. Selden's new epilogue assesses criticisms of the original edition, concedes that it neglected the 'dark side', reaffirms its perspectives, and reviews the state of the field.

298 **The Chinese Communists' road to power: the Anti-Japanese National United Front, 1937-1945.**
Shum Kui-kwong. Oxford: Oxford University Press, 1988. 312p.
bibliog.

Argues that the wartime United Front constituted the key turning point in the road to power, since the Chinese Communist Party necessarily came to terms with national bourgeoisie, rich peasants, patriotic landlords and enlightened gentry. Shum criticizes earlier studies for concentrating on peasant mobilization and for accepting the accusation that Wang Ming (a former General Secretary of the CCP) was a Soviet tool; Wang was vilified because he was Mao's chief rival at the time, but actually made important practical and theoretical contributions. The analysis concentrates on policy and statements from leaders, rather than local studies of policy implementation, and emphasizes unity of intention rather than struggle over control. Lyman P. Van Slyke, *Enemies and friends: the United Front in Chinese Communist history* (Stanford, California: Stanford University Press, 1967. 330p. bibliog.) follows the development of the United Front concept in the thought of Lenin, the First United Front in the 1920s, the Second United Front 1937-45, to the post-1949 campaigns to found the new China. Appendices contain documents describing official policy.

299 **Mobilizing the masses: building revolution in Henan.**
Odoric Y. K. Wou. Stanford, California: Stanford University Press,
1994. 477p. bibliog.

Using internal documents recently made available, this work traces the twists and turns of Chinese Communist Party strategy in Henan, a key inland province, from 1925-49. Wou emphasizes the development of appeals to urban workers, rural religious sectarians, rural gentry, student idealists, soldiers and, most important, the peasantry. Party strategy adapted to the needs and views of each of these groups, and mobilized them successfully with community action and reform programmes which built the political power needed to win the eventual Civil War of the 1940s.

300 **Red star over China.**
Edgar Snow. London: Victor Gollancz (Left Book Club); New York:
Random House, 1937. 464p.; New York: Grove Press, 1968. rev. ed.
543p.

A journalistic classic which conveys the militant optimism on the eve of the Sino-
Japanese war. Mao had been reported dead, and Snow's uncensored reports of social
revolution were major revelations even for Chinese readers; highlights include Mao's
'Autobiography', interviews with other leaders, and the epic account of the 1934-35
Long March. Snow recounts the political rivalry between the Nationalists and the
Communists, the life of the 'Young Marshall' Zhang Xueliang and the dramatic 1936
Xi'an Incident, in which Chiang Kai-shek was kidnapped and came to lead the new
United Front against Japan. For Snow's life and politics, see John Maxwell
Hamilton's readable *Edgar Snow: a biography* (Bloomington, Indiana: University of
Indiana Press, 1988. 343p.).

The People's Republic of China (1949-)

301 **New ghosts, old dreams: Chinese rebel voices.**
Geremie Barmé, Linda Jaivin. New York: Times Books, a Division
of Random House, 1992. 515p.

A companion and successor to *Seeds of fire: Chinese voices of conscience*, edited by
Geremie Barmé, John Minford (New York: Hill & Wang, 1988. 491p. 'Substantial
portions of this book were first published by Far Eastern Economic Review, Hong
Kong, 1986'). Both volumes are extraordinarily powerful, copiously illustrated
anthologies which weave selections from literature, visual arts, cinema, philosophy
and polemic into an integrated but complex overview of Chinese reform culture. The
earlier volume catches the 1980s mood of democracy and dissent among 'urblings', as
Barmé translates *zhiqing* (intellectual youth); the second explores the rebel scene
following the 1989 crackdown. In each, selections are grouped thematically, and
accompanied by sharply opinionated introductions and commentary by the editors.

302 **Wild lily, prairie fire: China's road to democracy, Yan'an to
Tian'anmen, 1942-1989.**
Edited by Gregor Benton, Alan Hunter. Princeton, New Jersey:
Princeton University Press, 1995. bibliog.

Contains sixty-eight documents with notes and an extensive introduction, aimed at
students and general readers. Benton and Hunter argue that there is a line of
intellectuals' dissent and protest which has grown in sophistication and strength.
Chapter one comprises Wang Shiwei's 1942 'Wild Lily', which criticized the élitism
and inflexibility of the Party, and essays by Ding Ling and Luo Feng. Chapters two and
three cover the critical arguments developed during the Hundred Flowers period (1957)
and the Cultural Revolution (1966-76), while chapter four covers 'China Spring'.
Chapter five, 'Prairie Fire, 1989', includes essays by students and workers, while
chapter six, 'Intellectuals' Critique', comprises essays by the leading dissident thinkers.

303 **Alive in the bitter sea.**
Fox Butterfield.   New York: Times Books, 1982. 468p.
An exposé portrait of China in the early 1980s by one of the first American correspondents to live in China since 1949. Other well regarded accounts also give readable, comprehensive, well-informed coverage and illustrate the emergence of a more realistic, first-hand view of China and the debates over 'socialism with Chinese characteristics': Richard Bernstein's thoughtful and disenchanted *From the center of the earth: the search for the truth about China* (Boston, Massachusetts: Little, Brown, 1982. 260p.); Roger Garside, *Coming alive: China after Mao* (New York: McGraw-Hill, 1981. 458p.), which provides a dramatic account of the transition from Mao to Hua Guofeng to Deng, including the brief flowering of Democracy Wall in 1978 as a forum for critical debate; and Jay and Linda Mathews' more affable *One billion: a China chronicle* (New York: Random House, 1983. 353p.).

304 **People's China: a brief history.**
Craig Dietrich.   New York; Oxford: Oxford University Press, 1994.
2nd ed. 362p. maps. bibliog.
A concise survey aimed at the advanced undergraduate and general reader, which describes the 'extraordinary historical scenes as the People's Republic sought to achieve social change, economic development, and power'. Ten chronologically ordered chapters cover political events and ideas, with an emphasis on policies, personalities and conflicts. The 'Suggested Readings' section offers an extensive, lightly annotated list of works in English, arranged by topic and period.

305 **China's intellectuals: advise and dissent.**
Merle Goldman.   Cambridge, Massachusetts; London: Harvard
University Press, 1981. 276p. bibliog.
Discusses intellectuals and politics from the end of the Great Leap Forward (1958), a programme of rapid economic expansion, to the Cultural Revolution, sketching many lives and careers. Goldman shows how academic, journalistic and literary 'liberal intellectuals', whose bureaucratic patrons included Zhou Enlai, criticized radical political programmes in the early 1960s and again in the early 1970s, working toward Western style modernization. On both occasions, 'radical intellectuals', whose patrons included Mao, counterattacked, espousing programmes of populist mobilization. Goldman's *Literary dissent in Communist China* (Cambridge, Massachusetts: Harvard University Press, 1967. 343p. bibliog. [Harvard East Asia Series, no. 39]) portrays Party campaigns and writers from 1940s Yan'an (especially Ding Ling and Wang Shiwei) to the One Hundred Flowers campaign of 1956 and the Great Leap Forward, especially Lu Xun's disciple, Hu Feng, and the novelist Xiao Jun.

306 **Sowing the seeds of democracy in China: political reform in the Deng Xiaoping era.**
Merle Goldman.   Cambridge, Massachusetts; London: Harvard
University Press, 1994. 426p. bibliog.
Political reform under Deng did not match the achievements made in economics; Goldman's clearheaded study explains why. Deng's protégé Hu Yaobang (1913-89) nurtured an intellectual network which came to advocate free press, an effective legislature, rule of law and competitive elections. Goldman charts the alternating

course between political openness and literary repression, especially the attacks on the writer Bai Hua, the Spiritual Pollution and Bourgeois Liberalism Campaigns, and the cycle of openness and repression which cumulatively evolved important revisions in ideology. Solidification of loyal opposition in the late 1980s provided the context for democratic élite support of the pro-democracy movement, which saw the emergence of a new type of democratic activist, the non-party student or worker.

307 China's establishment intellectuals.
Carol Lee Hamrin, Timothy Cheek. Armonk, New York; London: M. E. Sharpe, 1986. 266p. bibliog.

Analyses non-dissident intellectuals who accepted the party state but who tried at the same time to assert professional standards and the legitimacy of private interest; their opposition was not based on democratic theories of liberal pluralism, but was moralistic and Confucian. The introduction explores 'collaboration and conflict' in Chinese Communist Party history. Individual studies are grouped according to the degree of collaboration. Part one, 'At the Center', focuses on Peng Zhen (1902-), Party leader of Beijing deposed in the Cultural Revolution then rehabilitated to lead the overhaul of the legal system. Part two, 'Party Intellectuals', studies Yang Xiangzhen and Deng Tuo. Part three, 'Establishment Scholars', looks at Sun Yefang, a leader in the theory of socialist economics, and Wu Han (1909-69), historian, playwright and Mayor of Beijing. Part four includes a chapter on Bai Hua, a film writer on the Army's payroll, and a study of growing alienation among Chinese youths. *China's intellectuals and the state: in search of a new relationship*, edited by Merle Goldman, with Timothy Cheek, Carol Lee Hamrin (Cambridge, Massachusetts: Council on East Asian Studies, Harvard University, distributed by Harvard University Press, 1987. 374p.) is a symposium which explores various intellectual roles: as mouthpieces for official ideology, as members of the professional élite, and as a critical example.

308 The People's Republic of China, 1949-1979: a documentary survey.
Edited by Harold C. Hinton. Wilmington, Delaware: Scholarly Resources, 1980. 4 vols.

A comprehensive standard selection of published documents, taken largely from official press and radio sources, with brief commentaries from the editor. Hinton warns that these represent official propaganda to a high degree, but are essential in investigating policies and official intentions. The coverage continues in *The People's Republic of China, 1979-1984: a documentary survey* (Wilmington, Delaware: Scholarly Resources, 1986. 2 vols.). *The People's Republic of China: a documentary history of revolutionary change*, edited, with an introduction by Mark Selden, with Patty Eggleston (New York; London: Monthly Review Press, 1979. 718p. bibliog.) provides a briefer selection of official and unofficial documents, such as: major laws and directives; the four constitutions of the People's Republic; documents on the Five Year Plans; Mao's major theoretical statements; and documents defining the working class struggle, the women's movement and education. Selden provides a substantial interpretative introduction.

309 **The People's Republic, Part 1: the emergence of revolutionary China, 1949-1965.**
Edited by Roderick MacFarquhar, John K. Fairbank. Cambridge, England; New York; Port Chester, New York; Melbourne; Sydney: Cambridge University Press, 1987. 680p. bibliog. (Cambridge History of China, vol. 14).

Provides detailed chapter-length treatments of major political, economic and social developments; together with the following item, this work comprises the most comprehensive survey of the People's Republic. The editor's 'The Reunification of China' discusses the problem of unity in history, the role of modernization, and the problem of local control. Part one, 'Emulating the Soviet Model, 1949-1957', has chapters on establishing and consolidating the régime; economic recovery and the First Five Year Plan; education; the Party and intellectuals; and foreign relations. Part two, 'The Search for a Chinese Road, 1958-1965', has chapters on the Great Leap Forward and the split in the Yan'an leadership; the economy; education and the Great Leap Forward; the Party and intellectuals; and the Sino-Soviet split. The volume concludes with a magisterial essay on the basic sources, their limitations, and the English-language secondary literature.

310 **The People's Republic, Part 2: revolutions within the Chinese Revolution, 1966-1982.**
Edited by Roderick MacFarquhar, John K. Fairbank. Cambridge, England; New York; Port Chester, New York; Melbourne; Sydney: Cambridge University Press, 1991. 1,108p. bibliog. (Cambridge History of China, vol. 15).

Continues the previous item. An introductory chapter covers Mao's thought, 1949-76. Part one, 'The Cultural Revolution: China in Turmoil, 1966-1969', includes chapters on the confrontation with the Soviet Union; the Cultural Revolution and the struggle for succession, 1969-82; the opening to America; and the aftermath of the Cultural Revolution. Full chapters are devoted to: economic policy and performance; the educational revolution, its negation, and the 'Chinese model' in a Third-World perspective; and the relation between politics and creativity. The section 'Life and Letters under Communism' comprises chapters on: daily life in the countryside; urban life; and literature under Communism from the One Hundred Flowers campaign to the Cultural Revolution. A section covers Taiwan under Nationalist rule, 1949-82, and the epilogue considers the 'onus of unity'. Bibliographical essays describe primary sources, major themes of interpretation, and leading works, primarily in English and Chinese.

311 **Mao's China and after: a history of the People's Republic.**
Maurice Meisner. New York: Free Press; London: Collier Macmillan, 1986. rev. expanded ed. 534p. bibliog. (Transformation of Modern China Series).

A full general survey which provides a lucid analysis of Marxist-Leninist ideology, economic development strategies and political conflict. Meisner presents these developments 'through the prism of their own socialist aims', rather than in terms of 'modernization'. After chapters describing pre-1949 society and the development of Mao's revolutionary strategy, Meisner analyses the post-1949 'new order' in the cities, land reform ('the bourgeois revolution in the countryside'), collectivization and the social and political consequences of industrialization. The Great Leap Forward, the Cultural Revolution, and their accompanying campaigns are analysed as social as well as ideological and political conflicts. An epilogue discusses socialism and modernization in the post-Maoist era. A select bibliography lists works cited or consulted.

312 **China in our time: the epic saga of the People's Republic, from the Communist victory to Tiananmen Square and beyond.**
Ross Terrill.   New York; London; Toronto; Sydney; Tokyo, Singapore: Simon & Schuster, 1992. 366p.

A sympathetic but critical overview of China since 1949, painted with a broad brush and portraying vivid personalities. The narrative is woven around the three 'great dramas' fashioned by Mao: the Liberation in 1949; the Great Leap Forward of the 1950s; and the Cultural Revolution, 1966-76. The writing is vivid with anecdotes and dialogues, based on scholarship, with many observations on national personalities and local human consequence. Terrill has reflected upon China and socialism since the time of his first visit as an Australian student in 1964; his other books of travel and reportage include *800,000,000: the real China* (Boston, Massachusetts: Little, Brown, 1972. 235p.) and *Flowers on a iron tree: five cities of China* (q.v.).

Foreigners in China

313 **Empire of the sun.**
J. G. Ballard.   London: Victor Gollancz; New York: Simon & Schuster, 1984. 279p.

A novel, based on the author's boyhood experiences in Shanghai during the Second World War and imprisonment by the Japanese in Lunghua Civilian Assembly Centre, 1942-45. 'Jim', the young protagonist, son of a British resident, is lost in the tumult of the 1941 Japanese invasion and forced to fend for himself in the camp. Ballard uses his saga of humiliation, adaptation and survival to mirror and mock the end of the British Empire in Asia as it gives way to the Americans and Mao.

314 **Barbarians and mandarins: thirteen centuries of western travelers in China.**
Nigel Cameron.   New York; London: Weatherhill, 1970. maps. 443p.
Reprinted, Chicago; London: University of Chicago Press, 1976.

Contains engaging and well illustrated accounts of people who travelled to China, why they went, and their adventures. Cameron, who was a journalist in Asia during the 1950s and 1960s, begins with mediaeval religious sojourners, then goes on to cover: Marco Polo, John of Montecorvino, and Odoric of Perdenone; visitors who arrived during the Ming dynasty, including Tomaso Pirès and Matteo Ricci; those who arrived under the Qing, including Catholic missionaries, Lord Elgin and Mrs Archibald Little; and a bevy of modern travel writers.

315 **Spoilt children of empire: Westerners in Shanghai and the Chinese revolution of the 1920s.**
Nicholas R. Clifford. Hanover, New Hampshire; London: Middlebury College Press, published by University Press of New England, 1991. 361p. bibliog.

Portrays the 1920s foreign community in Shanghai – 'Shanghailanders' – and their reactions to the anti-imperialist Nationalist Revolution. Four chapters first describe the haphazard building of foreign institutions in Shanghai, such as the Shanghai Municipal Council, business and missionary enterprises, and social clubs. The May 30 1925 Incident mobilized Chinese radicals and horrified foreign hardliners; Shanghailanders demanded gunboat intervention, earning them the sobriquet the 'spoilt children of empire'. After 1927, foreign and Chinese cosmopolitans in Shanghai discovered common interests against 'parochials' on either side and against Nationalist government ambitions. Clifford considers whether Shanghai's model of Western society was an 'imperialist parasite' or 'China's future'.

316 **The missionary enterprise in China and America.**
Edited, with an introduction by John K. Fairbank. Cambridge, Massachusetts: Harvard University Press, 1974. 442p. bibliog. (Harvard Studies in American-East Asian Relations).

Contains twelve essays, with a substantial summary introduction by the editor. Part one, 'Protestant Missions and American Expansion', discusses: a comparison of the American China establishment with that of the Near East; the Student Volunteer Movement and the structure of recruitment and support for China missions; and the 'liberal search for an exportable Christianity', describing the reworking of Protestant Social Gospel theology. Part two, 'Christianity and the Transformation of China', concerns: the theology of American missions in China; an early mission newspaper in Chinese; the role of Chinese Christian reformers along the 'littoral' from Shanghai to Canton; and Yenching University. Part three, 'China Mission Images and American Policies', describes: mission justification of the use of force in early 19th-century China; why missions stayed in the face of 1920s Chinese nationalism; and a substantial theoretical essay by Arthur Schlesinger, Jr., 'The Missionary Enterprise and Theories of Imperialism'. James Reed, *The missionary mind and American East Asia policy 1911-1915* (Cambridge, Massachusetts: Council on East Asian Studies, Harvard University, distributed by Harvard University Press, 1983. 258p. bibliog. [Harvard East Asian Monographs, no. 104]) sees a missionary imprint on images and policy. Alvyn J. Austin, *Saving China: Canadian Missionaries in the Middle Kingdom, 1888-1959* (Toronto; Buffalo, New York; London: University of Toronto Press, 1985. 395p.) is a well researched and readable survey which deals with many topics common to Canadian and other mission efforts.

317 **China stands up: ending the western presence, 1948-1950.**
Beverly Hooper. Sydney; London; Boston, Massachusetts: Allen & Unwin, 1986. 246p. bibliog. (East Asia Series).

A lively history and analysis of how the new government dealt with Europeans, Americans and their institutions and eventually eliminated most of them. Chapters summarize a century of imperialism and the coming of the Communists, then describe the demise of Western institutions in business, missions, education and culture, and diplomacy. Some observers speculated that the decisive expulsion came only with the Korean War in 1950, but Hooper concludes that the logic of the Chinese government's nationalism and socialism would have forced a break in any case.

318   **Foreign devils on the Silk Road.**
Peter Hopkirk.   London: Murray, 1980. Reprinted, Oxford: Oxford
University Press, 1984; Amherst, Massachusetts: University of
Massachusetts Press, 1984. 252p. maps.

A well told account of the scholarly adventurers who raced across present-day
Xinjiang and Gansu in the early 20th century searching for lost treasures and
imperialist influence. These archaeological raiders bought or seized countless wall-
paintings, manuscripts, sculptures and other treasures, especially the library at
Dunhuang. Whether they rescued them from destruction or simply stole them for
museums of Europe, America and Japan is still a matter of some debate. Hopkirk first
sketches the rich history of trade and Buddhism on the Silk Road, then tells of six
men, including: Sven Hedin of Sweden; Sir Aurel Stein of Britain; Albert von le Coq
of Germany; Langdon Warner of the United States; and Count Otani of Japan.

319   **The gospel of gentility: American women missionaries in
turn-of-the-century China.**
Jane Hunter.   New Haven, Connecticut; London: Connecticut: Yale
University Press, 1984. 318p. bibliog.

An attractively written study which combines women's history, history of American
culture, and Chinese history. Hunter uses letters, diaries and published sources to
present individual lives, discussing the female culture of Protestant American women
missionaries, their dilemmas in choosing between responsibility to Chinese clients and
their own families, their reception and effect on Chinese women, and how Christianity
was changed by the context of American imperialism in China.

320   **Life along the South Manchurian Railroad.**
Itō Takeo, translated by Joshua A. Fogel.   Armonk, New York;
London: M. E. Sharpe, 1989. 241p. bibliog.

An autobiographical account. The Research Bureau of the South Manchurian Railway
was founded as the academic intelligence base for the Japanese empire in China, but
ironically became a hot-bed of radical social analysis (researchers sang the
Internationale to see off a colleague). Itō also describes the rural investigations they
carried out in 1920s and 1930s China. *Japanese agent in Tibet: my ten years of travel
in disguise*, by Hisao Kimura, as told to Scott Berry (London: Serindia, 1990. 232p.)
is a shrewd and charming memoir by a leading scholar who was trained during the
1930s in Western China for intelligence work and describes his adventures and
Chinese politics.

321   **China reporting: an oral history of American journalism in the
1930s and 1940s.**
Edited by Stephen R. MacKinnon, Oris Friesen.   Berkeley, California;
London: University of California Press, 1987. 230p. bibliog.

Brings together edited dialogues from a 1982 reunion conference of American
reporters and scholars who covered wartime China. John Fairbank called their
attempts to portray China a 'first-class disaster'. A reporter disagreed: 'we did a pretty
goddam good job'. John Hersey recounts his experiences with Henry Luce, who
monitored China reportage in *Time* and *Life*. Participants then recall the excitement
and problem of reporting from Shanghai and Hankow in the 1930s; dealing with

censorship and war conditions in Chungking; the editorial 'gatekeepers' who, like Henry Luce, chose what to allow into print; political objectivity and personal judgements; missed stories; and the relations of press coverage, American government policy and public opinion. The 'Selected Additional Readings' section lists books and articles in English.

322 The correspondence of G. E. Morrison.

George E. Morrison, edited by Lo Hui-min.   Cambridge, England;
New York: Cambridge University Press, 1976, 1978. 2 vols. maps.
bibliog.

Morrison (1862-1920) was the *Times* of London correspondent in China at the time of the 1911 Revolution, and Yuan Shikai then made him a paid adviser to the Chinese government, both key positions for meeting Chinese leaders and influencing foreign public opinion. His voluminous and lively correspondence with a wide range of Chinese and Europeans reflects British ambitions in China, all carefully annotated by Professor Lo. Morrison's first trip through China is described in the still readable late-Victorian travel book, George E. Morrison, *An Australian in China, being the narrative of a quiet journey across China to British India* (London: Cox, 1895. Reprinted, Hong Kong; Melbourne: Oxford University Press, 1985. 299p.). Cyril Pearl, *Morrison of Peking* (Sydney: Angus & Robertson, 1967. 431p.) provides a genial account of the man's life and times.

323 Foreigners within the gates: the legations at Peking.

Michael J. Moser, Yeone Wei-chih Moser.   Hong Kong: Oxford
University Press, 1993. 158p.

A brief history, which focuses on the physical setting of the Beijing foreign legation community, with photographs and maps, from its small-scale beginnings in the 19th century, and the Boxer siege, to the ensuing growth into an almost self-contained Legation Quarter. A final 'postscript' portrays the surviving remains and experience of buildings under the People's Republic. Personal memoirs of life in pre-revolution Beijing – then called 'Beiping' – include: George N. Kates, *The years that were fat: the last of old China* (New York: Harper, 1952. Reprinted, with a preface by John Fairbank, Cambridge, Massachusetts; London: M. I. T. Press, 1967. 268p.); John Blofeld, *City of lingering splendour: a frank account of old Peking's exotic pleasures* (London: Hutchison, 1961. Reprinted, Boston, Massachusetts; Shaftesbury, England: Shambala, 1989. 255p.); and David Kidd, *Peking story* (New York: Clarkson, 1988. 207p.).

324 China hands: the adventures and ordeals of the American journalists who joined forces with the Great Chinese Revolution.

Peter Rand.   New York: Simon & Schuster, 1995. 384p. map. bibliog.

Rand, whose father Christopher covered China for *New Yorker* magazine in the 1940s, tells a sympathetic but shrewd story of reporters who covered revolution and war, and their impassioned debates over how to save the China they loved. Figures discussed here include: Thomas Millard, the Missouri born founder of American journalism in Shanghai; Rayna Prohme, the romantic red-head who joined China's revolution in the 1920s as press agent for Sun Yat-sen's Nationalists, only to die in Moscow; Anna Louise Strong; Harold Isaacs, the author of *Tragedy of the Chinese revolution* (q.v.); Agnes Smedley, the impassioned revolutionary reporter; Edgar Snow, whose *Red star over China* (q.v.), scooped the world on Mao's revolution in 1937; and Theodore White and Annalee Jacoby, authors of *Thunder out of China* (q.v.), whose reporting on wartime corruption helped to discredit the Nationalist régime.

325 Escape to Shanghai.
James R. Ross.   New York: Free Press, 1994. 298p. bibliog.

During the 1930s, Shanghai was one of the few cities to accept Jewish refugees from fascist Europe. Here Ross uses published sources and interviews to tell their story for a general audience, including the efforts of the local community to assist them, wartime hardships under Japanese occupation, individual experiences and later careers. David Kranzler, *Japanese, Nazis, and Jews: the Jewish refugee community of Shanghai, 1938-1945* (New York: Yeshiva University Press, 1976. 644p.) is a more detailed study of the subject.

326 Shanghai: collision point of cultures, 1918-1939.
Harriet Sargeant.   London: Cape; New York: Crown, 1990. 371p. maps. bibliog.

A sprightly social history of Shanghai between the wars, written for a general audience. George Spunt, *A place in time* (New York: Putnam, 1968. 377p. map) provides a memoir of a family of Russian Jews who emigrated to Shanghai in 1904 and became cotton mill entrepreneurs; Spunt shrewdly characterizes both glittering social life and the context of Chinese misery and revolution. Vicki Baum, *Shanghai '37*, a translation of *Hotel Shanghai* (London; New York: Doubleday, 1939. Reprinted, Hong Kong: Oxford University Press, 1986 [Oxford in Asia]) is a popular novel reflecting images of romantic Shanghai in the 1930s. Noel Barber, *The fall of Shanghai* (New York: Coward, McCann, & Geoghegan, 1979. 248p. bibliog.) gracefully relates Shanghai 1945-51 experiences leading to 'liberation' (in the revolutionary view) or 'fall' (in the view of the foreign community on which Barber focuses). Sam Tata, *Shanghai 1949: the end of an era* (London: Batsford, 1989. 143p.) features photographs of street sights and people in the candid style of Henri Cartier-Bresson.

327 The stubborn earth: American agriculturalists on Chinese soil, 1898-1937.
Randall E. Stross.   Berkeley, California; Los Angeles; London: University of California Press, 1986. 272p.

These seven lively studies use diaries, letters and journals to discuss the stories and significance of men who brought American techniques to the world's largest agricultural economy; their frustrations reflect cultural differences, nationalistic touchiness and American blindnesses. Stross first compares attitudes toward agriculture in the two countries, then describes: the US Department of Agriculture's excursions into China; early advisers, 1890s-1910s; Joseph Bailie and his technical schools; Christian mission efforts; John Lossing Buck and his agricultural surveys at Nanking University; and the setbacks suffered by the Americans' 'star pupil', Shen Zonghan (1895-?), trained at Cornell School of Agriculture. James C. Thomson, Jr. *While China faced West: American reformers in Nationalist China, 1928-1937* (Cambridge, Massachusetts; Harvard University Press, 1969. 310p. [Harvard East Asia, no. 38], gracefully analyses liberal missionary and Rockefeller Foundation efforts in rural reconstruction under Chiang Kai-shek's régime.

111

Western and Central Asians in China under the Mongols: their transformation into Chinese.
See item no. 163.

Entering China's service: Robert Hart's journals, 1854-1863.
See item no. 802.

Bulls in the China shop and other Sino-American business encounters.
See item no. 962.

Foreign views of China

328 **The dragon and the eagle: the presence of China in the American enlightenment.**
A. Owen Aldridge. Detroit, Michigan: Wayne State University Press, 1993. 287p.

Surveys the 'American Enlightenment' from roughly 1706 to 1826 and disputes the earlier assumption that the 18th-century American perception of China was 'innocent and uninstructed'. During colonial times, China was a 'mirage or a reflection' of European writers who had never seen Asia, but after the Revolution many Americans actually walked on Chinese soil; Robert Waln, a Philadelphia merchant became the 'American Marco Polo'. Wide-ranging speculation came from Franklin, Jefferson, Philip Freneau and others. An appendix gives a 'List of American Imprints Concerning China Before 1826'. Stuart Creighton Miller, *The unwelcome immigrant: the American image of the Chinese, 1785-1882* (Berkeley, California: University of California Press, 1969. 259p.) provides many detailed examples of racist images leading up to exclusion of Asian immigration in 1882, indicating that the negative image was not confined to California or to workers threatened by cheap Chinese labour.

329 **The good earth.**
Pearl S. Buck. New York: John Day, 1931. Reprinted with an introduction by Peter Conn, New York: Pocket Books, 1995.

This novel was long the most widely read English-language book on China; in translations, it introduced even Chinese and Japanese readers to the Chinese village. Buck grew up in China as the daughter of missionary parents and married John Lossing Buck, who conducted the first extensive surveys of the Chinese farm economy. The novel's protagonists, Wang Lung, a farmer, and his wife, Olan, are presented as sympathetic human figures struggling to earn a living from the 'good earth'. Buck also portrays famine, patriarchal family values, and Wang's resistance to Christian missions and radical revolution. The book is not a completely trustworthy introduction to these topics, but recaptures an informed and once influential view.

330 **The Chinese chameleon: an analysis of European conceptions of Chinese civilization.**
Raymond Dawson. London; New York; Toronto; Oxford: Oxford University Press, 1967. 235p.

An urbane, standard survey of travellers, scholars and opinion makers showing how prevailing characterizations of China changed with the era: Marco Polo saw 'ritcheness and plentiffullnesse', the Jesuits a 'model even for Christians', but 19th-century historians saw a 'people of eternal standstill', while missionaries saw heathens and the public bought Chinoiserie willow-pattern. A recent survey is Colin Mackerras, *Western images of China* (Hong Kong: Oxford University Press, 1989. 337p.). Andrew L. March, *The idea of China* (New York; Washington, DC: Praeger, 1974. 165p.) provides a neglected but fruitful analysis of how the concept 'Asia' was historically constructed and how it shaped geographic interpretations of Chinese culture.

331 **Scratches on our minds: American views of China and India.**
Harold R. Isaacs. New York: John Day, 1958. 416p. Reprinted, Westport, Connecticut: Greenwood Press, 1973. Reprinted, with a new preface, Armonk, New York; London: M. E. Sharpe, 1980.

One of the most influential books in Western study of China, still feisty and insightful. Isaacs worked as a journalist in Shanghai during the early 1930s, producing *Tragedy of the Chinese revolution* (q.v.). In the 1950s he interviewed American opinion makers and read standard accounts to identify and explain how Americans saw China and India. His periodization for China has been widely followed, the 'ages' being six: *Respect* (18th century); *Contempt* (1840-1905); *Benevolence* (1905-37); *Admiration* (1937-44); *Disenchantment* (1944-49); and *Hostility* (1949-). *America views China: American images of China then and now*, edited by Jonathan Goldstein, Jerry Israel, Hilary Conroy (Bethlehem, Pennsylvania: Lehigh University Press; London; Toronto: Associated University Presses, 1991. 310p. bibliog.) collects articles on American views during the period 1840-1989, accompanied by an extensive bibliography; subjects include Charlie Chan, Carl Crow, Edgar Snow, and the insightful 'From China with Disdain', which analyses the growing disillusionment with China after 1972.

332 **Asia in the making of Europe.**
Donald Lach. Chicago; London: University of Chicago Press, 1965- . 3 vols. (five projected), each in two or more books. maps. bibliog.

Provides a detailed description and documentation, with copious bibliographical references, of the influx of ideas, technology, flora and fauna, art objects, and artifacts from all parts of Asia and the influences in Europe on arts, institutions, literatures and ideas. Volume one, 'The Century of Discovery' (in two books), deals with what Europe had come to know about Asia before 1600; volume two, 'A Century of Wonder' (in three books), covers the 17th century; and in volume three, 'A Century of Advance' (in four books), Lach, now with Edwin J. van Kley, describes in book one commercial trade, religious missions, and travel writing, while succeeding books depict European images of particular regions (Book Four covers East Asia).

333 **Writings on China.**
Gottfried Wilhelm Leibniz, translated, with an introduction, notes, and commentaries by Daniel J. Cook, Henry Rosemont, Jr. Chicago; La Salle, Illinois: Open Court, 1994. 157p. bibliog.

Leibniz, the influential 17th-century German philosopher, wrote widely on China as part of his ecumenical concerns; their high level of civilization made the Chinese prime candidates for conversion to Christianity, models for rational government, and inspiration for new philosophy. Cook and Rosemont bring together Leibniz' writings on China, with an extensive introduction to situate and explicate them. Included are 'Preface to NOVISSIMA SINICA, (1697/99)'; 'On the Civil Cult of Confucius' (1700); 'Remarks on Chinese Rites and Religion' (1708); and 'Discourse on the Natural Theology of the Chinese' (1716). *Moral enlightenment: Leibniz and Wolff on China*, edited and with an introduction by Julia Ching, Willard Oxtoby (Nettetal: Steyler Verlag, 1992. 299p. [Monumenta Serica Monograph, no. 26]) includes further essays by Leibniz and Christian Wolff (1679-1754).

334 **Asia in western fiction.**
Edited by Robin W. Winks, James R. Rush. Manchester, England: University of Manchester Press; Honolulu: University of Hawaii Press, 1990. 229p. bibliogs.

These chapter essays, by various hands, describe fiction (mostly in English or French) written about Asian countries. China is covered in Donald F. Lach, Theodore Foss, 'Images of Asia and Asians in European Fiction, 1500-1800', and Jonathan Spence, 'Chinese Fictions in the Twentieth Century', whose references include: Pearl Buck, *The good earth* (q.v.); Ernest Bramah's humorous novel of mythical scholars, *Kai Lung unrolls his mat* (New York: Doubleday, 1928. 320p.); André Malraux's politically involved novel of 1920s revolution, *La condition humaine*, translated by Haakon Chevalier as *Man's fate* (New York: Modern Library, 1936. 360p.); and Victor Segalen's *René Leys* (Paris, 1922; Paris: Gallimard, 1971; New York: Overlook, 1988. 222p.), an enigmatic tale of a mysterious Belgian adventurer who claimed inside connections with the Manchu court at the time of the 1911 Revolution.

Biographies and Autobiographical Accounts

Collective biography and dictionaries

335 **In the service of the Khan: eminent personalities of the early Mongol-Yuan period (1200-1300).**
Edited by Igor de Rachewiltz, Hok-lam Chan, Hsiao Ch'i-ch'ing, Peter W. Grier. Weisbaden, Germany: Harrasowitz, 1993. 808p.

Provides substantial, short, scholarly biographies of thirty-seven high ranking imperial servants, including empresses, soldiers, advisers and bureaucrats. Examples of each are selected for each reign period in the early part of the dynasty. Chinese characters are included, as well as extensive notes, bibliographic references and indexes.

336 **Sung biographies.**
Edited by Herbert Franke. Weisbaden, Germany: Franz Steiner Verlag, 1976. 4 vols. (Müchener Ostasiatische Studien).

These scholarly biographical entries cover 406 notables from the 9th-13th centuries, with extensive references and scholarly apparatus; some important figures were omitted because suitable authors could not be found. Entries are in English, German or French. Volume four is devoted to painters.

337 **A Chinese biographical dictionary.**
Herbert Giles. London: Quaritch; Shanghai: Kelly & Walsh, 1898. Reprinted, Taipei: Ch'eng-wen Publishing Company, 1966. 1,022p.

Although much of the scholarship is dated and the selection does not reflect current interests, this is still the only biographical work for the whole sweep of Chinese history and lists many figures not mentioned in other Western texts, especially for the periods before the Yuan dynasty, which are not covered in the other works listed in this section. Giles compiled the entries from standard Chinese reference works which reflect late imperial concerns and emphases.

338 **Dictionary of Ming biography, 1368-1644.**
Edited by Luther Carrington Goodrich, Fang Chao-ying. New York;
London: Columbia University Press, 1976. 2 vols.

The editors have compiled 659 substantial biographical articles on various types of persons, including emperors, scholars, scientists, soldiers and statesmen; much of the history of the dynasty is described along the way. Not covered are those who lived on into the Qing and are included in *Eminent Chinese of the Ch'ing period* (q.v.). Entries include Chinese characters and a short bibliography of writings by or about the subject.

339 **Eminent Chinese of the Ch'ing period, (1644-1911).**
Edited by Arthur W. Hummel. Washington, DC: United States
Government Printing Office, 1943, 1944. Reprinted, New York:
Paragon, 1964; Taipei: Ch'eng-wen, 1967. 2 vols.

Contains more than 800 biographical articles in 1,103 pages of text, on Chinese, Manchu and Mongol notables who died before 1912; the selection is weighted toward government figures but also includes rebels, poets, scholars, playwrights and Christian leaders. This represents a history of the Qing dynasty through biography, as material on many further figures and events is incorporated into the articles. The indexes of names, books and subjects make this a basic reference.

340 **Biographic dictionary of Chinese communism, 1921-1965.**
Donald W. Klein, Anne B. Clark. Cambridge, Massachusetts: Harvard
University Press, 1971. 2 vols. (Harvard East Asian Series, no. 57).

Contains biographical entries on 416 men and 17 women down to the outbreak of the Cultural Revolution. Most are Party, government or military notables, but some are cultural or medical leaders, athletes, provincial officials, diplomats or labour leaders. The articles remain largely reliable even though much additional material was 'liberated' by 1960s Red Guards or made public by 1980s reformers. Ninety-six appendices classify the subjects by: personal data (e.g. birth dates); early activities and organizations; participation in important events, army units and later Communist Party organizations; government organs; travel abroad; and fields of work. Entries give English references, and a selected bibliography lists important works. The glossary-index includes those mentioned in entries. Wolfgang Bartke, *Who's who in the People's Republic of China* (Armonk, New York: M. E. Sharpe, 'A Publication of the Institute of Asian Affairs, Hamburg', 1981. 729p.) covers current (as of 1980) active leadership in government, party, military and cultural organs; an appendix includes important deceased and purged cadres.

341 **Mountain of fame: portraits in Chinese history.**
John E. Wills, Jr. Princeton, New Jersey: Princeton University Press,
1994. 403p.

Conveys the sweep of history in China through twenty chapter-length biographies. Starting with Yu, the mythical founding ruler, and Confucius, Wills chooses emperors and an empress (the First Emperor of Qin, Empress Wu Zetian, Qianlong Emperor), historians (Sima Qian, Ban Zhao), reformers (Wang Mang, Liang Qichao), soldiers (Zhuge Liang, Yue Fei, Zheng Chenggong [Coxinga]), religious leaders (Hui Neng the Sixth Patriarch, Qiu Chuji the Daoist), poets (Su Dongbo, or Su Shi), and philosophers (Wang Yangming), with closing chapters on the Nationalist legacy, Mao Zedong, and 'Names in the News'.

342   **Confucian personalities.**
Edited by Arthur F. Wright, Denis Twitchett.   Stanford, California:
Stanford University Press, 1962. 411p.

A symposium which discusses and demonstrates the writing of Chinese biography. Wright's 'Values, Roles, and Personalities' and Twitchett's 'Problems of Chinese Biography' are clear and sophisticated expositions of the conventions, prejudices and biases found in traditional Confucian biographies. Among the individual essays are studies of: Feng Dao (882-954), a paragon of Confucian loyalty; Yue Fei (1103-41), the Song dynasty general whose betrayal by capitulationist rivals made him an emblem of nationalism in later times; Yelu Chucai (1189-1243), the statesmen credited with saving China under the Yuan; and Jia Sidao (1213-75), the archetypical 'bad last minister'. Earlier biographical symposia are *The Confucian persuasion*, edited by Arthur F. Wright (Stanford, California: Stanford University Press, 1960. 390p.), and *Confucianism in action*, edited by David Nivison, Arthur F. Wright (Stanford, California: Stanford University Press, 1959. 380p.).

343   **Chinese lives: an oral history of contemporary China.**
Zhang Xinxin, Sang Ye, edited by W. J. Jenner, Delia Davin, translated
by the editors and Cheng Lingfang, Gladys Yang, Judy Burrows,
Jeffrey C. Kinkley, Geremie Barmé, preface by Studs Terkel.
London: Macmillan London Ltd.; New York: Pantheon Books,
1987. 368p. map.

In 1984 Zhang (1953-) and Sang (1955-) travelled across China interviewing all sorts of people and artfully writing up their autobiographical talk as newspaper pieces; their eventual book was called *Beijingren* (Shanghai, China: Shanghai Cultural House, 1986), or 'Peking men', that is, descendants of their famous cave-ancestor. The result is a mosaic portrait of China, modelled on the books of Studs Terkel, in which many voices seem to speak directly to the reader. A less well-edited translation is *Chinese profiles* (Beijing: Panda Books, 1986. 276p.).

Directory of officials and organizations in China: a quarter century guide.
See item no. 1443.

Imperial China

344   **Confucius and the Chinese way.**
Herlee Glessner Creel.   New York: Harper, 1960. 363p.

An attractively written, broad biographical interpretation based on traditional written sources. Creel sets the scene of Confucius' time (?551-?479 BCE), recounts what is known of his life, presents his thought, and relates these to changing Confucian influences through later times, emphasizing the humanist and rational side. The work was originally published as *Confucius the man and the myth* (New York: John Day, 1949. 363p.).

345 **Koxinga and Chinese nationalism: history, myth, and the hero.**
Ralph C. Croizier.   Cambridge, Massachusetts: Harvard University
Press, 1977. 116p. (Harvard East Asian Monographs, no. 67).
Zheng Chenggong (1624-62), known in Europe as Koxinga or Coxinga, defied the
conquering Manchus to hold Taiwan as an independent multi-ethnic kingdom loyal to
the defunct Ming. Croizier studies how Zheng's historical reputation was formed and
re-formed by later Chinese nationalist patriots, and incorporates a good deal of
biographical information. For a short biography of Zheng, see Wills, *Mountain of
fame* (q.v.).

346 **Word, image, and deed in the life of Su Shih.**
Ronald C. Egan.   Cambridge, Massachusetts: Harvard University
Press, 1994. 474p. (Harvard-Yenching Institute Monographs, no. 39).
A comprehensive life of Su Shi, also called Su Dongpo (Su Shih; Su Tung-p'o; 1037-
1101). Su was a great poet and essayist, a political activist, government official, and
thinker. Egan relates him to Song dynasty Confucian thought, including Chan (Zen)
and Pure Land Buddhism, and, most important, explores his poetry and prose. Michael
A. Fuller, *The road to East Slope: the development of Su Shi's poetic voice* (Stanford,
California: Stanford University Press, 1990. 384p.) includes much background in a
study which focuses on literary craftsmanship. Beatta Grant, *Mt. Lu revisited:
Buddhism in the life and writings of Su Shih* (Honolulu: University of Hawaii Press,
1994. 249p.) is an illuminating study. Lin Yutang, *The gay genius: the life and times
of Su Tung-p'o, 1036-1101* (New York: John Day; London: Heineman, 1947.
Reprinted, Westport, Connecticut: Greenwood, 1971. 427p.) views Su in evocative but
anachronistic political terms. Burton Watson, *Su Tung-p'o: selections from a Sung
dynasty poet* (New York; London: Columbia University Press, 1965. 139p.) is the
fullest translation; much is also represented in standard anthologies.

347 **Son of heaven: founder of the T'ang dynasty.**
C. P. Fitzgerald.   Cambridge, England: Cambridge University Press,
1933. Reprinted, New York: AMS, 1971. 232p.
A straightforward presentation of the establishment of the Tang dynasty through a
political biography of Li Shimin (598-649), the ruthless, imaginative military talent
who organized the founding of the Tang and placed his father, Li Yuan (565-635) on
the throne before taking it over for himself. Fitzgerald uses the official dynastic
histories to recreate dramatic scenes, military campaigns, and the Han Chinese and
Turkic elements in the multi-cultural north-west frontier on which the Li family rose.

348 **The Empress Wu.**
C. P. Fitzgerald.   London: Cresset Press; Vancouver, Canada:
University of British Columbia Press, 1968. 2nd ed. 263p.
A colourful, historically well-read life and times of the only Chinese woman to rule as
emperor in her own name. Wu Zetian (630?-705) came to the palace as a concubine,
rose by intelligence and cunning tenacity, and contributed to historic shifts in political
structure and style. R. W. L. Guisso, *Wu Tse-T'ien and the politics of legitimation in
T'ang China* (Bellingham, Washington: Western Washington University Press, 1978.
355p.) examines how Wu manipulated political and religious appeals. More popular,
and occasionally even lurid, is Lin Yutang's fluent historical novel, *Lady Wu* (New
York: Putnam's, 1965. 255p.).

349 **The invention of Li Yu.**
Patrick Hanan. Cambridge, Massachusetts: Harvard University Press, 1988. 272p.

Li Yü (c. 1610-80) was a brilliant writer whose career spanned the Ming-Qing transition. One of the first professional literary men, he wrote innovative short stories, novels, plays, essays and criticism, and led a flamboyant, iconoclastic life. Hanan's sprightly biography portrays Li's literary life and outlook convincingly, giving extensive excerpts in readable translations. Translations of Li's work include the pornographic *The carnal prayer mat* (q.v.) and *Twelve towers: short stories*, retold by Nathan Mao (Hong Kong: Chinese University Press, distributed by University of Washington Press, 1979. 2nd ed. 1979. 149p.).

350 **Monarchy in the emperor's eyes: image and reality in the Ch'ien-lung reign.**
Harold L. Kahn. Cambridge, Massachusetts: Harvard University Press, 1971. 314p. (Harvard East Asian Series, no. 59).

Explores tensions between the images of the Qianlong Emperor (1711-99) as the 'brush and ink creature' of Chinese writers and as the 'flesh-and-blood maker of history'. Part one discusses 'the imperial image' in official writings of the time, in private historiography, and in the 'fractured image' of gentry criticism and popular novels. Part two, 'The Self-image: A Prince's View', vividly depicts the educative process in relation to his mother, his brother, and his tutors, showing how he was disciplined psychologically as well as politically. Part three, 'Self-image At The End', portrays a sanguine, eccentric Qianlong, who abdicated out of ostentatious filial deference to his grandfather's memory, leaving his throne and image in the control of the corrupt official, Ho-shen. Seventeen illustrations show the emperor in various roles.

351 **The poet Kao Ch'i (1336-1374).**
Frederick W. Mote. Princeton, New Jersey: Princeton University Press, 1962. 261p.

An elegant study of Ming dynasty cultural and intellectual worlds, as seen through the life of a leading poet, Gao Qi. Mote sketches the founding of the Ming dynasty, then tells in detail of the rise and disastrous shifts in the career of the young poet and his relations with literary circles in Suzhou (Soochow), the lower Yangzi centre of commerce and cultural innovation. The many readable translations of poetry (especially in the *shi* form) present the writings of Gao and his friends.

352 **Khubilai Khan: his life and times.**
Morris Rossabi. Berkeley, California; London: University of California Press, 1988. 322p.

The career of Khubilai (1215-94) spanned the apogee and decline of the Mongol empire; although a Mongol and not Chinese, he became emperor of China, and was the first Mongol to effectively rule, rather than simply control, China. Rossabi paints a vivid portrait of an intelligent and rapacious man and of his equally intelligent and independent wife. Khubilai's reign witnessed the construction of a capital city; the development of a legal code; new written scripts for languages in the Mongol domain; and court patronage of the theatre, the arts and crafts, and science and medicine. The biography thus constitutes a wide-ranging picture of China and Asian culture under Mongol rule in the 13th century.

353   **A madman of Chu: the Chinese myth of loyalty and dissent.**
Laurence A. Schneider.   Berkeley, California; London: University of
California Press, 1980. 270p.

Qu Yuan, a 3rd-century BCE court official serving the mid-Yangzi state of Chu, wrote
Songs of the south (q.v.) while in exile. Losing hope that the king would heed his
advice, he threw himself into the Milo River; the Dragon Boat races in south China
are (unhistorically) said to commemorate this sacrifice. Schneider's book studies the
process by which the historical figure became a legend with multiple and shifting
meanings: under the empire, he was a symbol of Confucian loyalty; in the New
Culture Movement of the 1920s, he became a symbol of artistic genius in conflict with
popular vulgarity; and after 1949, some considered him a 'people's poet', while others
saw him as a feudal aristocrat. Schneider studies folklore, various genres of writing,
and local customs to trace these changes.

354   **The death of Woman Wang.**
Jonathan D. Spence.   New York: Viking, 1978. 169p.

An extraordinary social history and slice of life in a Shandong village between 1668
and 1672; particularly intriguing is the portrait of 'Woman Wang', known to history
only because her death was recorded by the local government magistrate. Spence
weaves together the sparse information provided in this legal report with literary
evidence provided by the tales of Pu Songling, which are set in a neighbouring county.
The result is a speculative, provocative but entrancing biography, both about the life
of a 17th-century woman and about the process of writing history.

355   **Emperor of China: self-portrait of K'ang-hsi.**
Jonathan Spence.   New York: Alfred A. Knopf, 1974. 217p.

Selects and arranges the public and private writings of the Kangxi Emperor (1654-
1722) to form a mosaic self-portrait which offers a unique insight into his 1661-1722
reign. Chapters cover: the emperor's daily activities from hunting and writing poetry
to interviewing officials; the problems of ruling; philosophy and politics; growing old;
and choosing an heir and successor, no less vexing a problem for imperial rulers than
for those of the present day. Spence's *Ts'ao Yin and the K'ang-hsi emperor:
bondservant and master* (New Haven, Connecticut; London: Yale University Press,
1966. 329p.) studies the personal and political relations of the emperor with a trusted
personal servant whom he placed in a responsible bureaucratic position. The
succession problem is vividly analysed in Silas Wu, *Passage to power: K'ang-hsi and
his heir apparent, 1661-1722* (Cambridge, Massachusetts; London: Harvard
University Press, 1979. 252p.).

356   **Pan Chao: foremost woman scholar of China.**
Nancy Lee Swann.   New York; London: Century, 1932. Reprinted,
New York: Russell & Russell, 1968. 179p.

A straightforward biography of Ban Zhao (45-114?), a prominent member of the Han
dynasty Ban family, and best known for her contribution to writing history. Swann
first portrays the age, its literature, Ban's family, and her life. Sections also examine
her share in the *Hanshu* (Han History), and her poems, and describe her as 'a
representative Chinese woman'.

357   **The life and times of Po Chu-yi, 772-846.**
Arthur Waley.   London: Allen & Unwin, 1949. 238p.
A charming and learned literary biography of Bo Juyi (also pronounced Bai Juyi), the
most celebrated poet of the late Tang dynasty. Waley sketches the political and
religious background of the imperial court in which the poet served as a minor official,
at a time when the Tang empire went from tragic decline following the mid-century
rebellions to near dissolution. The narrative incorporates documents of the poet's life
and translations of about a hundred poems, with discussions of which poems were
moral commentary on politics and which represented individual expression. In his
Translations from the Chinese (q.v.), Waley translates an additional selection.

358   **The poetry and career of Li Po, 701-762 A.D.**
Arthur Waley.   London: Allen & Unwin; New York: Macmillan,
1950. 123p.
A brief biography, with many translations. The romantic, bibulous Li Bo (also
pronounced Li Bai), contrasts with his close but more austere friend Du Fu to make a
classic pair; they epitomize for many Chinese the Golden Age of the mid-Tang period.
Waley selects from more than a thousand poems attributed to Li, more of which
appear in most standard anthologies.

359   **Yuan Mei: eighteenth century Chinese poet.**
Arthur Waley.   London: Allen & Unwin, 1956; New York: Grove
Press, 1970. 227p. map.
A genial, well-read biography of Yuan Mei (1716-98), an elegant scholar, poet,
gourmet and influential essayist. Waley finds him a 'lovable, witty, generous,
affectionate, hot-tempered, wildly prejudiced man' and a 'writer of poetry that even at
its lightest always has an undertone of deep feeling and at its saddest may at any
moment light a sudden spark of fun'. Yuan was born in Hangzhou, where a prosperous
commercial gentry supported and participated in Confucian scholarly pursuits. Waley
follows Yuan's career under the Qianlong Emperor, and discusses his scholarship,
cooking, medicine and, most important, his poetry.

360   **The Confucian's progress: autobiographical writings in traditional
China.**
Wu Pei-yi.   Princeton, New Jersey: Princeton University Press, 1990.
283p.
Discredits the misconception that autobiography was not a characteristic Chinese
concern. Although there was no single form which corresponded to the Western
'autobiography', Wu excerpts and comments perceptively on: writings from Sima
Qian and Tao Qian; the breakthroughs in Chan (Zen) Buddhist writings of the 13th
century; Ming travel writings, which used the metaphor of the journey to explore the
development of the self; and the 'golden age' of autobiography in the disintegrating
Ming world of the 17th century.

Ssu-ma Ch'ien: grand historian of China.
See item no. 129.

Neo-Confucian thought in action: Wang Yang-ming's youth (1472-1509).
See item no. 560.

Tu Fu: China's greatest poet.
See item no. 1202.

20th century

General and to 1949

361 **The last Confucian: Liang Shuming and the Chinese dilemma of modernity.**
Guy S. Alitto.   Berkeley, California; London: University of California Press, 1979. 396p.

Liang Shuming (1893-1988), labelled conservative for criticizing facile Westernization and modernization, was a philosopher who turned to the countryside as a source for 'Confucian modernization'. Alitto's psychological and intellectual biography starts with Liang's relation with his father, Liang Ji, who drowned himself to protest against China's weakness. Participation in the famous 'debate between Eastern and Western cultures' brought Liang prominence, but the example of the radicals' Peasant Training Institute in Canton led him to the village; he founded an Institute in Shantung in the tradition of the village school and Confucian academies. In the 1930s, he and James Yen led a Rural Reconstruction Movement. In the 1940s, Liang was prominent in the Democratic League, which tried to form a Third Force. After 1949, he initially supported the new government, which he saw as carrying out his rural reforms, but soon became a prominent target for Mao's vicious attacks.

362 **Fei Xiaotong and sociology in revolutionary China.**
R. David Arkush.   Cambridge, Massachusetts; London: Council on East Asian Studies, Harvard University, distributed by Harvard University Press, 1981. 386p. bibliog. (Harvard East Asian Monographs, no. 98).

Fei (sometimes Hsiao-tung or Hsiao-t'ung; 1910-) was a Westernized intellectual who played three roles: social scientist, as China's most prominent anthropologist, whose 1930s village studies, e.g. *Peasant life in China* (q.v.), were among the first of any complex society; political journalist, particularly in the years just before 1949, when his essays advocating rural reform, e.g. *Earthbound China* (q.v.), influenced popular conceptions; and cultural intermediary between China and the West. However, Arkush holds that Fei was no 'marginal man' in limbo between East and West, but at the heart of China's intellectual transition. Fei was denounced in the mid-1950s as a 'rightist', as documented in James P. McGough, *Fei Hsiao-t'ung: the dilemma of a Chinese intellectual* (White Plains, New York: M. E. Sharpe, 1979. 159p.).

363   The last emperor.
Edward Behr.   Toronto; New York: Bantam Books, 1987. 336p.
The hapless scion of the Manchu imperial tree, Henry Puyi (P'u-i; 1906-67), was
mostly an onlooker to history: he succeeded to the throne when barely old enough to
walk, only to be deposed in 1911; was installed as head of the Japanese puppet
régime, Manchukuo in the 1930s; was jailed first by the Soviets and then by the new
People's Republic; and ended up as a gardener in his former holdings and subject of
Bertolucci's 1987 block-buster movie, *The last emperor*. Behr's attractive book, like
others on the topic, is based on Puyi's own *From emperor to citizen: the
autobiography of Aisin-Gioro Pu Yi* (Beijing: Foreign Languages Press, 1964-65. 2
vols.), which has the unvarnished poignancy of an induced 'self-criticism'.
Reginald F. Johnstone, with a preface by the Emperor, *Twilight in the Forbidden City*
(London: Gollancz, 1934. Reprinted, Hong Kong: Oxford University Press, 1985.
486p. [Oxford in Asia]) is a sharply observed memoir by the British
scholar/administrator who served as Puyi's English teacher and mentor (rather
different from the romantic young man in the movie!).

364   **Wild swans: three daughters of China.**
Chang Jung.   New York; London; Toronto; Sydney; Tokyo,
Singapore: Simon & Schuster, 1991. 524p.
A dramatic and widely read family history of modern China. Ms Chang, born in 1952,
relates a century of Chinese history through the stories of three generations of her
family. Her grandmother was first the concubine of a powerful general in Manchuria,
then married a kindly doctor. In the mid-1940s, her mother joined the student
underground where she met and finally married a young revolutionary – her father,
who had walked to Yan'an in 1938 to join the Communist Party and lead anti-
Japanese guerrillas. Chang Jung grew up as a privileged student in the New China;
when her parents were criticized and purged, she joined the Cultural Revolution as a
rampaging Red Guard, worked as peasant, then became a 'barefoot doctor',
steelworker and electrician, before going to Britain to study English.

365   **Yuan Shih-k'ai.**
Jerome Ch'en.   Stanford, California: Stanford University Press, 1972.
2nd ed. 258p. bibliog.
Yuan Shikai (1859-1916), a key military and political figure in late Qing and
Republican politics, was long blamed for destroying the Republic with his imperial
aspirations. Ch'en's scholarly biography goes beyond traditional moralism to set Yuan
in the context of Chinese and world history. Chapters cover the various periods of
Yuan's life: youth (1859-1882); as the Chinese imperial representative in Korea (1882-
95); in the army (1895-99); his role in the reforms of 1898 and the Boxer uprising
(1899-1901); as viceroy of Zhili province (1901-07); his eclipse when forced to retire
by the Empress Dowager (1908-11); in the revolution (1911); as the President (1912-
13); as the 'strong man' (1913-15); as the Emperor (1915-16); and his downfall (1916).

366   **The man who lost China.**
Brian Crozier, with Eric Chou.   New York: Scribner's, 1976. 430p.
Chiang Kai-shek (Jiang Jieshi; 1887-1975), one of the most consequential figures of
the century, still has no full scholarly biography. Crozier covered Asia in the 1960s
for the London *Economist*, and provides an energetic biography which tries to

reconcile chaotic secondary sources. *The early Chiang Kai-shek* by Pichon P. Y. Loh (New York; London: Columbia University Press, 1971. 216p.), looks carefully at the youthful years spent in Zhejiang and Shanghai, concentrating on psychology. Keijii Furuya, *Chiang Kai-shek: his life and times* (New York: St. John's University, 1981. 978p.) is a massive, uncritical account. *Chiang Kai-shek's secret past: the memoir of his second wife*, by Ch'en Chieh-ju, edited with an introduction by Lloyd E. Eastman (Boulder, Colorado; San Francisco; Oxford: Westview Press. 1993. 273p.) is a lively, long suppressed personal account of the period 1919-27. *The storm clouds clear over China: the memoir of Ch'en Li-fu 1900-1993* (Stanford, California: Hoover Institution, 1994. 359p. [Studies in Economic, Social, and Political Change]) presents the detailed recollections of Chen Lifu, a key adviser and organizer of the CC Clique, a powerful political faction led by Chen and his brother.

367   **Qian Mu and the world of seven mansions.**
Jerry Dennerline.   New Haven, Connecticut: Yale University Press, 1988. 192p.

Qian Mu (Ch'ien Mu; 1895-1990) was a Confucian scholar and educator, a creative and forward-looking conservative, who was 'plagued' by the problem 'Chinese or Western culture, which is right and which is best?' Dennerline's biography first presents Qian's own understanding of the 'spirit' or 'living truth' of Chinese culture. Part two portrays the social world of Qian's youth, and Seven Mansions, his ancestral home in Wuxi. Dennerline sketches the 'economic mold' of this world (covering landlords, granary and inheritance), and the 'small peasant cosmos' of rituals, festivals and beliefs which held the family system together. One striking episode is a recent widow's defence of widow chastity against suggestions that she remarry. The third section is Qian's 'Reminiscences of My Parents at the Age of Eighty'. Dennerline concludes with reflections on how the 'small cosmos' has changed.

368   **A latterday Confucian: reminiscences of William Hung (1893-1980).**
Susan Chan Egan.   Cambridge, Massachusetts: Council on East Asian Studies, Harvard University, distributed by Harvard University Press, 1987. 262p. (Harvard East Asian Monographs, no. 131).

A charming and insightful biography, based on Hung's extensive talks with the author. Hung (Hong Ye) was an influential teacher and scholar (see his biography of the Tang poet Du Fu – q.v.), a devout but not institutional Christian, and a shrewd academic administrator who in the 1920s helped to transform Yenching University into China's foremost Christian educational institution and centre of modern sinology. His reminiscences cover his early education and life in a wealthy Confucian family in Fuzhou, his education in the United States in the 1910s, his extensive social and political network in China 1920s-40s, and his exiled but productive life at the Harvard-Yenching Institute in Cambridge, Massachusetts. Egan also provides a bibliography of Hung's works and descriptions of his rich scholarly contributions.

369   **Liang and Lin: partners in exploring China's architectural past.**
Wilma Fairbank.   Philadelphia, Pennsylvania: University of Pennsylvania Press, 1994. 207p.

A shrewd, loving biography of Liang Sicheng and his wife, Lin Huiyin, which describes their work and personal fates from the 1920s to the Cultural Revolution. Liang was the son of the reformer Liang Qichao; Fairbank and her scholar husband

John met the couple in the early 1930s, and joined them as they toured the hinterlands in search of material for Liang's *Pictorial history of Chinese architecture* (q.v.). Fairbank describes Liang's work, the friendship between the two families, their experience in the war, and how the Liangs stayed after 1949 to serve their China.

370 **Chen Duxiu, founder of the Chinese Communist party.**
Lee Feigon. Princeton, New Jersey: Princeton University Press, 1982. 279p.

A political and intellectual biography. Chen Duxiu (Ch'en Tu-hsiu; 1879-1942) went from being a journalist and academic intellectual to being the first Secretary-General of the Chinese Communist Party in the 1920s, then back to being an independent intellectual after his expulsion from the Party as a Trotskyite. Feigon first describes his early career as Commissioner of Education in Anhui, Chen's home province; he goes on to cover Chen's time as a leader and editor of *New Youth* magazine during the early years of the New Culture Movement, when he determined to introduce 'Mr. Democracy' and 'Mr. Science' to replace Confucius, and as Dean of Peking University. Two central chapters describe his political career in founding the Party. A final chapter explains his Trotskyite critique of the Party and his final years.

371 **Crippled tree.**
Han Suyin. New York: Putnam's, 1965. 461p.

Han's compelling memoirs, sub-titled 'China, Autobiography, History', present the epic of modern China through her own life and through the lives of the Zhous, her Sichuan Hakka family. *Crippled tree* concerns the period 1885-1913, and includes a vivid view of the social unrest of the 1911 revolution in Sichuan and the poignant, difficult marriage of her Chinese father, who trained in Belgium as an engineer, and her Belgian mother, who never reconciled herself to China. *A mortal flower* (New York: Putnam's, 1966. 423p.) continues her story to 1928-38, to her education at Yenching University and medical study in Belgium. *Birdless summer* (New York: Putnam's, 1968. 347p.) focuses on her unhappy marriage with a Nationalist army officer, her life in Chongqing during the war with Japan, and going to London, a story which she originally told (from a rather different view) in the best selling *Destination Chungking* (London: Jonathan Cape, 1944. 287p.).

372 **A modern China and new world: K'ang Yu-wei, reformer, and utopian, 1858-1927.**
Hsiao Kung-ch'uan. Seattle, Washington; London: University of Washington Press, 1975. 669p.

A detailed biography and intellectual history of Kang Youwei (1858-1927), which describes his youth in Guangdong, his Buddhist studies, his development into an innovative thinker who saw 'Confucius as a Reformer', his time as the teacher of Liang Qichao, and his role as a hero of the One Hundred Days Reform débâcle of 1898. On the subject of Kang's *Datong shu* (Book of Great Peace), a socially radical utopian blueprint not published until after his death, see *Ta T'ung Shu: the one world philosophy of K'ang Yu-wei*, translated, with an introduction by Laurence G. Thompson (London: Allen & Unwin, 1958. 300p.). Lo Jung-pang, a respected scholar and Kang's grandson, edited *K'ang Yu-wei: a biography and a symposium* (Tucson, Arizona: University of Arizona Press, 1967. 541p. [Association for Asian Studies Monographs and Papers, no. 23]); in addition to Kang's 'Chronological Autobiography', there are six essays on various aspects of his thought.

373   The house of Confucius.

Kong Demao, translated by Rosemary Roberts, edited with an introduction by Frances Wood.   London; Sydney; Auckland; Toronto: Hodder & Stoughton, 1990. 180p. maps.

The descendants of Confucius, the Kong family, were supported by the emperor's government in their ancestral mansion. complex in the country town of Qufu, in Shandong. Kong Demao, born in 1917 into the seventy-seventh generation, charmingly recounts the last years of this unique and troubled family, complete with incidents of poisonings, household intrigue, the family reaction to the anti-Confucian student movements of the 1920s, and detailed descriptions of family rituals. The text is edited and rearranged from *In the mansion of Confucius' descendants* (Beijing: New World Press, 1984. 292p.).

374   Zhou Enlai: the early years.

Chae-Jin Lee.   Stanford, California: Stanford University Press, 1994. 241p.

A discussion of the personal, educational and political experiences of Zhou Enlai (1898-1976) through the early 1920s. According to the author, Zhou's family life was happier and more stable than previously thought. His education at Nankai Middle School gave him a solid grounding in Chinese philosophy and Western learning, as well as experience in organizational leadership, journalism and theatre. Lee also covers: his studies in Japan, which introduced him to Marxism via Japanese translations; the May Fourth Movement, which established him; and the Work-Study Movement in France, which developed his talents as a radical but pragmatic leader. Han Suyin, *Eldest son: Zhou Enlai and the making of modern China, 1898-1976* (New York: Hill & Wang, 1994. 483p.) is a sympathetic biography using material gathered in China.

375   Two self-portraits: Liang Ch'i-ch'ao and Hu Shih.

Liang Ch'i-ch'ao and Hu Shih, edited and with an introduction by Li Yu-ning, translated by Li Yu-ning, William Wycoff.   Bronxville, New York: Outer Sky Press, 1993. 263p.

Liang and Hu were among the leaders of China's intellectual renaissance, and both promoted the writing of Western style autobiography. Here Li Yu-ning presents their two partial autobiographies: Liang's 'My Autobiographical Account at Thirty'; and Hu's 'An Autobiographical Account at Forty', along with several of Hu's shorter reminiscences. A helpful introduction provides background on the two men and the problem of biographical writing in modern China.

376   Legacies: a Chinese mosaic.

Betty Bao Lord.   New York: Knopf, 1990. 245p.

While she was the wife of the American Ambassador in Beijing, Ms Lord, who was born in China, met many fellow Chinese who spoke freely to her about their lives. Here she tells a group of their stories, mostly in their own words, to convey the mixture of history and hope of China in the 1980s, especially the events of 1989 from the point of view of reform democrats and government officials.

377   **The adventures of Wu: the life cycle of a Peking man.**
H. Y. Lowe, edited with an introduction by Derk Bodde.   Princeton,
New Jersey: Princeton University Press, 1983. 512p.

Originally published in 1940 (Peiping: Henry Vetch), this is a novelistic but basically autobiographical picture of life in a an old Beijing family which was rich in tradition but not in wealth. The account of everyday life, covering the period 1915-36, depicts both individual personalities and patterns of culture, including religious practices and festivals. Bodde's introduction to the reissue (which also adds a useful index) calls the reader's attention to aspects which the text does not highlight, and provides background for the general reader.

378   **Daughter of Han: the autobiography of a Chinese working woman.**
Ida Pruitt, from the story told her by Ning Lao T'ai-'t'ai.   New Haven,
Connecticut; London: Yale University Press, 1945. Reprinted, with an
index, Stanford, California: Stanford University Press, 1967. 254p.

An illiterate working woman with a genius for story and character relates her rich, troubled life in late 19th- and early 20th-century China. Mrs Ning's story, as gathered and presented by Ida Pruitt, embodies Confucian family values, quiescent Buddhist recognition of worldly pain, and Daoist ritual used for birth, weddings and death. As a woman she is beset by bound feet, an opium addicted husband, and a politically disintegrating China, yet she actively uses Chinese culture and draws on history for meaning and support; she does not call for social change, but social reconstruction. Family is transcendent not as the conjugal unit of the present generation but as the chain of ancestors and descendants in which the individual is only a link.

379   **Legacies of childhood: growing up Chinese in a time of crisis,
1890-1920.**
Jon L. Saari.   Cambridge, Massachusetts: Council on East Asian
Studies, Harvard University, 1990. 379p. (Harvard East Asian
Monographs, no. 136).

Draws on Erik Erikson's life-cycle psychology to probe the last generation 'to have the world of Confucian learning etched into their memories as school children, yet the first as a group to confront the intrusive Western world'. Lucian Pye and Richard Solomon's interpretations stressed issues of authority and dependency; however, Saari's fertile study stresses successful personal development defined in Chinese terms. New Culture adolescents experienced decaying families and a beset China, but they created 'respectable work' in scholarship and political office; these new but elusive identities provided a way out by 'breaking the hold of the group'. Lu Xun and Guo Moro, two writers, fulfilled themselves by 'leading the group beyond the tradition'.

380   **The Soong dynasty.**
Sterling Seagrave.   New York; London: Harper & Row, 1985. 537p.

A gossipy portrait of the Soong (Song) family, consisting of the father, Charles, the Soong sisters – Soong Ch'ing-ling (Song Qingling; 1893-1981), who married Sun Yat-sen; Soong Ai-ling (Song Ailing; 1890-1973), who married H. H. Kung (Kong Xiangxi; 1888-1967); and Soong May-ling (Song Meiling; 1897-), who married Chiang Kai-shek – and their brother, T. V. Soong (Song Ziwen; 1894-1971). Early chapters describe 'Charlie's' college years in Georgia, his return as a Methodist missionary to Shanghai, his marriage into the Ni family, and the founding of his real estate fortune. Later chapters cover the colourful careers of his children. T. V. Soong, sometime Minister of Finance, Foreign Minister and Premier, is personally blamed by Seagrave for the corruption and political decay of wartime China; while creating China's modern financial system in the 1930s, Soong amassed a huge personal fortune and was a wheeler-dealer in wartime Washington. Scholars have accused Seagrave's book of being biased, inaccurate and hostile.

381　The great road: the life and times of Chu Teh.
Agnes Smedley.　New York: Monthly Review Press, 1956. 461p. map.

Zhu De (1886-1976) was Mao's most important pre-1949 collaborator. He and Mao joined forces after the Nanchang Uprising of 1 August 1927, an event which was considered the founding of the Red Army, built by Zhu into a major revolutionary force. Smedley became close to him in the early 1930s; her extensive interviews and first-hand observations make this a major source for Zhu's life. She relates his view of growing up in a poor peasant family in Sichuan, his training in the Yunnan Military Academy, his participation as a soldier in the 1911 Revolution, and experience in Europe, where he joined the Communist Party. The account of the early years of the agrarian revolution and the 1930s is especially vivid.

382　Memoirs of a Chinese revolutionary.
Wang Fan-hsi, translated, with an introduction, by Gregor Benton.
New York: Columbia University Press, 1991. 300p. (Morningside Edition).

Wang, who joined the Chinese Communist Party in the 1920s, sought refuge in Moscow, where he discovered Trotsky, returned to China, opposed Mao's leadership and was eventually expelled from the Party and jailed as a Trotskyite. He set out in his memoirs to show 'how Stalinism and its Maoist variant were born, began to flourish, and eventually triumphed in both the Soviet Union and in China'. He dramatically and insightfully portrays the personalities of the Party leadership and their struggles, and argues that they betrayed true socialism. The translation is based on Wang's *Shuang-shan hui yi lu* (Hong Kong, 1958), previously published as *Chinese revolutionary: memoirs* (Oxford; New York: Oxford University Press, 1980), and translated into French, German and Japanese. More voluminous and concerned with rivalries and high party politics is Chang Kuo-tao, *The rise of the Chinese Communist Party: the autobiography of Chang Kuo-tao* (Lawrence, Kansas: University Press of Kansas, 1971-72. 2 vols.).

383　The dragon empress: the life and times of Tz'u-hsi, Empress Dowager of China, 1835-1908.
Marina Warner.　New York: Macmillan, 1972. 271p.

An intelligent popular biography of the stateswoman central to most political decisions of the Manchu government from the 1860s to her death. Ci Xi played the role of scapegoat as often as that of authentic villain, as in her support of the Boxer Uprising of 1900, but more often was overpowered by history. Like other biographers, Warner is handicapped by the forgeries (exposed in Trevor-Roper's *Hermit of Peking*, q.v.) and sexist gossip provided by Chinese sources. Sterling Seagrave, *Dragon lady: the life and legend of the last empress of China* (New York: Knopf, 1992. 601p. maps. bibliog.)

entertainingly exposes the fraud, forgery and bigotry which fabricated the image of sexual and political depravity, and sketches her life based on English-language sources. For the beginning of a scholarly reassessment, see Sue Fawn Chung, 'The Much Maligned Empress Dowager: A Revisionist Study of the Empress Dowager Tz'u-hsi (1835-1908)', (*Modern Asian Studies*, vol. 13, no. 2 [1979], p. 177-96).

384 **Search for modern nationalism: Zhang Binglin and revolutionary China, 1869-1936.**
Young-tsu Wong.   Hong Kong; Oxford; New York: Oxford University Press, 1989. 233p.

A deep study of a scholar and political activist whose influential nationalism evolved in terms of Confucian morality, anti-Manchu racism, and Buddhist dialectics. The life of Zhang Binglin (Chang Ping-lin; 1869-1936), his relations with contemporaries such as Liang Qichao, and his nationalist agitation show that his erudition in 'traditional' culture did not conflict with taking part in 'modern' discourses. In particular, Zhang's ideas on race and ethnic identity unfolded over his long life. See also: Kauko Laitinen, *Chinese nationalism in the late Qing dynasty: Zhang Binglin as an anti-Manchu propagandist* (London: Curzon Press, 1990. 209p. [Scandinavian Institute of Asian Studies, no. 57]), a concise introduction to Zhang's thought before 1911; and Shimada Kenji, *Pioneer of the Chinese Revolution: Zhang Binglin and Confucianism*, translated by Joshua Fogel (Stanford, California: Stanford University Press, 1990. 169p.).

Time for telling truth is running out: conversations with Zhang Shenfu.
See item no. 246.

To the people: James Yen and village China.
See item no. 254.

After 1949

385 **Prisoner of Mao.**
Bao Ruo-wang (Jean Pasqualini), Rudolph Chelminksi.   New York: Coward, McCann, & Geoghegan, 1973. 318p. Reprinted, Penguin Books.

One of the first, and still one of the most chilling, eye-witness accounts of the state labour camp system to receive wide circulation in the West. Bao, whose father was Corsican and mother Chinese, worked with American Marines in the 1940s, and was arrested as a Rightist Bourgeois Element in December 1957. After interrogation produced a 700-page 'confession', he entered prison to emerge only in 1964 as part of French diplomatic recognition of the People's Republic. Bao describes the years of privation in harrowing detail yet with surprising equanimity; during 1959-61, few in China had enough to eat, but prisoners ate 'experimental food' – paper pulp and swamp scum – and picked grains from horse droppings. Other prison accounts include: Pu Ning, translated by Tong Chung-hsuan, *Red in tooth and claw: twenty-six years in communist Chinese prisons* (New York: Grove/Atlantic, 1994. 272p.); Harry Wu, Carolyn Wakeman, *Bitter wind: a memoir of my years in China's Gulag* (New York: Wiley, 1994. 290p.); and Wu Ningkun, *A single tear: a family's persecution, love, and endurance in Communist China* (New York: Atlantic Monthly Press, 1993. 367p.).

386 **The claws of the dragon: Kang Sheng – the evil genius behind Mao – and his legacy of terror in People's China.**
John Byron, Robert Pack. New York: Simon & Schuster, 1992. 560p. maps.

Kang Sheng (1899-1975) was one of Mao's staunchest collaborators, an intimate comrade of Jiang Qing, and a particularly despised Party elder. From the 1940s, Kang built the state security apparatus to remorselessly purge anyone who questioned Mao or challenged Kang's followers or could be suspected of doing either. 'John Byron' is the pseudonym of a diplomat who worked in Beijing in the 1980s; he obtained a copy of an internal Party biography of Kang Sheng prepared as part of a political campaign. In spite of the lurid title and sometimes breathless style, the resulting book presents much information not available elsewhere and tries to sort out uncheckable and sometimes conflicting sources.

387 **Life and death in Shanghai.**
Nien Cheng. New York: Grove Press, 1986. 547p.

A best selling memoir of the author's Cultural Revolution ordeal and spiritual survival. Ms Cheng [Zheng] and her diplomat husband chose to remain in New China, but in 1966, Red Guards ransacked the comfortable Shanghai home of the recently widowed Cheng. Her seven-year confinement and the strength of character with which she upheld her innocence are compelling. However, Cheng saw little of the broader development of the Cultural Revolution, which she read about in the newspapers after her release. *Six chapters from my life 'down under'*, by Yang Jiang, translated by Howard Goldblatt (Hong Kong: Chinese University Press; Seattle, Washington: University of Washington Press, 1982. 111p.) is in contrast a poetically understated vignette of a hard life and little victories in a rural labour camp during the Cultural Revolution after she and her husband, writer Qian Zhongshu, were arrested as 'Rightists'. Another translation is *A cadre school life: six chapters*, translated by Geremie Barmé (Hong Kong: Joint Publishing Company, 1982. 91p.).

388 **Deng Xiaoping and the Chinese revolution: a political biography.**
David S. G. Goodman. London: Routledge, Kegan Paul, 1994. 209p.

A standard political biography of Deng (1904-), covering his childhood, his political career both before and after 1949, and in particular his role in the reform programmes following Mao's death in 1976. There is a chapter on the sources and Deng's writings. Richard Evans, *Deng Xiaoping and the making of modern China* (New York; London: Viking Penguin, 1994. rev. ed. 339p.) draws on the author's experience as a British diplomat in China to present an equable and sympathetically critical biography. *Deng Xiaoping*, by Uli Franz, translated by Tom Artin (New York: Harcourt, Brace, Jovanovich, 1988. 340p.) is a sharper political study by an experienced journalist. Deng Mao Mao, *Deng Xiaoping: my father* (New York: Basic Books, 1995. 498p.) comprises a daughter's view of the pre-1949 period, which incorporates much new material. *Deng Xiaoping: portrait of a Chinese statesman*, edited by David Shambaugh (Oxford: Clarendon; New York: Oxford University Press, 1995. 172p.) is a symposium originally published in *China Quarterly*, no. 135 (September 1993). Deng's works available in English translation include *Selected works of Deng Xiaoping* (Beijing: Foreign Languages Press, 1984. 2 vols.).

389 **Born red: a chronicle of the Cultural Revolution.**
Gao Yuan, foreword by William A. Joseph.   Stanford, California:
Stanford University Press, 1987. 380p.

A vivid first-person account of a Red Guard, which covers the period 1966-69, as well as his boyhood and middle school days in a dusty North China town where Gao's father was a scrupulous revolutionary official. The style captures the colloquial Chinese mix of colourful vulgarity, sharp proverb, and literary allusion. His well-told story catches the slide from initial enthusiasm for Mao's promised egalitarian and participatory society, to attack on authority and 'bourgeois traitors', to berserk warfare between factions, each waving Maoist banners. Appendices and a glossary identify people and terms. Other vivid accounts include: Ling Ken, English text prepared by Miriam London, Lee Ta-ling, *The revenge of heaven: journal of a young Chinese* (New York: Putnam, 1972. 413p.); Gordon Bennett, Ronald N. Montaperto, *Red guard: the political biography of Dai Hsiao-ai* (Garden City, New York: Doubleday, 1971. 267p.); Anchee Min, *Red azalea* (New York: Pantheon, 1994. 306p.), a young woman's story of rural exile, making movies and love; and Yuan-tsung Chen, *The dragon's village: an autobiographical novel of revolutionary China* (New York: Pantheon, 1980. 285p.), which vividly portrays a student who participated in the land reforms of the 1950s.

390 **Mr. China's son: a villager's life.**
He Liyi, with Claire Anne Chik.   Boulder, Colorado; San Francisco;
Oxford: Westview Press, 1993. 271p.

He Liyi is a member of the Bai Nationality, an officially designated minority group in Yunnan Province. As a youth he learned two foreign languages, Mandarin Chinese and English, and was taught to look down upon his native Bai culture. In 1960, he was criticized as a 'rightist' for knowing English, lost his job as a translator, and spent the remaining Maoist years in prison camp. After rehabilitation, however, although he was caught in a village struggling to survive as a useless intellectual, he resolved to revive his English and write his autobiography – this book. Along the way, Mr He informs the reader of his ultimate reconciliation with Bai culture and portrays the economy and changing daily life in the countryside.

391 **Son of the revolution.**
Liang Heng, Judith Shapiro.   New York: Knopf, 1983. 301p.

A popular autobiography. Liang was born in 1954 in Changsha, Hunan, Mao's hometown; his parents called him 'Chairman Mao's good little boy'. When Liang's mother was denounced as counter-revolutionary, his father was still sure that the Party knew best. Liang neatly personified the Cultural Revolution experience. First, as a Red Guard, he toured China on a new Long March, then went with his still loyal father to the countryside, to see villagers inanely accused of capitalism for raising ducks. Liang's skill on a factory basketball team conferred comfort and privileges. Finally, numbed by meaningless violence and chaos, he entered college and met American 'Teacher Xia', his future wife, Judith Shapiro.

392   **A higher kind of loyalty: a memoir by China's foremost journalist.**
Liu Binyan, translated by Zhu Hong.   New York: Pantheon Books,
1990. 294p.
An autobiographical memoir, which describes the passage of Liu Binyan (Liu Pin-yen;
1925-) from being a favoured writer and journalist in the 1950s, to being imprisoned
as a rightist for his critical writings during the One Hundred Flowers period in 1956,
then being freed in the 1980s as a critical intellectual still sympathetic to the ideals of
socialism. Liu's other writings include: *China's crisis, China's hope: essays from an
intellectual in exile*, translated by Howard Goldblatt (Cambridge, Massachusetts:
Harvard University Press, 1990. 150p.); and, with Ruan Ming, Xu Gang, *Tell the world
what happened in China and why* (New York: Pantheon Books, 1989. 195p.).

393   **Almost a revolution.**
Shen Tong, with Marianne Yen.   Boston, Massachusetts: Houghton
Mifflin, 1990. 342p.
In the spring of 1989, Shen was an undergraduate at Beijing University, a proud native
of Beijing, a romantic poet, and a leader of the student movement which was 'almost a
revolution'. Like many autobiographical accounts listed in this section, this book was
written for a Western audience, and combines shrewd family and individual
portraiture with insightful eyewitness history; it does not give a 'balanced' overview
or analyse the dilemmas of thwarted reform and political structure. However, readers
do get a vivid insider's view of the chaos, optimism, egotism and promise of the
student movement which led up to the 1989 Beijing Massacre. Shen's account implies
that better student strategy would have averted the confrontation which neither
responsible young leaders nor government reformers wanted.

394   **The white-boned demon: a biography of Madame Mao Zedong.**
Ross Terrill.   New York: Simon & Schuster, 1984. Reissued, with a
new postscript, 1992. 466p.
Madame Mao took the stage name Jiang Qing (Chiang Ch'ing; 1913-91) – 'pure river'
– in the 1930s before travelling to Yan'an to join the revolution and marry Mao. She
was relegated to the background until Mao elevated her at the start of the Cultural
Revolution in 1965; she then became leader of the radical faction which was
eventually arrested and stigmatized as the Gang of Four after Mao's death in 1976.
Terrill mines the revelations published in China in the 1980s, interviews many leading
figures (including her first husband), and consults a wide range of published sources to
provide as reliable account as is now possible for a figure at once so remote and so
feared. Roxane Witke, *Comrade Chiang Ching* (Boston, Massachusetts: Little, Brown,
1978. 549p.) is based on interviews in which Jiang presents her own view and version
of many events.

395   **Enemies of the people.**
Anne F. Thurston.   New York: Knopf, 1987. 323p.
A sweeping, accessible account of the Cultural Revolution, told through the lives of
roughly half a dozen victims. Thurston uses interviews and published sources to
chronicle the ordeal of intellectuals from the glory days of the early 1950s, through
the Cultural Revolution, to the spontaneous mass commemoration at Tiananmen of
Zhou Enlai's death in 1976. She records the reverence for authority with which even
these victims started, their absence of an internalized moral code, the legitimization of

violence, the creation of classes by class labelling, the reliance on mob action rather than due process, and the dominance of politics in daily life and career building. Thurston brings both political and psychological theory to bear, but the major points are made through vivid personal stories.

396 **A Chinese odyssey: the life and times of a Chinese dissident.**
Anne F. Thurston.   New York: Scribner's; Toronto: Maxwell Macmillan Canada; New York; Oxford; Singapore; Sydney: Maxwell Macmillan International, 1991. 440p.

Ni Yuxian (1945-) was a leading activist in the 1980s Democracy Movement. Ni recounted his life to Thurston, a seasoned China scholar; she then visited his family and the relevant sites to give the book both personal and scholarly perspective. Ni emerges as cantankerous and self-righteous but ultimately in the right. He first clashed with authority as a young PLA soldier, then as a factory worker, gradually reading more and more the widely available classical Marxist texts. As he lived through the major events of the Cultural Revolution, vividly recounted here, and spent two years in jail, he developed his own critique of Chinese society and finally escaped to the West.

397 **To the storm: the odyssey of a revolutionary Chinese woman.**
Yue Daiyun, Carolyn Wakeman.   Berkeley, California; London: University of California Press, 1985. 405p.

A well-shaped memoir of the tribulations of typical intellectuals initially sympathetic to Mao and revolution. Yue and her husband joined the Party as students at Beijing University in the late 1940s, then took part in the early 1950s land reform campaigns. They joined the faculty at their alma mater, but as their family grew through the 1950s, Yue was accused of being a rightist. At first trusting the Party to protect her, she was expelled and sentenced to labour with a peasant family. Allowed to resume teaching in the early 1960s, she was caught again in the storm of the Cultural Revolution, Gang of Four, and Democracy Movements. Eventually Yue was restored to her university post and Party membership.

Chinese lives: an oral history of contemporary China.
See item no. 343.

Foreigners in China

398 **My several worlds: a personal record.**
Pearl S. Buck.   New York: John Day, 1954. 407p.

Buck grew up in China as the daughter of missionaries and became the most widely read American voice on China, starting with her 1931 book, *The good earth* (q.v.). This autobiography, written just after the Korean War pitted her Chinese and American worlds against each other, is a partial but significant account of her life in China and America. She describes her missionary parents more critically in *Fighting angel: portrait of a soul* (New York: John Day, 1936. 302p.) and *The exile* (New York: John Day, 1936. 315p.). Long deferred scholarly appraisal of Buck is begun in thirteen essays from a 1992 conference: *The several worlds of Pearl S. Buck*, edited by Elizabeth J. Lipscomb, Frances E. Webb, Peter Conn (Westport, Connecticut; London: Greenwood Press, 1994. 163p.).

399 **China called me: my life inside the Chinese revolution.**
Percy Chen. Boston, Massachusetts: Little Brown, 1979. 423p.

Chen's father, Eugene Chen, was a Jamaican overseas Chinese lawyer who in the 1920s became Sun Yat-sen's foreign minister. As a young man, Chen therefore witnessed the Great Revolution of 1925-27, and writes vividly of Sun, Michael Borodin, Madame Sun Yat-sen (Soong Qingling), and their coterie of friends, including Anna Louise Strong.

400 **John Fairbank and the American understanding of modern China.**
Paul M. Evans. Oxford; New York: Basil Blackwell, 1988. 366p.

An intellectual biography. John King Fairbank (1907-91) was a Harvard professor, State Department bureaucrat in wartime China, public pundit, policy adviser, and a leader in establishing 'area studies' and the study of China as an academic field. The Red Scare of the 1950s emerges as a key turning point in Evans' account; Fairbank came to view Chinese-Western relations as the tragic clash of two largely incompatible cultures. Evans sketches each of Fairbank's major works against this background. Fairbank's own *Chinabound: a fifty year memoir* (New York: Harper & Row, 1982. 481p.) is a more digressive personal account. *Fairbank remembered*, compiled by Paul A. Cohen, Merle Goldman (Cambridge, Massachusetts: Harvard University Press, 1992. 289p.) consists of memoirs from family, friends, students and colleagues.

401 **Nakae Ushikichi in China: the mourning of spirit.**
Joshua A. Fogel. Cambridge, Massachusetts: Council on East Asian Studies, Harvard University, distributed by Harvard University Press, 1989. 313p. (Harvard East Asian Monographs, no. 139).

A life and intellectual times of a Japanese scholar who both participated in Chinese politics from the 1911 Revolution to 1942 and contributed importantly to the debate over how to conceptualize Chinese history. Nakae (1889-1942) came from a prominent Japanese scholarly family. His life was transformed by becoming part of the Japanese expatriate community in Beijing and witnessing the May Fourth Movement; he saw his scholarly contributions as part of his service to the Chinese revolution. Fogel assesses: the influence of German idealism; Nakae's thought on Ancient China, especially the questions of Asiatic society and whether China had feudalism; and his 'expatriate vision' of Japan and of China.

402 **The call.**
John Hersey. New York: Knopf, 1985. 701p. map. bibliog.

A novel written in the form of a scholarly biography of a fictional American Protestant missionary, 'David Treadup', a composite of five actual missionaries, including Hersey's father. Treadup first mounts YMCA science campaigns in the 1910s, then after the nationalistic anti-Christian campaigns of the 1920s, goes to the village for Rural Reconstruction, working with 'Johnny Wu' (based on the actual James Yen). He undergoes the horrors of the Japanese invasion in the 1930s and internment in the 1940s only to emerge into a revolutionary China where he has no home. Shrewd, charming missionary accounts include: Grace Service, edited, introduced by her son, John Service, *Golden inches: the China memoir of Grace Service* (Berkeley, California; Los Angeles; Oxford: University of California Press, 1989. 346p.); and John Espey, *Minor heresies, major departures: a China mission boyhood* (Berkeley, California; Los Angeles; Oxford: University of California Press, 1994. 357p.), which reprints chapters from *Minor heresies* (1945), *Tales out of school* (1947) and *The other city* (1949).

403 **Our ordered lives confess: three nineteenth-century American missionaries in east Shantung.**
Irwin Hyatt.   Cambridge, Massachusetts: Harvard University Press, 1976. 323p. (Harvard Studies in American-East Asian Relations, no. 8).

Three linked biographies form a vivid portrait of the first generation of American Protestant missions on a cross-cultural frontier. Tarleton Perry Crawford (1821-1902), of the Southern Baptist Mission, was a harsh critic of Chinese culture and ultimately a depressing failure. Charlotte (Lottie) Diggs Moon (1840-1912), also a Baptist, was a fabulous success; her celebrated 'women's work for women' was a feminist vision of sacrifice for her American admirers (and fundraisers) and a model for her Chinese girls. Calvin Wilson Mateer (1836-1908), a Presbyterian, was the 'missionary as entrepreneur'; he built a thriving middle-school as the basis of a local Chinese Christian community and was an influential educator. Throughout, Hyatt balances appreciation for character, cultural analysis and development of Chinese history.

404 **Borodin: Stalin's man in China.**
Dan Jacobs.   Cambridge, Massachusetts: Harvard University Press, 1981. 369p.

Michael Borodin (1884-1953), a comrade of Lenin's dating back to 1905, was central in the Soviet global strategy to train an anti-imperialist ally in China. He collaborated with Sun Yat-sen and Chiang Kai-shek to reorganize the Nationalist Party and, almost incidentally, the fledgling Communists. This biography, based mostly on Russian published sources, provides a picture of Borodin's international career, from Moscow to Chicago to Mexico to Canton. Memoirs of other Soviet advisers include Vladimirovna Vishnakova-Akimova, *Two years in revolutionary China, 1925-1927*, translated by Steven I. Levine (Cambridge, Massachusetts: East Asian Research Center, distributed by Harvard University Press, 1971. 352p.).

405 **Agnes Smedley: the life and times of an American radical.**
Janice R. MacKinnon, Steven MacKinnon.   Berkeley, California: University of California Press, 1988. 425p.

A lively, well-researched biography. Smedley (1892-1950) left America to join and report as a journalist on the world revolution and ended up in China by way of Germany, India and Moscow. In China, she soon made a wide circle of friends, including many Chinese Communists, as well as Joseph Stilwell and Madame Sun Yat-sen. Her engaged reports from the front-line of the revolution include: *Battle hymn of China* (New York: Knopf, 1943. 528p. Reprinted, [n.p.]: Book Find Club, [n.d.]); *China correspondent* (London: Methuen, 1984); *The great road* (q.v.); and *Portraits of Chinese women in revolution*, edited by Jan MacKinnon, Steve MacKinnon (New York: Feminist Press, 1976. 203p.).

406 **Prisoners of liberation.**
W. Allyn Rickett, Adele Rickett.   San Francisco: China Books, 1981.
new ed. 343p.

The Ricketts, as Fulbright scholars beginning sinological careers in Beijing after the war, decided to stay on after the 1949 Liberation; they were subsequently arrested, given thought reform, and spent four years in prison. This memoir, originally published shortly after their release (New York: Cameron Associates, 1957. 288p.), records their soul-searching when confronted with charges of cultural imperialism and chronicles their spiritual growth in harsh circumstances.

407 **The man who stayed behind.**
Sidney Rittenberg, Amanda Bennett.   New York; London; Toronto:
Simon & Schuster, 1993. 476p.

Rittenberg went to China in the 1940s as a radical American GI and stayed on after 1949 to work for the new Revolution and become a Party member; for his troubles, he was imprisoned both in the 1950s and again during the Cultural Revolution. This reflective and readable autobiography provides a ringside view of politics and personalities, with revealing glimpses of Mao Zedong, Zhou Enlai and other leaders. The insightful account of the Cultural Revolution shows the descent from idealism to disaster; as an initial and knowledgeable enthusiast, Rittenberg's reflections on the reasons for its failure are moving and pertinent.

408 **A memoir of China in revolution: from the Boxer Rebellion to the People's Republic of China.**
Chester Ronning.   New York: Pantheon, 1974. 306p.

Ronning's parents were Norwegian immigrants to Canada who went as missionaries to Xiangyang, on the Yangzi in Hubei, where the future Ambassador was born in 1894. His charming and candid memoir first recounts his childhood in China, education in Minnesota, and return to China to teach in the 1920s. In 1945 he joined the Canadian Foreign Service, representing Canada in China as Chargé d'Affairs until 1951. Ronning describes the colourful decadence of Chiang Kai-shek's régime and the attractions of the new revolution and its leaders. He vividly sketches the long process of bringing Canada to recognize the PRC in 1971; his career as Ambassador to Norway and India; Canada's diplomacy between the United States and China from the Korean War to the Vietnam War; and his returns to the PRC.

409 **An American missionary in China: John Leighton Stuart and Chinese-American relations.**
Yu-ming Shaw.   Cambridge, Massachusetts: Council on East Asian
Studies, Harvard University, distributed by Harvard University Press,
1992. 381p. (Harvard East Asian Monographs, no. 158).

Stuart (1876-1962) was born to American missionary parents in Hangzhou, spoke fluent Chinese, but as a college student in Virginia initially resisted the call to return to China and evangelize. When the Social Gospel movement changed mission tactics to emphasize reform rather than proselytizing, Stuart returned to his native China. He worked with Chinese colleagues to develop Chinese Christian theology, and became President of Yenching University, which he developed as a sino-western Christian institution offering middle-class professional training. He spent the period 1941-45 in a Japanese prison camp, and in 1946 became Ambassador to China. Shaw's scholarly biography critically evaluates American Protestant missions in China and assesses US diplomacy, questioning whether there was a 'lost chance' to save China.

410 **To change China: western advisers in China, 1620-1960.**
Jonathan Spence.   Boston, Massachusetts: Little, Brown, 1969.
British edition, *The China helpers: Western advisors in China,*
1620-1960, London: Bodley Head, 1970. 335p. maps.

Provides deft short portraits of sixteen men who brought technical expertise to share with China; they 'speak to us still . . . about the ambiguities of superiority, and about that indefinable realm where altruism and exploitation meet'. Subjects include: Adam Schall and Ferdinand Verbeist, Jesuits who brought astronomy and God to the Manchu court; Peter Parker, the 1840s Protestant missionary doctor; Frederick Townsend Ward and Charles 'Chinese' Gordon, freebooting soldiers who fought the Taipings; Robert Hart; missionary educators W. A. P. Martin and John Fryer; Edward Hume, physician and head of Yale-in-China; Mikhail Borodin; O. J. Todd, an engineer who set out to tame the Yangzi; Norman Bethune, the Canadian doctor; Joseph Stilwell; and Soviet advisers in the 1950s.

411 **The memory palace of Matteo Ricci.**
Jonathan Spence.   New York: Viking; Harmondsworth, England:
Penguin, 1984. 350p. map. bibliog.

Ricci (1552-1610) was the Italian Jesuit missionary who brought Christianity to the officials and literati of Ming China. Spence masterfully weaves his complex story around four images from Ricci's 1596 book which presented a system of mnemonics; each image evokes an aspect of Ricci's career and of the China which he saw and described in far clearer detail than Marco Polo. *East meets west: the Jesuits in China, 1582-1773*, edited by Charles E. Ronan, S. J., Bonnie B. C. Oh (Chicago: Loyola University Press, 1988. 332p. maps. bibliog.) is a scholarly symposium. Sections include essays on Jesuit activity (Ricci and his predecessors, Chinese art and the Jesuits), the Chinese reaction (Yang Tingyun, Xu Guangqi), and the Jesuit interpretation of China to the West. The standard earlier work is George H. Dunne, *Generation of giants: the first Jesuits in China* (London: Burns & Oates; South Bend, Indiana: University of Notre Dame Press, 1962. 389p. maps. bibliog.).

412 **Right in her soul: the life of Anna Louise Strong.**
Tracy B. Strong, Helene Keyssar.   New York: Random House, 1984.
339p.

Strong (1885-1970), who graduated from Oberlin in 1905, the first woman to earn a PhD from the University of Chicago, left home to write up China's revolution as a journalist and be a 'friend of the Chinese people'. The authors of this sympathetic scholarly biography, one of whom is her grand nephew, lucidly chronicle her journey from Protestant reform to committed revolutionary reporting. Strong aligned herself with the Communist international movement in Moscow and China, obtained the famous interview in which Mao labelled the atom bomb a 'paper tiger', and ended up retiring in Beijing as a guest of the People's Republic.

413 **Hermit of Peking: the hidden life of Sir Edmund Backhouse.**
Hugh Trevor-Roper. London: Eland, 1993, with a new appendix by the author. 405p.

Backhouse (1873-1944), taken for an expert because he lived in Beijing and knew Chinese, is here exposed as a fraud who peddled political romance to suit early 20th-century Western tastes. His still beguiling *China under the Empress Dowager* (London: Heinemann, 1912. 525p.) and *Annals and memoirs of the court of Peking* (London: Heinemann; Boston, Massachusetts: Houghton Mifflin, 1914. Reprinted, New York: AMS Press, 1970. 531p.), both written with J. O. P. Bland, were long used as primary sources; the atmospheric detail is still evocative and the photographs undeniable, but the political gossip is skewed. Trevor-Roper gleefully traces Backhouse's career of gainful lying (including claims of an affair with the Empress Dowager) and gullibility (buying forged documents) in terms of Western racist naiveté and Chinese need for self-financing go-betweens. The work was first published as *A hidden life: the enigma of Sir Edmund Backhouse* (London: Macmillan, 1976; New York: Knopf, 1977).

414 **Stilwell and the American experience in China, 1911-1945.**
Barbara Tuchman. New York: Macmillan, 1970. 621p. Published in England as *Sand in the wind: Stilwell and the American experience in China*, London: Macdonald Futura.

A massive popular biography of America's leading military expert on China. Joseph Stilwell (1893-1946), a West Point graduate, was selected for language training in 1920s Beijing as the army's China specialist; eventually he became Chiang Kai-shek's chief-of-staff and commander of American forces in the wartime China-Burma-India theatre. Tuchman sympathetically describes Stilwell's successful training of Chinese troops, his dilemma when faced with Chiang's political concerns and Communist military capacity, disputes over strategy, and his disagreement with Chiang, whom he privately called 'the Peanut'. In 1944 Chiang forced Stilwell's recall.

The devil soldier: the story of Frederick Townsend Ward.
See item no. 232.

Edgar Snow: a biography.
See item no. 300.

Population, Demography and Family Planning

415 Slaughter of the innocents: coercive birth control in China.
John S. Aird. Washington, DC: AEI Press, 1990. 196p.
(AIE Studies).

Recounts the cycles of repression and liberalization in the history of China's post-1949 birth control objectives and policies, with some consideration of their implementation and impact. Aird argues that these policies violate the right to reproductive freedom and that the United States should oppose international funding for them. *A mother's ordeal: one woman's fight against China's one-child policy*, by Stephen Mosher (New York: Harcourt Brace Jovanovich, 1993. 335p.) develops much the same argument, using personal testimony and the life of one mother.

416 China's changing population.
Judith Bannister. Stanford, California: Stanford University Press, 1987. 488p.

A turning point in the study of Chinese population, which investigates all aspects of population, reliability of sources, and technical problems of analysis. Bannister uses the 1982 census, the most reliable in China's history, although in some areas she relies on earlier and less sound numbers. Topics discussed include fertility, mortality, late marriage, family planning and the one-child policy, age structure, population distribution, internal migration, health care and ethnic groups. Less technical is Penny Kane, *The second billion: population and family planning in China* (Harmondsworth, England: Penguin, 1987. 264p. maps).

417 China's one-child family policy.
Edited by Elisabeth Croll, Delia Davin, Penny Kane. London: Macmillan, 1985. 237p.

A symposium of reports and scholarly analyses of the first years of the one-child policy's implementation, problems and re-organization. Although specifics are no longer current, the discussion of effects and factors in policy-making are still relevant. Essays consider: the policy in the countryside and in the city; provincial fertility patterns; birth control methods and organization; implications for old-age security; the state and fertility motivation in Singapore and China; and the single-child family in Beijing.

418 **Migration and urbanization in China.**
Edited by Lincoln Day, Ma Xia. Armonk, New York; London: M. E. Sharpe, 1994. 293p. (Studies in Chinese Environment and Development).

Contains ten papers by scholars from the People's Republic, United States and Australia based on a large-scale survey of migration from the countryside to the cities conducted in 1986. The introduction explains that China's experience is remarkable for the level of government intervention, but that reliable statistics were not previously available because of decentralized record keeping and troublesome definitions of terms. The essays explore patterns of internal migration, motivations, demographic characteristics of the migrants, fertility and comparisons with Southeast Asia. There are statistical tables, maps and charts, and lists of books, reports and articles on China and world migration.

419 **Chinese historical microdemography.**
Edited by Stevan Harrell. Berkeley, California; Los Angeles; London: University of California Press, 1995. 236p. (Studies on China, no. 20).

Explores recent breakthroughs in demographic theory. Harrell builds on *Family and population in East Asian history*, edited by Susan Hanley, Arthur P. Wolf (Stanford, California: Stanford University Press, 1985. 360p.), a ground-breaking symposium which posited a distinctive Chinese 'demographic régime' of early and universal marriage, fairly high fertility and joint or extended families (differing from both Europe and Japan). Harrell's brisk and stimulating introduction critiques earlier aggregate national studies based on tax records (e. g. Ho, *Studies on the population of China*, q.v.) and summarizes the volume's use of genealogies and regional studies. He finds that mortality, rather than marriage or fertility, determined growth rates, which were not subject to extensive mortality crises, and that contrary to earlier assertions, the big family was indeed widespread and characteristic of all economic levels. Individual studies range over the last 1,000 years and various regions of China.

420 **Studies on the population of China, 1368-1953.**
Ping-ti Ho. Cambridge, Massachusetts: Harvard University Press, 1959. 341p.

A pioneering exploration of population history and the factors that went into it. Ho sees steady but erratic growth, in which population rises and declines with the prosperity of a dynasty. G. William Skinner, 'Sichuan's population in the nineteenth century: lessons from disaggregated data' (*Late Imperial China*, vol. 8, no. 1 [1987], p. 1-79), shows that officials produced figures for population 'growth' by adding a satisfactory percentage to each previous year's figures. Hans Bielenstein, 'Chinese historical demography, A. D. 2-1982' (*Bulletin of the Museum of Far Eastern Antiquities*, no 59 [1987], p. 1-288), challenges Ho's assumption that population periodically declined. Harrell's *Chinese historical microdemography* (q.v.) substantially modifies the demographic model by looking at regional and family records rather than aggregate numbers.

421 **Famine in China, 1959-1961: demographic and social implications.**
Penny Kane. London: Macmillan; New York: St. Martin's Press,
1988. 164p.

The 'three bad years' of 1959-61 in China saw the greatest famine in modern times;
experts now estimate that deaths ran to 25-30 million above normal. Kane first
discusses famines in China's history and elsewhere. Her account of the origins of the
famine which followed the Great Leap Forward emphasizes peasant overconsumption,
weather and the precipitous withdrawal of Soviet support, all factors outside the
control of leaders. Thomas Bernstein, 'Stalinism, famine, and Chinese peasants: grain
procurement during the Great Leap Forward' (*Theory and Society*, vol. 13, no. 3 [May
1984], p. 339-77), emphasizes the leadership blunders and anti-rightist campaigns
which prevented the gathering of honest information, the imposition of military
discipline in the communes, and the abolition of private plots and rural markets.
Kane's demographic analysis summarizes demographic work on the structure of the
tragedy.

422 **The population atlas of China.**
Compiled and edited by the Population Census Office of the State
Council of the People's Republic of China and the Institute of
Geography of the Chinese Academy of Sciences. Hong Kong: Oxford
University Press, 1987. 217p.

Provides details of the official population, as well as economic and social information
from the 1982 census, expressed in sumptuous maps, tables and brief essays.
Coverage includes Hong Kong and Taiwan, although not all data is measured
compatibly. Maps giving data at the county level cover: population distribution;
ethnicity, sex and age; population change; education and literacy; employment; and
family, marriage and fertility. A series of maps portrays population distribution for
eight periods of history beginning with the Han. See also *Diet, lifestyle, and mortality
in China: a study of the characteristics of 65 Chinese counties*, edited by Chen Junshi
(Ithaca, New York: Cornell University Press, with Oxford University Press, People's
Publishing House, 1990. 894p.).

423 **The population of modern China.**
Dudley L. Poston, Jr., David Yaukey. New York; London: Plenum
Press, 1992. 757p. (The Plenum Series on Demographic Methods and
Population Analysis).

Contains assorted English-language articles and chapters on the population of
mainland China. Most concern the 1980s, when the editors feel that the Chinese, for
all practical purposes, joined the international demographic community in policy
objectives and statistical coverage. Twenty-eight studies by Chinese and foreign
authors are grouped in eleven sections, dealing with: population and population
studies in China; size, growth and distribution; international migration; mortality;
fertility, abortion and contraceptive trends; fertility differentials; fertility policy; age
and sex structure; marriage and family; ethnic composition; and internal migration and
urbanization. There are many tables, graphs and lists of English and Chinese books
and articles on the subject.

424　**China's strategic demographic initiative.**
H. Yuan Tien.　New York; Westport, Connecticut; London: Praeger Publishers, 1991. 312p.

A sequel to the author's *China's population struggle: the demographic decisions of the People's Republic, 1949-1969* (Columbus, Ohio: Ohio State University Press, 1973. 405p.), which chronicled the demographic debates and policies of the 1950s and 1960s. The present volume, based this time on interviews with policy makers, personal observation and extensive research carried out in the PRC, analyses the SDI ('Strategic Demographic Initiative') which resulted when the control of population was declared an official government function in the 1978 Constitution.

425　**Population and development planning in China.**
Edited by Jiye Wang, Terence H. Hull.　Sydney: Allen & Unwin, 1991. 311p.

A symposium of Chinese and foreign specialists. An introductory chapter outlines the generally sympathetic approach taken by the contributors. Topics covered in chapter essays include: the historical context; sterilization and abortion; changes effected by increasing urbanization; resources and environment; and aging and social security.

426　**Family dynamics in China: a life table analysis.**
Zeng Yi.　Madison, Wisconsin: University of Wisconsin Press, 1991. 197p. (Life Course Studies).

Profiles and models contemporary population trends and family structure in the People's Republic. Professor Zeng, Deputy Director at the Institute of Population Research at Peking University, mathematically models the multi-generational structure more common in China than described in existing models. Chapter one provides a brief review of population trends and an explanation of the major demographic sources available, such as the 1982 census and subsequent surveys. Chapters two and three describe the Chinese family and its demographic determinants, such as family size and structure, and rural-urban, ethnic and regional differences. Following sections develop an extension of the Bongaarts life table methods, and apply the new model to family dynamics in China. Chapter twelve discusses the 'remarkable demographic differences' between the Chinese countryside and the city, with policy implications.

Man and land in Chinese history: an economic analysis.
See item no. 901.

Population and the environment in China.
See item no. 1020.

Cities

To 1949

427 **Urban change in China: politics and development in Tsinan, Shantung, 1890-1949.**
David D. Buck. Madison, Wisconsin; London: University of Wisconsin Press, 1978. 296p. bibliog.

Analyses the pre-1949 history of Jinan, a provincial centre in Shandong, both to discover how one Chinese city developed and also to help assess the general role of cities. Chapter one, 'Tsinan and the Question of the City In Modern Chinese History', describes theoretical questions and places the material in the context of urban history in the modern world. Succeeding chapters present a political and social history to analyse how economy and society in the urban network changed as warlord generals gave way to Japanese attack and Guomindang (Nationalist) rule. The final chapter, 'Politics and Development in Tsinan, 1890-1949', describes a 'failure to modernize'.

428 **Peking: a tale of three cities.**
Nigel Cameron, Brian Brake, foreword by L. Carrington Goodrich.
New York; Evanston, Illinois: Harper & Row, 1965. 263p. maps. bibliog.

An urbane recounting of Beijing in history, under the Mongols, the Ming, and finally in the 20th century, with colourful maps, illustrations and photographs. Roderick MacFarquhar, *The Forbidden City* (New York: Newsweek, 1972. 172p. [Wonders of Man]), is an illustrated history of the imperial complex, called 'forbidden' because commoners were forbidden to enter. MacFarquhar describes: Chinese capitals from the Tang; the Mongol founding of Beijing in the 13th century; early Ming emperors who fixed its present size and structure (as they did for the Great Wall); Manchu remodelling to suit their boisterous taste; and decline and restoration in the 20th century. L. C. Arlington, William Lewisohn, *In search of old Peking* (Peking: Henri

Vetch, 1935. Reprinted, New York: Paragon, 1967; Hong Kong: Oxford University Press, 1988. 382p. maps) and the more penetrating Juliet Bredon, *Peking: a historical and intimate description of its chief places of interest* (Shanghai, China: Kelly & Walsh, 1931. 3rd ed. Reprinted, Hong Kong: Oxford University Press, 1982. 571p.) are works of amateur scholars who loved and transcribed their exotic vanishing China.

429   **The Chinese city between two worlds.**
Edited by Mark Elvin, G. William Skinner.   Stanford, California: Stanford University Press, 1974. 458p. bibliog. (Studies in Chinese Society).

Twelve papers by historians and social scientists investigate the modernization of traditional urban forms in the period 1842-1949. Elvin's introduction provides an important theoretical and historical framework and summary. Topics include: 'The Treaty Ports and China's Modernization'; late imperial merchant organizations in Shanghai and Canton; Chungking as a centre of warlord power, 1926-37; educational modernization in Jinan, Shantung; the politically powerful Chambers of Commerce and the reforming YMCA; and the administration of Shanghai, 1905-14.

430   **Native place, city, and nation: regional networks and identities in Shanghai, 1853-1937.**
Bryna Goodman.   Berkeley, California; Los Angeles; London: University of California Press, 1995. 367p. maps. bibliog.

'Native place associations' (*huiguan*) organized support for people from the same region while they were away from home; they might provide lodging, insider business contacts, and influence peddling or cultural activities, such as home town opera and cooking. Goodman imaginatively analyses their growth and changing activities in Shanghai urban society from the Opium Wars and the 1853 Small Sword Uprising to the eve of the war with Japan. Chapters deal with: community, hierarchy and authority in making native-place culture; charity, modern enterprise, the city and the state; foreign authority, popular nationalism and anti-imperialism; the effects of warlord government; and state building in the Republican period. The conclusion looks at culture, modernity and sources of national identity, showing how localist identities paradoxically helped to build nationalism.

431   **Shanghai: revolution and development in an Asian metropolis.**
Edited by Christopher Howe.   Cambridge, England: Cambridge University Press, 1981. 444p. maps. bibliog.

A productive symposium which reflects recent research perspectives. Part one considers 'The Other China: Shanghai from 1919 to 1949'. Three essays in part two, 'Political Life', consider aspects of post-1949 politics, and Shanghai dockers in the Cultural Revolution. Part three contains essays on industrialization, the quest for food self-sufficiency, and changes in the standard of living of industrial workers, 1930-73. Part four looks at urban-suburban relations. Part five includes essays on the emergence of 'worker-writers' and Shanghai radicalism.

432   **Cities of Jiangnan in late imperial China.**
Edited by Linda Cooke Johnson.   Albany, New York: State University
of New York Press, 1993. 310p. bibliog. (SUNY Series in Chinese
Local Studies).

'Jiangnan', literally 'south of the river', is the rich lower Yangzi valley area, only
slightly smaller in size than France. These five scholarly papers, along with a scene-
setting preface by the editor and introduction by William Rowe, use geographical and
social science concerns to show that from the Southern Song dynasty to the mid-Qing
period (1150-1840), the cities in this area were not anomalies in a basically rural
China, but normal and integral parts of the social economy. Two studies show Suzhou
to have been a trading centre which developed 'roots of capitalism' on which a
bourgeoisie could later build. Hangzhou is studied as an example of urban reform in
the Ming, and another chapter treats Yangzhou as a Qing dynasty 'central place'.
Shanghai, contrary to the British colonial image, was not a sleepy fishing village
before contact with the West, but a long established commercial centre.

433   **Shanghai: from market town to treaty port, 1074-1858.**
Linda Cooke Johnson.   Stanford, California: Stanford University
Press, 1995. 440p. maps. bibliog.

Johnson engagingly argues that, contrary to the colonialist mythology that the city was
a sleepy fishing village before the coming of the British, Shanghai was a commercial
centre whose rise and evolution from the 11th to the 19th centuries illuminates the
world comparative study of cities. Six chapters first discuss theoretical considerations
and earlier work, then chart the historical development of Shanghai and the cities of
the Yangzi delta: Ming Shanghai, city of temples and gardens; Qing Shanghai and the
role of merchant guilds; and trade and commerce. The last six chapters deal with: the
arrival of the British and the China trade; the internationalization of Shanghai, 1846-
53; the 'Small Swords Rebellion' of 1853; the creation of the foreign Inspectorate of
Customs; and the emergence of the 'dual city', 1854-58.

434   **The dragons of Tiananmen: Beijing as a sacred city.**
Jeffrey F. Meyer.   Columbia, South Carolina: University of South
Carolina Press, 1991. 209p.

'Tiananmen' – the 'Gate of Heavenly Peace' – was the physical centre of Beijing and
the focus of religious beliefs and practices; therefore the late imperial capital was not
only an administrative but also a spiritual centre. Meyer deploys geography,
anthropology, urban planning and folklore to explain how this was so. The chapter
entitled 'The Chinese Capital in Historical Perspective' uses city plans and
architectural renderings to show how the city during the Ming and Qing periods
functioned as a cosmic diagram of a moral universe centred on the emperor; Meyer
focuses in particular on the rites or ceremonies which made local places sacred. He
also shows how common people used the yearly cycle of holidays and ceremonies to
give a sacred aura to their local places within the city.

435   **Hankow: commerce and society in a Chinese city, 1796-1889.**
William Rowe.   Stanford, California: Stanford University Press,
1984. 436p.

Together with its sequel, *Hankow: conflict and community in a Chinese city, 1796-
1895* (Stanford, California: Stanford University Press, 1989. 440p.), this work

constitutes a key social and economic history. Rowe demonstrates that Hankow, a mid-Yangzi river port and regional centre of commerce, developed a distinctive urban structure before the Europe-dominated age of global industry and trade. The city underwent significant economic development under the Qing dynasty and (contrary to earlier theory) was not passively subsumed under state control. Part one of the 1984 volume, 'The Emporium', treats formal structure and economy, including trade, credit and finance, and the relation of the state to commerce. Part two, 'Urban Social Organization', looks at the importance of place-of-origin organizations and the structure and effects of guild organization. These organizations did not create a 'bourgeois' revolution, but were powerful enough to negotiate with government officials. The 1989 volume examines the people, their social and cultural formations, and political ramifications.

436 **The city in late imperial China.**
Edited by G. William Skinner. Stanford, California: Stanford University Press, 1977. 820p. (Studies in Chinese Society).

A seminal theoretical and historical symposium. The work features Skinner's 'Introduction: Urban development in Imperial China' and 'Cities and the Hierarchy of Local Systems', which constitute a basic exposition of his influential theory of macroregions, an application of central place theory (for which see also Skinner's *Marketing and social structure in rural China*, q.v.). Essays describe: Nanjing, 1350-1400; the cosmology of the Chinese city; academies in Qing dynasty Guangdong; the morphology of walled capitals; and Qing urban guilds. Three essays treat Taiwan during the Qing dynasty.

437 **Chinese imperial city planning.**
Nancy Shatzman Steinhardt. Honolulu: University of Hawaii Press, 1990. 228p.

A wide-ranging history of the cultural ideals, politics and physical layout of dynastic capitals from earliest times to the 20th century, especially Chang'an (present-day Xi'an), Loyang, Bianliang (present-day Hangzhou), Nanjing and Beijing. Earlier scholarship saw all Chinese capitals as following an unvarying ancient model; however, Steinhardt shows that this model changed as successive dynasties both acknowledged the legitimizing power of precedent and responded to new needs and opportunities. The introduction explains the basic enduring characteristics of Chinese capital cities, sites and terminology. Chapters then follow the development of the imperial city dynasty by dynasty, including the Mongols, who founded modern Beijing. Many charts, plans and maps accompany the text.

438 **Shanghai: crucible of modern China.**
Betty Pei-t'i Wei. Hong Kong; New York: Oxford University Press, 1987. 299p. bibliog.

A colourful, broadly painted social and political history of Shanghai from the days of the Opium War to the Communist takeover of 1949. Wei's *Old Shanghai* (Hong Kong: Oxford University Press, 1993. 65p. [Images of Asia Series]) is an illustrated sketch of Shanghai life and society. Chapters cover: people and government; commerce, industry and finance; lifestyle; the Jewish community; and vestiges which have survived into the present. A selected list of sources in English is also included.

439 **The pivot of the four quarters: a preliminary enquiry into the origins and character of the ancient Chinese city.**
Paul Wheatley.   Chicago: Aldine; Edinburgh: Edinburgh University Press, 1971. 602p. maps. bibliog.

A pioneering study of ancient Chinese society and the earliest urban growths in Shang and Zhou China, especially Zhengzhou and Anyang. Part one argues that religious concerns and cosmology were more important than political or economic imperatives and that the Chinese pattern of urbanism was not imported from Western Asia. Part two looks at the early Chinese city in comparison with urban forms in other parts of the ancient world, and considers the ancient Chinese city as a 'cosmo-magical symbol'.

After 1949

440 **Cities with invisible walls: reinterpreting urbanization in post-1949 China.**
Kam Wing Chan.   Hong Kong: Oxford University Press, 1994. 193p. bibliog.

In imperial China, cities were sealed off by physical walls; after 1949, the government erected 'invisible walls' of policy and regulation to keep city and country apart. Chan first reviews Western research and finds 'grim misunderstandings' which accepted Maoist myths of an agrarian utopia. He then revises definitions of urbanization and assesses statistics to yield new understanding. He argues that the low growth in the Maoist era followed not from an anti-urban emphasis on rural development but from Soviet-style policies of promoting industrialization while containing costs of infrastructure. Urbanization policies in the post-Mao era continue many of these relationships. The conclusion summarizes the argument and considers future prospects. An earlier study is Richard J. Kirkby, *Urbanization in China: town and country in a developing economy, 1949-2000 AD* (London: Croom Helm; New York: Columbia University Press, 1985. 289p.).

441 **Urbanizing China.**
Edited by Gregory Eliyu Gulden, foreword by Fei Xiaotong.   New York; Westport, Connecticut; London: Greenwood, 1992. 256p. (Contributions in Asian Studies, no. 2).

These nine essays, intended for the interested general reader and student, provide an overall view of the recent phenomenal increase in the urban population, which by some definitions approached fifty per cent by the late 1980s. Part one contains essays on the role of great cities in China, an overview of post-1949 trends, and details of urbanization under economic reforms. Part two is devoted to small towns and the urbanizing countryside. Part three focuses on the Pearl River Delta of Guangdong as an advanced area of urbanization. There is a helpful 'Guide to Further Reading', listing books and articles in English on urbanization in China, Asia and the Third World. *Urban anthropology in China*, edited by Gregory E. Gulden, Aidan Southall, (Leiden, the Netherlands; New York: Brill, 1993. 429p. [Studies in Human Society, no. 6]) includes twenty-one papers from a large-scale 1989 conference held in Beijing; subjects include urban society and culture as well as economics and demography.

442 Chinese urban reforms: what model now?
Edited by R. Yin-wang Kwok, William L. Parish, Anthony Gar-on Yeh, with Xu Xueqiang. Armonk, New York; London: M. E. Sharpe, 1990. 256p. bibliog. (Studies on Contemporary China).

Geographers, sociologists, economists and an anthropologist assess urban development in a command economy once central regulations are relaxed. Their 1987 conference surveyed the results of urban planning policies, city growth, and rates and patterns of urbanization. Most of the twelve essays also deal with the burgeoning 'townships', which replaced the commune as the local unit of administration, and which are the locus for rural non-agricultural economic growth.

443 The fading of the Maoist vision: city and country in China's development.
Rhoads Murphey. New York; London; Toronto: Methuen, 1980. 169p. maps.

A broad overview and evaluation of the problems of development, urban planning and balancing urban-rural interests in revolutionary China, which makes many comparisons with India. The opening essays 'Cities and the Developing World' and 'China's Urban and Anti-urban Past' provide broad comparative context. Succeeding chapters describe policies and problems after 1949 ('Controlling and Dispersing Urban Growth', 'Walking on Two Legs', 'Planning for a New Urban China', and 'Tensions'). The book closes with 'China's Development Effort in Comparative Context' and conclusions, which develop a comparison with the Indian experience.

444 Beijing: the nature and planning of a Chinese capital city.
Victor Sit. Chichester, England; New York; Brisbane, Australia; Toronto; Singapore: Wiley, 1995. 389p. maps. bibliog. (Belhaven World Cities Series).

Uses Beijing's historical development and experience under socialism as a case-study for the Chinese city. The opening chapters discuss the previous literature, theory, and Beijing through the Ming and Qing periods. Detailed chapters then explore the city's post-1949 experience in terms of the following subjects: urban planning; spatial growth; economic development; population growth and its spatial pattern; housing and housing reforms; environment and preserving the old city; transport; and social areas. The conclusion summarizes chapter findings and asks 'Is There a Chinese Socialist City Model?' There are extensive references to Chinese and English primary and secondary works.

445 China's coastal cities: catalysts for modernization.
Edited by Yue-man Yeung, Hu Xu-wei. Honolulu: University of Hawaii Press, 1992. 330p. maps.

Contains thirteen essays, with a helpful introductory overview and conclusion, which place cities of the developing coast in present economic and historical geographic perspective. In the 1980s reforms and global interchange, these cities, two of which are Special Economic Zones (SEZs), burgeoned, but now face the problems that accompany success. The cities discussed include: Dalian (formerly called Dairen); Tianjin; Qingdao (Tsingtao), from colonial port to export base; Shanghai, as world city and SEZ; Ningbo, as rising industrial port; Wenzhou, a lower Yangzi town in late imperial history and today; Fuzhou, historically a gateway to the Southeastern frontier; Xiamen (Amoy), another SEZ; Guangzhou; Shenzhen, the model Special Economic Zone; and Taizhong (Taichung) in Taiwan.

Flowers on an iron tree: five cities of China.
See item no. 71.

Daily life in China on the eve of Mongol invasion, 1250-1276.
See item no. 153.

Migration and urbanization in China.
See item no. 418.

Urban life in contemporary China.
See item no. 606.

Chinese earth-sheltered dwellings: indigenous lessons for modern urban design.
See item no. 1310.

Minorities and Ethnic Relations

446 China's far west.
A. Doak Barnett. Boulder, Colorado; San Francisco; Oxford:
Westview Press, 1993. 688p.
Barnett covered China in the 1940s as a respected journalist; his *China on the eve of Communist takeover* (Boulder, Colorado; San Francisco; Oxford: Westview Press, 1985. 371p.) includes some of his reporting from that time. In the 1980s he returned to the provinces of Gansu, Qinghai and Xinjiang and here recounts in detail interviews with local officials and observations on the changes brought to the area by national unification, trade and communication with other parts of China, socialism, and economic development.

447 China's forty millions: minority nationalities and national integration in the People's Republic of China.
June Teufel Dreyer. Cambridge, Massachusetts: Harvard University Press, 1976. 333p.
Focuses on policy problems and conflicts as seen from Beijing, but with a consideration of the situation of the ethnic minorities and Muslims. Dreyer begins with a sketch of the imperial and Republican practices and Soviet policies, on which PRC officials drew. The main body of the book deals with successive post-1949 attempts to define what a 'nationality' is and how to integrate them, showing how Chinese practice differed from Soviet models.

448 Muslim Chinese: ethnic nationalism in the People's Republic.
Dru C. Gladney. Cambridge, Massachusetts; London: Council on East Asian Studies, distributed by Harvard University Press, 1991. 473p. bibliog. (Harvard East Asian Monographs, no. 149).
A methodologically innovative investigation of the Hui people, one of the ten officially recognized Muslim groups. Their ethnic identity formed and changed in interaction with their own evolving situation, Han majority culture, and government

policy. Gladney uses his own field observations and photographs to give vigorous portraits of four Hui communities in quite different situations: a Northwestern Sufi community; an urban enclave; a Hui autonomous village; and a Southeastern lineage. He discusses: the history of Islam in China; 'ethnogenesis', the political formation of ethnic groups; ethnic patterns in everyday life; ethnic pluralism in Chinese society; and the Chinese government's handling of ethnic nationalism in recent politics.

449 **Cultural encounters on China's ethnic frontiers.**
Edited by Stevan Harrell. Seattle, Washington; London: University of Washington Press, 1995. 379p. maps. bibliog.

These scholarly essays, with a substantial introduction, explore China's treatment of its ethnic minorities, especially the attempts of the Qing, Nationalist and Communist governments and Western missionaries over the last few centuries to culturally define, objectify and 'civilize' them. The editor's 'Introduction: Civilizing Projects and the Reaction to Them' compares the Christian missionizing project, which involved classifying and scaling the world's races, with the Confucian and Communist projects. Essays in part one discuss ways in which scholars and officials have construed the following: the Naxi of Northwest Yunnan province; the Yi peoples of Yunnan; Ming, Qing and contemporary views of the Miao, to whom the Hmong of Southeast Asia are related; the Yao; and the Gni-P'a. Essays in part two discuss the process of ethnic formation of the Miao, Mongols and the Dai.

450 **China and its national minorities: autonomy or assimilation?**
Thomas Heberer, translated by Michael Vale. Armonk, New York; London: M. E. Sharpe, 1989. 164p.

A survey of the issues and policies toward the fifty-five official minorities, based on official sources and definitions. Heberer discusses: the history of China's nationality policy; the 1950s problems of choosing which peoples to identify as 'minority'; policy clashes during the Cultural Revolution; policies towards economic growth, population planning and religions in Yunnan province, which contains twenty-four minorities; and Tibet. This English translation is an updated but abridged version of the German original.

451 **Creating Chinese ethnicity: Subei people in Shanghai, 1850-1980.**
Emily Honig. New Haven, Connecticut; London: Yale University Press, 1992. 174p.

In Shanghai, 'Subei people' (those from the poor and backward North Jiangsu area called 'Jiangbei') are stigmatized as rickshaw drivers, beggars, sweepers and honey-cart pullers, even though Zhou Enlai and former Shanghai Mayor (eventually President) Jiang Zemin are both from that area. Honig artfully applies sociological theories of identity and social invention of ethnic identity and racial prejudice to this phenomenon. Chapters analyse the society and economy of Jiangsu in the 19th century, migration to Shanghai, labour and employment, popular culture, self-defence organizations in squatter settlements, and the victimization of Subei people both during the Second World War and after 1949.

452 **Muslims in China: a study in cultural confrontations.**
Raphael Israeli. London: Curzon; Atlantic Highlands, New Jersey:
Humanities Press, 1980. 272p. (Scandinavian Institute of Asian Studies
Monographs, no. 29).
Deals with differences and conflicts between Han Chinese and Muslim Chinese first in
the period between the 13th and the 19th centuries, and then the period of 19th- and
20th-century rebellions.

453 **Mandarins, Jews, and missionaries: the Jewish experience in the
Chinese empire.**
Michael Pollak. Philadelphia, Pennsylvania: Jewish Publication
Society of America, 1980. 436p.
Part one deals with the 'discovery' of Chinese Christians and Jews in 1605 by Matteo
Ricci and European reactions to this sensational news. Part two synthesizes the
scattered scholarship on the origins, historic experience and eventual cultural
absorption of these Jewish communities. Donald Leslie, *The survival of the Chinese
Jews: the Jewish community of Kaifeng* (Leiden, the Netherlands: E. J. Brill, 1972.
270p. [T'oung Pao, Monographie, no. 10]) is a careful, scholarly study which
introduces and translates sources concerning the Jewish community in Kaifeng,
starting from the 10th century. A sympathetic novel on Kaifeng Jews in 1850 is Pearl
S. Buck, *Peony* (New York: John Day, 1948. Reprinted, with an afterword by Wendy
Abraham, New York: Biblio Press, 1990. 312 + 22p.). William Charles White,
Chinese Jews (Toronto: University of Toronto Press, 1942. 3 vols. Reprinted in one
volume, New York: Paragon, 1966) reproduces early English-language studies and
reminiscences.

454 **China's minority nationalities.**
Edited by Ma Yin, translated by Li Qizhong. Beijing: Foreign
Languages Press, 1989. 450p.
A more or less official compendium, written by scholars at the Central Institute for
Nationalities in Beijing, with encyclopaedia-type articles on each of fifty-five
officially designated minorities. Each article describes the history, religion, customs
and economic development of the group, emphasizing the progress made in recent
times under Chinese leadership. Observers note that 'minority' in official terms tends
to refer to groups which have come to be perceived ethnically and does not include
groups such as Jews, *tanka* (boat people), Subei or Jiangbei peoples in Shanghai, or
other 'sub-Han' rather than 'non-Han' minorities.

455 **China's minorities: integration and modernization in the twentieth
century.**
Colin Mackerras. Hong Kong: Oxford University Press, 1994. 355p.
Surveys the modern history of China's fifty-five non-Han minorities, including
Tibetans, Uygurs, Mongolians, Zhuang and Koreans, paying particular attention to
their degree of integration into Nationalist or Communist China, and their economic
modernization. Part one discusses problems of definition, concepts, sources and pre-
20th-century history. Part two, 'Tradition and Foreign Impact, 1900-1949', deals with:
the attempts, especially of the Tibetans and the Uygurs, to become independent; the
foreign, especially Soviet, impact; and economic and populations trends. Part three,

'Socialism Within Tradition: The People's Republic, 1949-1993', analyses policy evolution, foreign relations, and economic and population trends. The notes and bibliography which conclude the work supply extensive references.

The Ili rebellion: the Moslem challenge to Chinese authority in Xinjiang, 1944-1949.
See annotation to item no. 271.

Warlords and Muslims in Chinese Central Asia.
See item no. 271.

Mythology and folklore of the Hui, a Muslim Chinese people.
See item no. 1245.

Islam in China: a critical bibliography.
See item no. 1464.

Overseas Chinese

456 **Aiiieeeee! an anthology of Asian American writers.**
Edited by Jeffrey Paul Chan, Frank Chin, Lawson Frank Inada, Shawn
Wong. Washington, DC; Howard University Press, 1974. Reprinted,
with a new preface, New York: Mentor Books, 1991. 294p.

A pioneering anthology of fiction and poetry, followed by *The big aiiieeeee! an
anthology of Chinese American and Japanese American literature* (New York:
Meridian/Penguin Books, 1991. 619p.), edited by the same team. The 1974 volume
includes writing by writers of Filipino, Japanese and Chinese backgrounds, with an
extensive introduction, 'Fifty Years of Our Voice'. The 1991 volume contains only
Chinese American and Japanese American writers; the introduction, 'Come All Ye
Asian American Writers of the Real and the Fake', attacks Maxine Hong Kingston and
Amy Tan for writing 'to the specifications of the Christian stereotype of Asia being as
opposite morally from the West as it is geographically' and for preparing the way for
imperialism by accepting a Western feminist critique of Chinese culture.

457 **From China to Canada: a history of the Chinese communities in
Canada.**
Edited by Edgar Wickberg. Toronto: McClelland & Stewart in
Association with the Multiculturalism Directorate, Department of the
Secretary of State and the Canadian Government Publications Centre,
1982. 369p. bibliog.

A wide-ranging symposium on history and present conditions, with essays on the
current scene and aspects of history. David Chuenyan Lai, *Chinatowns: towns within
cities in Canada* (Vancouver, Canada: University of British Columbia Press, 1988.
347p. maps. bibliog.) focuses on Vancouver, the largest community. Family histories
in this Chinatown are poetically portrayed in a novel by Sky Lee, *Disappearing moon
cafe* (Vancouver, Canada; Seattle, Washington: Seal Press, 1990. 237p.). Chan Kwok
Bun, *Smoke and fire: the Chinese in Montreal* (Hong Kong: Chinese University Press,
1991. 338p.) interviews emigrants from the Canton area in Montreal about their
struggle to preserve cultural traditions and their dealings with Canadian racism.

458 **Entry denied: exclusion and the Chinese community in America, 1882-1943.**
Edited by Chan Sucheng.   Philadelphia, Pennsylvania: Temple University Press, 1991. 286p. (Asian American History and Culture).
These eight scholarly essays deal with the period following the passage of the 1882 Chinese Exclusion Law. This law, which effectively ended the immigration of Asians on grounds of race, was renewed, made permanent in 1904, and only rescinded as part of the wartime alliance with China against Japan in 1943. Four essays deal with the legal efforts of Chinese to fight racist laws in court, and another four with the effects on Chinese communities. Topics include: the exclusion of Chinese women; Chinatown organizations and the anti-Chinese movement, 1882-1914; the Guomindang (Nationalists) in Chinese-American communities before the Second World War; and Chinese Protestants in the San Francisco Bay area.

459 **Donald Duk.**
Frank Chin.   Minneapolis, Minnesota: Coffee House Press, 1990. 173p.
A cheeky, poignant novel in which a San Francisco Chinatown boy – Donald Duk – at first resents his father's Chineseness, but then dreams and re-experiences the history of Chinese in America, such as their obscured role in building the trans-continental railroad. Donald meets the God of War Kuan Kung and comes to terms with Chinese culture and American racism. Chin's *Gunga Din Highway* (Minneapolis, Minnesota: Coffee House Press, 1994. 404p.) takes up many of the same themes.

460 **China and the overseas Chinese: a study of Peking's changing policy, 1949-1970.**
Stephen Fitzgerald.   Cambridge, England: Cambridge University Press, 1972. 268p.
A scholarly study of the tension in China's policies between using overseas Chinese to promote revolution and the danger which this policy made for them as citizens of the countries Peking thus attacked. Fitzgerald, later Australia's Ambassador to the People's Republic, finds that revolutionary policies were carried out largely through the Party's relations with local Communist parties, while more normal relations continued to work on a government-to-government basis through the Ministry of Foreign Relations.

461 **Woman warrior: memoir of a girlhood among ghosts.**
Maxine Hong Kingston.   New York: Knopf, 1976; London: Allen Lane, 1977. 209p.
Contains evocative stories about an American of Chinese descent growing up in Stockton, California and coming to grips with her family and Chineseness. Kingston's *China men* (New York: Alfred Knopf, 1980. 308p.) contains stories of severe and suffering fathers, wayward or Confucian sons, and Chinese identities in America. In Kingston's *Tripmaster monkey: his fake book* (New York: Vintage, 1989. 342p.), Wittman Ah Sing – named for Walt Whitman and the 'heathen Chinese' Ah Sin? – becomes the legendary culture hero Monkey to recreate a China rooted culture in America. Other well received novels by Americans examining their Chinese heritage include: Amy Tan, *The Joy Luck Club* (New York: Putnam's, 1989. 288p.) and *The Kitchen God's wife* (New York: Putnam's, 1991. 415p.); Gish Jen, *Typical American* (Boston, Massachusetts: Houghton Mifflin, 1991. 296p.); and Gus Lee, *China boy* (New York: Dutton, 1991. 322p.).

462 **Revolutionaries, monarchists, and Chinatowns: Chinese politics in the Americas and the 1911 revolution.**
Eve Armentrout Ma. Honolulu: University Press of Hawaii, 1990. 228p.

Examines the history and political activities of Chinese communities in Hawaii, California and British Columbia. The contending groups in these communities first supported the monarchist organizations of the reformers Liang Qichao and Kang Youwei, but after 1908 Sun Yat-sen gained popular support. Yu Renqiu, *To save China, to save ourselves: the Chinese Hand Laundry Alliance of New York* (Philadelphia: Temple University Press, 1992. 253p. [Asian American History and Culture]) shows Chinese organizing themselves both for better conditions and to support China.

463 **Sons of the Yellow Emperor: a history of the Chinese diaspora.**
Lynn Pan. Boston, Massachusetts: Little, Brown, 1990. 444p. bibliog.

A lively, well-informed popular history of emigrant Chinese communities around the world. Pan describes: why and how emigrants left China; their political and cultural adaptations in the face of almost universal hostility; and their roles in the present world. The panorama ranges in time over four centuries and in place from the Philippines, Peru and Cuba to Malaya, France and North America. Pan clarifies a potentially confusing 'big picture' by interspersing opinionated anecdotes and gossipy biographies, as well as a savoury chapter on the role of Chinese food and another on the comparative anatomy of various Chinatowns. Pan's autobiography, *Tracing it home* (London: Martin Secker & Warburg, 1992; New York: Kodansha America, 1993. 229p.) recounts her own family's diaspora experience. Timothy Mo, *The redundancy of courage* (London: Chatto & Windus, 1991; New York: Vintage, 1992. 408p.) is a fast-moving novel concerning the political and identity problems of a gay Chinese hotel keeper in an invaded tropical island resembling East Timor.

464 **The Chinese experience in America.**
Henry Tsai. Bloomington, Indiana: Indiana University Press, 1986. 223p.

A careful survey of the 19th and 20th centuries, organized around the varying experiences in America of the 'sojourner', the 'ABC' (American Born Chinese), and student immigrants. The subject is also freshly and vigorously presented in Sucheng Chan, *Asian Americans: an interpretive history* (Boston, Massachusetts: Twayne, 1991. 242p. bibliog.), with an excellent bibliographic essay, and Ronald Takaki, *Strangers from a different shore: a history of Asian Americans* (Boston, Massachusetts: Little, Brown, 1989. 570p. map), a vigorous and groundbreaking survey. William Wei, *The Asian-American movement* (Philadelphia: Temple University Press, 1993. 355p.) focuses on 1960-1990s cultural and political organizations.

465 **China and the Chinese overseas.**
Gungwu Wang. Singapore: Select Books, 1991. 312p. maps.

Contains essays, lectures and papers by a leading scholar, dealing mainly with the Chinese communities in Southeast Asia. One group covers the history of immigration from China, how Chinese have been portrayed, their enterprises and business practices, and the various ways in which Chinese communities evolved in Singapore, Thailand, Malaysia and the Philippines. Another group deals with more contemporary issues, such as conflicts between loyalty of Overseas Chinese to lands of residence and to their Chineseness.

466   **Blood, sweat, and mahjong: family and enterprise in an overseas Chinese community.**
Ellen Oxfeld.   Ithaca, New York: Cornell University Press, 1993.
291p. maps. bibliog. (Anthropology of Contemporary Issues).
Vividly analyses the interplay of ethnicity, entrepreneurial strategies and family structure in a Hakka Chinese community in Calcutta, India, which came to dominate the leather tanning trade after the Second World War. Oxfeld's fieldwork and interviews bring to life the tension between the prudent frugality of family values and risk-taking instincts shown in gambling and business; in this way theory and story come together. *Emigration and the Chinese lineage: the Mans in Hong Kong and London*, by James L. Watson (Berkeley, California; Los Angeles; Oxford: University of California Press, 1975. 242p. map) studies the family and commercial networks which spread from Hong Kong to London, and how a South China culture adapted to life in Great Britain without losing its roots.

467   **Hidden heritage: historical archeology of the Overseas Chinese.**
Compiled, edited by Priscilla Wegars.   Amityville, New York:
Baywood Publishing Company, 1992. 430p.
These scholarly articles use both archaeological evidence and historical documents to examine the daily lives of Chinese immigrants in the 19th century, primarily in North America. The five sections discuss: rural contexts; urban contexts; work and leisure; analytic techniques in archaeology; and comparative/theoretical studies. The studies show that those Chinese in rural settings, such as Idaho miners, assimilated to new conditions much more quickly than their urban Chinatown counterparts. An innovative article, 'Chinese Opium Smoking Techniques and Paraphernalia', uses opium equipment excavated in America to show the diversity of social use in China and America and to explore its social significance.

468   **Trade and society: the Amoy network on the China coast, 1683-1735.**
Ng Chin-keong.   Singapore: Singapore University Press, 1983. 318p.
maps. bibliog.
An examination of the origins of the great migration from coastal Fujian to Southeast Asia. Ng's social and economic history covers rural society, the rise of Amoy (Xiamen) as a commercial port, the origins of the entrepreneurial frontier in Southeast Asia, merchant organization, and the role of Qing officials. *The Chinese in Philippine life 1850-1898*, by Edgar Wickberg (New Haven, Connecticut: Yale University Press, 1965. 280p.) analyses the transition of the Philippines from a Spanish trading outpost surrounded by outlying village communities and served by isolated Chinese merchants into a colonial society led by a multi-racial élite made up of affluent members of each component group. G. William Skinner, *The Chinese in Thailand* (Ithaca, New York: Cornell University Press, 1957. 459p.) analyses the distinctive factors in the relative integration of the Chinese into Thai economic and political life.

Writing diaspora: tactics of intervention in contemporary cultural studies.
See item no. 1113.

Dictionary of Asian-American history.
See item no. 1442.

The Asian-American encyclopedia.
See item no. 1448.

A history reclaimed: an annotated bibliograpy of Chinese language materials on the Chinese of America.
See item no. 1465.

Language

General

469 **Learn to write Chinese characters.**
Johan Björkstén. New Haven, Connecticut: Yale University Press, 1994. 120p. (Yale Language Series).
A succinct, engaging introductory manual which demonstrates the fundamentals of writing Chinese characters and their nature. Björkstén peppers his lessons with stories of Chinese life and culture to promote a practical understanding of the history of the characters, how they changed, and the various scripts in use today. *Fun with Chinese characters*, edited by the Straits Times Collection, cartoonist Tan Huay Peng (Singapore, Kuala Lumpur, Hong Kong: Federal Publications, 1980- . 4 vols.) is a cartoon illustrated series. The imaginative etymologies may not please the earnest scholar, but students may feel that anything to help remember a character is fair. Cecilia Lindqvist, *China: empire of living symbols*, translated from the Swedish by Joan Tate (Reading, Massachusetts: Addison-Wesley, 1989. 424p.) more soberly explicates characters, shown in oracle bone, bronze and modern forms, and relates them to traditional and modern life. Julie Mazel Sussman, *I can read that! a traveler's introduction to Chinese characters* (San Francisco: China Books, 1994. 176p.) is brief and practical.

470 **The origin and early development of the Chinese writing system.**
William G. Boltz. New Haven, Connecticut: American Oriental Society, 1993. 205p. bibliog.
A technical yet clear presentation of the development of the system of Chinese characters for writing, from earliest times to the Qin unification. Briefer and somewhat less technical is David N. Keightley, 'The origins of writing in China: scripts and cultural contexts', in *The origins of writing*, edited by Wayne M. Senner (Lincoln, Nebraska: University of Nebraska Press, 1989, p. 171-202). *Chinese characters: their origin, etymology, history, classification, and signification* by L. S. J. Wieger,

translated by L. Davrout, S. J. (Hsien Hsien, China: Catholic Mission Press, 1927. 2nd ed. Reprinted, New York: Paragon, 1965; New York: Dover Publications, 1965. 820p.) presents outdated 1920s scholarship.

471 Aspects of Chinese socio-linguistics.
Yuen Ren Chao, edited by Anwar S. Dil.   Stanford, California: Stanford University Press, 1976. 415p. bibliog.

Chao was not only the most influential scholar of the Chinese language in his generation, but also a gifted essayist, who often conveyed innovative analysis in a gracefully witty style. The topics of essays selected here include: 'My Linguistic Autobiography'; language and dialects (Wu, Changchow, Cantonese); dimensions of fidelity in translation; problems in lexicography; phonology; language problems of Chinese children in America; philosophical perspectives on Chinese grammar and logic; and structural perspectives (terms of address, plant words, chemical analogies). A bibliography lists Chao's published work, 1915-76.

472 The Chinese language: fact and fantasy.
John DeFrancis.   Honolulu: University of Hawaii Press, 1984. 330p. bibliog.

A provocative description of the Chinese language and its writing systems, intended for the public and specialists on China or on linguistics. The introduction reprints DeFrancis' wartime hoax, 'The Singlish Affair', a purported 'Japanese' proposal for writing English with characters. Part one, 'Rethinking the Chinese Language', more straightforwardly presents the considerable problems in defining 'Chinese' and 'language' (rather than 'idiolect', 'dialect', or 'regionolect'), and explains the principles of spoken Chinese. The sections 'Rethinking Chinese Characters' and 'Demythifying Chinese Characters' argue that characters are not essentially pictographs or ideographs, and discuss myths of 'universality', 'emulatability', 'monosyllabic', 'indispensability', and 'successfullness'. Part four discusses reforms in speech and writing before and after 1949, concluding that writing Chinese alphabetically can only happen when Chinese no longer speak regional languages. A 'Suggested Reading' section lists works on the Chinese language and general linguistics. *Speaking of Chinese* by Raymond Chang, Margaret Scroggin Chang (New York; London: W. W. Norton, 1978. 197p.) is a lively but not entirely reliable introduction; Richard Newnham, *About Chinese* (Harmondsworth, England: Penguin Books, 1971. 189p.) provides a non-technical discussion.

473 Nationalism and language reform in China.
John DeFrancis.   Princeton, New Jersey: Princeton University Press, 1950. Reprinted, New York: Octagon Books, 1972. 306p. bibliog.

A linguist's history of pre-1949 efforts to reform the Chinese language and replace characters with an alphabetic system. DeFrancis shows that the impulse to abolish characters was based more on a revulsion against traditional culture than on a rational assessment of costs and benefits. Especially interesting is the discussion of the Soviet Russian origins of *pinyin*, originally called *Latinxua*, and the ultimately unsuccessful campaigns for its universal adoption in the 1930s. *Language reform in China: documents and commentary*, edited with an introduction by Peter J. Seybolt and Gregory Kuei-ke Chiang (White Plains, New York: M. E. Sharpe; London: Dawson, 1979. 410p.) represents the controversy from the 1950s to the Cultural Revolution.

474 **Chinese.**
Jerry Norman. Cambridge, England: Cambridge University Press,
1988. 292p. bibliog. (Cambridge Language Surveys).
An authoritative survey, designed for the general reader and student. Norman first discusses the origins of Chinese as one of the early languages in North China, all of which interacted. He then summarizes the historical development of phonology, especially the work and accomplishments of Bernhard Karlgren in establishing the pronunciation of the Ancient (now called Middle) Chinese of the Tang dynasty, and the Archaic (now called Old) Chinese of the Zhou period. Further chapters describe the writing system, the grammar of Classical Chinese, and the evolution of particular grammatical forms. Two chapters deal with modern standard Chinese, so-called Mandarin. Two chapters then describe regional dialects, followed by a concluding chapter on the unifying cultural and linguistic structure beneath them.

475 **The languages of China.**
S. Robert Ramsey. Princeton, New Jersey: Princeton University
Press, 1989. 353p. maps. bibliog.
Presents the history, structure and social context of languages and dialects found within present-day China, including so-called 'minority languages'. Part one describes the history of the Chinese languages, the vernacular reform movement, writing systems, and six major spoken dialects. Ramsey expounds a significant hypothesis that the extreme linguistic diversity of modern South China resulted from the overlay of northern languages on a foundation of non-Chinese languages. This hypothesis highlights the political significance of the struggle in which Northern Mandarin was installed as the 'national' or 'common language' (*guoyu* or *putonghua*). Thematic maps indicate the history and distribution of languages. Part two surveys the languages of minority groups.

476 **Doing things with words in Chinese politics: five studies.**
Michael Schoenhals. Berkeley, California: Institute of East Asian
Studies, University of California, 1992. 135p. bibliog. (China Research
Monograph, no. 41).
Anatomizes not just what words *mean* but what they *do* in Chinese revolutionary politics. Essays analyse formalized language as a kind of power in order to show the ways in which Party manipulated 'terms' (*tifa*) during the Cultural Revolution to control discourse and to restrict what it was thus possible to say. Other topics discussed are: party circulars on terminology; ghost writers; Hu Qiaomu's 1955 instructions to newspaper editorial writers; and censorship, humanities and social sciences. The bibliography lists both sources and theoretical works.

477 **Modern Chinese characters.**
Yin Binyong, John S. Rohsenow. Beijing: Sinolingua; San Francisco:
China Books, 1994. 397p. bibliog.
By far the most lucid, rigorous and comprehensive description written for the language student or serious general reader. Topics include: the creation, evolution and number of characters; frequency of use; simplification and standardization schemes; characters frequently miswritten; pronunciation; the meanings of characters and how they developed; synonymous and antonymous characters; systems for arranging characters in order; writing characters (strokes, stroke order); and dictionaries and

reference works. James McCawley, a leading linguist, has written *The eater's guide to Chinese characters* (Chicago: University of Chicago Press, 1984. 248p.), to enable non-Chinese who enjoy Chinese food to better exploit Chinese restaurants; most readers will not read menus on the basis of this book, but may enjoy and profit from the brief practical explanation of the writing system.

478 **Crosstalk and culture in Sino-American communication.**
Linda W. L. Young. Cambridge, England: Cambridge University Press, 1994. 215p. bibliog. (Studies in Interactional Sociolinguistics).

Difficulties in American-Chinese communication often arise from differences in 'communicative behavior' – ways of organizing and linking ideas – not just vocabulary and grammar, much less Chinese 'inscrutability'. Using clearly explained techniques of sociolinguistics, Young analyses examples from Confucian philosophy and current business conversations. Differences include: interaction based more on open-endedness, aesthetics and harmony than individual assertion, agency and rationality; strategies of 'face', that is, public shame or social enhancement; how Chinese visualize and enact social relations; what sorts of information conversationalists rely upon to signify intent and decipher messages; and how these signals function in the cross-cultural interpretation of meanings. Kaidi Zhan, *The strategies of politeness in the Chinese language* (Berkeley, California: University of California Institute of East Asian Studies, 1992. 106p. [China Research Monograph]), contrasts 'speaker based' cultures with 'hearer based' cultures such as Chinese.

Sources of Shang history: the oracle-bone inscriptions of bronze age China.
See item no. 86.

Sources of Western Zhou history: inscribed bronze vessels.
See annotation to item no. 86.

Dictionaries

479 **Concise English-Chinese Chinese-English dictionary.**
Edited by A. P. Cowie, A. Evison, Zhu Yuan et al. Hong Kong: Oxford University Press; Beijing: Commercial Press, 1986. 600p.

A standard, pocket-size dictionary. The English-Chinese section contains roughly 20,000 entries, and the Chinese-English section gives a corresponding number listed by character, with combinations under them. The work is sufficient for beginning students and contemporary everyday usage. Simplified characters are used, supplemented with full characters and pinyin. The type size is quite small. *Learner's Chinese-English dictionary* (Singapore: Nanyang Siang Pau, Umum Publishers, 1990. rev. ed. 666p.) lists 5,000 'words' (i.e. characters) and 15,000 phrases and idioms, with pinyin pronunciations. Jerome P. Hu, Stephen C. Lee, *Basic Chinese vocabulary* (London: Longmans, 1989; Lincolnwood, Illinois: Passport Books, 1992. 389p.) lists words (in pinyin) in nineteen thematic groups, with English-Chinese and Chinese-English glossaries.

480 Oxford advanced learner's English-Chinese dictionary.
A. S. Hornby. Oxford: Oxford University Press, 1994. 1,910p.

Designed for Chinese students in their study of English. This standard reference contains roughly 50,000 entries, which cover English words, names and places, with more than 1,000 pictures and charts. Entries give the Chinese characters (with no pronunciation) and a brief definition.

481 Lin Yutang's Chinese-English dictionary of modern usage.
Lin Yutang. Hong Kong: Chinese University Press, distributed by McGraw-Hill, 1972. 1,720p.

Lists and translates words and phrases that a modern reader is likely to encounter in general, educated usage, including many classical references, proverbs and idioms. Lin's mastery of both Chinese and English frequently produces translations which catch nuances missed in other dictionaries. Arrangement is by Lin's own 'instant index system'; the work's acceptance was probably limited by this idiosyncratic but perfectly functional scheme. There is an index of English words.

482 Mathews' Chinese-English dictionary.
R. H. Mathews. Cambridge, Massachusetts: Harvard University Press, 1963. rev. ed. 1,226 + 186p.

Originally published by the China Inland Mission and Presbyterian Mission Press (Shanghai, 1931), this long, basic dictionary was reworked at the outset of the Second World War as the fullest coverage (more than 7,000 characters and 100,000 combinations) of 20th-century written Chinese. Although it does not reflect contemporary writing or spoken language, it is still valuable for its original purposes.

483 A Chinese-English dictionary of enigmatic folk similes (*xiehouyu*).
John S. Rohsenow. Tucson, Arizona: University of Arizona Press, 1991. 324p. bibliog.

Introduces and catalogues some 4,000 examples of a delightful and characteristic vernacular form, the two-part folk saying whose 'tail' changes the meaning of its 'head'. For instance, one might criticize a tiresome speech by saying 'it's like an old lady's foot bindings – long and smelly'. Often earthy, frequently punning, these will be entertaining to the novice, useful to those seeking cultural background, and informative to linguists. Rohsenow lists examples alphabetically, gives a translation and explication (with an English equivalent when possible), cites sources and provides indexes.

484 The pinyin Chinese-English dictionary.
Edited by Wu Jingrong. Hong Kong: Commercial Press; New York: Wiley, 1979. 976p.

The most widely used dictionary of contemporary usage. Roughly 6,000 character entries contain more than 50,000 combinations, arranged by pinyin pronunciation, with an index by radicals.

Grammar and description

485 A handbook of old Chinese phonology.
William H. Baxter. Berlin; New York: Mouton de Gruyter (formerly Mouton, the Hague), 1992. 922p. bibliog. (Trends in Linguistics: Studies and Monographs, no. 64).

A comprehensive summation of modern scholarship. Linguists now generally view Old Chinese as the spoken and written language of the Zhou dynasty, which eventually gave way to the Middle Chinese of the Sui and Tang dynasties. Baxter describes the methods and sources which he used to analyse the phonetic system, rhyme schemes and the writing system. Most Western scholars agree that Old Chinese had no tones, and here Baxter explains 'tonogenesis', the process by which tones were developed in Middle Chinese from consonant syllable endings. There is also a discussion of the Qing dynasty scholarship on the subject.

486 A grammar of spoken Chinese.
Yuenren Chao. Berkeley, California; Los Angeles: University of California Press, 1968. 847p.

A systematic analysis of the modern national language, intended for scholars and students. The work is technical but lively, and well grounded in general linguistic concerns. Charles N. Li, Sandra Thompson, *Mandarin Chinese: a functional reference grammar* (Berkeley, California; Los Angeles; London: University of California Press, 1981. 691p.) is a comprehensive analysis of modern spoken Chinese. Helen T. Lin, *Essential grammar for modern Chinese* (Boston, Massachusetts: Cheng & Tsui, 1981. 304p.) reworks recent scholarly grammatical analysis into practical chapters for language students and teachers.

487 Cantonese: a comprehensive grammar.
Stephen Matthews, Virginia Yip. London; New York: Routledge, 1994. 366p.

Cantonese is the language of fifty-five million speakers in parts of Guangdong, Hong Kong and some overseas communities. In this book, Matthews and Yip provide an analysis of the phonology and grammar, with a view to helping teachers and students. The introduction describes the language and tools for learning it. Siew-Yue Killingley, *Cantonese* (Munich, Germany; Newcastle, England: Lincom Europa, 1994. 50p. [Languages of the World/Materials, no. 6]) provides a succinct description, with chapters on phoneme inventory and romanization, morphology (form and structure) and syntax. The bibliography lists books, articles and texts. Keith S. T. Tong, Gregory James, *Colloquial Cantonese* (London; New York: Routledge, 1994. 248p.) comprises a brief course in the spoken language.

488 Outline of classical Chinese grammar.
Edwin G. Pulleyblank. Vancouver, Canada: University of British Columbia Press, 1995. 192p.

A concise, topically arranged reference grammar of the written language of the Zhou period. Pulleyblank summarizes and systematizes recent scholarship in the field for the linguist and for the student wishing to read classical texts. *Aspects of classical Chinese syntax*, by Christoph Harbsmeier (London; Malmö, Sweden: Curzon Press,

1981. 303p. [Scandinavian Institute of Asian Studies Monograph, no. 45]) introduces and analyses classical language through studies of specific topics (such as negation, pronouns and conditionality) and more than 1,000 sentence examples.

Textbooks and learning aids

489 Practical Chinese reader: elementary course.
Beijing Language Institute.   Boston, Massachusetts: Cheng & Tsui, 1990. 2 vols. (C & T Asian Language Series).

An edition, using traditional (full) characters, of the introductory textbook developed first in the 1970s at the Beijing Language Institute and originally published by the Commercial Press. Each of fifty lessons consists of a simple dialogue in pinyin romanization and characters, a list of new words, notes, some grammatical explanation, and pieces of cultural background. The American publishers have issued accompanying volumes of exercises for patterns and writing, as well as supplementary materials, videotapes and texts for succeeding years.

490 Chinese primer.
Ta-tuan Ch'en, Perry Link, Yih-jian Tai, Hai-tao Tang.   Cambridge, Massachusetts; London: Harvard University Press, 1989. 4 vols.

An introductory text which builds on Y. R. Chao's classic *Mandarin primer* (Cambridge, Massachusetts: Harvard University Press, 1948) in emphasizing strong foundation work, internalization of dialogues, use of humour, and varied grammatical patterns. Volume one provides foundation work and practical descriptions of pronunciation, dialogue lessons in romanization and English, and appendices describing romanization, the historical development of the language and script, and glossary-index. Volume two covers grammar and culture notes and exercises. Volume three comprises a character workbook, and volume four gives texts of the lessons in both traditional and simplified characters. Separate versions of the set are published in pinyin and in GR (*Gwoyeu Romatzyh*); the latter is an initially intimidating but extremely effective and highly recommended system which spells each of the four tones differently.

491 Gateway to the Chinese classics: a practical guide to literary Chinese.
Jeanette Faurot.   San Francisco: China Books, 1995. 130p.

A systematic introduction to the vocabulary and structure of *wenyan* – classical literary Chinese – through poems, essays and classical prose, emphasizing the type of classical language incorporated into modern written Chinese.

492 Mutant Mandarin: a guide to new Chinese slang.
Zhou Yimin, James J. Wang.   San Francisco: China Books, 1995. 170p.

Both a reference book of slang (much of it sexual, abusive or violent) and a source of information about a changing China, especially hip urban youth. The guide lists several hundred terms with definitions, examples (in simplified characters and pinyin), translations and hints on usage. Appendices give foreign loan words (e.g. AIDS, miniskirt, yuppie) and computer terms (e.g. batch file, login, modem). James J. Wang, *Outrageous Chinese: a guide to Chinese street language* (San Francisco: China Books, 1994. 124p.) provides the language student with the words not found in the textbooks; areas include how people in China actually address each other, terms for love and sex, expletives, food and drink, toilet terms, terms of abuse, getting sick, and weddings and funerals.

A little primer of Tu Fu.
See item no. 1202.

Religion and Philosophy

General

493   **Understanding the Chinese mind: the philosophical roots.**
Edited by Robert E. Allinson.   Hong Kong: Oxford University Press,
1989. 316p. bibliog.

Nine Chinese and Western scholars introduce and explore Chinese thought in the light
of techniques and concepts taken from Western philosophy. Essays include: 'An
Overview of the Chinese Mind'; 'Interpreting Across Boundaries'; 'The Chinese Case
in a Philosophy of World Religions'; 'Chinese Aesthetics'; and 'On Understanding
Chinese Philosophy'. Other essays discuss 'truth' and related concepts in early
Chinese thought; contrasting Chinese and European concepts of language and
language theory; Confucian and Daoist insights into the nature of reality; and
Confucian moral theory. The bibliography lists works cited.

494   **China and the search for happiness: recurring themes in four**
thousand years of Chinese cultural history.
Wolfgang Bauer, translated from the German by Michael Shaw.   New
York: Seabury Press, 1976. 502p.

A wide-ranging thematic treatment of the search for happiness in popular thought,
religious visions, philosophical inquiry and cosmology from earliest times to Mao
Zedong, originally published as *China und die hoffnung auf glück* (Munich, Germany:
Carl Hanser, 1971). Part one, 'Defining the Dimensions (ca. 1500-200 B. C.)',
discusses: classical thinkers, and 'unity of this world and beyond'; the turning away
from the present to a Golden Age; Confucian utopias; the escape from society;
hedonism; and individualism. Succeeding parts systematically explore evolving and
contending attempts under the empire to find happiness through politics, escape,
spirituality, madness and utopia, as seen in groups and in individual bureaucrats,
Daoist hermits, drunks, Buddhist messianic rebels and schismatic Confucians. Part
five, 'In the Twilight (since ca. 1800)', covers Taiping rebels, Sun Yat-sen, the
'conversation between Marx and Confucius', and Mao Zedong.

495 **Essays on Chinese civilization.**
Derk Bodde, edited, introduced by Charles Le Blanc, Dorothy Borei.
Princeton, New Jersey: Princeton University Press, 1981. 454p.
bibliog.
Contains twenty-one essays published from the 1930s to the 1970s by a leading
sinologist. Section topics include: the formation of Chinese culture ('The Chinese
Language as a Factor in Chinese Cultural Continuity', 'Myths of Ancient China',
'Feudalism in China'); law and society ('Types of Chinese Categorical Thinking',
'Basic Concepts of Chinese Law . . .', 'Prison Life in Eighteenth Century Peking',
'Henry Wallace and the Ever-normal Granary'); science ('Chinese "Laws of Nature":
A Reconsideration', 'The Chinese View of Immortality . . .'); and textual studies of
Confucian and Daoist texts. The work also includes a bibliography of Bodde's
published writings.

496 **Yüan thought: Chinese thought and religion under the Mongols.**
Edited by Hok-lam Chan, William Theodore de Bary. New York;
London: Columbia University Press, 1982. 545p. (Neo-Confucian
Studies).
These ten scholarly essays, together with a general introduction set the context and
summarize findings. Topics include: the historical thought of Ma Duanlin, author of
Wenxian tongkao, an encyclopaedic history of institutions; law, statecraft and the
Confucian *Spring and autumn annals*; Zhu Xi (1130-1200) and Yuan Neo-
Confucianism; Confucian hermits of the Yuan; Confucianism, local reform and
centralization; adaptations of Chinese Buddhism in Ta-tu, the Mongol capitol; Chan
(Zen) Buddhism in the Yuan; and 'Three teachings' syncretism of Confucianism,
Buddhism and Daoism.

497 **A source book in Chinese philosophy.**
Translated, compiled by Wing-tsit Chan. Princeton, New Jersey:
Princeton University Press, 1963. 856p.
The standard compendium of dominant ideas and formal thought, in fresh translations,
covering all periods and giving proportional treatment to Buddhism, Neo-Daoism,
20th-century thinkers, and the course of Neo-Confucianism, as well as the classical
thinkers. Whenever practicable, whole pieces are translated. Chan's scholarly
commentaries form a virtual survey on their own, while the translations are learned
and reliable. An appendix discusses translations of Chinese philosophical terms, and
the bibliography lists and lightly annotates hundreds of books and articles in Western
languages. Chan's *An outline and an annotated bibliography of Chinese philosophy*
(New Haven, Connecticut: Far Eastern Publications, Yale University, 1969. 220p.
[Sinological Series, no. 4]) is an invaluable guide, in which topical sections list books,
articles and sections of books.

498 **Chinese religions.**
Julia Ching. London: Macmillan Press; Maryknoll, New York: Orbis
Books, 1993. 275p. bibliog.
A sophisticated, succinct, clear introduction which emphasizes world religion and
comparative perspectives. Part one examines: indigenous traditions, including
ancestral cults and divination; Confucianism as 'religious humanism'; the legalist and
Mohist rivals of Confucius; and Daoism, first as 'religious philosophy', and after the

Han dynasty as 'salvation religion'. Parts two and three cover: foreign religions (Buddhism, Islam and Christianity); the Chinese response (Buddhist mysticism and devotion, Neo-Confucianism and the dilemma of Chinese Christianity); and the legacy of syncretism, especially in popular religion. The extensive bibliography lists recommended translations, general and special studies, as well as comparative work in Christian and other religions. Ching's other work includes *Confucianism and Christianity: a comparative study* (Tokyo; New York: Kodansha International, 1977. 234p.), and, with Hans Küng, *Christianity and Chinese religions* (New York: Doubleday, 1989. 309p.).

499   **Ideas across cultures: essays on Chinese thought in honor of Benjamin I. Schwartz.**
      Edited by Paul A. Cohen, Merle Goldman.   Cambridge,
      Massachusetts: Council on East Asian Studies, distributed by
      Harvard University Press, 1990. 400p. (Harvard East Asian
      Monographs, no. 150).

A compilation of ten essays by former students honouring Professor Schwartz and reflecting his breadth of interests in intellectual and cultural history. They include reflections on: the 'axial age breakthrough' in relation to classical Confucianism; a language of continuity in Confucian thought; Yan Fu's utilitarianism; the moral world of village opera; constitutional alternatives and democracy in the revolution of 1911; and the place of values in cross-cultural studies, with reference to the example of democracy in China.

500   **Chinese thought from Confucius to Mao Tse-tung.**
      Herlee Glessner Creel.   Chicago: University of Chicago Press,
      1953. 293p.

A standard, older history, written with charm and intelligence, and still useful for its sympathetically imaginative reading of the canonical texts. Creel tends to accept the self-conception of Confucian scholars as rational humanists and to emphasize orthodox thought.

501   **Self and society in Ming thought.**
      William Theodore de Bary and the Conference on Ming Thought.
      New York; London: Columbia University Press, 1970. 550p. (Studies
      in Oriental Culture).

Brings together a dozen essays which show changing scholarly approaches to Neo-Confucianism after the Song dynasty. Among the topics discussed are: the early Ming forms of Neo-Confucianism; the development of the concept of the moral mind from Wang Yangming to Wang Ji; individualism and humanitarianism in late Ming thought; the thought of Tang Xianzu (T'ang Hsien-tsu; 1550-1616), the dynasty's greatest playwright and influential intellectual, and his play, *Mudanting* (Peony pavilion); Daoist self-cultivation; Confucianism and popular educational works, looking at the unorthodox encyclopaedias compiled by commercial publishers for a new mass public; Confucian legalism and realism; Zhuhong's one mind of Pure Land and Chan (Zen) Buddhism; and a Daoist immortal.

502 **Religion and society in T'ang and Sung China.**
Patricia Buckley Ebrey, Peter N. Gregory. Honolulu: University of Hawaii Press, 1993. 379p.

A rich symposium on religion, thought and history. The editors' opening chapter, 'The Religious and Historical Landscape', authoritatively reviews recent findings which show how religion both reflected and shaped the epochal economic and political changes from the 7th to 12th centuries. Buddhism was indigenized (especially by Chan [Zen] Buddhism), popular cults and sects arose, and Confucianism began to reform. Essays treat: the rise of the Wenchang cult; Indian influences on lay religion; the growth of the idea of purgatory; myth, ritual and monastic practice in Song Chan (Zen) Buddhism; the official response to popular funeral practices, such as cremation; and Song academies as sacred places.

503 **The imperial metaphor: popular religion in China.**
Stephan Feuchtwang. London; New York: Routledge, 1992. 201p.

A general description and analysis, based on field observation in Taiwan. The author argues that popular religion in China differs from 'religion' in Europe: it is not the religion of a book, but is popular, based on locally specific cults and festivals, with elements from Buddhism, Daoism and official cults, and therefore different from the better studied ancestral and clan practices.

504 **A history of Chinese philosophy.**
Fung Yu-lan, translated with introduction, notes, bibliography, and index by Derk Bodde. Princeton, New Jersey: Princeton University Press, 1952, 1953. 2 vols. bibliog.

A comprehensive survey, with copious quotes and excerpts, and much background material, translated from *Zhongguo zhexueshi* (Shanghai: Commercial Press, 1934). Feng Youlan (1890-??), one of the first Chinese to be trained in both Western formal philosophy and the Confucian classics, rethought Chinese philosophical tradition in light of his new concerns. Volume one covers the thinkers of the classical period. Volume two deals with the period of 'classical learning', from the Han to the 20th century, with three chapters devoted to Buddhist philosophy. Chinese characters are supplied in the text and index. Fung Yu-lan, *A short history of Chinese philosophy*, translated by Derk Bodde (New York: Macmillan, 1948. 368p.) is an independent introduction, rather than a condensed version of the above.

505 **An intellectual history of China.**
He Zhaowu, Bu Jinzhi, Tang Yuyuan, Sun Kaitai, revised and translated by He Zhaowu. Beijing: Foreign Languages Press, 1991. 620p. (China Knowledge Series).

This detailed survey introduction, which discusses the development of 'the Chinese ideology' from 'primitive society' before the Xia dynasty to 1919, is a revised translation of *Zhongguo sixiangshi* (Beijing: 1985). Four parts, each with several chapters, cover ideology: in the pre-Qin period; in the 'early middle ages' (3rd century BCE-10th century CE); in the later middle ages (960-1840); and in modern times (1840-1919). The authors explain that they worked under the tutorship of the eminent Marxist historian Hou Wailu at the Institute of History, Academia Sinica, in Beijing. They emphasize the interaction of thought, material civilization, political structure, and social relationships of the people, with emphasis on economic thought. Throughout the work, they provide many quotations and particular examples, with references in English to works in Chinese.

506 **The development and decline of Chinese cosmology.**
John B. Henderson. New York; London: Columbia University Press, 1984. 331p.

A broad intellectual history of a basic subject. By the Han dynasty, Chinese thinkers had woven diverse earlier schools into a unified theory: this held that the 'cosmos' was a reverberant whole which harmonized the individual, the family, government, the observable physical universe and the further world of spirits. This web of 'correlative thought' included the idea of cosmic resonance, the fives phases (*wuxing*) of physical being, and mathematical magic. Cosmology and correspondence theory was a unified basis for government (the body politic), physical science and medicine (the physical body) and divinatory sciences, as well as literary endeavours such as history writing, literary criticism, Neo-Confucian philosophy and religious belief. All shared the same philosophical base and vocabulary. In late imperial times there was a reaction against this cosmology and a decline in its vigour.

507 **Chinese ideas of life and death: faith, myth, and reason in the Han period (202 BC-AD 220).**
Michael Loewe. London: Allen & Unwin, 1982. 226p. bibliog.

A clear summary presentation for general readers of Han religion and spiritual life, which emphasizes the balance between tradition and innovation. Chapters describe: the four attitudes of mind (rather than the anachronistic division into 'schools' of Confucianism, Daoism, etc.); the gods; nature; the universe and the shape of the heavens; the earth and its creatures; omens and miracles; shamans and intermediaries; funeral and burial practices; imperial cults; imperial sovereignty and the purposes of government; and the Han formation of the canon which resulted in the codification of thought into the 'schools' recognized in later times. Loewe's *Ways to paradise: the Chinese quest for immortality* (London: Allen & Unwin, 1979. 270p.) thematically surveys a longer sweep of history.

508 **Intellectual foundations of China.**
Frederick W. Mote. New York: Alfred A. Knopf, 1989. 2nd ed. 130p. (Studies in World Civilization Series).

A sprightly, concise survey which focuses on those intellectual features of ancient China which endured to influence later times. Mote draws on 'Myths of Ancient China' (in Derk Bodde, *Essays on Chinese civilization*, q.v.), which argues that the Chinese did not need creation myths of an external creator; rather they saw a 'spontaneously self-generating cosmos' based on concepts of organismic wholeness and the interconnectedness of all things. Mote traces the implications of this cosmogony, or theory of the creation of the universe, in sections on: the attitudes toward spirits and gods; the impact on institutions; the problem of evil in a world without sin; sources of authority in a secular harmonious world; and time-space concepts. Chapters treat: early Confucianism and Daoism; the philosopher Mozi; the problem of knowledge (epistemology); and Legalism in the creation of the Chinese empire. A lightly annotated bibliography lists books, articles and translations in English.

509 **Individualism and holism: studies in Confucian and Taoist values.**
Edited by Donald J. Munro. Ann Arbor, Michigan: University of
Michigan Center for Chinese Studies, 1985. 399p. (Michigan
Monographs in Chinese Studies).

Fifteen papers from a 1981 conference explore the ways in which Confucians and
Daoists balanced individualism with various wholes (family, clan, state, Dao or
nature). Munro's valuable introduction defines conceptual problems and summarizes
the papers, with references to useful writings. The Chinese did tend to emphasize the
family or state, Munro agrees, but this was also typical of European thought until the
18th century; the contrast is not 'East' vs. 'West', but between various ideas and
practices found in both. Confucians seek 'self-realization' through individual paths to
long-agreed upon goals; polar oppositions, often seen in modern Western thought,
between reason and emotion, body and mind, self and society, were in Chinese thought
mutually sustaining, representing *yin* and *yang* harmony. Daoists only superficially
resemble post-Romantic Europeans who developed individualism as a philosophic,
psychological and legal construct; Daoists sought to merge themselves in a universal
whole, not to seek expression of their uniqueness, privacy, autonomy and dignity.

510 **Religions of China: the world as a living system.**
Daniel Overmyer. San Francisco: Harper & Row, 1986. 125p.
(Religious Traditions of the World Series).

A concise introduction to Chinese religions as lived and practiced as well as
conceived. Beginning with a survey of developments of Chinese beliefs and values
over time, Overmyer examines: the world view; sacred space and sacred time;
symbols of superhuman power; rituals (including divination and exorcism);
meditation; and institutionalized religion, including leadership, organization, ethical
teachings and related cultural activities. A chapter on 'dynamics' looks at Chinese
religion as practiced, including the Spring Festival, Buddhist enlightenment, and the
exorcism of harmful ghosts. The book concludes with a consideration of Chinese
religion today in Taiwan and the People's Republic and thoughts on the lessons of
Chinese religion for today. A selected reading list is also included.

511 **The spirits are drunk: comparative approaches to Chinese
religion.**
Jordan Paper. Albany, New York: State University of New York
Press, 1995. 315p. (SUNY Series in Chinese Philosophy and Culture).

Contains nine essays which challenge earlier views of Confucianism as monolithic
and as a religion in the European sense. Paper explores: the ecstatic (shamans,
mediums); female gods; the symbolism of the religious masks in the Shang and Zhou
periods; and the representation of nature in Chinese art, especially in poetry, painting
and rock gardening.

512 **Chinese religion: an introduction.**
Laurence G. Thompson. Belmont, California: Wadsworth, 1988.
4th ed. 184p.

A standard college level text and survey introduction, with ample bibliographical
references. Other well regarded texts include Christian Jochim, *Chinese religions: a
cultural perspective* (Englewood Cliffs, New Jersey: Prentice-Hall, 1986. 202p.).

513 **The religions of China: Confucianism and Taoism.**
Max Weber, translated by Hans H. Gerth, introduction by C. K. Yang.
Glencoe, Illinois: Free Press, 1964. 308p.
As C. K. Yang's introduction to the 1964 paperback edition makes clear, the fact that
Weber's specific views and information have been supplemented, revised, or surpassed
does not invalidate this historical masterpiece as a starting point and stimulus. Weber's
work, such as his thesis that a 'Protestant ethic' eased the rise of capitalism in Europe,
virtually created the field of historical and religious sociology. This study makes a
subtle and tenacious argument about religion, the role of the literati, cities and
ideology. See also Weber's essay, 'The Chinese Literati', in *From Max Weber*, edited
by Hans Gerth, C. Wright Mills (New York: Oxford University Press, 1946).

514 **Religion and ritual in Chinese society.**
Edited by Arthur P. Wolf.   Stanford, California: Stanford University
Press, 1974. 377p. (Studies in Chinese Society).
Contains fourteen scholarly papers from a formative conference. Social scientists and
historians of religion met to learn how to focus on local and folk beliefs and practices
rather than restricting study to élite philosophical texts and nation-wide doctrines. The
initial paper, 'On the Sociological Study of Chinese Religion', by Maurice Freedman,
is a basic introduction to the intellectual problems and historical development of the
field. The editor's influential piece, 'Gods, Ghosts, and Ancestors', shows how local
practice treated these three entities as related but different forms of religious power.
Other studies look at localities in Taiwan and Hong Kong to understand how Chinese
religious philosophy included but was changed by common people. A comparison
with Japan concludes the volume.

515 **Religion in Chinese society: a study of contemporary social
functions of religion and some of their historical factors.**
C. K. Yang.   Berkeley, California: University of California Press,
1961. 473p. Reissued, Prospect Heights, Illinois: Waveland, 1991.
Remains a stimulating and informative survey using the sociological approach of
Talcott Parsons and Max Weber. Yang explains that he will examine the 'functional
basis for the development of religious life and the organizational system by which the
religious element in traditional living was propagated and perpetuated'. Chapters
explore: religion in the integration of the family; popular cults; the political role of
religion and state control; political rebellion; and diffused and institutional religion in
Chinese society, which argues that religion was not institutionalized. The final chapter
examines Communism as a new faith.

Sources of Chinese tradition.
See item no. 4.

A survey of Taoist literature: tenth to seventeenth centuries.
See item no. 569.

The encyclopedia of religion.
See item no. 1437.

Chinese religion in Western languages.
See item no. 1474.

Guide to Chinese religion.
See item no. 1481.

A select bibliography on Taoism.
See annotation to item no. 1481.

Classical thought

Translations

516 **The Ijing or Book of Changes.**
Rendered into English by Cary F. Baynes from the Richard Wilhelm translation into German, foreword by C. G. Jung (1949), preface by Hellmut Wilhelm. Princeton, New Jersey: Princeton University Press, 1967. Reprinted, with corrections, 1968. 3rd ed. 740p. (Bollingen Series, no. 19).

The Ijing (the book, or classic, of change) was a divination manual probably drawn together before the time of Confucius; the accrued commentaries and interpretations of its trigrams and hexagrams put it at the heart of later cosmology and philosophy. The Baynes translation has been considered as standard. *The Classic of Changes: a new translation of the* I Ching *as interpreted by Wang Bi*, translated by Richard John Lynn (New York; London: Columbia University Press, 1994. 596p. [Translations from the Asian Classics]), is freshly rendered for both the scholar and the fortune telling initiate. Hellmut Wilhelm, *Change: eight lectures on the* I Ching (Princeton, New Jersey: Princeton University Press, 1973. 130p.) methodically explains the form and meanings of the work. Kidder Smith, Jr., Peter K. Bol, Joseph A. Adler, Don J. Wyatt, *Sung dynasty uses of the* I Ching (Princeton, New Jersey: Princeton University Press, 1990. 275p.) considers how Su Shi, Shao Yong, Zhu Xi and Cheng I re-invented the classic.

517 **Complete works of Chuang-tzu.**
Chuang-tzu, translated by Burton Watson. New York; London: Columbia University Press, 1968. 394p.

Zhuangzi, or 'Master Zhuang', was a formative Daoist thinker in the 'one hundred schools' of the third century BCE. He drew on the then unorganized precepts of Daoism for a series of literarily striking and philosophically appealing essays, later edited into the book, *Zhuangzi* (The [book] of Master Zhuang). This work was later grouped with *Daodejing* and the *Liezi* as founding texts of classical Daoism. Useful selections of his work include: *Chuang Tzu: basic writings*, translated by Burton Watson (New York; London: Columbia University Press, 1964. 148p. [Translations from the Oriental Classics]); and A. C. Graham, *Chuang-tzu the seven inner chapters, and other writings* (London; Boston, Massachusetts: Allen & Unwin, 1981. 293p.). Robert Allinson, *Chuang-tzu for spiritual transformation: an analysis of the inner chapters* (Albany, New York: State University of New York Press, 1990. 203p. [SUNY Series in Philosophy]) analyses structure and metaphor to argue that it is a coherent philosophical text.

518   **Confucius: the analects.**
Confucius, translated by D. C. Lau.   Harmondsworth, England: Penguin Books, 1979. 249p.

The *Lunyu* (usually translated as 'The Analects') is a compendium put together by the followers of Confucius (c. 551-479 BCE) after his life of frustrated search for political influence. In it, the Master replies to questions with aphoristic observations on his troubled age. His basic claim – 'I do not create, I only transmit' – reveals his conservative intentions; in order to promote social cohesion, however, he did make philosophical innovations. In addition to excerpts in standard anthologies, translations include: *Confucius: the analects*, translated with an introduction and notes by Raymond Dawson (Oxford; New York: Oxford University Press, 1993. 110p. [World's Classics]); *The analects of Confucius*, translated by Arthur Waley (London: Allen & Unwin, 1938; New York: Macmillan, 1939. Reprinted, New York: Anchor Books, [n.d.]. 257p.); and James Legge, in *The Chinese classics* (1893-95. Reprinted, Hong Kong: Hong Kong University Press, 1960. 5 vols. Vol. 1 reprinted, New York: Dover, 1971).

519   **Han Fei Tzu: basic writings.**
Han Fei-tzu, translated by Burton Watson.   New York; London: Columbia University Press, 1964. 134p. (Translations from the Oriental Classics).

Han Fei (280?-233 BCE) pulled away from the realistic Confucianism of his teacher Xunzi, in order to fashion a 'realist' (or Legalist) doctrine out of earlier disparate thoughts on bureaucratic efficiency, state power and the Daoist faith in awesome kingly majesty. Han Fei's series of witty and persuasive essays was originally intended to instruct the sovereign in pragmatic rulership and state building. These sardonic treatises, later edited into *Hanfeizi* (The [book of] Master Hanfei), ridiculed traditionalistic Confucian morality in favour of the ruthless statism with which the Qin dynasty unified China in 221 BCE and developed a reputation much like Machiavelli's *The prince*.

520   **Tao te ching.**
Lao-tzu, translated by D. C. Lau.   Middlesex, England: Penguin Books, 1963. 191p.

Laozi – 'the venerable one' – was a possibly apocryphal thinker, probably contemporary with Confucius in the 5th century BCE. He is associated with the *Daodejing*, a poetic, powerful, deliberately obscure set of writings central to the traditions of Daoism. Translations bring out quite different aspects of the textually jumbled work, an early text of which was recently excavated at Mawangdui; there can therefore be no one definitive interpretation. Other reputable renditions include: Wing-tsit Chan, *The way of Lao Tzu* (Indianapolis, Indiana: Bobbs-Merrill, 1963. 285p. [Library of Liberal Arts]); Robert Henricks, *Lao-tzu: Te-tao ching: a new translation based on the recently discovered Ma-wang-tui texts* (New York: Ballantine, 1989. 282p.); Michael La Fargue, *The Tao of the Tao-te Ching* (Albany, New York: State University of New York Press, 1992. 270p.); Victor Mair, *Tao Te Ching: the classic 'Book of Integrity and the Way'* (New York: Bantam Books, 1990. 168p.), which also uses Mawangdui texts; Arthur Waley, *The way and its power: a study of the Tao Te*

Ching and its place in Chinese thought (London: Allen & Unwin, 1934. Reprinted, New York: Grove Press, 1958. 262p.); Lin Yutang, *The wisdom of Laotse* (New York: Random House, 1948. 325p.); not to mention Benjamin Hoff, *The Tao of Pooh* (New York: Dutton, 1982. 158p.).

521   **The book of Lieh-tzu: a classic of the Tao.**
Lieh-tzu, translated by Angus Graham.   London: John Murray, 1960.
Reissued, New York; London: Columbia University Press, 1990. 192p.
(Translations from the Asian Classics).
An anthology of Daoist stories and essays. Although the work was traditionally attributed to one Lie Yukou ('Master Lie') of the 5th century BCE, it is now agreed that the present text dates from the 3rd or 4th century CE, after the fall of the Han (many of the tales show a Buddhist influence). The work includes a chapter on the non-Daoist hedonist, Yang Zhu, known for his boast that he would not sacrifice one hair from his arm to save the world.

522   **Mencius.**
Mencius, translated by D. C. Lau.   Hong Kong: Chinese University
Press, 1984. 2 vols.
Meng Ke, known in the West as Mencius, was the 4th-century BCE disciple of Confucius who did most to expand the ideas of Confucius, emphasizing the innate moral nature of mankind, moral psychology, political economy and the nature of rulership. Lau's full translation includes appendices giving chronology, textual redaction and argumentation. Lau's standard earlier version is *Mencius* (Harmondsworth, England: Penguin Books, 1970. 280p.).

523   **Mo Tzu: basic writings.**
Mo Tzu, translated by Burton Watson.   New York; London: Columbia
University Press, 1963. 140p. (Translations of Oriental Classics).
Mo Di known as Mozi, or 'Master Mo' (c. 468-376 BCE), was the founder of the Mohist school of philosophy and organizer of close-knit bands of disciples. He preached the doctrine of universal, ungraded love, in contrast to the Confucian idea of hierarchical loyalties. His bands of 'wandering knights' (*youxia*) worked to control the warfare of the day; they used rhetoric to argue for peace at royal courts and military technique to defend endangered states. Watson's selections, with an introduction and index, include the chapters on universal love (*bo'ai*), moderation in funerals, explaining ghosts, and those against offensive warfare, music, fatalism and Confucians. Angus Graham, *Later Moist logic, ethics, and science* (Hong Kong: Chinese University Press; London: School of Oriental and African Studies, 1978. 590p.) comprises a rigorous examination of texts, terminology and philosophical problems.

524   **Xunzi: a translation and study of the complete works.**
Xunzi, translated by John Knowblock.   Stanford, California: Stanford
University Press, 1990-94. 3 vols. Volume 1: Books 1-6. Volume 2:
Books 7-16. Volume 3: Books 17-32.
Xunzi, or Master Xun (312?-238 BCE), adapted and developed Confucian teachings for the state-eat-state struggles of his time. In the Han dynasty his ideas were

appropriated into an Imperial Confucianism, and later idealist Confucians blamed this 'realistic Confucian' for imperial authoritarianism. The accusers misunderstood Xunzi to say that human nature was essentially and irredeemably evil; actually, he still felt goodness could be acquired through learning and ritual. Knowblock's is the first complete translation, with substantial introductions, notes and explanatory material. *Hsün Tzu: basic writings*, translated with introduction, notes, index by Burton Watson (New York; London: Columbia University Press, 1963. 177p. [Translations from the Oriental Classics]) includes the essays on encouraging learning, heaven, music and rites, military affairs, regulations of a king, and man's evil nature. Other studies include: Edward J. Machle, *Nature and heaven in the Xunzi: a study of the* Tian Lun (Albany, New York: State University of New York Press, 1993. 224p. [SUNY Series in Chinese Philosophy and Culture]), which considers whether 'heaven' (*tian*) was neutral or purposive and moral; and A. S. Cua, *Ethical argumentation: a study in Hsün Tzu's moral epistemology* (Honolulu: University of Hawaii Press, 1985. 228p.).

The *tso chuan*: selections from China's oldest narrative history.
See item no. 121.

The Book of Lord Shang: a classic of the Chinese school of law.
See item no. 874.

The book of songs.
See item no. 1209.

Studies and surveys

525   Thinking through Confucius.
Roger Ames, David Hall.   Albany, New York: State University of New York Press, 1987. 393p.

Ames and Hall, a sinologist and a philosopher, follow the thought of Confucius through his life: 'At fifteen I set my heart on learning, at thirty I took my stance, at forty I was no longer of two minds, at fifty I knew the mandate of heaven, at sixty my ear was attuned, and at seventy I could follow the desires of the heart-mind' (*Analects* 2:4). Chapters meditate on Confucius' thought and on related problems in European philosophy: 'Thinking, Personal Articulation, Aesthetics, Cosmology, and Communication'. Each chapter explains terms and concepts, such as *xue* (study), *si* (thinking) and *zhi* (knowledge). Confucius emerges as more creative and individualistic than in other accounts, such as Herbert Fingarette (q.v.). Ames and Hall conclude with 'The Failings of Confucius'.

526   The art of rulership: a study of ancient Chinese political thought.
Roger T. Ames, foreword by Harold D. Roth.   Albany, New York: State University of New York Press, 1994. 277p.

Presents the *Huainanzi*, a Han dynasty politico-religious compendium. Ames' opening chapter outlines Confucian and Daoist concepts, then shows how Han thought merged and blurred them for Legalist purposes. Chapters discuss the following concepts: *wuwei* (non-action/doing nothing/acting naturally); *shi* (strategic advantage/political purchase), in military and legalist usage; *fa* (penal law); *yongzhong* (utilizing the people); and *limin* (benefitting the people). Ames then translates all of *Huainanzi* book nine, 'The Art of Rulership (*zhushu*)'. Text, transmission and ideas are examined in Harold D. Roth, *The textual history of the* Huai-nan tzu (Ann Arbor, Michigan: Association for Asian Studies, 1992. 470p.), and *Mythe et philosophie à l'aube de la Chine impériale: études sur le Huainan Zi* (myth and philosophy at the dawn of imperial China: studies of the Huainanzi), edited by Charles Le Blanc, Rémi Mathieu (Montreal; Paris: Les Presses de l'Université de Montréal, 1992. 240p.). John S. Major, *Heaven and earth in early Han thought: chapters three, four, and five of the Huainanzi* (Albany, New York: State University of New York Press, 1993. 388p. [SUNY Series in Chinese Philosophy and Culture]) translates key chapters and provides a general introduction to Han cosmology and correspondence theory.

527 **The Confucian creation of heaven: philosophy and the defense of ritual mastery.**
Robert Eno. Albany, New York: State University of New York Press, 1990. 349p. (SUNY Series in Chinese Philosophy and Culture).
Eno innovatively defines the earliest Confucians as 'masters of dance' and discusses their philosophy by explaining the evolving concept of *tian* (heaven) in the texts of Confucius, Mencius and Xunzi. He argues that the reputation of Confucians for austere political pronouncements and puritanism came later, under the empire. The original Confucians – here called by their Chinese name, the *Ru* – had a philosophy which was not analytical in that it did not distinguish between theory and practice, but placed ritual practice at its centre; they danced, chanted, played drums and formed an ethical community defined through a comprehensive ritual choreography. They 'created' heaven by developing a philosophy to explain and defend their ritual mastery.

528 **Confucius: the secular as sacred.**
Herbert Fingarette. New York: Harper Torchbooks, 1972. 84p. bibliog.
A scholar of contemporary philosophy presents a seminal, controversial reading of the *Analects* as a more spiritual and philosophical system than the enlightenment pragmatic rationalism in earlier Western portrayals. Fingarette argues that Confucius pre-figured modern philosophy by seeing 'human community as holy rite', ordered by ritual (*li*), in harmony with greater, cosmic *dao*. The title phrase, the 'secular as sacred', is now taken as a standard point of departure. The thesis is sympathetically critiqued in Schwartz, *The world of thought in ancient China* (q.v.).

529 **Myth and meaning in early Taoism: the theme of chaos (*hun tun*).**
Norman Girardot. Berkeley, California; Los Angeles; Oxford: University of California Press, 1983. 422p.
Studies the concept of 'chaos' in the early Daoist vision by meticulous textual analysis and background study of the *Daodejing*, *Zhuangzi*, *Huainanzi* and *Liezi*.

530 **Disputers of the Tao: philosophical argument in ancient China.**
A. C. Graham. La Salle, Illinois: Open Court, 1989. 502p. bibliog.
A major general history of Chinese philosophy in the Classical age (500-200 BCE). Each of the chief schools is first presented in relation to a breakdown of the Zhou dynasty 'world order decreed by heaven': a conservative reaction (Confucius); a radical reaction (Mozi); a retreat to private life (Yang-ists); idealization of small, agrarian community in a 'farmers' school (*nongjia*); and the sharpening of rational

debate among the Chinese Sophists, or dialecticians. The following developments of the founders' thoughts represent a shift 'from social to metaphysical crisis': Mencius; Mozi's followers, who re-grounded morality in rational utility; and Zhuangzi, who used spontaneity as a value to reconcile with heaven and assault reason. The next stage – Laozi, Xunzi and Legalism ('an amoral science of statecraft') – let 'heaven and man go their own ways'. Finally, the Qin and Han dynasties unified not only the political empire but also re-established the philosophical unity of heaven and man; this urge to oneness is seen in the Cosmologists, who based their science on correlative thinking. Confucianism is then reformulated as the philosophy of empire. Appendix one looks at the logical structure of quasi-syllogism. Appendix two is 'The Relation of Chinese Thought to the Chinese Language'. A bibliography lists translations, books and articles in Western languages.

531 **A Daoist theory of Chinese thought: a philosophical interpretation.**
Chad Hansen. New York; Oxford: Oxford University Press, 1992.
448p. bibliog.

Reinterprets Chinese philosophy of the classical age, describing its central concerns and major writings from a Daoist point of view. Hansen rejects the 'orthodox' pro-Confucian stereotypes of most studies for being 'romantic' and for seeing Chinese thought as based on intuition and mysticism rather than analytical reason. Using concepts from contemporary Western philosophy, Hansen finds rather a radically different theory of language and mind in classical China, one which reveals a 'unified philosophical point of view that develops and matures until banned, buried, and burned by [Han] imperial authority'. He argues that Daoism was philosophically lucid in seeing language as social practice whose basic function is to guide action. This focus on the relation of language to action unites philosophers of the period, and distinguishes them from classical Greek and early modern European philosophers.

532 **Language and logic in ancient China.**
Chad Hansen. Ann Arbor, Michigan: University of Michigan Press,
1983. 207p. (Michigan Studies on China).

Innovatively (and controversially) appraises the logical techniques and linguistic theories in classical Chinese philosophy, especially the logician Gongsong Longzi. Hansen deploys the tools of modern linguistic philosophy on Chinese thinkers in order to expand the understanding of both. A symposium inspired by Hansen's themes is *Epistemological themes in classical Chinese philosophy*, edited by Hans Lenk, Gregor Paul (Albany, New York: State University of New York Press, 1993. 194p. [SUNY Series in Chinese Philosophy and Culture]). Topics in this work include: conceptions of knowledge in ancient China; validity in Zhou thought; equivalent axioms of Aristotelian, or traditional European, and later Mohist logic; and historical speculation in Zhou China.

533 **Confucian moral self-cultivation.**
Philip J. Ivanhoe. New York: Peter Lang, 1993. 115p.

An illuminating series of 1992 lectures in summation of a recent trend of analysis; they are aimed at an audience of philosophically inclined people with little China background or those interested in China with little knowledge of philosophy. Western philosophers have been more concerned with defining what good *is* while Chinese philosophers focused on how to *become* good – moral self-cultivation. Ivanhoe provides an account of moral self-cultivation from the Shang dynasty, through Confucius, to the Qing dynasty; secondary works are systematically cited and briefly evaluated.

534 The concept of man in early China.

Donald J. Munro. Stanford, California: Stanford University Press, 1969. 256p.

A lucid, basic study of the concept of human nature in the works of the classic Confucian and Daoist thinkers from the point of view of comparative philosophy. Munro is interested in the Confucian tension between concepts of equality and hierarchy, as seen in discussions of heredity, education and self-cultivation, and provides a thematic account of how the classic philosophers handled these issues.

535 Knowing words: wisdom and cunning in the classical traditions of China and Greece.

Lisa Raphels. Ithaca, New York: Cornell University Press, 1992. 273p.

Classical Greece and China both distinguished between two types of knowledge, one as a matter of words and linguistic discourse ('wisdom'), another as a matter of skills, tricks and results (*metos*, or 'cunning'). Raphels uses this distinction to mine a neglected tradition of 'cunning knowledge' in China which included Daoists, military strategists and Legalist tacticians. She also looks at strategists as represented in two Ming dynasty novels, Zhuge Liang in *Romance of the three kingdoms* and 'Monkey' in *Journey to the West* (q.v.).

536 The world of thought in ancient China.

Benjamin I. Schwartz. Cambridge, Massachusetts: Harvard University Press, 1985. 490p. bibliog.

A major reinterpretation and systematic discussion of the classic thinkers to 221 BCE. Inspired partly by Karl Jasper's concept of an 'axial age', Schwartz sees the parallel emergence of 'creative minorities' in the high civilizations of the ancient Near East, Greece, India and China. These thinkers no longer simply accepted the rules of orthodoxy, but questioned, developed and re-invented them, thereby creating conscious cultural life and transcendence. Although covering much of the standard material by close reading of the texts, Schwartz provides a fresh interpretation through his comparative approach and sensitivity to contemporary cultural philosophy. Heiner Roetz, *Confucian ethics of the axial age: a reconstruction under the aspect of the breakthrough toward postconventional thinking* (Albany, New York: State University of New York Press, 1993. 373p. bibliog. [SUNY Series in Chinese Philosophy and Culture]) is a more technical analysis.

537 Three ways of thought in ancient China.

Arthur Waley. London: Allen & Unwin, 1939; Garden City, New York: Doubleday, 1956; Stanford, California: Stanford University Press, 1982. 216p.

For many years a standard and still serviceable non-technical brief introduction to the three major schools – Confucianism, Daoism and Realism (a.k.a. Legalism). Waley's perceptive, empathetic but impressionistic presentation of the thinkers and their social situation is interspersed with thoughtfully selected translations from their writings. Scholars now point out that the 'schools' were actually set up by Han dynasty bibliographers in need of distinct classification.

538 **Mencius and Aquinas: theories of virtue and conceptions of courage.**
Lee H. Yearley. Albany, New York: State University of New York Press, 1990. 280p. (SUNY Series, Toward a Comparative Philosophy of Religions).

Investigates both 'thin' and 'real' resemblances between the moral philosophies of Mencius and Aquinas; this 'comparative philosophy of religious flourishings' approach is debated in *Journal of the History of Religious Ethics*, vol. 21, no. 2 (Fall 1993). Yearley first outlines the concepts and methods of comparative philosophy; chapters then descriptively analyse the context of Mencius and Aquinas's theories of virtue, the theories of virtue, and conceptions of courage. *Mencius on the mind: experiments in multiple definition* by I. A. Richards (London: Kegan, Paul; New York: Harcourt, 1932. 131p.) is an early, still suggestive study by a brilliant British poet and literary philosopher who lived in China for a time.

Popular religion

539 **Festivals in classical China: New Year and other annual observances during the Han dynasty, 206 B.C.–A.D. 220.**
Derk Bodde. Princeton, New Jersey: Princeton University Press; Hong Kong: Chinese University of Hong Kong, 1975. 439p. bibliog.

An examination of Han dynasty society and cosmological thought as seen through its round of twenty-one major festivals. An introduction for the general reader sketches the sources, the Chinese calendar and chronology, and the Han World View. Part one details the pre-Han history and Han development of the four major New Year festivals. Part two delineates other annual observances, including imperial ploughing, the first sericulturalist, the lustration (bathing) festival, the midsummer festival, registration of households, and competitive hunting. Most of these festivals declined after the Han. Carol Stepanchuk, Charles Wong, *Mooncakes and hungry ghosts: festivals of China* (San Francisco: China Books & Periodicals, 1991. 145p.) is a well illustrated, popular survey of festivals celebrated in China today (including national minorities) and among overseas Chinese.

540 **Guilt and sin in traditional China.**
Wolfram Eberhard. Berkeley, California: University of California Press, 1967. 141p. bibliog.

Some comparativists believed that the East Asian national character was shaped by other-directed 'shame' rather than inner-directed guilt and sin; Eberhard contests this Freudian theory by examining folk religion, popular literature and élite writing. He describes: Chinese traditional concepts of guilt, sin and sex; social sin; sins against property and religion; the concept of the structure, population and administration of various hells; and suicide. He concludes that the question of social class was crucial and problematic: élite texts, written 'for' but not 'by' the masses, cannot tell us which moral systems were popularly internalized. Among the people, Buddhism gradually became Confucianized by absorbing concepts of retributive morality. Among élites, Confucian shame operated in much the same way as Christian guilt. By the 19th century, however, the upper class lost its sense of mission, duty and responsibility, leading some reform moralists to adopt the Christian concept of guilt.

541 **The religion of the Chinese people.**
Marcel Granet, edited, translated, with an introduction by Maurice Freedman. Oxford: Basil Blackwell, 1975. 200p.

The translation of a classic early essay, *La religion des Chinois* (Paris: Presses Universitaires de France, 1922), still valued for its empathetic interpretation and feel for how elements fit together. Granet (1884-1940) was much influenced by the French sociologist Marcel Durkheim; his interpretations often reflected concern with deep connections of myth, social structure and psychology as well as a spark of wit and insight. Freedman's important introductory essay explores Granet's life and contributions to the study of religion. Chapters present: peasant, feudal and official religion; religious revivals; and religious sentiment in modern China.

542 **Changing gods in medieval China, 1127-1276.**
Valerie Hansen. Princeton, New Jersey: Princeton University Press, 1990. 256p. bibliog.

A sophisticated study of how changes in popular religion reflect and affect general developments in society; the make-up of the pantheon of gods to be worshipped reflected new ideas and new religious publics. Adherents of 'textual religions' tended to be literate élites; to avoid their bias, Hansen uses documentary evidence and a 12th-century collection of popular tales of strange happenings – dreams of gods, hells, ghosts, exorcisms and miracles. Pragmatic commoners accepted new gods if they were effective, and Hansen traces the spread of city gods, Guanyin (the so-called Goddess of Mercy), and new cults along trade routes in disregard of Confucian canonical rules. Terry F. Kleeman, *A god's own tale: the Book of Transformations of Wenchang, the Divine Lord of Zitong* (Albany, New York: State University of New York Press, 1994. 335p. [SUNY Series in Chinese Philosophy and Culture]) describes the development of a 4th-century Sichuan city official into a nationwide cult, Wenchang, the God of Literature, whose 'autobiography', translated here, was transcribed in the 12th century by 'spirit writers' who went into trances to take dictation from the gods.

543 **Pilgrims and sacred sites in China.**
Edited by Susan Naquin, Chün-fang Yü. Berkeley, California; Los Angeles; Oxford: University of California Press, 1993. 445p. bibliog. (Studies on China, no. 15).

The substantial introduction to this symposium places pilgrimage for spiritual and earthly reasons into a comparative setting. The editors provide a selected Western-language bibliography on religion and pilgrimage in China, and another on pilgrimage in other cultures. Then nine specialized essays explore these pilgrimages, especially to the five sacred mountains, Taishan [T'ai Shan], Wutaishan [Wu-t'ai Shan], Putoshan [P'u-t'o Shan], Huang Shan and Miaofengshan [Miao-feng-shan]. Another study examines the Chairman Mao Memorial Hall in Beijing as a pilgrim destination.

544   **Folk Buddhist religion: dissenting sects in late traditional China.**
Daniel L. Overmyer.   Cambridge, Massachusetts; London: Harvard
University Press, 1976. 295p. (Harvard East Asian Series, no. 83).
Chinese officials and earlier Western scholars viewed popular Buddhist sects as
politically rebellious and culturally deviant. Overmyer respectfully explores their
religious beliefs, leadership, scriptures and rituals, and compares them cross-
culturally. He also discusses the issues of intellectual methodology, and describes the
White Lotus, White Cloud and Lo sects from the Yuan to the early Qing dynasties.
B. J. Ter Haar, *The White Lotus teachings in Chinese religious history* (Leiden, the
Netherlands; New York, Köln: E. J. Brill, 1992. 343p. bibliog. [Sinica Leidensia])
describes the 11th-century origins of White Lotus religions devoted to the Amitabha
Buddha which opened the forms of monastic Buddhism to laymen. Ter Haar
concludes that there was no unitary 'White Lotus' tradition but rather diverse local
groups, some of which were confusedly labelled as White Lotus by officials relying on
set terms found in official regulations.

545   **Fortune-tellers and philosophers: divination in traditional Chinese
society.**
Richard J. Smith.   Boulder, Colorado; San Francisco; Oxford:
Westview Press, 1991. 434p. bibliog.
A multi-faceted intellectual and social history which emphasizes the late imperial
period; divination was central to a spiritual cosmic philosophy which united China
across economic and geographic lines. Smith first provides a sprightly, short history of
divination from antiquity to the present, followed by chapters on various forms:
cosmology (the nature and structure of the universe); the *Ijing* (Book of Changes);
fengshui (siting, or geomancy); fortune telling; and spirit mediums and spirit writing.
Cynthia Brokaw, *The ledgers of merit and demerit: social change and moral order in
late imperial China* (Princeton, New Jersey: Princeton University Press, 1991. 287p.)
shows how controversy over Buddhist and Daoist morality handbooks reflected
changing ideas of gentry social roles and intellectual values. Richard Smith, *Chinese
almanacs* (Hong Kong: Oxford University Press, 1992. 93p. [Images of Asia])
constitutes a concise, illustrated introduction to the popular calendars which presented
the Chinese cosmological system in a form useful for fixing auspicious days,
astrological predictions and divination.

546   **The ghost festival in medieval China.**
Stephen Teiser.   Princeton, New Jersey: Princeton University Press,
1988. 275p. bibliog.
The ghost festival, once celebrated widely in East Asia on the fifteenth day of the
seventh lunar month, wove together elements of early Chinese religion, focusing on
family and ancestors, Daoist concern with cosmos, and Buddhist rituals and church
organization inherited from India. Teiser shows that its rise during the 3rd to the 9th
centuries was part of an 'epochal realignment of Chinese society', and studies this
transformation in mythology, especially the story of the hero Mu-lian, who travelled
to hell to rescue his mother. Teiser also discusses shamanism, cosmology and family
religion.

Domesticated deities and auspicious emblems: the iconography of everyday life in village China.
See item no. 1247.

Ritual opera, operatic ritual: 'Mu-lien rescues his mother' in Chinese popular culture.
See item no. 1336.

Confucianism: Tang to Ming

547 **Transition to Neo-Confucianism: Shao Yung on knowledge and symbols of reality.**
Anne D. Birdwhistell.   Stanford, California: Stanford University Press, 1989. 317p.

An intellectual history of Shao Yong (1011-77). Shao's 11th-century mathematical and philosophical treaties used Buddhism and Daoism in a way that prepared for the following century's Neo-Confucian synthesis, in which he was then retrospectively included. Birdwhistell surveys both the general thought of his era and the scholarship concerning it.

548 **'This culture of ours': intellectual transitions in T'ang and Sung China.**
Peter Bol.   Stanford, California: Stanford University Press, 1992. 520p.

After the Tang dynasty, political authority shifted from hereditary aristocratic-military social clusters to an imperially sponsored élite chosen in competitive examinations and supported by landholding and bureaucratic positions. Culture changed accordingly: the Song *shi* ('literati', or educated gentlemen) cultivated moral values by the earnest study of Confucian textual traditions; they promoted moral action both by political conduct and by creating literary texts to serve as moral templates. Bol challenges Wm. Theodore de Bary's presentation of 'Neo-Confucianism' (a term which Bol avoids): thinkers in the 11th-century school of 'Dao Learning' (*daoxue*), particularly Ouyang Xiu, Wang Anshi, Sima Guang, Su Shi and Cheng I, were transfixed by the problems of 'culture' as presented by their new social and political positions; rather than developing along lines set by their predecessors, as often argued, they broke away from them.

549 **Chu Hsi: life and thought.**
Wing-tsit Chan.   New York: St. Martin's Press, 1987. 212p.

The life and thought of Zhu Xi (1130-1200), an important figure in the Song reformulation of Confucian thought and social practice, whom Chan calls 'undoubtedly the most influential thinker in Chinese history since Confucius and Mencius'. Chan's *Chu Hsi: new studies* (Honolulu: University of Hawaii Press, 1989. 628p.), gathers together his studies, roughly one third of which are devoted to Zhu

Xi's life, one third to his thought, and one third to his associates and pupils. Chan translates and introduces a central text intended for traditional students in *Reflections On Things At Hand: the Neo-Confucian anthology compiled by Chu Hsi and Lü Tsu-ch'ien* (New York; London: Columbia University Press, 1967. 441p.). *Chu Hsi and Neo-Confucianism*, edited by Chan (Honolulu: University of Hawaii Press, 1986. 644p.) contains essays drawn from a massive conference of Chinese, Japanese and Western scholars on all aspects of the master. *Images of human nature: a Sung portrait*, by Donald Munro (Princeton, New Jersey: Princeton University Press, 1988. 332p. bibliog.) lucidly examines the evolving philosophical discourse on human nature among Song dynasty thinkers, especially Zhu Xi and his followers.

550 **Liu Tsung-yüan and intellectual change in T'ang China, 773-819.**
Chen Jo-shui. Cambridge, England: Cambridge University Press,
1992. 221p. (Cambridge Studies in Chinese History, Literature, and
Institutions).

A wide-ranging study of Liu Zongyuan, who is usually grouped with Han Yü as a precursor of Neo-Confucianism. Chen first assesses the recent controversy on Neo-Confucianism and interprets Tang-Song literati and thought, then argues that Liu actually revived older forms rather than prefiguring new ones, but that Liu's literary and moral philosophy did pave the way. T. H. Barrett, *Li Ao: Buddhist, Taoist, or Neo-Confucian?* (Oxford: Oxford University Press, 1992. 178p. bibliog. [London Oriental Series, no. 39]) studies Li Ao (773?-836?) through a translation and commentary on his *Fuxingshu* (Writings on returning to one's true nature). Barrett examines the relations between the return to Confucian roots, Buddhism, and mystical (*xuanxue*) traditions, concluding that the work was basically Confucian.

551 **The liberal tradition in China.**
William Theodore de Bary. Hong Kong: Chinese University Press;
New York: Columbia University Press, 1983. 122p. (Neo-Confucian
Studies).

Delivered as the 1982 Ch'ien Mu Lectures at New Asia College of the Chinese University of Hong Kong, this is part of de Bary's larger project to defend Neo-Confucianism against the charge that it was authoritarian, élitist and fixed. After briefly sketching the origins of Neo-Confucianism, he reviews the careers of the Song dynasty's Zhu Xi and the Ming dynasty's Huang Zongxi with regard to liberal and popular education and especially the underemphasized role of individualism. An epilogue, 'China and the Limits of Liberalism', draws thoughtful points for an understanding of China's present dilemmas. See also the analytical review by Paul Cohen, with de Bary's reply, *Philosophy East and West*, no. 35 (July 1985), p. 305-10 and (October 1985), p. 399-412.

552 **Learning for oneself: essays on the individual in Neo-Confucian thought.**
William Theodore de Bary. New York; London: Columbia
University Press, 1991. 461p.

Surveys the thought of Zhu Xi and of his adherents. De Bary argues that despite a wide range of diverse concerns, thinkers worked within a conscious Confucian context which valued individuality and independent thought, not only 'face', community, or other-directedness. After assessing thinkers of the Yuan dynasty, de Bary delineates intellectual developments from Wang Yangming, who stressed an active concept of *xin* ('mind and heart'), through Wang Gen (1483-1540), founder of the Taizhou School, whose thought resembled egalitarian individualism, to Qing thinkers whose orthodox Neo-Confucianism was politically radical in its anti-Manchu activism. De Bary's *Neo-Confucian orthodoxy and the learning of the mind-and-heart* (New York; London: Columbia University Press, 1981. 267p.) contains earlier essays on this heritage. His *The message of the mind in Neo-Confucianism* (New York; London: Columbia University Press, 1989. 292p.) follows the concept of *xin* – mind/heart – in the tradition started by Zhu Xi and extended into the 19th century; he defends, perhaps too strongly, Wang Yangming from earlier charges of extreme idealism.

553 **The trouble with Confucianism.**
William Theodore de Bary.   Cambridge, Massachusetts: Harvard University Press, 1991. 132p.

The sociologist Max Weber saw Protestantism as critical, self-transforming and nature-conquering, whereas he felt that Confucianism was a philosophy of acceptance and accommodation. In these lectures, de Bary defends Confucianism against these charges, arguing that the ideal gentleman (*zhunzi*) was actually obliged to speak as a prophet for the people; the 'trouble' was that this fostered a two-class system where the people could not speak for themselves. De Bary begins with an analysis of sage kings and prophets in classical times, looks at the 'noble man' in the *Analects* of Confucius, then describes the dilemma of the Confucian in later times, including the present. Confucianism emerges as a style of thought with relevance to the present world rather than a fixed set of orthodoxies.

554 **Chu Hsi and the *Ta hsüeh*: Neo-Confucian reflection on the Confucian canon.**
Daniel K. Gardner.   Cambridge, Massachusetts: Council on East Asian Studies, Harvard University, 1986. 181p.

Zhu Xi followed Confucius in claiming that he did not originate, only transmit; much of his thought is found in his hermeneutic commentaries on the Classics, in this case the *Daxue*, or 'Great learning'. Gardner first sketches Zhu Xi's life and times, shows how the *Four Books* (of which the *Daxue* was one) came to replace the *Five Classics* as canonical texts, discusses Zhu's interpretation of the book, and then gives an annotated translation of the *Daxue* which reflects Zhu's interpretation. *Learning to be a sage: selections from the* Conversations of Master Chu, Arranged Topically, *by Chu Hsi*, translated by Daniel K. Gardner (Berkeley, California; Los Angeles; London: University of California Press, 1990. 217p.) translates Zhu's chief work on the central concept of 'learning'.

555 **Two Chinese philosophers: the metaphysics of the brothers Ch'eng.**
Angus Graham, foreword by Irene Bloom.   La Salle, Illinois: Open Court Press, 1992. 201p.

The brothers Cheng – Cheng Mingdao or Cheng Hao (1032-85) and Cheng Iyuan or Cheng I (1033-1107) – are thinkers whose philosophical and ethical work inspired the slightly later Zhu Xi, with whom they are often grouped. The so-called 'Cheng-Zhu school', in English often called 'Neo-Confucianism', was fixed by later dynasties as the philosophy to be memorized for the civil service exams. Graham's early but still basic work, first published as *Two Chinese philosophers: Ch'eng Ming-tao and Ch'eng Yi-ch'uan* (London: Lund Humphries, 1958), puts the brothers in their 11th-century context, then takes up the philosophy of each separately. The presentation is structured around important concepts, such as: *li* (here translated as 'principles', though in Graham's later work it is often 'pattern'); *qi* or 'ether'; the criticism of Buddhism; good and evil; and other basic terms. Appendices cover technical matters and bibliography, and there is a new index. Ira E. Kasoff, *The thought of Chang Tsai (1020-1077)* (Cambridge, England: Cambridge University Press, 1984. 209p.) explores this cluster of concepts with reference to a contemporary of the Cheng brothers.

556   **Escape from predicament: Neo-Confucianism and China's evolving political culture.**
Thomas A. Metzger.   New York: Columbia University Press, 1977. 303p. (Studies of the East Asian Institute).

A seminal, controversial study, which challenges earlier charges that Chinese intellectuals had to reject traditional Confucianism in order to modernize. Metzger builds on Max Weber's sociology and psychological dependence theory, exemplified in the work of Lucian Pye, but rejects their contention that Confucianism did not feel a Faustian tension between morality and society, and therefore did not evolve. Rather, according to Metzger, Neo-Confucianism embodied a tragic contradiction between responsibility for the political world and an inability to fulfil it. Modern cosmopolitanism offered techniques to resolve this 'predicament' but did not offer spiritual satisfaction. Metzger reinterprets philosophers such as Tang Chunyi (T'ang Ch'un-yi; 1907-78), the range of Chinese thought from Confucius to Mao, and philosophical terms and spiritual principles.

557   **Confucian discourse and Chu Hsi's ascendancy.**
Hoyt Cleveland Tillman.   Honolulu: University of Hawaii Press, 1992. 328p.

A lucid, comprehensive rethinking of Confucianism in the Southern Song; the 'Confucian fellowship' evolved from diversity to officially proclaimed orthodoxy. Tillman reinforces recent scholarship which no longer sees Neo-Confucianism simply as a rationalization for the emperor's rule or the examination system orthodoxy. He distinguishes three key levels: speculative philosophy; cultural value; and policy debate. After a brief synopsis of Confucian thought, Tillman describes Zhu Xi's 'Learning of the Way' (*daoxue*) community in Fujian (perhaps modelled on the Buddhist monastery) as one element in an emerging mainstream. Subsequent chapters analyse, period by period, the relationships and interchanges with Confucian communities in other regions. See Tillman's 'A New Direction in Confucian Scholarship: Approaches to Examining the Differences Between Neo-Confucianism and *Tao-hsueh*' (*Philosophy East and West*, vol. 42, no. 3 [July 1992], p. 455-74).

558   **Utilitarian Confucianism: Ch'en Liang's challenge to Chu Hsi.**
Hoyt Cleveland Tillman.   Cambridge, Massachusetts: Harvard University Press, 1982. 304p. (Harvard East Asian Monographs, no. 101).

By 1127, the Song dynasty had lost North China to the Jurchen conquerors and Confucians had lost their renaissance faith that reform and scholarship could perfect society. In the resulting reformulation of Confucianism, Zhu Xi represented an ethic of personal virtue and metaphysics, while Chen Liang (1143-94) represented an equally Confucian ethic of practical results, seen in the emperors of the Han and Tang. Tillman vividly portrays the two contrasting personalities, the letters and visits exchanged in their debates over the period 1182-93, and resonances with earlier and succeeding thinkers. He explores the usefulness in cross-cultural understanding of Western middle-level concepts such as 'utilitarian', 'nationalism' and 'materialistic'. See also Tillman's *Ch'en Liang on public interest and the law* (Honolulu: University of Hawaii Press, 1994. 150p. [Society for Asian and Comparative Philosophy, Monograph no. 12]).

559 **Confucian thought: selfhood as creative transformation.**
Tu Wei-ming. Albany, New York: State University of New York Press, 1985. 203p.

This work cogently argues that Confucianism is not a millstone weighing China down, preventing modernization, but rather a wellspring, facilitating creative adaptation to the modern world. See also: Tu Wei-ming, 'Confucius and Confucianism' in *Encyclopedia Britannica* (Chicago, 1988. 15th ed. Macropedia 16, p. 653-62); Tu Wei-ming, *Centrality and commonality: an essay on Confucian religiousness* (Albany, New York: State University of New York Press, 1989. 168p.), a revised and enlarged edition of *Centrality and commonality: an essay on* Chung-yung (Honolulu: University of Hawaii Press, 1976), which reinterprets the *Zhongyung*, or *Doctrine of the Mean*, as a central thread running through Confucian thought in later ages down to the present; and Tu Wei-ming, foreword by F. W. Mote, *Way, learning, and politics: essays on the Confucian intellectual* (Singapore: Institute of East Asian Political Economy, 1989; Albany, New York: State University of New York Press, 1993. 202p. [SUNY Series in Chinese Philosophy and Culture]), which collects Tu's 1982-87 writings and includes a 'Bibliography of Tu Wei-ming'.

560 **Neo-Confucian thought in action: Wang Yang-ming's youth (1472-1509).**
Wei-ming Tu. Berkeley, California; Los Angeles; Oxford: University of California Press, 1976. 218p.

Examines the early years of Wang Yangming, the radical Ming dynasty re-shaper of Neo-Confucian thought. Using the approach of the psychologist Erik Erikson, Tu explores Wang's 'quest for self-realization', looking at psychological development as well as philosophy. Julia Ching, *To acquire wisdom: the way of Wang Yang-ming* (New York; London: Columbia University Press, 1976. 373p.) presents and analyses Wang's thought in the context of his life.

561 *Instructions for practical living* **and other Neo-Confucian writings by Wang Yang-ming.**
Wang Yang-ming, translated, with notes by Wing-tsit Chan. New York; London: Columbia University Press, 1963. 358p. bibliog. (Records of Civilization: Sources and Studies; UNESCO Collection of Representative Works, Chinese Series).

The distinguished translator states that this work is 'indisputably the most important Chinese philosophical classic since the early thirteenth century'. Wang Yangming represents the idealist or intuitionist wing of Neo-Confucianism, which rose in the

Ming period to attack and for several centuries overshadow Song Neo-Confucianism. Wang's *Quanxilu* (Instructions for practical living) records his tutorials with students on a wide range of philosophical questions; the translator provides a meaty introduction and translations of eight other texts. *Knowledge painfully acquired: the 'K'un-chih chi' by Lo Ch'in-shu*, edited, translated by Irene Bloom (New York; London: Columbia University Press, 1987. 266p.) presents a philosophical tract by Lo Qinshu, a more orthodox contemporary, with twenty letters from Lo to Wang Yangming.

Ordering the world: approaches to state and society in Sung dynasty China.
See item no. 155.

The rise of Confucian ritualism in late imperial China: ethics, classics, and lineage discourse.
See item no. 198.

Classicism, politics, and kinship: the Ch'ang-chou school of New Text Confucianism.
See annotation to item no. 199.

From philosophy to philology: intellectual and social aspects of change in late imperial China.
See item no. 199.

Neo-Confucian education: the formative stage.
See item no. 1030.

Later Daoism

562 **Transcendence and divine passion: the Queen Mother of the West in medieval China.**
Suzanne E. Cahill. Stanford, California: Stanford University Press, 1994. 303p. map.
Studies the great Daoist goddess, Queen Mother of the West (*Xiwangmu*), the development of her myths and cult in Tang dynasty popular religion, her image in Tang literary and religious texts, and the questions these raise about the goddess and the society that revered her. The immortal Queen's life is presented first in Tang hagiography and then in more than 500 Tang poems and art; in the myth. she met (and coupled with) the great rulers and converted the great Daoist masters, reinterpreting China's history in terms of Daoist morals. Cahill explores the problems that the goddess' femaleness, creativity and individual power raised for a society in which family, patriarchy and hierarchy were the rule.

563 **Vitality, energy, spirit: a Taoist sourcebook.**
Thomas Cleary. Boston, Massachusetts: London: Shambala, 1991.
280p.

Presents excerpts for the general reader in reliable, readable but not sinological interpretations. Cleary's other attractive translations include many of the classics, as well as less well known texts, such as *Understanding reality: a Taoist alchemical classic by Chang Po-tuan* (Honolulu: University of Hawaii Press, 1987. 203p.). *The secrets of Chinese meditation: Taoist yoga, alchemy and immortality*, by Charles Luk (K'uan-yu Lu) (London: Rider, 1964, 1970; New York: Weiser, 1971. 270p.) is a guide to meditation by a committed practitioner. Although he presents some translations of texts, Luk writes that historical, linguistic and geographical data have 'nothing to do with' the 'profound meanings' of Chan, Mahayana and Daoist schools, which are 'beyond space and time'.

564 **Lao-tzu and Taoism.**
Maxime Kaltenmark, translated by Roger Greaves. Stanford,
California: Stanford University Press, 1969. 158p.

This slightly expanded translation of *Lao tseu et le taoïsme* (Laozi and Daoism), (Paris: Editions du Seuil, 1965) provides a succinct yet comprehensive history and analysis of the lives and ideas of Laozi and Zhuangzi, the later Daoist Holy Man, and the Daoist Religion, such as the Shangqing and Lingbao sects. Articles on 'Taoism' in the *Encyclopedia of religion* (q.v.) also present recent scholarship and history of religious studies, with references to recent scholarship and translations. Holmes Welch, *The parting of the way: Lao Tzu and the Taoist movement* (Boston, Massachusetts: Beacon Press, 1957. Revised, 1965. 204p.) is an evocative exposition of the classic texts, although no longer up-to-date on popular and religious Daoism.

565 **Early Chinese mysticism: philosophy and soteriology in the Taoist tradition.**
Livia Kohn. Princeton, New Jersey: Princeton University Press,
1992. 218p.

From the time of the *Daodejing* and Zhuangzi to the Tang dynasty, there were Daoist traditions of philosophy and mysticism ignored by Confucians and long unknown in the West. Kohn distinguishes three major types, each with a textual tradition: quietistic and naturalistic 'dark studies' (*xuanxue*, often translated as 'metaphysics') in cosmology and medicine which drew on Laozi and Zhuangzi; ecstatic and escapist shamanism seeking direct encounters with gods and immortals; and Buddhist insight meditation and interpretation of body and mind. The central text of this early mysticism, *Xisheng jing*, is translated and annotated in Livia Kohn, *Taoist mystical philosophy: The scripture of Western Ascension* (Albany, New York: State University of New York Press, 1991. 345p.). Livia Kohn, *Laughing at the Tao: debates among Buddhists and Taoists in Medieval China* (Princeton, New Jersey: Princeton University Press, 1995. 281p.) is a readable translation, with a substantial introduction and extensive annotation, of *Xiaodao lun*, a polemical attack on Daoism completed in the year 570.

566   **Taoist meditation and longevity techniques.**
Edited by Livia Kohn.   Ann Arbor, Michigan: University of Michigan
Center for Chinese Studies, 1989. 384p. (Center for Chinese Studies
Publication, no. 61).

Provides scholarly articles on topics including the Chinese perspective on body and
mind; drug taking and immortality; contemplative meditation; insight meditation; the
ancient tradition in Daoist gymnastics; longevity techniques in Lingbao texts and in
the Tang; and *qigong* (neo-traditional forms of martial arts and breath control) in
contemporary China;

567   **The Taoist experience: an anthology.**
Livia Kohn.   Albany, New York: State University of New York Press,
1993. 391p. (SUNY Series in Chinese Philosophy and Culture).

Brief introductions and about sixty texts in translation make an attractive scholarly
presentation of the range of Daoist schools and practices for students of religion and
serious general readers. The work begins with ancient concepts of the Dao and its role
in the creation of heavens and the world, before moving on to an outline of overall
teachings on 'long life and eternal vision' (as the *Daodejing* describes its central
concern), and immortality. The texts are taken from many periods and cover all the
major schools down to the present revival in the People's Republic.

568   **Taoist ritual in Chinese society and history.**
John Lagerwey.   New York; London: Macmillan, 1987. 364p.

Introduces the spiritual message and ritual expression of Daoism through a detailed
transcription and explication of basic rituals transcribed from performance in present-
day Taiwan. Part two vividly depicts the liturgy for the living and liturgy for the dead,
with a choreography of the physical movements, vestments, altar configurations,
ceremonies and texts, with specific explanations of the significance of each. The
introduction and parts one and three make exaggerated claims for the unchanging
nature of Daoism over the centuries and explain Daoist liturgy, including Chinese
numerology, liturgy in time (the calendar) and liturgy in space (the Daoist altar).

569   **Taoism and Chinese religion.**
Henri Maspero, translated by Frank A. Kierman, Jr., introduction
by T. Barrett.   Amherst, Massachusetts: University of Massachusetts
Press, 1981. 578p.

Contains pioneering essays by a master French sinologist based on his exploratory
readings in the massive *Daozang* or Daoist canon. The canon, first published in 1442,
gathered more than 1,000 works going back to Laozi and Zhuangzi; it included
medical and pharmacological treatises, lives of saints, ritual and magic texts,
expositions of the *Ijing* (Book of Changes), alchemy handbooks, and moral
exhortations. Maspero began the task of surveying this jumbled, uninventoried, but
not incoherent, body of texts. Barrett's introduction describes Maspero's significance
and the growth of Daoist studies. Judith Boltz, *A survey of Taoist literature, tenth to
seventeenth centuries*, (Berkeley, California: Center for Chinese Studies, University of
California, 1987. 417p. maps [China Research Monographs, no. 32]) describes the
contents of the *Daozang* topic by topic, with a general introduction. This constitutes
an invaluable reference for the scholar and an engrossing survey for the interested
general reader who wishes to go beyond introductory surveys.

570 **Taoist meditation: the Mao-shan tradition of great purity.**
Isabelle Robinet, translated by Norman Girardot, Julian F. Pas, with a foreword by Norman Girardot, a new afterword by Isabelle Robinet. Albany, New York: State University of New York Press, 1993. 285p. map. bibliog. (SUNY Series in Chinese Philosophy and Culture).

A synthetic overview of the Daoist esoteric and mystical techniques of the Shangqing, or 'Great Purity', tradition. This school, centred on Mt. Mao (Mao Shan) near Nanjing in Jiangsu, sprang from revelations given through Lady Immortal Wei in the 4th century, flourished in the Tang, and was absorbed into Lingbao Daoism after the Song. Its meditative visualizations involved both inner voyages (bodily symbolism) and outer (astral) journeys. Robinet's exposition of these labyrinthine texts and important commentaries is necessarily technical. Girardot's foreword introduces the work of Maspero, Kaltenmark and Robinet. This English version augments Robinet's original *Méditation taoïste* (Daoist meditation), (Paris: Dervy Livres, 1979), and adds a bibliography, illustrations and list of citations.

571 **Histoire du taoisme des origines au XIVe siècle.** (History of Daoism from its beginnings to the 14th century.)
Isabelle Robinet. Paris: Cerf, 1991. 269p. bibliog. (Patrimoines).

Summarizes the pathbreaking findings of French scholarship in this field. Robinet describes how classical Daoism provided inspiration and legitimation for a vast, later, range of organized Daoist religion and spiritual practices not found in the texts of Laozi and Zhuangzi. Various semi-independent traditions, which competed with but preceded Buddhism, sprang up in the spiritual crisis of late Han and Six dynasties period, with later heights of creativity in the Tang, Song and Ming. Their traits included popular salvation, gods and saints, ritualism and collective devotion, inner and outer alchemy, and mystic practice.

572 **The master who embraces simplicity: a study of the philosophy of Ko Hung (A.D. 283-343).**
Jay Sailey. San Francisco: Chinese Materials Center, 1978. 658p.

Ge Hong, known as 'Baopuzi' – 'the master who embraces simplicity' – was one of the first important thinkers to rework classical Daoism as a philosophical basis for hermit life; he pursued medical and alchemical experiments and the magical control of nature. James Ware, *Alchemy, medicine, and religion in the China of A. D. 320: the Nei P'ien of Ko Hung* (Cambridge, Massachusetts: Massachusetts Institute of Technology Press, 1966. Reprinted, New York: Dover, 1981. 388p.) is a readable translation, but makes a questionable equation of *Dao* with 'God'.

573 **The Taoist body.**
Kristofer Schipper, translated by Karen C. Duval. Berkeley, California; Los Angeles; London: University of California Press, 1993. 273p.

Schipper trained both as an academic historian of religion and as a Daoist priest in Taiwan. Here he presents a unified interpretation of Daoist beliefs, originally published as *Le corps taoïste* (Paris: Fayard, 1982). The body in Daoist practice is not simply a physical framework, he argues, but a site for developing inner knowledge. The body simultaneously represents the social body of ritual participants, the physical body of individuals (especially those practicing 'inner alchemy'), and the cosmic body representing the universe. This presentation draws on the classic texts of Laozi and Zhuangzi and Schipper's own participant observations, rather than the Daoism of any particular time or place. For a discussion of this approach, see Norman Girardot, 'Let's Get Physical: The Way of Liturgical Taoism' (*History of Religions*, no. 23 [1983], p. 169-80).

574 **Facets of Taoism: essays in Chinese religion.**
Edited by Holmes Welch, Anna Seidel.   New Haven, Connecticut; London: Yale University Press, 1979. 301p.

A pivotal international symposium which shows new respect for Daoist spirituality and learning; Western scholars long accepted the Confucian disdain for Daoism as irrational and assumed that popular religion was a dilution of classical texts. An essay on religious Daoism and popular religion from the 2nd to the 4th centuries CE explains how the two creatively interacted. Another essay explores the textual problems and egalitarian ideology of the *Taipingjing* ('Classic of Heavenly Peace' or 'Scripture of General Welfare'), attributed to the Yellow Turban uprising of 184 CE. Daoist learning is explored in essays on the alchemy of Tao Hongjing (456-536), a follower of Ge Hong (q.v.), and Kou Qianzhi (363-448), who lobbied the court to suppress Buddhism and promote Daoism. Further essays explore Daoist monastic life, the formation of the Daoist canon and Daoist studies in Japan.

Art of the bedchamber: the Chinese sexual yoga classics.
See item no. 644.

Doctors, diviners, and magicians of ancient China.
See item no. 667.

Chemistry and chemical technology: part 2: spagyrical discovery and invention: magisteries of gold and immortality.
See item no. 1080.

Buddhism

575 **Buddhism in China.**
Kenneth K. S. Ch'en.   Princeton, New Jersey: Princeton University Press, 1964. 560p. (Princeton Series in the History of Religion).

A standard comprehensive historical survey of Buddhism in China for 'those who do not have the time or the linguistic equipment to read the research literature'. Originally delivered as a series of lectures, Ch'en's narrative of people, events, ideas and institutions is detailed but clear, with extensive references. The bibliography lists and lightly annotates work in Western languages, Chinese and Japanese. A glossary and list of Chinese names and titles give Sanskrit equivalents and Chinese characters.

576 **The Chinese transformation of Buddhism.**
Kenneth K. S. Ch'en.   Princeton, New Jersey: Princeton University Press, 1973. 345p.

Analyses, with many examples and particulars, the ways in which Buddhism adapted and was transformed over the ages and how Chinese culture was changed in successive ages by the Buddhist traditions. Chapters are devoted to: ethical life, such as changes in conceptions of filial piety by a religion which sought to escape from the burden of earlier existences; political life; economic life, particularly the institutional and technological developments of monastic Buddhism in the Tang; literary life, particularly in the life and poetry of the Tang poet Bo Juyi; and educational and social life.

577 **Chan insights and oversights: an epistemological critique of the Chan tradition.**
Bernard Faure. Princeton, New Jersey: Princeton University Press, 1993. 322p.

Together with Faure's *The rhetoric of immediacy: a cultural critique of Chan/Zen Buddhism* (Princeton, New Jersey: Princeton University Press, 1991. 400p.), this work forms a controversial, highly regarded reinterpretation and overview of Chan (Zen) Buddhism using *au courant* social and critical theory. Faure examines not only individual Chan thinkers, but also their paradigmatic systems, metaphors and terms; meanings were not fixed by the founding masters for all time, but historical contingency and context continued to generate new insights. Faure's *La volonté d'orthodoxie dans le bouddhisme chinois* (The will to orthodoxy in Chinese Buddhism) (Paris: Éditions du Centre National de la Recherche Scientifique, 1988. 318p.) reinterprets the establishment of Chan orthodoxy in the 7th and 8th centuries, and questions the claims to predominance of the so-called Southern School.

578 **Buddhism in Chinese society: an economic history from the fifth to the tenth centuries.**
Jacques Gernet, translated by Franciscus Verellen. New York; London: Columbia University Press, 1995. 441p.

A revision of *Les aspects économiques du bouddhisme dans la société chinoise du cinquième au dixième siècle* (Paris: Ecole Français d'Extreme-Orient, 1956). This classic work describes and analyses the social, economic and organizational history of Buddhism and the Buddhist Church in its most flourishing and prosperous era, when monasteries and temples controlled much land and handled extensive investments. Gernet traces economic thought and practice, such as the introduction of the pawnshop as a credit institution. The translator has supplied updated references, a bibliography and an index for this translation.

579 **Tsung-mi and the Sinification of Buddhism.**
Peter N. Gregory. Princeton, New Jersey: Princeton University Press, 1991. 368p.

Tsung-mi (780-841) was a key thinker in the late Tang maturation of distinctively Chinese forms of Buddhism. Part one of Gregory's technical but lucid study outlines Tsung-mi's life and conversion; he first espoused Chan (Zen), then moved to Huayan doctrines. Parts two and three analyse the history of these doctrines in Chinese Buddhism and explain Tsung-mi's innovations. Part four describes Confucian and Daoist elements in this process. Other studies of the production of a Chinese Buddhism include: Kenneth K. Tanaka, *The dawn of Chinese Pure Land Buddhist doctrine: Ching-ying Hui-yuan's commentary on the* Visualization Sutra (Albany, New York: State University of New York Press, 1990. 304p. [SUNY Series in Buddhist Studies]); and Paul Swanson, *Foundations of T'ien-t'ai philosophy: the flowering of two truths theory in Chinese Buddhism* (Berkeley, California: Asian Humanities Press, 1989. 399p.).

580 **The Zen teachings of Master Lin-chi: a translation of the *Lin-chi lu*.**
I-hsüan, translated, with an introduction, by Burton Watson. Boston,
Massachusetts; London: Shambala, 1993. 140p.

Ixuan (d. 866), known as Master Linji (Japanese, 'Rinzai'), was the final major
formulator of Chan (Zen) Buddhist thought in China before it took root in Japan.
Chan Buddhism did not hold so much with doctrinal theology as with lively, personal,
sometimes baffling direct teaching using 'cases' (*gongan*; Japanese, *kōan*). This
record (*lu*) of the Master's sermons and conversations with his students was a basic
text for Chinese and Japanese followers, and is presented here in a clear and lively
translation.

581 **The northern school and the formation of early Chan Buddhism.**
John McRae. Honolulu: University of Hawaii Press, 1987. 393p.
(Kuroda Institute Studies in East Asian Buddhism, no. 3).

A detailed history of the leaders and ideas which later became known as the Northern
School. McRae follows the leaders and ideas from the 6th century until the full
emergence in the 8th-century Tang dynasty. Robert E. Buswell, Jr., *The formation of
Ch'an ideology in China and Korea: the 'Vajrasamadhi-Sutra', a Buddhist
apocryphon* (Princeton, New Jersey: Princeton University Press, 1989. 315p.), focuses
on the 7th- and 8th-century production of new texts which were accepted as ancient –
apocrypha – and their role in the emergence of Chan (Zen) Buddhism.

582 **Buddhism under the T'ang.**
Stanley Weinstein. Cambridge, England; London; New York:
Cambridge University Press, 1987. 236p. (Cambridge Studies in
Chinese History, Literature, and Institutions).

A detailed institutional and political history of the Buddhist church, paying particular
attention to relations with the central government. Sections cover: developments reign
by reign, showing that imperial patronage was both a boon and a stumbling block;
monasteries; translations of scriptures; clerical privileges; land holding; and temples
that were at various times supported, controlled or suppressed. New tendencies
included Chan (Zen) Buddhism, which was largely non-scriptural, and Pure Land
Buddhism, which allowed laymen to directly worship the Amitabha Buddha by
chanting his name. The suppressions at the end of the dynasty virtually destroyed the
institutions of the monastic and scripturally based sects, which had flourished with
imperial patronage; their disappearance left the way open for devotional popular sects,
such as Pure Land and Chan.

583 **The practice of Chinese Buddhism, 1900-1950.**
Holmes Welch. Cambridge, Massachusetts: Harvard University
Press, 1967. 568p. (Harvard East Asian Series, no. 26).

A lucid history of the tumultuous but comparatively rapid adjustment of Buddhist
doctrine and organization to a modernizing China. This volume deals with men,
organizations and events; sections describe the monastic institutions (people, layout,
observance of the food and sexual rules, the abbot, rites and economy) and the
individual Buddhist (the monastic career, the lay Buddhist). Welch's *The Buddhist
revival in China*, with a section of photographs by Henri Cartier-Bresson (Cambridge,
Massachusetts: Harvard University Press, 1968. 385p. [Harvard East Asian Series, no.
33]) discusses the following topics: the career of Yang Wenhui; the rival Buddhist

associations of the 1920s; the lay Buddhist movement; the building of new monasteries and publishing houses; social action and social welfare by the sangha (the monastic order); foreign contacts; sects and dissension; and the problem of Christian stereotypes and Buddhist realties. Chan Sinwai, *Buddhism in late Ch'ing political thought* (Hong Kong: Chinese University Press, 1985. 192p.) treats the philosophical influences, especially with reference to the reformist Tan Sitong. Welch's *Buddhism under Mao* (Cambridge, Massachusetts: Harvard University Press, 1972. 666p.) covers monks and monasteries from 1949 to the Cultural Revolution, using Hong Kong interviews and published sources.

584   **Buddhism in Chinese history.**

Arthur F. Wright.   Stanford, California: Stanford University Press, 1959. 144p.

A masterly 'reflective interpretation', delivered originally as a lecture series. Wright first sketches the thought and society of Han China, whose disintegration gave way to a period of preparation for Buddhism, then to a period in which believers found ways to domesticate originally outlandish concepts and practices. The Sui and Tang dynasties saw independent growth, followed by a thousand years, to 1900, in which Buddhism evolved as one of the domestic Chinese religious systems. The closing discussion of the 'legacy' includes a comparison with Marxism in China. There is a list of 'Suggested Further Readings'. Wright's *Studies in Chinese Buddhism*, edited by Robert M. Somers (New Haven, Connecticut; London: Yale University Press, 1990. 204p.) brings together his biographical studies and essays on Buddhism and Chinese culture.

585   **The renewal of Buddhism in China: Chu-hung and the late Ming synthesis.**

Yü Ch'un-fang.   New York; London: Columbia University Press, 1981. 353p.

Zhuhong (1535-1615) was the head of the Yunqi monastery in Hangzhou where he amalgamated Pure Land and Chan (Zen) Buddhism in the closing years of the Ming, and taught lay Buddhist practices. Yü describes the general impact and significance of these religious changes. *The syncretic religion of Lin Chao-en,* by Judith A. Berling (New York: Columbia University Press, 1980. 348p. [Neo-Confucian Studies; Buddhist Studies and Translations; IASWR]) describes the parallel efforts of Lin Zhaoen (1517-98).

586   **The platform sutra of the sixth patriarch.**

Translated by Philip B. Yampolsky.   New York: Columbia University Press, 1967. 216p. (Records of Civilization).

A pioneering translation, with helpful commentary and analysis, of the basic text of Tang dynasty Chan (Zen) Buddhism. Chan Buddhism stressed meditation and wordless understanding, and claimed to have been transmitted directly from Buddha. Huineng (d. 713) was the head, or 'patriarch', of a monastery and tradition; his sacred text, or 'sutra', was influential in developing the so-called Southern School which stressed 'sudden enlightenment' (Japanese: *'satori'*), as opposed to the so-called Northern School, which emphasized gradual enlightenment.

587 **The Buddhist conquest of China: the spread and adaptation of Buddhism in early medieval China.**
Erik Zürcher.   Leiden, the Netherlands: E. J. Brill, 1972. rev. ed.
2 vols.

A thoroughly documented scholarly history, first published in 1959, which covers the period from the fall of the Han dynasty to the Tang. Buddhism was at first seen as a foreign intruder which attacked Confucian ideas of filial piety, lured believers away from family and defied political authority. Zürcher describes how these objections were overcome first among the exiled élite of the South, and then focuses on the monasteries as both spiritual and worldly institutions. *Lives of the nuns: biographies of Chinese Buddhist nuns from the fourth to sixth centuries*, translated and introduced by Kathryn Ann Tsai (Honolulu: University of Hawaii Press, 1994. 188p.) translates an anthology of sixty-five biographies compiled in the 6th century CE.

Ennin's travels in Tang China.
See item no. 66.

Praying for power: Buddhism and the formation of gentry society in late-Ming China.
See item no. 173.

Millenarian rebellion in China: the Eight Trigrams uprisings of 1813.
See item no. 220.

Folk Buddhist religion.
See item no. 544.

Islam, Judaism and Christianity

588 **Singing of the source: nature and god in the poetry of the Chinese painter Wu Li.**
Jonathan Chaves.   Honolulu: University of Hawaii Press, 1993. 208p.
(SHAPS Library of Translations).

The first study and translation in any language of the poetry of Wu Li (1632-1718), previously known primarily as an early Qing orthodox painter. The book goes on to deal with Christianity in 17th-century China, as Wu was one of the first Chinese Jesuit converts and Catholic priests. His poetry was completely conventional in form, but boldly experimental in creating Chinese Christian images and content. Chaves' presentation of this sincere religious faith implies that Christianity was not culturally incompatible with Chinese thought.

589　China and the Christian impact: a conflict of cultures.
Jacques Gernet, translated by Janet Lloyd.　Cambridge, England;
New York; Port Chester, New York; Melbourne; Sydney: Cambridge
University Press, 1985. 310p.

A major study of Jesuits in 17th- and 18th-century China and their critical reception by the sophisticated Neo-Confucian literati, originally published as *Chine et Christianisme* (China and Christianity), (Paris: Gallimard, 1982). Some Chinese intellectuals accepted Christianity but Gernet concludes that the impact was not wide and that assimilation did not follow. His argument is not that the literati were xenophobic or conservative, but that European modes of thought and language were structured differently from Chinese. Erik Zürcher, like Gernet also a scholar of Buddhism, in *Bouddhisme, Christianisme, et société chinoise* (Buddhism, Christianity and Chinese society), (Paris: Julliard, 1990. 93p.), emphasizes political factors, primarily the insistence from Rome on the centralized control of Christianity in China. John D. Young, *Confucianism and Christianity: the first encounter* (Hong Kong: Hong Kong University Press, 1988. 182p.) studies the writings of Matteo Ricci and Xu Guangqi, Yang Guangxian's attacks, and the Kangxi emperor's ultimate rejection. Nicholas Standaerdt, *Confucian and Christian in late Ming China* (Leiden, the Netherlands: E. J. Brill, 1981. 263p. [Sinica Leidensia, no. 19]) is a solid intellectual biography of the Christian thinker Yang Tingyun (1562-1627).

590　The forgotten Christians of Hangzhou.
D. E. Mungello.　Honolulu: University of Hawaii Press, 1994. 248p.

In the generations following Matteo Ricci (1552-1610), Christianity did not spread widely, but Mungello argues here that some orthodox Confucians saw Christianity as complementary to Confucianism and even transcending it in some respects. Using archives only recently made available, Mungello tells a lively tale, sometimes using an imaginative recreation of the thoughts of the Jesuit missionaries (primarily Martino Martini) and the Chinese literati in the lovely lakeside city of Hangzhou. Between 1611 and 1731 they built an impressive church, a seminary for training Chinese priests, a library, a publishing house, and a Jesuit cemetery, only to be closed down by the Yongzheng emperor. Mungello argues that this was evidence of political, not cultural, incompatibility.

591　Unfinished encounter: China and Christianity.
Bob Whyte.　London: Collins, 1988. 537p. maps. bibliog.

A history of Christianity in China from the 7th century to the 1980s and the endeavour to find Christian spiritual forms appropriate for China; missions and foreign contributions are considered only inasmuch as they participated in this enterprise. The early period is summarized in the opening chapters, with somewhat more attention paid to the first part of the 20th century, when Chinese Christians sought independence. The heart of the book deals with Christianity's confrontation with Marxism; Whyte finds that the best and most altruistic minds turned to revolution, rather than to Christianity. After 1949, Christian churches accommodated to the new government's 'Three Self' policy, which required autonomy from foreign finance and control.

Curious land: Jesuit accommodation and the origins of Sinology.
See item no. 97.

The memory palace of Matteo Ricci.
See item no. 411.

Muslims in China: a study in cultural confrontations.
See item no. 452.

Mandarins, Jews, and missionaries: the Jewish experience in the Chinese empire.
See item no. 453.

The survival of the Chinese Jews: the Jewish community of Kaifeng.
See annotation to item no. 453.

Islam in China: a critical bibliography.
See item no. 1464.

Contemporary China

592 **Taoist ritual and popular cults of southeast China.**
Kenneth Dean.   Princeton, New Jersey: Princeton University Press, 1993. 290p.
Describes a post-Mao reinvigoration of Daoist popular religion and practice, such as ecstatic possession and bloody sacrifice as well as sophisticated liturgies and refined doctrine. In the mid-1980s, just as central political control relaxed and the reform economy burgeoned, Dean travelled widely through impoverished rural Fujian province on the southern coast and found that political suppression had not destroyed 'feudal superstition': money raised locally and among Overseas Chinese was used to rebuild temples and revive local cults even before many villages had televisions or refrigerators. Dean traces this vigour to the Daoism of late imperial times, which was built on an interaction of government officials, merchants, gentry or local élites, and Daoist ritual specialists.

593 **Protestantism in contemporary China.**
Alan Hunter, Kim-kwong Chan.   Cambridge, England: Cambridge University Press, 1993. 291p. map. bibliog. (Cambridge Studies in Ideology and Religion).
A rich, balanced survey aimed both at readers with no background in China and at scholars of religion. The less restrictive government policy of the 1980s led to a revival in religious life of many sorts. Hunter and Chan, scholars with training both in Chinese studies and religious history, focus on the Protestant community, its historical legacy, relations with Buddhists and Catholics and, most originally, an exploration of Chinese religious culture and varieties of Christian life. Throughout the work, the

authors present both the varying experiences of individuals and comparative analytical perspectives. Ample footnotes and a bibliography provide references to English articles and books.

594   **Inheriting tradition: interpretations of classical philosophers in Communist China, 1949-1966.**
Kam Louie.   Hong Kong: Oxford University Press, 1986. 272p.
After sketching the historical and intellectual framework of the New China and describing the debate over definitions, methods and criticism in the 1950s, Louie devotes chapters to controversies in interpreting individual schools of philosophy. Topics include: Confucius, slave-owner mentality or paragon of teachers?; use and abuse of Laozi and Zhuangzi in the escape from Communism; Mozi: commoner or fanatic?; and reconstructing minor traditions (Mencius, Xunzi, Han Feizi).

595   **Religion under socialism in China.**
Edited by Zhufeng Luo, translated by Donald E. MacInnis, Zheng Xi'an, introduction by Donald E. MacInnis, foreword by Bishop K. H. Ting.   Armonk, New York; London: M. E. Sharpe, 1991. 243p. (Chinese Studies on China Series).
These nine studies from the Shanghai Academy of Social Sciences present semi-official views. The introductory chapter, apparently written by an editorial committee, reviews the history of missions, Catholic and Protestant organizations in China, relations with the Vatican, ties to the Nationalist government, and the formation of Christian and Buddhist patriotic and self-supporting bodies after 1949. The studies are based on field interviews with local authorities, who tend to see the phenomenon of religion under socialism as a 'problem' which will wither away.

596   **Religion in China today: policy and practice.**
Donald E. MacInnis.   Maryknoll, New York: Orbis Books, 1990. 448p.
An anthology of policy documents, excerpts from newspaper and magazine articles, public statements by designated religious leaders, and interviews with them by MacInnis. The introduction provides a general background to the subject. This volume continues the coverage provided in *Religious policy and practice in Communist China: a documentary history*, edited by Donald E. MacInnis (London: Hodder & Stoughton, 1967. 392p.).

597   **The turning of the tide: religion in China today.**
Edited by Julian F. Pas.   Hong Kong: Oxford University Press, for the Hong Kong Branch of the Royal Asiatic Society, 1989. 378p.
Thirteen brief scholarly papers give a feel for the diversity of religious development in the People's Republic. Topics include: recent Chinese research publications on religious studies; a review of Chinese interpretations of peasant rebellions; a revival of religious practice in Fujian; Buddhist and Daoist monasteries; symbolic amulets and jewelry in popular culture; a revival of temple worship and popular religious traditions; a revival of Confucian ceremonies; the Catholic church; the Protestant church; folk religion; and Buddhism in Hong Kong and the New Territories. Two extensive bibliographies list books and articles in English and Chinese.

598   **The Catholic Church in modern China: perspectives.**
        Edited by Edmond Tang, Jean-Paul Wiest.   Maryknoll, New York:
        Orbis Books, 1993. 260p. bibliog.

A selection of testimonies, interviews, articles and research papers, some specially translated for this volume, on the situation of the Catholic Church in China after 1949, particularly the relations between the open, government sanctioned public church and the underground church communities. The various authors and informants discuss such topics as the relationship of the Church to historical imperialism, the relationship between the universal and local church, the question of religious freedom, and future prospects. Jean-Paul Wiest, *Maryknoll in China: a history, 1918-1955* (Armonk, New York; London: M. E. Sharpe, 1988. 591p.) is a detailed study of the first American Catholic foreign mission in China. Beatrice Leung, *Sino-Vatican relations: problems in conflicting authority 1976-1986* (Cambridge, England: Cambridge University Press, 1992. 415p. [LSE Monographs in International Studies]) summarizes the Vatican's relationship with imperial China, with Soviet Communism, and with the People's Republic, then goes on to analyse relations in the first decade of post-Mao reform.

Society and Social Conditions

General

599 Chinese society on the eve of Tiananmen: the impact of reform.
Edited by Deborah Davis, Ezra Vogel. Cambridge, Massachusetts:
Council on East Asian Studies, distributed by Harvard University
Press, 1990. 401p. bibliog. (Harvard Contemporary China Series).

A 1988 conference exploring how decollectivization, privatization and commodification had changed relations between the party-state and Chinese society. In part one papers consider: the fate of the collective after the commune; political reform and rural government; and the politics of migration in a market town. Part two surveys urban job mobility; micropolitics and the factory director responsibility system, 1984-87; income distribution in Tianjin, 1976-86; and urban private business and social change. Part three includes studies of changes in mate choices; new options for the urban elderly; and the spiritual crisis of China's intellectuals. Part four surveys the increased inequality in health care and the impact of reform on youth attitudes. Appendices provide a glossary, chronology, and selected bibliography of books and articles.

600 Urban spaces in contemporary China: the potential for autonomy and community in post-Mao China.
Edited by Deborah Davis, Richard Kraus, Barry Naughton, Elizabeth
J. Perry. Washington, DC: Woodrow Wilson Center; Cambridge,
England; New York: Cambridge University Press, 1995. 449p. maps.
bibliog. (Woodrow Wilson Center Series).

A key symposium which describes and assesses contemporary China. The introduction describes how the political economy altered personal autonomy, social interactions, and community institutions, asking whether a 'civil society' is emerging. Essays in part one explore the economic and political forces that structure urban space, the

202

economic system, the regulatory state, and the floating population of internal immigrants. Part two, 'Urban Culture and Identities', looks at changing leisure patterns, artists between the plan and the market, films and their audience, avant-garde painters and poets. Part three, 'Urban Associations', covers labour's battle for political space, dissident and liberal legal scholars, the craze for *qigong* forms of martial arts, and student associations and mass movements. 'Conclusions: Historical Perspectives' considers attempts of earlier cities to deal with comparable problems of social order, livelihood, cultural representation and the role of state power.

601   **Family, field, and ancestors: constancy and change in China's social history, 1550-1949.**
Lloyd E. Eastman.   New York; Oxford: Oxford University Press, 1988. 267p. maps. bibliog.

A synthesis text which covers: population and demography (growth, structure and migration); the family and the individual; agriculture and the problem of 'peasant immiseration'; commerce and the geography of trade; capitalism and manufacturing (a 'failed industrial revolution?'); commerce and manufacturing under the impact of the West; new social classes, such as new merchants, the transformation of Confucian 'scholar-gentry' into intellectuals and professionals, new military, the new urban working class, and the resulting 'challenge to familism'; and the '*yin*' or underside of society (secret societies, bandits and feuds). Chapter bibliographies provide selective references to English-language books, articles and chapters.

602   **The study of Chinese society.**
Maurice Freedman, selected, introduced by G. William Skinner.
Stanford, California: Stanford University Press, 1979. 491p.

Provides twenty-four essays, collected posthumously, with an introduction assessing Freedman's contribution in the founding of China anthropology in the West. Sections concern: 'The Chinese in Southeast Asia'; 'Chinese Society in Singapore'; 'Social Change in the New Territories of Hong Kong'; 'Kinship and Religion in China'; and 'On the Study of Chinese Society'. Included are all of Freedman's major sinological work that does not appear in his books, *Lineage organization in southeastern China* (London: Athlone Press; New York: Humanities Press, 1958, 1965. 151p.) and *Chinese lineage and society: Fukien and Kwangtung* (London: Athlone Press, 1966. 207p.). *An old state in new settings: studies in the social anthropology of China in memory of Maurice Freedman*, edited by Hugh D. R. Baker, Stephen Feuchtwang (Oxford: JASO, 1991. 286p.) includes an obituary and bibliography.

603   **Village and family in contemporary China.**
William L. Parish, Martin King Whyte.   Chicago: University of Chicago Press, 1978. 417p.

Together with Whyte and Parish, *Urban life in contemporary China* (q.v.), this work forms a sociological portrait and analysis of Chinese society at the end of the Maoist period, focusing on Guangdong, but relevant nationally. In part one, the authors outline the Marxist, totalitarian and modernization models of social change which they go on to test. Chapters in part two assess material equality and inequality, health, education, and welfare policies, status and power, and peasant satisfaction. Part three deals with 'Family Organization and Ritual Life', whereas part four, 'Communities and Change', looks at changing patterns of cooperation and conflict within the commune. *Chinese rural development: the great transformation*, edited by William L. Parish (Armonk, New York; London: M. E. Sharpe, 1985. 278p.) constitutes a lively symposium which evaluates early reforms.

604 **Village life in China.**
Arthur Smith, with an introduction by Myron Cohen. New York: Fleming Revell, 1899. 360p. Reprinted, Boston, Massachusetts: Little, Brown, 1970. 278p.

Smith lived in a North China village as a Protestant missionary for twenty years before writing this classic 19th-century account, still valued for its detailed and acerbic observations. Part one describes 'The Village, Its Institutions, Usages, and Public Characters', including village theatre, schools and education, temples, markets and fairs, weddings and funerals, bullies, and headmen. Part two, 'Village Life', is a critical account of boys and men, women, family, and 'the vacuity of village life'. Part three asks 'What Can Christianity Do For China?' R. F. Johnston, *Lion and dragon in Northern China* (London: Murray, 1910. Reprinted, with an introduction by Pamela Atwell, Hong Kong: Oxford University Press, 1986. 461p. map) is another characterful view and detailed description of the British leased territory at Weihaiwei, Shandong, where Johnston served as District Officer and Magistrate. Paternalistic affection and a sharp eye animate his descriptions of village customs and his defence of Chinese religions against missionary censure.

605 **Death ritual in late imperial and modern China.**
Edited by James L. Watson, Evelyn S. Rawski. Berkeley, California: University of California Press, 1988. 334p. (Studies on China, no. 8).

These twelve scholarly essays explore sociological meaning and historical changes in funerals, burials, mourning, graves, memorials and other death rites. Watson's anthropological introductory perspective, 'The Structure of Chinese Funerary Rites: Elementary Forms, Ritual Sequence, and the Primacy of Performance', argues that while Europe became fragmented in the early modern period, China was culturally unified because of the homogenization of ritual *practice* ('orthopraxy'). Rawski's introductory perspective differs in emphasizing uniform *belief* ('orthodoxy'). Further essays explore the competitive weight of practice and belief: funerals in North China; death, food and fertility; funeral laments of Hakka women; gender and ideological differences; conflicting themes in popular culture; graves and politics in Southeastern China; Ming and Qing emperors and death ritual; death rituals for Mao, Sun Yat-sen and Chiang Kai-shek; and death in the People's Republic.

606 **Urban life in contemporary China.**
Martin King Whyte, William L. Parish. Chicago; London: University of Chicago Press, 1984. 408p.

A companion volume to Parish and Whyte's *Village and family in contemporary China* (q.v.). Whyte and Parish survey sociological theory and comparisons with other Socialist countries to test whether the 'Chinese model' of urbanism in the 1950s-70s avoided Western-style inequality and social disorder. Part one, 'The Urban Political Economy', describes political and economic structures, including low residential mobility, bureaucratic penetration, the work-unit (*danwei*), and the handling of problems. Part two, 'Family Behavior', looks at mate choice and marriage, families, and the position of women. Chapters in part three discuss: crime and social control;

political control; religion and social values; and personal relations. The authors conclude that the distinctive features of the Chinese city rest on a degree of bureaucratic control which would not be acceptable in liberal societies.

Community studies

607 **Chen village under Mao and Deng.**
Anita Chan, Richard Madsen, Jonathan Unger.   Berkeley, California; London: University of California Press, 1992. rev. expanded ed. 345p.

Combines scholarly, moral and political concerns in telling the dramatic story of 'Chen Village', near Canton, from the early 1960s and through the Cultural Revolution, the troubled 1970s, and the 'Midas touch' of 'entrepreneurs and gamblers' under Deng's reforms. The 1984 edition, *Chen village*, was one of the earliest studies to use Hong Kong interviews to highlight one village; first-hand research in the village now confirms and deepens the original understandings. The authors reveal the micro-politics of family and personal rivalries which interact with debates over social policy and morality, and are especially careful to present different points of view within the village, including sent-down intellectuals, Party cadres, village youths, and elders.

608 **Peasant life in China: a field study of country life in the Yangtze valley.**
Fei Hsiao-t'ung, with a preface by Bronislaw Malinowski.   London: Routledge & Kegan Paul, 1939. 300p. (International Library of Sociology and Social Reconstruction).

A classic work. Fei (also written Fei Xiaotong; 1910-), among the first social scientists trained in China, carried out fieldwork in Kaixiangong, a delta village near Shanghai, then went to London to study with Malinowski. This influential book is a readable, structuralist analysis of the geographic, economic and social factors affecting the radical transformation of village life; the aim is as much reformist as scientific. Fei's *Rural development in China: prospect and retrospect* (Chicago: University of Chicago Press, 1989. 240p.) reprints 1980s essays from his *Small towns in China: functions, problems, prospects* (Beijing: New World Press, 1986. 374p.), together with descriptions of Kaixiangong in 1957 and 1981 reprinted from his *Chinese village close-up* (Beijing: New World Press, 1983. 269p.). Fei's *China's gentry: essays in rural-urban relations* (Chicago: University of Chicago Press, 1953. 290p.) contains graceful essays on pre-1949 life and social structure.

609 **Ting Hsien: a North China rural community.**
Sydney Gamble, foreword by Y. C. James Yen, fieldwork directed by Franklin Ching-han Lee.   New York: Institute of Pacific Relations, 1954. Reissued, Stanford, California: Stanford University Press, 1968. 472p. maps.

A social survey of Dingxian, a county in Hebei, made in 1926-33 as part of James Yen's Ting Hsien Experiment in Rural Reconstruction. Gamble went to China before the First World War as a YMCA Secretary and stayed on to help found the academic profession of sociology. Chapters and tables focus on statistics, rather than social structures or personalities, but present unique information on all aspects of society, including government, economy, religion and history. There are many photographs. Gamble's *North China villages: social, political, and economic activities before 1933* (Berkeley, California; London: University of California Press, 1963. 352p.) covers eleven further villages. His *Chinese village plays from the Ting Hsien region . . .* (Amsterdam: Philo Press, 1970. 762p.) translates forty-eight *yangge*, or 'rice-sprout songs' (actually village plays).

610　Under the ancestors' shadow: kinship, personality, and social mobility in village China.
Francis L. K. Hsu.　New York: Columbia University Press, 1948; London: Routledge & Kegan Paul, 1949. 313p. Reprinted: Stanford, California: Stanford University Press, 1967. rev. expanded ed. 370p.

A rich pioneering community study of 'West Town' in Yunnan, Southwest China, in which Hsu focuses on family and religious life, personality formation, and applicability to Chinese society as a whole. As in his *Religion, science, and human crises* (q.v.), Hsu views historical culture as powerful but malleable. Chapters describe and analyse: graveyards, family shrines and temples; relationships in the family home; betrothals, weddings and matrilocal marriage; the big family as a frustrated ideal; the spirit world of the ancestors; communion with ancestors; and birth, care and education of children. Theoretical summary chapters discuss the implications for culture and personality. The 1967 edition adds a chapter on kinship, personality and mobility in China, arguing that older patterns have been affected but not destroyed by socialism.

611　The spiral road: change in a Chinese village through the eyes of a Communist Party leader.
Huang Shumin.　Boulder, Colorado; San Francisco; Oxford: Westview Press, 1989. 222p.

The vivid saga of a village in Fujian, South China. Huang discusses land reform in the early 1950s, the formation of cooperatives and communes, the beginnings of market reform and the breakup of the collectives. He then relates and analyses these developments from the point of view of his chief informant, the canny local leader, Party Secretary Ye. Local cadres were often caught between personal ties (*guanxi*) in the local community and the demands of the higher ranks. Villagers had mixed reactions to Maoism and its demise, and Huang helpfully sorts out the material he presents.

612　Sex, death, and hierarchy in a Chinese city: an anthropological account.
William R. Jankowiak.　New York: Columbia University Press, 1993. 345p.

Uses the theory of symbolic interactionism to explore contemporary urban culture. Jankowiak reports on the dynamic process of politics, personal ethics and morality in Huhhot, the capital of Inner Mongolia, a Chinese city with a large Mongol population. Chapters focus on: the rise of ethnic antagonism and 'objectification of ethnicity'; 'Urban Hierarchy: Honor, Power, and Morality'; 'Locality, Neighbors, and Urban Crime'; social control and dispute management; 'Gender Images, Sexual Attraction and Mate Selection'; 'Romance in Daily Life'; the family; and the Socialist transformation of mortuary rites.

613 **Morality and power in a Chinese village.**
Richard Madsen.   Berkeley, California; London: University of California Press, 1986. 283p.

A reflective exploration of the moral and philosophical world of Chinese village life and revolutionary politics. The work draws on Chan et al. *Chen Village* (q.v.), of which Madsen is a co-author, but the purpose and focus are different. The book meditates on the experience of the village under Mao, explores the relationship between official ideology and individual action, and probes moral discourse, social change and political process. Parts one to three discuss the Confucian tradition and its Maoist transformation into a synthesis which emphasized community values of individual sacrifice and service. Part four describes the subsequent 'triumph of utilitarian morality'. The conclusion portrays grass-roots political leaders found in the village, who represent four character types, and their reliance on various moral visions.

614 **Report from a Chinese village.**
Jan Myrdal, translated from the Swedish by Maurice Michael, illustrated with photographs by Gun Kessle.   London: Heineman; New York: Pantheon Books, 1965. 374p.

Contains chapter-length, autobiographical accounts recorded in August 1962 on a month-long visit to Liu Ling, a poor village in Shaanxi province. Myrdal, a well-known Swedish writer and critic of capitalism, says he was a 'sympathetic listener to plebeian, peasant, democratic and puritan remembrances'; critics claimed that he was taken in by a myth of revolution. In any case, the village stories in this book were widely read and represent one serious but disputed version of the 'feudal' oppression of China's old days and the struggle to build a socialist village China.

615 **Cowboys and cultivators: the Chinese of Inner Mongolia.**
Burton Pasternak, Janet W. Salaff.   Boulder, Colorado; San Francisco; Oxford: Westview Press, 1993. 280p.

Han Chinese have expanded into Inner Mongolia for over a century, and brought with them 'the Chinese way' in intensive grain farming and patrilineal-patrilocal family organization. Pasternak and Salaff interviewed immigrant families and here delineate their changing organization of labour, gender differences, and family structure; recollections describe the now disbanded commune system and collective labour. They find that Chinese men continued their pattern of patriarchal dominance of the family, unlike pastoral Mongols, even when they abandoned settled farming.

616 **China's peasants: the anthropology of a revolution.**
Sulamith Heins Potter, Jack M. Potter.   Cambridge, England: Cambridge University Press, 1990. 358p.

A ethnographic description of a Canton delta village which highlights the viewpoints of the villagers. The Potters argue that Mao's agrarian socialism grew out of traditional village and Confucian moral values and was an historical necessity, given the decay of 'feudal' society; that land reform and collectivization in the 1950s was based on mobilizing the self-interest of the poor peasant majority, who were empowered by Party work teams; that the Great Leap Forward communes did not succeed in increasing production but did leave a legacy of water control, roads and small factories; and that Maoist collective institutions drew on deep traditional faith in the power of moral thought to transform society. Critics have asked why, then, the Maoist-Confucian synthesis disappeared so quickly in the 1980s.

617 **A Chinese village: Taitou, Shantung province.**
Martin C. Yang. New York: Columbia University Press, 1945. 275p. maps.

A detailed, affectionate memoir by an anthropologist of his home village before the Pacific War, which describes social life first in the family, then in the wider village. Chapters discuss: the village site; population; agriculture; the standard of living; the family as an economic and ceremonial group; marriage; child training; rise and fall of a family; village organization; conflicts and conflict resolution; leaders; and intervillage relations. The book closes with 'The Story of Tien-sze', which follows the maturation of a village boy, and 'The Village of Tomorrow'.

The dragon's village: an autobiographical novel of revolutionary China.
See item no. 389.

Fanshen: a documentary of revolution in a Chinese village.
See item no. 993.

Family and kinship

618 **Chinese family and kinship.**
Hugh D. R. Baker. London: Macmillan; New York; London: Columbia University Press, 1979. 243p. bibliog.

Surveys pre-20th century structures for the student or general reader from an anthropologist's point of view. Chapters cover major topics, including family composition, functions of the individual, lineage and clan, ancestor worship, fictive kinship, and changes in modern times.

619 **Chinese families in the post-Mao era.**
Edited by Deborah Davis, Stevan Harrell. Berkeley, California; London: University of California Press, 1993. 370p. bibliog. (Studies on China, no. 17).

Eleven papers from a 1990 conference explore household composition, marriage patterns (especially dowry and bride price), childbearing, mental sickness and old age. The introduction summarizes the findings: post-1949 state orthodoxy intended to replace Confucianism but did not destroy the 'feudal' family, for public health policies meant that the numbers of babies and elderly increased; restrictions on internal migration meant that men stayed home; marriage and divorce laws undercut but did not destroy patriarchy; and land reform transfigured the family farm. Post-1978 reforms re-transfigured the countryside with the uneven distribution of new wealth, foreign popular culture, a draconian birth control campaign, and party dominance. Global theories, such as those of sociologist William Goode, do not fit China's combination of state power and social independence. See also: Martin King Whyte, *Dating, mating, and marriage* (New York: Aldine, 1990. 325p.), which analyses recent surveys from Chengdu, Sichuan; and Elisabeth Croll, *The politics of marriage in contemporary China* (Cambridge, England: Cambridge University Press, 1981. 210p.).

620 **Kinship organization in late imperial China, 1000-1940.**
Edited by Patricia Ebrey, James L. Watson. Berkeley, California; Oxford: University of California Press, 1986. 319p. maps. (Studies on China, no. 5).

Presents nine scholarly essays on historical change and regional variation in formal kinship organizations (kinship here does not include the nuclear family). The essays modify the influential model of Maurice Freedman, e.g. in *Study of Chinese society* (q.v.), which they argue is limited and regional. The introduction lucidly sets out the terminology and outlines the 'repertoire' of kinship organizational forms, such as ritual (e.g. death rituals), patrilines, welfare funds for widows and orphans, property holdings and schools. Essay topics include: the early stages of development of descent groups; marriage, descent groups and localist strategy in the Song and Yuan; and marriage, adoption and charity in the development of lineages in Wuxi, Jiangsu province.

621 **Chinese views of childhood.**
Edited by Anne Behnke Kinney. Honolulu: University of Hawaii Press, 1995. 352p. bibliog.

Eleven scholarly essays open up the study of children, parents and Chinese images of them from the Han dynasty to the 1960s. After a comparative introduction, part one contains essays on: Han dynasty notions of the moral development of the child; famous childhoods; private love and public duty found in images of children in art; and filial paragons and spoiled brats in the 3rd-century anthology, *Shishuo xinyu*. Essays in part two deal with: the middle and late imperial period: parents and children, 800-1700; the body from birth to death as depicted in Chinese medicine; infanticide and dowry in the Ming and Qing; and an adolescent world, as seen in the 18th-century novel, *Hongloumeng*. Part three covers: the modern period: relief institutions for children in the 19th century; early 20th-century stories of childhood; and the psychology of rebel youth, 1966-67.

622 **Daughters of the Canton delta: marriage patterns and economic strategies in South China, 1860-1930.**
Janice E. Stockard. Stanford, California: Stanford University Press, 1989. 221p.

Han Chinese in the Canton delta were influenced by the unique ecology of the area and by indigenous non-Han peoples, a situation which is reflected in their distinctive marriage patterns. Stockard, an anthropologist, describes 'delayed transfer marriage', a phenomenon not common elsewhere. An anti-marital bias, linked to women's economic independence and their participation in sericulture, led to alternatives to marriage and the rise of distinctive institutions, such as sworn spinsterhood, compensation marriage and spirit marriage.

623 **Getting an heir: adopting and the construction of kinship in late imperial China.**
Ann Waltner. Honolulu: University of Hawaii Press, 1991. 226p.

The continuation of the family into the next generation was so central that adoption became an important and much debated strategy. Waltner uses a wide range of sources to follow changing values and practices in Ming and Qing China by analysing the debates on controversial points.

624 **Marriage and inequality in Chinese society.**
Edited by Rubie S. Watson, Patricia Buckley Ebrey. Berkeley, California: University of California Press, 1991. 402p. (Studies on China, no. 12).

An up-to-date conference volume, accompanied by an excellent summary introduction and an afterword, 'Marriage and Gender Inequality'. Topics include: élite marriages in the Spring and Autumn period, showing that ancient rulers often had more than the one wife theoretically allowed; imperial marriage in native Chinese and non-Han states, from the Han to the Ming dynasties; the important shift from bride price to dowry, from the 6th to 13th centuries; marriages of Song imperial clanswomen; imperial marriage and the problems of rulership; brides and wives in the mid-Qing period; wives, concubines and maids in the Hong Kong region, 1900-40; prostitution and the market for women in early 20th-century Shanghai; marriage and mobility under rural collectivism; and women, property and law in the People's Republic.

625 **Marriage and adoption in China, 1845-1945.**
Arthur P. Wolf, Huang Chieh-shan. Stanford, California: Stanford University Press, 1980. 426p.

This basic study of historical demography demonstrates that there were many common patterns of marriage in addition to 'orthodox', patrilocal marriage. In particular, Wolf and Huang examine the unexpectedly widespread practice of *tongyang xi*, or adopted daughters-in-law, in which the prospective bride lives with and labours for the future husband's family. Although the research was richest for Taiwan, where Japanese household registers are abundant and reliable, the authors argue that their findings also apply to much of South China.

626 **The Chinese family in the Communist revolution.**
C. K. Yang. Cambridge, Massachusetts: M. I. T. Press, 1959. 246p. Reprinted, together with *A Chinese village in early Communist transition* (Cambridge, Massachusetts: M. I. T. Press, 1959. 276p.), as *Chinese Communist society: the family and the village* (Cambridge, Massachusetts: M. I. T. Press, 1965).

This classic sociological description of the early years of the People's Republic is based on the author's long knowledge of the situation and observation in 1951 of the first months of the Communist takeover in Guangdong. Yang first describes the Chinese family in traditional society and the modern family revolution, then devotes chapters to: the post-1949 freedom of marriage; divorce; the crumbling of age hierarchy; the ascendancy of the status of women in the family; the women's movement; changing family economic structure; the secularization of the family institution; and the disorganization of the clan. A final chapter discusses the Great Leap Forward and long-term trends.

Chinese family law and social change in historical and comparative perspective.
See item no. 865.

Women and gender studies

627 **The unfinished liberation of Chinese women, 1949-1980.**
Phyllis Andors. Bloomington, Indiana: Indiana University Press, 1983. 212p.

Traces party doctrine, government policies and local implementation with reference to the position of women in China. Andors argues that party and government leaders were sincere in their belief that women would be liberated under socialism. During the radical phases of the Great Leap Forward and Cultural Revolution, top leaders worked toward gender equality and were not committed to patriarchal values in themselves. However, they were frustrated by bureaucratic inertia, local government footdragging and opposition from male family members. Judith Stacey, *Patriarchy and socialist revolution in China* (Berkeley, California; Oxford: University of California Press, 1984. 324p.) critiques socialist and feminist theory for not dealing with the failed liberation of Chinese women. Stacey argues that the revolution appealed to patriarchal village leaders and that socialism cannot co-exist with patriarchy.

628 **Feminism and socialism in China.**
Elisabeth Croll. London; Boston, Massachusetts; Henley, England: Routledge & Kegan Paul, 1978. 363p. bibliog.

A key survey of the 20th century. The introduction explains the erosion of the author's original view that socialist revolution would liberate women. Chapter two portrays the ideological, physical and economic oppression of women at the turn of the century. Four chapters then identify stages of reform and revolution: early 1900s feminists promoted patriotism and the right to vote, resisted imperialism, but accepted Western middle-class individualism, freedom and self-fulfilment; feminists in the 1920s were taken into the Nationalist or Communist parties; and the period 1928-37 saw the 'development and fate of the women's movement within a decaying semi-feudal society', and a Chinese 'feminine mystique'. Chapters seven to ten follow the conflict between socialism and feminism from 1949 to the Cultural Revolution, with a concluding chapter, 'A political solution: socialism and feminism'.

629   **The inner quarters: marriage and the lives of Chinese women in the Sung period.**
Patricia Buckley Ebrey.   Berkeley, California; Oxford: University of California Press, 1993. 332p. bibliog.

A balanced, lucid and well-illustrated portrayal of family, gender, kinship and marriage in the formative period from the 10th to 13th centuries. Ebrey describes the inequities of concubinage, traffic in women, footbinding, female infanticide and gender hierarchy, but avoids making judgemental ethnocentric or modernist views. She tells not only of victims, virtuous daughters-in-law, and chaste widows, but also of active women: jealous or manipulating wives, scheming concubines, and the widows who frequently defied orthodoxy by remarrying. Other topics include such elusive issues as sexuality, jealousy and gender symbolism, as well as dowries, matchmaking, rites and celebration, and new roles enabled by the commercialization of cloth production. The discussion of the origins and spread of footbinding is the most balanced and thorough yet available.

630   **Engendering China: women, culture, and the state.**
Edited by Christina Gilmartin, Gail Hershatter, Lisa Rofel, Tyrene White.   Cambridge, Massachusetts: Harvard University Press, 1994. 454p. (Harvard Contemporary China Series, no. 10).

Sixteen scholars persuasively deploy feminist theories to illuminate historical and contemporary issues. Chapters examine: learned women in the 18th century; the changing status of present-day village women; sexuality and child-bearing; prostitution as modernizing sex in early 20th-century Shanghai; a critique of modernist sexology in the work of Van Gulick (q.v.); women's consciousness and writing in fiction from the late Ming to the contemporary period; government policies toward birth planning and women workers; and the concept 'woman' in the construction of a Chinese nation. Although the style is scholarly, the arguments are lucid and the views varied, with many references to the theoretical and historical literature. See also Mark Elvin, 'Female Virtue and the State in China' (*Past and Present*, no. 104 [1984], p. 111-52).

631   **Women in China: current directions in historical scholarship.**
Edited by Richard W. Guisso, Stanley Johannesen.   Youngstown, New York: Philo Press, 1981. 238p.

A pioneering collection which includes discussions of: early Buddhist monastic orders for women; female infanticide; women in the Song; widows and remarriage in Ming and early Qing; Daoism and the androgynous ideal; and anti-footbinding movements.

632   **Personal voices: Chinese women in the 1980s.**
Emily Honig, Gail Hershatter.   Stanford, California: Stanford University Press, 1988. 387p.

The everyday experience of 'growing up female' in 1980s China is told through vivid individual stories and broader analysis. Honig and Hershatter, taking into account feminist theory and comparisons with other countries, see in post-reform China a reinvigoration of male dominance: women's sexuality is denied and inhibited, their careers restricted into 'women's' occupations, and their bodies battered by males. Families, teachers, friends and the official Women's Federation reinforce these restrictions. On the other hand, women's newspapers and magazines print 'feminist outcries', and report that some Chinese women are aware of the gap between official claims of gender equality and the actuality of discrimination.

633 **Women and Chinese patriarchy: submission, servitude, and escape.**
Edited by Maria Jaschok, Suzanne Miers. Hong Kong: Hong Kong University Press; London; Atlantic City, New Jersey: Zed Books, 1994. 294p. maps.

Brings together a combination of scholarly essays and personal testimony. The introduction analyses forms of exploitation in the Chinese patriarchal system, Western imperialism and Asian women, and Chinese and Western concepts of women's and individual rights. Sections examine: girls' houses and working women in the Pearl River Delta, 1900-41; child betrothals in the New Territories of Hong Kong; prostitution in Singapore; and servant women's bondage. Section three, 'Social Remedies and Avenues of Escape', includes essays on social work in Singapore, the protection of women in 19th-century Hong Kong, and missionary and Chinese Christian organizations set up to save women. An epilogue considers the recent trade in women and children in China and the international exploitation of women. Maria H. A. Jaschok, *Concubines and bondservants: the social history of a Chinese custom* (London: Zed Books, 1988. 156p.) provides a description and oral history of the *mooi-jai*, or female bondservants of Hong Kong and the South China Coast.

634 **Women, the family, and peasant revolution in China.**
Kay Ann Johnson. Chicago: University of Chicago Press, 1983. 282p.

A discussion of the evolution of party and government policy from the 1940s Yan'an period to the beginnings of late 1970s reforms, and the effect of these policies on family organization, patterns of authority within the family, the role of women in local society, marriage decisions, and female autonomy. Johnson finds that male party functionaries consistently sacrificed the interests of women in favour of production, political stability and the preservation of social equilibrium – patriarchy. This relationship is also explored in Delia Davin, *Woman-work: women and the party in revolutionary China* (Oxford: Clarendon Press, 1976. 244p.).

635 **Gender and power in rural North China.**
Ellen Judd. Stanford, California: Stanford University Press, 1994. 295p.

The reforms of the 1980s dismantled rural collectivism and commune organization in favour of household production and township government, but paid no specific attention to the economically and culturally central roles which women played in agriculture, local industry and social life. Judd's field research in Shandong focused on how reforms restructured the household, relations between men and women, and the way in which women are attempting to organize themselves. Chapters provide a detailed analysis of the process of 'dividing the land' (ending the communes), village enterprises and 'Socialist commodity production' (village industry), then go on to examine the gender consequences.

636 **Teachers of the inner chambers: women and culture in seventeenth century China.**
Dorothy Ko.   Stanford, California: Stanford University Press, 1994. 395p.

Ko portrays the new community of women in the commercializing and urbanizing 17th-century lower Yangzi valley, and presents new ways of understanding traditional Chinese society by rethinking gender relations. Chinese women were not merely silent victims, as had been patronizingly charged in China from the time of the 1920s New Culture Movement; rather women were writers, readers, editors, poets and teachers who took part in the new 17th-century world of commercial publishing. They creatively (though ultimately in vain) built their own domestic, social and public communities within the network of traditional family life. Ko shows, for instance, that to some women, footbinding was not defined as oppression or suffering, but rather as participation in patriotic resistance to non-Chinese invaders.

637 **Chinese women through Chinese eyes.**
Edited by Li Yu-ning.   Armonk, New York; London: M. E. Sharpe, 1992. 251p.

An anthology of twenty-three previously published essays and memoirs which give a vivid historical picture of the range and variety of women's experience up to 1949. Part one, 'Historical Interpretations', reprints seven major essays by Chinese historians, including: 'Women's Place in Chinese History' (Hu Shi); 'Female Rulers In Ancient China' (Yang Lien-sheng); 'Feminist Thought In Ancient China' (Lin Yutang); 'Chinese Women's Fight For Freedom' (Soong Ch'ing-ling); and 'Historical Roots of Changes in Women's Status' (Li Yu-ning). Part two, 'Self-Portraits of Women in Modern China', reprints personal essays by 20th-century women, from a village teacher and a factory worker to the last consort of the last emperor. *The position of women in early China*, by Albert Richard O'Hara (Taipei: Meiya, 1971. 302p.) translates portions of the Han dynasty works, Liu Xiang's *Biographies of great women* (*Lienu zhuan*) and Ban Zhao's *Admonitions for women*, to provide a summary of the ideals presented to upper-class women in early imperial times.

638 **Women in Chinese society.**
Edited by Margery Wolf, Roxane Witke.   Stanford, California: Stanford University Press, 1975. 315p. (Studies in Chinese Society).

A pathbreaking symposium. Essays include: the influence of women's literacy on 16th-century thought; Margery Wolf's important 'Women and Suicide in China'; marriage resistance in rural Guangdong, a study of unmarried women who formed substitute families; women as writers in the 1920s and 1930s; and 'The Power and Pollution of Chinese Women', the anthropologist Emily Ahern's insightful analysis. *Women in China: studies in social change and feminism,* edited by Marilyn Young (Ann Arbor, Michigan: Center for Chinese Studies, University of Michigan, 1973. 259p.) is another useful early collection and includes the powerful 'Mao Tse-tung, Women, and Suicide'.

639 **Revolution postponed: women in contemporary China.**
Margery Wolf.   Stanford, California: Stanford University Press, 1985. 285p.

Presents Chinese women speaking in individual voices, arguing that at every turning point since 1949 the priorities of the state and building socialism has deflected a feminist agenda and delayed the liberation of women. Chapters focus on: women workers in the city; in the countryside; being and becoming a proper Chinese women; marriage in new China; family organization; urban domestic relationships; rural domestic relationships; and the birth limitation programme. A final chapter, 'The Other Revolution', assesses the future possibilities of feminism.

Chinese women in a century of revolution, 1850-1950.
See item no. 255.

Views from jade terrace: Chinese women artists, 1300-1912.
See item no. 1291.

Women in China: bibliography of available English language materials.
See item no. 1457.

Sexual life

640   **Sexual life in ancient China: a preliminary survey of Chinese sex and society from ca. 1500 B. C. till 1644 A. D.**
R. H. van Gulik.   Leiden, the Netherlands: E. J. Brill, 1961, 1974. 392p.

Translates many sexual texts (some spicy passages into Latin) and reproduces explicit pictures, arguing that Chinese sexual norms, unlike those of Victorians, were not perverse or repressed, but healthy and non-Puritanical. Van Gulik holds that after the Song dynasty, sexual latitude was replaced by a neo-Confucian orthodoxy which repressed women and pleasure. Charlotte Furth, 'Re-thinking Van Gulik', in Gilmartin, et al. *Gendering China: women, culture, and state* (q.v.), argues that van Gulik represents Freudian 'sexology' and a modern focus on sexuality as erotic pleasure, whereas Chinese sexual doctrine did not deal with pleasure as much as with male health, Daoist mysticism, longevity, family reproduction, male rulership and cosmic nature.

641   **Sex, culture, and modernity in China: medical science and the construction of sexual identities in the early Republican period.**
Frank Dikötter.   London: C. Hurst; Honolulu: University of Hawaii Press, 1995. 233p. bibliog.

An intellectual and social history of the early 20th century using recent cultural theory. Dikötter shows how the Chinese took categories of analysis and perception of body, medicine and health, including 'race', 'sex', 'woman', or 'youth' from European discourse, but used them in ways conditioned by Chinese thought and society. Chapters examine: the naturalization of gender distinctions; sexual desire and procreation; the emergence of population and eugenic studies; the new cultural meanings of disease, including venereal disease, masturbation and homosexuality; and the cultural construction of youth.

642 **Passions of the cut sleeve: the male homosexual tradition in China.**
Brent Hinsch. Berkeley, California: University of California Press,
1990. 256p.

Arising from an amorous dalliance, a Han dynasty emperor cut off the sleeve of his
robe rather than disturb his sleeping male lover; this 'cut sleeve' thus became a
symbol of male homosexual love. Hinsch surveys male same-sex love from earliest
times, with excerpts from dynastic histories, erotic novels, Buddhist tracts, poetry,
legal cases and joke books. After summarizing theoretical debates between
'essentialists', who hold that homosexuality is a cross-cultural essence, and 'social
constructionists', who hold that sexuality is contingent and local, Hinsch introduces a
typology of homosexualities: transgenerational, trans-genderal, class-structured and
egalitarian. The book tries to break free from censorious Western preconceptions,
though it sees a conscious Chinese tradition where some see only discrete incidents.
An appendix discusses the scanty sources available on lesbianism.

643 **Chinese footbinding: the history of a curious erotic custom.**
Howard S. Levy. New York: Bell, 1967. reprint. 352p.

Pulls together the secondary sources available in Chinese, Japanese and English to
provide a well-illustrated preliminary survey. For many Westerners, the 'curious'
custom of footbinding, along with the Great Wall and eating dogs, epitomized exotic
Chinese culture; ideas of its significance were based more on myth than on
investigation. Levy traces the origins of the custom to Tang dynasty court dancers;
Neo-Confucian thinkers promoted it, but evidence (pending further research) for its
widespread practice does not appear until perhaps the Ming. The book ends with a
survey of both missionary and far larger Chinese anti-footbinding campaigns in the
20th century.

644 **Art of the bedchamber: the Chinese sexual yoga classics, including
women's solo meditation texts.**
Douglas Wile. Albany, New York: State University of New York
Press, 1992. 293p.

Confucius observed that 'eating and sex illustrate our intrinsic natures'. In his
extensive introduction, Wile compares sexual ideals and practices in the East and
West, expounds the ethos of Chinese sexual practices, explores the relation to Chinese
medicine and to Daoism, and discusses the development of Western sexology. Part
two translates, with extensive notes and commentary, the 'Chinese Sexual Yoga
Classics'. Texts are taken from the Han dynasty, the Sui-Tang period, medical
manuals and handbooks for householders, and the elixir literature of sexual alchemy.
Wile argues that these practices constitute a tradition quite different from the West,
for the male is concerned primarily with health, through the conservation of vital
essences, and with female pleasure. The volume concludes with previously
untranslated texts of 'women's practices'.

Social problems and social welfare

645 **Long lives: Chinese elderly and the Communist revolution.**
Deborah Davis. Stanford, California: Stanford University Press,
1993. 2nd ed. rev. expanded. 174p. bibliog.

China's post-1949 success in the lowering of death rates has meant that more people live to old age. Davis briskly explores: problems, attitudes and policies, with chapters on work and retirement; living arrangements; relations with children; funerals and filial piety; intergenerational conflict; and the childless elderly. A final chapter considers 'Old age under communism'.

646 **Beautiful merchandise: prostitution in China, 1860-1936.**
Sue Gronewold. New York: Institute for Research in History and
Haworth Press, 1983. 114p.

A brief, energetic, preliminary description, based on English-language sources, of the trade in women, their victimization as prostitutes, and early reform movements. Gronewold discovers shifts over the period under discussion, as families came to prefer pawning goods to outright sale (thus increasing their profit) and society developed more ambivalent attitudes towards prostitution.

647 **Class conflict in Chinese socialism.**
Richard Kurt Kraus. New York: Columbia University Press, 1981.
243p. (Studies of the East Asian Institute).

Maoists have debated whether social inequality continued even after 1949, fighting about its theoretical significance and about how to counteract its political and social consequences. The radical Maoist programme attacked sources of privilege and aimed to consolidate the advancement of the working masses; however, Deng Xiaoping and his circle (and Mao at one point) felt that class conflict in China had been basically curbed with the creation of socialist institutions in 1956. Kraus argues that there were two models of class stratification: after 1956 a property-based system (landlords, capitalists) was replaced by a political system, based on occupation, in which bureaucrats had power over workers and peasants. He analyses the debate over terms, concepts and ideology, to show how it reflected contending visions of society.

648 **Violence in China: essays in culture and counterculture.**
Edited by Jonathan Lipman, Stevan Harrell. Albany, New York:
State University of New York Press, 1990. 249p. (SUNY Series in
Chinese Local Studies).

Uses cross-cultural and historical perspectives to explore the uses and significance of violence. Essays focus on: Guangdong and Fujian lineage feuds in the Qing dynasty; Han-Muslim conflicts in Gansu; religious sects, including White Lotus; the Cultural Revolution; and violence against women. R. J. Rummel, *China's bloody century: genocide and mass murder since 1900* (New Brunswick, New Jersey: Transaction Publishers, 1991. 333p.) is a less theoretical summary of the massive loss of life due to non-natural causes.

649   **Madness in late imperial China: from illness to deviance.**
       Vivien Ng.   Norman, Oklahoma; London: University of Oklahoma
       Press, 1990. 204p.

This monograph argues that under the Manchus the conceptualization and treatment of the mentally ill changed from a medical to a legal basis; the Qing government was primarily concerned with enforcing hierarchy by controlling threats to the social and moral order. Ng first sketches Chinese writings on madness, beginning with Han dynasty medical texts, and explains customary understandings based on popular fiction and plays. These popular theories, based on classic correspondence theory, saw madness as the result of either demons to be exorcised or of bodily imbalances to be restored. Trial records and official memorials reveal that 18th-century emperors gradually expanded the legal system, ordering the protective registration and confinement of the mentally anomalous; however, murderers who lacked 'awareness' were given lesser sentences.

650   **Class and social stratification in post-revolution China.**
       James L. Watson.   London: Cambridge University Press, 1984. 289p.

The editor's introduction, 'Class and Class Formation in Chinese Society', gives helpful theoretical and comparative background. The following nine essays cover: 'Chinese Views of Social Classification', which provides historical background; 'Classes, Old and New, in Mao Zedong's Thought, 1949-1976'; destratification in China; 'The Class System in Rural China: A Case Study'; 'Sexual Inequality Under Socialism: the Chinese Case in Perspective'; and sociological, anthropological and political studies of post-1949 class structure.

651   **Resistance, chaos, and control in China: Taiping rebels, Taiwanese
       ghosts, and Tiananmen.**
       Robert P. Weller.   Seattle, Washington: University of Washington
       Press, 1994. 255p.

Weller, an anthropologist who works in the fields of religion and social theory, looks at three cases of popular resistance to dominant culture – the mid-19th-century Taiping rebels; ghost worshipers in 1980s Taiwan; and, more briefly, the 1989 demonstrators in Tiananmen Square. He is concerned with the theoretical problem of how everyday patterns of tacit resistance can in certain situations turn into open or organized rebellion. Weller holds that neither theories of hegemonic cultural domination nor views of ubiquitous resistance are convincing; rather an analysis of historical specifics shows contradictory and shifting perspectives, for which even the participants themselves are not able to fix a single interpretation.

Culture and social relations

652 From the soil: the foundations of Chinese society.
Fei Xiaotong, with an introduction and epilogue by Gary G. Hamilton, Wang Zhen. Berkeley, California; Los Angeles; Oxford: University of California Press, 1992. 160p.

A translation of Fei's 1947 *Xiangtu Zhongguo*, whose fourteen essays introduced the Chinese public to Fei's concept of Chinese culture as 'fundamentally rural', or 'from the soil'. The introduction, 'Fei Xiaotong and the Beginnings of Chinese Sociology', sketches the intellectual context of the 1930s and 1940s, and maintains, with many references, that Western sociology does not match Fei's insights into distinctive Chinese society or even the West. Fei's essays argue that power in Chinese society is configured by networks of *chaxugeju*, or 'differential mode of association', rather than Western social classes. Other essays analyse village society, social psychology, bringing literacy to the countryside, gender and family relations, and regionalism. The editors' epilogue discusses 'Sociology and the Reconstruction of Rural China'.

653 The Chinese hospital: a socialist work unit.
Gail E. Henderson, Myron S. Cohen. New Haven, Connecticut; London: Yale University Press, 1984. 183p.

A sociological analysis of a hospital and the 'work unit' (*danwei*), which is not only a workplace but also an administrative unit which unifies the control of salary, housing, food and recreation. The authors, a medical sociologist and a physician, worked in a hospital in Wuhan, Hubei province. They first describe private daily routines and family life, the control exerted by the work unit, and the routine of work. They depict the infectious disease ward of the hospital, and place it in the larger administrative structure, examining the role of leadership, the hierarchy of management and the issue of work autonomy. The final section focuses on patients in the ward, their interactions with the medical practitioners, and the way in which control is exercised. A final chapter explores the sociological and medical significance of the *danwei* for the modernization of medicine.

654 Americans and Chinese: passages to difference.
Francis L. K. Hsu. Honolulu: University of Hawaii Press, 1981. 3rd ed. 534p.

A pioneering, provocative comparison of the life-styles, cultures and psychology of Americans and Chinese, written by one of the first Chinese to be a professional anthropologist. Hsu maintains that the Chinese are more 'situation oriented', while Americans are more individualistic, selfish and autonomous. These distinctions are applied in many areas, including: sex and relationships between the genders; religion, with a contrast between monotheism and polytheism; childraising; and the particular strengths and weaknesses of the two cultures. Throughout the work, Hsu draws examples from the 1950s, when the book was conceived.

655 Encountering the Chinese: a guide for Americans.
Hu Wenzhong, Cornelius L. Grove. Yarmouth, Maine: Intercultural Press, 1991. 192p. map. bibliog.

An approachable presentation of Chinese culture for those studying, teaching or doing business in China, which draws on both experience in China and the scholarship of cross-cultural studies. Part one consists of practical essays based on cross-cultural analysis: Chinese titles, names and forms of address; greetings, conversations and farewells; dining; time-use patterns; modesty and humility; making friends; education and being a student or a teacher; negotiating and institutional decision making; and the concept of 'face'. Part two goes into more day-to-day detail on the subjects. The 'Recommended Readings' section describes useful books and articles.

656　**To see ourselves as others see us: comparing traditional Chinese and American cultural values.**
Zhongdang Pan, Steven H. Chaffee, Godwin C. Chu, Yanan Ju.
Boulder, Colorado; San Francisco; Oxford: Westview Press, 1994.
258p. bibliog.

Compares surveys of 2,000 Shanghai-area residents and 2,500 US citizens in order to examine the extent to which Confucian values persist in China after forty years of revolution and whether there is an erosion of American traditional values. Pan, Chaffee, Chu and Ju compare changes in culture systems which deal with family and kinship, relations between the sexes, and interpersonal relations, and find that both societies have changed over recent generations, but along different paths. After explaining definitions and procedures, the authors give detailed breakdowns of social and demographic characteristics, communication influences, individual differences, and make comparisons with Taiwan and Korea.

657　**Small groups and political ritual in China.**
Martin King Whyte.　Berkeley, California; Los Angeles; London: University of California Press, 1974. 271p. (Michigan Studies on China).

A ground-breaking description of how 'small groups' (*xiaozu*) are organized in the Communist Party, factories, schools, communes and labour camps; the post-1949 network of social control depended on this lowest level of organization. Whyte first explores the significance of the 'small group', political rituals, and the techniques of 'study' (*xuexi*) and 'criticism' (*piping*), then shows how general forms are adapted to varying conditions.

658　**Gifts, favors, and banquets: the art of social relationships in China.**
Mayfair Mei-hui Yang.　Ithaca, New York: Cornell University Press, 1994. 370p. bibliog. (The Wilder House Series in Politics, History, and Culture).

Analyses the social networks built by exchanging gifts and favours – *guanxi*. Yang's introduction probes post-modernist theorists, such as Michel Foucault, and the politics of fieldwork anthropology. Part one provides a ethnographic description, covering the following topics: words and concepts used in discussing *guanxi*; scope and use-contexts; ethics, tactics and etiquette of giving and receiving; the roots in history (back to the Confucian classics); and the post-revolutionary decline and re-emergence of *guanxi*. Part two, 'Theoretical Formulations', examines whether *guanxi* networks are the fabric of an underground economy and an emerging Chinese civil society which subvert the state and support individualism. The English bibliography lists books and articles on theory and Chinese society.

Mooncakes and hungry ghosts: festivals of China.
See item no. 539.

The psychology of the Chinese people.
See item no. 660.

Dealing with the Chinese: a practical guide to business etiquette.
See item no. 961.

The great wall in ruins: communication and cultural change in China.
See item no. 1368.

Psychology

659 **Beyond Chinese face: insights from psychology.**
Michael Harris Bond. Hong Kong: Oxford University Press, 1991.
125p.

A lucid introduction which summarizes recent work in the field. After explaining the perils and necessity of cross-cultural observation, chapters examine both Chinese uniqueness and shared humanity: 'how Chinese think'; socializing the Chinese child; the social actors in Chinese society; the sense of self and social world; social behaviour; organizational life; psychopathology, Chinese style; and modernization and the loss of Chineseness. Bond sees a number of 'golden threads' running through these themes: the naturalness of hierarchy, seen as based on achievement; personal judgement as superior to legislated law; the interdependence of people in society; and the need of children to master the writing of Chinese characters, which develops attention to detail, memory and holistic thinking.

660 **The psychology of the Chinese people.**
Edited by Michael Harris Bond. Hong Kong; Oxford; New York:
Oxford University Press, 1986. 366p.

Contains seven substantial essays by Hong Kong and Taiwan based scholars which review recent research, explain and compare theoretical models, and summarize current hypotheses on a wide range of topics. These include: patterns of socialization; perceptual processes, including reading; cognition; personality and personality change; psychopathology; social psychology; and the psychology of organizational behaviour, such as management and the influence of Confucianism.

661 **Children of Mao: personality development and political activism in the Red Guard generation.**
Anita Chan. Seattle, Washington; London: University of Washington Press, 1985. 254p.

A psychological and political study, based on in-depth interviews with fourteen young activists from the Cultural Revolution. Chan finds that they displayed an 'authoritarian personality', marked by a fear of authority and a willingness to submit, combined with a strong desire to dominate others.

662   **Dialectic of the Chinese revolution: from utopianism to hedonism.**
Ci Jiwei.   Stanford, California: Stanford University Press, 1994. 281p.
Ci presents the history of China after 1949 not in an historian's way but in what he calls 'the philosopher's way', as a history of consciousness, or psychological and spiritual stages. He presents a narrative informed by philosophical concepts in order to grasp the vital things more open to introspection than documentation. He begins with the invention in 1949 of a new set of utopian meanings based on classical Marxism, Maoism and asceticism, in which group sacrifice would lead to material abundance. In the 1960s and 1970s, this type of utopianism produced its dialectical opposite, nihilism, then in the 1980s and 1990s hedonism, defined as selfish individual pleasure, capitalism and consumerism.

663   **Chinese patterns of behavior: a sourcebook of psychological and psychiatric studies.**
Edited by David Yau-Fai Ho, John A. Spinks, Cecilia Siu-Hing Yeung. New York: Praeger, 1989. 502p.
Lists and summarizes 3,549 items, organized by category, including articles, books and sections of books in English and Chinese. Topics, which cover Chinese people in all parts of the world, include: general psychology; psychometrics; experimental psychology; physiological psychology; communications systems, covering linguistics and the Chinese language; developmental psychology; personality; social psychology, covering 'face', aggression, family and social attitudes; educational psychology; applied psychology; physical, psychological and psychiatric disorders; assessment, treatment and prevention; and professional personnel and professional issues. There are extensive indexes.

664   **Social origins of distress and disease: depression, neurasthenia, and pain in modern China.**
Arthur Kleinman.   New Haven, Connecticut; London: Yale University Press, 1986. 264p.
A key inquiry into the social and cultural origins of mental and physical distress, or psychobiology, in China. Kleinman, trained both as a psychiatrist and an anthropologist, holds that depression and neurasthenia are expressed in bodily terms – somatization – in ways which change in response to change. The first chapters furnish the history and theory of neurasthenia, depression and somatization. Two following chapters focus on thirteen cases Kleinman investigated at Hunan Medical College in the early 1980s. These patients illustrate how psychology, local milieu and cultural and political patterns affect psychobiology; recently patients are more likely to define their distress in psychological rather than purely physical terms. An epilogue draws tentative conclusions for further testing.

Psychology

665 Normal and abnormal behavior in Chinese culture.
Edited by Arthur Kleinman, Lin Tsung-yi. Dordrecht, the
Netherlands; Boston, Massachusetts: Reidel, 1981. 463p.

A wide-ranging symposium of anthropologists, historians and psychologists which
explores the different ways in which mental illness manifests itself in particular
cultures, historical periods and segments of society. One section covers child
development and child psychopathology, another family studies. Typical chapter titles
include 'Suicide and the Family in Pre-modern Chinese Society' and 'Love, Denial,
and Rejection: Responses of Chinese Families to Mental Illness'.

666 Chinese culture and mental health.
Edited by Wen-shing Tseng, David Y. H. Wu. Orlando, Florida:
Academic Press, 1985. 412p.

A report volume from a 1982 Honolulu conference of mental health professionals
from all over the world, representing the fields of psychology, psychiatry, sociology
and anthropology. Twenty-nine diverse papers are divided into sections: culture,
society and personality; family and child; adjustment in different settings; mental
health problems; management and prevention of mental illness; and summary and
suggestions for the future. Especially striking are the psychiatric reports from the
People's Republic, which discuss alcoholism, family disorders and somatization (the
manifestation of distress in bodily terms). Other papers debate the social, cultural and
psychological causation of psychopathology, outline a theory for a Chinese
psychiatry, and report on new findings of depression, anxiety and phobic disorders in
post-Cultural Revolution China.

Americans and Chinese: passages to difference.
See item no. 654.

The spirit of Chinese capitalism.
See item no. 943.

**Chinese negotiating style: commercial approaches and cultural
principles.**
See item no. 960.

Preschool in three cultures: Japan, China, and the United States.
See item no. 1028.

The paradox of power in a People's Republic of China middle school.
See item no. 1054.

Medicine and Health

General and to 1911

667 **Doctors, diviners, and magicians of ancient China.**
Kenneth J. DeWoskin. New York; London: Columbia University Press, 1983. 224p.

Provides brief biographies from Sima Qian's *Shiji*, primarily those of ascetics and wandering healers during the Han dynasty who have been claimed as the first active Daoists. These magico-technicians worked for individual cultivation, immortality and direct access to the world of gods and natural forces. To accomplish these feats they used all manner of magic, such as: divination; acupuncture; medicinal plants, minerals, dietetics and other medical techniques; and spirit-mediumship. Readers should be aware that our knowledge of the technical terms involved is unreliable.

668 **Religion, science, and human crises: a study of China in transition and its implications for the West.**
Francis L. K. Hsu. London: Routledge & Kegan Paul, 1952. 142p. (International Library of Sociology and Social Reconstruction).

A classic anthropological field study of a cholera epidemic in a wartime town in Yunnan. Hsu explores the reaction to the epidemic as a confrontation between old ideas and a new challenge; Western medicine and traditional Chinese medicine each mix science with magic, and scientific medicine can only be accepted when it is integrated with local beliefs and needs.

669 **Forgotten traditions of ancient Chinese medicine: a Chinese view from the eighteenth century (*The I-hseh Yan Liu Lun*).**
Hsü Ta-ch'un, translated by Paul U. Unschild. Brookline, Massachusetts: Paradigm Publications, 1990. 416p. bibliog.

A scholarly translation, with an introduction and extensive annotations, of 100 brief essays commenting on all aspects of medicine and disease, including foundations of life, illness, therapeutic principles, and treatments for specific problems. Xu Daqun (1693-1771) was a scholar of Chinese medical learning and practice in the prosperous lower Yangzi valley during the 18th-century rejection of Song 'Neo-Confucian' learning in favour of Han classical studies. He presents one among many possible versions of 'traditional' Chinese medicine. Unschild also provides some background, translates a life of Xu by the famous literatus Yuan Mei, lists Xu's works, and appends a bibliography of modern studies, mostly in Chinese.

670   **The web that has no weaver: understanding Chinese medicine.**
Ted J. Kaptchuk.   New York: Congdon & Weed, 1987. 402p.

The most reliable and helpful of the many popular works available on this subject. Kaptchuk, who has training in a school of traditional medicine, first presents a clear, simple outline of Chinese medicine, then goes on to argue, with many illustrations, that its practice should be combined with modern scientific medicine to form a more powerful synthesis. *Chinese medicine*, by Pierre Huard, Wong Ming, translated by Bernard Fielding (New York; Toronto: McGraw Hill, 1969. 256p. [World University Library]) is a useful, nicely illustrated, but casual survey which indicates the range and significance of Chinese medical thought and practice but not the distinctions between various traditions and eras; some aspects are romanticized or misunderstood. Likewise, Felix Mann, *Acupuncture: the Chinese art of healing* (New York: Random House, 1963. 178p.) is thoughtful, but based more on surmise than on a knowledge of Chinese doctrine and practice.

671   **Celestial lancets: a history and rationale of acupuncture and moxa.**
Lu Gwei-djen, Joseph Needham.   Cambridge, England: Cambridge University Press, 1980. 427p.

Draws on research carried out for *Science and civilisation in China* (q.v.) to provide an authoritative description of the origins, development and practice before c. 1600 of the two most celebrated techniques of treatment in pre-modern Chinese medical practice, with extensive quotations, illustrations and historical context. Lu Gwei-djen, Joseph Needham, *Clerks and craftsmen in China and the West: lectures and addresses on the history of science and technology* (Cambridge, England: Cambridge University Press, 1970. 470p.) includes 'Proto-endocrinology in Medieval China', 'Hygiene and Preventative Medicine in Ancient China', 'China and the Origins of Qualifying Examinations in Medicine', and 'Medicine and Chinese culture', which brilliantly speculates on the influence of social structures on science.

672   **The washing away of wrongs: forensic medicine in thirteenth-century China.**
Brian E. McKnight.   Ann Arbor, Michigan: Center for Chinese Studies, University of Michigan, 1981. 181p. (Science, Medicine, and Technology in East Asia).

The imperial government, in the person of the county magistrate, took responsibility for redressing crimes of murder – the 'washing away of wrongs'. This is an annotated translation of the oldest surviving manual of forensic medicine, *Xiyuan jilu*, by Song Ci (Sung Tz'u), which helped the magistrate arrest and punish perpetrators by accurately describing and interpreting the clues offered by the *corpus delicti*. Lu Gwei-djen, Joseph Needham, 'A History of Forensic Medicine in China' (*Medical History*, no. 32 [October 1988], p. 357-400) contains much useful medical information.

673   **Medicine in China: a history of ideas.**
Paul U. Unschild.   Berkeley, California; Los Angeles; Oxford:
University of California Press, 1985. 423p.

Focuses on the concepts, rather than the practice, of Chinese medicine, introducing a preliminary selection of basic texts and ideas, with personal interpretations. Unschild includes translations of medical theory texts from the (purported) Yellow Emperor to the present day, with comments on their textual history and the way in which they responded to the changing spirit of their times. Manfred Porkert, *The theoretical foundations of Chinese medicine: systems of correspondence* (Cambridge, Massachusetts: M. I. T. Press, 1974. 328p. [East Asian Science Series]) is a reliable, scholarly investigation of the basis in correspondence theory and cosmology of medical terminology and physiological concepts as found in the *Inner Canon (Neijing)* tradition. *The essential book of traditional Chinese medicine*, edited by Liu Yanchi (New York: Columbia University Press, 1987. 2 vols.) provides a comprehensive summary from the Beijing College of Traditional Chinese Medicine, intended for an audience of Chinese readers. Volume one is devoted to theory, and volume two to clinical practice.

674   **Medicine in China: a history of pharmaceutics.**
Paul U. Unschild.   Berkeley, California; Los Angeles; Oxford:
University of California Press, 1986. 366p.

The rich tradition of Chinese medicinal herbs and concoctions was embodied in a vast literature of pharmaceutics, known as the *bencao (pen-ts'ao)* texts. These writings changed from age to age in aim and technique, despite the efforts of commentators and editors to assert unity and continuity. Unschild provides information from Chinese and Japanese references on the structure, contents and textual history of selected *bencao* texts, with illustrations and translated selections. A companion volume, *Medicine in China: Nan-ching – the Classic of Difficult Issues, with commentaries by Chinese and Japanese authors from the third through the twentieth century*, translated and annotated by Paul U. Unschild (Berkeley, California; Los Angeles: University of California Press, 1986. 760p.) is a fully annotated translation of one of the most widely read classics of pulse theory and acupuncture.

675   **History of Chinese medicine: being a chronicle of medical
happenings in China from ancient time to the present period.**
K. Chimin Wong, Wu Lien-te.   Shanghai, China: National Quarantine
Service, 1936. Reprinted, New York: AMS Press, 1973; Taipei: South
Wind Press, [n.d.]. 906p.

A detailed pioneering history. Sections on medicine in imperial China present a biased and poorly informed history; however, sections on the 20th century offer useful information and reveal attitudes toward the introduction of Western professional medicine from the point of view of distinguished 1930s medical doctors. The work translates many anecdotes and excerpts from early texts.

20th century

676 **An American transplant: the Rockefeller Foundation and Peking Union Medical College.**
Mary Brown Bullock. Berkeley, California; Los Angeles; Oxford: University of California Press, 1980. 280p.

Explores the cultural and political strains created when the Rockefeller Foundation brought professionalized Western medicine, taught entirely in English, to a country with a huge population and a proud medical tradition. The Peking Union Medical College (PUMC) opened in 1921 but only 329 students graduated before 1949. However, John D. Grant, called a 'medical Bolshevik' for his insistence on public health, fostered the village health experiments of C. C. Chen (Chen Zhiqian) and James Yen at Ting Hsien which helped create a new medicine which was both scientific and Chinese. C. C. Chen, *Medicine in rural China: a personal account* (Berkeley, California; Los Angeles; London: University of California Press, 1989. 218p.) also indicates his influence on the post-1949 public health programme. Karen Minden, *Bamboo stone: the evolution of a Chinese medical élite* (Toronto; Buffalo, New York; London: University of Toronto Press, 1994. 201p.) tells a parallel story for Canadian missionaries and the West China Union College in Chengdu.

677 **Traditional medicine in modern China: science, nationalism, and the tensions of cultural change.**
Ralph Croizier. Cambridge, Massachusetts: Harvard University Press, 1968. 325p. (East Asian Series, no. 39).

A study of the history of ideas. During the New Culture Movement of the 1910s and 1920s, intellectuals debated whether 'traditional' Chinese medicine was a cultural treasure to be developed or a feudal superstition to be destroyed. Croizier carefully presents these debates and explores the cultural tensions between a concern for truth, as embodied in 'scientific' medicine, and value, as perceived in traditional practices.

678 **Knowing practice: the clinical encounter of Chinese medicine.**
Judith Farquhar. Boulder, Colorado; San Francisco; Oxford: Westview Press, 1994. 260p. (Studies in the Ethnographic Imagination).

A sophisticated anthropologist analyses the relationship of theory, as now taught in colleges of traditional medicine, to actual practice, seen in her field observations in Guangdong. Farquhar describes the doctor moving from specific diagnosis to abstract description back to specific prescription by use of categories supplied by theory. She relates this 'clinical encounter' to the yin/yang type relation between theory and practice which is also seen in contemporary structuralism and post-structuralism, and shows how these findings test and revise Western theory.

679 **The politics of medicine in China: the policy process 1949-1977.**
David M. Lampton. Boulder, Colorado; San Francisco; Oxford: Westview Press, 1977. 301p.

Analyses the 'two-line struggle' between the ideologists and the professionals, a political and ideological battle to see which factions and policies would control the

Ministry of Health. During the 1950s, the professionals developed both public health and intensive scientific medicine; however, the Cultural Revolution attacked these policies as élitist, urban and expensive, and promoted public health initiatives, such as the barefoot doctors, which claimed to be democratic, village based and cheap.

680   **Chinese medical modernization: comparative policy continuities, 1930s-1980s.**
AnElissa Lucas.   New York: Praeger, 1982. 188p.
A suggestive analysis of the national policy choices and debates which developed in the 1920s, began to be put into practice in the 1930s, and shaped public health and government organization of medicine to the 1970s. Chinese medical planners realized from early on that they could not duplicate the professionalized, urban, curative, high-tech medical system of the West; therefore they sought to create a distinctively Chinese scientific medicine which was politically organized, preventative, rural and self-supporting. These debates were not peculiar to Mao or the Cultural Revolution; in the work of doctors such as C. C. Chen, they could be traced back to the 1920s. 'Barefoot doctors' were a distortion of this line of thought, rather than a creative culmination of it.

681   **A barefoot doctor's manual.**
Edited by the Revolutionary Health Committee of Hunan Province.
Bethesda, Maryland, 1974; Philadelphia: Running Press, 1977. rev. and enlarged ed. 942p.
During the Cultural Revolution, Mao's followers attacked professionals and bureaucrats for élitism and urban leanings; to compensate, massive numbers of village health workers – barefoot doctors – were given quick, basic training to expand medical treatment and bring it to every village. This manual, reliably translated here, was compiled to instruct them in all aspects of scientific and traditional Chinese medicine, complete with diagrams.

682   **Serve the people: observations on medicine in the People's Republic of China.**
Victor W. Sidel, Ruth Sidel.   Boston, Massachusetts, New York:
Josiah Macy Foundation, 1973. 317p. maps. bibliog.
The authors, an American doctor and a psychiatric social worker, visited China twice during the later stages of the Cultural Revolution; here they describe what they saw and learned sympathetically but not uncritically. Chapters describe: the development of health services; health care in the cities and the countryside, including barefoot doctors; the role of the community and patient; medical education; the integration of traditional and modern medicine; and mental illness. A bibliography lists books and articles in English. Joshua Horn, *Away with all pests: an English surgeon in People's China, 1954-1969* (London: Hamlyn; New York: Monthly Review, 1969. 192p.) is an enthusiastic eye-witness account of the spread of public health and the development of scientific medicine.

683   Traditional medicine in contemporary China: a partial translation
       of *Revised outline of Chinese medicine* (1972) with an introductory
       study on change in present-day and early medicine.
       Nathan Sivin.   Ann Arbor, Michigan: Center for Chinese Studies,
       University of Michigan, 1987. 550p. bibliog. (Science, Medicine, and
       Technology in East Asia).
An extremely useful translation and annotation of a 1972 medical text widely used in
the People's Republic. The introduction lucidly surveys traditional medicine and its
study in the West, focusing on its place in contemporary China but largely devoted to
earlier theory and practice and their evolution. The body of the book is an accurate
translation of a 1972 Chinese medical reference text, describing general diagnostic
doctrine taught to professional primary health workers at that time. Extensive
bibliographies list Asian and Western books and articles, with brief annotations,
including useful comparative and theoretical studies.

**Sex, culture, and modernity in China: medical science and the
construction of sexual identities in the early Republican period.**
See item no. 641.

The Chinese hospital: a socialist work unit.
See item no. 653.

Politics and Government

General and to 1949

684 The bureaucracy of Han times.

Hans Bielenstein. Cambridge, England: Cambridge University Press, 1980. 262p. (Cambridge Studies in Chinese History, Literature, and Institutions).

Analyses the structure and development of the government of the first long-lived dynasty (202 BCE-220 CE) covering: central administration; local administration; the military, with a brief but thorough description of the army organization and command; recruitment, discipline and salary of bureaucrats; and civil service and governmental power. Bielenstein argues that this constitutes a Weberian rational bureaucracy.

685 The government and politics of China, 1912-1949.

Ch'ien Tuan-sheng. Cambridge, Massachusetts: Harvard University Press, 1950. 544p. Reprinted, Stanford, California: Stanford University Press, 1970.

Long the standard treatment of formal government for the 20th century to the eve of the 1949 revolution. The author provides detailed analytical summaries of Nationalist government structures, political history (especially of the period from 1927 to the war), and legal activity.

686 Local government in China under the Ch'ing.

Ch'ü T'ung-tsu. Cambridge, Massachusetts: Harvard University Press, 1962. (Harvard East Asian Studies, no. 9). Reprinted, Stanford, California: Stanford University Press, 1969. 360p. bibliog.

Comprehensively describes, analyses and interprets the government of the Qing (Manchu) dynasty at the *zhou* (department) and *xian* (county) levels. Ch'ü outlines the formal structure, and describes the roles of the magistrate (the lowest official

231

appointed and supervised by the emperor), and his clerks, 'runners', and private secretaries. Chapters then analyse the administration of justice, taxation, population registration, public works, welfare, education and ceremonial observances. Finally Ch'ü examines the informal power of the local 'gentry', who could make or break the theoretically all-powerful magistrate. The conclusion holds that central control predominated, and that there was no local autonomy. *Village and bureaucracy in Southern Sung China*, by Brian McKnight (Chicago: University of Chicago Press, 1971. 219p. bibliog.) analyses government influence in affairs at the local level, beneath the reach of the formal bureaucracy, and the efforts of landowners to resist it. John R. Watt, *The district magistrate in late imperial China* (New York; London: Columbia University Press, 1972. 340p.) examines the office to argue that Chinese society was becoming more egalitarian, efficient, socially managed, less bound by ancestral precedent, in short, more 'modern'. *A complete book concerning happiness and benevolence:* Fu-hui ch'üan-shu, *a manual for local magistrates in seventeenth century China*, by Huang Liu-hung, translated by Djang Chu (Tucson, Arizona: University of Arizona Press, 1984. 656p.) provides an important insight into the magistrate's job.

687 **The origins of statecraft in China.**
Herlee Glessner Creel.   Chicago: University of Chicago Press, 1970.
Vol. I, *The Western Chou empire*; Vol. II not yet published.

Creel argues that the competitive struggle for existence in the late Zhou period forced the state of Qin to evolve a bureaucracy and rationalized government, develop innovative and effective military organization, and anticipate modern bureaucratic norms. Statesmen such as Shang Yang regularized the concept of *fa* (law), and their followers were later called *fajia* (Legalists). Chapter topics include the Mandate of Heaven (the spiritual authority of the Emperors to rule), the rise of the Zhou, and the origin of the deity *tian*. Creel's lucidly presented argument is perhaps extreme, but reviews much interesting material.

688 **A history of Chinese political thought.**
K. C. Hsiao, translated by Frederick W. Mote.   Princeton, New Jersey: Princeton University Press, 1979. 2 vols.

A masterpiece by one of modern China's leading scholars, which analyses specifically political thought, which was the occasion for Chinese philosophy much as epistemology was in the European tradition. Hsiao summarizes vast areas of knowledge, with copious and shrewdly chosen excerpts. He starts with the pre-Confucians of antiquity, through the leading (and many lesser) political thinkers of dynastic China, to the important but lesser known thinkers of late imperial China (on whom this work is often the first and best reference). Mote's elegant volume supplies standard and reliable translations of many elusive Chinese terms.

689 **The censorial system of Ming China.**
Charles Hucker.   Stanford, California: Stanford University Press, 1966. 406p. bibliog.

The Ming emperors developed the institution of the 'censorate', which was staffed by 'censors'. This was parallel to, but separate from, the military and civilian bureaucracies, and reported on them directly to the emperor. Censors, by their surveillance and impeachment, were supposed to ensure honesty and loyalty, but often used their powers in factional disputes or became tools of capricious despotism. Hucker analyses the precedents, structure and techniques of the system and its role in history.

690 **Chinese government in Ming times.**
Edited by Charles O. Hucker. New York; London: Columbia University Press, 1969. 285p. (Studies in Oriental Culture).
Contains seven scholarly studies on aspects of Ming government stemming from a 1965 conference. Lien-sheng Yang's study, 'Ming Local Administration', discusses 'feudalism and centralism in the Chinese tradition', pointing out that *fengjian*, usually misleadingly translated as 'feudalism', actually meant decentralized or local government, quite different in significance from European 'feudalism'. Other studies analyse: the Mongol origins of the *wei-so* military system of organization; policy formation and decision making on war and peace issues; fiscal administration; educational intendant or local school officials; academies and politics, especially the Donglin Academy; and background forces in the bureaucracy.

691 **The Communist Party of China and Marxism, 1921-1985: a self portrait.**
Laszlo Ladany, with a foreword by Robert Elegant. Stanford, California: Hoover Institution, 1988. 588p.
For three decades, Father Ladany, a Hungarian Jesuit who came to in China in the 1940s, combed Chinese sources, interviewed refugees, and applied a critical intelligence to publish heavily documented essays in his *China News Analysis* (q.v.). This book draws on much of that published material, forming a 'concatenation of first hand sources'. The judgements are independent and pungently phrased, often using vivid images and examples to argue that Mao and his revolution destroyed Chinese culture and replaced it with chaos. Chapters follow the CCP's development period by period, with many anecdotes and fresh analysis. Ladany's *Law and legality in China: the testament of a China-watcher* (Honolulu: University of Hawaii Press, 1992. 179p.) is an essay on Chinese culture, China's legal system, and Mao's attack on it, edited after Ladany's death in 1990 by Marie-Luise Näth.

692 **Governing China: from revolution through reform.**
Kenneth Lieberthal. London; New York: Norton, 1995. 298p. bibliog.
A comprehensive description and analysis of government in China for the student and general reader. Part one, 'Legacies', briefly traverses the imperial and Republican periods. Part two, 'Politics and Policies Since 1949', describes the system of policy ideas and governance during the Maoist and reform eras. Part three, 'The Political System', describes the organization of political power first from the outside, in a formal analysis, and then from the inside, explaining informal channels and personal relations. A chapter is devoted to the 1990s succession problem. Part four, 'The Challenges Ahead', looks at contentious issues, such as economic development, the environment, and state and society. A selection of key documents, footnotes and a bibliography conclude the volume. Other standard texts on the subject include: June Teufel Dreyer, *China's political system* (New York: Paragon House, 1993. 448p); Lucian Pye, *China: an introduction* (Boston, Massachusetts; Toronto: Little, Brown, 1986. 3rd ed. 400p.); Suzanne Ogden, *China's unresolved issues: politics,*

development and culture (Englewood Cliffs, New Jersey: Prentice-Hall, 1989. 375p.); and James Townsend, Brantly Womack, *Politics in China* (Boston, Massachusetts; Toronto: Little, Brown, 1986. 3rd ed. 464p.).

693 **The Chinese civil service: career open to talent?**
Edited with an introduction by Johanna M. Menzel. Boston, Massachusetts: DC Heath, 1963. 110p. bibliog. (Problems in Asian Civilizations).
Provides excerpts from scholarly writings selected for undergraduate research papers. The introduction outlines the problem, historical background and the development of major scholarly points of view. Sections of excerpts from works by historians and sociologists then cover 'The Chinese Civil Service and Social Mobility', 'Recruitment and the Struggle for Power' and 'The Attempt to Measure Talent'. The section entitled 'Suggestions for Additional Reading' comprises an annotated bibliographical essay.

694 **Chinese eunuchs: the structure of intimate politics.**
Mitamura Taisuke, translated by Charles Pomery. Rutland, Vermont: Tuttle, 1970. 176p.
A survey written for the Japanese general audience, incorporating much anecdotal detail and some general analysis. Mitamura explains that emperors needed certifiably pure heirs; accordingly, access to women's quarters was restricted to those who were no threat in that respect. Therefore eunuchs were the only adults to know the imperial women, their children and future emperors. Particularly in the Tang and Ming dynasties, eunuchs took advantage of their intimate position, but for political rather than for sexual engrossment.

695 **Foundations and limits of state power in China.**
Edited by Stuart Schram. Hong Kong: Chinese University Press, 1987. 367p.
A wide-ranging symposium which ponders the state exercise of political, religious, and symbolic power, mostly in dynasties from Qin to Qing, but also including Nationalist and Chinese Communist attempts to build a nation-state. Benjamin Schwartz's theme-setting discussion avoids the word 'state' to talk of the primacy of a broad 'political order' in East Asian societies. Other essays agree that the term 'state' is restricting, emphasizing the religious and ritual aspects of state definition and legitimation. A study of the Liao, Jin and Yuan dynasties sees the state as only one element in these polyethnic societies. In the 20th century, state power came to include popular foundations and the use of legal systems to construct a nation-state. The editor's long essay shows how Mao pulled together traditional and modern themes, as well as European and Chinese.

696 **Government and politics in Kuomintang China, 1927-1937.**
Tien Hung-mao. Stanford, California: Stanford University Press, 1972. 226p.
A systematic analysis of the Nationalist (Guomindang) government in its first decade of power. Part one, 'The Central Government', covers: the establishment of the party-state in Republican China; the organization of the régime; factions such as the Blue Shirts and the C. C. Clique; and government revenues and expenditures. Chapters in part two,

'The Provinces', deal with: the structures of provincial and county government; the special 'Bandit' (i.e. Communist) Suppression Zones; the educational background of the provincial élites; their social composition and turnover; and provincial revenues and expenditures. Tien's conclusion argues that it was not possible to have predicted the future success of the Communists but criticizes Nationalist failure to build party membership, address rural problems, or develop a legitimate decision making structure. The Nationalist government, according to Tien, was militarized, dominated by cliques, weakened by regional power groups and fiscally ineffective.

Autocratic tradition and Chinese politics.
See annotation to item no. 100.

Oriental despotism: a comparative study of total power.
See item no. 100.

Ordering the world: approaches to state and society in Sung dynasty China.
See item no. 155.

An introduction to the civil service of Sung China: with emphasis on its personnel administration.
See item no. 159.

The Book of Lord Shang: a classic of the Chinese school of law.
See item no. 874.

The life and thought of Sun Yat-sen (1866-1925)

697 **All under heaven: Sun Yat-sen and his revolutionary thought.**
Sidney H. Chang, Leonard H. D. Gordon. Stanford, California: Hoover Institution Press, 1991. 253p. (Studies in Economic, Social, and Political Change: The Republic of China).

A sympathetic general treatment of Sun's life (1866-1925) and an analysis of his thought. The authors place his agitation at the centre of the 1911 Revolution, his thought at the centre of democratic reform in the early years of the century, and his legacy at the centre of the Republic of China's economic development on Taiwan. The authors examine Sun's writings in detail, especially the *Sanmin zhuyi*, 'Three People's Principles' of nationalism, socialism and democracy. *Bibliography of Sun Yat-sen in China's Republican Revolution, 1885-1925* (Lanham, Maryland: University Press of America, 1991. 349p.), compiled and edited by Sidney H. Chang, Leonard H. D. Gordon, is a comprehensive, topically arranged, multiply indexed listing of published and unpublished works and documents by and about Sun in many languages.

698   **The Japanese and Sun Yat-sen.**
Marius Jansen.   Cambridge, Massachusetts: Harvard University Press,
1954. 294p. (Harvard Historical Monographs, no. 27).

Sun's Japanese friends helped him to organize anti-Manchu revolution, especially his
1905 party, the Tongmenghui, and supported him after 1911. They held in common
ideas of Pan-Asianism, nationalism and racism; Sun looked to Japan for investment
and moral support against European imperialism. Jansen deftly relates the story of
Sun's adventures in Japan and the nature of his Japanese admirers. The 1902
autobiography of one of these Japanese supporters is *My thirty-three years' dream*, by
Miyazaki Tōten, translated by Marius Jansen, Etō Shinkichi (Princeton, New Jersey:
Princeton University Press, 1982. 298p.).

699   **Sun Yat-sen: reluctant revolutionary.**
Harold Z. Schiffrin.   Boston, Massachusetts: Little, Brown, 1980.
290p. bibliog. (Library of World Biography).

A one-volume biography, aimed at the general reader, and covering Sun's full life and
activities, with some historical background. Schiffrin draws on the research done for his
more detailed *Sun Yat-sen and the origins of the Chinese Revolution* (Berkeley,
California; London: University of California Press, 1968. 412p.), the first of two
projected volumes. *Sun Yat-sen, his life and its meaning: a critical biography* by Lyon
Sharman (New York: John Day, 1934. Reissued, with a preface by Lyman P. Van Slyke,
Stanford, California: Stanford University Press, 1968. 420p.) did not have access to
archival material or recent scholarship, but sets out to rescue Sun from the political cult
which turned the active, contradictory man into a 'lacquered image'. Thus the book,
begun shortly after Sun's death, in 1926, is 'critical' not in the sense of disparaging, but
in the sense of examining Sun's successes and failures openly. *Sun Yat-sen*, by Marie-
Claire Bergère (Paris: Fayard, 1994. 538p.) is a lucid biography, due to be translated
into English, which nicely summarizes knowledge of Sun's life and significance.

700   **Prescriptions for saving China: selected writings of Sun Yat-sen.**
Edited with an introduction, notes by Julie Lee Wei, Ramon H. Myers,
Donald G. Gillin, translated by Julie Lee Wei, E-su Zen, Linda Chao.
Stanford, California: Hoover Institution Press, Stanford University,
1994. 328p. (Studies in Economic, Social, and Political Change: the
Republic of China).

An anthology of more than forty of Sun's essays and speeches spanning his active
career, 1894-1924. An introduction and an extensive chronology outline Sun's life and
its significance. Section one, 'To Overthrow the Manchu Regime', starts with Sun's
1894 memorial to Viceroy Li Hongzhang, describing needed reforms; other selections
show the origins of the 'Three People's Principles'. Section two covers the years 1912-
13, which saw the establishment and frustration of the Chinese Republic. Section three,
'Launching a New Revolution', deals with Sun's writings during the period 1916-24.

701   **Sun Yat-sen: frustrated patriot.**
C. Martin Wilbur.   New York; London: Columbia University Press,
1976. 410p. (Studies of the East Asian Institute).

A basic political study. Wilbur's first chapter, 'Molding Influences and Career Line',
examines Sun's early career and character. Succeeding chapters then carefully discuss:

the finances of the revolution, in particular the support from Overseas Chinese; the search for foreign aid up to 1911; attempts to harness foreign power after 1911, especially American and Japanese; negotiating Soviet aid and working with Comintern agents such as Michael Borodin; frustrations with the revolutionary situation in the early 1920s; and 'the final quest', covering the last, cancer-ridden months of his life.

The rise of the Chinese Communist Party (1921-49)

702   Revolutionary discourse in Mao's Republic.

David E. Apter, Tony Saich.   Cambridge, Massachusetts; London: Harvard University Press, 1994. 403p.

The Communist Revolution before 1949, like the French and Russian Revolutions, produced a revolutionary discourse (a set of key words, metaphors and myths), which was 'inversionary in purpose, rupturing in intent, and morally transformational'. The authors deploy post-modern culture theory to show how Mao, as a 'storyteller', mobilized moral values to build a symbolically powerful 'revolutionary simulacrum' and created texts to form a 'revolutionary syllabus'. After an explanatory section, 'Toward a Discourse Theory of Politics', chapters follow the early history of the Communist Party, showing the transformation from a party of intellectuals to one of activists. Part two, 'Yan'an as a Mobilization Space', traces the 1937-45 construction of 'Mao's republic', an ostensible moral centre of revolution. Part three, 'The Power of Symbolic Capital', returns to theory to discuss 'Foucault's paradox', in which the 'inversionary' appeal of revolution becomes the 'hegemonic' power of repression.

703   Mao's China: party reform documents, 1942-44.

Translation, introduction by Boyd Compton.   Seattle, Washington: University of Washington Press, 1952. 278p.

A selection of speeches, articles and resolutions originally published in Yan'an as a study handbook for the 1942 *zhengfeng yundong*, or 'rectification campaign'. Millions of Party members and cadres studied this handbook and other basic writings of Marxism as an important stage in the development of a Chinese style of revolution. The campaign and its contents are described in the preface and introduction. Included here are basic writings of Mao Zedong, Chen Yun and Liu Shaoqi; works by Lenin and Stalin are omitted, as is Mao's 'Talk to the Yan'an Forum on Art and Literature', since they are easily available elsewhere.

704   Wang Shiwei and 'Wild Lilies': rectification and purges in the Chinese Communist Party, 1942-1944.

Dai Qing, edited, with an introduction by David E. Apter, Timothy C. Cheek.   Armonk, New York; London: M. E. Sharpe, 1993. 204p.

Dai Qing, herself a member of the political élite, wrote piercing journalistic histories in the 1980s to expose Party abuse of intellectuals. One of her subjects was Wang Shiwei, an idealistic writer who went to Yan'an in the 1930s but came to question party omniscience. His story, 'Wild Lilies', punctured the myth of revolutionary egalitarianism; as a result he was arrested in the 1942 rectification campaigns, pilloried and eventually beheaded. This book translates Dai's work on Wang, and includes a selection from Wang's other writings: official attacks on him; details of his eventual rehabilitation; and interviews conducted by Dai in the 1980s. An introduction analyses Wang's case and Dai's exposé.

705   **The origins of Chinese Communism.**
       Arif Dirlik.   New York; Oxford: Oxford University Press, 1989. 315p.

A detailed reinterpretation of the social and intellectual origins of the Chinese Communist Party in the 1910s and 1920s. Basing his work on wide primary and theoretical reading, Dirlik argues that the diffuse radicalism of the period was more often anarchist than Marxist; anarchists not only offered a detailed programme of social change but also created new organizations and reordered their daily lives. This new culture ferment was precipitated into Chinese Communism when the international Communist movement offered better organizational tools, not deeper political understanding or theoretical analysis. Thus Bolshevism displaced anarchism and its democratic and socialist ideals, leading to the triumph of the CCP by the Second Party Congress in 1922. See also Michael Y. L. Luk, *The origins of Chinese Bolshevism: an ideology in the making, 1920-1928* (Hong Kong; Oxford; New York: Oxford University Press, 1990. 366p.).

706   **Single sparks: China's rural revolutions.**
       Edited by Kathleen Hartford, Steven M. Goldstein.   Armonk, New
       York; London: M. E. Sharpe, 1989. 216p. maps. (Studies of the East
       Asian Institute Columbia University).

Mao declared in 1927 that 'a single spark can start a prairie fire', but his strategy of relying on the spontaneous combustion of poverty and oppression fizzled in the short run. This conference volume of five local studies examines the painful development of the revolution in the countryside before 1949. The editors' introduction is a careful and imaginative historiographical review of successive generations of interpretation from the 1940s to the 1980s. Chapters by individual authors then examine: the successful Guomindang (Nationalist) suppression of Communist bases in the early 1930s; Communist guerrilla bases left behind in Southeast China by the Long March; repression and Communist success in Jin-Cha-Ji base area, 1938-45; Nationalist guerrillas in Shandong province; and 1940s military organization building as the basis for rural revolution in Manchuria.

707   **The broken wave: the Chinese Communist peasant movement,
       1922-1928.**
       Roy Hofheinz.   Cambridge, Massachusetts: Harvard University Press,
       1977. 355p. (Harvard East Asian Series, no. 90).

Argues that the basis for Mao's revolution developed in the early 1920s in Guangdong, long before the Red Army or the anti-Japanese war, and that the eventual success was for organizational and political reasons, not because of class structure, economics or demography. Part one, 'Strategy', describes rural revolution and Mao as a strategist. Part two, 'Organization', covers the development of the Peasant Movement under Comintern tutelage, in which Mao was trained. Part Three, 'Practice', details Peng Pai's 'people's war' in Guangdong. Peasant uprisings, including Mao's 1927 Uprisings, failed, argues Hofheinz, because they had not laid political and organizational foundations. Hofheinz puts various theories to the quantitative test, with useful maps, in his 'The ecology of Chinese Communist success . . .' in *Chinese Communist politics in action*, edited by A. Doak Barnett (Seattle, Washington: University of Washington Press, 1969. 620p. maps. p. 3-77).

708 **Peasant nationalism and Communist power: the emergence of revolutionary China, 1937-1945.**
Chalmers Johnson. Stanford, California: Stanford University Press, 1962. 256p. maps.

An influential, controversial study which argues that Chinese Communist mass support in the villages was based not so much on land reform and class conflict but on anti-imperialist nationalism aroused by the Japanese invasion of North China. For comparison, Johnson assesses the mass nationalism of the Yugoslav partisan movement during the Second World War. His thesis is disputed by Donald Gillin in 'Peasant Nationalism in the Study of Chinese Communism' (*Journal of Asian Studies*, vol. 23, no. 2 [February 1964], p. 269-89), which argues that appeals to social justice founded a mass base even before the war. Johnson considers the controversy in 'Chinese Communist Leadership and Mass Response . . .' in *China in crisis, vol. I*, edited by Ping-ti Ho, Tsou Tang (Chicago: University of Chicago Press, 1968), and 'Peasant Nationalism Revisited: The Biography of a Book' (*China Quarterly*, no. 72 [1977], p. 766-85).

709 **Anvil of victory: the communist revolution in Manchuria, 1945-1948.**
Steven I. Levine. New York: Columbia University Press, 1987. 314p. (Studies of the East Asian Institute).

A key monograph which analyses the Civil War in the Northwest (Manchuria), where victory put the Communists on the threshold of national power. Levine concludes that contrary to revolutionary mythology, success was uncertain until the last moment; in addition, victory was military, based on organizational strength, coercion and terror, rather than ideological attraction, populism or even peasant self-interest. The first three chapters set the Civil War in the context of Soviet-American rivalry and describe the base of Communist power in Manchuria, including anti-Japanese guerrillas in the 1930s. Chapters four to six describe: the Civil War in the Northeast, 1945-48; the political economy of the Civil War, showing that military supply was the basic objective; and revolution in the countryside, showing that organizational expansion, not social justice, was the motivation for land reform. The earlier period is carefully examined in Chong-sik Lee, *Revolutionary struggle in Manchuria: Chinese Communism and Soviet interest, 1922-1945* (Berkeley, California: University of California Press, 1983. 366p.).

710 **The origins of the first United Front in China: the role of Sneevliet (alias Maring).**
Tony Saich. Leiden, the Netherlands; New York; Copenhagen; Köln: E. J. Brill, 1991. 2 vols.

Sneevliet was a Dutch agent of Comintern – Lenin's Communist International. Saich presents first a detailed narrative of his career before and after coming to China, where he worked from 1921-25, then translates and annotates extensive documents found in the Sneevliet Archive in Holland, many available for the first time. These documents provide detail on relations with Sun Yat-sen, Sneevliet's conclusion that Nationalist organizers were stronger than Communists, especially in the strikes and labour movements, and Comintern's low opinion of China's revolutionary potential.

711   **New perspectives on the Chinese Communist Revolution.**
Tony Saich, Hans van de Ven.   Armonk, New York; London: M. E. Sharpe, 1995. 414p.

Twelve cutting-edge papers from a 1990 Leiden conference use newly available sources to rethink Party history. Part one, 'Early Organizational Trends', covers: the emergence of the 'text-centered party'; the politics of gender in the making of the party; and recent reinterpretations of Li Dazhao (one of the founding fathers of Chinese marxism). Part two, 'Regional Variations', asserts that the 'Leninist' Party actually evolved many local variations: chapters explore the 'Futian incident' (a revolt directed against Mao), the experience of party members left behind after the 1934 Long March, the Chinese Communist Party in rural Hebei from 1921-36, and peasant responses to Chinese Communist Party mobilization, 1937-45. Part three, 'The Making of Victory', studies: Yan'an as a political and symbolic capital; intellectual service in Chinese Communist Party propaganda institutions, 1937-45; the financially crucial participation of the CCP in the opium trade; the 1945 'resolution on Party history' which installed Mao's interpretations; and how changing leadership showed a change from a Leninist to a charismatic party, 1937-45.

712   **The rise to power of the Chinese Communist Party: documents and analysis, 1920-1949.**
Edited by Tony Saich, with a contribution by Benjamin Yang.
Armonk, New York; London: M. E. Sharpe, 1994. 1,500p.

An extensive and systematic selection of key documents, with annotations and analysis, showing the development of ideology in the service of politics. Documents show debate, formulation and communication for all major policies from the 1920s to 1949. *A documentary history of Chinese Communism*, edited by Conrad Brandt, Benjamin Schwartz, John K. Fairbank (Cambridge, Massachusetts; London: Harvard University Press, 1952. 552p.) gives official documents on policy and ideology from 1921-50. Stephen Uhalley, Jr., *A history of the Chinese Communist Party* (Stanford, California: Hoover Institution Press, 1988. 340p.) provides a narrative analysis.

713   **Chinese Communism and the rise of Mao.**
Benjamin I. Schwartz.   Cambridge, Massachusetts: Harvard University Press, 1951. 258p.

One of the first studies to subject the ideas of Chinese Communism to scholarly analysis, this remains a useable introduction. Chapters one to four discuss the origins of Marxism-Leninism in China before and after the May Fourth Movement of 1919, the founding of the Party, and collaboration with the Guomindang (Nationalists). Chapters five to eleven analyse the controversies over strategy under Party leaders Qu Qiubai, Li Lisan and Wang Ming. Chapters twelve to thirteen conclude with the triumph of Mao and an analysis of the essential features of the Maoist strategy in the late 1920s; this strategy was not planned by Moscow and even ran against orthodoxy, representing Marxism's 'slow but steady process of decomposition'. Schwartz' views were famously contested by Karl August Wittfogel in *China Quarterly*, no. 1 (1960), which contends that Mao's ideas were not creative, autonomous and indigenous, but rather derived from the international Communist movement.

714 **From friend to comrade: the founding of the Chinese Communist Party, 1920-1927.**
Hans J. van de Ven.   Berkeley, California; London: University of California Press, 1991. 373p.

Uses newly opened archives and recent rethinking to trace the stages by which Communists developed from a loose social grouping of intellectuals into a disciplined, text centred, Leninist party by the time of their suppression in 1927. Early activists, many of whom had studied in Europe, organized local study groups and youth organizations. Van de Ven devotes considerable space to showing how the United Front with the Nationalists, Northern Expedition and mass mobilization of 1925-27 transformed regional and provincial groups into a national Bolshevist organization capable of revolutionary discipline; however, party leaders neglected the military. Thus the Leninist CCP which finally came to power in 1949 was not truly formed until after 1927.

Anarchism and Chinese political culture.
See item no. 248.

The life and works of Mao Zedong (1893-1976)

715 **The writings of Mao Zedong, 1949-1976.**
Edited by John K. Leung, Michael Y. M. Kau.   Armonk, New York; London: M. E. Sharpe, 1986- .

A scholarly edition which will, when completed, include post-1949 published writings and speeches, edited and checked for accuracy, with explanatory notes and comparative sources. The index contains proper names and some terms and concepts. The official *Selected works* (q.v.) is, in the words of editors Leung and Kau, 'incomplete and extremely selective in relation to the total corpus of Mao's works'. Along with Schram's *Mao's road to power* (q.v.), these volumes will reliably present the sweep of Mao's thought and public presence. Volume one covers September 1945-December 1955, and volume two January 1956-December 1957.

716 **The private life of Chairman Mao.**
Li Zhisui, with Anne Thurston, foreword by Andrew J. Nathan.   New York: Random House, 1994. 682p.

A devastating, engrossing first-hand portrait of an autocrat as edited by a careful American scholar. Dr Li, a graduate of West China Union Medical College, was Mao's physician from the early 1950s for the rest of his life (and after - Li performed the embalming). He convincingly exposes poor hygiene – Mao didn't believe in baths or brushing his teeth – sexual turpitude, and corruption by absolute power. The focus is unremittingly personal, however, not entirely reliable in its judgements of Mao's associates, and blames Mao individually for all evils (just as he had earlier been credited with all glorious achievements).

717   **The secret speeches of Chairman Mao: from the Hundred Flowers to the Great Leap Forward.**
Edited by Roderick MacFarquhar, Timothy Cheek, Eugene Wu, with contributions by Merle Goldman, Benjamin I. Schwartz.   Cambridge, Massachusetts; London: Council on East Asian Studies, Harvard University, distributed by Harvard University Press, 1989. 561p. bibliog. (Harvard Contemporary China Series).
Provides new texts of selected speeches of 1957 and 1958, the period of Mao's prodigious initiatives. As Mao was 'allusive, tangential, colloquial, earthy', the editors have provided explanatory footnotes, five analytical essays, an essay, 'Contemporary China Studies: The Question of Sources', and a bibliography. Editions of individual works with notes and introductions include: Roger R. Thompson, *Report From Xunwu* (Stanford, California: Stanford University Press, 1990. 278p.), Mao's 1930 socio-political analysis of Xunwu, a village in Jiangxi province; *Mao Zedong and the political economy of the Border Regime: a translation of Mao's economic and financial problems*, edited by Andrew Watson (Cambridge, England; New York; Port Chester, New York; Melbourne; Sydney: Cambridge University Press, 1980. 271p.); *Mao Zedong on dialectical materialism*, edited by Nick Knight (Armonk, New York; London: M. E. Sharpe, 1990. 295p.), a 1937 essay showing Mao's ideological development; and Bonnie S. McDougall, *Mao Zedong's 'Talks at the Yan'an Conference on Literature and Art': a translation of the 1943 text with commentary* (Ann Arbor, Michigan: Center for Chinese Studies, University of Michigan, 1980. 112p. [Michigan Papers in Chinese Studies, no. 39]).

718   **Selected works of Mao Tse-tung.**
Mao Zedong.   Beijing: Foreign Languages Press, volumes 1-3, 1965, volume 4, 1971, volume 5, 1977.
The official selection and translation, edited to meet political needs at the time of publication, but still reasonably useful for following Mao's evolving thought. Volume one covers the First United Front and early uprisings (1924-32); volumes two and three cover the War of Resistance Against Japan (1937-45), including Mao's ideological writing from Yan'an; volume four deals with the 1945-49 Civil War; and volume five, published after Mao's death, contains patchy choices from the sensitive post-1949 period. Official selections, all with various reprints, include: *Selected readings from the works of Mao Tsetung* (Peking: Foreign Languages Press, 1971. 504p.); *Quotations from Chairman Mao Tsetung* (Beijing: Foreign Languages Press, 1966. 312p. Reprinted, San Francisco: China Books, 1990), a.k.a. the 'Little Red Book' originally edited at Lin Biao's behest for PLA study; and *Selected military writings* (1967), which contains some material not included in *Selected works*. Jerome Ch'en, *Mao and the Chinese revolution* (New York: Oxford University Press, 1965. 419p.) includes translations of thirty-seven of Mao's poems.

719 **Marxism, Maoism, and utopianism.**
Maurice Meisner. Madison, Wisconsin: University of Wisconsin
Press, 1982. 255p. bibliog.

Meisner, a thoughtful, sympathetic critic of Mao's thought, notes that the 1980s
Communist Party joined earlier Western scholars in condemning Mao as recklessly
utopian and irrationally anti-modern. He reprints and revises eight of his own 1980s
essays on the intellectual history of Mao's utopian deviations from Marxism and
Leninism. Topics include: utopian themes in the relation between town and
countryside; perspectives on populism; images of the Paris Commune; the cult of
Mao; and Chinese Marxism and the ritualization of utopia in the post-Maoist era. The
bibliographic notes discuss Mao's texts and the secondary literature on chapter topics.

720 **The thought of Mao Tse-tung.**
Stuart R. Schram. Cambridge, England: Cambridge University Press,
1989. 242p.

Contains two essays by the leading Western scholar of Mao, providing a close
analysis of texts, political manoeuvres and evolving political thought, reprinted from
Cambridge history of China, vols. 14 and 15. The first covers the period 1919-49 and
the second 1949-76. Schram's *The political thought of Mao Tse-tung* (New York;
Washington, DC; London: Praeger Publishers, 1969. rev. and enlarged ed. 479p.) is a
thematic anthology of Mao's writings, arranged topically, with extensive commentary.
John Bryan Starr, *Continuing the revolution: the political thought of Mao* (Princeton,
New Jersey: Princeton University Press, 1979. 366p.) interprets themes in Mao's
ideology treated as a whole, especially the theory of continuing revolution. Frederic
Wakeman, Jr., *History and will: philosophical perspectives of Mao Tse-tung's thought*
(Berkeley, California; Los Angeles; London: University of California Press, 1973.
392p.) develops Chinese and European philosophical comparisons. Brantly Womack,
The foundations of Mao Zedong's political thought, 1917-1935 (Honolulu: University
of Hawaii Press, 1982. 238p.) analyses thought and political contexts; and Raymond
F. Wylie, *The emergence of Maoism: Mao Tse-tung, Chen Po-ta and the search for
Chinese theory, 1935-1945* (Stanford, California: Stanford University Press, 1980.
351p.) also studies Mao's first exploration of Marxist classics and Stalinist primers.
Joshua A. Fogel, *Ai Ssu-chi's contribution to the development of Chinese Marxism*
(Cambridge, Massachusetts: Council on East Asian Studies/Harvard University, 1987.
145p. [Harvard Contemporary China Series, no. 4]) shows how Mao in the 1937-45
period used a popularized textbook writer, Ai Siqi (1910-66). Helmut Martin, *Cult and
canon: the origins and development of state Maoism* (Armonk, New York: M. E.
Sharpe, 1982. 233p.) creatively traces the systematization and ossification of Mao's
thought in the 1940s and 1950s.

721 **Mao's road to power: revolutionary writings, 1912-1949.**
Edited by Stuart R. Schram, Nancy J. Hodes, Associate Editor.
Armonk, New York; London: M. E. Sharpe, 1994- .

This edition of Mao's pre-1949 writings will be the most comprehensive in any
language; it will include a translation of every item whose Chinese text can be
obtained (some are still kept in archives). Items include not only Mao's published
articles, but letters, classroom notes, and even marginal annotations in books he read.
Introductions to the series and to the individual volumes provide the general reader
with brief but up-to-date information and background on the period. Extensive notes
and references serve both specialists and those interested in Mao from other

perspectives. The volumes published so far are: volume one, *The pre-Marxist period, 1912-1920* (1994); volume two, *National revolution and social revolution, December 1920-June 1927* (1995); and volume three, *From the Jingganshan to the establishment of the Jiangxi Soviets, July 1927-December 1930* (1995).

722   **Mao's revolution and the Chinese political culture.**
Richard H. Solomon.   Berkeley, California; Los Angeles; London: University of California Press, 1971. 604p. bibliog. (Michigan Studies on China).

An ambitious, necessarily controversial analysis which expands on Lucian Pye's cultural approach (q.v.). Solomon's introduction outlines China's political culture (ambivalence toward authority and avoidance of conflict) and the study's procedures, including extensive interviewing. Part two contains chapters on: 'Confucianism and the Chinese Life-Cycle'; childhood socialization into relations with authority; 'Emotional Control'; and the 'Pains and Rewards of Education'. Part three concerns: 'Adult Perceptions of Social Relations: "Confusion" (*luan*) and the Need for Strong Authority'. Parts three and four relate Mao's career and his Revolution. The selected bibliography covers personality formation, socialization and social change, as well as Chinese culture and politics.

723   **Mao: a biography.**
Ross Terrill.   New York: Harper & Row, 1980. Reissued, with new introduction, postscript, and bibliographic note, New York: Touchstone Books/Simon & Schuster Trade Paperback, 1993. 524p.

A biography aimed at general readers. The 1980 edition was translated into six languages, and finally appeared in the People's Republic in 1988 after years of Party opposition and sold 50,000 copies in the first month. Stuart Schram, *Mao Tse-tung* (Harmondsworth, England; Baltimore, Maryland: Penguin Books, 1967. rev. ed. 372p.), still the fundamental scholarly biography, sees Mao as basically consistent throughout his life and as a loyalist to international Leninism. Terrill believes rather that there is an ad hoc aspect to Mao's ideology, which he often 'reshaped, compromised or even set aside'. Terrill had access to material exposed in Red Guard publications of the Cultural Revolution and the memoir literature following Mao's death. Edward E. Rice, *Mao's way* (Berkeley, California; Los Angeles; London: University of California Press, 1972. 596p.) is a thorough political biography, with emphasis on the Cultural Revolution. Rice uses materials and a view gathered when he was American Consul-General in Hong Kong.

The People's Republic (1949-)

General

724 **China: politics, economics, and society: iconoclasm and innovation in a revolutionary socialist country.**
Marc Blecher. London: Frances Pinter; Boulder, Colorado: Lynne Rienner, 1986. 232p. maps. bibliog. (Marxist Regimes Series).
Analyses and describes China's post-1949 development in comparison with other revolutionary régimes, treating Chinese socialism seriously and critically. Chapter topics include: imperial legacy, capitalist failure and socialist triumph; Chinese socialist development, 1949-85; the state and politics; society and socialism; class and gender; political economy; and domestic and foreign policy in the age of modernization.

725 **Power and policy in China.**
Parris H. Chang. University Park, Pennsylvania: Pennsylvania State University, 1978. 2nd ed. Dubuque, Iowa: Kendall Publishing Company, 1990. 3rd ed. with an added chapter. 352p.
A basic study which provides a detailed analysis of the policy-making process and policy disputes at the decision-making level of the Communist Party and central government. The following topics are covered: the 1950s disputes over the agricultural programme and communization in the countryside; the Great Leap Forward and the subsequent retreat; the Socialist Education Campaign and the emerging 'pluralistic' policy-making process; the Cultural Revolution as the Maoist 'last stand', and the downfall of the radicals; and 'de facto de-Maoization'. The third edition adds a section on 'Deng's half-hearted reform' down to 1989.

726 **China's continuous revolution: the post-Liberation epoch, 1949-1981.**
Lowell Dittmer. Berkeley, California; Los Angeles; London: University of California Press, 1987. 320p.
A careful, clearly explained analysis of the political process in the People's Republic, with an emphasis on the interaction of ideology, leadership and politics. Dittmer sees mass movements, steered by charismatic leaders, as the vehicle of continuous revolution which aimed at combining economic development with social revolution. Other standard studies include John Gittings, *China changes face: the road from revolution, 1949-89* (Oxford: Oxford University Press, 1989. 290p.).

727 **The government and politics of the PRC: a time of transition.**
Jürgen Domes. Boulder, Colorado; London: Westview Press, 1985. 316p. bibliog.
Domes has presented the results of his China watching in a series of volumes: *The internal politics of China, 1949-1972* (London: C. Hurst; Berkeley, California: University of California Press, 1976. 283p.); *China after the Cultural Revolution: politics between two party congresses* (London: C. Hurst, 1976; Berkeley, California:

University of California Press, 1977. 283p.); and this volume, which follows the transition from Mao's appointed successor, Hua Guofeng, to Deng Xiaoping and his early reforms. Domes focuses on élite politics, but also supplies the reader with background on history (back to the origins of the Han peoples), geography, economics and society, in order to provide a complete picture. This volume begins with an essay on the methodology of China watching, including the 'Ten Commandments' drawn up by Father Laszlo Ladany (q.v.); he argues that ignoring these rules was the downfall of a number of China watchers.

728   **Chinese intelligence operations.**
Nicholas Eftimiades.   Annapolis, Maryland: Naval Institute Press, 1994. 169p.

A brief depiction, largely based on published sources, of the structure, operations and methodologies of China's intelligence services, mainly overseas operations. Eftimiades describes their origins, bureaucratic structure, goals and cases where Chinese intelligence agents have come to light. He concludes that 'like much of the PRC government, China's intelligence services just do not work – or at least not very well'. Richard Deacon, *The Chinese secret service* (London: Grafton, 1989. rev. ed. 443p.) relates gossipy anecdotes of espionage and intrigue in ancient and modern times. Roger Faligot, Rémi Kauffer, *The Chinese secret service* (London: Headline, 1989; New York: Morrow, 1990. 527p.) focuses on Kang Sheng (Director of Security in the 1930s and 1940s) and secret police operations inside the party and out; their account of this shadowy subject is probably the least unreliable.

729   **From bandwagon to balance-of-power politics: structural constraints and politics in China, 1949-1978.**
Avery Goldstein.   Stanford, California: Stanford University Press, 1991. 366p.

Argues that although the political actors remained basically the same, China from 1949-66 was a hierarchic arena which can be explained by 'bandwagon theory', but that the period of the Cultural Revolution was an anarchic realm best explained by 'balance-of-power' theory. Goldstein begins with a discussion of competing theories, claiming that totalitarian, 'Mao-in-command', or factionalism models illuminate only partially. The body of the book applies the balance-of-power and 'bandwagon' models to the political history to produce structural explanations of actions, administrative consequences and phenomena such as purge politics, agricultural policy and coalition formation.

730   **Organizing China: the problems of bureaucracy, 1949-1976.**
Harry Harding.   Stanford, California: Stanford University Press, 1981. 418p.

A history of debates and experiments in organizational policies for Party and state to the eve of Deng's reforms. Chinese leaders sometimes tried to rationalize the bureaucracy, sometimes tried to replace it with more participatory forms, but always returned to a basic strategy of recruitment on political reliability and control of bureaucracy through indoctrination and rectification. The price was conformity, lack of creativity and low technical and managerial skills. Harding follows the debates and experiments period by period, looking at each political development from this vantage point. *Cadres, bureaucracy and political power in Communist China* by A. Doak

Barnett, with Ezra Vogel (New York: Columbia University Press, 1967. 563p.) is a classic, detailed presentation of the structure and functions of the various bureaucracies before 1966 at the national, county and commune levels, using extensive interviews with former cadres in Hong Kong.

731 **Building a nation-state: China at forty years.**
Edited by Joyce Kallgren. Berkeley, California: Institute of East Asian Studies, University of California, 1990. 205p. (China Research Monographs, no. 37).

Seven essays assess the Chinese state to the late 1980s. Specialists raise issues, relate important developments and suggest further readings in key areas: foreign policy; political development, especially ideology, leadership and politics; political institutions, turning points and transformations; the legacy of Chinese socialism left by Mao, his goals and experience; Party-State versus society, examining changes in how the Chinese live; the intelligentsia, as viewed in literature; and social change and choice on the eve of the 1990s. Another well balanced set of essays is *China at forty: mid-life crisis?*, edited by David S. G. Goodman, Gerald Segal (Oxford: Clarendon Press, Oxford University Press, 1989. 178p.).

732 **The politics of China, 1949-1989.**
Edited by Roderick MacFarquhar. Cambridge, England: Cambridge University Press, 1993. 534p.

Five substantial overview essays provide a detailed and judicious narrative introduction to and analysis of the politics of the People's Republic, with copious notes and references. Four chapters are reprinted from *Cambridge History of China*, vol. 14: 'The Establishment and Consolidation of the New Regime, 1949-57'; 'The Great Leap Forward and the Split in the Yan'an Leadership, 1958-65'; 'The Chinese State in Crisis, 1966-9'; and 'The Succession to Mao and the End of Maoism, 1969-82', with an added fifth chapter, 'The Road to Tiananmen: Chinese Politics in the 1980s'. A series of eight new appendices covers party leaders and meetings. References give a list of sources cited.

733 **The dynamics of Chinese politics.**
Lucian W. Pye. Cambridge, Massachusetts: Oelgeschlager, Gunn & Hain, 1983. 307p. bibliog.

A systematic presentation of the political culture model of politics. Pye believes that a basic contradiction exists between the cultural imperative of conformity/consensus and the perhaps stronger cultural imperative to form particularistic networks of personal relations; his analysis looks at factions, ideology, policy contention and the resulting cyclical rhythm of politics. Topics include the nature of factions, the role of generations, attitudes toward authority (dependence), the symbolic use of issues, the power of words, and how Deng's politics could replace those of Mao. Pye's other works include: *Asian power and politics: the cultural dimensions of authority* (Cambridge, Massachusetts: Harvard University Press, 1985. 414p.); *The spirit of Chinese politics: a psychocultural study of authority crisis in political development* (Cambridge, Massachusetts: M. I. T. Press, 1968. 255p.); and *The mandarin and the cadre* (Ann Arbor, Michigan: University of Michigan Center for Chinese Studies, 1988. 204p.).

734 **The new emperors: China in the era of Mao and Deng.**
Harrison Salisbury.   Boston, Massachusetts: Little, Brown, 1992.
544p. maps.
Salisbury, a long-time overseas New York *Times* correspondent, used his contacts to gather inside views of Mao, Zhou Enlai and Deng Xiaoping, and many other actors in key situations. The gossipy, personalized view of politics presented in this energetic volume corresponds to one held by many Chinese, and provides an attractive narrative of politics and personalities during the period 1949-89.

735 **Ideology and organization in communist China.**
Franz Schurman.   Berkeley, California; Los Angeles: University of California Press, 1968. expanded ed. 642p.
An important discussion of Mao's organizational approach, which was long considered the basic analysis of how the Communist Party used a 'consistent yet changing ideology' to create a web of organization which covered and penetrated all of Chinese society. Chapter one, 'Ideology', distinguishes pure from practical ideology and outlines Mao's 'dialectical conception' of Chinese society. Following chapters apply these concepts to: party; government; management of factories and bureaucracy; control systems, economic and political control and purges; cities; and villages, from traditional China to the Great Leap Forward. Schurman argues that inherited Chinese modes were replaced in the early 1950s by Soviet-style, centralized bureaucracy and factory management; the Great Leap Forward then attacked Soviet styles but developed a dialectical synthesis. The second edition appends a section on the early Cultural Revolution and the military.

736 **The reach of the state: sketches of the Chinese body politic.**
Vivienne Shue.   Stanford, California: Stanford University Press, 1988. 175p.
Contains four conceptual, critical, experimental essays on how to think about Chinese state, society and politics. 'State, Society, and Politics under Mao' reviews recent studies in order to question the totalitarian model in understanding Maoist China. In 'Peasant Localism and the Chinese State: A Center-Periphery Approach to the Evolution of State Socialism Under Mao', 'The Reach of the State: A Comparative Historical Approach to the "Modernization" of Local Government in China', and 'Honeycomb and Web: The Process of Change in Rural China', Shue argues that the Maoist political system did not, contrary to widespread assertion, exert full control in the countryside, and in fact often evoked subtle but powerful resistance; however, the reforms of the 1980s may enhance state authority in the countryside.

737 **Canton under Communism: programs and politics in a provincial capital, 1949-1968.**
Ezra F. Vogel.   Cambridge, Massachusetts: Harvard University Press, 1969. 448p. (Harvard East Asian Series, no. 41).
A narrative analysis of the political conquest of society in the city of Guangzhou and the countryside of surrounding Guangdong province. After introductory sections on the decay of the imperial order, the rise of Communism, and Guangdong before Communism, Vogel constructs a detailed account and analysis of successive campaigns, from attempts to establish local urban control in 1949 to the first stage of

the Cultural Revolution in 1968. A main theme is the tense interaction between Beijing policy-makers and provincial administrators, particularly the old-time revolutionary Tao Zhu.

The People's Republic of China, 1949-1979: a documentary survey.
See item no. 308.

Party-military relations in the PRC and Taiwan: paradoxes of control.
See item no. 856.

China builds the bomb.
See item no. 860.

China's strategic seapower: the politics of force modernization in the nuclear age.
See item no. 861.

Political developments (1949-65)

738 **Bureaucracy, economy, and leadership in China: the institutional origins of the Great Leap Forward.**
David Bachman. Cambridge, England; New York; Port Chester, New York; Melbourne; Sydney: Cambridge University Press, 1991. 262p.

A detailed and theoretically oriented study of the policy-making process of the mid-1950s. Bachman argues that the disastrous Great Leap Forward did not issue from Mao's fevered ideological brow, as has been widely assumed, but from a bureaucratic power struggle in which Chen Yun and Li Xiannian of the Ministry of Finance vied with the Ministry of Industry, led by Li Fuchun and Bo Yibo. Top leaders were constricted by the options presented to them, particularly when planners pushed policies of national self reliance, industrial aid to agriculture, decentralization and building medium- and small-scale factories. Bachman's 'new institutionalism' perspective is criticized for belittling individual choice but praised for analysing the structure of decision making.

739 **The origins of the Great Leap Forward: the case of one Chinese province.**
Jean Luc Domenac, translated by A. M. Berrett. Armonk, New York; London: M. E. Sharpe, 1995. 212p. map. bibliog. (Transitions: Asia & Asian America).

The province of Henan in Central China was a testing ground and national model for the Great Leap Forward. Domenac uses local materials to generate an understanding of the general phenomenon, especially the interplay of central policy, provincial politics, and local response and initiative. Opening sections describe the early 1950s as a possible period of reason, but one which came to economic and social straits in 1956-57. The ensuing political crisis of the spring and summer of 1957 spawned a rectification campaign, which is analysed here as a 'political error'. Further sections detail the emergence of 'Henan radicalism', which brought both great achievements and disaster in 1958.

Politics and Government. The People's Republic (1949-). The Great Proletarian
Cultural Revolution (1965-76)

740   The origins of the Cultural Revolution.
       Roderick MacFarquhar.   London: Oxford University Press; New
       York: Columbia University Press, 1974, 1983. 2 vols.
These two richly detailed and often dramatically narrated volumes (a third volume is
projected) help to explain the Cultural Revolution by analysing its roots in the decade
preceding it. Volume one, *Contradictions among the people, 1956-1957*, explains the
unravelling of the period of relative harmony following the initial unification, the
Hundred Flowers Movement, and the ensuing anti-Rightist campaigns. Volume two,
The Great Leap Forward 1958-1960, recounts the origins and disastrous consequences
of the movements to organize communes, increase factory production, and achieve
socialism in one fell swoop.

741   Politics and purges in China: rectification and the decline of party
       norms, 1950-1965.
       Frederick C. Teiwes.   Armonk, New York; London: M. E. Sharpe,
       1993. 2nd ed. 593p.
Teiwes first analyses the rectification campaigns and high level élite purges from 1949
up to the start of the Cultural Revolution, then provides a broader examination of the
decline of norms which had shaped the inner life of the Chinese Communist Party
during its rise to power. Finally Teiwes presents an overall reinterpretation of pre-
1966 politics which challenges the widespread 'two-line' struggle theory in favour of
a 'dominant Mao interpretation'. Teiwes developed this approach in his *Politics at the
court of Mao: Gao Gang and party factionalism in the early 1950s* (Armonk, New
York; London: M. E. Sharpe, 1990. 326p.).

The Great Proletarian Cultural Revolution (1965-76)

742   China in ferment: perspectives on the Cultural Revolution.
       Edited by Richard Baum, with Louise B. Bennet.   Englewood Cliffs,
       New Jersey: Prentice-Hall, 1971. 246p. bibliog.
A basic compilation of published articles and documents presenting a range of views,
on the assumption that the Cultural Revolution had played out by 1969. Included are
Lin Biao's Report to the 9th Party Congress and contending scholarly essays. Thomas
W. Robinson, editor, *The Cultural Revolution in China* (Berkeley, California; Los
Angeles; London: University of California Press, 1971. 509p.) comprises five
scholarly essays whose topics include: power, policy and ideology in the making of
the Cultural Revolution; Maoist theories of policy making and organization; Zhou
Enlai's role; foreign affairs and the Foreign Ministry; and the Cultural Revolution in
the countryside, the anatomy of limited rebellion.

743   Up to the mountains and down to the villages: the transfer of youth
       from urban to rural China.
       Thomas Bernstein.   New Haven, Connecticut: Yale University Press,
       1977. 371p.
Between 1968 and 1975, some twelve million urban 'intellectual youth' (*zhiqing*) –
secondary school graduates – were sent 'up to the mountains and down to the villages'
(*shangshan xiaxiang*). The announced aims were to give them revolutionary

experience, to close the rural-urban gap by developing backward areas, to relieve
overpopulated cities and probably to scatter restive youth. Bernstein reviews goals and
politics, describes the organization, appeals and pressures of the mobilization
campaigns and explains the problems and realities of adapting to rural life (locals did
not welcome unskilled, hungry strangers). He also evaluates their contributions, and
considers the stability of the settlement and possibilities of youth returning home. A
final chapter asks if this was a model for the Third World. Peter J. Seybolt, editor, *The
rustication of urban youth in China: a social experiment* (Armonk, New York;
London: M. E. Sharpe, 1977. 200p.) translates articles from a Chinese investigation
and evaluation of the movement.

744   **Liu Shao-ch'i and the Chinese Cultural Revolution: the politics of
mass criticism.**
Lowell Dittmer.   Berkeley, California: University of California Press,
1974. 386p.

A political biography of Liu Shaoqi (1898-1969), an organizer in the Chinese
Communist Party from the 1920s. He was named Mao's 'close comrade in arms and
successor' after the failure of the Great Leap Forward, attacked at the start of the
Cultural Revolution as 'China's Khrushchev' and a 'capitalist roader', and eventually
left to die of untreated pneumonia on the floor of his unheated jail cell. Radicals
claimed that Liu's 'bourgeois reactionary line' opposed Mao's 'proletarian
revolutionary line'. Dittmer first describes 'Liu's China and China's Liu' from the
1920s to the 1960s; he shows how this history shaped Liu's attempt to 'combine order
with revolution and equality with economic efficiency and technocratic values'. Liu's
vision of socialist modernization did diverge from Mao's, but Dittmer recounts
Cultural Revolution struggles to show that the allegations of a 'two line struggle' were
largely polemical.

745   **Rebellion and factionalism in a Chinese province: Zhejiang,
1966-1976.**
Keith Forster.   Armonk, New York; London: M. E. Sharpe, 1990.
338p. (Studies on Contemporary China).

A detailed political study of the bitter, sometimes violent, political struggles in
Zhejiang, especially its capital, Hangzhou. Forster, who taught in Hangzhou shortly
after, finds that these struggles were unusually closely tied to factional divisions in
Beijing and lasted for a full ten years, long after other provinces had become
exhausted or reconciled.

746   **Shanghai journal: an eyewitness account of the Cultural
Revolution.**
Neale Hunter.   New York: Praeger, 1969; Boston, Massachusetts:
Beacon Press, 1971. 311p.

Hunter and his wife taught in Shanghai from 1965-67, when the city was the centre of
radical politics and Red Guard activity. He begins with the observation that 'Great
Proletarian Cultural Revolution' would better be translated as 'full-scale revolution to
establish working class culture'. His lively narrative is well-informed and sympathetic
to the original anti-bureaucratic and populist impulses of Mao and the Red Guards, but
confirms the existence of excesses and factional wars. Other ground-level accounts
include: Victor Nee, *The Cultural Revolution at Peking University* (New York:

Politics and Government. The People's Republic (1949-). The Great Proletarian Cultural Revolution (1965-76)

Monthly Review, 1969. 91p.); William Hinton, *Hundred day war: the Cultural Revolution at Tsinghua University* (New York: Monthly Review Press, 1972. 288p.); and David and Nancy Milton, *The wind will not subside: years in revolutionary China, 1964-1969* (New York: Pantheon, 1976. 397p.).

747   **The critique of ultra-leftism in China, 1958-1981.**
William A. Joseph.   Stanford, California: Stanford University Press, 1984. 312p.

The Cultural Revolution polarized the 'revolutionary line' of the Maoists and 'revisionism'; radical charges against the revisionists as modernizers and capitalists are widely known, but critiques of ultra-Leftism are less so. This lucid study redresses the balance by presenting the ideas and values resisting the Great Leap Forward, the Cultural Revolution, and the Gang of Four; the focus is not on ultra-Leftism as such, but on the evolving accusations that it betrayed Marxism-Leninism and weakened Chinese socialism, on the role of Mao, and on the politics of the critique. Joseph shows that ultra-Leftism drew from Mao's emphasis on relations of production, class struggle, continuous revolution and the contradiction between theory and practice. Political thinkers associated with Liu Shaoqi, Zhou Enlai, Deng Xiaoping and sometimes Mao, criticized it for perverting Mao's thought with petty-bourgeois dogmatism, subjectivism and sectarianism.

748   **New perspectives on the Cultural Revolution.**
Edited by William Joseph, Christine W. Wong, David Zweig. Cambridge, Massachusetts: Council on East Asian Studies, Harvard University, distributed by Harvard University Press, 1991. 351p. bibliog. (Harvard Contemporary China Series, no. 8).

A dozen articles take advantage of copious new information from China, recent scholarship and the literature in comparative socialism (all amply referenced) to reassess the politics, economics and culture of the 1966-76 decade. Authors find that the real but fearfully exaggerated threats from the Soviets in the North and Americans in the south led Mao to launch the ultimately disastrous Great Proletarian Cultural Revolution (GPCR). Mao's strategy in so doing was to destroy internal enemies and promote a 'Third Front' to decentralize and evacuate industry to inaccessible regions. Chapters deal with: individuals, areas and policies; the GPCR in post-Mao politics; GPCR radicalism as a variation on a Stalinist theme; agrarian radicalism; the unintended results of administrative policies; the Maoist model and political economy as 'neither plan nor market'; arts policies and model operas; and industrial policy.

749   **The Lin Piao Affair: power politics and military coup.**
Edited by Michael Y. M. Kau.   White Plains, New York: International Arts and Sciences Press, 1975. 591p.

In 1969 Lin Biao (1907-71) was officially proclaimed 'Comrade Mao Zedong's close comrade in arms and successor'; however, in 1971 he fled China and is presumed to have died in a fiery plane crash. Subsequently he was officially accused of plotting a military coup and Mao's assassination. The seventy-three official documents translated here show Lin's background, rise and destruction, and are accompanied by a substantial interpretive introduction. Part five is devoted to an extensive selection of Lin's own writings, including the famous 1965 'Long Live the Victory of People's War!' and speeches and talks expounding the radical line of the Cultural Revolution.

Beijing partisan gossip fuels Yao Ming-le's novel, *The conspiracy and death of Lin
Biao* (New York: Knopf, 1983; published also as *The conspiracy and murder of Mao's
heir* [London: Collins, 1983]).

750   **The politics of the Chinese Cultural Revolution: a case study.**
Hong Yung Lee.   Berkeley, California; Los Angeles; London:
University of California Press, 1978. 369p.

A basic political analysis of the Cultural Revolution during the period 1965-68. Lee
argues that the Cultural Revolution can be best described as 'Mao's attempt to resolve
the basic contradictions between the egalitarian view of Marxism and élitist
tendencies of Leninist organizational principles', that is, a struggle between radicals
with a mass following drawn from underprivileged groups, and conservatives, largely
in power, who developed mass followings of their own. Chapters trace: the
development from a politics of bureaucracy (October 1965-August 1966); the politics
of mass manipulation (August-December 1966); the politics of the masses (January-
August 1967); and the politics of factionalism (after September 1967). Byung-joon
Ahn, *Chinese politics and the Cultural Revolution: dynamics of policy processes*
(Seattle, Washington; London: University of Washington Press, 1976. 392p.)
comprises the most thorough structural analysis of the years which generated the
Cultural Revolution.

751   **Red guard factionalism and the Cultural Revolution in Guangzhou
(Canton).**
Stanley Rosen.   Boulder, Colorado: Westview Press, 1982. 320p.

Rosen innovatively explains the savage factionalism among Red Guards of mid-1960s
Guangzhou not by alleged ideological differences derived from élite factions in
Beijing, but by cleavages generated locally when middle schools became instruments
to determine university entrance and lifetime job assignments. Part one describes pre-
Cultural Revolution classrooms and school systems. Part two portrays the 'rebels',
who tended to have 'bad' class backgrounds to overcome, and 'conservatives', who
tended to spring from cadre and military families vulnerable to ideological attack.
Middle school students were the fiercest contenders; advancement to university was
already denied to 'sent-down youth' and already gained by university students (whose
motivations Rosen finds more ideological). In addition to class origin, patterns varied
according to geographical origin and whether one attended a top, next-best, middle
grade or neighbourhood school.

752   **The Cultural Revolution and post-Mao reforms: a historical
perspective.**
Edited by Tang Tsou.   Chicago; London: University of Chicago Press,
1986. 351p.

Brings together eight essays by a leading scholar on the Chinese Communist
movement written over the previous eighteen years. Tsou's introduction concerns
methodology and frames of analysis, with reflections on the state of knowledge in the
field. The essays, all from the point of view of a political scientist with deep historical
knowledge, include an analysis of: the Cultural Revolution and the Chinese political
system; informal groups in Communist Party politics; Mao Zedong thought and the
struggle for succession; the responsibility system in agriculture; and reflections on the
formation and foundation of the party-state. Professor Tsou's students pay tribute in

Contemporary Chinese politics in historical perspective, edited by Brantly Womack (New York: Cambridge University Press, 1991. 334p.); essays, with Professor Tsou's comments in reply, focus on the situation of China after 1989, including the search for democracy, industrial reform, an analysis of competition among political élites, and the roles of ideology.

753 **Policies of chaos: the organizational causes of violence in China's Cultural Revolution.**
Lynn T. Whyte, III. Princeton, New Jersey: Princeton University Press, 1989. 344p.

Explains the massive and ubiquitous violence of the Cultural Revolution, not in terms of general culture or historical conjunctures, but in terms of organization and ideology. Whyte holds that the work unit (*danwei*) locked people into permanent groups; that the system of class labels established permanent 'castes' and 'enemies' who were allowed no humanity; and that the established succession of campaigns (*yundong*) meant that conflict came to be anticipated. Violence as a means of public humiliation of class enemies inured people to suffering by making it seem needed and even progressive, and rewarded participants through peer pressure and group responsibility.

Born red: a chronicle of the Cultural Revolution.
See item no. 389.

Son of the revolution.
See item no. 391.

The man who stayed behind.
See item no. 407.

Children of Mao: personality development and political activism in the Red Guard generation.
See item no. 661.

The politics of medicine in China: the policy process, 1949-1977.
See item no. 679.

Understanding Communist China: Communist China studies in the United States and the Republic of China, 1949-1978.
See item no. 1491.

Deng's reforms (1976-89)

754 **Reform and reaction in post-Mao China: the road to Tiananmen.**
Edited by Richard Baum. New York; London: Routledge, Chapman & Hall, 1991. 209p.

Scholars examine the decade of the 1980s as 'the anatomy of incomplete reform', and analyse what went wrong with 'gentle revolution' in China. Essays take various views and focus on: socialist reform and Sino-Soviet convergence; economic reform, social mobilization and democratization; the rise (and fall) of public opinion; urban private businesses; urban reform and the transition from plan to market; market reform and disintegrative corruption in urban and rural China; and permanent technological revolution and democratizing Leninism. The editor contributes a substantial introduction and epilogue. Another effective symposium is *State and society in China: the consequences of reform*, edited by Arthur Lewis Rosenbaum (Boulder, Colorado; San Francisco; Oxford: Westview Press, 1992. 240p.).

755 **Burying Mao: Chinese politics in the age of Deng Xiaoping.**
Richard Baum. Princeton, New Jersey: Princeton University Press, 1994. 489p.

Recounts the 'vicissitudes of China's recent political history through the prismatic lens of élite conflict', covering the period 1975-93. Baum focuses on 'key political actors, ideological issues, factional controversies, and events in the center of the Chinese political system', rather than the institutional mechanics of policy making, bureaucratic bargaining or policy implementation. Baum sees some half-dozen cycles of reform in which liberal 'letting go' (*fang*) alternated with conservative 'tightening up' (*shou*), eventually arriving at a marketized Marxism which was far from Mao's revolutionary vision. Deng, who both sponsored market reforms and repressed the 1989 Democracy Movement, emerges as a manipulator presiding over intergenerational and factional battles of older orthodox revolutionaries against younger and more innovative Marxists.

756 **Verdict in Peking: the trial of the Gang of Four.**
David Bonavia. New York: Putnam; London: Burnett Books, 1984. 219p.

Bonavia uses testimony given at the trial of the Gang of Four to reconstruct the machinations of Jiang Qing, Yao Wenyuan, Wang Hongwen, Zhang Junchiao and Chen Boda in propaganda and myth-making, performing arts and persecution of intellectuals. He also looks at Hua Guofeng and Zhou Enlai's personality cults and Lin Biao's plot to kill Mao. The official version is *A great trial in Chinese history: the trial of the Lin Biao and Jiang Qing counter-revolutionary cliques* (Beijing: New World Press; Elmsford, New York: Pergamon Press, 1981. 234p.).

757 **Chinese Marxism in the post-Mao era.**
Bill Brugger, David Kelly. Stanford, California: Stanford University Press, 1990. 223p.

Argues that Marxist thinkers in China of the late 1970s and early 1980s developed concepts of 'Marxism without Leninism' and possibly 'Marxism without Marx', but were tragically ignored by political leaders intent on economic development; the 1989 massacres resulted from government failure to develop sources of legitimacy. Brugger and Kelly sympathetically present and critique the debates surrounding the Marxist humanists Su Shaozhi and Wang Ruoshui and the non-Marxist dissident Fang Lizhi. *The philosophical thought of Mao Zedong: studies from China, 1981-1989*, edited by Nick Knight (Armonk, New York; London: M. E. Sharpe, a special issue of *Chinese Studies in Philosophy*, vol. 23, nos. 3-4 [Spring-Summer 1992], 288p.) selects and provides a substantial introduction for essays exploring aspects of Mao's philosophy and its practical application in the 1980s, including Su Shaozhi's overview, 'The Study of Mao Zedong Thought in Contemporary China'. *Marxism and the Chinese experience: issues in contemporary Chinese socialism*, edited by Arif Dirlik, Maurice

Meisner (Armonk, New York: M. E. Sharpe, 1989. 384p. bibliog. [Political Economy of Socialism]) contains critical essays in the Marxist tradition concerning theory and descriptions, for instance, of workers' movements.

758 **The Chinese Communist Party's nomenklatura system.**
John P. Burns.   Armonk, New York; London: M. E. Sharpe, 1989.
166p. (Chinese Studies On China).
The 'nomenklatura system', adopted from the Soviet Communist Party model, consists of lists of the leading positions over which party units exercise the power to make appointments and dismissals. Burns' extensive introduction explains the history and workings of the system, and how reformers in the 1980s set out to replace it. The system was left intact but Burns shows that central Party control has been substantially undercut by decentralization, local patronage and political dealing. The body of the book provides translations of documents from the 1980s on the process of cadre management, on the responsibilities of central committee departments, and a case-study of nomenklatura in the People's Bank of China.

759 **Policy conflicts in post-Mao China: a documentary survey, with analysis.**
Edited by John P. Burns, Stanley Rosen.   Armonk, New York;
London: M. E. Sharpe, 1986. 372p.
A college anthology, with useful introductions and commentaries, of primary sources concerning issues discussed by reformist public opinion, giving useful insight into the nature of the sources. Documents include newspaper articles, letters to the editor, and cartoons. Issues include political socialization, participation, industry, agriculture, education, corruption, bureaucratism, and the role of intellectuals. The editors begin with an essay on the nature, location and traits of sources; they also give a chronology of political events during the period 1976-85, further readings, charts of organizations and definitions of key terms.

760 **China under reform.**
Lowell Dittmer.   Boulder, Colorado; San Francisco; Oxford:
Westview Press, 1994. 228p. (Politics in Asia and the Pacific:
Interdisciplinary Perspectives).
A well-organized overview of the political consequences of economic reform. Dittmer argues that the third generation leadership after Deng will have to either reshape its ideology and political strategy or risk squandering a sterling economic performance. Chapters first rehearse development from revolution to reform and the lineage of reform socialism, then describe in detail and analyse political leadership and succession in the 1990s.

761 **Dilemmas of reform in China: political conflict and economic debate.**
Joseph Fewsmith.   Armonk, New York; London: M. E. Sharpe, 1994.
289p. (Socialism and Social Movements).
This detailed analytical narrative traces the politics of China's economic reforms from the late 1970s, especially rural reform and enterprise reform. Conflicts emerged when young economists pressured for comprehensive reform and conservatives criticized them, leading to fissures among reformers. The reform leader Zhao Ziyang tried to

outmanoeuvre conservative resistance, leading to the collapse of the reform process, 1988-89. Fewsmith is attentive throughout to power conflicts among the leaders, but also emphasizes the genuine disagreements on economic policy and social doctrine.

762 **China in the era of Deng Xiaoping: a decade of reform.**
Edited by Michael Ying-mao Kau, Susan H. Marsh. Armonk, New York; London: M. E. Sharpe, 1993. 506p. bibliog. (Studies on Contemporary China).

Brings together sixteen papers which were prepared for a 1987 conference at Brown University, many of which were revised after 1989. Part one covers: the theory and practice of reform socialism under Deng; political and administrative reforms, 1982-86; institutionalizing a new legal system; recasting the economic system in agriculture and industry; foreign trade, capital inflow and technology transfer; performance and trends in economic growth; educational reform; intellectuals in the Deng era; reorganizing and modernizing the military; China's search for a security strategy; reorienting China's foreign policy; and Deng's quest for 'modernization with Chinese characteristics' and the future of Marxism-Leninism. Each is followed by expert comments. Part two includes public addresses by diplomats from the United States, China, Japan and Russia.

763 **Policy implementation in post-Mao China.**
David M. Lampton. Berkeley, California; Los Angeles; London: University of California Press, 1987. 439p.

Revised papers from a 1983 conference present early but still cogent analyses. The editor's introduction analyses the disparity between the intentions of Deng's reform leadership, organizational behaviour, and actual results. Chapters then examine the general contents of reform programmes, institutional structures and sociopolitical context. Sections discuss the following topics: economic policy (control over investment, politics of price control, tax policy); resource policy (water management, energy policy, tree planting); rural policies, including one-child-per-couple policies; and education and science, including the restoration of the policy of designating key secondary schools which had been rejected during the Cultural Revolution.

764 **From revolutionary cadres to party technocrats in socialist China.**
Hong Yung Lee. Berkeley, California; Los Angeles; Oxford: University of California Press, 1991. 437p.

An analysis of changes in party ruling élites, their make-up and social origins, their factional groupings and the cadre system which organizes them. Lee uses an extensive database to explore the reasons why these élites persevered when Soviet and East European élites disintegrated, the nature of personnel conflict in the Cultural Revolution and during post-Mao reforms, and the rise of technocratic élites to supplant cadres from earlier generations. The restructuring of the Chinese Communist Party as part of the reforms is analysed in Ch'i Hsi-sheng, *Politics of disillusionment: the Chinese Communist Party under Deng Xiaoping, 1978-1989* (Armonk, New York; London: M. E. Sharpe, 1991. 328p. bibliog. [Studies on Contemporary China]), which concludes that the introduction of new faces did not substantially change the quality or functioning of personnel. Melanie Manion, *Retirement of revolutionaries in China: public policies, social norms, private interests* (Princeton, New Jersey: Princeton University Press, 1993. 196p.) elegantly describes the tortuous process of creating new social and political norms, using the example of personnel policy.

765 **Bureaucracy, politics, and decision making in post-Mao China.**
Edited by Kenneth Lieberthal, David M. Lampton. Berkeley,
California; Los Angeles: University of California Press, 1992. 379p.
(Studies on China, no. 14).

Eleven rich papers from a 1988 conference look at the key bureaucratic decision-making level, sandwiched between top leaders and the localities. The introduction categorizes these bureaucracies into six core clusters – economic, propaganda and education, organization and personnel, civilian coercive, military, and Party territorial – and sketches a 'fragmented authoritarianism' model in relation to other models. Part one, 'National Issues', contains two essays, on bureaucratic politics and on the political strategy of economic reform. Part two, 'The Center', analyses the party leadership system and information flows. Part three, 'Bureaucratic Clusters', provides essays on the military system, educational policy process, the cadre retirement process, and relations with private enterprises. In part four, 'Subnational Levels', essays analyse provinces as competitors for power, urban industrial finance, and urbanization in rural China.

766 **Policy making in China: leaders, structures, politics, and processes.**
Kenneth Lieberthal, Michel Oksenberg. Princeton, New Jersey:
Princeton University Press, 1988. 445p. bibliog.

An influential, basic study aimed at policy-makers, businessmen and political scientists. The authors interviewed Chinese participants and American, European and Japanese observers, used extensive documentary sources, and deployed comparative political science models to present actual policy-making processes not found in formal descriptions. Chapters one to four survey the Western literature on Chinese policy process, introduce the bureaucratic structure, outline the commissions and ministries of the central government, and note the salient characteristics of the structure of power (fragmented structure of authority, integrative mechanisms, behavioural consequences). Chapters five to seven provide detailed cases-studies: the development of the petroleum industry from national autonomy to multinational partnership, 1959-84; the Three Gorges Dam Project; and energy development. Chapter eight, 'Some Implications for Comparative Communist Studies', also speculates about the evolution of the bureaucratic structure and its capacity for reform. *Decision-making in Deng's China*, edited by Carol Lee Hamrin, Suisheng Zhao (Armonk, New York; London: M. E. Sharpe, 1995. 255p. [Studies in Contemporary China]) contains eighteen essays by former Chinese government officials and policy intellectuals; they describe the leadership and executive systems, bureaucratic structure and experiments in system reform.

767 **Political reform in post-Mao China: democracy and bureaucracy in a Leninist state.**
Barrett L. McCormick. Berkeley, California; Los Angeles; London:
University of California Press, 1990. 256p. bibliog.

A lucid exploration of the prospects for democracy and reform in China, based on a description of PRC politics since 1966. McCormick critiques Lenin's theories of the state and uses Max Weber's concept of patrimonial rulership to argue that the post-Mao state rationalization failed to reconcile an alienated society with recalcitrant institutions. Chapter one describes the common anti-state nature of Cultural Revolution incidents – the Shanghai Commune (1967) and the Nanjing Incident

(1976), which presaged later Democracy Movements. Subsequent chapters analyse the contradictory attempts to reconcile party leadership with 'socialist law', elections to local People's Congresses, and Party rectification.

768 **Reform without liberalization: China's National People's Congress and the politics of institutional change.**
Kevin J. O'Brien.   New York; Cambridge, England: Cambridge University Press, 1990. 263p. bibliog.

The National People's Congress (NPC) is designated by the Constitution as the 'highest organ of state power', but has never been effectual. O'Brien first traces parliamentary bodies over the last century, which were discredited by their factionalism and petty bickering; in the Anti-Rightist Campaigns of the mid-1950s the NPC lost its initial role as a forum for presentation and explanation of policy. The bulk of the book focuses on the NPC since 1978, when reformers tried to revitalize the body as a way to promote their legitimacy, rebuild the united front, recruit able talent and stabilize reform. Reforms were 'self-limiting', as the NPC could not discuss forbidden questions and was not even convened during the tumultuous spring of 1989.

769 **From reform to revolution: the demise of communism in China and the Soviet Union.**
Pei Minxin.   Cambridge, Massachusetts; London: Harvard University Press, 1994. 253p.

Among the fullest and most theoretically *au courant* of the many comparative political science studies of régime transition from Communism. Pei compares the development of the private sector and the liberalization of the media in the two régimes, finding that democracy by itself does not reform the economy, and that conversely economic success does not bring democracy. Lively, sophisticated scholarly symposia include: *The crisis of Leninism and the decline of the Left*, edited by Daniel Chirot (Seattle, Washington; London: University of Washington Press, 1991. 245p. [Jackson School Publications in International Studies]); *Remaking the economic institutions of socialism*, edited by Victor Nee, David Stark, with Mark Selden (Stanford, California: Stanford University Press, 1989. 405p.); and *Market reforms in socialist countries: comparing China and Hungary* (Boulder, Colorado: Lynne Reiner, 1989. 322p.).

770 **The political economy of reform in post-Mao China.**
Edited by Elizabeth J. Perry, Christine Wong.   Cambridge, Massachusetts: Council on East Asian Studies, Harvard University, distributed by Harvard University Press, 1985. 331p. (Harvard Contemporary China Series, no. 2).

Brings together ten sound and imaginative essays from a conference on the first years of reform, explaining still significant problems and successes. The editors' introduction summarizes the causes, content and consequences of the reforms. Part one, 'Agriculture', features a key essay on the demise of the commune, 'Socialist Agriculture is Dead; Long Live Socialist Agriculture!' as well as helpful essays on: the economic theory of the restoring of the peasant household as farm production unit; rural marketing and exchange; peasant income; the single-child family; implications for rural cadres; and rural collective violence. Part two, 'Industry', contains essays on the politics of industrial reform, financial reforms, and the impact on local industries of material allocation and decentralization.

771 **Deng Xiaoping, chronicle of an empire.**
Ruan Ming, translated and edited by Nancy Liu, Peter Rand, Lawrence
R. Sullivan, with a foreword by Andrew J. Nathan. Boulder,
Colorado; San Francisco; Oxford: Westview Press, 1994. 288p.

Ruan, a 1980s reform insider, uses his knowledge of key personalities and incidents to tell the story of how Deng accommodated conservative, even Stalinist forces, on the economy, foreign affairs and ideology. The original edition is *Deng Xiaoping: chronique d'un empire, 1978-1990* (Paris: Editions Philippe Picquier, 1992). Ruan details a fiercer political struggle than appears in earlier Western accounts; Deng pragmatically juggled factions not in order to break free from the Maoist past or build economic efficiency, but simply to stay on top; China gained economically but lost a chance to build political regularity and democracy. Another insider analysis, focusing on the ideological clash between the party and intellectuals, is X. L. Ding, *The decline of communism in China, 1977-1989* (Cambridge, England: Cambridge University Press, 1994. 230p.).

772 **The political logic of economic reform.**
Susan Shirk. Berkeley, California; Los Angeles; Oxford: University
of California Press, 1993. 399p.

A wide-ranging interpretation of Chinese politics under Deng. Shirk's model emphasizes institutional politics within the central, provincial and party bureaucracies; a 'selectorate' decides important issues, and potential successors to Deng must 'play to the provinces'. Part one sketches the argument, describes the pre-reform Chinese economy, and analyses how the decision to initiate market reforms was made. Part two, 'Chinese Political Institutions', describes authority relations, leadership incentives (political succession and reciprocal accountability), the government bureaucracy as a bargaining arena, and delegation by consensus. Part three examines in detail how political decisions were made at the various stages of reform: fiscal decentralization; creating vested interests and the take-off of industrial reform, 1978-81; leadership succession and the choice between profit contracting and substituting tax-for-profit, 1982-83; building bureaucratic consensus, 1983-84; and abortive price reform and the revival of profit contracting, 1985-88. The conclusion summarizes the political lessons.

773 **China's transition from socialism: statist legacies and market reforms, 1980-1990.**
Dorothy Solinger. Armonk, New York; London: M. E. Sharpe, 1993.
292p. (The Political Economy of Socialism).

Provides eleven pieces originally published during the 1980s, with a summary introduction and an afterword. Solinger deals with attempts to use market mechanisms to supplement state planning: the urban state economic bureaucracy; restructuring relations between city, province and region; and relations between state cadres and urban entrepreneurs. She holds that 'statism' is behind the reform effort; reform of the economy was not, in itself, a goal. Rather, reform was a contingent means to 'the modernization, invigoration, and enhanced efficiency of the national economy and its consequent heightened capacity to boost both productivity and returns to the central state treasury', as well as to improve the state's capacity to address social needs and ensure social stability. When 'capitalism' emerges in China, it will be distinctive.

774   **One step ahead in China: Guangdong under reform.**
Ezra Vogel, with a contribution by John Kamm.   Cambridge,
Massachusetts: Harvard University Press, 1989. 510p. bibliog.
Continues the narrative started in *Canton under Communism* (q.v.), the story of sixty
million Cantonese in the decade 1978-88, emphasizing the interactions between
economic, social and political transformations. Part one, 'The Winds of Change',
summarizes the experience of Guangdong in the Cultural Revolution and the way in
which nearby Hong Kong shaped the reforms. Part two, 'Patterns of Change', looks at
the Special Economic Zones (SEZs) and varying experiences in the capital, the delta,
the mountain counties and Hainan Island. Part three, 'Agents of Change', covers
entrepreneurs, statesmen, scramblers and 'niche seekers'. Kamm's chapter discusses
'Reforming Foreign Trade'. Part four provides an overview of 'Society in Transition'
and 'take-off' in the Hong Kong-Guangdong region. A selected bibliography lists
major known works on Guangdong since 1949.

The Chinese army after Mao.
See item no. 859.

Chinese business under socialism.
See item no. 945.

Peasant power in China: the era of rural reform, 1979-1989.
See item no. 994.

**State and peasant in contemporary China: the political economy of
village government.**
See item no. 997.

**Beijing street voices: the poetry and politics of China's democracy
movement.**
See item no. 1222.

The crisis of 1989 and after

775   **Black hands of Beijing: lives of defiance in China's democracy
movement.**
George Black, Robin Munro.   New York: Wiley, 1993. 390p.
Presents the personal lives and public careers of three activists accused by the Beijing
government of being the 'black hands' – instigators – behind the 1989 Democracy
Movement. Chen Zeming and Wang Juntao participated in the April 1976
demonstrations at Tiananmen to commemorate the death of Zhou Enlai; they then
became editors of the dissident journal *Beijing Spring* and prominent critics of reform.
Han Dongfang was a leader in organizing the non-government Beijing Workers
Autonomous Federation. Black and Munro use the experience of these individuals to
bring the complexities of the Democracy Movement to life.

776 **Neither gods nor emperors: students and the struggle for democracy in China.**
Craig Calhoun. Berkeley, California; Los Angeles; London: University of California Press, 1994. 333p. maps. bibliog.

Tells the story of the student movement of spring 1989, based on accounts gathered by the author, a comparative social theorist and historian then a visiting professor at Beijing University. Calhoun argues that the democracy movement was not inevitably doomed, and was 'creative, vital, and full of possibilities'. Chapters in part two then analyse: the dynamics and social base of the movement; its role as part and product of China's halting development of a public sphere and civil society; the role of foreign newspapers and television journalism; the nature of China's cultural crisis; the meanings of democracy for the students and for other Chinese; and the students' struggle for personal and collective respect and the sources of their heroism.

777 **Beijing turmoil: more than meets the eye.**
Che Muqi. Beijing: Foreign Languages Press, 1990. 232p.

A virtually official government interpretation and response to international criticism by a senior journalist. Che describes the background and events of spring 1989 in detail, and concludes that the student demonstrations may have started as a patriotic movement but ended up as anti-government turmoil.

778 **Behind the Tiananmen massacre: social, political, and economic ferment in China.**
Chu-yuan Cheng. Boulder, Colorado; San Francisco; Oxford: Westview Press, 1990. 256p.

A full-scale narrative analysis. Chapters topics include: 'from economic reform to social unrest'; ideological schism and power struggle; intellectual challenge and student movements; the military and politics; the making of the massacre; the impact of the bloodshed; and the road from Tiananmen. Appendices provide a chronology, profiles of fifty major figures, and five major documents.

779 **Chinese democracy and the crisis of 1989: Chinese and American reflections.**
Edited by Roger Des Forges, Luo Ning, Wu Yen-bo. Albany, New York: State University of New York Press, 1993. 371p.

Provides sixteen substantial essays, some previously published, with a brief introduction. Part one, 'Historical Perspectives', includes 'The Formation and Characteristics of China's Existing System', by Su Shaozhi, and covers the following topics: democracy in Chinese history; civil society and public sphere in modern Chinese history; political and ideological origins of the crisis; and the social origins and limits of the Democratic Movement. Part two, 'The Rise and Demise of the Movement', 1986-89, comprises essays on: the dilemmas of participation in political reform; economic problems in the industrial sector; student organization; the role of Chinese workers in the movement; and why the army fired on the people. Part three, 'Culture, Values, and the Media', includes essays on: 'The River Elegy' (*Heshang*); the performance of the Chinese media during the spring of 1989; 'professionalism' in China's press corps; and some reasons why Party propaganda failed on this occasion.

780 **National identity and democratic prospects in socialist China.**
Edward Friedman. Armonk, New York; London: M. E. Sharpe, 1995.
359p. bibliog.

Argues that creative politics could lead China on a political path of democracy and that deep historic structures do not preclude China from democratic possibility. Essays in part two, 'National Identity Crisis', explore: whether nationalist identities can hold China together as one nation; a 'failed Chinese modernity'; the split between Mao's 'Northern project', which emphasizes patriarchy and control, and a Southern style of openness and reform; and whether the present 'dictatorial, overly centralized régime' can find a substitute for Mao's once effective ideology of 'militarized, anti-imperialist self-reliance'. Part three, 'After Socialist Anti-Imperialism', discusses: foreign policy; Confucian Leninism and patriarchal authoritarianism; and 'was Mao Zedong a Revolutionary?' Part four focuses on the problem of defining Chinese democracy and charting its prospects in Leninist states.

781 **China deconstructs: politics, trade, and regionalism.**
Edited by David S. G. Goodman, Gerald Segal. London; New York:
Routledge, 1994. 364p. maps. bibliog.

Scholars and journalists examine how the decentralization of economic decision making and increasing foreign trade affect the relationship between the central government and the regions. The general conclusion is that regions are growing in power, that Beijing must now negotiate with the regions, but that the centre retains influence. Two opening essays set the stage and warn that China has gone through many periods of decentralization in the past without disintegrating – reports of China's 'death' are greatly exaggerated. Individual chapters then focus on: the role of the provinces in foreign trade; Guangdong and the greater Hong Kong region; Fujian; Shanghai and the lower Yangzi; North China and Russia; Xinjiang; and Yunnan. The emphasis is on economics and politics, but questions of national cultural identity also arise.

782 **The broken mirror: China after Tiananmen.**
Edited by George Hicks. Chicago; London: St. James Press,
Longman Group, 1990. 526p.

The events of June 1989 'broke the mirror that the West always held up to itself when it thought it was looking at China'. Twenty-five committed scholars and friends of China try to 'seek relief from the sense of anger, impotence, and frustration caused by the massacre'. Their polemical, well-informed essays reject the optimism of the 1980s, doubt the achievements of reform, and condemn as 'illusion' the idea that Deng's reforms would lead to a democratic political system. They treat economic, political, diplomatic and social questions, with appendices on 'A Chronology of Selected Documents and Statements' and 'Who was Who During Beijing Spring'.

783 **China wakes: the struggle for the soul of a rising power.**
Nicholas D. Kristof, Sheryl WuDunn. New York: Times Books,
1994. 501p. maps.

Two reporters for the New York *Times* provide impressions and vignettes from their stay in China; the book opens with a powerful description of the spring of 1989. Kristof and WuDunn, husband and wife, present alternating chapters and sometimes differing views on issues from the status of women to village life under the reforms.

China emerges as a country torn between Deng's successful economic strategy and frustrated political reform and human rights. A chapter describes the establishment of China as a rising military force on the international scene.

784 **China after Deng Xiaoping: the power struggle in Beijing since Tiananmen.**
Willy Wo-lap Lam. Singapore; New York; Chichester, England; Brisbane, Australia; Toronto: Wiley, 1995. 497p. bibliog.

Draws together Lam's detailed political coverage as chief China-watcher for Hong Kong's *South China Morning Post*. Basing his work on a careful reading of official sources, extensive interviewing and travel, and meticulous sifting of gossip and rumours, Lam assesses the role of personality, factional rivalry, and the clash of ideology and economic interest. Chapters cover: Deng's legacy and contributions; economic reform, the 'quasi-capitalist road', and rules of the game in the socialist market economy; the residual influences of the Maoists; the expanding role of the People's Liberation Army; political reform and the future of the Party; post-Deng leadership; the tension between Beijing and the regions; and the rise of private entrepreneurs.

785 **China's crisis: dilemmas of reform and prospects for democracy.**
Andrew J. Nathan. New York: Columbia University Press, 1990. 242p. (Studies of the East Asian Institute).

Provides ten previously published essays, with a new introduction, 'Setting the Scene: Confessions of a China Specialist'. Part one includes Nathan's influential and controversial essay, 'A Factionalism Model for CCP Politics', originally published in an abridged form in *China Quarterly*, no. 53 (January-March 1973). Parts two to four are devoted to: 'American Views of China'; 'The Crisis of Reform', on paradoxes of reform at the late 1980s crossroads; 'Political Change in Taiwan'; and 'Prospects for Chinese Democracy', considering whether the events of 1989 represented another in a series of failures or conceivably the beginning of success.

786 **China's search for democracy: the student and mass movement of 1989.**
Edited by Suzanne Ogden, Kathleen Hartford, Lawrence Sullivan, David Zweig. Armonk, New York; London: M. E. Sharpe, 1992. 451p.

A documentary history of the 1989 popular movements, with more than 200 handbills, wall posters, songs, poems, speeches, newspaper articles and radio broadcasts, with substantial commentaries. There are six sections, each with an explanatory essay by one of the editors: part one, 'Summer 1988-Spring 1989', provides views from the reform debates; part two, 'April 15-April 27: The Movement Begins'; part three, 'April 28-May 12: The Conflict Escalates as the Students Defend Their Patriotism'; part four, 'May 12-May 19: The Hunger Strike: From Protest to Uprising'; part five, 'Sliding Toward Tragedy: Martial Law'; and part six, 'The Beijing Massacre and its Aftermath'. Official documents and leadership points of view are collected in a companion volume: *Beijing Spring 1989: confrontation and conflict: the basic documents*, edited by Michel Oksenberg, Lawrence R. Sullivan, Marc Lambert (Armonk, New York; London: M. E. Sharpe, 1990. 403p.).

787 **The Chinese people's movement: perspectives on spring 1989.**
Edited by Tony Saich. Armonk, New York; London: M. E. Sharpe,
1990. 207p. bibliog.

A compilation of seven essays, with an appendix, 'Chronology of the 1989 Student
Movement', and a bibliographical note on sources and publications in Chinese and
Western languages. Two essays present analytical narratives: 'Student protests and the
Chinese tradition, 1919-1989'; and 'When Worlds Collide: The Beijing People's
Movement of 1989'. 'The Political Economy Behind Beijing Spring' is a
sophisticated, lucid analysis of the economic tensions and political consequences
produced by post-Mao reforms. 'Learning How to Protest' and 'Petitioners,
Popperians, and Hunger Strikers: The Uncoordinated Efforts of the 1989 Chinese
Democratic Movement' analyse the experience of the 'bystander' and of contending
factions within the movement. 'The Emergence of Civil Society in China, Spring
1989' argues that an historical corner was turned. 'The Changing Role of the Chinese
Media' constitutes an excellent brief overview of Chinese journalism in the 1980s.

788 **Mandate of Heaven: a new generation of entrepreneurs, dissidents,
bohemians, and technocrats lays claim to China's future.**
Orville Schell. New York; London; Toronto; Sydney; Tokyo;
Singapore: Simon & Schuster, 1994. 464p.

The political crackdown of 1989 was followed by an economic boom and cultural
resurgence in the non-government sector. Schell conveys in sharp vignettes how local
leaders turn a blind eye to a 'gray' cultural area of pop entrepreneurs in publishing,
film, rock music, nightlife and small business. The emerging middle class concentrates
on getting rich, rather than on politics, but could rival a post-Deng government for
control of society. Schell has provided an ongoing narrative in other readable and
well-informed reports: *In the People's Republic* (New York: Random House, 1977.
269p.), a sympathetic first-hand account of working on the Dazhai commune and in a
factory; *Watch out for the foreign guests: China encounters the West* (New York:
Pantheon Books, 1980. 178p.); *To get rich is glorious: China in the 1980s* (New York:
Pantheon Books, 1984. 210p.); and *Discos and democracy: China in the throes of
reform* (New York: Pantheon Books, 1988. 384p.), which describes new
commercialism, loyal democratic reformers (Fang Lizhi, Liu Binyan, Wang
Ruowang), the student Democracy movement of 1986, and the subsequent crackdown.

789 **Tiananmen square.**
Scott Simmie, Bob Nixon. Vancouver, Canada: Douglas & McIntyre;
Seattle, Washington: University of Washington Press, 1989. 212p.
maps.

Two experienced journalists have gathered careful, compelling, largely first-hand
stories of the fifty days of the Democracy Movement of spring 1989 and the Beijing
Massacre of 4 June. Other first-hand accounts by well-informed observers include:
Michael S. Duke, *The iron house: a memoir of the Chinese democracy movement and
the Tiananmen massacre* (Layton, Utah: Gibbs Smith, 1990. 180p.); Lee Feigon,
China rising: the meaning of Tiananmen (Chicago: Ivan Dee, 1990. 269p.); and Yi
Mu, Mark V. Thompson, *Crisis at Tiananmen: reform and reality in modern China*
(San Francisco: China Books, 1989. 283p.). Extensive photographic coverage is
included in *Children of the dragon: the story of Tiananmen square* (New York:
Macmillan, 1990. 223p.), by Human Rights in China, and *Beijing spring* (New York:
Workman, 1989. 175p.), by David C. Turnley.

790   **China since Tiananmen: political, economic, and social conflicts –
an East Gate reader.**
Edited by Lawrence R. Sullivan.   Armonk, New York; London: M. E.
Sharpe, 1995. 331p.

Sullivan has compiled more than one hundred primary documents for college study
from Chinese and Hong Kong media, arranged to illustrate contrasting images and
perspectives within China, 1989-94. The documents are divided into four parts:
politics (including leadership struggles, foreign policy, corruption and a case-study of
the Three Gorges Dam); economics; society and culture (including social changes,
women and population policy, public health and environment, AIDS, intellectuals,
journalism, and the arts); and science and technology. The editor supplies
introductions, suggestions for further reading, organizational charts, a chronology for
the period 1989-94, and a biographical glossary.

791   **The pro-democracy protests in China: reports from the provinces.**
Edited by Jonathan Unger.   Armonk, New York; London: M. E.
Sharpe, 1991. 239p.

Provides thirteen detailed reports by foreign scholars, many based on eye-witness
accounts, as well as interviews and published accounts, of Democracy Movements and
their suppression in all parts of the country. After an introduction and a background
section recounting the rise and fall of the People's Movement in the capital, sections
describe events in Manchuria, Xi'an, Chengdu, Chongqing, a Hunan backwater county
town, Fujian, Hangzhou and Shanghai. Ten of the chapters first appeared in the
Australian Journal of Chinese Affairs.

792   **Popular protest and political culture in modern China.**
Edited by Jeffrey N. Wasserstrom, Elizabeth J. Perry.   Boulder,
Colorado; San Francisco; Oxford: Westview Press, 1994. 2nd ed.
350p. bibliog.

Scholars look at political symbolism, public language, and the varieties of ritual in
modern China, especially the events of 1989. An influential essay by Wasserstrom and
Joseph Esherick, reprinted from *Journal of Asian Studies*, vol. 49, no. 4 (November
1990), examines the 1989 student demonstrations as 'political theater', with an added
commentary on the narratives of these events as 'myth'. Other essays discuss: the
difference between commemoration and historical memory in 4 May 1919 and in
1989; the village compact of the Communist Party; the changing role of intellectuals,
from priesthood to professionals; styles of urban protest; the historical relationship
between US and Chinese journalism; the male domination of the 1989 student
movements; the bifurcation of urban and rural identities; and historical comparisons of
modern student protest movements.

The tyranny of history: the roots of China's crisis.
See item no. 8.

Almost a revolution.
See item no. 393.

Quelling the people: the military suppression of the Beijing democracy movement.
See item no. 859.

A splintered mirror: Chinese poetry from the Democracy Movement.
See item no. 1222.

Foreign Relations

General and to 1800

793   China and Russia: the 'great game'.
O. Edmund Clubb.   New York; London: Columbia University Press,
1971. 578p. maps. bibliog.

Surveys diplomatic relations and frontier rivalry between the Chinese and Russian
empires from the 16th to the 20th centuries, with particular emphasis on the recent
period. Mark Mancall, *Russia and China: their diplomatic relations up to 1728*
(Cambridge, Massachusetts: Harvard University Press, 1970. 396p. [Harvard East
Asian Series, no. 61]) chronicles relations between expanding Czarist Russia and the
newly established Manchu empire as a successful diplomatic interaction leading up to
the long-lasting Treaty of Khiakhta in 1728. Eric Widmer, *The Russian ecclesiastical
mission in Peking during the eighteenth century* (Cambridge, Massachusetts: East
Asian Research Center, Harvard University, 1976. 262p. [East Asian Monographs, no.
69]) describes the first officially accepted foreign mission in China and the
information it provided.

794   The Chinese world order: traditional China's foreign relations.
Edited by John King Fairbank.   Cambridge, Massachusetts: Harvard
University Press, 1968. 416p. maps. bibliog. (Harvard East Asian
Series, no. 32).

A pioneering and influential symposium volume. Fairbank's introduction and a
historical note by Yang Lien-sheng summarize traditional views of the 'tribute
system', under which foreign powers submitted tribute and paid homage to Peking.
Essays treat: relations with Southeast Asia; the Qing tribute system; Sino-Korean
tributary relations; the Liu-ch'iu (Ryukyu) islands; Inner Asia (the Xiongnu and
Tibet); Vietnam during the Tayson rebellion; and Qing relations with the Dutch. No
single book has replaced this overview, but subsequent scholarship has challenged the
analysis as Sino-centric and for not making clear that the 'tribute' system characterized
only the Ming and early Qing dynasties and was not typical of earlier periods.

268

795   **China considers the Middle East.**
Lillian Craig Harris.   London; New York: I. B. Tauris, distributed in
North America by St. Martin's Press, 1993. 345p.
A careful survey. The substantial opening section, 'The Historical Foundation',
discusses the mutual influences of the great Islamic and Chinese empires. Harris then
evaluates modern China's relations with Arabs, Persians and Israelis from 1949 to the
1990s. China has long seen the Middle East as an extension of its Central Asian
security buffer zone, sometimes emphasizing revolutionary rhetoric, sometimes
economic interest. From the 1950s to the 1970s, China could play the balancing power
between Middle Eastern countries and the superpowers; after the collapse of the
Soviet Union and the Cold War world order, the Gulf Crisis of 1990-91 showed the
need for an independent Chinese foreign policy.

796   **Antiforeignism and modernization in China, 1860-1980: linkage
between domestic politics and foreign policy.**
Liao Kuang-sheng.   Hong Kong: Chinese University Press; New
York: St. Martin's, 1984. rev. ed. 333p.
Analyses more than a century of popular and government debate over how to handle
foreign threats and the effects on policy formation. Topics include: the Self-
Strengthening and anti-Christian movements in the 19th century; the role of
xenophobic forms of nationalism and anti-imperialism in 20th-century foreign policy
decision making; and the decline of anti-foreignism. John Gittings, *The world and
China, 1922-1972* (New York; Evanston, Illinois; London: Harper & Row, 1974.
303p.) is a thoughtful history of the ideas behind China's foreign policy, particularly
Mao's widely accepted argument that revolution at home was linked to anti-
imperialism abroad.

797   **China at the center: 300 years of foreign policy.**
Mark Mancall.   New York: Free Press, 1984. 540p. (Transformation
of Modern China Series).
A survey text which links the basic policies of the Manchu Qing empire to those of
subsequent régimes using an approach centred on the Chinese world-view and
cognitive patterns, rather than on Western preconceptions.

798   **China among equals: the Middle Kingdom and its neighbors
10th-14th centuries.**
Edited by Morris Rossabi.   Berkeley, California; Los Angeles;
Oxford: University of California Press, 1983. 419p. maps.
This accessible symposium volume challenges traditional views of China as the centre
and dominant organizer of international relations. The editor's lucid introduction
argues that Song dynasty China realistically dealt with 'barbarian' neighbours on a
basis of equality within a multi-state system; the Europeans were not the first
challenge to an eternal 'Chinese world order' based on the 'tribute system'. Specific
essays analyse: the foreign policy of the Wu Yueh state which preceded the Song; the
Song as a 'lesser empire' (than the Tang); trade as a factor in foreign policy; images
of the Khitan as 'barbarians' or 'Northerners'; foreign embassies; and Tibetan
relations with China and the Mongols. Two papers concern Mongol hegemony, and a
final paper examines the long-term context of the China-Manchuria-Korea triangle.

799 **China and Inner Asia from 1368 to the present day.**
Morris Rossabi. London: Thames & Hudson, 1975. 320p. maps.
bibliog.
Surveys Chinese diplomatic and commercial relations with Mongolia, Manchuria and
Central Asia (but not Tibet) starting with the Ming. Rossabi argues that contrary to the
avowals of dynastic Chinese officials, Inner Asia was of strategic and economic
importance to China even before Russian expansion in the 17th century. Ming policies
and attitudes towards the pastoral empires were basically defensive. After the
Manchus conquered China, they adopted a forward policy of conquest to meet
Russia's parallel expansion, culminating in the 1728 Treaty of Khiakhta. Qing 19th-
century decay led to widespread revolts and eventually Japanese infiltration and
Russian ascendancy, with control from China not re-established until the 1950s. Notes
and a bibliography refer to the extensive literature available in English.

800 **The star raft: China's encounter with Africa.**
Philip Snow. London; New York: Weidenfield & Nicolson, 1988.
250p. maps. Reprinted, Ithaca, New York: Cornell University Press,
1989.
A lively account, intended for the non-specialist, of interactions between China and
Africa from the Ming dynasty to the 1980s. Snow begins with the Ming explorations
of the coast of Africa by the admiral Zheng He, then describes Chinese traders and
mine workers during the period of European colonization. Support by the People's
Republic for liberation movements was balanced by a rivalry with Taiwan for
diplomatic recognition, which required dealing with established governments. After
1958, China offered economic aid and a model of Third World economic
development. The book concludes with a well-rounded account of African students
brought to study in China and their often hostile reception.

801 **Trade and expansion in Han China.**
Ying-shih Yü. Berkeley, California; Los Angeles; Oxford: University
of California Press, 1967. 251p. maps. bibliog.
A monographic study of the politics and economics of Han China as seen in military
and economic relations with Central Asia. Yü studies the Han military expansion,
especially the expeditions of Zhang Qian, and the interaction of the Chinese and
Central Asian economies. Xinru Liu, *Ancient India and ancient China: trade and
religious exchanges, AD 1-600* (Delhi; New York: Oxford University Press, 1988.
231p. maps) discusses commercial routes, commercial centres, items of trade and
possible links with Buddhism. Charles Backus, *The Nan-chao kingdom and T'ang
China's southwestern frontier* (Cambridge, England: Cambridge University Press,
1981. 224p.) constitutes a full-scale history which emphasizes diplomatic and military
relations with independent kingdoms in present-day Yunnan.

The perilous frontier: nomadic empires and China.
See item no. 162.

Alien regimes and border states, 907-1368.
See item no. 166.

Peace, war, and trade along the Great Wall: nomadic-Chinese interaction through two millennia.
See item no. 167.

When China ruled the seas: the treasure fleet of the dragon throne, 1403-1433.
See item no. 181.

The Great Wall of China: from history to myth.
See item no. 186.

19th century to 1949

With the West

802   **Entering China's service: Robert Hart's journals, 1854-1863.**
Edited, with narratives by Katherine F. Bruner, John K. Fairbank, Richard J. Smith.   Cambridge, Massachusetts: Council on East Asian Studies, Harvard University, 1986, 1991. 2 vols. (Harvard East Asian Monographs, nos. 125 and 155).

Robert Hart went to China shortly after the Opium Wars in the service of her Britannic Majesty, Queen Victoria; he eventually won the confidence of Chinese court officials and served the equally majestic Empress Dowager. He was appointed Inspector General of the China Imperial Maritime Customs Service, a position in the Qing bureaucracy, and became the most influential Westerner in China until his death in 1907. Volume two is *Robert Hart and China's early modernization: his journals, 1863-1866*, edited by Richard J. Smith, John K. Fairbank, Katherine F. Bruner. Fairbank, Bruner, and Elizabeth MacLeod Matheson also edited *The I. G. in Peking: letters of Robert Hart, Chinese Maritime Customs, 1868-1907* (Cambridge, Massachusetts: Belknap Press of Harvard University Press, 1975. 2 vols.). In all these volumes Hart's own words are annotated and prefaced, providing the reader with a detailed chronicle of an important life.

803   **China and the West: society and culture, 1815-1937.**
Jerome Ch'en.   London: Hutchinson; Bloomington, Indiana: Indiana University Press, 1979. 488p. bibliog. (History of Human Society).

A richly documented, thoughtful, disjointed survey of China's cultural and social contacts with Western Europe and America, particularly at the level below the state. Part one analyses image makers and their activities in the following activities: education, medicine, social work, anti-Christian movements, Chinese Christian theology and growth of autonomy; scholars and students (study abroad, Western thought, translation); and traders and emigrants (traders in Shanghai, Chinese in San Francisco). Part two includes 'Politics and the Law' (constitutions and law reform, political parties, the mixed courts of Shanghai and extraterritoriality, modern courts),

'The Economy' (imports, exports, foreign concessions, railroads, failure of industrialization), and 'Society' (family revolution, emancipation of women, the labour movement). A select bibliography annotates books and articles in English and Chinese.

804 **Trade and diplomacy on the China coast: the opening of the treaty ports, 1842-1854.**
John King Fairbank. Cambridge, Massachusetts: Harvard University Press, 1953; one volume edition, 1964. 489p. (Harvard Historical Studies, no. 62).

Fairbank provides basic, early coverage of the diplomatic and political aspects of the Opium Wars and the establishment of the treaty system and extraterritoriality. Part one, 'China's Unpreparedness for Western Contact', expounds on China's response to the West, the growth of trade, and the Canton system. Parts two to five then recount in detail: the collapse of the Canton system and the Opium Wars; the negotiation and conclusion of treaty settlements; the opening of the Treaty Ports; the creation of the foreign Inspectorate of Customs at Shanghai, 1850-54; the policies of British and Manchu diplomats; and a conclusion, 'The Treaties Succeed the Tribute System'. Volume two contains extensive reference notes and scholarly apparatus.

805 **Cherishing men from afar: Qing guest ritual and the Macartney embassy of 1793.**
James L. Hevia. Durham, North Carolina; London: Duke University Press, 1995. 292p.

A vigorous, methodologically innovative study of the rituals which organized relations between Qing and British rulers. A critical introduction reviews previous studies, such as those by Fairbank, Peyrefitte and Wills (qq.v.), and suggests how insights from critical theory and anthropology explain Qing and British practices and frameworks. Macartney's mission is often seen as prefiguring a cultural collision between a rational, dynamic modern West and a stagnant and isolated East; Hevia instead sees interaction between two multi-ethnic imperial formations. The body of the book analyses: Qing rulership and court ritual, including the Kowtow; British conceptions of civil society (and lack of applicability for China), trade, diplomacy and China; and competing accounts of the 1793 Embassy in Qing and British records. A final chapter glosses subsequent historical accounts to suggest new views of China's modern history. *Ritual and diplomacy: the Macartney mission to China, 1792-1794*, edited by Robert A. Bickers (London: British Association for Chinese Studies, Wellsweep Press, 1993. 93p.), is a lively symposium.

806 **Imperialism and Chinese politics, 1840-1925.**
Hu Sheng. Beijing: Foreign Languages Press, 1981. 332p.

A translation of the sixth edition of *Diguozhuyi yu Zhongguo zhengzhi* (Beijing: Renmin chubanshe, 1978). Long the orthodox treatment of Western involvement in Chinese domestic politics during the heyday of imperialism, now outdated in sources and approaches, this remains a powerful presentation of a widely held view, with many quotations and examples. Chapters cover: the 'establishment of new relationships' (1840-64) with subsequent 'toadying to the foreigners'; 1900 and the I He Tuan (Boxers); the 'strong man' (Yuan Shikai); and 'revolution and counter-revolution' (1919-24). Roberta Allen Dayer, *Bankers and diplomats in China,*

1917-1925: the Anglo-American relationship (London; Totowa, New Jersey: Frank Cass, 1981. 295p.) uses English-language sources to argue that monied interests exercised enormous influence over Chinese politics in the warlord period.

807 **Germany and Republican China.**
William Kirby. Stanford, California: Stanford University Press, 1984. 361p.

A vigorous, multi-faceted examination of Sino-foreign interaction, which challenges the view of Nationalist China as passive and stagnant and of Germany as simply imperialist. Kirby first sketches the efforts of Sun Yat-sen and his generation to learn from foreign models and 'isms', and German initiatives in China before 1925. The heart of the book comprises chapters on the Nationalist industrial strategy, in which Chiang Kai-shek's government used the German 'model' to industrialize the economy and mobilize and discipline the people. Chiang turned to German military, ideological and economic advisors for a programme of frugality, fascism and New Life. The Japanese invasion of 1937 and alliance with Hitler ended the relationship.

808 **Wei Yuan and China's rediscovery of the maritime world.**
Jane Kate Leonard. Cambridge, Massachusetts: Council on East Asian Studies, Harvard University, 1984. 276p. bibliog. (East Asian Monographs, no. 111).

Studies the conceptual development of a leading 19th-century official. Wei Yuan (1794-1856) worked in the statecraft (*jingshi*) tradition which called for administrative reform to enrich the people and supported an aggressive foreign policy based on a strong navy. He also continued in a Confucian belief that the basic problem of government was not creating new institutions or expanding the economy but recruiting talented and moral scholars into the bureaucracy. Fred W. Drake, *China charts the world: Hsu Chi-y and his geography of 1848* (Cambridge, Massachusetts: East Asian Research Center, Harvard University, 1975. 272p. bibliog. [East Asian Monographs, no. 64]) details the remarkably successful efforts of an official turned geographer and cartographer, Xu Jiyu (1795-1874), to gather intelligence information concerning Western countries; his book and Wei's were studied in 1850s Japan to prepare for the expected confrontation with the West.

809 **The outsiders: the western experience in India and China.**
Rhoads Murphey. Ann Arbor, Michigan: University of Michigan Press, 1977. 299p. maps. bibliog.

A wide-ranging study which probes and assesses both the impact of European 'outsiders' on Asia and of Asia on the Europeans living there. Some theorists argue that Asian cultures and economies were destroyed by imperialism; Murphey, trained in history and geography, describes China and India as more resilient and less damaged, but as differing greatly from each other in the style and results flowing from their interactions with the new world economy.

810 **The immobile empire.**
Alain Peyrefitte, translated by Jon Rothschild. New York: Knopf, 1992. 630p.

A narrative of George Macartney's 1792-94 diplomatic mission to the court of the Qianlong Emperor. Peyrefitte, a former French diplomat in Beijing, views the Chinese rebuff to Macartney as a portent of China's irrational refusal to understand and emulate the modernizing West. Peyrefitte's *Un choc de cultures: la vision des Chinois* (Culture shock: the Chinese vision) (Paris: Fayard, 1991. 522p.) develops this grand historical vision, popularized also in Christopher Hibbert, *The dragon wakes: China and the West, 1793-1911* (New York: Harper & Row; London: Longmans, 1970. 427p.). Many scholars now criticize this view for treating China as an unchanging and homogeneous culture and idealizing the 'West'; see Hevia (q.v.). George Macartney, *An embassy to China: being the journal kept by Lord Macartney during his embassy to the Emperor Ch'ien-lung, 1793-94*, edited, with an introduction and notes by J. L. Cranmer-Byng (London: Longmans, 1963. 421p. maps. Reprinted, St. Clair Shores, Michigan: Scholarly Press, 1972) is a day-by-day account, with extensive notes. A well-edited journal of a succeeding mission (originally Edinburgh: Blackwood, 1859. 2. vols.), is Laurence Oliphant, *Elgin's mission to China and Japan in the years 1857, '58, and '59*, with an introduction by J. J. Gerson (Hong Kong; New York: Oxford University Press, 1970. 2 vols. maps [Oxford in Asia]).

811 **Imperialism and Chinese nationalism: Germany in Shantung.**
John Schrecker.   Cambridge, Massachusetts: Harvard University Press, 1971. 322p. (Harvard East Asian Series, no. 58).
A discussion of the diplomacy, politics and economics of imperialism, which describes the German seizure and administration of territory in Shandong, 1894-1914, and the surprisingly effective Chinese responses. The initial German intervention was both military and diplomatic, precipitated by violence against German missionaries and by railway ambition, but moved on to commerce, finance and education. Chinese government and private reaction, ranging from canny diplomacy and the Boxer uprising to entrepreneurial creativity, undermined the German sphere of influence while appropriating what was profitable (e.g. Tsingtao beer). The parallel French effort is studied in Robert Lee, *France and the exploitation of China, 1885-1901: a study in economic imperialism* (Oxford: Oxford University Press, 1989. 358p.). British imperialism of the time is covered most recently in: E. W. Edwards, *British diplomacy and finance in China, 1895-1914* (Oxford: Oxford University Press, 1987. 212p.); and Pamela Atwell, *British mandarins and Chinese reformers: the British administration of Weihaiwei (1898-1930) and the Territory's return to Chinese rule* (Hong Kong: Oxford University Press, 1985. 302p.).

812 **China's response to the West: a documentary survey, 1839-1923.**
Edited by Ssu-yü Teng, John King Fairbank, with E-tu Zen Sun, Chaoying Fang, and others.   Cambridge, Massachusetts: Harvard University Press, 1954. 296p.
An influential early interpretation. The editors have selected letters, official documents, proclamations and published essays to show 'the way in which the scholar-official class of China, faced with the aggressive expansion of the modern West, tried to understand an alien civilization and take action to preserve their own culture and their political and social institutions'. Sections include: 'The Problem and its Background' (intellectual tradition); 'Recognition of China's Need to Know the West, 1839-1860', including the Opium War and the theory of 'self-strengthening'; 'The Desire for Western Technology, 1861-1870'; 'Efforts at Self-Strengthening, 1871-1896'; 'Reform Movements through 1900'; 'Reform and Revolution, 1901-1912'; and 'Ideological Ferment and the May Fourth Movement, 1912-1923'. For a respectful critique and references, see Cohen, *Discovering history in China* (q.v.).

813   **Pepper, guns, and parleys: the Dutch East India Company and China, 1662-1681.**
John E. Wills.   Cambridge, Massachusetts: Harvard University Press, 1974. 232p. (Harvard East Asian Series, no. 75).

A lively scholarly investigation of a pivotal era. In order to handle foreign relations in the early years of the Qing dynasty, the Manchus adopted the 'tribute system', recently developed by the Ming, with its sino-centric emphasis on ritual and outward obeisance; the court's handling of the Dutch and other powers, described here, developed an illusion of success which lasted until the 19th century. Wills' *Embassies and illusions: Dutch and Portuguese envoys to K'ang-hsi, 1666-1687* (Cambridge, Massachusetts: Council on East Asian Studies, distributed by Harvard University Press, 1984. 303p. [Harvard East Asian Monographs, no. 103]) continues the argument that the 'tribute system' (described in an introductory chapter) is not the best key to a comprehensive understanding of traditional foreign relations. These volumes combine colourful and detailed diplomatic history with long-term perspective.

814   **China in the international system, 1918-1920: the Middle Kingdom at the periphery.**
Yongjin Zhang.   New York: St. Martin's Press, 1991. 262p.

Uses rich Chinese sources to show that the much reviled warlords and officials of the rump government in Beijing actually shared the aspirations of emerging popular nationalism; all yearned to defy imperialism and restore China to a leading role on the world stage. Although this book does not force a major revision in previous views of China's post-First World War diplomacy, Zhang shows that China's diplomats argued ably but unavailingly at the Peace Conference in Versailles, setting the scene for somewhat better achievements at the Washington Conference of 1922.

Pirates of the South China Coast, 1790-1810.
See item no. 207.

The opium war, 1840-1842.
See item no. 215.

Spoilt children of empire: Westerners in Shanghai and the Chinese revolution of the 1920s.
See item no. 315.

Shanghai: from market town to treaty port, 1074-1858.
See item no. 433.

With Japan and international relations

815   **China and Japan at war: the politics of collaboration, 1937-1945.**
John Hunter Boyle.   Stanford, California: Stanford University Press, 1972. 430p.

A political history in which Boyle first describes Japanese attempts to avert war, find Chinese allies among the Nationalists, and deal with the 'China problem'. After 1937, factions among both the Nationalists and the Japanese still sought accommodation. Wang Jingwei (1883-1944) agreed in 1940 to head the government in Nanjing, one of several Japanese sponsored régimes. Like Quisling (Norway) and Laval (France) in Europe, Wang felt that he was doing his patriotic duty; after all, he had been a follower of Sun Yat-sen long before Chiang Kai-shek, and believed that China and Japan shared Mao and Stalin as enemies. Wang failed, however, to understand emerging wartime popular nationalism and Japanese arrogance.

816 **Facing Japan: Chinese politics and Japanese imperialism, 1931-1937.**
Parks M. Coble. Cambridge, Massachusetts: Council on East Asian Studies, Harvard University, distributed by the Harvard University Press, 1991. 492p. (East Asian Monographs, no. 135).

A study of the domestic politics of foreign policy. Chiang Kai-shek's dilemma was that fighting the Japanese was militarily suicidal, but realistic appeasement was politically disastrous. Coble's even-handed and meticulous analysis argues that Chiang was frightened by mass public opinion, which grew more restive with each crisis, and that he used the Japanese threat to blackmail and undercut provincial warlords. Playing internal Nationalist factions against each other, he eventually brought even the Communists to support him as the only leader capable of unifying China in the Second United Front, which lead to the disastrous war he rightly feared. Donald Jordan, *Chinese boycotts versus Japanese bombs: the failure of China's 'revolutionary diplomacy', 1931-1932* (Ann Arbor, Michigan: University of Michigan Press, 1991. 363p.) argues that economic attacks on Japan were provocative bluster and destroyed hopes of earlier generations for Pan-Asian cooperation. An unheeded realist critique, prepared for the American State Department, was *How the peace was lost: the 1935 memorandum Developments Affecting American Policy in the Far East*, by John Van Antwerp MacMurray, edited with an introduction by Arthur Waldron (Stanford, California: Hoover Institution, Stanford University, 1992. 165p. bibliog.).

817 **China and Japan: search for balance since World War I.**
Alvin D. Coox, Hilary Conroy, introduction by Robert Scalapino. Santa Barbara, California: ABC-Clio; Oxford: European Bibliographical Centre-Clio Press, 1978. 468p.

Seventeen essays, written for this volume by Chinese, Japanese and American scholars, deal with official relations between China and Japan from the first World War to the 1970s. Subjects include: Japanese unobstructed development in Shandong during the 1910s; Chinese diplomacy of resistance at that time; how China was presented in Japanese textbooks approved by the Ministry of Education; the Communist Party and 1930s anti-Japanese agitation in Manchuria; the Japanese-sponsored North China Autonomy Movement of the mid-1930s; the Sino-Japanese War of 1937-45; the peace negotiations and treaty between Japan and the Republic of China on Taiwan in the early 1950s; and the way in which Prime Minister Tanaka negotiated the establishment of diplomatic relations with the People's Republic in 1972.

818 **The Japanese informal empire in China, 1895-1937.**
Edited by Peter Duus, Ramon Myers, Mark Peattie. Princeton, New Jersey: Princeton University Press, 1989. 454p. maps.

A conference volume of essays on political, economic and diplomatic aspects of Japanese imperialism in China before the outbreak of war in 1937. Sections concern: 'Trade and investment', including the South Manchurian Railway, cotton mills and economic development in Manchukuo; 'Culture and Community', which analyses

Japanese treaty port settlements, schools for training Japanese experts on China and the Foreign Ministry's use of the Boxer Indemnity; and 'Experts and Subimperialists', which treats China initiatives in the army, the Foreign Ministry and the effects of anti-Japanese boycotts. A companion volume, *The Japanese colonial empire, 1895-1945* (Princeton, New Jersey: Princeton University Press, 1984. 540p.), analyses the background of imperialism and colonialism in Korea and Taiwan.

819   **Chinese-Soviet relations 1937-1945: the diplomacy of Chinese nationalism.**

John W. Garver.   New York: Oxford University Press, 1988. 301p. maps. bibliog.

Garver argues that national interest, rather than socialist solidarity, animated wartime relations between Stalin, Mao and Chiang Kai-shek. Soviets ruthlessly promoted their state interests, not revolution in China. Chiang and Mao understood this perfectly; although they had less power than Stalin, they played the power game and resisted Soviet imperialism skilfully. Garver begins by describing the negotiations between Chiang and Stalin at the beginning of the anti-Japanese war in 1937. Stalin supported Chiang in order to divert Japan, leaving out the Chinese Communists, and demanding territory in Manchuria in return. Chiang preserved Chinese rule in Xinjiang, but lost Mongolia. Mao was appalled by Stalin's territorial demands, and developed a knack for resisting Stalin while extolling Moscow; when Stalin demanded an all-out anti-Japanese offensive, Mao pursued his own style of guerrilla war.

820   **After imperialism: the search for a new order in the Far East, 1921-1931.**

Akira Iriye.   Cambridge, Massachusetts: Harvard University Press, 1965. 375p. (Harvard East Asian Series, no. 22). Reprinted, Chicago: Imprint Publications, 1990. map.

An influential study of American, British, Japanese and Chinese diplomacy and the international system from the Washington Conference to the Manchurian crisis. After the First World War the United States, Japan and China attempted to replace the discredited 19th-century 'diplomacy of imperialism', which had provided Europe with a century of peace and global dominance; conflict between Chinese nationalism and Japanese assertion of national interests led to the 1931 war. Iriye analyses the earlier system in *Pacific estrangement: Japanese and American expansion, 1897-1911* (Cambridge, Massachusetts: Harvard University Press, 1972. 290p. [Harvard Studies in American-East Asian Relations, no. 2]). Reprinted, Chicago: Imprint, 1994); his basic study *Power and culture: the Japanese-American war, 1941-1945* (Cambridge, Massachusetts: Harvard University Press, 1981. 304p.) argues that wartime conflict gave way to postwar cooperation because the two powers shared Wilsonian cultural assumptions.

821   **The Chinese and the Japanese: essays in political and cultural interactions.**

Edited with an introduction by Akira Iriye.   Princeton, New Jersey: Princeton University Press, 1979. 368p.

Sixteen scholarly essays deal with political and cultural interactions at both the private and governmental levels in the period 1800-1945. Topics include: conceptions of

'China' in Tokugawa Japanese thought, 1600-1868; the Chinese community in mid-19th century Japan; Chinese reactions to the war with Japan, 1894-95; Japanese support of Chinese reformers and revolutionaries in the decade leading up to the 1911 Revolution; a biographical study of Japanese friends of China (Konoe Atsumaro, Naitō Konan, Ishibashi Tanan, Ugaki Kazushige) and one of their Chinese friends, Cao Rulin; Chinese Quislings; and Japanese atrocities, 1937-45.

822   **Japan and China: from war to peace, 1894-1972.**
      Marius B. Jansen.   Chicago: Rand McNally, 1975. 547p. 6 maps.
      bibliog.

In form, this is a text-survey of the period from the Sino-Japanese war of 1894 to the exchange of formal diplomatic recognitions in 1972; in content, these are twelve richly detailed interpretive essays on the development of Sino-Japanese ties into an integrated East Asia. The unifying theme is the contrasting responses of the two societies to European imperialism, industrial economics and mass politics. The framework is of wars and diplomacy, but 'deeper currents were those of cultural influence, revolution, and reconstruction, and the students and their books count for as much as the soldiers and their guns'. One chapter is devoted to Japan and Korea. A concluding twenty-five-page section, 'Sources', provides an annotated selective bibliography of scholarship. Jansen's *China in the Tokugawa world* (Cambridge, Massachusetts: Harvard University Press, 1992. 137p.), the 1988 Edwin O. Reischauer lectures, evokes the shifting image of China from culture source to inferior political rival.

823   **China and the origins of the Pacific War, 1931-41.**
      Youli Sun.   New York: St. Martin's Press, 1993. 244p.

The foreign policy of China in the 1930s is analysed in terms of the international system and the ideas of Chinese diplomats, politicians and public opinion. Sun finds that the Chinese 'belief system' consisted of two major perceptions: that Japan's aggression threatened Western powers and conflict was inevitable; and that foreign allies were desirable both to defend China and to allow the government to use military resources on domestic enemies. After a discussion of changing conceptualizations of imperialism and the international system in the 1920s and 1930s, Sun analyses frustrated Chinese diplomacy after the 1931 Manchurian Incident; the policy of avoiding confrontation with Japan should not be called 'appeasement' but 'gradualism' in building military and industrial power for resistance. Popular nationalism and Soviet popular front strategy prevented Sino-Japanese accommodation, and after 1937 the only hope became American intervention. Akira Iriye, *Origins of the Second World War in Asia and the Pacific* (London; New York: Longman, 1987. 202p. maps. bibliog. [Origins of Modern Wars]) is a succinct international history.

China's bitter victory: the war with Japan.
See item no. 282.

Life along the South Manchurian Railroad.
See item no. 320.

The Japanese and Sun Yat-sen.
See item no. 698.

With the United States

824 **East Asian art and American culture: a study in international relations.**
Warren I. Cohen. New York: Columbia University Press, 1992. 264p. bibliog.

A specialist in diplomatic history tells the story of American collectors of Chinese and Japanese art in the first half of the 20th century and analyses foreign relations (and imperialism) on the cultural level. Art patrons and collectors such as Langdon Warner and Charles Freer participated in the process which formed taste (particularly for certain types and periods), institutionalized Asian art in museums, and professionalized its study. Some were free-booters – Cohen tells of the looting of the Longmen caves – while others were genuine and creative in developing cultural relations based on equality and mutual understanding.

825 **Pacific passage: the study of American-East Asian relations on the eve of the twenty-first century.**
Edited, with an introduction, by Warren I. Cohen. New York: Columbia University Press, 1995. bibliog.

Provides state-of-the-field essays on recent scholarship on the US relations with China, Japan, Korea, Philippines and Vietnam, sponsored by the Committee on American-East Asian Relations. Topics include: 'Sino-American Relations Studies in China', which describes the development of academic study in the 1980s and 1990s; 'Asian Immigrants and American Foreign Relations'; recent scholarship on pre-1900 Sino-American relations; 'The Open Door Raj: Chinese-American Cultural Relations 1900-1945'; 'Sino-American Relations in Comparative Perspective, 1900-1949'; and 'Continuing Controversies in the Literature of U.S.-China Relations Since 1945'. This work forms a series with: *New frontiers in American-East Asian relations*, edited by Warren I. Cohen (New York: Columbia University Press, 1983. 294p. bibliog.); and *American-East Asian relations: a survey*, edited by Ernest R. May, James C. Thomson, Jr. (Cambridge, Massachusetts: Harvard University Press, 1972. 425p. [Harvard Studies in American-East Asian Relations, no. 1]). *Sino-American relations since 1900*, edited by Priscilla Roberts (Hong Kong: Centre of Asian Studies, Hong Kong University, 1991. 563p.) contains conference essays reflecting and evaluating recent work on the subject.

826 **The making of a special relationship: the United States and China to 1914.**
Michael Hunt. New York: Columbia University Press, 1983. 419p. bibliog.

A broad survey of two interacting components of 19th- and early 20th-century Sino-American relations: the development of an American 'Open Door constituency' of missionaries, traders and diplomats, with a common commitment to penetrating China and propagating at home a 'paternalistic vision' of defending and reforming China; and high-level government policy, characterized by the 'desperate ploys of embattled Chinese' on the one side and mounting American pretensions on the other. Also described is the American racist reaction against, and Chinese government protection of, Chinese immigrants in the United States. The notes incorporate brief essays on the secondary scholarship and primary sources.

827 **Across the pacific: an inner history of American-East Asian relations.**
Akira Iriye, introduction by John K. Fairbank. New York: Harcourt, Brace, and World, 1967. 361p. bibliog. Reprinted, with two new chapters, Chicago: Imprint Publications, 1990.

A pioneering survey of relations among the United States, Japan and China from 1780 to the 1960s. Iriye was influential in expanding the study of foreign relations from diplomatic history to include culture and ideas as well as diplomacy. Part one, 'The Initial Encounter, 1780-1880', describes 'East Asia in America' (concepts and immigrants). Part two, 'Imperialism, Nationalism, and Racism', has four chapters analysing: late 19th-century changes in the international system; Japanese and American imperialism; the genesis of American-Japanese antagonism; and Chinese nationalism and the United States. Part three, 'Sino-American Co-operation Against Japan', covers the origins, diplomacy and outcome of the Pacific War. Finally, part four describes the post-1949 Sino-American military confrontation and hopes for peace.

828 **The United States and China in the twentieth century.**
Michael Schaller. New York; Oxford: Oxford University Press, 1990. 2nd ed. 247p. map. bibliog.

A synoptic text, with an emphasis on diplomacy, intended for the college undergraduate or general reader. Chapters are devoted to: images of China; the origins and diplomacy of the Pacific War, 1937-45; the wartime Chinese-American alliance; the United States confrontation with the Chinese Revolution before and after 1949; the agony of Vietnam; the Sino-American détente; and the politics of normalization. A broader survey of political and cultural relations from the 1840s is Warren Cohen, *America's response to China: an interpretive history of Sino-American relations* (New York; London: Columbia University Press, 1990. 3rd ed. 241p.). Hugh Deane, *Good deeds and gunboats: two centuries of America-Chinese encounters* (San Francisco: China Books & Periodicals, 1990. 258p.) presents a lively narrative which emphasizes individual contributions and China's anti-imperialist struggle.

829 **America's failure in China, 1941-50.**
Tsou Tang. Chicago; London: University of Chicago Press, 1963. 614p.

A detailed critique of the failure of American policy toward China between Pearl Harbor and China's involvement in the Korean War. Tsou, developing a realist critique, finds an imbalance between ends and means, an unwillingness either to use military power to achieve political objectives or to abandon unattainable goals. After a review of America's Open Door policy and a critique of American images (including that of Chinese Communism), Tsou analyses the breakdown of American wartime policies of limited assistance to Chiang, the Civil War and the mission of General George Marshall. Michael Schaller, *The American crusade in China, 1938-1945* (New York: Columbia University Press, 1979. 364p.) describes diplomatic and military interaction. *Sino-American relations, 1945-1955: a joint reassessment of a critical decade*, edited by Harry Harding, Yuan Ming (Wilmington, Delaware: Scholarly Resources, 1989. 343p.) is a symposium of papers by scholars from the US and the People's Republic from a post-Cold War perspective.

830 **Patterns in the dust: Chinese-American relations and the recognition controversy, 1949-1950.**
Nancy Bernkopf Tucker.   New York; London: Columbia University Press, 1983. 396p. (Contemporary American History Series).
In 1949, the US State Department expected to wait for the 'dust to settle' before recognizing Beijing. Here Tucker deploys a wide range of American and Chinese sources to appraise America's traditional China policy, the international context, and the new Chinese government's unexpected policy of openness following the Nationalist downfall and withdrawal to Taiwan. The American China Lobby opposed recognition; a surprising number of missionaries were prepared for reconciliation with Beijing; journalists and the media, for their part, went in all directions. The public, Congress and scholars searched for a way through the dilemma, wanting neither to rescue Chiang nor countenance Mao. The State Department and President Truman were further frustrated by the outbreak of the war in Korea, which froze relations until Nixon's visit to Beijing in 1972.

Thunder out of China.
See item no. 288.

An American missionary in China: John Leighton Stuart and Chinese-American relations.
See item no. 409.

Stilwell and the American experience in China, 1911-1945.
See item no. 414.

After 1949

831 **The making of foreign policy in China: structure and process.**
A. Doak Barnett.   Boulder, San Francisco; Oxford: Westview Press, 1985. 160p.
A systematic description of how foreign policy decisions were made in the 1980s, based both on an extensive series of interviews with policy-makers and on research in published sources. Barnett does not deal so much with content or intentions, but rather analyses the roles of party and government organizations, ministries and the military establishment. Barnett's *China and the major powers in East Asia* (Washington, DC: Brookings Institution, 1979. 416p.) remains an important work, particularly for the thorough, policy-oriented, historical surveys of China's relations with Japan, the United States and the Soviet Union. *The agreements of the People's Republic of China with foreign countries, 1949-1990*, edited by Wolfgang Bartke (München; New York: Saur, 1992. 2nd rev. and enlarged ed. 231p.) is a standard reference which lists official government agreements year by year.

832 **Friends and enemies: the United States, China, and the Soviet Union, 1948-1972.**
Gordon H. Chang.   Stanford, California: Stanford University Press, 1990. 383p. (Modern America Series).

A revisionist study which uses newly declassified American archives and published Chinese and Russian documents. Chang argues that American policy-makers of the 1950s and 1960s, especially Dulles, Eisenhower and Nixon, publicly castigated the Moscow-Beijing monolith while privately advocating steps to crack it. Blind anti-Communism did not drive these leaders; their dilemma was that they could neither antagonize nor accommodate China. Chang finds: that China followed pragmatic policies independent of Soviet direction in the Korean War and the crises over threats to the Quemoy islands (which, according to Chang, are misrepresented in Eisenhower's memoirs); that Kennedy explored with the Russians a pre-emptive strike on Chinese nuclear facilities; and that American racial fear, ethnocentric ignorance and stereotypes consistently warped decisions, including that to intervene in Vietnam.

833 **China's road to the Korean War: the making of the Sino-American confrontation.**
Chen Jian.   New York: Columbia University Press, 1994. 339p. (The U.S. and Pacific Asia: Social, Economic, and Political Interaction).

Earlier analyses of the Korean War saw China as reacting to Korean adventurism, US initiative or Stalin's orders; however, recent work adds Chinese policy and cultural concerns. After a review of the scholarly literature, in part one Chen analyses China's emergence as a revolutionary power, its commitments to international Communism and its security concerns. Part two, which covers the period November 1948-June 1950, chronicles US debate over the recognition of 'Red' China and the formation of the Sino-Soviet alliance. Part three details Beijing's response to the start of the war in Korea and argues that Mao had already decided to intervene before UN troops crossed the 38th parallel and that no US course of action would have forestalled Chinese intervention. Shu Guang Zhang, *Mao's military romanticism: China and the Korean War, 1950-1953* (Lawrence, Kansas: University Press of Kansas, 1995. 338p. [Modern War Studies]) emphasizes culture and historical consciousness. Zhang argues that hurt national pride led Mao to intervene against overwhelming odds and to draw misleading lessons from seeming success; Americans were correspondingly misled by convictions of technological invincibility. Russell Spurr, *Enter the dragon: undeclared war against the U.S. in Korea, 1950-51* (New York: Newmarket Press, 1988. 335p.) interviews Chinese soldiers and leaders to describe individual experiences as well as policy. Other basic studies include Mark A. Ryan, *Chinese attitudes toward nuclear weapons: China and the United States during the Korean War* (Armonk, New York: M. E. Sharpe, 1989. 327p.). US policy is emphasized in: Rosemary Foot, *The wrong war: American policy and the dimensions of the Korean conflict, 1950-1953* (Ithaca, New York: Cornell University Press, 1985. 290p.); and William Whitney Stueck, Jr., *The road to confrontation: American policy toward China and Korea, 1947-1950* (Chapel Hill, North Carolina: University of North Carolina Press, 1981. 326p.).

834 **Sino-Soviet normalization and its international implications, 1945-1990.**

Lowell Dittmer.   Seattle, Washington; London: University of Washington Press, 1992. 373p.

A meticulous analysis of the course of the Sino-Soviet alliance, which pays careful attention to the internal motivations, relations with other members of the bloc, and reasons for the bitter relations of the 1960s-1980s. Most attention is given to the step-by-step normalization following the death of Mao in 1976. *China, the United States and the Soviet Union: tripolarity and policy making in the cold war*, edited by Robert S. Ross (Armonk, New York; London: M. E. Sharpe, 1993. 204p. [Studies on Contemporary China]) explores the 'strategic triangle' in the 1970s and 1980s.

835 **Reluctant adversaries: Canada and the People's Republic of China, 1949-1970.**

Edited by Paul M. Evans, B. Michael Frolic.   Toronto; Buffalo, New York; London: University of Toronto Press, 1991. 268p.

Ten essays for general readers examine the sources and content of Canadian policy towards the PRC in the period before diplomatic recognition in 1970, asking why Ottawa followed the lead of Washington even though few Canadians endorsed policies of military containment and isolation. Topics include: origins and the Canadian missionary connection; policy problems in the 1950s (recognition, membership in the United Nations); policy-makers; Lester Pearson, Prime Minister in the 1960s; Chester Ronning, a former missionary who represented Canada in China in 1945 and later lobbied against US policies; Alvin Hamilton; and recognizing the PRC (Prime Minster Pierre Trudeau's initiative, recognition and the Toronto Chinese Community, and de-recognition of Taiwan).

836 **The practice of power: U.S. relations with China since 1949.**

Rosemary Foot.   Oxford: Clarendon Press, Oxford University Press, 1995. 291p. bibliog.

A concise and balanced diplomatic history, based on published scholarship and records, as well as interviews in the United States and China. Robert S. Ross, *Negotiating cooperation: the United States and China, 1969-89* (Stanford, California: Stanford University Press, 1995. 349p. bibliog.) looks in more depth at a key period. Ross analyses the political process within each bureaucracy as their governments moved toward diplomatic contact; reached a *modus vivendi*, resulting in the Shanghai Communiqué of 1972; accomplished the entrance of the People's Republic into the United Nations and the eventual diplomatic recognition from the US; and reached the end of the era in June 1989.

837 **Foreign relations of the People's Republic of China.**

John W. Garver.   Englewood Cliffs, New Jersey: Prentice-Hall, 1993. 346p. bibliog.

A comprehensive text which surveys the period 1949-92. Coverage is broken down into six interrelated dimensions, rather than chronologically: pre-1949 experiences and traditions, including the 'myth of national humiliation', traditional world order and Chinese nationalism; relations with the Soviet and American superpowers, dealing with the formation and collapse of the Sino-Soviet alliance, the *détente* with the United States, and triangular disengagement; development as the centre of world revolution and retreat; international economic relations; national security, including military objectives in the confrontations with the US and USSR; and China in the 21st century. Chapter notes include extensive bibliographical references to books and articles in English.

838   **Uncertain partners: Stalin, Mao, and the Korean War.**
Sergei Goncharov, John Lewis, Xue Litai.   Stanford, California: Stanford University Press, 1994. 393p.

Uses new Russian and Chinese sources and interviews to portray in careful detail the Sino-Soviet alliance and the triangular dynamics of Chinese-Soviet-Korean relations leading up to the Korean War. The authors argue that Stalin saw China as the basis of his world strategy; he not only wanted to test and distract American military attention with a war in Korea, but also to drive a wedge between the Americans and the new People's Republic. Moscow endorsed Kim Il-sung's initiative, but offered limited support, preferring that China shoulder the burden.

839   **A fragile relationship: the United States and China since 1972.**
Harry Harding.   Washington, DC: Brookings Institution, 1992. 458p.

An analytical history of how the US and China created not only governmental but also cultural and business relations after Nixon's visit to Beijing. Harding puts post-1949 relations into four phases: an initial period of hostility, lasting to the Vietnam War; strategic alignment against the Soviets to the 1980s; roughly a decade of cooperation in modernization and reform ending in 1989; and the present period of distrust and confusion. The relationship was 'fragile' because each side had mistaken images and expectations of the other. According to the author, differences over Taiwan, Hong Kong, and relations with the Soviet Union were partially resolved and partly papered over, whereas differences over human rights and trade, exacerbated by American proselytizing attitudes, remain. Two final chapters outline future scenarios.

840   **China and the world: new directions in Chinese foreign relations.**
Edited by Samuel S. Kim.   Boulder, Colorado; San Francisco; Oxford: Westview Press, 1993. 2nd fully rev. ed. 339p. bibliog.

Provides essays which focus on foreign policy in the Deng decade (1978-88), when China was entering the global political system. In part one, 'Theory and Practice', three essays look at domestic sources of foreign policy, Maoist and post-Maoist conceptualizations. In part two, essays look at Sino-American relations, Sino-Soviet relations, and China and the Second and Third worlds. Part three examines policies and issues such as defence policy, the political economy of China's opening up, policy toward multi-lateral institutions, and the changing role of science and technology in foreign relations. Part four examines foreign policy options in the 1990s. An extensive bibliography, arranged by topic, covers Chinese and foreign books and articles in English, largely those published since 1972.

841   **Sovereignty and the status quo: the historical roots of China's Hong Kong policy.**
Kevin P. Lane.   Boulder, Colorado: Westview Press, 1990. 167p.
(Westview Special Studies on China and East Asia).

A succinct review and balanced analysis of Beijing's policies towards Hong Kong, which considers both domestic and international factors. *The Hong Kong Basic Law:*

blueprint for 'stability and prosperity' under Chinese sovereignty? edited by Ming K. Chan, David J. Clark (Armonk, New York: M. E. Sharpe, 1991. 328p.), and *Precarious balance: Hong Kong between China and Britain, 1842-1992*, edited by Ming K. Chan (Armonk, New York; London: M. E. Sharpe, 1994. 235p. bibliog.), both volumes in the Hong Kong Becoming China series, address current political concerns with scholarly tools; the second volume contains ten essays on the history of London-Canton-Beijing-Hong Kong relations.

842   **Chinese foreign policy: theory and practice.**
Edited by Thomas W. Robinson, David Shambaugh.   Oxford:
Clarendon Press, Oxford University Press, 1994. 644p. (Studies on
Contemporary China).

A comprehensive team survey, with extensive bibliographic references, of People's Republic foreign policy; the twenty authors also evaluate earlier views and suggest issues for future research. Section one considers domestic sources ('traditions of centrality, authority, and management', 'perception and ideology', 'economic development strategy', and 'elite politics'). Section two deals with 'China and the International Strategic System' and 'International Science and Technology'. Section three covers bilateral and regional relationships with United States, Russia, Europe, Africa and the Middle East, and China as an Asian power. Section four analyses patterns of behaviour (China's cooperative behaviour, international organizational behaviour, and negotiating behaviour). Section five examines 'International Relations Theory and the Study of Chinese Foreign Policy'. Section six provides a summary 'Conclusion'. An appendix suggests new bibliographical sources.

843   **The Indochina tangle: China's Vietnam policy, 1975-1979.**
Robert S. Ross.   New York: Columbia University Press, 1988. 392p.

The Second Indo-China War started when America's Vietnam War finished; China and Vietnam, flushed by victory, fought over (and in) Cambodia, over the issue of overseas Chinese in Vietnam, over the question of boundaries, and, probably most fundamentally, over Vietnam's relation with Russia. Ross analyses this regional (or sub-regional) war in a scholarly mode as a problem in Chinese foreign policy analysis, providing historical background, various possible interpretations, and methodological considerations. The war and its diplomacy are brought to life in another work by a respected diplomatic journalist who covered it for the *Far Eastern Economic Review*: Nayan Chanda, *Brother enemy: the war after the war* (San Diego, California; New York; London: Harcourt Brace Jovanovich, 1986. 479p.).

844   **Beautiful imperialist: China perceives America, 1972-1990.**
David Shambaugh.   Princeton, New Jersey: Princeton University
Press, 1991. 326p.

Anatomizes the field of America-watching in China, which burgeoned after Nixon's visit in 1972. Shambaugh explores interactions between images and decision making in international relations, and finds that a surprising diversity of interpretation developed among Chinese central government bureaucracies, professional research institutes, newspapers, and universities. However, he finds that there is still much unfamiliarity, misinformation, and misreading even among China's most knowledgeable 'America watchers'. The diversity comes partly from being positioned in different institutions, varying ideological and intellectual traditions, and formative experiences. *The Chinese view of the world*, edited by Hao Yufan, Huan Guocan (New York: Pantheon, 1989. 350p.) presents unofficial but well-informed views from young Chinese scholars with graduate training in the United States; they assess Chinese official attitudes and policies, including security, strategic, and economic aspects.

845   **Taiwan, Hong Kong and the United States, 1945-1992.**
       Nancy Bernkopf Tucker.   New York: Twayne; Toronto: Maxwell
       Macmillan Canada; New York; Oxford; Singapore; Sydney: Maxwell
       Macmillan International, 1994. 337p. bibliog. (Twayne's International
       History Series, no. 14).

Argues that American relations with the People's Republic were conditioned by 'uncertain friendships' with Taiwan and Hong Kong. After Nixon's visit to the PRC in 1972, the new economic and political strength of the two smaller entities, described in some detail here, earned them the right to be treated on their own. Tucker's vivid and persuasive story covers not only crises and treaties, commerce, and military strategy, but also the trans-Pacific cultural, personal and social webs which affected 'images' and psychology. The analysis encompasses Chinese-American immigrants, novels and movies, and scholarly relations, and concludes with an assessment of 'Greater China's' role in the developing Pacific Rim. A detailed bibliographical essay of secondary works and sources is also included.

846   **Cold war and revolution: Soviet-American rivalry and the origins of the Chinese civil war, 1944-1946.**
       Odd Arne Westad.   New York: Columbia University Press, 1993.
       260p. (The U.S. and Pacific Asia: Studies in Social, Economic, and
       Political Interaction).

A monographic reinterpretation of how developments in China affected Soviet-American rivalry and how their competition critically shaped the emerging Chinese civil war. After briefly reviewing earlier interpretations, chapters deal with: the end of the war, the Yalta Conference, and Roosevelt and Stalin's support for Chiang Kai-shek; Chiang's welcome of the Yalta agreement and Soviet support; Mao Zedong's foreign policy 1944-45; the growing tension in relations on the four sides, especially the Soviet-American Cold War; and a detailed analysis of Russian vacillation and American military and diplomatic interventions, which eventually led Chiang to choose a military solution in a new international system which offered him no effective support.

847   **China eyes Japan.**
       Alan S. Whiting.   Berkeley, California: University of California
       Press, 1989. 221p. bibliog.

Looks at the Sino-Japanese relationship in the light of China-Japan-US triangular relations. Whiting asks whether the rational, present-minded approach advocated by professional foreign policy officials in China and Japan (which should benefit the United States) can prevail over historic feelings of cultural resentment and political rivalry. Atavistic antagonism, after all, produced nearly a century of war, sharply remembered in both countries, especially China. Whiting recounts the relations between the two governments since 1945 in clear detail; his conclusions, often based on talks with high officials in China and Japan, are thought-provoking on many issues. Chae-jin Lee, *China and Japan: new economic diplomacy* (Stanford, California:

Hoover Institution, 1984. 174p.) explores Japan's role in the Baoshan complex and the steel industry, oil development and the Bohai oil fields, and Japanese government loans and grants.

848 **The Chinese calculus of deterrence: India and Indochina.**
Alan S. Whiting. Ann Arbor, Michigan: University of Michigan Press, 1975. 299p.

A study of China's foreign policy aims and methods, which focuses on protecting interests in Vietnam and the 1962 Himalayan war with India. Neville Maxwell, *India's China war* (London: Cape, 1970. 475p.) is a circumstantial diplomatic and military account, which is critical of Nehru's diplomacy for being both naive and provocative. Jay Taylor, *The dragon and the wild goose* (Westport, Connecticut: Greenwood, 1987. 289p. [Contributions to the Study of World History]) is a generalist's presentation of relations between China and India from the time of Buddha and Confucius to the days of Gandhi and Mao.

849 **Deterrence and strategic culture: Chinese-American confrontations, 1949-1958.**
Zhang Shuguang. Ithaca, New York: Cornell University Press, 1993. 302p. (Cornell Studies in Security Affairs).

Uses American and Chinese published sources (some newly declassified), American archives (Chinese archives are not yet open), and interviews on both sides of the Pacific to study seven major crises. These include: Truman's 1950 decision to place the Seventh Fleet in the Taiwan Straits; the military conflict in Korea; Eisenhower's search for a truce in 1953; the Indo-China war and Geneva settlement; and the confrontations of 1954 and 1958 which threatened nuclear war. 'Neither side had the aggressive intentions that the other feared', Zhang concludes in his evaluation of the political science theory of mutual deterrence.

China and the overseas Chinese: a study of Peking's changing policy, 1949-1970.
See item no. 460.

Chinese arms transfers: purposes, patterns, and prospects in the new world order.
See item no. 857.

China builds the bomb.
See item no. 860.

China's participation in the IMF, the World Bank, and GATT: toward a global economic order.
See item no. 953.

The China-Hong Kong connection: the key to China's Open-Door policy.
See item no. 963.

Military and Defence

To 1949

850 **Cultural realism: strategic culture and grand strategy in Chinese history.**
Alastair Iain Johnston. Princeton, New Jersey: Princeton University Press, 1995. 307p. maps. bibliog.

Analyses ideas and behaviour in Chinese military classics (*bingshu*) and Ming dynasty strategic decision making. Theorists in current international relations make predictions based on structural realpolitik and rational policy judgements which operate across cultures; area studies relativists argue that cultural assumptions about conflict, the nature of the enemy, and the efficacy of violence affect strategic priorities. Johnston considers these conflicting theories, devises empirical models to test them, and concludes that there is a Chinese strategic culture but that its components are not self-evidently unique. Topics include: questions of methodology; Chinese ideas of righteous war, efficacy of violence, and 'not fighting and still subduing the enemy'; the Ming security *problematique*; and Ming security culture.

851 **Chinese ways in warfare.**
Edited by Frank A. Kierman, Jr., John K. Fairbank. Cambridge, Massachusetts: Harvard University Press, 1974. 401p. (Harvard East Asian Series, no. 74).

Contains eight scholarly essays, with a substantial introduction, entitled 'Varieties of the Chinese Military Experience'. Topics include: phases and modes of combat in Zhou dynasty China; the campaigns of Han Wudi; the siege and defence of towns in Song and Yuan China; inland naval warfare in the founding of the Ming dynasty; and the disastrous 'Tumu incident' of 1449, in which a eunuch general led a disastrous expedition against the Mongols, leading to the capture of the emperor.

852   **The pursuit of power: technology, armed force, and society since A.D. 1000.**
William McNeil.   Chicago: University of Chicago Press; Cambridge, England: Basil Blackwell, 1982. 405p.

A history of the role of military force in the making of the modern world. Chapter two, 'The Era of Chinese Predominance, 1000-1500', analyses Chinese military technology and organization and the repercussions of Chinese commerce throughout the world. The remainder of the book examines reasons for the loss of dominance and the rise of the military industrial complex in Europe. Geoffrey Parker, *The military revolution: military innovation and the rise of the West* (Cambridge, England; New York; Port Chester, New York; Melbourne; Sydney: Cambridge University Press, 1988. 234p.) also includes a description of China's early modern technological predominance.

853   **China's struggle for naval development, 1839-1895.**
John L. Rawlinson.   Cambridge, Massachusetts: Harvard University Press, 1967. 318p.

Examines the first generation of Self-strengtheners who bought Western military technology to save Confucian China. Regional leaders, evading conservative bureaucrats in the central government, used traditional institutions to develop competing regional navies. However, their initial success in building these fleets undermined any chance to build a national navy and led to the débâcles of 1884 and 1895. Thomas L. Kennedy, *The arms of Kiangnan: modernization in the Chinese ordinance industry, 1860-1895* (Boulder, Colorado; San Francisco; Oxford: Westview Press, 1978. 246p.) studies the arsenals in the lower Yangzi valley. Kennedy claims that the eventual failure to form an independent Chinese arms industry was caused by the low quality of foreign experts and government inability to stop meddling in technical decisions or to eliminate corruption and waste.

854   **The seven military classics of ancient China.**
Translation, commentary by Ralph D. Sawyer, with Mei-chün Sawyer. Boulder, Colorado; San Francisco; Oxford: Westview Press, 1993. 568p. bibliog. (History of Warfare Series).

By the Song dynasty, military thought, like much derived from the ancient Classics, had become standardized in a set of texts – the *Wujing qishu*, or Seven Military Classics, translated here. The Sawyers include a thorough set of introductions and notes to help readers interested in military history but not much background in China. An extensive bibliography of secondary works includes sections on general background, weapons, technology (such as transport), and military history. The most famous of the manuals, *The art of war* (*Sunzi bingfa*), written by Sunzi (Sun Tzu), a rough contemporary of Confucius, influenced combatants from Mao Zedong to corporate executives; Sawyer's translation is re-issued separately (Boulder, Colorado; San Francisco; Oxford: Westview Press, 1994. 375p. [History and Warfare]). Other sound translations include: *The art of war*, translated, with an introduction by Samuel B. Griffith (London; Oxford; New York: Oxford University Press, 1963. 197p. bibliog.); and *The art of war*, translated by Thomas Cleary (Boston, Massachusetts: Shambala Publications, 1991. 2nd abridged ed. 120p.) which discusses the book as a Daoist text.

855 **Eighth voyage of the dragon: a history of China's quest for seapower.**
Bruce Swanson.   Annapolis, Maryland: Naval Institute Press, 1982.
348p. bibliog.

A broad military and political history of Chinese naval power, with an emphasis on
the pre-1949 period, based on English-language sources. Swanson discusses the Ming
navy and its voyages, 19th-century build-up and destruction from the Opium Wars to
the 1895 Sino-Japanese War, and the naval plans and achievements of Nationalist
China and the People's Republic to 1980.

Rebellion and its enemies in late imperial China: militarization and social structure, 1796-1864.
See item no. 218.

Mercenaries and mandarins: the Ever-Victorious Army in nineteenth century China.
See item no. 232.

China at war, 1901-1949.
See item no. 258.

Chemistry and chemical technology: part 6: military technology: missiles and sieges.
See item no. 1084.

After 1949

856 **Party-military relations in the PRC and Taiwan: paradoxes of control.**
Cheng Hsiao-shih.   Boulder, Colorado: Westview Press, 1990. 178p.
(Westview Special Studies on China and East Asia).

Analyses the functions of the commissar system, which exerts civilian (i.e. Party)
control over the military on either side of the Taiwan Strait, both of which adopted
this Leninist system in the 1920s. After a thorough review of the theoretical literature,
Cheng examines the system in the People's Republic and the Republic of China on
Taiwan. He concludes that although the danger of military coup is minimal, the
commissar system does not in fact ensure civilian control, as the commissars are fixed
in the military hierarchy. The analysis shows that during the 1960s and 1970s, the
relative power of generals and party leaders waxed and waned.

857 **Chinese arms transfers: purposes, patterns, and prospects in the new world order.**
R. Bates Gill.   New York; Westport, Connecticut; London: Praeger
Publishers, 1992. 248p.

Argues that in transferring weapons to foreign countries, China's aims have often been
more strategic than ideological or economic. In the 1950s, free arms were given to

North Korea and North Vietnam as a defence against the US; in the 1960s the USSR became the primary rival leading to free weapons for client states in Africa and Asia; in the 1980s, Iran and Iraq received their share. Other scholars give more emphasis than Gill does to economic motives, and stress the rise of a commercial minded military-industrial complex outside the control of Beijing's political and security bureaucracies.

858   **From swords to plowshares? defense industry reform in the PRC.**
       Paul Humes.   Boulder, Colorado: Westview, 1992. 297p.
Humes examines the effects of the 1980s reforms and the rethinking of defence strategies on the political economy of the military industrial complex. He uses both published sources and interviews in China to describe national policy and the experience of particular factories in Beijing, Shanghai, Xi'an and Chongqing. Humes finds that there was success both in converting factories to civilian production and in selling weapons abroad; military allocations in the published budget fell under the reforms, but total actual expenditure may well have kept pace with inflation or even risen. Problems include resistance from military professionals, retraining former soldiers and workers, finding domestic and foreign markets, and excess capacity.

859   **The Chinese army after Mao.**
       Ellis Joffe.   Cambridge, Massachusetts: Harvard University Press, 1987. 210p.
A clear description and policy analysis of changes in organization and strategy of the People's Liberation Army after 1978. Joffe first summarizes the 1950-76 period of Soviet tutelage when Mao kept the military politically subordinate. Although it fought well in Korea, the People's Liberation Army fell behind evolving world standards in doctrine, organization and weapons, and during the Cultural Revolution was demoralized by a bickering and politicized officer corps. After 1978, reformers campaigned to professionalize and modernize officers, their doctrines and their weaponry. Maoist guerrilla doctrine was forgotten, while the restoration of morale and technical expertise used 1950s styles. Standard studies include: Harvey W. Nelson, *The Chinese military system: an organizational study of the Chinese People's Liberation Army* (Boulder, Colorado: Westview Press, 1981. 2nd ed. rev. and updated. 285p.); William W. Whitson, with Huang Chen-hsia, *The Chinese high command: a history of communist military politics, 1927-71* (New York: Praeger Publishers, 1973. 638p.); Lee Ngok, *China's defense modernization and military leadership* (Sydney: Australian National University Press, 1989. 395p.). *Quelling the people: the military suppression of the Beijing democracy movement*, by Timothy Brook (New York: Oxford University Press, 1992. 265p.) is a readable, detailed narrative of the People's Liberation Army's role in the June 1989 suppression of the democracy movement, with much background material on the role and ideology of the military.

860   **China builds the bomb.**
       John Wilson Lewis, Xue Litai.   Stanford, California; Stanford University Press, 1988. 329p.
A political and institutional history of early nuclear weapons policy debate and development, paying particular attention to the 1964 uranium bomb and the multi-stage nuclear weapon of 1967. Lewis and Xue mine published memoirs, interviews and public documents, but had no access to Chinese archives or classified documents. The opening chapters describe the political background of the 1950s decision to invest

in nuclear exploration. The middle chapters provide a detailed narrative of the search for uranium, the production of fissions grade material, and the design and production of the first uranium bomb in 1964. The authors assess: the impact of strategic and defence policies on political development; the role of Soviet assistance (though American technology and American trained experts were equally important); the problems caused by political campaigns; and the contributions of Mao and Zhou (which were minimal compared to those of the scientific leaders).

861   **China's strategic seapower: the politics of force modernization in the nuclear age.**
John Wilson Lewis, Xue Litai.   Stanford, California: Stanford University Press, 1994. 393p. maps. bibliog.

Discusses the interaction of politics and technology in strategic force modernization from 1958 to the reforms of the 1980s, continuing the history of the strategic weapons complex begun in *China builds the bomb* (q.v.). Mao in the heat of the Great Leap Forward was snubbed by the Soviets and determined to develop nuclear power. After the near-total shift to solid-propellant rockets and the development of sea-based and new mobile ballistic missiles, efforts focused on submarine-launched ballistic missiles and building up a fleet of nuclear powered submarines, programmes which were disrupted by radical Cultural Revolution elements. Part one, 'The Submarine', contains chapters on nuclear propulsion, design, military industry, and building and deployment. Part two analyses 'the missile'. Part three, 'Strategy', explores strategic uncertainty and rationale and reason in the nuclear era.

862   **Defending China.**
Gerald Segal.   New York; Oxford: Oxford University Press, 1987. 364p. maps. bibliog.

A topical history of wars and confrontations since 1949, focusing on the policy debates and adaptation of strategies. Chapters treat relations (particularly military and near military confrontations) with Vietnam, India, Korea, Japan and the Soviet Union. *Chinese defense policy*, edited by Gerald Segal, William T. Tow (Urbana, Illinois: University of Illinois Press, 1984; London: Macmillan, 1986. 286p.) and *China's military reforms: international and domestic implications*, edited by Charles D. Lovejoy, Jr., Bruce W. Watson (Boulder, Colorado: Westview Press, 1986. 142p.) are symposia which provide a range of analysis of policy and developments.

Law, Democracy and Constitutions

General and to 1949

863 **Civil law in Qing and Republican China.**
Kathryn Bernhardt, Philip C. C. Huang.   Stanford, California:
Stanford University Press, 1994. 340p.

Contains conference papers which challenge the generalization that civil law (dealing with disputes among the people) has been less important in China than criminal or administrative law. Basing their findings on newly opened local archives in China, the authors show how Qing and Republican courts dealt consistently, and in accordance with written codes, with land rights, debt, marriage, inheritance and commercial transactions. Two opening chapters authoritatively summarize issues in history and theory, with useful theoretical disquisitions and bibliographical references. One paper deals with lawyers and the legal profession during the Republican period. Throughout the work, the authors examine the society in which the law operated, thereby working in the fields of both social and legal history.

864 **Law in imperial China, exemplified by 190 Ch'ing dynasty cases.**
Translated from the *Hsing-an hui lan*, with historical, social, and
juridical commentaries.
Derk Bodde, Clarence Morris.   Cambridge, Massachusetts: Harvard
University Press, 1967. Reprinted, Philadelphia, Pennsylvania:
University of Pennsylvania Press, 1973. 615p.

A pioneering introduction to the cross-cultural study of Chinese law. Part one surveys: the concepts and history of Chinese law and its role in government and society; the Qing code (*xingan huilan*); the penal system (punishments by imprisonment, fines, beating with bamboo); and the judiciary system. Part two translates, with the Qing interpretations, 190 cases from the code. Appendices analyse the cases and give sources and references. The basic statutes are given in *The Great Qing Code*, translated by William C. Jones, with the assistance of Tianquan Cheng, Yongling

Jiang (Oxford: Clarendon Press; New York: Oxford University Press, 1994. 441p.), which provides both a view of the intentions of the dynasty and a set of standard English translations for legal terms.

865   **Chinese family law and social change in historical and comparative perspective.**
Edited by David Buxbaum.   Seattle, Washington: University of Washington Press, 1978. 553p. (University of Washington School of Asian Law Series, no. 3).

Contains fifteen pioneering essay, whose topics include: marriage and divorce in Han China, in which Ban Zhao's often quoted *Admonitions for women* is shown to be advice to women, not descriptive of them; divorce in traditional Chinese law; family property and the law of inheritance in traditional China; and family partition in Taiwan. Essays make comparisons with Soviet, post-revolutionary Indonesian, Indian and Hindu family law.

866   **Law and society in traditional China.**
Ch'ü T'ung-tsu.   Paris, The Hague: Mouton, 1965. rev. reprint. 304p. bibliog. (Le Monde d'Outre-mer, Passé et Présent, Première Série, no. 4).

Argues that from the Han to the Qing dynasties, government used law to advance Confucian social ideals, especially in the field of family law. Although later scholars modify Ch'ü's thesis that the legal structure did not change over two thousand years, the descriptions of laws, judicial rulings, and the manner of enforcement make this volume worth consulting. Both Confucians and Legalists agreed on ideals, though Confucians only gradually came to accept political means of enforcement: family harmony and social stability depended on strengthening the *zu* (the patrilineal unit) and on reinforcing the powers of the father as head of family.

867   **Essays on China's legal tradition.**
Edited by Jerome Alan Cohen, R. Randle Edwards, Fu-mei Chang Chen.   Princeton, New Jersey: Princeton University Press, 1980. 438p. bibliog.

Provides ten ground-breaking scholarly essays. The editors' introduction presents problems and describes the state of the field. Topics include: institutions and procedures of the Zhou dynasty; the administration of justice in the Song; age, youth and infirmity in Qing law; Qing judicial decisions; Qing legal jurisdiction over foreigners; and slavery at the end of the Qing.

868   **Policing and punishment in China: from patriarchy to 'the people'.**
Michael R. Dutton.   Cambridge, England; New York; Melbourne: Cambridge University Press, 1992. 391p. bibliog.

A dense, theoretically oriented interpretation of Chinese law and political power in light of Michel Foucault's theories. Dutton describes the great changes in 'technologies of power' – law and enforcement – from late imperial times to the 1980s, but finds that Foucault's analysis of the European modernization of law and society does not fit China. The relation between the individual, the group, law, and political power were quite different, even as a powerful modern national power emerged in China. Both the traditional and contemporary systems were expected to promote social harmony, not individual rights, but Dutton describes equally great discontinuities in aims and techniques, and doubts that the economic reforms of the 1980s will produce political individualism, liberal self-realization, or Western concepts of human rights.

869 *T'ang-yin pi-shih*, 'Parallel cases from under the pear tree': a 13th century manual of jurisprudence and detection.
Translated by R. H. van Gulik. Leiden, the Netherlands: E. J. Brill, 1956. 198p. bibliog. (Sinica Leidensa).

County magistrates in China had responsibility for all aspects of local government, in that they both investigated the crime and judged the perpetrators. This manual of illustrative cases, accompanied here by an introduction and commentary, was widely used in late imperial China. Magistrates could supposedly find guidance by perusing these examples; in any case, they could enjoy the stories. R. H. van Gulik, a Dutch diplomat-Orientalist, was obviously intrigued by this informative and charming book, and went on to write his own detective stories featuring Judge Dee (see *Celebrated cases of Judge Dee*, q.v.).

870 Remnants of Ch'in law.
A. F. P. Hulsewé. Leiden, the Netherlands: E. J. Brill, 1985. 242p. bibliog.

Provides annotated translations of recently excavated fragments of laws and regulations from the 3rd century BCE. Hulsewé's *Remnants of Han law* (Leiden, the Netherlands: E. J. Brill, 1955. 2 vols.) interprets the nature of law in the Han dynasty, with a translation of the chapter on 'punishments' in Ban Gu's *Hanshu*. Hulsewé's 'Ch'in and Han Law' in *Ch'in and Han empires, 221 BC-AD 220* (q.v.) sets the law in its historical and political context. For later codes, see: Wallace Johnson, *The T'ang code: volume I, general principles* (Princeton, New Jersey: Princeton University Press, 1979. bibliog. [Harvard Studies in East Asian Law, no. 10]), which reconstructs as much as possible of the Tang codes, with a substantial introduction and commentaries; and Paul H. Ch'en, *Chinese legal tradition under the Mongols: the code of 1291 as reconstructed* (Princeton, New Jersey: Princeton University Press, 1979. 205p. bibliog. [Harvard University Series in East Asian Law]), in which Ch'en argues that the Mongols made a contribution to Chinese legal tradition. This work also includes a complete translation of the 1291 legal code.

871 Traditional Chinese penal law.
Geoffrey MacCormack. Edinburgh: Edinburgh University Press; New York: Columbia University Press, 1991. 309p. bibliog.

A detailed introduction to the evolution of penal law, based on an examination of the written codes, primarily in the period from Tang to Qing. MacCormack describes the following subjects: the judicial system; punishments; exemptions on the basis of family position or status; the central role of confessions, which demonstrated repentance and were required in capital cases; and how family law (far more than in the West) was used to enforce family values and practices, such as mourning and inheritance. The conclusion compares Chinese and Western law and offers tentative explanations for the basic principles of Chinese law.

872 **The quality of mercy: amnesties and traditional Chinese law.**
Brian McKnight. Honolulu, Hawaii: University of Hawaii Press,
1981. 172p. bibliog.
The emperor and his minions developed the practice of granting amnesty (often seasonal) for both ritual and practical considerations. McKnight traces this practice from the Zhou dynasty to the Qing; after the Song dynasty amnesty was granted less often by increasingly rigid and autocratic governments. Another judicial device is brought to life in rich social and political context by Joanna Waley-Cohen, *Exile in mid-Qing China: banishment to Xinjiang, 1758-1820* (New Haven, Connecticut: Yale University Press, 1991. 267p.).

873 **Law and order in Sung China.**
Brian E. McKnight. Cambridge, England: Cambridge University
Press, 1992. 557p. maps. bibliog. (Cambridge Studies in Chinese
History, Literature and Institutions).
A social history of law, law enforcement, criminality and the penal system during the Song dynasty (960-1279). McNight writes broadly, informing the serious general reader of the historical context of the Song as a commercializing and urbanizing civilization which was developing from a military to a civilian government, with attendant changes in the role of law. Chapter topics include: crimes and criminals; formal and informal law enforcement; personnel problems; urban crime and security; the penal system; prisons and jailers; and the death penalty.

874 **The Book of Lord Shang: a classic of the Chinese school of law.**
Shang Yang, translated, edited by J. J. L. Duyvendak. London:
Probsthain, 1928. Reprinted, Chicago: University of Chicago Press,
1963. 346p.
Shang Yang (c. 390-338 BCE) – Lord Shang – reformed the Qin state, which led to the unification of empire; his book expounds the administrative practices of Legalism. *Shang Yang's reforms and state control in China*, edited and with an introduction by Li Yu-ning (White Plains, New York: M. E. Sharpe, 1977. 271p. [China Book Project]) translates a Cultural Revolution monograph, *Shang Yang bianfa*, by Yang Kuan (Shanghai: Renmin, 1973). Li's meaty introduction describes the historical sources, then explains Shang Yang's reputations as either rational bureaucrat or totalitarian technician, and why Yang Kuan's book was controversial. An appendix translates the biography from Sima Qian's *Shiji*. *Guanzi: political, economic, and philosophic essays from early China*, by Guan Zhong (Kuan Chung), translated by W. Allyn Rickett (Princeton, New Jersey: Princeton University Press, 1985- ; vol. I, *A study and translation*) is a pre-Han miscellany of political and cosmological texts.

875 **Order and discipline in China: the Shanghai Mixed Court,
1911-1927.**
Thomas B. Stephens. Seattle, Washington; London: University of
Washington Press, 1992. 159p. bibliog.
Extraterritoriality exempted foreigners in Shanghai from Chinese law, and meant that Chinese could not be tried in foreign courts. Agreements established the Mixed Court of the International Settlement in which Chinese judges and foreign consular representatives prosecuted crimes and adjudicated disputes. Thomas reviews various

studies of Chinese law and social theory to argue that this Court cannot be evaluated in terms of traditional jurisprudence; he offers a new perspective, that of 'disciplinary theory' which provides a more apt understanding of the 'order without law' which he sees as the Court's achievement.

Getting an heir: adoption and the construction of kinship in late imperial China.
See item no. 623.

The washing away of wrongs: forensic medicine in thirteenth-century China.
See item no. 672.

A history of Chinese political thought.
See item no. 688.

The People's Republic (1949-)

876 **The criminal process in the People's Republic of China, 1949-1963: an introduction.**
Jerome Alan Cohen.   Cambridge, Massachusetts: Harvard University Press, 1968. 706p. bibliog. (Harvard Studies in East Asian Law, no. 2).
A detailed description, which includes both theory and practice, presented through cases, documents, commentaries and annotations. The reforms of the 1980s did not completely change these procedures, and many of the laws and regulations described here remain as a basis or reference point for post-Mao reforms. Leng Shao-chuan, with Hungdah Chiu, *Criminal justice in post-Mao China: analysis and documents* (Albany, New York: State University of New York Press, 1985. 330p.) is another case textbook, offering more recent statutes, commentaries and annotations.

877 **Basic principles of civil law in China.**
Edited by William Jones.   Armonk, New York; London: M. E. Sharpe, 1989. 378p. bibliog.
The 1986 General Provisions of Civil Law was promulgated with the understanding that it was to be supplemented with semi-official commentaries and treatises for law schools and working jurists. One of these is *Minfa yuanli* (Beijing, 1987), roughly two-thirds of which is translated here. Jones' introduction explains that the text represents both an indispensable reference work and a partisan policy statement on the role of law in Chinese society; the text ostentatiously favours socialist ownership in order to counter anti-reformist attacks on 'bourgeois law'. The organization and principles are modelled on the German Code, which assumes that individuals should use contracts and organize collective entities to promote economic growth. Topics include: the legal position of citizens; partnerships and joint ventures; property, in the sense of German 'sachen'; obligations; and contracts (including foreign).

878   **Law without lawyers: a comparative view of law in China and the United States.**
Victor Li. Boulder, Colorado: Westview Press, 1978. 102p. bibliog.

A broad comparison of values and practices, with a critical evaluation of then favourable views of law in China. Many held that economic justice and social organization could produce civil order without professional lawyers and an autonomous police system, and that in any case, people from other cultures were not in a position to condemn China.

879   **Domestic law reforms in post-Mao China.**
Edited by Pitman Potter. Armonk, New York; London: M. E. Sharpe, 1994. 311p. bibliog. (Studies on Contemporary China).

Six essays, with an overview introduction, evaluate the initial accomplishments of Chinese law reform, the mixed intentions behind them, and the difficulties they face. Essays in part one place reforms into historical, comparative and legal perspectives. Part two, 'Economic and Civil Law', examines the Supreme People's Court and the development of contracts, asking whether they are legal institution, administrative device or foreign import. In part three, essays examine the draft press law ('to protect or restrict?') and the administrative litigation law as judicial review and bureaucratic reform. Contributors to the volume include Stanley Lubman, Edward J. Epstein, Murray S. Tanner, William C. Jones, James V. Feinerman, Judy Polumbaum and Pitman B. Potter.

880   **The economic contract law of China: legitimation and contract autonomy in the PRC.**
Pitman B. Potter. Seattle, Washington; London: University of Washington Press, 1992. 234p. bibliog.

The Economic Contract Law of the PRC was promulgated as part of the 1980s reforms to create a market economy. Potter first explains the theoretical issues involved in choosing which legal tools to use in resolving contract disputes and how China's approaches resemble and differ from those tried in the West. Using a case by case explication, he then shows that during the 1980s the tools of the command economy and administrative supervision were gradually but not completely replaced by market principles and legal autonomy. He describes the institutions such as the State Administration of Industry and Commerce and the Notarial Offices, which are under the Ministry of Justice, and provides almost sixty pages of tables of cases and of regulations.

881   **Laogai: the Chinese Gulag.**
Harry Hongda Wu, translated by Ted Slingerland, foreword by Fang Lizhi. Boulder, Colorado: Westview, 1990. 247p. maps.

A committed, passionate, meticulous exposé and analysis of the prison labour camp system in the People's Republic by one of its former inmates. Wu maintains that *laogai* (reform through labour) and prison labour camps are essential parts of the government economic system; he provides a detailed history of their origin, theoretical basis, structure, conditions and economic significance. Wu shows that convict labour, 're-education through labor' (*laojiao*), and 'forced job placement' are regular and official parts of the legal control system. A final chapter considers reforms under Deng Xiaoping, concluding that the two main purposes of the system – 'violent suppression' and 'production by slaves' – have not changed. Appendices supply maps, lists of commodities, and further statistics on 990 labour reform camps.

Foreign trade, investment and the law in the People's Republic of China.
See item no. 957.

The People's Republic of China: a bibliography of selected English language legal materials.
See item no. 1498.

Democratic thought and human rights

882 China: punishment without crime: administrative detention.
Amnesty International.   London; New York: Amnesty International Publications, 1991. 62p.

Amnesty International is a non-governmental worldwide movement; it works globally for the release from detainment for prisoners of conscience, fair and early trials for all political prisoners, opposes the death penalty or torture for any prisoner, and issues frequent regional reports to the public. This 1991 report details post-Tiananmen violations. Earlier reports, which offer background essays, references and documentation, pictures, charts and maps, include: *Political imprisonment in the People's Republic of China* (New York; London: Amnesty International, 1978. 176p.); and *China: violations of human rights: prisoners of conscience and the death penalty in the People's Republic of China* (London: Amnesty International 1984. 129p.). See also *Punishment season: human rights in China after martial law*, by Asia Watch Committee (New York: Human Rights Watch, 1990. 173p.). An official response is China State Council, *Human rights in China* (Beijing: Information Office, State Council, November 1991. 86p.). *China: the massacre of June 1989 and its aftermath* (London: Amnesty International, 1990) uses eye-witness accounts to establish the sequence of events and numbers of victims.

883 On socialist democracy and the Chinese legal system: the Li Yizhe debates.
Edited by Anita Chan, Stanley Rosen, Jonathan Unger.   Armonk, New York; London: M. E. Sharpe, 1985. 310p. bibliog.

After the fall of Lin Biao, the Defence Minister whose attempted coup in 1971 was unsuccessful, authorities encouraged public criticism. 'Li Yizhe', a group pseudonym for three former Canton Red Guards newly released from prison, responded with a series of Big Character Posters which landed them back in jail. Their 'On Socialist Democracy and the Legal System', widely circulated in handwritten copies, called for the rule of law, due process, political participation, and an end to personal rule. Translated here also are the documents surrounding their arrest in 1974 and vindication after the fall of the Gang of Four, along with essays showing their evolving thought, such as 'Mao Zedong and the Cultural Revolution'. Also critical from a Marxist view is Chen Erjin, translated by Robin Munro, *Crossroads socialism* (London: Verso; New York: Schocken Books, 1983. 263p.). The early phases of the movement are critically analysed in Peter Moody, *Opposition and dissent in China* (Stanford, California: Hoover Institution Press, 1977. 342p.).

884 **Between freedom and subsistence: China and human rights.**
Ann Kent. Hong Kong: Oxford University Press, 1993. 293p. bibliog.
Assesses the overall condition of human rights in China since 1949 at the formal institutional level and at the informal level of practice. The work also develops a comparative theoretical framework relating China's particular situation to historic international standards. Prevailing international definitions of human rights include both the civil and political rights emphasized in Western political democracies and the social, economic and developmental rights stressed by socialist, developing nations like China. Kent argues that a realistic moral analysis can avoid both cultural relativism and ethnocentric moralism. Chapters examine these problems in chronological periods from imperial China to the 1989 Democracy Movement.

885 **Human rights in contemporary China.**
R. Randle Edwards, Louis Henkin, A. J. Nathan. New York; London: Columbia University Press, 1986. 193p. bibliog.
Surveys the history and status of human rights in China. Henkin's essay looks at China from the comparative perspective of both Marxist and democratic examples. Edwards examines civil and social rights in current Chinese legal theory. Nathan first discusses the continuing but changing concern with rights of citizenry in eleven Chinese constitutions from 1912 to 1982, then explores 'Sources of Chinese Rights Thinking'. Timothy Gellat, Lawyers Committee for Human Rights, *Criminal justice with Chinese characteristics* (New York: Lawyers' Committee for Human Rights, 1993. 89p.) is a well-crafted brief for the practicability and benefit of finding Chinese counterparts for Western legal concepts. *Human rights in post-Mao China*, by John F. Copper, Franz Michael, Yuan-li Wu (Boulder, Colorado; San Francisco, California; Oxford: Westview Press, 1985. 117p.) begins with a self-proclaimed 'western bias' in defining human rights as something which the Marxist-Leninist tradition cannot absorb; the authors see Deng's reforms as inconsequential, but hold out the hope that humane elements in China's legal tradition could nurture modern Chinese democratic institutions.

886 **Cries for democracy in China: writings and speeches from the 1989 Chinese democracy movement.**
Edited by Han Minzhu, Hua Sheng, preface by Yan Jiaqi, introduction by Jonathan D. Spence. Princeton, New Jersey: Princeton University Press, 1990. 401p.
The two pseudonymous editors select, translate and comment on writings and speeches from the 1989 Democracy Spring in Beijing and other cities. They include flyers, big character posters, handbills, poems, articles from underground journals, government statements, and transcriptions of tapes. The selections are arranged chronologically, along with a number of photographs, to tell the story and recreate the atmosphere of that spring.

887　**China's struggle for the rule of law.**
Ronald C. Keith.　London: Macmillan; New York: St. Martin's, 1994.
290p. bibliog.

A detailed but not unduly technical overview of Chinese legal aspirations. The 1980s
debate over the 'rule of law' (*fazhi*) asked whether a socialist law could shape and
curb the political system rather than simply implementing its decisions. Keith explains
that problems arose over the use of foreign concepts, the nature of a socialist market
economy, new patterns of ownership, and the legal structure of 'socialism with
Chinese characteristics'. Chapter one outlines the Chinese debate, Western
perspectives, and the history of the concepts. Succeeding chapters describe:
comparative legal cultures, including imperial Confucian and Legalist approaches;
civil law and civil society; law, contracts and ownership rights; political and criminal
law change under reform; Hong Kong and the rule of law across 'two systems'; and
the changes and continuities after Tiananmen. Appendices include a select glossary of
Chinese terms and a bibliography.

888　**Chinese democracy.**
Andrew J. Nathan.　New York: Alfred A. Knopf, 1985. Reprinted,
Berkeley, California: University of California Press, 1990. 313p.

A basic study. The Democracy Movement of the mid-1980s, which anticipated that of
1989 is appraised through interviews and writings of participants and through an
analysis of the landmark local elections of 1980. Chapters then trace Chinese
democratic tradition back nearly a century to Liang Qichao, founder of the Progressive
Party in 1913. Liang, like Mao and many contemporary Chinese Democrats, saw
democracy not as a self-justifying good for embodying individual human rights, but as
instrumental in gathering information for policy-makers, communicating state policies
once formed, and enlisting support for their efficient execution. Nathan shows that the
numerous post-1911 constitutions grandly created rights but conditioned them on state
need and expedience. Chapters also study the rise of propaganda and mass media
developed for the service of the state. The conclusion broadly discusses 'Chinese
Democracy and Western Values'.

889　**Toward a democratic China: the intellectual autobiography of Yan
Jiaqi.**
Yan Jiaqi, translated by David S. K. Hong, Dennis Mair, foreword by
Andrew J. Nathan.　Honolulu, Hawaii: University of Hawaii Press,
1992. 285p. (School of Hawaiian Asian & Pacific Studies Library of
Translations).

Yan Jiaqi (1942-) was one of the élite theorists of Deng Xiaoping's government in the
1980s; his autobiography (a translation of *Wo de sixiang zijuan* [Hunan, China:
People's Press; Hong Kong: Joint Publishing, 1989]) explains his ideas with passion
and imagination. One of the essays takes a 'time trip' to interview European thinkers
of the Enlightenment, and other essays explore democracy in the socialist world. The
introduction to *Yan Jiaqi and China's struggle for democracy*, edited, translated, with
an introductory essay by David Bachman, Dali Yang (Armonk, New York; London:
M. E. Sharpe, 1991. 201p. [Chinese Studies on China]), a volume of Yan's essays,
argues that Yan's concept of Chinese style democracy is based on a tradition which
emphasizes collective spirit and works toward social cooperation; the (Western)
pluralist view is that procedural process regulates and constrains autonomous
individuals.

Chinese democracy and the crisis of 1989: Chinese and American reflections.
See item no. 779.

China's crisis: dilemmas of reform and prospects for democracy.
See item no. 785.

Economy

General economic history and to 1949

890　**Big business in China: Sino-foreign rivalry in the cigarette industry, 1890-1930.**
Sherman Cochran.　Cambridge, Massachusetts; London: Harvard University Press, 1980. 332p. (Harvard Studies in Business History).
A broad economic, cultural and social study of competition between the British-American Tobacco Company (BAT), a multinational conglomerate, and the Chinese-owned Nanyang Brothers Tobacco Company. The introduction assesses theories of imperialism, economic nationalism and entrepreneurship. Cochran then describes 19th-century Chinese merchants' defeat of foreign attempts to enter Chinese markets; however, early 20th-century foreign investors took advantage of treaty protection, access to foreign capital, technology, and entrepreneurial expertise. On the other hand, Chinese firms knew local markets, exploited nationalism and used cheaper labour. In the 1920s, Nanyang contested BAT's lucrative monopoly, which integrated tobacco growing, processing, and distribution, but found that it could only survive, not prosper. The conclusion assesses this test case and the overall situation.

891　**The pattern of the Chinese past.**
Mark Elvin.　London: Eyre Methuen; Stanford, California: Stanford University Press, 1973. 346p. maps. bibliog.
A controversial and influential interpretation by a wide-ranging economic historian. Part one examines 'the formation of the world's largest enduring state' – asking in effect 'why is China so big?' Elvin shows that the mediaeval state's near-monopoly on force prevented true feudalism; that a Sino-barbarian synthesis in north China led to a 'middle empire' by the Tang; that China had 'manorialism without feudalism'; and that iron and gunpowder were harnessed by the Mongols, leading to the 'supremacy of logistics' under the Ming. Part two portrays a 'medieval economic revolution' in

farming, water transport, money and credit, market structure, urbanization, and science and technology. These led to 'economic development without technological change', delineated in part three.

892 **Foreign investment and economic development in China, 1840-1937.**
Hou Chi-ming.   Cambridge, Massachusetts: Harvard University Press, 1965. 306p.

The author rebuts the following charges: that foreign intrusion wrecked the traditional economy by destroying handicrafts, disrupting agriculture, and allying with feudal forces to retard capitalism; that foreign trade drained the Chinese economy by fixing unfavourable terms of trade; and that foreign enterprises in China were efficient and backed by foreign power, so that Chinese modern enterprises were smothered. Chapters examine: the structure and quantity of the foreign obligations of the Chinese government; foreign direct investment in China; and the determinants of investment. Hou argues that China's 'failure to modernize' was due more to internal factors than to foreign oppression. China was split into a 'dualistic economy'; the modern grew without destroying the traditional, and sometimes actually benefitted it.

893 **The dragon and the iron horse: the economics of railroads in China, 1876-1937.**
Ralph William Hueneman.   Cambridge, Massachusetts; London: East Asian Research Center, distributed by Harvard University Press, 1984. 347p. maps. bibliog. (Harvard East Asian Monographs, no. 109).

Relates the story of the spread and impact of railways, the 'anguished ambivalence' of Chinese statesmen to the costs and benefits of this development, and an appraisal of theories of economic imperialism. Hueneman rebuts pessimistic arguments; he shows that economic benefits were great in spite of foreign profits, costs of transition, and market volatility. Chapters first present econometric theories and controversies, then describe the politics of economic exploitation and Chinese response under late Qing and Nationalist governments. Other topics include: the dynamics of exploitation; the structure of railway costs; and the causes of financial distress. The conclusion summarizes arguments for benefit and harm. Appendices and tables provide statistical backing. Tim Wright, *Coal mining in China's economy and society, 1895-1937* (Cambridge, England: Cambridge University Press, 1984. 249p.) also analyses technology, patterns of growth, foreign investment, Chinese entrepreneurs and the state, working and living conditions of workers, and the labour movement.

894 **To achieve wealth and security: the Qing imperial state and the economy, 1644-1911.**
Edited by Jane Kate Leonard, John R. Watt.   Ithaca, New York: Cornell University East Asia Program, 1993. 189p. (Cornell East Asian Series, no. 56).

Eight scholarly articles describe how the Qing state acted variously in 'regulatory', 'participatory', and 'command' modes to achieve social, strategic and political objectives in the economy. In regulating and encouraging household production of silk, for instance, the Qing built upon successful policies from earlier dynasties; moreover, since silk was made by women, government policies had gender consequences. Further studies look at: merchant influence on government trade policy with Korea; successful government policy toward the Grand Canal; and contrasting policies toward Central Asia and coastal areas as seen in the tea trade.

895 **The Chinese economy, past and present.**
Ramon H. Myers.   Belmont, California: Wadsworth, 1980. 278p. maps. bibliog.

An introductory text designed to supplement history and economics courses. Myers focuses on three key questions: What kind of economic system enabled China to more than double its population from the 17th to the 19th centuries without modern technology? Why was industrial development and agricultural revolution so long in coming? How did China achieve such high rates of growth in the period 1949-78? Part one explains concepts of economic growth and analytic frameworks. Part two, 'Premodern Economic Growth', examines the state and the private sectors, with emphasis on geographical basis and historical change. Part three, 'Early Modern Economic Development', analyses the foreign impact, treaty ports, imperialism, and hinterland response, and the economy under Nationalist rule. Part four, 'Modern Economic Growth', discusses the structure of socialism, economic policy, and economic performance during the period 1949-78. Each chapter is accompanied by notes and selected readings, and there are reference appendices and an index.

896 **Nourish the people: the state civilian granary system in China, 1650-1850.**
Peter C. Perdue, R. Bin Wong, with James Lee, contributions by Jean C. Oi, Pierre-Étienne Will.   Ann Arbor, Michigan: University of Michigan Center for Chinese Studies, 1991. 631p. (Michigan Monographs in Chinese Studies).

An economic and institutional study which demonstrates how the Qing granary system successfully alleviated famine and balanced out fluctuations in food supply and local grain prices, probably to the eve of the destructive 19th-century rebellions. Earlier studies, such as *Rural China: imperial control in the nineteenth century* (q.v.), claimed that the government interfered with and perhaps stunted the market and failed to feed the population. Perdue and Wong argue that officials bought and sold through the expanding inter-regional market, countering instability with loans, sales and grants.

897 **China's modern economy in historical perspective.**
Edited by Dwight Perkins.   Stanford, California: Stanford University Press, 1975. 344p.

Contains nine articles from a conference held in 1973. The editor's introduction discusses whether tradition was a hindrance or an aid to economic development; he finds that Chinese pre-modern experience with complex organizations nurtured entrepreneurs and workers who were effective when given an opening, but that government was largely a hindrance. Articles cover the following topics: the role of foreigners in China's economic development, 1840-1949; surplus and stagnation in modern China; skills and resources in late traditional China; the growth and structure of China's 20th-century economy; modern cotton textile industry and competition with handicrafts; producer's industries, 1900-71; the 'standard market' of traditional China; cooperation in traditional agriculture and its implications for team farming in the People's Republic of China; and the Yan'an origins of current economic policies.

898 **Economic growth in pre-war China.**
Thomas G. Rawski. Berkeley, California; Los Angeles; Oxford:
University of California Press, 1989. 448p.

A persuasive revisionist study which disputes assumptions that the Chinese economy stagnated in the period 1890-1937 or was ruined by imperialism. Rawski focuses on the modern sector, primarily cotton textile factories, rail and steamship transport, and western-style commercial banking. He argues that Qing and Nationalist government interference was only mildly retarding; what was more debilitating was their inability to assure property rights, establish monetary standards, build infrastructure, and maintain political stability. Strong complementarities between the modern and the inherited sectors promoted growth; the strength of the inherited economy at first slowed modern innovation, which eventually spread by using, rather than displacing, existing markets, financial institutions and technologies. Rawski finds that aggregate output rose by roughly two per cent per year over the period 1918-37; that the national product was probably forty per cent larger in 1937 than during the First World War; and that the average level of individual consumption rose by nearly one-tenth.

899 **Economic organization in Chinese society.**
Edited by W. E. Willmott. Stanford, California: Stanford University
Press, 1972. 461p. (Studies in Chinese Society).

A multi-disciplinary symposium on traditional and modern economic organization. Chapters discuss: sericulture and silk textile production in Qing China; cotton culture and manufacture in early Qing; traditional (*qian zhuang*) banks in Ningbo, 1750-1880; the high level equilibrium trap and the decline of invention in the traditional Chinese textile industries; and the commercialization of agriculture in modern China.

Commerce and society in Sung China.
See item no. 160.

Community, trade, and networks: southern Fujian province from the third to the thirteenth century.
See item no. 161.

Agriculture (1368-1976)

900 **Commercialization and agricultural development: Central and Eastern China, 1870-1937.**
Loren Brandt. Cambridge, England; New York; Port Chester, New
York; Melbourne; Sydney: Cambridge University Press, 1989. 232p.

Disputes the charge that commercialization and foreign trade of the late 19th and early 20th centuries injured the Chinese economy by depressing growth, increasing poverty and widening gaps in income distribution. Brandt analyses available statistics to argue that the results of commercialization were actually the opposite. The historian David Faure, *The rural economy of pre-Liberation China: trade expansion and peasant livelihood in Jiangsu and Guangdong, 1870-1937* (Hong Kong: Oxford University Press, 1989. 283p.) finds supportive evidence. R. Bin Wong, 'Chinese Economic History and Development: A Note on the Myers-Huang Exchange' (*Journal of Asian Studies*, vol. 51, no. 3 [August 1992], p. 600-11) assesses arguments raised in Ramon Myers, 'How Did the Modern Chinese Economy Develop? – A Review Article', and Philip C. Huang's reply, *Journal of Asian Studies*, vol. 50, no. 3 (August 1991), p. 604-33.

901 **Man and land in Chinese history: an economic analysis.**
Kang Chao.   Stanford, California: Stanford University Press, 1986.
268p.

A key analysis of China's agricultural economy and demography from ancient to early modern times. Chao persuasively argues that this economy, far from being 'feudal', was characterized by free population movement, private land ownership and legally protected property rights, division of labour by economic rather than social or political means, inter- and intra-regional markets supported by the state, and market and price penetration of all parts of the economy and society. The critical limitations on economic growth were population pressure on arable land, ecological degradation, and decay of infrastructure; growth stagnated precisely because of free market success in exploiting land to its limits before industrialization. Chao also discusses population levels and factors in growth. *Development versus stagnation: technological continuity and agricultural progress in pre-modern China*, by Gang Deng (New York; Westport, Connecticut; London: Greenwood Press, 1993. 263p. [Contributions in Economics and Economic History]) examines traditional agricultural manuals (*nongshu*) to argue that officials were concerned with agriculture and contributed to China's early modern productivity growth.

902 **Agriculture in China's modern economic development.**
Nicholas R. Lardy.   Cambridge, England; New York: Cambridge
University Press, 1983. 285p. maps. bibliog.

A lucid economic analysis of planning and agricultural growth from the 1950s to the early 1980s. Lardy concludes that fertilizer, high-yield seeds, and irrigation brought growth in the 1950s; however, bureaucratic control and Maoist ideology stifled this growth, leading to famine in the late 1950s, low growth and debate. Chapter one discusses agriculture in Chinese history and socialist strategy. Chapter two traces the evolution of planning, showing that state extraction of rural surpluses resulted both from ideological opposition to markets and a commitment to heavy industry; communes promoted regional self-sufficiency in grain thus slighting secondary products, local markets and inter-regional trade. Chapters three to five analyse changes in prices and intersectoral resource transfers, allocation of investment, living standards, distribution of income, and prospects for reform. Y. Y. Kueh, *Agricultural instability in China, 1931-1991: weather, technology, and institutions* (Oxford: Clarendon Press, 1995. 387p. bibliog. maps) is an important, innovative, technical but accessible analysis.

903 **Land reform and economic development in China: a study of institutional change and development finance.**
Victor D. Lippit.   White Plains, New York: International Arts and
Sciences Press, 1974. 181p. bibliog.

Argues that development became possible only when the revolution used land reform to redirect farm surpluses into capital formation; Lippit claims that such surplus existed, was wasted, but could have been redeployed. Chapter one, 'Property Ownership, Class Relations, and the National Savings-investment Ratio', presents the theoretical framework. Following chapters discuss the traditional property share in the rural sector, estimate the size and nature of the surplus, and investigate the revolutionary redistribution of that surplus after 1950. Chapter four puts China's land reform into international and historical context. A 'Statistical Appendix' pulls together various sources into statistical tables. The bibliography lists selected works in Chinese and English.

904 **The Chinese peasant economy: agricultural development in Hopei and Shantung, 1890-1949.**
Ramon Myers. Cambridge, Massachusetts: Harvard University Press, 1970. 394p. (Harvard East Asia Series, no. 47).
Myers uses survey data gathered by Japanese researchers of the South Manchurian Railway Research Bureau in North China villages during the 1930s and 1940s, in order to argue that the foreign commercial and industrial presence in North China did not destroy traditional agriculture, but rather brought growth in new patterns. Myers begins with a brief review of the historical and economic literature, then provides a detailed picture of village agriculture. Myers' chapter, 'The Agrarian System' in *Republican China, 1911-1969, Pt 2* (q.v.), argues that the rural economy grew from the mid-19th-century to the 1920s, but that political chaos, breakdown in transport, and the depression destroyed the village's ability to market in the cities, creating a crisis then perceived as 'feudalism'.

905 **Agricultural development in China, 1368-1968.**
Dwight H. Perkins, with the assistance of Yeh-chien Wang, Kuo-ying Wang Hsiao, Yung-ming Su. Chicago: Aldine; Edinburgh: Edinburgh University Press, 1969. 395p. maps.
A basic economic study. Mining local histories and official documents, Perkins makes a economic analysis of pre-modern and 20th-century agriculture. He argues that production rose over the period at roughly the rate of population growth. Chapter two, 'Six Centuries of Rising Grain Production', provides a précis of the argument. Succeeding chapters cover: improved seeds, changing crop patterns and new crops; farm implements, water control and fertilizer; the distribution of land and the effects of tenancy; rural marketing and its effects on farm output; urbanization, famine and the market for grain; and centralized government and the traditional economy. Statistical appendices summarize Chinese Population Data, Cultivated Acreage, and Crop Acreage (1914-57).

The agriculture of China.
See item no. 980.

The food of China.
See item no. 1348.

The People's Republic (1949-   )

General and to 1976

906   **In praise of Maoist economic planning: living standards and economic development in Sichuan since 1931.**
Chris Bramall.   Oxford: Clarendon Press, Oxford University Press, 1994. 385p. (Studies on Contemporary China).

Mao's egalitarian state planning is now commonly dismissed as disastrous, but Bramall seeks a more mixed judgement. He first reviews the political economy theories of Carl Riskin, Mark Selden and Peter Nolan, then uses the approach to analyse development in Sichuan from the 1930s to the 1980s. Incomes grew modestly (more rapidly than in developing countries generally) and were more equally distributed across class and space; standards of living rose in non-material ways; and a foundation was laid for industrialization. Bramall concludes that success was vitiated by the unprecedented, needless famines of 1959-61, but that the 'miracle' of the 1980s would have been impossible without the preceding Maoist economic development.

907   **The distribution of income in China.**
Edited by Keith Griffin, Zhao Renwei.   Basingstoke, England; London: Macmillan; New York: St. Martin's, 1993. 359p.

Eight essays present the initial results of a large-scale multi-national research programme conducted by the Institute of Economics of the Chinese Academy of Social Sciences, with a summary introduction by the editors. In addition to wages, their nation-wide household survey (described in an appendix) included value of income in kind, production for self-consumption, and imputed values for government subsidized goods and services. Part one, 'The Distribution of Income', includes essays on household income and its distribution and 'three features of the distribution of income during the transition to reform'. Part two, 'Income and Wealth in Rural China', comprises three essays. Part three, 'Employment and Human Capital', provides essays on workers in China's rural industries, on why urban wages differ in China, and on the determinants of educational attainment.

908   **The foundations of the Chinese planned economy: a documentary survey, 1953-1965, Volume I.**
Christopher Howe, Kenneth R. Walker.   New York: St. Martin's, 1989. 370p.

Provides thirty-seven major speeches, directives and policies documents, as well as some out-of-the-way materials which illustrate practical insights into the system, designed to provide basic coverage for students and researchers in Chinese economics, comparative economic systems, economic development or economic planning. Sections of eight to a dozen documents are devoted to 'Strategy and Planning', 'Industrial Development and Organization', 'Agricultural Development', and 'Population, Labour, and Urbanisation'. A second volume is planned.

909 **The phoenix and the lame lion: modernization in Taiwan and mainland China, 1950-1980.**
Alan P. L. Liu. Stanford, California: Hoover Institution, 1987. 182p.

Compares the 'dazzling success' in Taiwan with the frustration in the PRC through the early years of reform. Liu uses economic analysis, but writes for a general audience. Chapters discuss: a comparison of Mao Zedong and Chiang Kai-shek; economic élites in Taiwan and the mainland ('cosmopolitans' vs. 'parochials'); popular politicians vs. totalitarian cadres; the rise of the business class in Taiwan and its fall on the mainland; and strategies for modernization. Alvin Rabuska, *The new China: comparative economic development in mainland China, Taiwan, and Hong Kong* (Boulder, Colorado: Westview, 1987. 254p.) also presents broad comparisons.

910 **The economic development of China: a comparison with the Japanese experience.**
Ryōshin Minami, translated by Wenran Jiang, Tanya Jiang, with assistance from David Merriman. New York: St. Martin's Press, 1994. 262p.

A comprehensive introduction to the Chinese economy since 1949, with particular reference to the period after 1978. Professor Minami, a leading Japanese economic scholar, applies extensive quantitative analysis to economic problems and how they can be understood comparatively. He first presents a detailed comparison of the economic experiences of China and Japan over the last century. He argues that China is not now at the stage of Japan after the Second World War, but rather that China can learn from Japan's prewar experiences. Finally, Minami presents policy recommendations.

911 **China's political economy: the quest for development since 1949.**
Carl Riskin. Oxford; New York: Oxford University Press, 1987. 418p. map.

A basic study which focuses on the intersection of society, economics and politics, analysing links between what Marx called the 'forces' and the 'relations' of production. Riskin first discusses the advantages of various theoretical approaches, with copious citations and statistical tables. Chapters then analyse: China's pre-1949 situation and the initial steps to control and rehabilitate the economy; mobilization and development under the first Five Year Plan and the beginnings of cooperative agriculture; socialist transformation and administrative decentralization; and the ascendancy and crisis of 'late Maoism', 1958-76, encompassing the transition from Soviet influence in industry and the speed-up of collectivization in the Great Leap Forward, the formation of communes, and the famine years. Three chapters deal with economic conflict and Cultural Revolution, self-reliance, and egalitarian distribution. The post-Mao period is covered in four substantive chapters, which include a discussion of the dismantling of the commune and the Open Door international economic policy.

912 **The political economy of Chinese socialism.**
Mark Selden. Armonk, New York; London: M. E. Sharpe, 1988. 241p.

A major analytical evaluation of economic policy and practice under Chinese socialism, with a detailed and copiously documented examination of problems and achievements. Selden highlights two deeply rooted but divergent tendencies:

'voluntary cooperation' and social reform, developed in the 1950s (and perhaps in the 1980s); and Stalinist 'mobilizational collectivism', which Mao adopted in the Great Leap Forward and the Cultural Revolution. A chapter compares the accumulation of capital in Taiwan and the PRC, finding many resemblances in the way both squeezed agriculture to finance industry. Other chapters look closely at market reforms under Deng, especially the various forms of rights to use of land, rural income inequality, and the role of the state.

913　**Economic growth in China and India: a perspective by comparison.**
Subramanian Swamy.　New Delhi: Vikas Publishing House, 1989. 173p.

Swamy first sketches the two 19th-century economies, which were developed but not industrialized (commercialized agriculture, a monetary system and pre-modern banks). Despite differences in political control, their growth rates during the period 1870-1950 were roughly equal (less than one per cent per year); a lack of competent reform government (not imperialism) was the reason for this non-industrialization. The Chinese Revolution and Indian Independence brought popular governments in both countries. Over the period 1952-86, China's economy, based on an advantage in agriculture and a powerful political system, grew at 5.1 per cent a year, with a lower birth rate; India's initial advantage in industry and communications saw growth at 4 per cent. China also achieved higher efficiency in the allocation of resources and income distribution equity.

914　**The poverty of plenty.**
Wang Xiaoqiang, Bai Nanfeng, translated with an introduction by Angela Knox.　New York: St. Martin's Press, 1991. 193p.

This study, published in China as *Furao di pinkun* (1986), exposed a 'third world division' within China between prosperous eastern areas and the backward provinces of Yunnan, Guizhou, Ningxia, Qinghai, Inner Mongolia, Xinjiang and Tibet – all with high percentages of 'minority' peoples. Wang and Bai, now in exile, were close advisers to the reform leader Zhao Ziyang, who was deposed in 1989. They claim that these interior regions are overcontrolled and underfunded; most of the vaunted state 'subsidy' and investment actually go to support Han civilian and military immigration, state enterprises with little connection to the local economy, and the bloated bureaucracy. Extensive charts, graphs and statistics demonstrate underdevelopment, exploitation, and extraction of raw materials and plantation crops, but do not substantiate the authors' implication that uncivilized natives are partly to blame.

Reforms (1976-)

915　**The market mechanism and economic reforms in China.**
William A. Byrd.　Armonk, New York; London: M. E. Sharpe, 1991. 268p.

A technical but relatively clear application of the economic theory of markets to the case of China during the 1980s reforms. Socialism in many countries developed in conditions of shortage and a sellers' market; however, China in the 1980s had at least a partial buyers' market, which forced many enterprises to adapt in order to meet consumer demands. Therefore the 'market' performed in unique but understandable ways.

916 **Economic reform in China: problems and prospects.**
Edited by James A. Dorn, Wang Xi. Chicago; London: University of Chicago Press, 1990. 383p. (A Cato Institute Book).

Contains essays, mostly reprinted from *Cato Journal*, no. 8 (Winter 1989), which were originally presented at a 1988 conference in Shanghai. The volume opens with Milton Friedman's essay, 'Using the Market for Social Development', and is concluded by George Gilder's 'Let a Billion Flowers Bloom'. More specialized essays are grouped in the following sections: 'China in Transition: Setting a Framework for Reform'; 'Decentralization and Development; Economic Reform and Foreign Relations'; and 'The Road to China's Future'. Most essays include references to sources and further reading.

917 **China's economic reforms: the costs and benefits of incrementalism.**
Edited by Fan Qimiao, Peter Nolan. Basingstoke, England; London: Macmillan; New York: St. Martin's, 1994. 347p. (Studies on the Chinese Economy).

Nolan's introduction disputes the 'consensus view' which holds that former centrally planned economies must avoid the 'halfway house of market socialism' in order to rapidly establish private property rights, market fixed prices, and world integration. In the following articles of this symposium, Chinese and Western economists cover: China's economic system; problems of monetary control; the political economy of investment control; communes, the responsibility system and agriculture; state-owned enterprise reform; the effects of financial decentralization on industrial growth, 1952-88; lessons from the West on the stock market and industrial performance; rationing and consumer demand; regional variations in urban living standards; and death rates, life expectancy and economic reforms (a critique of A. K. Sen). *The Chinese economy and its future*, edited by Peter Nolan, Fu Reng Dong (Cambridge, England: Polity Press; Cambridge, Massachusetts, 1990. 283p.) contains analytical essays by economists.

918 **Chinese state enterprises: a regional property rights analysis.**
David Granick. Chicago; London: University of Chicago Press, 1990. 347p.

Intended for comparative economists but accessible to other serious readers, this work argues that China is a unique case; in spite of rural reform and private sector growth, the backbone of the industrial economy remains state-owned urban enterprise. The basic features of this economy persist from the 1950s: multiple level supervision of enterprises; easily filled quotas and access to resources to fill them; a multiple prices system; and the nomenklatura control of personnel decisions and appointments. Granick hypothesizes that these features are in effect form 'property rights' of regional governmental bodies, which constrain central control and will be slow to change. In developing this argument, Granick analyses twenty case-studies of reform enterprises gathered by the World Bank and Chinese Academy of Social Sciences, 1982-85, making frequent comparisons with Russia and Eastern Europe.

919 **Economic reform and state-owned enterprises in China, 1979-1987.**
Donald A. Hay, Derek J. Morris, Guy Liu, Shujie Yao.   Oxford:
Clarendon Press, 1994. 494p. (Studies on Contemporary China).

Based on detailed questionnaires, interviews with managers, and quantitative data, this volume provides an economic analysis of state-owned, large-scale industries. The authors conclude that the Chinese piecemeal process was more successful than East European 'big bang' reforms – although constrained by state ownership, enterprises now behave more like Western firms. Chapters in part one summarize the reform process, describe the behaviour of manufacturing enterprises, and characterize enterprise autonomy and incentives. Chapters in part two look at: employment and wages; productive efficiency and costs; profits and profit margins; flow of funds analysis; investment behaviour; interaction of financial and expenditure decisions; the 'soft' budget constraint; and a 'complete model' of the firms and policy simulations. Part three presents options for reform and discusses the need to transfer from state to share ownership.

920 **Rural China in transition: non-agricultural development in rural Jiangsu, 1978-1990.**
Samuel S. P. Ho.   Oxford: Clarendon Press, 1994. 352p. maps. bibliog.

An analysis and description of the collectively-owned and private industries and small-scale enterprises in a key province. Ho, in cooperation with the Jiangsu Provincial Academy of Social Sciences, carried out field surveys of Township and Village Enterprises (TVEs). The results are presented both in extensive tables and in brief summaries of significant findings. Ho shows that the TVEs dominate the sector, and are controlled by local township governments, and that private entrepreneurs are not as successful as government ones.

921 **Economic theories in China, 1979-1988.**
Robert C. Hsu.   Cambridge, England; New York; Port Chester, New York; Melbourne; Sydney: Cambridge University Press, 1991. 198p.

Presents, in largely non-technical terms, the economic debate in Deng's reform China over strategies of development, the role of the market and planning, price and wage tools, and ownership under socialism. Hsu allows that ideology and politics both influenced which policies were implemented, but is more concerned with discussions of theory in which think-tank economists, party officials and government planners gradually developed from an initial consensus for a socialist planned economy to a 'planned commodity economy', and then to a 'market socialist economy'.

922 **China: from revolution to reform.**
Hua Sheng, Luo Xiaopeng, Zhang Xuejun.   New York: Macmillan, 1993. 244p.

Chinese economists who participated in the process provide an overall view of the economic reforms of the 1980s. They explain why the initial rural reforms were successful in benefitting farmers, city people, and the government, and analyse the subsequent success in light industry and local enterprises. They give an inside but not overly detailed view of the economists' theoretical debates concerning pricing systems, ownership issues, later development of the farm sector, and how to reform administrative structures.

923   **Economic trends in Chinese agriculture: the impact of post-Mao reform.**
Y. Y. Kueh, Robert F. Ash, with a foreword by Lord Wilson of Tillyorn.   Oxford: Clarendon Press, Oxford University Press, 1993. 405p. (Studies on Contemporary China).

A volume in memory of Kenneth Richard Walker (1932-89), one of the founders of China studies in Great Britain. Ten papers, each by a leading economic specialist, deal with the results of reform policies in agriculture during the 1980s. Although subsequently published statistics suggest some revisions, these studies form a basically reliable analysis of the strong and widespread growth of farm production and income which formed the basis for further rural and urban development in light industry. Reforms included the break-up of the commune and production team in favour of household production through the land contract system, and also a reduced use of direct planning of production to management of prices and markets. Essays also study rural employment, technology change, agricultural trade, food consumption and income. Eight of the papers represent up-dates of essays first published in *China Quarterly* (December 1989). *Continuity and change in China's economic development: collective and reform eras in perspective*, by Louis Putterman (New York; Oxford: Oxford University Press, 1993. 379p.) contains detailed studies of rural economics, examining the continuities and breaks between the era of Mao and the era of Deng, based on research in a North China county.

924   **Growing out of the plan: Chinese economic reforms, 1978-1993.**
Barry Naughton.   Cambridge, England: Cambridge University Press, 1995. 379p. bibliog.

A comprehensive narrative and economic analysis, which draws comparisons with other Soviet-style economies. Heavy industry and macroeconomic policy debate, considered to be difficult areas, receive more attention than agriculture or foreign trade. Chapter one describes the economy on the eve of reform. Chapters two to five examine the early period, 1979-83, and the debates over the vague, Eastern European models of planned reform; in the ensuing 1984-88 phase a distinctive Chinese approach emerged. Chapters six and seven deal with this unpremeditated system, covering: the gradual, tentative but firm de-control of industry (rather than a 'big bang'); a transitional dual-track public-private balance; prices set by supply and demand; managerial reform; and high savings. Chapters eight and nine concern the period following 1989. A conclusion analyses lessons and limitations of the Chinese experience, and an appendix provides statistics for the period.

925   **Market forces in China: competition and small business – the Wenzhou debate.**
Edited by Peter Nolan, Dong Fureng.   London; New Jersey: Zed Books, 1990. 183p.

Wenzhou, a district of some six million people near Shanghai, gained fame in the 1980s for freeing individuals and local units to organize non-farm enterprises; the resulting commercial boom lifted the area from poverty. The core of this book consists of six articles by Chinese economists, published originally in Chinese, which detail policies, analyse increasing income differentials, and describe 'big labor-hiring households'. They also propose small town construction as an alternative path, and argue that socialism can encompass Wenzhou's privatization, marketization and polarization. Nolan's introduction places the reforms in a context of socialist experience going back to Bukharin's reforms in Russia in 1929. A chapter describes the general role of petty commodity production in the post-Mao era, and another by Chris Bramall evaluates the 'Wenzhou miracle'.

926   **The rise of China: how economic reform is creating a new superpower.**
William Overholt, introduction by Ezra Vogel.   New York; London: Norton, 1993. 431p. maps.

An energetic, optimistic portrait intended for the general reader, illustrated by charts and maps. Overholt credits the economic and political reforms of Deng Xiaoping with preparing China to become the next Japan. Chapters include: 'The Rise of China's Economy'; 'The Politics of Economic Takeoff'; 'The Emergence of Capital Markets'; and 'The Golden Age of Hong Kong and Guangdong'. The book finishes with chapters on 'The Diplomacy of Hong Kong's Transition', 'The Transformation of International Relations', and 'The United States and China'.

927   **China's economic dilemmas in the 1990s: the problems of reforms, modernization, and interdependence.**
Edited by the United States Congress. Joint Economic Committee, Congress of the United States.   Armonk, New York; London: M. E. Sharpe, 1992. 954p.

Since 1967, the Joint Economic Committee has regularly sponsored scholarly symposium volumes; they commission authoritative and diverse analyses for policymakers and the public. This volume is divided into sections of from four to a dozen papers, covering: 'The Context for Analyzing China; Reforms; Social and Human Factors'; 'Modernization in Agriculture, Industry, and Science and Technology'; 'Military'; and 'Interdependence' (foreign trade, investment, Special Economic Zones). Earlier volumes include: United States Congress [95th], Joint Economic Committee, *The Chinese economy post-Mao* (Washington, DC: US Government Printing Office, 1978. 2 vols.); United States Congress [97th], Joint Economic Committee, *China under the four modernizations* (Washington, DC: US Government Printing Office, 1982. 2 vols.); and United States Congress [97th], Joint Economic Committee, *China's economy looks toward the year 2000* (Washington, DC: US Government Printing Office, 1986. 2 vols.).

928   **Riding the tiger: the politics of economic reform in post-Mao China.**
Gordon White.   Hampshire, England: Macmillan; Stanford, California: Stanford University Press, 1993. 286p.

Discusses the interaction between political reform and economic development in the reform decade. An introductory chapter on the Maoist period explains the successes which laid the foundation and need for reform. Following chapters take up the growth of the market in the agricultural and industrial sectors. Succeeding chapters show the impact on social structure and institutions when prosperity encouraged participation in politics. The emergence of a 'civil society' provided an opening for legitimate dissent, more influence for already approved mass organizations (trade unions, street committees, village cooperatives), and the creation of social outlets based on market relations. The problem is for the existing state to dismount from the totalitarian 'tiger' and find a new seat, probably in 'state capitalism' of an authoritarian rather than totalitarian nature.

929 **China: reform and the role of the plan in the 1990s.**
World Bank. Washington, DC: World Bank, 1992. 291p. (World Bank Country Study).
The World Bank has worked closely with the Chinese government to gather data and develop policy analysis. Their sympathetic but not uncritical reports are up-to-date and thorough, aimed at presenting technical material in a form accessible to policy planners and the public. This 1992 summary assesses the 1980s and presents reform and development policies for the 1990s; particular attention is paid to fundamental areas, such as transport, and alternative 'scenarios' to describe possible results of various policy choices. One key chapter is reprinted in Peter Harrold, *China's reform experience to date* (Washington, DC: World Bank, 1992. 40p. [World Bank Discussion Papers]). Peter Harrold, Rajiv Lall, *China: reform and development in 1992-1993* (Washington, DC: World Bank, 1993. 52p. [World Bank Discussion Papers]) briefly updates this analysis. *The East Asian miracle: economic growth and public policy* (Oxford; New York: Oxford University Press, for the World Bank, 1993. 389p. maps. bibliog.) places China in the wider Asian perspective.

Dilemmas of reform in China: political conflict and economic debate.
See item no. 761.

The political economy of reform in post-Mao China.
See item no. 770.

The political logic of economic reform.
See item no. 772.

China's transition from socialism: statist legacies and market reforms, 1980-1990.
See item no. 773.

Private business in China: revival between ideology and pragmatism.
See item no. 941.

Chinese firms and the state transition in property rights and agency problems in the reform era.
See item no. 942.

China's foreign trade reforms: impact on growth and stability.
See item no. 952.

Foreign trade and economic reform in China, 1978-1990.
See item no. 955.

Green gold: the political economy of China's post-1949 tea industry.
See item no. 991.

The political economy of collective farms: an analysis of China's post-Mao rural reforms.
See item no. 996.

Economic and statistical yearbooks and annual surveys

930 Statistical yearbook of China 1994.

Edited by the State Statistical Bureau. Beijing: China Statistical
Publishing House, distributed by China Communications Center,
Somerset, New Jersey, 1994. 794p.

This official compilation has appeared in English-language editions, with various
distribution outside China, since 1981: *Statistical Yearbook of China* (Hong Kong:
Economic Information and Agency, 1981-87); and *China Statistical Yearbook* (Hong
Kong: International Centre for the Advancement of Science and Technology, 1988-
93). *China agriculture yearbook*, Editorial Board of China Agricultural Yearbook
(Beijing: Agricultural Publishing House, distributed by China International Book
Trading Corporation, 1986) cumulates statistics for the years 1949-86.

931 China's provincial statistics, 1949-1989.

Hsueh Tien-tung, Li Qiang, Liu Shucheng (et al.). Boulder,
Colorado; San Francisco; Oxford: Westview Press, 1993. 595p.

A systematic compilation of regional statistics (province, autonomous region, and
municipality). Part one, 'The Provincial Statistics', gives statistical tables for 100
economic and social variables separated into 15 categories: national output and
income; investment; consumption; public finance and banking; labour force;
population; agriculture; industry; transport; domestic trade; foreign trade; prices;
education; social factors; and natural environment. Part two, 'Exposition of the Key
Variables', explains the construction of the tables. There are indices for key variables
in English and Chinese alphabetical order.

932 Almanac of China's economy, 1981: with economic statistics for 1949-1980.

Xue Muqiao, editor in chief. Economic Research Center, State Council
of the People's Republic of China, State Statistical Bureau. Beijing:
Modern Cultural Company, distributed by New York; Hong Kong:
Ballinger Publishing, 1982. 1,144p.

A comprehensive compilation of official statistics, documents and articles on current
economic policy and performance; coverage goes back to 1949, with an emphasis on the
1978-81 period of initial reforms. Sections cover: a general survey of history, geography
and economics; major economic documents, policies and decrees from the period 1978-
81 in agriculture, industry, finance and taxes, banking, foreign investment, trade and
customs; monographs on current economic policy, including basic reform statements by
Xue Muqiao; a survey of China's economy, with eighty-six encyclopaedic articles on
major topics, from heavy industry and communications to culture and social services;
Chinese economic theory; and statistics, including economic development by province.
Nine appendices list and give addresses for major economic organizations, colleges and
periodicals. Later compilations will not be retrospective.

China Facts And Figures Annual.

See item no. 1429.

Finance and Banking

933 The inflationary spiral: the experience in China, 1939-50.
Chang Kia-ngau. Cambridge, Massachusetts: Wiley and the
Technology Press of the Massachusetts Institute of Technology, 1958.
394p. maps.

A classic analysis of the disastrous wartime inflation which destroyed the financial
(and social) base of the Nationalist government. Chang (Zhang Jia'ao) was a well-
connected government official and combines statistics with personal observation. See
also Chou Shun-hsin, *The Chinese inflation, 1937-1949* (New York; London:
Columbia University Press, 1963. 319p.).

934 The Chinese financial system.
Cecil R. Dipchand, Zhang Yichun, Ma Mingjia. Westport,
Connecticut; London: Greenwood Press, 1994. 223p. bibliog.
(Contribution in Economics and Economic History).

A joint research effort between scholars at Dalhousie University in Canada and at
Xiamen University in the People's Republic, which outlines the formal structure and
functioning of the Chinese financial system as it evolved in the 1980s. After a brief
description of the pre-1980 experience, succeeding chapters describe: People's Bank
of China; the Central Bank; specialized banks (such as the Industrial and Commercial
Bank, the Agricultural Bank of China, the Bank of China, the People's Construction
Bank of China, China Investment Bank, and the Housing Savings Bank); non-bank
and foreign exchange markets; securities markets; foreign banks in China; and the
outlook for China's financial system. Each chapter appends references which
bafflingly do not distinguish between works in English and those in Chinese.

935 **Monetary policy and the design of financial institutions in China, 1978-90.**
Leroy Jin. Basingstoke, England; London: Macmillan; New York: St. Martins, 1994. 255p.

Argues that the stop/go cycle of monetary expansion and contraction is the result of economic reforms which are only partial, for they involve no reform of ownership of enterprises by local government or development of capital markets. According to Jin, Beijing and the provinces play a 'game' which creates monetary expansion for political, rather than economic reasons. Chapters cover: successes and problems of reform; sources and the process of monetary expansion; credit expansion and the centre-locality game; local government ownership and incentive compatibility; a case-study of the banking system and its operation; and tight money in 1988-89. The concluding summary addresses policy implications, and the relevance of Western models and approaches, and advocates the 'second-best solution', in which the central government's 'game' would be to supervise the provincial governments and encourage provinces to integrate themselves economically.

936 **The history of the Hong Kong and Shanghai Banking Corporation.**
Frank H. H. King. Cambridge, England; New York: Cambridge University Press, 1987, 1988, 1988. 3 vols.

A magisterial, richly documented history of the banking corporation which was at the financial centre of China's foreign trade and government fiscal policy for nearly a century. Led by the legendary 'taipans', the Hong Kong and Shanghai Bank brokered trade deals, floated Chinese government loans, and even issued currency. This study, supported but not controlled by the bank, studies all aspects of these activities, based on the bank's own records and archives from the 1840s down to the time of publication.

937 **Money in the People's Republic of China.**
Gavin Peebles. Sydney; London; Boston, Massachusetts: Allen & Unwin; Concord, Massachusetts: Paul & Company, 1991. 289p. bibliog.

An analytical and empirical examination of money supply, output and prices for the period 1949-88. Peebles begins by explaining in clear terms the basics of monetary theory and history, controversies in the interpretation of monetary events in planned socialist economies, and the relevance of monetary theory for developing economies. He argues that the dominant paradigm of Western monetary economics, the Quantity Theory of Money, is not applicable to China, and offers a looser but more comprehensive theory based on purchasing power. The book then recounts policy history over the period 1952-85, taking pains to detail and evaluate statistical sources. Appendices give tables and bibliographic references by topic. The author's *A short history of socialist money* (Sydney; London; Boston, Massachusetts: Allen & Unwin, 1991. 170p.) presents a relatively non-technical survey.

938 **A monetary history of China (*Zhongguo huobi shi*).**
Peng Xinwei, translated by Edward H. Kaplan. Bellingham, Washington: Western Washington University, 1994. 2 vols. (East Asian Research Aids and Translations).

Peng began a career in banking, but after 1949 became a teacher at Fudan University in Shanghai and pursued his avocation as a collector of coins and numismatist. He died during the Cultural Revolution. Kaplan's translation of the 3rd edition (1965) of this richly documented historical compendium provides a brief preface, notes and tables, as well as photographs of the illustrations from the original. The narrative is wide-ranging, touching on daily life and ancient philosophers and late Qing picaresque novels. For each historical period, starting from the Bronze age, Peng describes coins and purchasing power, including gold, silver, grain and silk. He also recounts monetary theory of the time, describes credit systems and institutions, and follows the development of numismatics.

939 **Money, banking, and financial markets in China.**
Gang Yi.   Boulder, Colorado; San Francisco; Oxford: Westview Press, 1994. 311p.

A technical investigation of the financial sector since the establishment of the Central Bank (1984-93). Part one reviews how the all-inclusive monobank system, acting essentially as a passive accounting tool in central planning, became an active policy-maker. Part two, 'The Money Supply Process', examines monetary policies and interest rate theory and practice. Part three, 'The Demand for Money', analyses the velocity of money, including a review of: monetary theory applicable to China; the monetization process; inflation expectations and price instability; and the demand for money. Part four, 'Money and Inflation', examines: price reforms and inflation; models of inflation in China; and money and economic activity. Part five, 'Financial Markets in China', describes non-bank financial institutions, including the major national institutions, and the stock and bond markets. Katherine Huang Hsiao, *Money and monetary policy in Communist China* (New York; London: Columbia University Press, 1971. 308p.) and William Byrd, *China's financial system: the changing role of banks* (Boulder, Colorado; San Francisco; Oxford: Westview Press, 1983. 187p.) are standard studies of earlier periods.

The market mechanism and economic reforms in China.
See item no. 915.

Business, Management and Domestic Commerce

940 **Management in China during the age of reform.**
John Child. Cambridge, England: Cambridge University Press, 1994.
333p. (Cambridge Studies in Management).
A description and analysis of Chinese management during the 1980s, including foreign trade and investment, from both theoretical and practical viewpoints. Part one, 'The Context of Management in China', sketches the economy, culture and politics. The chapters in part two, 'Managing in Chinese Enterprises', cover the following topics: enterprise leadership; the levels and process of decision making; enterprise autonomy; management of marketing and purchasing; work roles of senior managers; and personnel practices and reward systems. Part three, 'Joint Ventures in China', provides both general discussion and case-studies. The conclusion is a cross-cultural and theoretical 'search for perspective' on reform and the development of a business system in China. Child explores the combination of Western precepts, Soviet models and Chinese historical practices which will define future patterns. There is a useful listing of English-language books and articles on management and cross-cultural organization.

941 **Private business in China: revival between ideology and pragmatism.**
Willy Kraus, translated from the German by Erich Holz. Honolulu, Hawaii: University of Hawaii Press; London: C. Hurst, 1991. 246p.
In this expansion and revision of the 1989 German original, Kraus argues that after 1949 ideological rigour sabotaged efficient private businesses; in 1978, they were freed from ideological fetters, but by 1988 were again thwarted. Chapters analyse:

official policies toward markets, market pricing and entrepreneurial initiatives, including taxes, licenses and permits; popular attitudes to private business; management issues; economic structure and organization, including capital supply and marketing; purchase of share rights in state and collective firms; social and political effects; and future prospects. Kraus follows the changes as individual businesses (firms with seven or fewer employees) grow into private businesses (with eight or more employees).

942 **Chinese firms and the state transition in property rights and agency problems in the reform era.**
Keun Lee. Armonk, New York; London: M. E. Sharpe, 1991. 210p.
(Studies on Contemporary China).

A technical and theoretical analysis, which grew out of a doctoral dissertation in economics, of the problems in post-1978 policies of factory management and enterprise law. Lee finds that no overall mechanism (market or other) emerged to replace tight central control. The ensuing distortion of resource allocation and unfair economic competition allowed irregular private gains to a favoured few, including corrupt bureaucrats, a major issue in 1988-89 discontent. Chapter two describes the contending views on socialist economic reform and enterprises in order to establish a framework for testing economic efficiency. Following chapters analyse three stages in the management structure of the 1980s, focusing on issues of state planning, manager responsibility, and the nature of property in a socialist system.

943 **The spirit of Chinese capitalism.**
S. Gordon Redding. Berlin; New York: de Gruyter, 1990. 267p.
(de Gruyter Studies in Organization).

Builds on Max Weber's general insight that sociocultural values affect business organization and management style, but doubts his theory that a lack of 'Protestant ethic' holds the Chinese back from capitalism or commercial success. The book is based on interviews in Taiwan, Hong Kong and Southeast Asia with Chinese businessmen outside China, who Redding considers to represent general Chinese values. In chapters three and four, he introduces the theories of Weber, Lucian Pye and Maurice Freedman, and examines the literature growing from them. He goes on to describe the successful Chinese style as small-scale, family owned and managed; paternalistic, personal and authoritarian; highly flexible and opportunistic; and able to take advantage of family and family-like networks, including access to capital.

944 **Organization and management in China, 1979-1990.**
Edited by Oded Shenkar. Armonk, New York; London: M. E. Sharpe, 1991. 181p. Previously published as vol. 20, nos. 1-2 of *Organization and Management in China, 1979-1990* (International Studies in Management and Organization).

Provides articles by scholars, largely from the United States and Hong Kong. Part one, 'Domestic Enterprises', includes chapters on: managerial leadership in industrial enterprises; enterprise autonomy and market structures; technical decision making; perceptions of desirable organizational reforms in state enterprises; the views of senior managers on the reasons for their success; and the 'little dragons' as role models. Part two, 'Foreign Affiliates and Trade', includes chapters on: Sino-foreign strategic alliance types and related operating characteristics; managerial roles of trade unions in joint ventures; the Chinese foreign trade environment; attitudes towards doing business with the US; and the PRC as an exporter. Each chapter includes extensive references.

945 Chinese business under socialism: the politics of domestic commerce, 1949-1980.

Dorothy J. Solinger. Berkeley, California; Los Angeles; London: University of California Press, 1984. 368p.

A description and theoretical analysis of 'socialist commerce' before the 1978 reforms, especially local commodity markets in farm products, light industrial goods for daily use and handicraft items. After 1949, the government discouraged the use of money; traditional local marketing systems were gradually restrained but not eliminated. Solinger describes the resulting struggle between individual, collective and state interest which played out locally and in state policy debates. There was also political conflict and competition for resources among commerce, industry and agriculture. Technological backwardness is analysed as a key restraint. Solinger highlights three lines, or 'tendencies': bureaucratic control through the plan; market autonomy; and radical mass participation. These tendencies respectively emphasize productivity, order and equality. The late 1970s legitimization of free markets allowed a resurgence of older marketing patterns.

946 Management reforms in China.

Edited by Malcolm Warner. New York: St. Martin's Press, 1987. 240p.

A useful early symposium of Chinese and Western scholars who draw on both theory and personal experience. Sections of essays deal with 'Reforming the Enterprise', 'Developing Management Skills', 'Adapting the Labour Market', and 'Widening the Debate'. These themes are further developed in Warner's *How Chinese managers learn: management and industrial training in China* (London, Macmillan; 1992. 211p.) and *Management in China during and after Mao in enterprise, government, and party* by Oiva Laaksonen (Berlin: de Gruyter, 1988. 375p. [de Gruyter Studies in Organization]).

947 Private business and economic reform in China.

Susan Young. Armonk, New York; London: M. E. Sharpe, 1995. 179p. bibliog. (Studies on Contemporary China).

A political and economic study, centred on Sichuan, of the re-emergence of private enterprise in the 1970-80s. Cultural Revolution radicals had taken the suppression of the private sector to extremes, but reform leaders experimented with local or individual initiative and market forces. Young puts this evolution of policy and response in a broad context, analysing the shifting balance of central party ideology and bureaucratic interest, local government responsibility for economic growth and enterprise initiative. The interaction between emerging small businesses, networks of entrepreneurs and local government in Chengdu is more specifically described in Ole Bruun, *Business and bureaucracy in a Chinese city: an ethnography of private business households in contemporary China* (Berkeley, California: Center for Chinese Studies, University of California Press, 1993. 273p.).

Local merchants and the Chinese bureaucracy, 1750-1950.
See item no. 193.

Policy making in China: leaders, structures, and processes.
See item no. 766.

The market mechanism and economic reforms in China.
See item no. 915.

Economic reform and state-owned enterprises in China, 1979-1987.
See item no. 919.

Industrial management and economic reform in China, 1949-1984.
See item no. 969.

International Trade and Business

948   **The political economy of China's Special Economic Zones.**
George T. Crane.   Armonk, New York; London: M. E. Sharpe, 1990.
205p. (Studies on Contemporary China, 1990).

In 1979, the government established four Special Economic Zones (SEZs), three in Guangzhou (Shenzhen, Zhuhai and Shantou) and one in Fujian (Xiamen), within which overseas investors had privileged economic status. These burgeoned into models of industrial development, but by 1984 were castigated for corruption and mismanagement. Crane describes and analyses the politics of the SEZs during the period 1979-87, successes, policy gyrations, shortcomings and the scholarly literature they spawned, relating them to liberal and Marxist paradigms. *China's Special Economic Zones: policies, problems, and prospects*, edited by Y. C. Jao, C. K. Leung (Hong Kong: Oxford University Press, 1986. 249p.) is a symposium of scholarly economic and political analysis.

949   **400 million customers: the experiences – some happy, some sad, of an American in China, and what they taught him.**
Carl Crow, drawings by G. Sapojnikoff.   New York; London:
Harpers, 1937. 317p.

A popular classic, cited by some as still amusing and relevant. Crow went to Shanghai at the time of the First World War, and became an advertising and merchandising agent. He recounts his adventures with verve and sometimes condescending wit, presenting China as exotic, amusing and profitable. A neglected but worthwhile novel is *Oil for the lamps of China* by Alice Tisdale Hobart (Indianapolis, Indiana: Bobbs-Merrill, 1931. 403p. various reprints), based on the disillusioning experience of a Standard Oil Company executive in China.

950 **China business: the portable encyclopedia for doing business with China.**
Edited by Christine Genzberger. San Rafael, California: World Trade Press, 1994. 418p. maps. bibliog. (World Trade Press Country Business Guides).

A one-volume reference. Chapters present cogent summaries, compiled from assorted publications or written by a team of editors. These cover background information (trade, investment, import and export policy, demographics, labour, business law), advice (business culture), reference (currency, foreign exchange, corporate taxation), directory information (trade fairs, financial institutions, ports and airports, important addresses), and other topics, with travel maps and city street plans.

951 **Foreign direct investment in China.**
Phillip Donald Grub, Jian Hai Lin. New York; Westport, Connecticut; London: Quorum Books, an imprint of Greenwood Publishing, 1991. 280p. bibliog.

A technical but clear description and analysis for international business managers and executives. Grub and Lin first describe the history and background of foreign investment since 1979. They then devote chapters to: reform Open Door policies, Special Economic Zones and opened cities; investment policies and incentives; motivations and modes of investment; foreign investment inflows; organizations involved; and negotiation and approval procedures. Chapters are then devoted to case-studies illustrating joint venture feasibility. Appendices provide sample contracts, regulations from the Shanghai Pudong New Area, and rules for implementation of the Wholly Foreign-Owned Enterprises Law. The 'Further Reading' section lists books and business journal articles. Nigel Campbell, *A strategic guide to equity joint ventures in China* (New York; London: Pergamon, 1989. 179p.) is pithier but covers much the same ground.

952 **China's foreign trade reforms: impact on growth and stability.**
John C. Hsu. Cambridge, England: Cambridge University Press, 1989. 221p.

Asks whether China's foreign trade serves as the engine of growth that it has done for Taiwan and Korea. The introduction sketches the role of foreign trade in economic development up to the reform period, with an appendix commenting on the nature and reliability of government statistics. Chapters are then devoted to foreign trade reforms and economic efficiency, trade incentives (such as the profit sharing scheme), and the commodity composition of China's foreign trade, 1978-85. Part two, 'Foreign Trade, Shortage, and Inflation', develops the argument that Chinese enterprises were slow to respond to changes in domestic and international markets, and that exposure to foreign markets exacerbated inflation. The conclusion maintains the need for further reforms of exchange rates, price reforms and incentive systems.

953 **China's participation in the IMF, the World Bank, and GATT: toward a global economic order.**
Harold K. Jacobsen, Michel Oksenberg. Ann Arbor, Michigan: University of Michigan Press, 1990. 199p.

Analyses the interaction of the People's Republic with the 'KIEOs' (keystone international economic organizations), such as the International Monetary Fund, the

World Bank and General Agreement on Trade and Tariffs. The authors use archival and published sources, as well as extensive interviews with Chinese and foreign officials, to examine the give and take in relations, which were basically well-managed until the 1989 Tiananmen Incident. Early chapters trace the origins and development of China-KEIO relations, including the implications for Hong Kong and Taiwan. Using organization theory and international relations theory, further chapters analyse the stages of mutual adjustment and accommodation. According to the authors, China has not gone capitalist nor have the KEIOs abandoned their liberal economics; future beneficial relations will depend on many contingent factors.

954 **China: business strategies for the '90s.**
Arne de Keijzer, with the collaboration of Allan H. Liu, case-studies contributed by US-China Business Council, Business International Asia/Pacific, Asia Pacific Resources Group, P. Richard Bohr, Julie Reinganum, Roy F. Grow, JETRO, A. T. Kearney. Berkeley, California: Pacific View Press, 1994. 2nd ed. 279p.

A practical and detailed framework for discussing whether a mid-sized or small company can find 'profitable niches' in China. Chapter one offers 'Seven Reasons Why China Might be Worth the Risk'. Succeeding chapters provide a 'fifteen minute China briefing' and 'trade and investment basics'. Part two gives more than two dozen pointed case-studies of trade, technology and equity ventures in many fields. Part three, 'The Lessons Learned', explains how to accomplish solid planning, sound positioning and effective negotiations. Appendices provide a 'China Business Bookshelf', which lists books, articles and recommended subscription publications, as well as 'Useful Organizations and Contacts'.

955 **Foreign trade and economic reform in China, 1978-1990.**
Nicholas R. Lardy. Cambridge, England: Cambridge University Press, 1992. 197p.

First introduces competing conceptions of trade and economic development and the pre-reform trade system (including organization of trade, pricing, exchange rates and exchange control), then describes the process of reform (decentralizing authority, finding new forms of trade, reorganizing licensing, use of tariffs and domestic tax rebates, and experiments in foreign exchange control). Lardy then assesses the economic efficiency of China's foreign trade in regard to planning, price structure and trade contracts. By 1990 Maoist control and self-reliance was replaced with 'openness', direct foreign investment, special export processing zones and dramatically higher foreign trade, all of which fostered general political and economic reform. Lardy's *China in the world economy* (Washington, DC: Institute for International Economics, 1994. 156p.) is an incisive summary of China's role in the world trading system, its participation in international capital markets, economics issues in US-China relations, and policy implications. A more technical analysis is Wang Hong, *China's exports since 1979* (New York: St. Martin's Press, 1993. 262p. [Studies on the Chinese Economy]).

956 **America's China trade in historical perspective: the Chinese and American performance.**
Edited by Ernest R. May, John K. Fairbank. Cambridge, Massachusetts: Committee on American-East Asian Relations of the Department of History in collaboration with the Council on East Asian Studies, distributed by Harvard University Press, 1986. 388p. maps. bibliog. (Harvard Studies on American-East Asian Relations, no. 11).

A symposium on US-China trade before 1949 and its significance for both countries. Fairbank's introduction concludes that trade between the two continental economies was never as big as imagined (less than five per cent of American foreign trade was with China). Articles in part one show how China's entrepreneurs built tea and silk into major exports but were thwarted by a lack of government support and by better organized Japanese competition. Part two analyses American imports into China – cotton textiles, tobacco and cigarettes, and petroleum. Part three contains two articles, 'The Minor Significance of Commercial Relations Between the United States and China, 1850-1931' and 'The Impact of American Multinational Enterprise on American-Chinese Economic Relations, 1786-1949'.

957 **Foreign trade, investment and the law in the People's Republic of China.**
Edited by Michael Moser. Hong Kong: Oxford University Press, 1987. 2nd ed. 603p.

Experts present both formal laws and regulations and their own experiences, in a volume aimed at potential investors and students of contemporary China. Three chapters describe the bureaucratic system (including customs and import-export controls), the tax system, and the legal framework. Further chapters analyse: the issues behind technology transfer, offshore oil and gas exploration, patent, trademark and environmental law; arbitration; the jurisdiction of Chinese courts over foreign disputes; and the law of sovereign immunity. For more technical matters, see: *China tax guide*, edited by Michael Moser, Winston K. Zee (Hong Kong: Oxford University Press, 1993. 2nd ed. rev. and enlarged. 316p.); and James L. Kenworthy, *Guide to the laws, regulations, and policies of the PRC on foreign trade and investment* (Buffalo, New York: W. S. Hein, 1989. 189p.).

958 **Doing business in China: the last great market.**
Geoffrey Murray. New York: St. Martin's Press, 1994. 350p.

An enthusiastic business journalist and consultant provides a jaunty snapshot of China's business and investment situation for the neophyte. Based on general English-language media and the author's observations, the opening section provides a cursory overview of reform and socialist modernization. Chapters then discuss: the business and investment features of Beijing, Shanghai, the coastal cities and inland provinces; the main options for investing; mistakes which have been made on both sides; the Chinese art of salesmanship; necessary negotiating skills; management and labour; China's financial system; and tax and taxation policy. *Foreign joint ventures in contemporary China* by Michael Franz Roehrig (New York: St. Martin's Press, 1994. 180p.) provides a quick treatment of the experience of foreign joint ventures, with emphasis on local experience rather than national policy. A 'List of references' cites books and periodical articles in English.

959 **Joint ventures in the People's Republic of China: the control of foreign direct investment under socialism.**
Margaret M. Pearson. Princeton, New Jersey: Princeton University Press, 1991. 335p.

Discusses the nature, role and development of JVs (Joint Ventures) in the People's Republic. Pearson tests the contention in dependency theory that foreign investments undermine domestic control of the economy. She claims that the strategies and politics of Beijing decision makers were influenced by four key areas: bargaining capacity; domestic politics; domestic economy; and the goals and motivations of foreign investors. Decision makers often had to accept compromises based on international standards, definitions and practices; localism, corrupt administration, economic problems and the prospect of international competition hampered implementation. An economic study of the first Joint Ventures is *China's open door policy: the quest for foreign technology and capital*, by Samuel P. S. Ho, Ralph W. Hueneman (Vancouver, Canada: University of British Columbia Press, 1984. 277p.). See also Alfred Kuo-liang Ho, *Joint ventures in the People's Republic of China: can capitalism and communism co-exist?* (New York: Praeger, 1990. 170p.).

960 **Chinese negotiating style: commercial approaches and cultural principles.**
Lucian W. Pye. New York; Westport, Connecticut; London: Quorum, 1992. 120p.

A revised edition of Pye's *Chinese commercial negotiating style* (1982), in which a political psychologist addresses the practicalities of commercial negotiations. Topics include: sources of difficulties, particularly cultural ones; the ambience of negotiations; opening moves (set general principles and details); tips on substantive negotiations ('horse trading is always a loser', obstinacy vs. flexibility, and asymmetrical empathy in which foreigners give more than they get); and the emotional basis for the Chinese negotiating style (a mixture of xenophobia and xenophilia, which leads to a web of dependency, 'face' and *guanxi* [connections]). Pye summarizes commercial and diplomatic negotiating principles: patience, restrained steadfastness, avoiding the trap of indebtedness, preventing exaggerated expectations, resisting efforts at shaming, limiting damages, and the ability to 'know cultural differences but be yourself'.

961 **Dealing with the Chinese: a practical guide to business etiquette.**
Scott D. Seligman. New York: Warner Books; London: Mercury Book, 1989. 213p.

A thoughtful and clearly presented guide to present-day Chinese business culture for the foreign entrepreneur. *Kevin B. Bucknall's cultural guide to doing business in China*, by Kevin B. Bucknall (Oxford; London; Boston, Massachusetts: Butterworth-Heineman, 1994. 169p.) contains briefer essays on business etiquette, focusing on situations such as meetings, negotiations, socializing and living in China. *Culture shock! China*, by Kevin Sinclair, Iris Wong Po-yee (Singapore, Kuala Lumpur: Times Books International, 1990. 270p.) provides an irreverent, well-informed background briefing. *Chinese etiquette and ethics in business*, by Boye de Menthe (Lincolnwood, Illinois: NTC Business Books, 1994. 230p.) offers gossipy, capricious opinions on all aspects of culture – history (some of which is reliable), 'living in a beehive society', rules and guidelines for business, eating and drinking etiquette – and is saved from ruinous condescension by the author's delight in his China experiences and sometimes unique insights.

962 **Bulls in the China shop and other Sino-American business encounters.**
Randall E. Stross.   New York: Pantheon Books, 1990. Reprinted, Honolulu: University of Hawaii Press, 1992. 330p.

A readable history of the process of opening China in the 1980s to American consumerism. The introduction, 'Salesman in Beijing', relates recent blunders and successes to deeper cultural and historical themes. Part one, 'Getting Reacquainted', tells of the Canton Trade Fairs of the 1970s and the American fad for China chic. Chapters then analyse American-run management training programmes, teaching marketing expertise (the 'marketing of marketing'), and getting Chinese consumers hooked on American products ('Coca-colonization'). *Beijing jeep: the short, unhappy romance of American business in China*, by Jim Mann (New York: Simon & Schuster, 1989. 333p.) describes the original good intentions and ensuing frustration in the collaboration between American Motors and the Chinese government in establishing a plant to manufacture an American designed jeep for Chinese use and export to other parts of Asia. *China takes off: technology transfer and modernization*, by E. E. Bauer (Seattle, Washington; London: University of Washington Press, 1986. 227p.) offers a Boeing engineer's engaging memoir of teaching how to service B-707s and B-747s. Other accounts include: *If everybody bought one shoe: American capitalism in Communist China*, by Graeme Browning (New York: Farrar, Strauss & Giroux, 1989. 239p.); and *China's opening to the outside world: the experiment with foreign capitalism*, by Robert Kleinberg (Boulder, Colorado: Westview Press, 1990. 277p.).

963 **The China-Hong Kong connection: the key to China's Open-Door Policy.**
Yun-wing Sung.   Cambridge, England: Cambridge University Press, 1991. 183p.

An examination of Hong Kong's role as global intermediator for the People's Republic in the 1980s and the political and economic effects. Sung, an economist at Hong Kong University, first sketches the history and characteristics of the Open-Door Policy and the pivotal role of Hong Kong, then devotes chapters to 'The Institutional Setting', which also examines decentralization in PRC trade, 'Evaluation of the Open-Door Policy' (import liberalization, economic decentralization, investments), 'Hong Kong as Financier', 'Hong Kong as Trading Partner', and 'Hong Kong as Middleman' (entrepôt role in indirect trade, re-exports, trans-shipment). The summary and conclusion assess the costs and benefits to China, and evaluate the future of Hong Kong's role after Tiananmen.

964 **China: foreign trade reform.**
World Bank.   Washington, DC: World Bank, 1994. 334p. (A World Bank Country Study).

A detailed economic analysis of policy problems and options, based on the work of a 1992 mission and the World Bank's highly regarded resident staff. Since the intended readership is international policy-makers, not all of whom have economics training, the analysis is clearly spelled out, is technical but not abstruse, and aims to be impartial but not uncritical. The World Bank Country Studies series consists of major studies, which are up-dated or supplemented by World Bank Discussion Papers.

Big business in China: Sino-foreign rivalry in the cigarette industry, 1890-1930.
See item no. 890.

Foreign investment and economic development in China, 1840-1937.
See item no. 892.

Harvesting mountains: Fujian and the China tea trade, 1757-1937.
See item no. 982.

Green gold: the political economy of China's post-1949 tea industry.
See item no. 991.

Industry

965 China's rural industry: structure development and reform.
Edited by William A. Byrd, Lin Qingsong. New York: Oxford
University Press for the World Bank, 1990. 445p.

The editors have compiled seventeen case-studies, with a substantial introduction,
using World Bank and the Economics Institute of the Chinese Academy of Social
Sciences surveys of the 'township, village, private' (TVP) sector. Chapters cover:
survey data and policy analysis on such topics as the early 1980s policy debates;
problems of ownership and property rights after the devolution of the commune;
labour training, wages and incentives, mobility and attitudes; the role of government;
and comparisons of TVPs in China with similar institutions in other socialist and
Asian countries. *China's rural entrepreneurs: ten case studies,* edited by John Wong,
Rong Ma, Mu Yang (Singapore: Times Academic Press, for the Institute of East Asian
Political Economy, 1995. 347p.) describes ten successful factories started by TVEs
(Township and Village Enterprise).

966 Chinese industrial firms under reform.
Edited by William A. Byrd. New York: Oxford University Press,
published for the World Bank, 1992. 438p.

Provides seven case-studies, drawn from a World Bank survey, of state-owned
industrial enterprises from 1978 to the mid-1980s which were among the first allowed
(or required) to face market discipline, though still under bureaucratic restraint.
Interviews with managers supply a lively perspective of success and frustration in
trying to manipulate the bureaucratic system and sometimes a genuine engagement
with the market. Included are the Chongqing Clock and Watch Company, a machinery
plant, a smelter, woollen and silk textile mills, the Anshan Iron and Steel Company,
and the Second Motor Vehicle Manufacturing Plant. An introductory chapter
describes the general industrial reform process and another draws conclusions from
the case-studies. The material represents an up-dated selection from a larger study of
twenty firms, *China's industrial reform*, edited by Gene Tidrick, Chen Jiyuan (New
York: Oxford University Press, 1987. 378p.).

967 China's automobile industry: policies, problems, and prospects.
Eric Harwitt. Armonk, New York; London: M. E. Sharpe, 1995.
208p. (Studies on Contemporary China).

Analyses the development of the automobile industry in the reform period both politically as an example of policy formation and economically as an example of China's use of foreign capital and technology. Harwitt first surveys the political science literature applicable to decision making in China, especially at the lower levels. Chapters are then devoted to: China's automotive history and policy development, 1949-93; political structures and individual leaders; the 'bumpy road' of the Beijing Jeep Corporation, the first Sino-foreign automotive joint venture; Shanghai Volkswagen's success through foresight and local cooperation; Guangzhou Peugeot; Panda Motors, the largest foreign owned Chinese company, whose failure came from its own mistakes rather than from competition or government bungling; and a conclusion which discusses the problem of measuring Chinese economic and policy progress.

968 Dream of a red factory: the legacy of high Stalinism.
Deborah A. Kaple. New York; Oxford: Oxford University Press,
1994. 163p. bibliog.

In the 1950s, the Chinese government set out to create an industrial system with socialist management, socialized workers and control of the masses. This book argues that the Chinese copied and adapted 'the worst of Stalinism', a system of personality cult, strict factory managers, carefully controlled mass campaigns and mass organizations, which created and manipulated a new Chinese working class. Kaple uses only published sources, especially Russian texts translated at the time into Chinese; she did not carry out any fieldwork or interviews to represent implementation and its problems.

969 Industrial management and economic reform in China, 1949-1984.
Peter N. S. Lee. Hong Kong: Oxford University Press, 1988. 335p.

A detailed study which develops a theoretical framework to analyse struggles over national policies of industrial management. Lee challenges the theory of 'two line struggle' which was developed during the Cultural Revolution and its conventional opposition between 'red' and 'expert'. Instead he sees a 'vicious cycle of alternative approaches': 'synoptic' policies (normative, comprehensive, led by planners) in the 1949-76 period were supported by followers of both Mao and Liu, but degenerated into bureaucracy, commandism and lack of control. After 1976, a 'strategic' model, using an economic approach, attacked the problems but produced the unintended consequences of overinvestment, inflation and corruption.

970 Rural small-scale industry in the People's Republic of China.
The American Rural Small-scale Industry Delegation, Dwight Perkins,
Chairman. Berkeley, California; Los Angeles; London: University of
California Press, 1977. 296p.

A delegation of American social scientists and engineers toured China in 1975. Their report assesses the 'Chinese model', which aimed at economic development without the social disruption of the European Industrial Revolution. Principles of the model included independence (both national and local), decentralization, reliance on worker creativity rather than managerial expertise, and the creation of appropriate new technologies. Chapters cover: socialist administrative systems and small-scale industry; worker incentives; economic theory; agricultural mechanization; small-scale chemical fertilizer technology; cement industry technology; service to agriculture; impact on Chinese society; and expanding knowledge and transforming attitudes. Their assessment of this model on the eve of reform is still useful as a benchmark study.

971 **China's transition to industrialism.**
Thomas G. Rawski. Ann Arbor, Michigan: University of Michigan Press, 1980. 211p.

Focuses on machine tools, metallurgy, chemical, building materials, energy and mining, treating each in the periods 1900-76. Rawski finds that a substantial base was built before 1949. For the 19th century, see Stephen C. Thomas, *Foreign intervention and China's industrial development, 1870-1911* (Boulder, Colorado; San Francisco; Oxford: Westview Press, 1984. 186p.).

972 **Industrial society in Communist China.**
Barry Richman. New York: Random House, 1969. 968p. map. bibliog.

Richman, an American professor of business management, toured Chinese factories for two months in 1966. He first presents a conceptual framework – 'Marxism, Management, and Economic Progress' – then sketches the historical environment and China's response in education, politics and economics. The heart of the book comprises a detailed analysis of: China's industrial performance to 1966; the structure and operations of Chinese industrial enterprise; managerial performance; and domestic and retail trade. A final chapter describes 'Communist China's capitalists', and the rise and fall (as of 1966) of private enterprise. William Brugger, *Democracy and organization in the Chinese industrial enterprise (1948-1953)* (Cambridge, England: Cambridge University Press, 1976. 374p.) presents a history of the initial period in which the socialist system of labour, management and production underwent experimentation and development. Stephen Andors, *China's industrial revolution: politics, planning, and management, 1949 to the present* (New York: Pantheon, 1977. 344p. [Pantheon Asia Library]) offers a sympathetic account of China's industrial system and Cultural Revolution policies which avoid the exploitation of workers.

973 **From lathes to looms: China's industrial policy in comparative perspective, 1979-1982.**
Dorothy J. Solinger. Stanford, California: Stanford University Press, 1991. 335p.

Looks in detail at a key period in which China turned away from a state command economy and set the goal of balancing light, heavy and agricultural sectors of the economy. Solinger first sets the stage with an examination of policy structures and the dilemmas which faced policy-makers in the late 1970s. She then combines an examination of published national sources with extensive interviews with officials in the industrial city of Wuhan to identify the pre-conditions for successful implementation of nationally determined reforms. The study concludes that policy consensus at the top was not enough, for there must be a sense of urgency and support at lower levels. This situation is compared to that of other recovering command economies.

974 **Communist neo-traditionalism: work and authority in Chinese industry.**
Andrew G. Walder.   Berkeley, California; Los Angeles; London:
University of California Press, 1986. 302p.

A close description of the factory as an institution and an important contribution to the general sociological understanding of cultures transformed by Marxism-Leninism. Walder argues that China is neither a 'rational-legal' society, in the terms of Max Weber, nor yet a traditional or pre-industrial one, but one in which the party-state dominates society, including the working class. Under 'Communist neo-traditionalism', petty managers, party supervisors, and workers in the factory work-unit are held together in a 'patrimonial' web of 'clientelism', which apportions jobs, wages, housing, medicine and education. Walder concludes that the Cultural Revolution failed to disturb the system; only the (extremely unlikely) end of socialism and party rule would do so.

Economic growth in pre-war China.
See item no. 898.

Chinese state enterprises: a regional property rights analysis.
See item no. 918.

Economic reform and state-owned enterprises in China, 1979-1987.
See item no. 919.

How Chinese managers learn: management and industrial training in China.
See item no. 946.

Agriculture and Rural Political Economy

General

975 **The rice economies: technology and development in Asian societies.**
Fransesca Bray. London; New York: Blackwell, 1986. Reprinted, Berkeley, California; Los Angeles; Oxford: University of California Press, 1994. 254p.

Explains why Asian wet-rice economies (principally China and Japan) fell behind Europe after 1800 despite earlier periods of Green Revolution in the Song and Ming. Avoiding Eurocentric models of historical change, Bray first describes the origins of the Asian rice-plant, then the historical paths of technical development in its cultivation, various water control technologies, and the implications of these for the wider economies of the countries involved. She concludes with a discussion of peasant, landlord and state, covering: changes in relations of production; land to the tiller programmes; group farming; and socialist land reform. She sees the postwar success of Japan and eventually China as growing from this historical difference from the European model. *The Chinese agricultural economy*, edited by Randolph Barker, Sinha Radhu, with Beth Rose (Boulder, Colorado; San Francisco; Oxford: Westview Press, 1982. 266p.) is a useful symposium which discusses nature, history and prospects of the farm economy.

976 **Han agriculture: the formation of early Chinese agrarian economy (206 B.C. – A.D. 220).**
Cho-yun Hsu, edited by Jack L. Dull. Seattle, Washington; London: University of Washington Press, 1980. 377p. (Han Dynasty China).

The Han dynasty produced the characteristic enduring pattern of Chinese agriculture – specialized, market oriented, intensive farming. Part one argues that government policy and local response repressed the pre-Qin mentality of an urban, profit-making, entrepreneurial and contractual economy. Chapters analyse: government response to

336

population pressure and land tenure problems; land as wealth; the farmer's livelihood; resources; methods and techniques; and non-agricultural alternatives. Part two, 'Documents of Han Agriculture', translates and annotates several hundred documents, some of which are quite vivid, arranged according to the topics in part one.

977 **Farmers of forty centuries or permanent agriculture in China, Korea, and Japan.**
F. H. King, preface by Liberty Hyde Bailey.   Madison, Wisconsin: privately printed, 1911. Reprinted, Emmaus, Pennsylvania: Rodale Press, 1989. 441p.

King taught agronomy at the University of Wisconsin and toured Asia early in the century. This book, illustrated with many photographs, describes Asian intensive farming techniques in such detail that it is reprinted as a practical guidebook for ecologically sound farming. King was charmed by what he saw as efficient and intensive agriculture, but did not make an economic or technical analysis.

978 **Understanding peasant China: case studies in the philosophy of social science.**
Daniel Little.   New Haven, Connecticut; London: Yale University Press, 1989. 322p.

Little, a philosopher of social science logic, evaluates rational choice models of explanation and Marxist theories of historical materialism in four case-studies: the 'moral economy debate' coming out of the challenge to James Scott's work; the 'macro-regions debate' coming out of the discussion of G. William Skinner's work (q.v.); the 'breakthrough debate' in which the economist Chao Kang's (q.v.) claim that pre-modern development was frustrated by overpopulation is controverted by Victor Lippit (q.v.), who holds that a rentier class engrossed a significant surplus; and the 'peasant rebellion' debate involving Susan Naquin (q.v.), who sees rebellion as part of a millenarian Buddhist world-view, Elizabeth Perry (q.v.), who argues that village self-defence strategies unintendedly evolved into rebellion, and Robert Marks (q.v.), who attributes revolution to landlord-tenant class conflict.

979 **Land and labor in China.**
R. G. Tawney.   London: Allen & Unwin, 1932. Reprinted, with an introduction by Barrington Moore, Jr., Boston, Massachusetts: Beacon Press, 1966. 207p.

Tawney, a prominent historian of mediaeval Europe and a Fabian Socialist, visited China in 1931, a time of economic trouble, political chaos and natural disaster. His elegant, influential, though now outdated, study first sketches the 'rural framework' and the 'problems of the peasant' (methods of cultivation, marketing, credit, land tenure, and poverty, war and famine). The chapter on 'the possibilities of rural progress' argues that science and education, cooperative farming, drought and flood control, and the development of industry could alleviate the farmer's misery, but warns that if rulers continued their heedless exploitation, 'the revolution of the peasant' will become likely and not undeserved. Two chapters analyse 'the old industrial order and the new' and 'politics and education'.

980   **The agriculture of China.**
Xu Guohua, L. J. Peel.   Oxford: Oxford University Press, 1991. 300p.
(Centre for Agricultural Strategy Series).
A descriptive rather than analytical geography, which provides background information and technical description. Eight chapters, all written by experts with positions in the People's Republic, cover: natural environment (including geographical setting and resources); historical and social background; the components of agriculture (crops, forestry and animal husbandry); the ten agricultural regions of China; infrastructure and agricultural inputs (irrigation, flood control, chemicals, feedstuffs, machinery, transport and energy); the rural economy (rural polices, non-agricultural enterprises and the life of the Chinese peasants); agricultural education, research, and extension. A concluding chapter summarizes the characteristics and problems of Chinese agriculture and prospects for the future. Chapter references list works in English and Chinese. Appendices define geographical, agricultural and economic terms, and provide statistics for 1986.

Early modern political economy

981   **Rents, taxes, and peasant resistance: the Lower Yangzi region, 1840-1950.**
Kathryn Bernhardt.   Stanford, California: Stanford University Press, 1992. 326p. bibliog.
A sophisticated technical analysis of local ecology in Jiangsu and Zhejiang, and the economics of production, taxation, land ownership, rents and local administration. Bernhardt argues that social relations were not understandable in conventional, abstract categories of 'peasant' and 'landlord', but that after the 1850s Taiping Rebellion, landlordism was undermined by dropping rents, rising taxes (especially under the Nationalist government) and tenant organization. The Communists confronted a diminished remnant, not immemorial feudalism.

982   **Harvesting mountains: Fujian and the China tea trade, 1757-1937.**
Robert Gardella.   Berkeley, California; Los Angeles; London: University of California Press, 1994. 259p.
Gardella first examines China's connection with the capitalist world economy before the Opium Wars, then asks whether foreign trade was an overall benefit or imperialist oppression and what was the role of government in organizing markets and supporting trade expansion. Chapters then show how commercial capitalism developed and the tea trade grew before the 1840s. The 'tea boom' of 1842-88 then produced 'extensive growth without structural change'. The challenge of capitalism, in the form of competition from colonial India and Ceylon, produced international market volatility while the political decline of the Qing meant that China did not have the resilience to respond. Reviving the tea trade became an issue for reformers and the Nationalist government during the period 1890-1937. The conclusion assesses 'A provincial trade in a global market, 1757-1937'.

983 **The peasant economy and social change in North China.**
Philip C. C. Huang.   Stanford, California: Stanford University Press, 1985. 369p.

Addresses basic questions of economic history from the 17th to the 20th centuries. Part one explores the issues, the sources and the ecological setting. Huang explains that there have been three traditions of peasant studies: formalist, such as the economist Theodore Schultz; substantivist, such as A. V. Chayanov, stressing household demography; and Marxist, emphasizing class relations. In parts two ('Economic involution and social change') and three ('The village and the state'), Huang offers an 'integrated analysis of a differentiated peasant economy', which covers population pressure, agricultural commercialization and social stratification. An early modern crisis resulted when petty capitalist households, who depended on both market farming and wage income, depressed wages and precluded capital accumulation. The state milked an economy which increased in size without transformation in structure until the reforms of the 1980s.

984 **The peasant family and rural development in the Yangzi delta, 1350-1988.**
Philip C. C. Huang.   Stanford, California: Stanford University Press, 1990. 421p.

A wide-ranging and influential history. Huang begins with a consideration of the theoretical traditions of Adam Smith and Karl Marx, then develops concepts of 'involutionary commercialization' and 'involutionary growth' – growth without structural change, intensified labour input, increased total output but decreasing marginal returns. This pattern of household agriculture endured through six centuries of capitalist market and commercial growth 1350-1950, a period also marked by imperialism, urban development and the formation of managerial agriculture. This household economy also survived three decades of socialist collective agriculture, 1950-80. In the reforms of the 1980s, Huang concludes, households finally diverted the investment of labour from farming into rural industries and profitable sidelines to produce structural transformation. A concluding chapter speculates on: China's population density; the social system and political economy, especially the question of landlordism and gentry hegemony; and the rural-urban gap.

985 **China's silk trade: traditional industry in the modern world, 1842-1937.**
Lillian M. Li.   Cambridge, Massachusetts: Harvard University Press, 1981. 288p. bibliog. maps. (East Asian Monographs, no. 97).

An examination of the production and manufacture of silk in the period when the international economic and political system challenged China. Li concludes that foreign investment was not large enough nor foreign political power focused enough to exert the degree of control claimed by critics of imperialism. Joe Eng, *Economic imperialism in China: silk production and exports, 1861-1932* (Berkeley, California: Institute of East Asian Studies, Center for Chinese Studies, 1986. 243p. bibliog. map [China Research Monographs, no. 31]) reviews much the same material, but concludes that the silk trade was heavily conditioned by the imperialist framework and strongly exhibited all the consequences of economic imperialism.

986 **Rural revolution in South China: peasants and the making of history in Haifeng County, 1570-1930.**
Robert Marks. Madison, Wisconsin: University of Wisconsin Press, 1984. 339p. maps. bibliog.

Marks discusses the development of a peasantry and eventual revolution. The first part of the book describes the growth of a freeholding peasantry by the beginning of the Qing, overthrowing the Ming manorial system. Commercial competition for money and power then led to deep-rooted violent vendettas, but also to the growth of strong local organizations, chiefly lineages and secret societies. This order was disrupted in the late Qing largely by integration into world trade, while local leaders came to ally themselves with the state to erode tenant land tenure rights. The second part of the book describes the ensuing revolutionary organization of the innovative organizer Peng Pai and the Communist Party, which responded to but did not create peasant demands.

987 **Exhausting the earth: state and peasant in Hunan, 1500-1850.**
Peter C. Perdue. Cambridge, Massachusetts: Harvard University, Council on East Asian Relations, 1987. 331p. bibliog. (Harvard East Asian Monographs, no. 130).

An ecological and political history. Hunan developed from an unprofitable frontier to a densely populated, rice-exporting commercial economy in the early modern period. Perdue argues that there were two cycles involving commercialization and overpopulation, enhanced by interaction between government officials and private actors: the early Ming government organized growth by fostering immigration, distributing land and providing seeds and tools; in the succeeding stage of this cycle, farmers and private entrepreneurs built dykes, dams and reservoirs, and introduced new techniques (early-ripening rice, crop rotation), which led to oversettlement, overcultivation, flooding and chaos. By the 17th century, this cycle of boom and bust reached bottom, to repeat from itself the 17th century to the 1850s.

988 **Xiang lake: nine centuries of Chinese life.**
R. Keith Schoppa. New Haven, Connecticut; London: Yale University Press, 1989. 283p. bibliog.

An innovative ecological, political and social history, interspersed with poetry and literary vignettes. Xiang Lake is a six thousand-acre artificial reservoir created in 1112 near Hangzhou, in Zhejiang. Access to its water and fertile shores was vital to local farmers, and a general good was created by irrigation and flood prevention; however, entrepreneurs with political clout wanted to drain it for private gain. Schoppa's 'drama of human struggle for life and for control of the environment' develops themes including ecology, the enlarging sphere of public claims on private interests, and the changing concepts of 'public' and 'private'. When the government could mobilize public spirit and local community, the lake was an economic boon and cultural symbol; however, in the politically decayed 19th and 20th centuries, the lake was largely destroyed.

989 **Agents and victims: accomplices in rural revolution.**
Helen F. Siu.   New Haven, Connecticut; London: Yale University
Press, 1989. 378p. maps. bibliog.
A multi-faceted study, covering the period from the early Qing dynasty to the present
day, of relations between local élites and national political power in Xinhui County, in
the Pearl River Delta area of Guangdong. In late imperial times, a mixed and
ecologically changing economy of agriculture, manufacturing and commerce spawned
complex, cross-cutting ties between villagers, local leaders and government. Elites
looked up to national superiors for cultural and political help in dominating those
below, but were restrained by kinship, community institutions and social competition.
After 1949, socialist revolution and land reform undercut old leaders and put local
Party cadres in a powerful but awkward new position. Siu argues that the post-1949
extension of state power combined with 'autarkic' local development to produce
'cellularization', that is, local self-sufficiency. Concluding chapters examine recent
reforms and the reanimation of old customs for new purposes.

The People's Republic (1949-)

990 **Revolution in a Sichuan village.**
Stephen Endicott.   London: L. B. Tauris; New York: New
Amsterdam, 1991. 261p.
In the early 1980s, Endicott returned as a China scholar to Sichuan, where his father
and grandfather had been Canadian Methodist missionaries. He used extensive village
interviews and fieldwork to follow social, economic and political struggles and
changes from the 1940s to the Cultural Revolution, including an effective description
of the Barefoot Doctors. As in the works of William Hinton (q.v.), his focus is on the
village and local leaders, not national policy; his analysis is evaluative, but less
critical than in *Chinese village, socialist state* (q.v.).

991 **Green gold: the political economy of China's post-1949 tea
industry.**
Dan M. Etherington, Keith Forster.   Hong Kong; Oxford; New York:
Oxford University Press, 1993. 270p.
Opens with chapters entitled 'What is Tea?' and a 'Brief History of Tea in China', and
proceeds to analyse the economic geography of its regional cultivation. The work also
discusses: the institutional framework of the industry; the policies and output of the
production system; constraints on growth, including inherent natural causes of low
yields and management problems; processing systems; and domestic and international
marketing. The authors, one an economist and one a specialist in politics, find that tea
growing is one area where the management reforms under the responsibility system of
the 1980s threatened productivity, as state farms growing tea outperformed the small-
holders.

992 **Chinese village, socialist state.**
Edward Friedman, Paul G. Pickowicz, Mark Selden, with Kay Ann
Johnson. New Haven, Connecticut: Yale University Press, 1991.
336p. maps.

A key socio-political portrait of Wugong, a village on the North China plain, from
1938 to 1961, which analyses state-society linkages, as well as economy, gender
relations, patriarchy and a culture of violence. In eighteen visits over ten years, the
authors learned how the Party's original 'silent revolution' and multi-class socialist
cooperation developed during the Anti-Japanese war, how the new government
adopted Soviet collective institutions after 1949 to control the village and raise capital
for industrialization, and how the commune system was imposed with disastrous
results. Wugong succeeded through political connections, but other communes
foundered; socialist revolution gave way to a rich-poor gap, economic chaos and
political repression. There are sixteen pages of photographs.

993 **Fanshen: a documentary of revolution in a Chinese village.**
William Hinton. New York: Monthly Review Press, 1966; New
York: Vintage Books, 1968. 637p.

A classic account of early land reform. *Fanshen* means 'to turn over', or to join the
anti-feudal, anti-imperialist revolution. Hinton accompanied a 1948 Party land reform
team to Longbow village, in Shaanxi. Here he presents a dramatic documentary of
how outside cadres establish trust with poor peasants, gradually and with difficulty
raise their consciousness, often manipulate violence, are reproved by Party officials
and instructed in Mao's 'mass line', and finally lead the overthrow of the gentry and
landlords. Hinton's *Shenfan* (New York: Random House, 1983. 785p.) follows
Longbow through the Great Leap Forward and Cultural Revolution. His *The great
reversal: agrarian reforms in China, 1978-1989* (New York; London: Monthly
Review Press, 1990. 143p.) reprints essays which claim that the post-Mao reforms
threw out the progressive baby with the ultra-leftist bath water by destroying *all*
cooperatives in favour of individualistic markets and high technology; the 1989
massacre was the result of Deng's authoritarian rejection of socialist ideas.

994 **Peasant power in China: the era of rural reform, 1979-1989.**
Daniel Kelliher. New Haven, Connecticut; London: Yale University
Press, 1992. 264p. bibliog.

Discusses the interaction between state reform and peasant initiative in the reform
era, examines competing theories and makes comparisons with other socialist
countries and third world economies. Kelliher holds that aggregate peasant choices
and participation in local politics pushed the party and state to accelerate market
reforms and to dismantle the commune system of state control of farming. Earlier
theorists doubted the capacity of peasants for collective action; however, Kelliher
highlights 'atomized mass action', in which concerted but unpremeditated peasant
reactions led the state to exercise ultimate control in a less direct, less resented way.
The standard study of village politics is John P. Burns, *Political participation in
rural China* (Berkeley, California; Los Angeles; London: University of California
Press, 1988. 283p.).

995   **Broken earth: the rural Chinese.**
Steven W. Mosher.   New York: Free Press, 1983. 317p.
A disillusioned portrait of village life and culture in the late 1970s and early 1980s.
Mosher was the first American social scientist allowed to undertake field observation
since 1949, and artfully describes the warmth of village life and the falseness of
Mao's statist vision of the commune, which had coloured foreign analysis. Chapters
evoke family life, child rearing, the role of women, the frustration of the rural
economy and the horrors of the one-child policy. Mosher was expelled from China
and from the Stanford Department of Anthropology PhD programme for ethical
breaches. The book and the expulsion controversy are discussed in Martin K. Whyte,
'The Rural Chinese and Steven Mosher' (*Peasant Studies,* vol. 11, no. 2 [Winter
1984], p. 111-18).

996   **The political economy of collective farms: an analysis of China's
post-Mao rural reforms.**
Peter Nolan.   Cambridge, England: Polity Press, 1988; Boulder,
Colorado, Westview Press, 1989. 259p. (Aspects of Political
Economy).
Considers the case for and against collective farms and repudiates the author's earlier
argument that they are usually appropriate for poor countries. Nolan sketches debates
on the subject in socialist countries going back to Stalin vs. Bukharin in the 1920s,
then examines the performance of Chinese agriculture under Maoist planning. Often
cooperation is socially and economically desirable, particularly in the fields of
irrigation, credit, purchasing, industrial production and marketing, but collective
ownership of farmland, animals and other farm assets is not practicable, and collective
income distribution is disputable. The success of the reforms in the 1980s shows that
many arguments for collective farms were mistaken, but that socialist ideals should be
reworked rather than abandoned.

997   **State and peasant in contemporary China: the political economy of
village government.**
Jean Oi.   Berkeley, California; Los Angeles; London: University of
California Press, 1989. 287p.
A detailed political and social analysis of state grain procurement policy in the Maoist
and post-Maoist periods, which reveals the extent of government confiscation, how it
evolved, and how it demonstrated the nature of the political system which was
originally thought to represent peasant interests. Oi sheds important light on the
'clientelist' nature of local government, where state confronts society; peasants
attempted to establish ties with village officials to resist the state, strengthening the
local officials. Kenneth R. Walker, *Food grain procurement and consumption in
China* (Cambridge, England: Cambridge University Press, 1984. 329p.) offers an
economist's analysis.

998 **Peasant China in transition: the dynamics of development toward socialism, 1949-1956.**

Vivienne Shue. Berkeley, California; Los Angeles; London: University of California Press, 1980. 394p.

Analyses the initial success in drawing peasants relatively quickly into socialist transformation, focusing on Hubei province. Part one, 'Class Struggle', describes land reform as the redistribution of wealth and the establishment of political control. Part two looks at attempts to ensure the equitable distribution of new wealth and a transition to socialism by policies which structured village self-interest (tax reform, market and credit structures, and the ideological encouragement of mutual aid teams). Part three follows the debate on rural development strategies down to the Great Leap Forward; chapters cover: rural trade, supply and marketing cooperatives, and the contract system for the unified purchase of grain; rural finance and credit cooperatives; and the decision to push elementary cooperatives into advanced forms. The conclusion enumerates the principles for success and their subsequent erosion.

999 **Marketing and social structure in rural China.**

G. William Skinner. Ann Arbor, Michigan: Association for Asian Studies, 1993. 399p.

A set of three influential articles, reprinted from *Journal of Asian Studies* (1964-65). Skinner borrows from geographers' central place theory to analyse 'local systems' defined by marketing areas, which organize rural society economically, culturally and socially; 1950s communes tended to coincide with pre-1949 marketing areas. G. William Skinner, Edwin A. Winckler, 'Compliance succession in rural Communist China: a cyclical theory', in *Complex organizations: a sociological reader*, edited by Amitai Etzioni (New York: Holt, Rinhart & Winston, 1969, 2nd ed., p. 410-38), explains campaign cycles by the succession of means: 'normative' (which appeals to a sense of right and wrong) developing into 'remunerative' (mainly economic), developing into 'coercive'. The authors apply this theory to rural campaigns of the 1950s and 1960s.

1000 **Agrarian radicalism in China, 1968-1981.**

David Zweig. Cambridge, Massachusetts; London: Harvard University Press, 1989. 269p. (Harvard East Asian Series, no. 102).

Analyses polemics, factional struggles and village responses in the attempt to create a new socialist countryside free of class oppression and inequality. Zweig doubts totalitarian explanations in favour of a more pluralist model. According to him, radicals were a minority in a divided leadership but outmanoeuvred moderate opponents by orchestrating media campaigns, manipulating provincial allies, and using Mao's well publicized political tours. Radical initiatives were modified or neutralized by bureaucratic politics and local implementation. Villagers were not passive; they determined success or failure of policies by calculating personal, family or community benefit. Topics include: production brigade, brigade accounting, and higher stages of socialism; restricting private plots; resource expropriation and equalization; and the making of a new rural order under reform. The conclusion is entitled 'The Failure of Agrarian Radicalism'.

Energy and Mining

1001 Minerals, energy, and development in China.
James P. Dorian. Oxford: Clarendon Press, Oxford University
Press, 1994. 288p.

A discussion of the structure and recent history of the mining industry, policy choices,
possible future developments and foreign involvement. 'Mining' includes minerals
(metals and non-metals) and energy (petroleum, coal, natural gas and products). Part one,
'Mining and Development Planning', describes the role of minerals in PRC economic
development, covering the history of geological exploration, centrally planned vs. free
market development, and the Five-Year Plans from the 1950s. Dorian discusses both
internal features (working practices, performance standards and criteria) and the workings
of state and inter-sectoral involvement. Part two, 'Economic Relations and Impacts',
examines the mining base and industry, the commodity trade and international
cooperation, and mining and the Chinese economy. *China's energy and mineral
industries: current perspectives*, edited by J. P. Dorian, D. J. Fridley (Boulder, Colorado;
San Francisco; Oxford: Westview Press, 1988. 162p.) includes essays by specialists.

1002 Fueling one billion: an insider's story of Chinese energy development.
Lu Yingzhong. Washington, DC: Washington Institute Press, 1993.
266p. bibliog.

A policy-oriented description, which summarizes the work carried out in the 1980s by
a team at Tsinghua University in Beijing, with copious charts, diagrams and statistical
tables. Part one describes: the evolution from pre-1980 'disastrous policy-making' to
'energy reality'; the scientific basis of policy; and political structures. The reforms of
the 1980s departed from the orthodox centralized, publicly owned economy to 'walk
on two legs', that is, to use public and private capital, large- and small-scale facilities,
modern and traditional technologies, and both domestic and foreign investment.
Chapter five sketches an Integral Energy Planning for the village, comprising
agricultural residues, biogas, firewood and minihydropower. Part two provides case-
studies. The bibliography gives no indication whether items were published in
Chinese or English.

1003　**Energy in China's modernization: advances and limitations.**
Vaclav Smil.　Armonk, New York; London: M. E. Sharpe, 1988.
250p.

Critically appraises the foundation and prospects of China's energetics, that is, the sources, structure and use of all forms of energy. The Chinese countryside is heavily dependent on biomass; fossil fuels and electricity are used inefficiently in industry. Smil discusses the potential of solar power, wind, biomass generation (such as methane gas), water power and reserves of hydrocarbons and fossil fuels. He concludes that hydropower has great potential, since there are many rivers which descend sharply from west to east. Future energy extraction will prove more difficult and expensive.

Policy making in China.
See item no. 766.

Coal mining in China's economy and society, 1895-1937.
See item no. 893.

Transport and Telecommunications

1004 **The Ming tribute grain system.**
Hoshi Ayao, translated by Mark Elvin. Ann Arbor, Michigan:
Center for Chinese Studies, University of Michigan, 1969. 112p.
maps. (Michigan Abstracts of Chinese and Japanese Works on
Chinese History).

During the Ming dynasty, 'tribute grain' for the imperial government was shipped
from the rich south to the capital, encouraging the intensification of existing river and
canal transport while European shipping focused on overseas trade and conquest.
Professor Hoshi's study, *Mindai söun no kenkyū* (Tokyo: Nihon gakujutsu shinko-kai,
1963), here presented in a summary translation, describes the nature and scale of
Chinese inland waterway transport, the imperial bureaucracy, the technology of
shipping and the type of goods transported.

1005 **The spatial economy of Communist China: a study on industrial
location and transportation.**
Wu Yuan-li. New York: Praeger; London: Pall Mall, for the Hoover
Institution on War, Revolution, and Peace, 1967. 367p.

Includes a sound description of the 1950s development of railways, waterways and
highways of China, accompanied by maps and statistics. *China, the transport sector*
(Washington, DC: World Bank, 1985. 127p.) analyses problems and policy choices in
the early years of reform.

1006 **Transport in transition: the evolution of traditional shipping in
China.**
Translations by Andrew Watson. Ann Arbor, Michigan: Center for
Chinese Studies, University of Michigan, 1972. 93p. (Michigan
Abstracts of Chinese and Japanese Works on Chinese History).

Provides four articles of interest to business historians and economic sociologists on
two main themes in the history of junks in Chinese shipping: the institutional

organization of the shipping business; and the forms of ownership and operation. The articles offer much detail on the lower Yangzi junk trade, showing its high level of development and economic importance.

1007 **The junks and sampans of the Yangtze.**
G. R. G. Worcester.   Annapolis, Maryland: United States Naval Institute Press, 1971. 626p.

A compilation of reprints, together with some other material; these include: Worcester's magisterial and renowned *Sail and sweep in China* (London: Her Majesty's Stationary Office, 1966); *The junks and sampans of the upper Yangtze* (Shanghai, 1940); and *The junks and sampans of the Yangtze* (Shanghai, 1947. 2 vols.). Worcester's passion was the physical structure and sailing characteristics of the many varieties of craft which plied the Yangzi until recently; here he lovingly sketches and describes them with the care of an ornithologist.

The dragon and the iron horse.
See item no. 893.

China takes off: technology transfer and modernization.
See item no. 962.

Physics and physical technology: part 3: civil engineering and nautics.
See item no. 1078.

Labour and
Employment

1008 **Work and inequality in urban China.**
Yanjie Bian.   Albany, New York: State University of New York
Press, 1994. 286p. bibliog. (SUNY Series in the Sociology of Work).
A systematic sociological analysis of the impact of work organization (especially allocation of jobs) on social stratification, based on surveys, interviews and official data from the industrial city of Tianjin. Bian argues that in addition to the structural allocation of status, other factors include status inheritance, educational achievement, political 'virtue' and connections (*guanxi*). Chapter topics include: structural segmentation and social stratification; structure and functions of work organization; urban employment policies and practices; the Chinese version of status attainment; *guanxi* and social resources in job searches; party membership; and wages. A final chapter discusses market reforms and social inequalities. Appendices give details of the surveys.

1009 **The Chinese labor movement, 1919-1927.**
Jean Chesneaux, translated by H. M. Wright.   Stanford, California:
Stanford University Press, 1968. 574p. maps.
A vivid social history of Chinese industrial labour up to the 1927 destruction of the Left, slightly revised from *Le mouvement ouvrier chinois de 1919 à 1927* (Paris, 1962). Based on research and interviews with workers in China during the 1950s, the book analyses workers' lives, economics and factory conditions, and describes the strikes and boycotts of the 1920s. Chesneaux, an eminent French Marxist, is criticized by later authors for placing the Party at the centre of the workers' story. Other works on the history of labour include: S. Bernard Thomas, *Labor and the Chinese revolution: class strategies and contradictions of Chinese communism, 1928-1948* (Ann Arbor, Michigan: Center for Chinese Studies, University of Michigan, 1983. 341p.); and Lynda Shaffer, *Mao and the workers: the Hunan labor movement, 1920-1923* (Armonk, New York; London: M. E. Sharpe, 1982. 251p.).

1010   **The workers of Tianjin, 1900-1949.**
Gail Hershatter.   Stanford, California: Stanford University Press,
1986. 313p.

A multifaceted social history. Official post-Liberation accounts portrayed factory
workers as class-conscious activists, waiting only for the Party to lead them; however,
Hershatter finds a more complex situation. Tianjin, near Beijing, was a major
international trading and industrial centre, but had only a small sector of modern
factories; production principally came from small, largely unmechanized workshops,
and workers mostly came directly from villages. Workers were organized by patron-
client ties with factory foremen, gang bosses and secret society lodge masters, and
operated within a culture of worker-on-worker violence. Party organizers had to adopt
new tactics and develop new strategies.

1011   **Sisters and strangers: women in the Shanghai cotton mills,
1919-1949.**
Emily Honig.   Stanford, California: Stanford University Press, 1986.
299p.

Contrary to predictions, Honig found 'almost no evidence' that women mill workers
of the 1920s were class-conscious revolutionaries. She describes Shanghai in history,
the role of women workers in the labour movement, the nature of their work and daily
lives, and social relations within the workplace. 'Localism' (place of origin) defined
workers' lives rather than class solidarity; patriotic unity did not arise in the face of
imperialist exploitation, as many workers preferred the better conditions in Japanese
factories. In addition, more feared than capitalists was the criminal underworld
organization, the Green Gang, which forcibly contracted and controlled women's
labour. The political education and literacy work of the YWCA was more effective
than 1920s Communist organizers, who focused on male workers. By the 1940s, the
CCP had learned from the YWCA that working-class consciousness was multifaceted;
militant women participated in strikes not so much as members of a working class, but
as activists in their own cause.

1012   **Labour and the failure of reform in China.**
Michael Korzec, foreword by Christopher Howe.   Basingstoke,
England; London: Macmillan; New York: St. Martin's, 1992. 108p.
(Studies on the Chinese Economy).

A critical inquiry into the main characteristics of the current Chinese labour system.
Korzec's aim is to explain how the reform of the system in the 1980s failed and why
the decay of Communist states is irreversible. Chapters cover: 'Administrative
Lawlessness', a situation which leaves enterprises as 'small states'; 'Occupational
Inheritance', which structures the lives of workers and their children; 'Flexible
Labour', the web of regulations which govern temporary workers, unemployment and
employment regulation; and 'Efficiency Wages and Enterprise Behaviour', which
discusses the structure of wages, the control of the wage fund, piece wages, planning
efficiency and the dilemmas of reform. Statistical appendices describe labour
productivity in the 1980s and the system of wages in state enterprises.

1013   **Shanghai on strike: the politics of Chinese labor.**
Elizabeth Perry.   Stanford, California: Stanford University Press,
1993. 327p.

A key work in labour and social history, which makes speculative comparisons with
other regions and countries. Perry focuses on the working classes of Shanghai from
the mid-19th century to 1949 as significant in themselves rather than as simply a part
of Mao's revolution. The first part, 'The Politics of Place, 1839-1919', analyses social
divisions between 'South China artisans' from Guangzhou or the lower Yangzi and
more rural 'North China proletarians'. The second part, 'The Politics of Partisanship,
1919-1949', deals with Communist and Nationalist organizers and the evolution of
systematic unionization. Perry finds that workers were divided by gender, place of
origin, trade and even gang affiliation, but united to seek economic benefit and support
the nation. The final section, 'The Politics of Production', examines differing
situations in the tobacco, textile and transport industries.

1014   **Industrial reformers in Republican China.**
Robin Porter.   Armonk, New York; London: M. E. Sharpe, 1994.
276p. (Studies on Modern China).

Discusses the efforts of the YMCA, YWCA, International Labour Organization (ILO),
and Chinese and foreign liberal industrial reform groups to improve working
conditions in China's factories during the 1920s and 1930s. Basing his work mainly
on archives in Geneva, Porter describes ILO investigations and reports, which often
provided the first solid information on the squalor and exploitation of the factories,
then details the frustrated efforts to form organizations powerful enough to bring
pressure to bear.

Communist neo-traditionalism: work and authority in Chinese industry.
See item no. 974.

**Historiography of the Chinese labor movement, 1895-1949: a critical
survey and bibliography of selected Chinese source materials at the
Hoover Institution.**
See item no. 1486.

Environment

1015　**Grasslands and grassland sciences in Northern China.**
　　　　Committee on Scholarly Communications with the People's Republic
　　　　of China.　Washington, DC: National Academy Press, 1992. 214p.
　　　　maps.
Ten natural and social scientists report on grasslands and the state of grasslands
science. They warn that degradation is rapid, accelerating and caused by human
intervention, particularly the extension of agriculture and overgrazing. Part one
describes ecology, society and land use in the arid and semi-arid areas of the
Northeast, Inner Mongolia, Gansu, Qinghai and Xinjiang. Part two comprises six
state-of-the-field essays on Chinese scholarship of particular areas, and one on social
science studies. Part three describes twenty-two Chinese scientific institutions and
their research programmes. Part four summarizes key issues in grassland studies: the
pastoral frontier in history; atmosphere-biosphere interactions; social dimensions;
desertification and degradation; rangeland management; and conservation and
wildlife. Throughout the volume there are copious references to Chinese and Western
works.

1016　**Water management in the Yellow River basin of China.**
　　　　Charles Greer.　Austin, Texas: University of Texas Press, 1979.
　　　　174p. maps. bibliog.
Analyses the attempts both in imperial times and in the 20th century to manage the
Yellow River (Huanghe, formerly the Hwangho) for flood control, irrigation and soil
conservation. Chapters cover the nature of the problem, historical management
strategies, early Western interest, Soviet assistance after 1949, reliance on traditional
methods, and new strategies. *Water conservancy and irrigation in China: social,
economic, and agrotechnical aspects* by E. B. Vermeer (The Hague: Leiden
University Press, 1977. 350p. bibliog.) is a scholarly analysis of the post-1949
organization of labour, education and research, and problems of irrigation,
salinization, state policy and finance in the major river basins (Yellow River, Huai
River and Yangzi). *Water management organization in the People's Republic of
China*, edited, with an introduction by James E. Nickum (Armonk, New York;

London: M. E. Sharpe, 1981. 269p.) brings together articles from PRC journals which discuss technical and socio-political aspects of river management and development. The editor's substantial introduction describes the historical background and the political aspects.

1017 **China on the edge: the crisis of ecology and development.**
He Bochuan, translated by Jenny Holdaway, Guo Jian-sheng, Susan Brick, Hu Si-gang, Charles Wong. San Francisco: China Books, 1991. 214p.

A passionate attack by a Chinese scholar-journalist on the environmental policies of the People's Republic. The Chinese original, *Shan ao shang di Zhongguo* (1986), was widely read, then suppressed. He Bochuan musters statistics, charts, graphs and tables to argue that China's environment 'has gone past the point of no return'. Agricultural and industrial pollution, together with overwhelming population growth, have ruined water, air, farmland and forest. Mao Zedong is blamed for opposing population control and for policies ranging from low fixed prices for scarce resources to politically inspired 'miracle' development campaigns. In addition, the free market policies of the Deng Xiaoping years have produced a grotesquely distorted development, built on export/import consumerism and exploitation which has damaged both society and the environment.

1018 **Megaproject: a case study of China's Three Gorges Project.**
Edited by Luk Shiu-hung, Joseph Whitney. Armonk, New York; London: M. E. Sharpe, 1993. 236p. (Chinese Environment and Development Series).

A collection of articles by Chinese engineers and planners published before the 1989 crackdown effectively ended open debate within China. See also Grainne Ryder, *Damming the Three Gorges: what dam-builders don't want you to know* (Toronto: Probe International, 1990. 135p.), a polemical, well-informed argument against the project, which accuses it of being larger than necessary, environmentally unsound and economically dubious.

1019 **Forest and land management in imperial China.**
Nicholas K. Menzies. Basingstoke, England; London: Macmillan; New York: St. Martin's, 1994. 175p. maps.

Investigates both deforestation in history and conditions under which stable systems of forest management occurred. Chapter one, 'Forests in China', outlines the historic processes and patterns of deforestation and the role of forests in Chinese culture; maps and tables describe the major forests and their history. Chapter two, 'Forest Stability and Decline', reviews how Chinese culture, institutions and economics affect the conditions for sustainable forestry. Six chapters then discuss case-studies of forest management in imperial China: an imperial hunting enclosure; temple and monastic forests; clan, community and commons; trees for profit in agriculture; economic forests (for fuelwood, sericulture and edible fungi); and logging old growth. A final chapter discusses the conclusions and implications for policy today, and the 'References' section lists useful comparative and historical material.

1020 Population and the environment in China.
Qu Geping, Li Jinchang, translated by Jiang Baozhang, Gu Ran, English-language edition edited by Robert B. Boardman. Boulder, Colorado: Lynne Rienner; London: Paul Chapman, 1994. 217p. bibliog.

Starting from the statement that 'the sustainable development – in fact, the very existence – of the whole Chinese nation depends on resolving its population and environmental problems', the authors present a heavily documented but clearly argued analysis of historical and contemporary issues. Dr Qu and Professor Li are administrators and advisers in the PRC's National Environmental Protection Agency, and draw on their insiders' knowledge and research. Chapters are devoted to: population and environmental issues in China's history; population and land availability; forest resources; mineral resources; water resources; energy resources; and the living environment. Three concluding chapters assess needs and programmes for the future. Unfortunately, the bibliography does not distinguish between Chinese and English-language publications.

1021 Forests and forestry in China.
S. D. Richardson. Washington, DC: Island Press, 1990. 352p.

Richardson toured China in 1963 and described the state of the forests and government management policies in *Forestry in Communist China* (Baltimore, Maryland: Johns Hopkins University Press, 1966. 237p.). He returned in the 1980s, and found that decentralization and market reforms had led to substantial forest destruction. This book catalogues forest and vegetation types, analyses the motivations for government policies, and argues that the incentives offered to individual tree farmers failed to provide for the long-term overall planning needed to encompass both village production and large-scale industry, such as paper mills. Harrison E. Salisbury, *The Great Black Dragon Fire: a Chinese inferno* (Boston, Massachusetts: Little, Brown, 1989. 180p.) dramatically narrates the faulty planning and bureaucratic bungling which led to China's most damaging forest fire.

1022 Environmental policy in China.
Lester Ross. Bloomington, Indiana: Indiana University Press, 1988. 240p.

A detailed, lucid analysis of the politics of environmental policies in forestry, water conservancy, natural hazards and pollution control. Ross finds that government statutes and official commentaries are written by legal scholars familiar both with China's needs and with world environmental law; the implementation of the laws, however, is more problematic, and little is done through courts or case law. Most action is taken through indirect or administrative means, and enforcement tends to have political rather than judicial aims. Ross advocates market-exchange solutions which would rely on self-interest for enforcement. Lester Ross, A. Silk Mitchell, *Environmental law and policy in the People's Republic of China* (New York: Quorum Books, 1987. 449p.) comprises a documentary collection which includes major statutes or proposed statutes in the area of environmental law, law review articles, newspaper articles and some other Chinese commentaries.

1023 China's environmental crisis: an inquiry into the limits of
national development.
Vaclav Smil. Armonk, New York; London: M. E. Sharpe, 1993.
257p.

An impassioned, detailed, but non-technical probing of the structural causes and
political factors behind impending catastrophe. Using Chinese government statistics,
Smil examines the mutual dependence of water, energy, land, food and labour; each
affects all the others, producing a vicious downward spiral of land exhaustion, energy
depletion and population pressure, all leading to raging pollution of land, air and
water. The pessimistic conclusion is that 'there are no solutions within China's
economic, technical, and manpower reach'. Smil's earlier and still powerful book, *The
bad earth: environmental degradation in China* (New York; London: M. E. Sharpe,
1984. 247p.) originally broke the story on China's environmental degradation.

Man and land in Chinese history: an economic analysis.
See item no. 901.

Exhausting the earth: state and peasant in Hunan, 1500-1850.
See item no. 987.

Education

General

1024 **The schooling of China: tradition and modernity in Chinese education.**
John Cleverly.   North Sydney, Australia: Allen & Unwin; Concord, Massachusetts: Paul & Company, 1991. 2nd ed. 378p. bibliog.
Argues that present-day education in China is a product of traditional Chinese thought, Communist practice and modern international influences. The first two chapters summarize Confucian education for a 'world of harmony' and schools in ancient China. Chapters three and four describe the founding of modern education and education under the Republic (1911-49). Chapters five and six look at Mao Zedong and education, the origins of Communist schooling, post-liberation schooling, useful Russian influence and the aftermath (1949-57). Chapters nine to thirteen cover the 'two-line struggle' which led to the rise and fall of the Cultural Revolution. The final chapters describe the anatomy of the present Chinese school system and the problems and prospects for Chinese education. The 'Sources' section provides an extensive but miscellaneous listing of references consulted.

1025 **Education and modernization: the Chinese experience.**
Edited by Ruth Hayhoe.   Oxford; New York: Pergammon Press, 1992. 393p. bibliog. (Comparative and International Education Series).
A multifaceted international symposium. Essays in part one examine historical topics, including: Confucius and traditional education; real and imagined continuities in the struggle for literacy; lessons from the Republican era; and modernization and revolution in the Great Leap Forward and the Cultural Revolution. Essays in part two examine the balance between formal and non-formal education systems. Part three is devoted to 'issues and groups in education and modernization', such as: moral political education; foreign language education; women, education and modernization; education of national minorities; and management training. An extensive select bibliography and research guide conclude the volume.

356

1026 **China's education reform in the 1980's: policies, issues, and historical perspectives.**
Suzanne Pepper. Berkeley, California: Institute of East Asian Studies, Center for Chinese Studies, 1990. 196p. (China Research Monograph).

Evaluates post-1976 education policies against an analysis of the reform tradition going back to the early 20th century. The book supplements and frames Pepper's chapters on education in the period 1949-79 in *People's Republic of China, Pt 1* and *Pt 2* (qq.v.), forming with them a major interpretive analysis of 20th-century Chinese education. Part one of this book traces the 'two-line struggle' in Chinese education back to the 1920s. Part two analyses educational reform in the 1980s, when 'two lines become one'.

1027 **Education in modern China.**
R. F. Price. London; Boston, Massachusetts; Henley, England: Routledge & Kegan Paul, 1979. 2nd ed. 345p. bibliog. (World Education Series).

An analysis sympathetic to Mao's aspirations, kindled by the author's experience teaching in China 1965-67, and first published as *Education in Communist China* (1970). Chapters one, 'Educational Aims and the Thoughts of Mao Zedong', and two, 'The Chinese Tradition – Background to Mao's Thoughts', set the stage for the following chapter topics: obstacles to educational reform (geography, family loyalties, economic factors, the influence of the pre-1949 school system and foreign influence); full-time and part-time schools; teachers; moral-political educators (CCP, PLA, Youth League, Young Pioneers and Red Guards); education and the Cultural Revolution; and education after Mao. There are references throughout, and the bibliography lists books, articles and pamphlets in English on education and general background.

1028 **Preschool in three cultures: Japan, China, and the United States.**
Joseph J. Tobin, David Y. H. Wu, Dana H. Davidson. New Haven, Connecticut; London: Yale University Press, 1989. 238p.

An insightful comparative study of child psychology, teaching styles, school organization and general cultural priorities. The method is 'dialogic' and 'multi-vocal', using not only field observation in all three countries, but also the insider voices of preschool teachers, parents and administrators, who each react to videotapes of the others' schools. Issues raised in the China section include: the school's role in correcting the 'spoiling' in the single child family; regimentation and the concept of *guan*, 'to govern', which has positive connotations in Chinese of 'to love', 'to care for'; working mothers; gender; and the historical role of preschool education in China, arguing that the emphasis on controlling the individual and promoting the collective good is not just a socialist phenomenon.

Chinese intellectuals and the West: 1872-1949.
See item no. 241.

The Chinese civil service: career open to talent?
See item no. 693.

Education under the Empire

1029 **The thorny gates of learning in Sung China.**
John Chaffee. Albany, New York: State University of New York
Press, 1995. new ed. 318p.

Song dynasty Emperors wanted a meritocratic education system in order to reward the deserving and provide reliable, pliable bureaucrats; literati wanted to do well for Confucius and family fortunes. In this social history, Chaffee explores the impact of the examination system on social life, and how the debate over merit and schooling reflected intellectual and political changes. Chapters trace the growth of the literati, the evolution of the exam system, regional differences and the culture of examinations. In the Northern Song, government schools educated many, if not most, of those ambitious to enter the bureaucracy. However, by the time of the later, Southern Song, many joined the statesman/philosopher Zhu Xi in attacking the government schools for sycophancy and sterility, and championing independent private academies (*shuyuan*) controlled by local lineages and literati. Chaffee concludes that a 'failure of fairness' doomed the meritocratic state. This work was originally published in 1985 (London: Cambridge University Press, 1985. 279p. maps. [Cambridge Studies in Chinese History]).

1030 **Neo-Confucian education: the formative stage.**
Edited by Wm. Theodore de Bary, John W. Chaffee. Berkeley,
California; Los Angeles; London: University of California Press,
1989. 593p. (Studies on China, no. 9).

Editors and fifteen scholars study the thought, educational practice and influence of statesman and philosopher Zhu Xi (1130-1200); his Neo-Confucian ideology is now credited with both the disciplined creativity of Asia's economic boom and also with neo-authoritarian government. The introduction summarizes contributions and provides a framework. Part one, 'The Background of Neo-Confucian Education', studies Buddhism and education in Tang times, Chan (Zen) education, and Song education before Zhu Xi. Part two contains five studies on the background, thought, aims and content of the master's own practice. Part three, 'Education in the Home', comprises studies on the formulation of family ritual, the education of children, and women's education. Part four, 'Education Beyond the Family', provides studies on: the 'community compact' (*xiangyue*), sponsored by officials to encourage education and morality; the scholarly academies (*shuyuan*) which acted as research centres, political think tanks and social gathering points; the politics of education; problems of the local community; and legal experts and learning.

1031 **Education and society in late imperial China, 1600-1900.**
Edited by Benjamin A. Elman, Alexander Woodside. Berkeley,
California; Los Angeles; London: University of California Press,
1994. 575p. (Studies on China, no. 19).

Fourteen social and intellectual historians view education in the 'ferment and achievement of a sprawling, multiethnic empire'. The editors' introduction and 'Afterword: The Expansion of Education in Ch'ing China', summarize and frame findings. Part one includes three studies on: the education of daughters; the roles of school teachers as seen in a Qing dynasty novel; and family education as practised by

Zeng Guofan, an important 19th-century official. Part two presents three studies on the official examinations and changing curricula. Part three, 'Technical Learning and Intellectual Challenge', covers the teaching of mathematics, legal education and education for Manchus. Part four, 'Theory and Practice of Schools and Community Education', includes studies on: lower Yangzi valley elementary education; frontier schools; a 19th-century Shanghai academy which developed an indigenous reform curriculum rather than Westernization; and 'the divorce between the political center and educational creativity'.

1032   **Imperial China's last classical academies: social change in the Lower Yangzi, 1864-1911.**
Barry C. Keenan.   Berkeley, California; Los Angeles; London: University of California Press, 1994. 199p. (China Research Monographs, no. 42).

After the Qing suppressed the mid-19th-century rebellions, Jiangsu élites in the area around Shanghai restored all levels of schools, especially the traditional Confucian academies. These academies, which taught no Western subjects, trained a local élite which the central government could not control. Keenan looks at these schools, their methods of teaching, and the developing rivalry between this local élite and the modernizing late Qing reformers in the central government.

1033   **Government education and examinations in Sung China.**
Thomas H. C. Lee.   Hong Kong: Chinese University Press; New York: St. Martin's Press, 1985. 327p.

An examination of the development, organization and practice of government schools and civil service examinations during the 10th to 13th centuries. Part one sketches education before the Song, the influence of Song education in later dynasties, and the problems and purposes of the study of Song education. Part two describes Song students, teachers, and institutions in higher education, local schools, and the history and functions of the civil service system. Part three analyses the social significance and moral purpose of the exams (impartiality, equality and social mobility). Lee explains how moral and political conflict arose because the government used schools as a device to recruit non-aristocratic élite children into a subservient bureaucracy. Anxiety over the lapse of a moral ideal contributed to the rise of private Neo-Confucian academies. Part four evaluates the significance and strength of Song government education.

1034   **Academies in Ming China: a historical essay.**
John Meskill.   Tucson, Arizona: University of Arizona Press, 1982. 203p.

Although much of the schooling in traditional China was conducted individually or in small-group tutorials, the academy (*shuyuan*) developed into a major institution for teaching, moral inquiry and scholarship; in 1595 Matteo Ricci compared them to the wide-ranging academies of his Renaissance Italy. Meskill describes the origins of the academies in the Ming, their role as cells of reform, and their part in the decline of the dynasty. On the Donglin Academy and its notorious political suppression and bitter factional warfare, see Meskill's 'Academies and Politics in the Ming Dynasty', in *Chinese government in Ming times* (q.v.). The Qing dynasty highest educational institution is studied in Adam Yuen-cheng Lui, *The Hanlin academy: training ground for the ambitious, 1644-1850* (Hamden, Connecticut: Archon, 1981. 284p.).

1035 **China's examination hell: the civil service examinations of imperial China.**
Miyazaki Ichisada, translation by Conrad Schirokauer. New York: John Weatherhill, 1976. Reprinted, in paperbound edition, New Haven, Connecticut: Yale University Press, 1981. 144p.

A portrayal of the zenith of the examination system in the Qing dynasty. The original edition, *Kakyō: Chūgoku no shiken jigoku* (Tokyo: Chūo koron, 1963), was written for the Japanese general public. Professor Miyazaki describes the cycle of the examination life from study and preparation, through the district and prefectural levels, to the provincial and metropolitan exams, culminating, for the lucky and assiduous few, in the palace examination. He also highlights the problems, such as systematic cheating, and the social implications, such as the family support required. Separate chapters describe the military and special exams. Chapter ten, 'An Evaluation of the Examination System', discusses the system's strengths, costs, and abolition in 1905. The translator adds a useful 'Suggestion for Further Reading' and a glossary-index. *The reform and abolition of the traditional Chinese examination system*, by Wolfgang Franke (Cambridge, Massachusetts: East Asian Research Center, distributed by Harvard University Press, 1968. 100p. [East Asian Monographs, no. 10]) describes the political and administrative changes leading to the 1905 abolition of the examination system, and is accompanied by extensive translations of Chinese documents.

1036 **Education and popular literacy in Ch'ing China.**
Evelyn Sakakida Rawski. Ann Arbor, Michigan: University of Michigan Press; Rexdale, Canada: Wiley, 1979. 294p. map. (Michigan Studies on China).

Chinese reformers and Western observers had long claimed that low literacy was a reason for China's failure to modernize; in this work, Rawski effectively challenges this view. If realistic measures of practical literacy are used instead of the ability to read abstruse classical texts, then male literacy was roughly twenty per cent or one literate person per family; this was approximately the same as the rate of Japan at that time, and was among the highest in the world. The book first surveys the popular elementary schools, their costs and availability, then describes popular education materials, showing how the nature of the Chinese writing system allowed many people with just an introductory education to read practical texts.

The ladder of success in imperial China: aspects of social mobility, 1368-1911.
See item no. 192.

The scholars.
See item no. 1134.

Modern education before 1949

1037　**Chang Chih-tung and educational reform in China.**
　　　William Ayers.　Cambridge, Massachusetts: Harvard University
　　　Press, 1971. 287p. (Harvard East Asian Series, no. 54).
Relates the life and education activities of one of the most effective late Qing reform officials. Zhang Zhidong (1837-1909) saw Western technology not as antithetical to Chinese culture, but rather as a way to develop and protect it. His best-selling pamphlet, unreliably translated by Samuel I. Woodbridge as *China's only hope* (New York: Revell, 1900), popularized the dichotomy between Confucian learning for 'principle' or 'substance' (*ti*) and Western learning for 'utility' or 'function' (*yong*). This formula challenged both those who wanted to abandon tradition and those who wanted to preserve it unchanged. Zhang sponsored new schools, military academies and agricultural reforms, leading up to the abolition of the examination system in 1905. Knight Biggerstaff, *The earliest modern government schools in China* (Ithaca, New York: Cornell University Press, 1961. 276p.) describes the educational efforts of the Self-strengtheners in the 1860s.

1038　**Reform the people: changing attitudes towards popular education**
　　　in early 20th century China.
　　　Paul Bailey.　Edinburgh: Edinburgh University Press; Vancouver,
　　　Canada: University of British Columbia Press, 1990. 296p.
An intellectual and social history. Before the 1911 Revolution, government officials and critical intellectuals agreed on the responsibility to educate the 'people', but differed on methods and goals. They reformed the formal school system and developed largely non-governmental popular education, consisting of half-day, literacy and vocational schools, lectures, and public libraries. In 1912 the Ministry of Education framed a Western-style school system; however, political disorder limited its development, and some doubted that it was suitable for China's traditions and needs. Local popular education movements sprang up to fill the gap, including a Work-Study Movement which sent workers to France during the First World War for practical education. Bailey relates these issues and experiments to later Nationalist and Communist educational methods.

1039　**Educational reform in early 20th century China.**
　　　Marianne Bastid, translated by Paul J. Bailey.　Ann Arbor,
　　　Michigan: Center for Chinese Studies, University of Michigan, 1988.
　　　331p. (Michigan Monographs in Chinese Studies).
Zhang Jian was a leading official who developed new schools as a basis for modernization. Bastid's *Aspects de la réforme de l'enseignement en Chine au début du XXè siècle d'après les écrits de Zhang Jian* (Aspects of the educational reform in China in the early 20th century according to the work of Zhang Jian) (Paris; La Haye, France: Mouton, 1971. 321p.), translated here, describes the political background, the collaboration between gentry élites and government officials, and the opposition to their new schools. Appended are a number of documents and essays in translation. For a study of Zhang's work as an industrialist, see Samuel Chu, *Reformer in modern China: Chang Chien, 1853-1926* (New York; London: Columbia University Press, 1965. 256p.).

1040 **Education and social change in China: the beginnings of the modern era.**
Sally Borthwick. Stanford, California: Hoover Institution Press, Stanford University, 1983. 216p. (Education and Society).

A rich analysis of the political debate and ideological controversy over the introduction of Western-style modern schools, 1890-1911. The 'traditional' schools, often known as *sishu*, were local, small-scale establishments, financed by villages or families, and taught by cheap, untrained Confucian scholars; though limited, these schools were effective in meeting local needs and expectations. Reformers introduced science, foreign languages and sports; these new schools were 'modern', but raised disquieting questions of social impact by being hierarchical, alien, urban and expensive. Borthwick explores curricula, social values and the changing role of the national state against a background of debate over freedom, social discipline and civilization.

1041 **Schoolhouse politicians: locality and state during the Chinese Republic.**
Helen R. Chauncey. Honolulu: University of Hawaii Press, 1992. 295p. (Studies of the East Asian Institute).

Examines provincial educational circles in Jiangsu province, 1900-49, as a way of understanding the relation between national and local politics. Chauncey argues, on the basis of comparative theory, that the authority of the national state depended on its ability to identify and incorporate local efforts to build from the bottom up. The direct focus of the book is on the growth of elementary and secondary schools and accompanying phenomena such as educational journals, teachers' assemblies, textbooks and even the physical management of public space in schoolhouses and exercise yards. Chauncey contrasts the Nationalist government of the 1930s with the emerging Communist power, which maintained a Central China Base Area from 1941.

1042 **The Dewey experiment in China: educational reform and political power in the early Republic.**
Barry Keenan. Cambridge, Massachusetts: East Asian Research Center, distributed Harvard University Press, 1977. 335p. (East Asian Monographs, no. 81).

John Dewey, the pre-eminent American philosopher of education and pragmatism, visited China in 1919, just as the May Fourth Movement was begining and young Chinese were looking abroad for inspiration. At the behest of former students such as Hu Shi, Tao Xingzhi and Jiang Menglin (Chiang Monlin), Dewey stayed on for nearly two years of lecture tours and teaching. Keenan describes Dewey's progressive thought, his lectures, the peak of American liberal influence on schools and education in the mid-1920s, and the reasons why this influence waned in the politicized period of 1925-27. The lectures are reconstituted in *John Dewey: lectures in China, 1919-1920*, translated from the Chinese, edited by Robert W. Clopton, Tsuin-chen Ou (Honolulu: University Press of Hawaii, 1973. 337p.).

1043   **China and the Christian colleges, 1850-1950.**
Jessie Gregory Lutz.   Ithaca, New York; London: Cornell University
Press, 1971. 575p.

The thirteen Protestant colleges founded by mission boards are here carefully
examined as both 'mediators of Western civilization' and 'participants in a continuing
Chinese revolution'. Although Christians never exceeded one per cent of China's
population, by the 1930s Christian colleges enrolled ten to fifteen per cent of China's
college population. Lutz describes Yenching University, Lingnan University, Cheeloo
University, Ginling College, St. John's University and Hangchow University, with
brief reference to their three Roman Catholic counterparts. She evaluates innovations
in women's education, medical training, rural programmes, liberal arts and social
sciences. A major part of the story deals with the competition of these liberal
institutions with radical revolution for the allegiance of students. Throughout the
work, copious references to Chinese and English-language materials are included.

1044   **Yenching University and Sino-Western relations, 1916-1952.**
Philip West.   Cambridge, Massachusetts; London: Harvard
University Press, 1976. 327p. (Harvard East Asian Series, no. 85).

Yenching University was founded in 1916 to provide patriotic Christian education for
China's emerging middle class; it was at the centre of Chinese and American attempts
to work out a liberal inter-cultural approach to China's national salvation. In 1951, the
patriotic nationalism of the Korean War snuffed out Yenching cosmopolitanism, and
Peking University took over the campus. West describes the original bonds between
Chinese, such as Wu Leiquan (Wu Lei-ch'üan), and Americans, such as President
John Leighton Stuart, which were both religious and political. He shows how
theology, curriculum, scholarship, student life and faculty politics responded to the
international and cultural crises of the 1920s and 1930s.

1045   **The alienated academy: culture and politics in Republican China,
1919-1937.**
Yeh Wen-hsin.   Cambridge, Massachusetts; London: Council on
East Asian Studies, Harvard University, distributed by Harvard
University Press, 1990. 449p. (Harvard East Asian Monographs,
no. 148).

Yeh describes how Western-style colleges and universities in Shanghai, Beijing and
Nanjing produced middle-class students who lacked the status and power which the
imperial exam system had conferred on their literati predecessors. The new
professionals searched for ways to turn their new cultural status into real social and
political power. Yeh studies 'campus culture' in contrasting universities (including St.
John's, Shanghai, Zhongshan [Chung-shan] and Yenching). The Nationalist
government sought to 'partify' education, while revolutionaries sought to recruit
activists. Students were torn over the introduction of new subjects, such as science and
German literature, and especially the cultural significance of the English language.
This 'alienated academy', produced a 'deracinated' élite which turned variously to
aestheticism, love, science and revolution. Ming K. Chan, Arif Dirlik, *Schools into
farms and factories: anarchists, the Guomindang, and the National Labor University,
1927-1932* (Durham, North Carolina: Duke University Press, 1991. 339p.) is
concerned with students and ideas at an anarchist Shanghai university first sponsored
by the Nationalist government, then eventually closed by it.

To the people: James Yen and village China.
See item no. 254.

An American transplant: the Rockefeller Foundation and Peking Union Medical College.
See item no. 676.

The People's Republic (1949-)

1046   **Chinese education since 1949: academic and revolutionary models.**
Theodore Hsi-en Chen.   New York; London: Pergamon Press, 1981. 304p.

A standard survey of education in China from 1949 to the Cultural Revolution. Chen sketches the historical background of the revolution, then analyses the developments in schools and universities in each of the successive periods. He sees a 'two line struggle' between a populist model typified by Mao and a professional model led by educators. John N. Hawkins, *Mao Tse-tung and education: his thoughts and teachings* (Hamden, Connecticut: Linnet Books, Shoestring Press, 1974. 260p.) is a respectful exposition; chapters take up Mao's educational thought in successive periods, then by topic, with extensive references and a partially annotated bibliography.

1047   **Chinese education: problems, policies, and prospects.**
Edited by Irving Epstein.   New York: Garland Press, 1991. 304p.

An authoritative collection of short essays organized to survey all aspects of education in the People's Republic, emphasizing the present day. Contributors use up-to-date research and approaches, and take a special interest in policy problems.

1048   **Chinese Communist education: records of the first decade.**
Compiled, edited by Stewart Fraser.   Nashville, Tennessee: Vanderbilt University Press, 1965. 542p. bibliog.

After an summary essay, 'Education, Indoctrination, and Ideology', the editor presents speeches, articles and documents from the 1950s, mainly from the translations series of the United States Consul General in Hong Kong and Foreign Languages Press in Peking. The bibliography (p. 413-96) comprises a topically arranged list of English-language and translated books, articles and documents on all periods of Chinese education. A briefer anthology is *Chinese education under Communism*, edited with an introduction by Chang-tu Hu (New York; London: Teachers College Press, Columbia University, 1974. 2nd ed. 229p.); more emphasis on education in the Cultural Revolution is included in *Toward a new world outlook: a documentary history of education in the P. R. C. 1949-1976*, edited by Hu Shiming, Eli Seifman (New York: AMS Press, 1976. 335p.).

1049   **To open minds: Chinese clues to the dilemma of contemporary education.**
Howard Gardner.   New York: Basic Books, 1989. 326p.

An engaging essay in which Gardner, a leading educational theorist, describes his four visits to China, the schools he saw and the philosophical issues raised. Progressive ('transformative') education, as practiced by Socrates and cultivated in America, centres on students and emphasizes individualism, creativity, spontaneity and freedom. Traditional ('mimetic') schooling, whether Confucian, Maoist or American, centres on teachers, and emphasizes hierarchy, discipline and rote learning. Gardner opposes the neo-conservative 'back to basics' programme for today's pluralistic America, and was surprised to find that Chinese mimetic pedagogy nurtured the artistic achievements of Chinese children; Chinese teachers did not believe in individual, transformative exploration, but in 'artistic activity as the recreation of traditional beautiful forms and the engendering of moral behavior'.

1050   **The saga of anthropology in China: from Malinowski to Moscow to Mao.**
Gregory Eliyu Gulden.   Armonk, New York; London: M. E. Sharpe, 1994. 298p.

Anthropology in China has experienced four successive approaches: before 1949, Western models were introduced by disciples of Malinowski; in the 1950s, these were attacked as bourgeois and not suited to China; the resulting Soviet style anthropology was itself attacked and transformed in the Maoist radical period; and finally, in the 1980s, a continuing pluralist debate emerged. Gulden follows the life and career of Liang Zhaotao, a senior anthropologist now at Zhongshan University, to show the development of a distinctive discipline from a China-centred viewpoint. *Anthropology in China: defining the discipline*, edited by Gulden (Armonk, New York; London: M. E. Sharpe, 1990. 217p. [Chinese Studies on China]) gathers 1980s articles from PRC journals which debate archaeology, palaeoanthropology, ethnology and ethno-linguistics. See also: Siu-lin Wong, *Sociology and socialism in contemporary China* (London: Routledge & Kegan Paul, 1979. 147p.); and Leo Douw, 'Chinese Rural Sociology of the 1930s: On the Acculturation of Social Scientists' Political Attitudes', in *China's modernisation: Westernisation and acculturation* (Stuttgart, Germany: Franz Steiner, 1993, p. 83-109).

1051   **China's universities and the open door.**
Ruth Hayhoe.   Armonk, New York: M. E. Sharpe, 1989. 249p. bibliog.

Focuses on higher education in the 1980s, when reformers revived systems from the 1950s but aspired to create democratic knowledge-power relations which would produce both social order and economic production. They re-encountered a persisting contradiction in 20th-century Chinese education between knowledge for modernization and knowledge for political order. In the 1950s, Soviet style hierarchical organization of universities and structure of knowledge in teaching echoed those of Confucian China. The Cultural Revolution violently attacked this regimentation, but failed to build new democratic institutions. The core of the book discusses the university curriculum reform of the 1980s, participation in global exchange, and the attempts to create a new relationship with foreign knowledge. The final chapter critically reviews World Bank educational projects of the 1980s. The bibliography provides an excellent selection of English-language works.

1052 Education in post-Mao China.

Jing Lin. Westport, Connecticut; London: Praeger, 1993. 131p.

Summarizes changes and problems in the decade of reform. Chapter topics include: changing means of socialization from the Cultural Revolution to the present; problems in rural education (drop-outs, teacher motivation, non-formal education); urban education (tracking students into academic or vocational education); reform and problems in educational administration; achievements and problems in educational research; and the student movement of 1989. See also: Stig Thörgersen, *Secondary education in China after Mao: reform and social conflict* (Aarhus, Denmark: Aarhus University Press, 1990. 168p.); and Suzanne Pepper, *China's universities: post-Mao enrollment policies and their impact on the structure of secondary education* (Ann Arbor, Michigan: Center for Chinese Studies, University of Michigan, 1984. 155p. [Michigan Monographs on Chinese Studies]).

1053 China learns English: language teaching and social change in the People's Republic of China.

Heidi A. Ross. New Haven, Connecticut; London: Yale University Press, 1993. 280p.

Ross carried out field research and taught at an élite Shanghai middle school which specialized in foreign language teaching. This book first delineates China's long-time need to master foreign languages without surrendering sovereignty, then traces this dilemma back to the 19th century and through the post-1949 twists and turns of language teaching policy. The central chapters focus on the psychology and role of teachers as both professionals and political victims, the experiences of students as they master English and challenge authority, and the attempts of bureaucrats and commissars to control and develop education. For a Chinese view of the middle school teacher's moral responsibility, see Liu Xinwu, 'The Teacher' (*Ban zhuren*), in *Prize-winning stories from China, 1978-1979* (Beijing: Foreign Languages Press, 1981, p. 3-26).

1054 The paradox of power in a People's Republic of China middle school.

Martin Schoenhals. Armonk, New York; London: M. E. Sharpe, 1993. 216p. (Studies in Contemporary China).

Basing this work on his field observation of student and teacher life in 'Third Middle School', the author discusses general Chinese social values in historical and sociological terms: *shame* (the expectation that the individual will be sensitive to others); and *face* (the public manifestation of that sensitivity). The author analyses family socialization and the politics of everyday school life to show how emotions structure social action. Deep anxiety over evaluation and criticism lead to a 'paradox of power' in which those of high status, such as teachers, are particularly vulnerable to loss of face when publicly criticized. The problems presented for Chinese youth culture are visible both in the schools witnessed by Schoenhals and in the 1989 Tiananmen crisis.

1055 Literacy in China: the effect of the national development context and policy on literacy levels, 1949-1979.

Vilma Seeberg. Bochum, Germany: Brockmeyer, 1990. 352p.

A statistically sophisticated analysis, which finds that there was very little improvement in school age and adult literacy between 1949 and 1979. Seeberg draws on United Nations definitions and comparisons with other Third World countries to evaluate China's series of authoritarian campaigns organized by the party and government, especially during the 1950s, and the experience of local governments and communes during and after the Great Leap Forward. The Confucian tradition predisposed villagers to education, but 'Maoist Radicalism' did not solve the low quality of teachers, inadequate capital investment, the difficult nature of the writing system and the sheer size of the problem. See also Charles W. Hayford, 'Literacy Movements in Modern China', in *National literacy campaigns: historical and comparative perspectives*, edited by Robert F. Arnove, Harvey J. Graff (New York; London: Plenum Press, 1987, p. 147-71).

1056   **Competitive comrades: career incentives and student strategies in China.**
        Susan Shirk.   Berkeley, California; Los Angeles; London: University of California Press, 1982. 231p.
Shirk began studying China when the Cultural Revolution was promising a socialist society without Stalinism and schools which would revolutionize human ideals and behaviour; her work demonstrated the negative consequences of Maoist programmes through careful scholarship rather than ideological denial. This book opens with a sympathetic explanation of Mao's egalitarian vision of the early 1950s, and goes on to describe city middle schools and their formal structure (including the *ban* [class by class organization]) to show how students competed not on merit ('meritocracy') but on political morality ('virtuocracy'). Students accepted egalitarian and collectivist values, but government policies structured their friendships, choice of career strategies (mainly whether or not to become activists), and social opportunities. The result of this was intense competition rather than the desired socialist cooperation.

1057   **Party and professionals: the political role of teachers in contemporary China.**
        Gordon White.   Armonk, New York: M. E. Sharpe, 1981. 361p.
Discusses the changing professional status of teachers as an example of the interplay between ideology, policy and social structure. The analytical chapters look at the social prestige of teachers, issues of income and material welfare, political status and teachers as a political interest group, and draw conclusions about the political nature of the teaching profession. The extensive appendix, parts of which were published in the journal *Chinese Education* (vol. 12, no. 4 [Winter 1979-80]), provides translated documents on the issues discussed, as well as on teachers' discontent and demands.

Up to the mountains and down to the villages: the transfer of youth from urban to rural China.
See item no. 743.

Red guard factionalism and the Cultural Revolution in Guangzhou (Canton).
See item no. 751.

Chinese Education: A Journal of Translations.
See item no. 1394.

Research guide to education in China after Mao, 1977-1981.
See item no. 1494.

Educational exchange, teaching and research in China

1058 Educational exchanges: essays on the Sino-American experience.
Edited by Joyce K. Kallgren, Denis Fred Simon. Berkeley,
California: Institute of East Asian Studies, University of California,
1987. 257p. (Research Papers and Policy Studies).

These thoughtful scholarly evaluations discuss the following topics: background and overview; the 'trajectory of cultural internationalism'; the role of the National Committee on US China Relations; American philanthropy; the goals and roles of universities; a comparison with US-Indian exchanges; European-Chinese relations; and particular disciplines. Leo Orleans, *Chinese students in America: policies, issues, and numbers* (Washington, DC: National Academy Press, 1988. 144p.) analyses evolving policies on study abroad, the 'brain drain' issue, and students and scholars in the United States.

1059 A relationship restored: trends in U.S.-China educational exchanges, 1978-1984.
Edited by David Lampton, with Joyce A. Madancy, Kristen M.
Williams for the Committee on Scholarly Communications with the
People's Republic of China. Washington, DC: National Academy
Press, 1986. 266p.

Describes the beginnings of cultural and scholarly relations between China and the United States, together with notes, tables and statistical appendices. Introductory chapters sketch Sino-American academic exchanges before 1950, Sino-Soviet exchanges during the period 1950-60, and academic exchange in the 1970s and 1980s. Following chapters cover: the characteristics of exchange students, programmes and sponsors; Chinese students and scholars on American campuses; language training in Chinese and English; and the consequences for Chinese studies, American studies, and such fields as physics, cancer epidemiology, seismology and agriculture. A conclusion assesses future opportunities.

1060 China bound, revised: a guide to academic life and work in the PRC.
Anne Thurston, with Karen Turner-Gottschang, Linda A. Reed.
Washington, DC: National Academy Press, 1995. 272p. paperbound
only.

A practical handbook for students, teachers and researchers, based on the extensive experience of the Committee on Scholarly Communication with China. Chapters cover: research fellowships and grants; practical information on daily life and professional work; research (planning and implementation, archives, surveys, laboratories); teaching (bureaucratic structure, working conditions, students, language lessons); study (American programmes, Chinese-language institutes, Chinese universities); and services available (US embassy, communications, medical, transport, travel). The work concludes with a glossary and listings of useful information. Also detailed and sensible is *Living in China: a guide to teaching and studying in China including Taiwan*, by Rebecca Weiner, Margaret Murphy, Albert Li

(San Francisco: China Books & Periodicals, 1991. 304p.), whose useful bibliography includes materials on the techniques of teaching English.

1061   **Teaching China's lost generation.**
         Tani E. Barlow, Donald M. Lowe.   San Francisco: China Books & Periodicals, 1987. 267p.

An insightful, politically aware memoir of teaching English to the first class of students admitted to the Shanghai Teacher's College after the Cultural Revolution. Barlow and Lowe are both scholars of China; Lowe was raised in Shanghai up to the age of nine. University conditions have changed since their experience, but their observations remain informative. This reissue adds several sections to their *Chinese reflections: Americans teaching in the People's Republic* (New York: Praeger, 1985). F. A. Kretschmer, *An American teacher in China: coping with cultures* (Westport, Connecticut; London: Bergin & Garvey, 1994. 164p.) reflects the cross-cultural experience of a scholar of comparative literature teaching in Beijing in the period leading up to 1989; his bibliographical essay comments freshly on much writing about China. Lois Muehl, Siegmar Muehl, *Trading cultures in the classroom: two American teachers in China* (Honolulu: University of Hawaii Press, 1993. 255p.) perceptively describes a teaching experience during the late 1980s.

The early arrival of dreams: a year in China.
See item no. 60.

Iron and silk.
See item no. 68.

Encountering the Chinese: a guide for Americans.
See item no. 655.

Science and Technology

To 1949

1062 Chinese thought, society, and science: the intellectual and social background of science and technology in pre-modern China.
Derk Bodde.   Honolulu: University of Hawaii Press, 1991. 441p.

A leading sinologist explores Chinese thought, society and language (though few scientific or medical texts) to see what aspects of Chinese culture might have aided or held back the development of science. Bodde claims in particular that the structure of the Chinese language was not conducive to scientific thought, an argument which has been widely challenged.

1063 American science and modern China: 1876-1936.
Peter Buck.   Cambridge, England: Cambridge University Press,
1980. 283p.

Studies the American missionary medical colleges, the China Medical Board of the Rockefeller Foundation, Cornell University, and a new class of professional Chinese scientists who brought 'modern' science to China. Buck uses mostly English-language sources to argue that American ideas and organizations were exploitative and inappropriate to a situation demanding populist and revolutionary changes. He sees 'backwardness and dependence', 'tragedy and farce' in the spread of specialized, laboratory based, professional science. Bullock's *An American transplant* and Reardon-Anderson's *Study of change* (qq.v.) claim that the foreign input led to China forming its own characteristic modern science after 1949.

1064   **China at work: an illustrated record of the primitive industries of China's masses, whose life is toil, and thus an account of Chinese civilization.**
Rudolph P. Hommel.   New York: John Day, 1937. Reprinted, Cambridge, Massachusetts; London: M. I. T. Press, 1969. 366p.

A classic book which provides detailed descriptions and numerous photographs of Chinese tools and implements, sometimes incorporating earlier accounts. During the 1920s Hommel lived and travelled in China; here he portrays a life in which, for some ungiven (and indefensible) reason, he assumed 'there has been no considerable change for thousands of years'. Chapters include: 'Tools to Make Tools'; 'Tools for Procuring Food' (ploughs, threshing, winnowing, mills, soy beans and bean curd, sugar making, etc.); 'Tools for Making Clothes' (spinning, dyeing, ironing, sewing, shoemaking, etc.); 'Tools for Providing Shelter' (axes, saws, carpentry, lighting, etc.); and 'Tools for Enabling Transport' (roads, wheelbarrows, carts, boats, etc.).

1065   **Scientism and modern Chinese thought.**
Danny Kwok.   New Haven, Connecticut: Yale University Press, 1965. Reprinted, New York: Biblo & Tannen, 1971. 231p.

When thinkers of the New Culture Movement sought to replace Confucius with democracy and science, they often fell into 'scientism' – an exaggerated belief in the transformative power of science. Kwok sketches the ideas of 'materialistic scientism' in Wu Zhihui (1865-1953) and Chen Duxiu (1879-1942); 'empirical scientism' in the thought of Hu Shi (1891-1962) and three scientists; and 'scientism triumphant' in the 1923 debate on 'science' vs. 'metaphysics'.

1066   **The study of change: chemistry in China, 1840-1949.**
James Reardon-Anderson.   Cambridge, England; New York; Melbourne: Cambridge University Press, 1991. 444p. bibliog. (Studies of the East Asian Institute, Columbia University).

Perceptively describes the introduction of Western chemistry, the professionalization of its study, the interaction with government and society, and the development of the chemical industry from the 19th century to the Communist Revolution. From 1840-95, missionary scientists and government officials collaborated to translate texts and establish school curricula; the Qing state and society set the limits of change. During the 'interregnum', 1895-1927, Chinese entrepreneurs and educators founded the chemical industry and organized scientific professions. Under the Nanking government, 1927-37, the state attempted to dominate research and the economy. During the war, 1937-45, new relations were established with the Nationalist and Communist governments. Reardon-Anderson discusses individual scientists, educators and entrepreneurs, providing an excellent insight into general social and economic modernization.

1067   **Pacing the void: T'ang approaches to the stars.**
Edward H. Schafer.   Berkeley, California; Los Angeles; London: University of California Press, 1977. 352p.

An engaging and many-sided sinological exploration of how Tang dynasty (617-907) poets, scientists and religious thinkers imagined the sun, moon and stars. Schafer shows that there were no clear distinctions between science, philosophy and literature in the Tang world of 1,300 years ago.

1068 **Researches and reflections: a selection of essays, reprinted, revised, and new.**
Nathan Sivin. Aldershot, England: Variorum; Brookfield, Vermont: Ashgate, 1995. 2 vols.

Volume one, *Science in ancient China: researches and reflections*, reprints from scattered original publications articles on: the Chinese conception of time; the cosmos and computation in mathematical astronomy; biographies of Shen Gua (1031-95) and Wang Xishan (1628-82) revised from the *Dictionary of scientific biography*; Copernicus in China; and general introductions and considerations. Volume two, *Medicine, philosophy, and religion*, covers: new articles comparing Greek and Chinese philosophy and science; emotional countertherapy; the myth of the 'naturalists'; and Daoism and science. Also reprinted are articles on: the 'first Neo-Confucianism' (in the Han dynasty); the word 'Daoist' as a source of perplexity; and the history of Chinese alchemy. Split between the volumes is the important 'introductory bibliography' of traditional Chinese science (Volume one) and medicine (Volume two) which evaluates books and articles in Western languages, updated from Shigeru Nakayama, Nathan Sivin, *Chinese science* (q.v.).

1069 **T'ien-kung k'ai-wu: Chinese technology in the seventeenth century.**
Sung Ying-hsing, translated by E-tu Zen Sun, Shiou-Chuan Sun. University Park, Pennsylvania; London: Pennsylvania State University Press, 1966. 372p. bibliog.

Sung Yingxing (c.1600-c.1660), a literatus-official, aimed to counter the abstract idealism of late Ming philosophy with this illustrated encyclopaedia, *Tiangong kaiwu* (1637), or 'The creations of nature and man', which surveyed all aspects of practical technology. Individual chapters, which include clear and sometimes charming woodblock print illustrations, are devoted to: the farming of grains; clothing materials; salt; sugar; ceramics; metal casting; boats and carts; hammer forging; calcination of stones; vegetable oils and fats; paper; metals; weapons; vermillion and ink; yeasts; and pearls and gems. Bibliographies cite Chinese sources and a valuable, topic-by-topic-list of Western-language books and articles is included.

1070 **The genius of China: 3,000 years of science, discovery, and invention.**
Robert Temple, introduced by Joseph Needham. New York: Simon & Schuster, 1986; British edition: *China: land of discovery and invention*. London: Patrick Stephens Ltd., 1986. 254p.

A popularised survey, accompanied by photographs, drawings and diagrams, in which chapters are organized invention by invention. Temple uses Needham's *Science and Civilisation in China* to the exclusion of subsequent works, is too eager to give primacy to Chinese inventions, and makes dubious interpretations. Sections describe: agriculture; astronomy and cartography; engineering; domestic and industrial technology; medicine and health; mathematics; magnetism; physical sciences; transport and exploration; sound and music; and warfare. *China: seven thousand years of discovery: China's ancient technology*, China Science and Technology Museum, China Reconstructs (Beijing: China Reconstructs; San Francisco: China Books, 1983. 80p.) describes a 1983 touring exhibition; it provides brief and colourfully illustrated articles on paper and printing, gunpowder, the compass, Chinese medicine, ceramics, bronze, architecture, silks and embroidery, and handicrafts, but does not use recent scholarship. Eva Wong, *Feng-shui: the ancient wisdom of harmonious living for modern times* (Boston, Massachusetts: Shambala, 1996. 276p.) includes both instructions for practice and extensive interpretations of modern theory.

1071   **Iron and steel in ancient China.**
        Donald B. Wagner.   Leiden, the Netherlands; New York; Köln: E. J. Brill, 1993. 573p. (Handbuch der Orientalistik/Handbook of Oriental Studies, no. 9).

Discusses the production and use of iron and steel in China from the earliest times to the beginning of the Han dynasty. Wagner gives central place to the scholarly problems of bringing together surviving written sources and recent archaeological discoveries, immersing the reader in clear discussions of technical detail. He concludes that iron was first used in partially sinified, non-Chinese areas of south-east China, perhaps in the 6th century BCE, when north Chinese bronze technology was adapted. In contrast to Europe, cast iron technology was developed before that of wrought iron. An iron industry dominated by rich men then quickly improved scale and quality for use in weapons, ploughs and instruments (including manacles and leg-irons).

1072   **Salt production techniques in ancient China: the *aobo tu*.**
        Yoshida Tora, translated, revised by Hans Ulrich Vogel.   Leiden, the Netherlands; New York; Köln: E. J. Brill, 1993. 309p.

The *Aobo tu*, 'Illustrated boiling of sea water', is a Yuan dynasty technical treatise which describes the stages of producing salt from sea water with prose, poetry and illustrations. Yoshida translated the work into Japanese, which Vogel translates into English and augments with an extensive introduction. The treatise demonstrates the technological sophistication developed during the Song and Yuan dynasties; it also discusses salt as a key to imperial finance as well as commerce, the social organization of production, and official involvement in production and technology.

Alchemy, medicine, and religion in the China of A.D. 320.
See item no. 572.

Chinese bridges.
See item no. 1313.

Carpentry and building in late imperial China: a study of the fifteenth century carpenter's manual, *Lu Ban Jing*.
See item no. 1318.

Science and Civilisation in China and related works

1073 **Introductory orientations.**
Joseph Needham, with research assistance of Wang Ling.
Cambridge, England: Cambridge University Press, 1954. 318p. maps.
bibliog. (Science and Civilisation in China, vol. I).

The grand opening of one of the great intellectual achievements of the century, this volume was intended to prepare readers in the 1950s for the study of Chinese civilization (the Chinese language, a geographical survey, sketches of Chinese history). Needham (1890-1995) emphasizes the mutual influence of ideas and techniques between China, the Arabs and Europe; 'modern' science was formed by confluence, not independent development, and is 'universal', rather than uniquely Western. Needham's well-documented interpretations and clearly argued hypotheses combine a tempered Marxian social analysis, British empiricism, and a principled tendency to give China the benefit of the doubt; however, his view that Daoism spawned proto-democracy and science has not been adopted by other researchers. The series is superbly fortified with maps, illustrations, charts, bibliographies in Chinese and Western languages, and indices; Chinese sources are meticulously listed and assessed.

1074 **History of scientific thought.**
Joseph Needham, with research assistance of Wang Ling.
Cambridge, England: Cambridge University Press, 1956. 697p. maps.
bibliog. (Science and Civilisation in China, vol. II).

Surveys Chinese thought from Confucius to the Ming dynasty, emphasizing scientific concepts, attitudes and terminology. This volume was influential in its attention to Mohists and Daoists as scientific thinkers, and is still full of insights, arguments, information and views, but is no longer a standard starting point. After chapters on the major schools of ancient thought, Needham devotes a long section to 'The Fundamental Ideas of Chinese Science'. There he discusses: the origins of important scientific words; correlative thinking and correspondence theory (starting with the Han); 'pseudo-sciences' (such as divination) and the skeptical tradition; Buddhist thought; later Daoist thought; and Song and Ming idealists and the affirmation of materialism. The final and seminal section is entitled 'Human Law and the Laws of Nature in China and the West'.

1075 **Mathematics and the sciences of the heavens and the earth.**
Joseph Needham, with research assistance of Wang Ling.
Cambridge, England: Cambridge University Press, 1959. 874p.
(Science and Civilisation in China, vol. III).

Section nineteen, Mathematics, surveys: mathematical works from antiquity to the Ming; arithmetica (including theory of numbers, magic squares, roots); mechanical aids to calculation (counting rods, abacus); artificial numbers; geometry (Mohist definitions, Pythagorean theorem, cone sections, the coming of Euclid, trigonometry); algebra (including quadratic equations, binomial theorem, calculus); and comparisons between East and West. Section twenty, Astronomy, includes: the history of the study of Chinese astronomy; cosmological ideas; the polar and equatorial character of Chinese astronomy; the mapping of the stars; astrological instruments (sighting-tube, armillary sphere, celestial globes); and the Jesuits. Section twenty-one covers Meteorology. Section twenty-two, Geography and Cartography, discusses: geographical classics and treatises; the interrupted tradition of scientific cartography in Europe and the continuous tradition in China; the role of the Arabs; and transmissions. Sections twenty-three to twenty-five cover Geology, Seismology and Mineralogy. Li Yan, Du Shiran, translated by John N. Crossley, Anthony W. C. Lun, *Chinese mathematics: a concise history* (Oxford: Oxford University Press, 1987. 290p.) provides a non-expert translation of a 1963 Chinese introductory textbook; a sophisticated account is Jean-Claude Martzloff, *Histoire des mathématiques Chinoises* (History of Chinese mathematics) (Paris: Masson, 1988. 375p.).

1076 **Physics and physical technology: part 1: physics.**
Joseph Needham, with research assistance of Wang Ling, special cooperation of Kenneth Girdwood Robinson. Cambridge, England: Cambridge University Press, 1965. 430p. (Science and Civilisation in China, vol. IV).

Section twenty-six, Physics, includes: waves and particles; mass, mensuration, statics and hydrostatics (Mohist contributions, the lever, balance, specific gravity, China and the metric system); dynamics; heat and combustion; light (Mohist optics, mirrors, lenses); acoustics (the concept of *qi* ['subtle matter', 'matter-energy']), classifications of sound, evolution of equal temperament; Western music and Chinese mathematics); magnetism and electricity; the compass; the magnet; divination; and chess.

1077 **Physics and physical technology: part 2: mechanical engineering.**
Joseph Needham, with research assistance of Wang Ling.
Cambridge, England: Cambridge University Press, 1965. 753p.
(Science and Civilisation in China, vol. IV).

Section twenty-seven, Mechanical Engineering, begins by discussing artisans and engineers in feudal-bureaucratic society, tools and materials. It then covers: basic mechanical principles (levers, hinges and linkworks); wheels, gear wheels, pedals and paddles; pulleys, driving belts and chain-drives; cranks and eccentric motion; screws, worms and helicoidal vanes; springs; conduits, pipes and siphons; valves, bellows and fans; and mechanical toys. Sub-sections then treat: types of machines and the balance of Jesuit novelty and transmissions (including the steam turbine); the locksmith's art; vehicles for land transport (chariots, wagons, wheelbarrow and sailing carriage, the hodometer, south pointing carriage); and power sources, including efficient harnesses, water raising machinery, water flow and descent (water wheels, reciprocating motion, trip hammers, water mills, and the problem of the spread of inventions). 'Clockwork: the hidden six centuries' puts a claim for early Chinese origins of clocks which is contested (not entirely convincingly) in David Landes, *Revolution in time: clocks and the making of the modern world* (Cambridge, Massachusetts: Harvard University Press, 1983. 482p.). Further sections cover the revolving bookcase, the windmill in East and West, and the 'pre-history of aeronautical engineering' (kites, helicopter tops, parachutes, balloons).

1078   **Physics and physical technology: part 3: civil engineering and nautics.**
Joseph Needham, with research assistance of Wang Ling.
Cambridge, England: Cambridge University Press, 1971. 927p.
(Science and Civilisation in China, vol. IV).

Section twenty-eight, Civil Engineering, analyses: the nature and expansion of the road network and post system; walls (including the Great one); building technology (the spirit of Chinese architecture, town and city planning, principles of construction, historical development, pagodas, triumphal gateways, imperial tombs); and bridges. The sub-section on hydraulic engineering discusses control, construction and maintenance of waterways, engineering and its social aspects in Chinese legend, and the Zhengguo and Guanxian (Dujiangyan) waterworks of the Qin dynasty, the Grand Canal of the Sui and Yuan, and techniques. Section twenty-nine, Nautical Technology, covers: comparative morphology and the evolution of sailing craft (junks, sampans); the Chinese ship in philology and archaeology, including flotillas used in the Ming voyages of Zheng He; navigation (star, compass and rutter); propulsion (sails, oars); control (steering, axial rudder and its transmission to Europe); and techniques of peace and war afloat (anchors, moorings, docks, caulking, hull sheathing, pumps, the ram, projectile tactics).

1079   **Chemistry and chemical technology: part 1: paper and printing.**
Tsien Tsuen-hsuin.   Cambridge, England: Cambridge University Press, 1985. 485p. (Science and Civilisation in China, vol. V).

Section thirty-two continues and advances the coverage of Tsien's *Written on bamboo and silk* (q.v.) to cover the origin, development and migration of paper and printing and the factors contributing to their early invention in China. Sub-sections analyse: the technology and evolution of papermaking, including raw materials; and uses of paper and paper products (graphic arts, stationery, medium of exchange, ceremonial, clothing and furnishing, wallpaper and household use, recreational). Further sub-sections then cover: the origin and development of printing in China – prehistory and beginnings; the incunabula of the Song; printing under the non-Han dynasties; new dimensions of Ming printing; prosperity and decline in the Qing; techniques and procedures of Chinese printing (woodblock and movable type, format, binding, inkmaking); woodcuts, multi-colour printing and New Year pictures; the spread of paper and printing to the West and southwards; and the contribution to world civilization, including the impact on Chinese scholarship and society.

1080   **Chemistry and chemical technology: part 2: spagyrical discovery and invention: magisteries of gold and immortality.**
Joseph Needham, with the collaboration of Lu Gwei-djen.
Cambridge, England: Cambridge University Press, 1974. 507p.
(Science and Civilisation in China, vol. V).

The first of four magisterial volumes, comprising section thirty-three of Needham's original plan, on the 'spagyric' (alchemy) tradition. This introductory volume first surveys the primary sources and secondary literature, and explains concepts, terminology and definitions (e.g. 'aurification', or 'making gold'). It also deals with: macrobiotics (seeking long life through diet); immortality theory and ideas of afterlife in East and West; and the *xian* ('immortal', earlier translated as 'fairy') and the

Chinese emphasis on material or physical, rather than spiritual, immortality. Further sections concern the metallurgical-chemical and physiological backgrounds to the search for immortality through external means (*wai dan*).

1081 **Chemistry and chemical technology: part 3: historical survey, from cinnabar elixir to synthetic insulin.**
Joseph Needham, with research assistance of Wang Ling.
Cambridge, England: Cambridge University Press, 1976. 478p.
(Science and Civilisation in China, vol. V).

This work continues section thirty-three and discusses the historical development of alchemy and early chemistry. Sub-sections concern: its origins in the Zhou, Qin and early Han dynasties; the Daoist sage Ge Hong, the *Baopuzi*, and systematizing alchemy; alchemy in the Daoist 'patrology' (*Daozang* or Daoist Canon); the Golden Age, from the 4th to the 9th centuries (including the Daoist Church at Maoshan, chemical theory and spagyrical poetry, chemical lexicography, and Buddhist echoes of Indian alchemy); the Silver Age, from the 9th to the 13th centuries (the first scientific printed book, from proto-chemistry to proto-physiology, alchemy in Japan, the laboratory of the National Academy, social aspects, Northern and Southern Schools of Daoism); alchemy in decline in Yuan, Ming and Qing; and the coming of modern chemistry (the failure of the Jesuit mission, mineral acids and gunpowder, the Kiangnan Arsenal, and the sinicization of modern chemistry).

1082 **Chemistry and chemical technology: part 4: apparatus, theories and gifts.**
Joseph Needham, with a contribution by Nathan Sivin. Cambridge, England: Cambridge University Press, 1980. 772p. (Science and Civilisation in China, vol. V).

A continuation of section thirty-three which first covers laboratory apparatus and equipment: the laboratory bench; stoves; reaction vessels; steaming apparatus, condenser tubes and temperature stabilizers; distillation and exaction (including evolution of the still); ardent water (alcohol); mineral acid; soluble salts; saltpetre and copperas as limiting factors in East and West; bacterial enzyme actions; and geodes and fertility potions. The virtually independent section on the theoretical background of elixir alchemy, written by Nathan Sivin, explores: how the alchemists understood and explained what they were doing (Needham's emphasis elsewhere is on the criterion of today's science); alchemical ideas and Daoist revelations; the role of time (organic development, planetary correspondences, subterranean evolution of natural elixir); the alchemist as an accelerator of the cosmic process; cosmic correspondence embodied in apparatus; and proto-chemical anticipations. The section ends with a detailed consideration of interactions and comparison among the Chinese, Hellenistic and Arabic worlds, and macrobiotics in the Western world.

1083 **Chemistry and chemical technology: part 5: physiological alchemy.**
Joseph Needham. Cambridge, England: Cambridge University Press, 1983. 574p. (Science and Civilisation in China, vol. V).

A further continuation of section thirty-three. Previous segments covered external alchemy (*wai dan*), which used materials matured in the earth or laboratory; physiological, or internal, alchemy (*neidan*), covered here, also sought bodily immortality, but by 'inner macrobiogens', or enchymoma. After descriptions of the terminology, European alchemy and basic theories, chapters here describe techniques: respiration control, aerophagy and salivary deglutition, which affect the circulation of *qi*; gymnastics, massage and exercise; meditation and mental concentration; sexuality and the role of theories of generation; the late literature of the Ming and Qing, such as the *Secret of the golden flower*; Chinese physiological alchemy (*neidan*) and Indian Yoga, Tantric and Hathayoga systems; and *neidan* as proto-biochemistry. A chapter gives a preliminary (and now outdated) account of: mediaeval preparations of urinary steroid and protein hormones; the use of sexual organs in Chinese medicine; proto-endocrinology; and the history of the technique. Needham's interpretation of *neidan* as 'proto-biochemistry' has been questioned for using modern positivistic criteria which leave out important aspects.

1084   **Chemistry and chemical technology: part 6: military technology: missiles and sieges.**
Joseph Needham, Robin D. S. Yates, with the collaboration of Krzysztof Gawlikowski, Edward McEwen.   Cambridge, England: Cambridge University Press, 1995. 601p. (Science and Civilisation in China, vol. V).

Discusses military technology and thought from the Zhou dynasty to the Ming, drawing comparisons with other traditions. Sections describe literature on the art of war, distinctive features of Chinese military thought, the bow, the cross-bow, ballistic weapons, and Chinese cities and poliocertics (the theory and practice of sieges), beginning with Mozi and Sunzi. Contributors speculate on cultural differences between Chinese and European attitudes towards warfare, the social use of force, and cultural definitions of the military, including heroes like Guan Gong, God of War. The rapid development of the cross-bow, for instance, was not matched by a development of body armour; vulnerable rulers, it is argued, were needful of compensatory Confucian justification, while military functions pervaded the government rather than being restricted to 'army' institutions. Needham's sections were written in the 1960s.

1085   **Chemistry and chemical technology: part 7: military technology: the gunpowder epic.**
Joseph Needham, with the collaboration of Ho Ping-yü [Ho Peng Yoke], Lu Gwei-djen, Wang Ling.   Cambridge, England: Cambridge University Press, 1986. 693p. (Science and Civilisation in China, vol. V).

Section thirty, covering Military Technology, and entitled 'The gunpowder epic', is a strikingly original, independent treatise. The first pages introduce the topic, describe the historical literature and sketch the ancestry of gunpowder (naphtha, 'Greek fire' and petrol flame-throwers). Sections then describe: gunpowder compositions; proto-gunpowder; fire-crackers and fireworks; bombs and grenades; land and sea mines; the fire lance, ancestor of all gun barrels; the eruptor, ancestor of all cannon; deflagration and detonation (rise in nitrate content, powder manufacture and theory); artillery; hand-guns (arquebus, musket, matchlocks, wheel-locks and flintlocks); the musket in China and Japan; gunpowder as a propellant (rocket arrows, winged rockets, military rockets); the peaceful uses of gunpowder; and inter-cultural transmissions.

1086   **Chemistry and chemical technology: part 9: textile technology.**
Dieter Kuhn.   Cambridge, England: Cambridge University Press,
1988. 497p. maps. (Science and Civilisation in China, vol. V).
This volume contains section thirty-one of the series. The introduction discusses:
sources and earlier scholarship; the significance of Chinese yarn and thread; and the
bast fibres (hemp, ramie, *pueraria thunbergiana*, banana, and others). Kuhn explains
that earlier scholarship overstressed Chinese uniqueness and lacked technical
precision, necessitating that this inclusive survey be done from original sources. Sub-
sections then describe: the origins of hand-spindle spinning in the neolithic period and
spindle-whorls of the Shang, Zhou and Han times; rope-making; sericulture (including
deities, silk in Neolithic and Shang archaeology), and the production of silk (mulberry
trees, silkworms, implements and equipment, storing and treatment of cocoons, silk-
reeling, and silk-reeling frames and roller systems); and silk machinery in East and
West. A follow-up volume on looms is expected.

1087   **Biology and biological technology: part 1: botany.**
Joseph Needham, with the collaboration of Lu Gwei-djen, special
contribution by Huang Hsing-tsung.   Cambridge, England:
Cambridge University Press, 1986. 708p. (Science and Civilisation in
China, vol. VI).
Represents section thirty-eight in the series. Introductory sections outline: the nature
of Chinese scientific achievement in botany; China's plant geography; and botanical
linguistics (plant terminology and nomenclature), where the nature of the Chinese
language may have lent advantages. A sub-section is devoted to the Chinese literature
and its contents – dictionaries, encyclopaedias, imperial florilegia, and especially the
'pandects of natural history', the *bencao* [*pen-ts'ao*] tradition of compiling and editing
botanical writings and natural histories. This tradition culminated in Li Shizhen
(1518-93), 'The Prince of Pharmacists', whose *Bencao gangmu* (printed in 1596)
noted nearly 2,000 medicinal plants and animals. Further sub-sections discuss
botanical monographs and tractates (citrus fruits, bamboos, peonies, chrysanthemums,
orchids, rosaceae), and plants and insects in man's service (natural plant insecticides,
biological pest control).

1088   **Biology and biological technology: part 2: agriculture.**
Francesca Bray.   Cambridge, England: Cambridge University Press,
1984. 713p. maps. (Science and Civilisation in China, vol. VI).
Section forty-one explores the technological basis of China's agrarian empire and its
general significance. Introductory chapters outline the general characteristics of
Chinese agriculture, agricultural regions by geography and principle crops, and the
origins of agriculture. Sources are reviewed in the next sub-section, including
agricultural calendars and imperial almanacs. Further sub-sections examine: field
systems (shifting cultivation, permanent fields of North and South); agricultural
implements and techniques (ploughs, hoes, mattocks, spades, rakes, harrows, rollers);
sowing; fertilization; weeding and cultivation; grain storage technology and public
grain storage; crop systems for millets, sorghum, maize, wheat, barley and rice;
legumes; and oil, tuber, fibre, vegetable and fruit crops. In conclusion, Bray explores
Asia's contributions to Europe's agricultural revolution, in 'Agricultural revolution in
China?', and 'development or change?'

1089 *Li, Qi, and Shu*: an introduction to *Science and civilisation in China.*
Ho Peng Yoke. Hong Kong: Hong Kong University Press, 1985.
262p. bibliog.

A serious but comprehensible introduction for the student or general reader by one of his collaborators, which presents Needham's work, without bringing in alternative and more recent approaches. Sections provide cogent surveys of fundamental concepts, mathematics, astronomy and alchemy. The bibliography lists the Chinese and English-language works cited. Qian Wen-yuan, *The great inertia: scientific stagnation in traditional China* (London: Croom Helm, 1985. 155p.) contests Needham. Qian, trained as a physicist in China, argues that cultural factors held science back until the opening of China to the modern world.

1090 Explorations in the history of science and technology in China.
Li Guohua, Zhang Mengwen, Cao Tianqin. Shanghai, China:
Shanghai Chinese Classic Publishing House, 1982. 835p. bibliog.

Provides essays in Chinese and English in honour of Needham by scholars from all parts of the world. Among the more significant essays in English are: 'The First Half-life of Joseph Needham', by Lu Gwei-djen, his collaborator and wife; 'Peregrinations with Joseph Needham in China, 1943-1944'; 'Why the Scientific Revolution Didn't Take Place in China – or Didn't It?', by Nathan Sivin; 'Siege Engines and Late Zhou Military Technology'; 'Chinese Mining: Where was the Gunpowder?'; and 'The Conceptual History of Psychiatric Terms in Traditional Chinese Medicine'. Bibliographies list Needham's voluminous publications over the period 1925-75.

1091 Chinese science: explorations of an ancient tradition.
Edited by Shigeru Nakayama, Nathan Sivin. Cambridge,
Massachusetts; London: M. I. T. Press, 1973. 334p. bibliog.
(East Asian Science Series, no. 2).

This volume, published in honour of Needham's seventieth birthday, contains essays which aim to help readers think critically about science in traditional China. The preface discusses intellectual and practical problems of study, attacks the pseudo-learned sentimentality and 'garden-variety ignorance' of much Western writing on Chinese science, and outlines the field. Needham contributes an insightful religious 'meditation' on the historian of science as 'ecumenical man'. Three useful essays introduce and evaluate Needham's life, work and ideas; six further essays explore particular topics. The important introductory bibliography evaluates books and articles in Western languages up to 1972; it is updated in Nathan Sivin, *Researches and reflections* (q.v.).

1092 The grand titration: science and society in East and West.
Joseph Needham. London: Allen & Unwin, 1969. 350p.

Needham was a generous and adept essayist and lecturer; these occasional summaries of his general thought and ongoing research are often more accessible and wide-ranging than the full presentations in *Science and Civilisation in China*. The eight essays presented here include: 'Poverties and Triumphs of the Chinese Scientific Tradition'; 'Science and China's Influence on the World', an especially valuable overview; 'On Science and Social Change'; several essays on the social background of science; 'Time and Eastern Man'; and 'Human Law and the Laws of Nature'.

Needham's Ch'ien Mu Lectures at Chinese University of Hong Kong, *Science in traditional China* (Cambridge, Massachusetts: Harvard University Press; Hong Kong: Chinese University Press, 1981. 134p.) comprise four lectures based on earlier publications, covering: the history of gunpowder and firearms; comparative macrobiotics; the history and rationale of acupuncture and moxibustion; and attitudes towards time and change as compared with Europe.

1093   **The shorter *Science and civilisation in China*.**
       Colin A. Ronan.   Cambridge, England: Cambridge University Press, 1978-   . 4 vols.
Abridges, without revising or updating, the original volumes of *Science and Civilisation in China* for non-scientific readers, accompanied by copious plates and illustrations. Mercifully, standard pinyin romanizations are substituted for Needham's idiosyncratic 'modified Wade-Giles'. Ronan's later volumes, which cover particular topics, are more useful than the earlier general surveys of thought. However, interested readers should not hesitate to plunge into the originals.

The People's Republic (1949-)

1094   **Science and technology in post-Mao China.**
       Edited by Merle Goldman, Denis Simon.   Cambridge, Massachusetts: Council on East Asian Studies, Harvard University, distributed by Harvard University Press, 1989. 461p. (Harvard Contemporary China Series).
Fourteen scholars examine the political role of science and technology. Chapters discuss: social and political factors; the experience and legacy of the Nationalist government, 1928-53; military research and development systems; the organization of technical advice; acquiring foreign technology and technology transfer; scientific studies of agriculture; the military; microelectronics; scientific education; and Chinese students trained abroad.

1095   **Science in contemporary China.**
       Edited by Leo Orleans.   Stanford, California: Stanford University Press, 1980. 599p.
Provides a 'map' of contemporary Chinese science in the form of encyclopaedic descriptions of the study of science and scientific institutions. Sections cover: science in China's past; science policy and organization, summarizing government policies before and after the Cultural Revolution; pure and applied mathematics; physics; chemistry; astronomy; geography; earth sciences; meteorology; fisheries, aquaculture and oceanography; basic biomedical research; clinical and public health aspects of biomedical research; plant breeding and genetics; plant protection; animal sciences; agricultural mechanization; engineering; energy; electronics; environmental science; and social sciences (linguistics, archaeology, history, economics, political science, law). Each section describes the national institutions, training and personnel, research

achievements and priorities, major projects and publications for each area. Appendices list research institutes, science and engineering societies, and scientific and technical journals.

1096 **China's science policy in the 1980s.**
Tony Saich. Manchester, England: Manchester University Press; Atlantic Highlands, New Jersey: Humanities Press International, 1989. 188p. (Studies on East Asia).

Studies the politics and organization of China's civilian science and technology in the post-Mao era, when leaders wanted both independence from foreign interference and also access to the latest international innovations. An opening chapter provides the political and policy background. Two chapters then look at organizational reform, in particular the problems of changing from military to civilian markets. Two more chapters discuss the problems of financing new organizations and the personnel system, and a final chapter deals with the place of science and technology in Deng Xiaoping's broad reforms.

1097 **Technological innovation in China: the case of Shanghai's electronics industry.**
Denis Simon, Detleff Rehn. Cambridge, Massachusetts: Ballinger Publishing Company, 1988. 206p.

The authors begin by reviewing the literature on technological innovation in socialist countries, China's historical experience and post-Mao reforms in science and technology. The body of the book presents a detailed description of the development of the electronics industry in China, in which Shanghai played a central role, drawing on the authors' extensive interviews and field visits. Topics discussed include: national policy-making; the organization and structure of the industry; a discussion of sectors such as integrated circuits, consumer electronics, military electronics, computers and communications; the 'Third Front' opened during the Cultural Revolution to protect the industry by moving it to the hills; and the recent development of private (*minban*) factories. Obstacles to growth include fragmentation, a difficulty in absorbing foreign technology, and questions of domestic market protection.

1098 **Research and revolution: science policy and societal change in China.**
Richard P. Suttmeier. Lexington, Massachusetts: Lexington Books, 1974. 188p.

Explores the interaction of science, politics and Chinese society through the early Cultural Revolution, asking whether there is a replicable or exportable 'Chinese model' for low income countries. Three chapters first describe the policy conflicts and experiments in organization-building for science during the period 1949-57, especially the Chinese Academy of Sciences (CAS). Chapters then explore competing models and radical approaches developed during the Great Leap Forward (1957-61) and the Cultural Revolution (1966-71); these mobilizational approaches tried to replace the professional and bureaucratic control with new institutions of mass participation.

1099　**Technology, politics, and society in China.**
Rudi Volti.　Boulder, Colorado: Westview Press, 1982. 225p.
bibliog. (Westview Special Studies on China and East Asia).
An examination of the technological policies of the Maoist period. Part one describes the Chinese model, the 'red vs. expert' dilemma, and Mao's 'walking on two legs' strategy. Part two studies: agriculture (water control, mechanization, seed varieties and insecticides); energy (coal, petroleum and electricity); surface transport (railways, roads and trucks); and medical technologies (rural care, schistosomiasis, traditional and modern medicine, and acupuncture). The conclusion considers technology, social inequality, indigenous development and the 'Chinese model'.

1100　**China's science and technology policy: 1949-1989.**
Wang Yeu-farn.　Aldershot, England; Brookfield, Vermont; Hong Kong; Singapore; Sydney: Avebury, 1993. 173p.
An analysis of the major issues in science and technology, development and modernization since 1949, which looks in particular at the relations with the state as well as the mediating institutions. Wang adopts a 'neo-Weberian approach'. She starts with a discussion of state-science-society relations in traditional China in order to analyse the long-term effects of socio-economic structures and institutional legacies. Subsequent chapters examine state planning and development strategies, period by period, from 1949-89. See also, *The technological transformation of China*, T. David McDonald (Washington, DC: National Defense University Press, for sale by the Superintendent of Documents, Government Printing Office, Washington, DC, 1990. 191p.).

1101　**Science and socialist construction in China.**
Xu Liangying, Fan Dainian, edited by Pierre M. Perrolle.　Armonk, New York; London: M. E. Sharpe, 1982. 224p.
A translation, with a new foreword by the authors and introduction by the editor, of *Kexue he woguo shehuizhuyi jianshe* (1957), which appeared in the period of 'Let A Hundred Flowers Bloom'. The authors present a liberal Marxist analysis of the nature of modern science and its development in China, arguing that in 'feudal' and 'semicolonial' China, science was constrained, but is now liberated in socialist China. The authors' argument that science, socialism and democracy are mutually sustaining is one to which scientists returned in the 1980s. *Lysenkoism in China: proceedings of the 1956 Qingdao genetics symposium*, edited by Laurence Schneider (Armonk, New York; London: M. E. Sharpe, 1988. 97p.) includes a selection of articles from Chinese sources, with an extensive introduction, examining the sorry history of China's encounter with Lysenko, Stalin's favourite geneticist.

China builds the bomb.
See item no. 860.

Literature

General guides and anthologies

1102 Anthology of Chinese literature.
Edited by Cyril Birch, with Donald Keene, associate editor. New York: Grove Press, 1965, 1972. 2 vols.

A comprehensive anthology which presents the sweep and scope of Chinese literature of periods from the Zhou dynasty onwards, primarily poetry, prose essays, history, fiction and drama. A limited number of writers are given extensive space as well as the distinctive voices of particular translators. Volume one, *From early times to the fourteenth century*, in addition to sections devoted to particular periods, includes chapters on a theme (e.g. death, the poetry of the recluse, etc), and others on individual authors. Volume two, *From the fourteenth century to the present day*, devotes sections to the fiction, poetry and drama of the late imperial period and 20th century.

1103 Literature of the People's Republic of China.
Edited by Kai-yu Hsu, Ting Wang, co-editor, with the special assistance of Howard Goldblatt, Donald Gibbs, George Cheng. Bloomington, Indiana: Indiana University Press, 1980. 976p. (Chinese Literature in Translation).

Comprises 200 selections, including poems, stories, essays, a *xiangsheng* (comic patter dialogue), excerpts from novels, plays, movie scripts and an opera, from 1942 to 1979. Selections are grouped chronologically and organized in relation to the major controversies, reflecting the relationship between literature and politics in the People's Republic. Part one covers 1942-55, beginning with Mao's talks to the Yan'an Forum and samples of socialist realism. Parts two and three cover the Hundred Flowers Movement and the Anti-rightist Campaign (1956-58) and the Great Leap Forward and Anti-revisionism (1959-61). Part four, 'The Socialist Education of the People (1962-1964)', leads up to the Cultural Revolution. Part five, 'The Great Proletarian Cultural

Revolution (1964-1970)', includes both those attacked as rightists and the writings of their radical antagonists. Part six, 'The Aftermath: The Fall of the Gang of Four – Returns and Reversals (1971-)', includes the beginnings of new directions, mostly officially published writings.

1104 **Morning sun: interviews with Chinese writers of the lost generation.**
Laifong Leung.   Armonk, New York; London: M. E. Sharpe, 1994. 392p. (Studies on Contemporary China).

The 'lost generation' born in the late 1940s or early 1950s, became Red Guards, but were sent 'down to the countryside' during the Cultural Revolution. Known as *zhiqing* ('intellectual', 'sent down' or 'rusticated' youth), they typically went from idealism to eye-opening struggle, then to dejection or cynicism; many turned to writing 'scar' literature (*shanghen wenxue*) which explored their wounding experiences, but emerged in the 1980s as inventive, sophisticated, popular writers. Leung here interviews twenty-six fiction writers (poets are not included) to get their stories first hand; she supplies an introduction, headnotes, bibliographies of published works, lists of translations into English, biographical notes and suggested readings. Included are authors represented in the anthologies edited by Link (q.v.), Barmé (q.v.), and *Mao's harvest: voices from China's new generation*, edited by Helen Siu, Zelda Stern (Stanford, California: Stanford University Press, 1983. 231p.), such as Cheng Naishan, Kong Jiesheng, Mo Yan, Shi Tiesheng, Wang Anyi and Zheng Yi.

1105 **Stubborn weeds: popular and controversial Chinese literature after the Cultural Revolution.**
Edited with an introduction by Perry Link.   Bloomington, Indiana: Indiana University Press, 1983. 292p.

The first of three coordinated anthologies edited by Link, with informative introductions; the coverage is modelled on Hsu's *Literature of the People's Republic of China* (q.v.). Link's *Roses and thorns: the second blooming of the hundred flowers in Chinese fiction, 1979-1980* (Berkeley, California; Oxford: University of California Press, 1984. 346p.) is the second. Together the two volumes represent and describe the first years of relative freedom of expression in the post-1978 reforms and explain the mechanics of publishing, the status of authors and audience response, the stories, poems and plays including the so-called 'scar literature' (*shanghen wenxue*), the first public and sanctioned expression of the widespread revulsion against the Cultural Revolution. Link's third volume, *People or monsters? and other stories from China after Mao by Liu Binyan*, introduction by Leo Ou-fan Lee (Bloomington, Indiana: Indiana University Press, 1983. 140p.), presents the 'report literature' (*baogao wenxue*) in which Liu exposed official corruption in the hope of improving Party behaviour. *After Mao: Chinese literature and society, 1978-1981*, edited by Jeffrey C. Kinkley (Cambridge, Massachusetts: Council on East Asian Studies, Harvard University, 1985. [East Asian Monographs, no. 115]) includes essays on science fiction, love stories, crime fiction, 'obscure' ('misty') poetry and the sociology of reading and publishing.

1106 **The Columbia anthology of traditional Chinese literature.**
Edited by Victor H. Mair. New York: Columbia University Press,
1994. 1,330p. (Translations from the Asian Classics).
A fresh, basic compilation of all genres of writing from antiquity to the 20th century.
Part one, 'Foundations and Interpretations', includes: early divination and
inscriptions; philosophy, thought and religion; and criticism and theory. Part two,
'Verse', covers: classical poetry; lyrics and arias; elegies and rhapsodies; folk and
folk-like songs; ballads; and narrative verse. Part three, 'Prose', encompasses:
documents; history; moral lessons; parallel prose; letters; prefaces and postfaces;
discourses, essays and sketches; travelogues and scenic descriptions; jokes; culinary
writing; biographies, autobiographies and memoirs; and fictionalized biographies. Part
four, 'Fiction', includes: rhetorical persuasions, parables and allegories; anecdotal
fiction; tales of the strange; classical language and vernacular short stories; and
novels. Part five, 'Oral and Performing Arts', comprises prosimetric storytelling and
drama. Mair provides a general preface, careful explanations of genres and literary
forms, and extensive annotations.

1107 **A selective guide to Chinese literature, 1900-1949.**
General editor, N. G. D. Malmqvist. Leiden, the Netherlands; New
York; Copenhagen; Köln: E. J. Brill, 1988-90. 4 vols.
The volumes, which cover a total of more than 300 works, are: volume I: *The novel*,
edited by Milena Dolezelova (1988. 238p.); volume II: *The short story*, edited by
Zbigniew Slupski (1988. 300p.); volume III: *The poem*, edited by Lloyd Haft (1989.
301p.); and volume IV: *The drama*, edited by Bernd Eberstein (1990. 347p.). Each
opens with a substantial introduction by the volume editor which interprets the history
and development of the particular genre. The body of each volume is comprised of
encyclopaedia-style entries on the major works in the genre, each entry containing a
detailed synopsis, comments on the author, brief evaluation, bibliographical details,
list of translations and further references on the author in both Chinese and Western
languages. Chinese characters are supplied.

1108 **Modern Chinese writers: self-portrayals.**
Edited by Helmut Martin, Jeffrey Kinkley. Armonk, New York;
London: M. E. Sharpe, 1993. 380p. bibliog. (Studies on Modern
China).
Provides personal reflections on society, writers as intellectuals and the creative
process by forty-three modern authors, with overview introductions by the editors and
extensive references. Sections include: contemporary writers in the People's Republic,
such as Bai Hua, Chen Rong (better known as Shen Rong), Chen Ruoxi, Chen
Yingzhen, Dai Houying, Feng Jicai, Gao Xiaosheng, Gu Hua, Han Shaoguang, Liu
Xinwu, Wang Anyi, Wang Meng, Wang Ruowang, Wu Zuguang, Wang Meng, Zhang
Jie, Zhang Xianliang, Zhang Xinxin and Zhong Acheng; writers from Taiwan; and
Republican era writers, such as Ba Jin, Ding Ling, Lao She, Lu Xun, Mao Dun, Shen
Congwen, Yu Dafu and Zhang Ailing. Bibliographies include translations and
scholarship in English books, anthologies and periodicals. There is also an extensive
glossary of terms, names and works. *Biographical dictionary of modern Chinese
writers* (Beijing: Foreign Languages Press, 1994. 1,165p.) is a comprehensive and
reliable reference to a wide selection of poets, writers of fiction, essayists, and others.

1109   **Literature of the Hundred Flowers.**
Edited by Hualing Nieh.   New York; London: Columbia University
Press, 1981. 2 vols.

In April 1956 Chairman Mao decreed 'let one hundred flowers bloom', inviting criticism and suggestions; writers responded with sincere criticisms, only to be attacked as 'rightists'. Volume one of this extensive selection, *Criticism and polemic*, which begins with a full introduction on the political and theoretical background, includes: Mao's original speech and the political sequelae; political criticism of literary problems; writings for and against 'socialist realism'; humanism (i.e. non-political concern) in literature, and its critics; and speeches from the anti-rightist campaign which withered the Hundred Flowers. Volume two, *Poetry and fiction*, repeats the introductions from volume one and includes: articles of theory and criticism on poetry; poems by and criticisms of Ai Qing, Bian Zhilin and eleven others; and a parallel selection of fiction and fables, with the political and literary polemics by and about Ai Qing, Ding Ling, Feng Xuefeng, Liu Binyan, Xiao Jun, Wang Meng, Wang Ruowang and others.

1110   **Early Chinese literature.**
Burton Watson.   New York; London: Columbia University Press,
1962. 304p.

A masterly introduction for the general reader, which embraces poetry, philosophy and history in the pre-Han period, especially the conceptions of Confucius and his followers. Watson sets the stage with a brief historical background, then examines, with extensive translations, each of the major genres, including poetry and history.

The Indiana companion to traditional Chinese literature.
See item no. 1447.

A guide to the Oriental classics.
See item no. 1459.

Guide to Chinese poetry and drama.
See item no. 1467.

Guide to Chinese prose.
See item no. 1470.

Theory and criticism

1111   **Gender politics in modern China: writing and feminism.**
Edited by Tani E. Barlow.   Durham, North Carolina; London: Duke
University Press, 1993. 307p. bibliog.

Contains fifteen studies of gender, sexuality and modernism in Chinese literature from the May Fourth Movement to the 1980s, expanded from *Modern Chinese Literature*, vol. 4, nos. 1-2 (1991). Authors discussed include Bing Xin, Can Xue, Dai Qing, Ding

Ling, Lu Xun, Mao Dun, Tian Han, Wang Anyi, Zhang Ailing (Eileen Chang) and Zhang Jie. Another exploration of the application of critical theory is *Gender and sexuality in twentieth century Chinese literature and society*, edited by Lu Tonglin (Albany, New York: State University of New York Press, 1993. 204p. bibliog. [SUNY Studies in Feminist Criticism and Theory]). This work provides nine essays on modern fiction, including Liu Heng's *Fuxi Fuxi* (on which Zhang Yimou's film *Judou* is based) and Mo Yan's *Red sorghum*, also made into a film by Zhang. Both volumes carry introductions which describe the current state and prospects of the field.

1112 **Women and Chinese modernity: the politics of reading between West and East.**
Rey Chow.   Minneapolis, Minnesota; Oxford: University of Minnesota Press, 1991. 197p. (Theory and History of Literature).

A re-examination of modern Chinese literature. Chow's self-proclaimed 'Westernized Chinese subjectivity' as a Chinese woman born in the colony of Hong Kong rejects both Chinese nativism and Westernization to search for the unstable but creative ground which encompasses and transcends both. Four essays probe and expand this stance: 'Seeing Modern China: Toward a Theory of Ethnic Spectatorship'; 'Mandarin Ducks and Butterflies: An Exercise in Popular Readings'; 'Modernity and Narration – In Feminine Detail'; and 'Loving Women: Masochism, Fantasy, and the Idealization of the Mother'.

1113 **Writing diaspora: tactics of intervention in contemporary cultural studies.**
Rey Chow.   Bloomington, Indiana: Indiana University Press, 1993. 223p. bibliog. (Arts and Politics of the Everyday).

Contains lively critical essays on literature and cultural theory, legacies of colonialism and imperialism, sexuality, the media, pedagogy and new 'solidarities'. The introduction discusses 'Orientalism and East Asia' as the persistence of a scholarly tradition, taking issue with Steven Owen, 'The Anxiety of Global Influence: What is World Poetry?' (*New Republic* [19 November 1990], p. 28-32) for its 'racist spirit'. Essays explore Chinese intellectuals in the 1990s, the politics and pedagogy of Asian literatures in American universities, and popular and rock music. The 'Works Cited' section lists sources and theoretical literature.

1114 **The transparent eye: reflections on translation, Chinese literature, and comparative poetics.**
Eugene Chen Eoyang.   Honolulu: University of Hawaii Press, 1993. 311p. (SHAPS Library of Translations).

A compilation of related essays, some previously published, on the nature and problems of literary translation. Eoyang sees translation both as a means of understanding the original works and also of forcing us to explore comparative poetics and culture. The preface and early chapters discuss the theory and history of translation, the study of literature and images of Chinese literature in English translation. Eoyang critiques translations of Chinese novels and poems and explains the problems involved in translating particular passages. Later chapters take up the theoretical framework of translation and the philosophy of comparative understanding of civilizations. Essays focus on particular examples, such as Ezra Pound and Arthur Waley as translators of Chinese poetry.

1115   **Politics, ideology, and literary discourse in modern China: theoretical interventions and cultural critique.**
Edited by Liu Kang, Tang Xiaobing, foreword by Frederic Jameson. Durham, North Carolina; London: Duke University Press, 1993. 316p.

Brings together a dozen articles from the first annual meeting of the American Association for Chinese Comparative Literature in 1990. They represent wide-ranging political agenda and theoretical approaches, including feminism, psychoanalytical criticism, post-structuralism, narrative analysis, Marxist critical theory and new historicism. Part one, 'Problematics of Subjectivity and Modernity', includes essays on subjectivity, Marxism and cultural theory in China. Part two, 'Representation, Realism, and the Question of History', deals with literary realism as an imported theory and *Red sorghum* as a novel and film. Part three contains four essays on cultural critique and ideology.

1116   **Chinese theories of literature.**
James J. Y. Liu.   Chicago: University of Chicago Press, 1976. 197p.

Introduces traditional Chinese thought about literature, especially poetry. The translations and commentaries are grouped in convenient categories, rather than chronologically or by philosophical school: metaphysical theories; deterministic and expressive theories; technical theories; aesthetic theories; and pragmatic theories. Liu's *Art of Chinese poetry* (q.v.) also applies this approach.

1117   **Readings in Chinese literary thought.**
Stephen Owen.   Cambridge, Massachusetts; London: Council on East Asian Studies, Harvard University, distributed by Harvard University Press, 1992. 674p. bibliog. (Harvard-Yenching Institute Monograph Series, no. 30).

An ambitious selection and explication of important or representative texts on the nature of literature from the time of Confucius to the 18th century. The aim is to introduce the material to theorists and scholars of other literatures and to help students of Chinese literature, who will appreciate the technical apparatus. Seven major works are translated in their entirety (including Lu Zhi's 'Remarks on literature' and Ouyang Xiu's 'Remarks on poetry'), together with many selections from shorter pieces; the Chinese text for each is given. Owen's commentaries set the context, provide comparisons with Western theory, and highlight structural and historical developments. A glossary of short entries translates and briefly explains basic terms. The selected analytical bibliography comprises works in Chinese and Japanese and selected English readings, with brief annotations.

1118   **The problem of a Chinese aesthetic.**
Haun Saussy.   Stanford, California: Stanford University Press, 1993. 296p.

These essays are united by a concern with problems of comparative philosophy and comparative literature; all depend on the close study of language and use a wide range of contemporary critical theory. Chapters treat: the contemporary theory of allegory compared with practice translations by 17th-century Jesuit missionaries and the philosopher Leibniz; the history of the *Shijing* or *Book of Odes* and its tradition of allegorical interpretation; the allegorical programme of the *Odes*; and 'Hegel's Chinese Imagination', which discusses the place of China in Hegel's conceptions of world history.

1119   **Poetry and personality: reading, exegesis, and hermeneutics in traditional China.**
Steven Van Zoeren.   Stanford, California: Stanford University Press, 1991. 333p.

Confucian readers, Van Zoeren argues, read the commentaries to the *Shijing* (*Book of Poetry*, or *Odes*) as an integral part of the text; this process of exegesis (explaining the text) and hermeneutics (understanding its moral message) was built over the centuries into a tradition of its own. Here Van Zoeren studies and explains the major commentaries. The earliest are layers of interpretation in the *Analects*, Mencius and Xunzi, which see the *Odes* as moral teachings in the development of personality rather than as mere musical texts designed to convey emotion. Further chapters examine Han dynasty editions and commentaries which incorporated the *Odes* into the canon of imperial Confucianism. Three final chapters examine the development of conscious hermeneutics among Song Neo-Confucians and a 'personal-devotional' approach to the Classics.

1120   **Diffusion of difference: dialogues between Chinese and Western poetics.**
Wai-lim Yip.   Berkeley, California; London: University of California Press, 1993. 246p.

These six essays, expanded from versions written during 1973-88, seek to correct the Eurocentrism found in the Western study of literature. As a poet himself, Yip was early dismayed by the 'formidable distortions of the Chinese indigenous aesthetic horizon in treacherous modes of representation'. His essays here demonstrate that no universal model or 'common poetics' can represent all literature; translation involves the 'confrontation, negotiation, and modification of cultural codes and systems'. Essays discuss: syntax and horizon of representation in classical Chinese and modern American poetry; the aesthetic consciousness of landscape in Chinese and Anglo-American poetry; and a theory for reading the Chinese poem. Yip's earlier contributions to this field include: *Ezra Pound's 'Cathay'* (Princeton, New Jersey: Princeton University Press, 1969. 259p.); and *Chinese poetry: major modes and genres* (Berkeley, California; London: University of California Press, 1976. 475p.), an anthology which introduces and translates the poetic tradition.

1121   **The tao and the logos: literary hermeneutics, East and West.**
Longxi Zhang.   Durham, North Carolina; London: Duke University Press, 1992. 238p. (Post Contemporary Interventions Series).

Provides essays which explore sophisticated literary theory, championing the humanistic strategy of hermeneutics (the interpretation of literary texts). Zhang eschews schemes such as deconstruction which hold that an unleapable gulf of difference exists between the 'Other' and the self or between East and West. To display the theory in action, Zhang shows how Chinese poets Tao Qian, Wang Wei and Li Shangyin use poetry – language itself – to probe the incapacity of language. Hermeneutics, as propounded by Hans-Georg Gadamer, overcomes this disability through an undogmatic appreciation for the genius of the author, a delight in literature and disciplined common sense. Zhang further explores French poetry and Chinese literature in order to demonstrate that perception of universal 'sameness' can overcome particular difference.

Theories of the arts in China.
See item no. 1248.

Classical fiction and prose

Translations

1122   **The plum in the golden vase, or,** *Chin P'ing Mei.*
Anonymous, translated by David Tod Roy. Volume One: *The*
gathering.   Princeton, New Jersey: Princeton University Press,
1993. 610p. (Princeton Library of Asian Translation).

China's most famous erotic novel, *Jinpingmei*, was first printed in the early 17th
century, and partially translated by Clement Edgerton as *The golden lotus* (London: G.
Routledge, 1939. 2 vols. Reprinted, London: Kegan Paul, 1994. 4 vols.) with spicy
passages omitted or translated into Latin. Roy's lively, scrupulous annotated
translation of the full text reveals it as a cynical, often comic, virtuosic pastiche of
detective novel, pornography and poetic romance. The anonymous author was one of
the first to use realistic novelistic techniques; however, by setting his novel in the 12th
century, he can pillory his own time in safety. Roy's substantial introduction argues
that its notorious eroticism cloaks a Buddhist allegory of sin and redemption. In this,
the first of five planned volumes of the translation, each of which can be read
independently, Merchant Ximen Qing (Hsi-men Ch'ing) plots both to advance
commercially and to sexually exploit the wife of his sworn brother.

1123   **Stories from a Ming collection.**
Translated by Cyril Birch.   Bloomington, Indiana: Indiana
University Press, 1958. 205p. (UNESCO Collection of Representative
Works).

Presents six stories from a late Ming collection brought together from various sources
by Feng Menglong (1574-1646). The stories use new realistic techniques and
colloquial language to describe a commercial and manipulative Ming society in the
prosperous lower Yangzi valley. In their world, poets, merchants and literati value
romance and the high life more than office or Confucian notions, and women take
amorous initiatives, but the tone remains moralistic. The best known stories are 'The
Pearl-sewn Shirt' and 'The Canary Murders'.

1124   **The story of the stone.**
Cao Xueqin, translated by David Hawkes.   Harmondsworth,
England: Penguin Books, 1973-86 (Penguin Classics); Bloomington,
Indiana: Indiana University Press, 1979. 5 vols. Volume I, *Golden*
days; volume II, *The crab flower club*; volume III, *The warning voice*;
volume IV, *The debt of tears*; volume V, *The dreamer wakes* (edited
by Gao E), translated by John Minford.

The supreme creation of Chinese fiction, *Shitouji*, known also as *Hongloumeng*
(Dream of the red chamber). Unfinished at the author's death in 1763, the manuscript
was circulated under various titles until publication in 1792, with a concluding section
(here volume V) of uncertain authorship. The multi-layered story is at base a deeply
sad, romantic, wise, Buddhist reincarnation allegory. Volume I may be read
independently as a psychologically realistic picture of a Chinese élite family at
doomed zenith – like the Chinese empire. The portrayal of women is almost feminist;

heroines range from wan romantics to viragos, while the males range from neurasthenic to coldly incompetent. Baoyu, the tender hero, and Daiyu, his *inamorata*, are known to Chinese audiences today from television and a theme park. Admirable translations are: Yang Hsien-yi, Gladys Yang, *A dream of red mansions* (Peking: Foreign Languages Press, 1978-80. 3 vols.); an abridgement by Florence McHugh, Isabel McHugh, *Dream of the red chamber* (New York: Pantheon, 1958. 582p. Reprinted, Westport, Connecticut: Greenwood Press, 1975); and a drastic abridgement by Chi-chen Wang, *Dream of the red chamber* (Garden City, New York: Doubleday, 1929. Reprinted, London: Vision, 1958. 574p.).

1125 **Flowers in the mirror.**
Li Ju-chen, translated, edited by Lin Tai-yi.   Berkeley, California;
Los Angeles: University of California Press, 1965. 310p.

A charming minor work, *Jinghua yuan*, here fluently translated and abridged, is often compared to *Gulliver's travels* for its worldly satire. Li Ruzhen (1763-1830) passed only the first level of the exams, and shows an amused contempt for Confucian scholars, an interest in popular Daoism, and flashes of feminism. The novel, set in the Tang dynasty, includes a famous incident in which Empress Wu commands all flowers in the empire to bloom. The hero, Tang Ao, is banished from the court, and his travels include a visit to a mythical Kingdom of Women where men bear all the burdens in China customarily borne by women: footbinding, childbearing, menstruation and servility. Mark Elvin discusses the novel in 'The Inner World of 1830', in *The living tree: the changing meaning of being Chinese today* (q.v.).

1126 **The carnal prayer mat (*rou putuan*).**
Li Yu, translated, with an introduction and notes by Patrick Hanan.
New York: Ballantine Books, 1990. 317p.

One of the liveliest in China's 16th- and 17th-century urban tradition of erotic novels, in which the hero has a penis transplanted from a dog and makes the most of it. Hanan, author of *The invention of Li Yu* (q.v.), argues in the preface to this translation that the Chinese erotic tradition was superior to its later counterparts in England and France: Chinese eroticism explored adultery as defying China's family-centred morality, rather than the European focus, defloration, which is an individualistic action; for Chinese writers, sexuality was a drive that 'had to lose when it collided with social values'. Chang and Chang, *Crisis and transformation in seventeenth century China* (q.v.) doubt Li's authorship of *Rou buduan*.

1127 **Three kingdoms: a historical novel.**
Luo Guanzhong (attrib.), translated with afterword and notes by Moss
Roberts.   Berkeley, California; Oxford: University of California
Press; Beijing: Foreign Languages Press, 1993. 1,096p.

The historical novel, *Sanguozhi yan'i*, which resembles Homeric epic in scope and influence, was brought together from earlier tales, probably by Luo Guanzhong (1330?-1400?). It chronicles the decline of the Han dynasty and its partition during the period 168-280 CE into the Three Kingdoms of Wei, Wu and Shu. Three young loyalists meet and pledge the famous 'Peach Garden Oath' to fight for the legitimate, doomed Han dynasty: Liu Bei a pious scion of royalty; Guan Yu, who was later apotheosized as the God of War; and Zhang Fei, a rash and selfless former pig-butcher. They are joined by Zhuge Liang, the wily, steadfast statesman (Premier Zhou

Enlai was often compared to him). Their rivals include General Cao Cao, an archetypical Machiavellian figure. All are familiar through opera, song and adage as exemplifying loyalty, political legitimacy and personal honour. This translation replaces the fusty though still serviceable C. H. Brewitt-Taylor, *San-kuo: the romance of the three kingdoms* (Shanghai, China: Kelly & Walsh, 1925. 2 vols.).

1128   **Traditional Chinese stories: themes and variations.**
Edited by Y. W. Ma, Joseph S. M. Lau.   New York; London:
Columbia University Press, 1978. 603p.

A magisterial anthology which provides balanced coverage for the student of Chinese literature. The organization differs from other anthologies in presenting the stories first by form: *biji* or 'jottings'; *chuanji*, typical of or modelled on Tang dynasty stories; *bianwen* stories, found in the Dunhuang excavations, used for popular Buddhist teaching; *huaben*, once thought to have been modelled on Song dynasty prompt books, but now designating any story typical of later dynasties; and *gongan*, court case fiction. Each form is illustrated by many themes (e.g. selfless friend, knight errant, heartless lover, superhuman maiden, ghosts, etc.) with ample annotation and supporting apparatus.

1129   **Selected tales of Liaozhai.**
Pu Songling, translated by Hsien-yi Yang, Gladys Yang.   Peking:
Panda Books, 1981. 151p.

Pu Songling (P'u Sung-ling; 1640-1750), an erudite scholar, built on a literary tradition of the exotic and the weird to create innovative literary ghost tales, black humour fables and realistic horror tales. Spence's *Death of Woman Wang* (q.v.) also translates selections of his work. An earlier selection is Herbert Giles, *Strange stories from a Chinese studio* (London: Thos. de la Rue, 1880. Reprinted, New York: Dover Press, 1969. 2 vols.). Judith Zeitlin, *Stories of the strange: Pu Songling and the Chinese classical tale* (Stanford, California: Stanford University Press, 1993. 332p.) is an imaginative, engrossing biography and detailed literary study.

1130   **Six records of a floating life.**
Shen Fu, translated with an introduction and notes by Leonard Pratt,
Chiang Su-hui.   Harmondsworth, England: Penguin Books, 1983.
170p. maps.

As a minor government clerk or painter, Shen Fu (1763-1809) never attained a gracious standard of living but became esteemed in China long after his death for this affecting autobiographical memoir, *Fusheng liu ji*, which unpretentiously evokes the love and cultured poverty shared by Shen and his wife. He depicts family life, the functioning of the magistrate's office, and the role of courtesans who much resembled the Japanese *geisha*. See Paul Ropp, 'Between two worlds: women in Shen Fu's *Six Chapters of a Floating Life*', in *Women and literature in China*, edited by Anna Gerstlacher (Bochum, Germany: Brockmeyer, 1985).

1131   **The outlaws of the marsh.**
Shi Nai'an, Luo Guanzhong, translated by Sydney Shapiro.   Beijing:
Foreign Languages Press, 1969. 3 vols.; Bloomington, Indiana:
Indiana University Press, 1981. 2 vols.

A rousing picaresque favourite, known to Chinese as a touchstone of moral rebellion, full of lusty, violent and vivid characters. The novel, cobbled together in the late Ming dynasty from earlier vernacular tales, concerns 108 male heroes forced by an unjust government into a life of righteous rebellion in the North China marshes, or 'water margin' which gives the title to the Chinese version – *Shuihu zhuan*. A conscientious earlier translation is Pearl S. Buck, *All men are brothers* (New York: John Day, 1933. 2 vols. Reprinted, New York: Grove Press, 1957). A fluid and colloquial translation is in progress: John and Alex Dent-Young, translators, *The broken seals*, part one of *The marshes of Mt. Liang* of Shi Nai'an and Luo Guanzhong (Hong Kong: Chinese University Press, 1994. 434p.).

1132   **Celebrated cases of Judge Dee (Dee goong an): an authentic eighteenth-century Chinese detective story.**
Translated with an introduction and notes by Robert van Gulick.
Tokyo, 1949. Reprinted, New York: Dover Publications, 1976. 237p.

Long before Edgar Allen Poe invented the Western genre, an 18th-century Chinese writer pulled together various story tellers' yarns to form a detective story based on an exemplary Tang dynasty official. Since the county magistrate was both investigator and judge, he was the natural hero of the popular Chinese story of detection, rather than a mere police officer or a private detective. In this tale, Judge Dee and his assistants unscramble a series of predicaments – a double murder among travelling merchants, the poisoning of a bride on her wedding night and a village imbroglio – giving a vivid glimpse of law in local practice. As a Dutch scholar-diplomat, van Gulick was too busy during the Second World War to pursue research, so created his own versions based on Chinese models; among the many is *Murder in Canton* (Chicago: University of Chicago Press, 1993. 207p.).

1133   **Journey to the west.**
Wu Cheng-en, translated, edited by Anthony C. Yu.   Chicago:
University of Chicago Press, 1977-83. 4 vols.

Xiyouji is a rambunctious, occasionally earthy, comic, but morally instructive masterpiece featuring some of the best loved characters in Chinese popular culture. Yu's complete translation is virtually definitive, but Arthur Waley's witty and charming abbreviated version, *Monkey* (London: Allen & Unwin, 1942; Penguin Books, [n.d.]. 351p. [Penguin Classics]), is a classic in its own right. The Tang dynasty hero, Tripitika, based on the actual scholar-monk Xuanzang (596-664), was dispatched to India ('the West') to bring back the Buddhist sutras, which he then spent the rest of his life translating. The novel adds three companions from folk legend, each representing a facet of humanity: 'Pigsy' (in Waley's translation) – earthy, stolid and selfish; 'Sandy' – the pious, narrow acolyte; and, most resoundingly, 'Monkey' (Sun Wukong), renowned in later opera and tale, the rebellious and inventive Monkey King who is pressed into service by the Buddha to expiate his sins.

1134   **The scholars.**
Wu Ching-tzu, translated by Yang Hsien-yi, Gladys Yang.   Beijing:
Foreign Languages Press, 1957; New York: Grosset & Dunlop, 1972;
New York: Columbia University Press, 1972. Reprinted with a preface
by C. T. Hsia, New York: Columbia University Press, 1992. 692p.

The novel *Rulin waishi* (more literally, 'unofficial history of the literati') was
completed in the mid-18th century but published only in 1957, after the author's
death. It presents a lively, satirical panorama of a newly prosperous bourgeois society;
the plot contrasts rich merchants with poverty raddled scholars and teachers who fall
comically short of Confucian ideals. Paul Ropp, *Dissent in early modern China: Ju-lin
wai-shih and Ch'ing social criticism* (Ann Arbor, Michigan: University of Michigan
Press, 1981. 356p.) studies Wu Jingzu (1704-54) as a sophisticated cosmopolitan who
satirizes social issues such as the lack of professional and intellectual autonomy,
schools and the examination system, feminist thought, and the skepticism of
intellectuals toward the supernatural in popular religion.

**Classical Chinese fiction: a guide to its study and appreciation: essays
and bibliographies.**
See item no. 1479.

History and criticism

1135   **Images and ideas in Chinese classical prose: studies of four
masters.**
Yu-shih Chen.   Stanford, California: Stanford University Press,
1988. 235p.

An examination of the interaction of history, ideas and prose style of Han Yu (768-824),
Liu Zongyuan (773-819), Ouyang Xiu (1007-72) and Su Shi (1037-1101), the four Tang
dynasty masters of the *guwen* – classical prose essay – which was at the heart of the
Neo-Confucian revival of thought and aesthetics. Chen describes the background and
setting, then devotes chapters to each of the writers.

1136   **The Chinese vernacular short story.**
Patrick Hanan.   Cambridge, Massachusetts: Harvard University
Press, 1981. 276p. bibliog. (Harvard East Asian Series, no. 94).

A lucid scholarly study of origins and development. Hanan first analyses Tang, Song
and Ming examples for language and narrative models (including court case fiction,
demon fiction and romance), then pays detailed attention to late Ming authors
including Feng Menglong and Li Yu.

1137   **The classic Chinese novel: a critical introduction.**
C. T. Hsia.   New York; London: Columbia University Press, 1968.
413p. (Companions to Asian Studies).

A key introduction for Western general readers to the six novels considered in China
to be the classics: *Three kingdoms (Sanguozhi yanyi)*; *Water margin (Shuihu zhuan)*;

Journey to the west (*Xiyouji*); *Golden lotus*, or *Plum in the golden vase* (*Jinpingmei*); *The scholars* (*Rulin waishi*); and *Story of the stone* (*Hongloumeng* or *Shitou ji*) (qq.v.). Hsia, an admired and learned literary critic, summarizes the historical background to each novel, introduces the authors, comments on the plots and characters, and highlights useful comparisons with Western novels.

1138   **From historicity to fictionality: the Chinese poetics of narrative.**
Sheldon Hsiao-peng Lu.   Stanford, California: Stanford University Press, 1994. 213p.

Lu deploys Western literary discourse from Aristotle to Roland Barthes to correct its own Eurocentrism and develop a truly comparative understanding by studying the 'poetics' – the theory of structure and function – of Chinese narrative. Chapters one and two examine the use of terms 'narrative', 'history', and 'fiction' in the West and China. Chapters three to five analyse the poetics of historiography and read Tang fiction as history, allegory and fantasy. Chapter six describes the emergence of a self-conscious poetics of fiction in the Ming and Qing. During this period the dominance of historical narrative gave way to a process of 'dehistoricization' in which critics and readers of *xiaoshuo* ('fictional narrative') came to define and accept the nature and characteristics of 'fictionality'; they moved from a concern with what actually happened to a concern with creating a vivid and morally significant world.

1139   **T'ang transformation texts: a study of the Buddhist contribution to the rise of vernacular fiction and drama in China.**
Victor H. Mair.   Cambridge, Massachusetts: Council on East Asian Studies, Harvard University, 1989. 286p. (Harvard-Yenching Institute Monograph, no. 28).

The author uses texts of *bianwen* – Buddhist folk transformation tales from the 8th and 9th centuries – excavated early in the 20th century at the Central Asian oasis at Dunhuang. Mair argues that forms and themes from India were significant in Chinese literary development, which Mair also studied in *Tun-huang popular narratives* (Cambridge, England: Cambridge University Press, 1983. 329p. [Cambridge Studies in Chinese History, Literature, and Institutions]). A number of the tales are translated in Arthur Waley, *Ballads and stories from Tun-huang: anthology* (London: Allen & Unwin, 1960. 273p.), including the legend of Meng Jiangnü (whose husband died building the Great Wall), Mu-lian Rescues his Mother, and Buddhist pieces.

1140   **Four masterworks of the Ming novel.**
Andrew H. Plaks.   Princeton, New Jersey: Princeton University Press, 1987. 595p.

A seminal exploration of 'literati novels'. Plaks argues that *Romance of the three kingdoms*, *Water margin* (or, *Men of the marshes*), *Journey to the west* and *Golden lotus* (or *Plum in a golden vase*), all written in the 16th century, collectively constituted a technical breakthrough reflecting new cultural values and intellectual concerns. Their educated authors appropriated earlier storytellers' conventions to fashion self-consciously ironic narratives whose seeming familiarity camouflaged a Neo-Confucian moral critique of late Ming decadence. Plaks explores: the textual history of the novels (all published after their author's death, usually anonymously); the major Chinese and Japanese commentaries; formal structures; and how the ironic and satiric devices of these novels paved the way for the great novels of the 18th century. *Chinese narrative: critical and theoretical essays,* edited by Andrew H. Plaks (Princeton, New Jersey: Princeton University Press, 1977. 365p.) is a pioneering scholarly symposium on these topics. Shelley Hsueh-lun Chang, *History and legend: ideas and images in the Ming historical novel* (Ann Arbor, Michigan: University of Michigan Press, 1990. 279p.) describes: the Ming world of fiction and ideas of historical change; the hero; social, political, cosmic order and morality; and reactions to the growth of imperial despotism.

1141   **How to read the Chinese novel.**
       Edited by David L. Rolston.   Princeton, New Jersey: Princeton
       University Press, 1989. 534p. bibliog.
Provides material for a 'poetics of the Chinese novel' independent of foreign frameworks and literary theory. Chinese critics of the 17th and 18th centuries wrote copious running commentaries – called *dufa* ('how to read') – interspersed with the text of the work to form one experience for the reader. Scholars in this volume translate and introduce the most important of these commentaries written for the six now classic *xiaoshuo,* ('small' or 'minor' narratives), conventionally translated as 'fiction' or 'novel'. Rolston's extensive introductory chapter explains the nature and history of the commentaries and construes their terminology. An extensive bibliographical section describes the relevant Chinese sources.

1142   **The story of stone: intertextuality, ancient Chinese stone lore, and
       the stone symbolism in the *Dream of the Red Chamber*, *Water
       Margin*, and *The Journey to the West*.**
       Jing Wang.   Durham, North Carolina; London: Duke University
       Press, 1992. 347p. (Post-Contemporary Interventions).
Wang applies close reading of texts as well as contemporary literary theory to explore the web of mutual references ('intertextuality'), to decode the changing significances of powerful symbols, and to explain mythic elements in three classic novels. In addition to the lore concerning stones, Wang explains the problem of the sources of Sun Wukong ('Monkey') in *Journey to the west* and fear and distrust of women in *Water margin.* Throughout the work, Wang is concerned with testing and expanding theory and concept in comparative literature.

Han Yü and the T'ang search for unity.
See item no. 141.

Modern fiction and prose

Translations

1143 Fortress besieged.
Ch'ien Chung-shu, translated by Jeanne Kelly, Nathan K. Mao.
Bloomington, Indiana; London: Indiana University Press, 1979. 377p.
(Chinese Literature in Translation).

The novel *Weicheng*, first published in 1947, established Qian Zhongshu (1911-) as one of modern China's most sophisticated writers. In their detailed introduction, the translators call the novel a 'comedy of manners with much picaresque humor, as well as a scholar's novel, a satire, a commentary on courtship and marriage, and a study of one contemporary man'. The event-filled plot centres on a man named Fang, who returns from study in Europe in 1937. He travels through China in the early stages of the war, witnessing gossipers and political schemers in Shanghai, decay in his home town of Wuxi, and pseudo-intellectual torpor in the universities. Fang, like the city of the title and China itself, is 'besieged'; unlike the author, he succumbs to nihilism.

1144 The rice-sprout song.
Eileen Chang. New York: Scribner's, 1955. 182p.

A novel, composed in English, of idealistic youths working in the villages in the early 1950s who are forced by political demands to suppress starving peasants. Without giving in to ideological crudity, Chang (Zhang Ailing; 1921-95) presents individual characters to dramatize her view that the political process brought personal and social tragedy. Although she lived in America after 1949, Chang's reputation as an international and sophisticated Shanghai writer of the 1930s made her influential in Taiwan when other modernist writers were not available. Her 1943 novella, 'The Golden Cangue' (*Jinsuo ji*) is included in Lau, *Modern Chinese short stories and novellas* (q.v.).

1145 The execution of Mayor Yin, and other stories from the Great Proletarian Cultural Revolution.
Chen Jo-hsi, translated by Nancy Ing, Howard Goldblatt, introduction by Simon Leys. Bloomington, Indiana; London: Indiana University Press, 1979. 220p. (Chinese Literature in Translation).

Contains stories widely read outside China by a Taiwan-born author who emigrated to the People's Republic during the Cultural Revolution. Chen (Chen Ruoxi; 1938-) was among the first to present a disillusioning picture of Maoist realities and social pettiness. The title story describes political intrigue in a small town. Included in addition to this story are: 'Chairman Mao is a Rotten Egg', in which a child's casual remark is turned into a political struggle; and 'Nixon's Press Corps', concerning the extensive preparations for a 'spontaneous' reception for the American President in 1972.

1146 **Stones of the wall.**
Dai Houying, translated by Frances Wood. London: Michael
Joseph; New York: St. Martin's, 1985. 309p.

This critical novel, published in Beijing in the 1980s, presents a panorama of the political campaigns culminating in the Cultural Revolution as seen in a Shanghai university. Dramatic, first-person vignettes are told by a variety of characters in their attempts to understand and rebuild their lives, each of whom retells the stories of the others. The characters debate the meaning of humanism in politics, love in personal life and the vicissitudes of history.

1147 **Born of the same roots: stories of modern Chinese women.**
Edited by Vivian Ling Hsu. Bloomington, Indiana: Indiana University
Press, 1981. 308p. bibliog. (Chinese Literature in Translation).

Provides stories from Taiwan and the People's Republic which illustrate the plight of women in modern Chinese history. *Seven contemporary Chinese women writers* (Beijing: Panda Books, 1982. 280p.) contains stories reflecting new, post-Cultural Revolution viewpoints, arguing that it is no longer enough to serve the revolution in the same way as men while remaining subordinate to them. The anthology includes some of the most popular writing of the 1980s, such as Shen Rong's 'At Middle Age' and Zhang Jie's 'Love Must Not Be Forgotten', as well as works by Ru Zhijuan, Huang Zongying, Zong Pu and Wang Anyi. Wang Anyi, *Lapse of time* (Beijing: Panda; San Francisco: China Books, 1988. 235p.) includes six short stories, a novella, and an autobiographical note. Wang portrays Shanghai in the Cultural Revolution with a remarkable lack of rancour, but examines new political class distinctions and petty political rivalries in daily life.

1148 **I myself am a woman: selected writings of Ding Ling.**
Ding Ling, edited by Tani E. Barlow, with Gary J. Bjorge,
introduction by Tani E. Barlow. Boston, Massachusetts: Beacon
Press, 1989. 361p.

A compilation of twelve celebrated short stories with a substantial historical and critical introduction. Ding Ling [Ting Ling, pseud. of Jiang Bingzhi; 1904-85] appeared in the 1920s as a 'modern girl', an anarcho-feminist product of new women's schools; her 1927 story, 'Miss Sophia's Diary', shocked readers with its (actually rather mild) eroticism. After her lover was executed by the Nationalist government, Ding Ling joined the Communists in Yan'an. There she defied party authorities with the (actually rather mild) politically critical 'When I was in Xia Village'. For a detailed literary study, see Yi-tsi Mei Feuerwerker, *Ding Ling's fiction* (Cambridge, Massachusetts: Harvard University Press, 1982. 196p.).

1149 **The sun shines over the Sanggan river.**
Ding Ling, translated by Yang Hsien-yi, Gladys Yang. Beijing:
Foreign Languages Press, 1954. 348p. Reissued, 1984. 379p.

A social documentary novel of the coming of the land revolution to a North China village, based on Ding Ling's own participation in a village land reform team in the 1940s. Rather than focusing on character development or individual personalities, the novel, which won the Stalin Prize in 1951, portrays the process of class struggle. The characters are poor peasants, petty-bourgeois intellectuals, rich peasants and landlords, described in terms and judgements supplied by Maoist political analysis.

1150   **Three inch golden lotus.**
Feng Jicai, translated by David Wakefield.   Honolulu, Hawaii:
University of Hawaii Press, 1994. 239p. (Fiction From Modern
China).

An energetic, technically daring satirical novel. Feng (1942-) was trained as a painter,
but during the Cultural Revolution turned to fiction. *San cun jinlian* (Tianjin, China:
Baihua, 1986) is set in the period 1890-1930, when footbinding came under attack by
missionaries and reformers. Women in the novel first have their feet broken to make
them sexually attractive, then are humiliated by iconoclastic reform ideologues. Feng
dramatizes the beautiful, oppressive literati tradition in contrast with ugly, liberating
modernity. A postscript describes the author and the history of footbinding. Feng's
stories are selected in *Chrysanthemums and other stories*, translated by Susan Wilf
Chen (San Diego, California: Harcourt, Brace, Jovanovich, 1985. 255p.).

1151   **Chairman Mao would not be amused: fiction from today's China.**
Edited with an introduction by Howard Goldblatt.   New York: Grove
Press, 1995. 321p.

These twenty stories, published between 1985-93, represent new writers breaking out
of official modes and experimenting with new forms. Authors include Can Xue, Duo
Duo, Kong Jiesheng, Mo Yan, Shi Tiesheng, Su Tong and Wang Meng. *Raise the red
lantern: three novellas*, by Su Tong, translated by Michael S. Duke (New York:
William Morrow, 1993. 268p.) contains intense portrayals of an almost mythical
'feudal' Chinese society, from one of which the plot for Zhang Yimou's 1992 film,
Raise the red lantern, was drawn. *Rice*, by Su Tong, translated by Howard Goldblatt
(New York: Morrow, 1995. 266p.) is a harrowing, urgent family tale of a rice-
merchant household undone by lust and greed. *Old floating cloud: two novellas* by
Can Xue, translated by Ronald Jansen, Jian Zhang, with a foreword by Charlotte Innes
(Evanston, Illinois: Northwestern University Press, 1991. 269p.) contains two novellas
of the early 1980s, *Yellow Mud Street* and *Old Floating Cloud*; they were among the
first experiments in surrealist and grotesque writing influenced by Western
modernism. Can Xue (1953-) sets her work in contemporary China and deals with
family and petty officialdom, but evokes atmosphere and emotion more than plot.
Three kings: three stories from today's China, by Ah Cheng (pseud. of Zhong
Acheng; 1949-), translated by Bonnie S. McDougall (London: Collins Harvill, 1990.
223p.) contains three realistic novellas of the mid-1980s, 'The King of Chess', 'The
King of Trees', and 'The King of Children', the last of which was made into a film by
Chen Kaige. *Old well*, by Zheng Yi, translated by David Kwan (San Francisco: China
Books, 1989. 154p.), the basis for the 1987 film of the same name, portrays the bleak
village life of north China where Zheng (1948-) was sent down.

1152   **The golden road.**
Hao Ran, translated by Carma Hinton, Chris Gilmartin.   Beijing:
Foreign Languages Press, 1981. 390p.

Hao Ran (pseud. of Liang Jinguang; 1932-) was born into the poverty ridden North
China which he presents in this popular documentary novel, *Jinguang dadao*. The first
of four planned volumes was published in 1972, a slightly abridged version of which
is translated here. The literary technique follows that of Ding Ling, Liu Qing, Zhao
Shuli and Zhou Libo (qq.v.); the story takes up where their novels leave off, with the
initial success of land reform in 1950 and the formation of cooperatives. Influenced by
the ideals of the Cultural Revolution, during which Hao Ran returned to the

countryside, the plot shows heroic Maoist cadres leading poor peasants to attack poverty by overcoming individualism and resurgent capitalism.

1153 **The field of life and death and Tales of Hulan river: two novels by Hsiao Hung.**
Hsiao Hung, translated by Howard Goldblatt, Ellen Yeung.
Bloomington, Indiana; London: Indiana University Press, 1979. 290p.
(Chinese Literature in Translation).

Xiao Hong (pseud. of Zhang Naiying; 1911-42), before her early death of tuberculosis in Japanese occupied Hong Kong, was victimized as a woman by family and lovers. Under the auspices of Lu Xun, she finally blossomed as a popular writer who created vivid characters and caustic social portraits. Her short novel, *The field of life and death* (*Shengsichang*) (Shanghai, China: Rongguang, 1935), was read for its anti-Japanese depiction of village life in the North-east, or Manchuria, where Xiao Hong grew up; the translators argue in their introduction that it is nonetheless more art than propaganda. *Tales of Hulan River* (*Hulan he zhuan*) (1942), her last work, is an autobiographical though not nostalgic story which explores the plight of the villager, the suffering of women and the scenic beauty of the country. A concise life and critical introduction is presented in Howard Goldblatt, *Hsiao Hung* (Boston, Massachusetts: Twayne, 1976. 161p. [Twayne Authors Series]).

1154 **Cat country: a satirical novel of China in the 1930s.**
Lao She, translated, with an introduction by William A. Lyell, Jr.
[n.p.]: Ohio State University Press, 1970. 295p.

Lao She (pseud. of Shu Qingqun; 1899-1966) wrote *Maocheng ji* (Shanghai, 1933), to express the scathing cultural pessimism felt after China's military defeats in 1931 and 1932. The novel is a purported 'travel diary' of an airplane trip to a country of cats on 'Mars', where the narrator crash lands and learns 'Felinese'. The satire is sometimes brilliant, but sometimes inclined to preach. The Felinese – like Chinese? – despise each other more than they hate foreign invaders, and attack all that is best in their past. They remain oblivious by eating 'reverie leaves', a drug introduced by foreigners, who also brought Free Love, 'Everybody Shareskyism', and 'brawls', as political parties are designated. Students are graduated on the first day of school for fear they might demonstrate against professors and examinations. As the book ends, the two last Felinese are in the process of killing each other.

1155 **Rickshaw: the novel *Lo-t'o Hsiang Tzu* by Lao She.**
Lao She, translated by Jean M. James.   Honolulu, Hawaii:
University of Hawaii Press, 1979. 249p.

One of modern China's most poignant and influential novels, often called Dickensian, and acclaimed for its sympathetic, unsentimental picture of the Beijing lower classes of the 1930s. The hero, fresh from the village, toils for years to earn his own rickshaw; however, he loses it overnight to marauding solders, from whom he then steals a team of camels, earning his nickname, 'Camel Xiangzi'. The novel portrays his search for love and ineluctable destruction in an atomistic, selfish society where cash is more important than values or loyalty. Other translations are: *Camel Xiangzi*, translated by Shi Xiaoqing (Beijing: Foreign Languages Press, 1981. 236p.); and Lau Shaw [sic], *Rickshaw Boy*, translated by Evan King (New York: Reynal & Hitchcock, 1945. 383p.), which is fitted with a happy ending. Ranbir Vohra, *Lao She and the Chinese revolution* (Cambridge, Massachusetts: East Asian Research Center, Harvard University Press, 1974. 199p. [East Asian Monographs, no. 55]) discusses the life and times of Lao She, relating the main works to his experience and evolving view of China.

1156 **Modern Chinese stories and novellas, 1919-1949.**
Edited by Joseph S. M. Lau, C. T. Hsia, Leo Ou-fan Lee. New York; London: Columbia University Press, 1981. 578p. bibliog. (Modern Asian Literature Series).

An extensive anthology of short fiction, with helpful introductions and notes. Although the realistic mode predominates, the compilation shows the remarkable range of technique and points of view in the period, which rejected domination by traditional forms and literary language. The extensive selected bibliography lists books and articles in English. Less comprehensive but valuable anthologies include: *Straw sandals: Chinese short stories, 1918-1933*, edited with an introduction by Harold Isaacs (Cambridge, Massachusetts: M. I. T. Press, 1974. 444p.); *Modern Chinese stories*, edited by W. J. F. Jenner (London; New York: Oxford Paperbacks, 1970. 271p.); and *Twentieth century Chinese stories*, edited by C. T. Hsia (New York: Columbia University Press, 1971. 230p.).

1157 **Travels of Lao Ts'an.**
Liu T'ieh-yün, translated by Harold Shadick. Ithaca, New York: Cornell University Press, 1952. Reissued, New York; London: Columbia University Press, 1990. 277p. (A Morningside Book).

Liu Tieyun (Liu E; 1857-1909) was an unconventional late Qing reformer and official who worked in the field of river control and engineering. During the Boxer Uprising he speculated in government rice, distributing it to the poor. He was cashiered for these efforts, but shrewd investments had left him wealthy enough to follow his pioneering archaeological studies and to write fiction. *Laocan youji* (1906), here translated with an introduction, is his most famous work. Thinly covering his own views in those of the physician hero, Liu satirically describes the rise of the Boxers in the countryside (inaccurately), the decay of the Yellow River control system, and the hypocritical incompetence of the bureaucracy. *The travels of Lao Can*, translated by Yang Xianyi, Gladys Yang (Beijing: Panda Books, 1983. 176p.) omits major sections on the questionable grounds that Liu could not have written them because they were superstitious.

1158 **Red crag.**
Lo Kuang-pin, Yang Yi-yen. Peking: Foreign Languages Press, 1978. 606p.

'Red Crag' was the site just outside Chongqing, in Sichuan, of a concentration camp run by Nationalist secret police trained by Americans during the war; when Communist troops were about to enter the city in 1949, leftist prisoners were slaughtered. In this widely read documentary novel, two ex-inmates of the camp dramatically present prison life as a parable of revolutionary virtue versus reactionary villainy, with American imperialism supporting the latter. After 1989, the novel was re-issued in China, perhaps because of its anti-American sentiment. Other popular novels of revolutionary history include Yang Mo's 1958 political and romantic *Song of youth* (*Qingchun zhi ge*) (Peking: Foreign Languages Press, 1964) and Liang Bin's

1957 *Keep the red flag flying* (*Hongqi pu*), translated by Gladys Yang (Peking: Foreign Languages Press, 1961), describing the North China student-peasant alliance in the 'pig rebellion' of the 1930s.

1159 Lu Xun: selected works.
Lu Xun, translated by Yang Xianyi, Gladys Yang. Peking: Foreign Languages Press, 1980. 2nd ed. 4 vols.

A reliable though slightly bookish translation of stories, essays and poetry by Lu Xun (pseud. of Zhou Shuren; 1881-1936), first published in 1965. Portions of these translations are published separately, including: *Selected stories of Lu Hsun* (Peking: Foreign Languages Press, 1960, various reprints), which contains eighteen stories including 'Preface to *Call to arms*', 'A madman's diary', 'Kung I-chi', 'Medicine', 'My old home', 'The true story of Ah Q', 'In the wine shop' and 'Divorce'; *The complete stories of Lu Xun* (Beijing: Foreign Languages Press; Bloomington, Indiana: Indiana University Press, 1981. 295p.); and *Old tales retold* (Peking, 1972. 137p.). Another respected selection is *Diary of a madman and other stories*, translated by William A. Lyell (Honolulu: University of Hawaii Press, 1990. 389p.).

1160 Midnight.
Mao Dun, translated by Xu Mengxiong, A. C. Barnes. Peking: Foreign Languages Press, 1957. Reprinted, Hong Kong: C & W, distributed by Cheng & Tsui, Boston, 1976. 524p.

A sprawling, energetic social satire, published in 1933 as *Ziye*, and sometimes referred to as *Twilight*. Mao Dun, a pen-name of Shen Yanbing (1896-1981), aimed to expose the nature of Shanghai bourgeois society and the rot of the capitalist order in a panoramic story of a capitalist family. Critics generally consider this to be one of modern China's few masterpieces of politically inspired literature. Mao Dun, *Spring silkworms and other stories*, translated by Sydney Shapiro (Beijing: Foreign Languages Press, 1956. Reprinted, New York: AMS, 1979. 278p.) dramatizes the exploitation of the peasant by the capitalist market.

1161 Rainbow.
Mao Dun, translated with an introduction by Madeleine Zelin. Berkeley, California; Los Angeles; Oxford: University of California Press, 1992. 235p.

Called by C. T. Hsia 'in many respects [Mao Dun's] finest', this 1929 novel depicts a young heroine's traversal from Western liberal individualism to revolutionary commitment in the years from May 4 1919 to the defeat of the left in 1927. The heroine leaves the husband selected for her by her family in Chengdu to become a school teacher; she is then installed as companion and tutor to a politically progressive, socially conservative Nationalist general. She joins revolutionary life and a new man in Shanghai, and finally is swept away in the Great Revolution. The vigour of the story reflects Mao Dun's political participation, the representation of psychology, and his growing literary skill. This fusion of politics, psychology and technique is explored in Yu-shih Chen, *Realism and allegory in the early fiction of Mao Dun* (Bloomington, Indiana: Indiana University Press, 1986. 262p.).

1162   **Red sorghum: a family chronicle.**
Mo Yan, translated by Howard Goldblatt.   London: Heinemann;
New York; London: Viking Penguin, 1993. 378p.

A riveting historical panorama, translated from *Hong gaoliang jiazu* (Beijing: Taipei, 1987), of tough, proud families in village Shandong, where the author was born. They fight invaders and each other over three generations from the 1920s through the Anti-Japanese war in the 1930s to the mid-1950s. Mo Yan (pen-name of Guan Moye; 1956-) mixes violence, romance, gruesome humour and magical realism to see in a different way the revolution's base in banditry and machismo. Zhang Yimou's film adaptation of 1989 used part of the story. Mo Yan, *Explosions and other stories*, edited by Janice Wickeri (Hong Kong: Chinese University Press, 1991. 214p.) contains six stories also depicting villagers, especially women. *The garlic ballads*, translated by Howard Goldblatt (New York: Viking Penguin, 1995. 290p.) chronicles the victimization of poor farmers by nature and officials when the market for their garlic is glutted.

1163   **Cold nights.**
Pa Chin, translated by Nathan K. Mao, Liu Ts'un-yan.   Hong Kong:
Chinese University Press; Seattle, Washington; London: University of
Washington Press, 1978. 181p.

Ba Jin (pseud. of Li Feigan; 1904-) was an influential anarchist of the 1920s; his fiction dramatizes the New Culture distrust of the traditional family as repressive and reactionary. This is a translation of *Hanye* (1947), considered to be the author's most skilfully constructed novel. The story is set in wartime Chongqing, and depicts the collapse of social values amid mounting inflation, high unemployment, epidemics of tuberculosis, starvation and loss of faith in government. The realistic plot indicts Chinese government and cultural values, while the protagonist, his mother and his wife, are artfully shown as both victims and participants in a changing, corrupt society.

1164   **Family.**
Pa Chin, introduction by Olga Lang.   New York: Anchor Books,
1972. 329p.

A tremendously popular 1931 novel, part of a trilogy drawing on the author's own life. Like *Story of the stone*, on which it draws, *Family* (*Jia*) foregrounds the suffering of youth and women, even suicide, but unlike its model, becomes maudlin. The plot concerns the struggles of three brothers in a patriarchal Sichuan extended family early in the century, especially the efforts of the youngest to find cultural liberation and romantic love. This American edition is based on the translation by Sidney Shapiro (Peking: Foreign Languages Press, 1958), but restores deleted passages. Olga Lang, *Pa Chin and his writings: Chinese youth between the two revolutions* (Cambridge, Massachusetts: Harvard University Press, 1967. 402p.) presents a detailed, sympathetic study of Ba Jin's life and times.

1165   **Imperfect paradise: stories by Shen Congwen.**
Shen Congwen, translated and edited by Jeffrey Kinkley.   Honolulu:
University of Hawaii Press, 1994. 537p. (Fiction from Modern China).

A fundamental compilation. Shen (Shen Ts'ung-wen; 1902-88), who largely withdrew from writing fiction after 1949, was one of the major talents of the pre-war scene; a masterful biography is Jeffrey Kinkley, *The odyssey of Shen Congwen* (Stanford,

California: Stanford University Press, 1987. 464p.). Kinkley shows how Shen became an innovative modernist, and even adopted Freudian theories, while using local material from his youth in western Hunan, where he was raised and roamed as a soldier among the rebellious Miao minority peoples. *The border town and other stories* by Shen Congwen, translated by Gladys Yang (Beijing: Panda Books, 1981. 195p.) includes: 'The Border Town', telling of an old ferryman, his granddaughter and her suitors; 'Xiaoxiao'; 'The husband'; and 'Guisheng'. *The Chinese earth*, by Shen Ts'ung-wen, translated by Ching Ti, Robert Payne (London: Allen & Unwin, 1947. Reprinted, New York: Columbia University Press, 1982. 292p.) provides an overlapping collection.

1166 **Furrows: peasants, intellectuals, and the state: stories and histories from modern China.**
Compiled, edited by Helen Siu. Stanford, California: Stanford University Press, 1990. 341p.

Brings together twenty-four stories, personal histories and essays which represent the changing images of peasants created by writers from the 1930s to the 1980s who 'consciously used the peasantry to condemn or support the political authorities'. The thoughtful introduction, 'Social Responsibility and Self-expression', together with headnotes to each section, provide a substantial analysis of the tense relation between 'literary imagination and political culture'. Pre-revolutionary Marxist critiques of abusive conditions in the countryside gave way after 1949 to critiques of how revolutionaries in power abused the peasantry.

1167 **Bolshevik salute: a modernist Chinese novel.**
Wang Meng, translated, with an introduction and critical essay, by Wendy Larson. Seattle, Washington; London: University of Washington Press, 1989. 154p.

Wang Meng (1934-) joined the Communist Party in 1948, but was denounced in the One Hundred Flowers period in 1957 for his story 'A Young Man arrives at the Organization Bureau' (see *Literature of the One Hundred Flowers Period*, q.v.), which criticized bureaucratism. He was criticized as Rightist, exiled to Xinjiang, but rehabilitated in 1979, eventually serving as Minister of Culture from 1986-89. This 1979 novel, *Buli*, uses modernist techniques to convey the psychology of a young man who goes through much the same political and emotional experiences as the author; episodes are fragmented but clear. Wang Meng, translated by Denis Mair et al., *Selected works of Wang Meng* (Beijing: Foreign Languages Press, 1989- . 2 vols.) includes 'The strain of meeting', 'Snowball' and other stories; there were no further volumes after 1989.

1168 **Hunger trilogy.**
Wang Ruowang, translated by Kyna Rubin with Ira Kasoff. Armonk, New York; London: M. E. Sharpe, 1991. 133p.

An autobiographical novella, based on Wang's three periods of ordeal and starvation: once in a Nationalist government jail in the 1930s; once fleeing Japanese soldiers in the 1940s; and once during Mao's Cultural Revolution in 1960s Shanghai. Rubin's introduction provides background information on Wang, discusses the political and literary uses of food and hunger symbolism, and shows how the modern experience of intellectual, nation and Party are drawn together in Wang's novel.

1169   **Chestnuts and other stories.**
Xiao Qian, translated by Xiao Qian, et al.   Beijing: Panda Books, 1984. 184p.

Xiao (Hsiao Ch'ien; 1910-), born in Beijing and educated at Yenching University, was a well-travelled cosmopolitan journalist. Here he writes evocative short stories of life in the old capital, often told from the point of view of children. Many were published in *The spinners of silk* (London: George Allen & Unwin, 1944). The stories 'The conversion' and 'Cactus flower' deal with the effect of missionary Christianity. 'The captive' and 'Shandong Deng' nostalgically evoke Chinese folk tradition, which is presented less favourably in 'When your eaves are low', 'A rainy evening' and 'Under the fence'. Other stories concern resistance to the Japanese aggression of the 1930s. Hsiao Ch'ien, *Traveller without a map*, translated by Jeffrey C. Kinkley (London: Hutchison; Stanford, California: Stanford University Press, 1990. 276p.) charmingly, and sometimes tartly, reminisces on his childhood, education and sojourn in wartime Britain, especially his warm relations with Arthur Waley and E. M. Forster.

1170   **Baotown.**
Wang Anyi, translated by Martha Avery.   New York; London: Norton, 1989. 144p.

Like many writers of her generation, Wang (1954-) was sent down to the countryside. Her 1985 novella, *Xiao bao zhuang*, explores China's rural roots and story-making traditions by relating the mythical origins of a village in Anhui province, its eccentric characters, and troubled present through famine, romantic love and political disaster. *A small town called Hibiscus* by Gu Hua (Beijing: Foreign Languages Press, 1983. 260p.) also explores a town's communal experience of the Cultural Revolution, but uses more realist techniques; the story was made into a film in 1986 by Xie Jin.

1171   **Schoolmaster Ni Huan-chih.**
Yeh Sheng-tao, translated by A. C. Barnes.   Peking: Foreign Languages Press, 1958. 2nd ed. 1978. 335p.

This eventful novel of educated youth during the Great Revolution of the 1920s gained great popularity when first serialized in 1929. The author, Ye Shengtao (a.k.a. Ye Shaojun; 1894-??), was a leading New Culture educator and literary innovator. The novel's hero, a young teacher named Ni, begins teaching in a village elementary school, and is gradually drawn into revolutionary struggle. The story follows his development to dramatize the conflict between the gradual, liberal, cultural approach favoured by American influenced educators such as Tao Xingzhi and the revolutionary political approach.

1172   **Half of man is woman.**
Zhang Xianliang, translated by Martha Avery.   New York; Middlesex: Viking, 1988. 252p.

This novella created a sensation at its publication in 1985 in the leading literary magazine *Shouhuo* as *Nanren de yiban shi nüren*; many readers and critics were shocked by its explicit sex, while others were excited by its rough, lyrical language and probing of the connection between politics and psychology. The plot spans the decade of the Cultural Revolution in which the narrator serves in a labour camp; he marries a fellow prisoner, but has been rendered sexually impotent (and by implication politically castrated). Zhang's emphasis, however, is on consciousness and character, rather than society, leading to wide debate over the nature and morality of the male and female protagonists. Zhang's *Grass soup*, translated by Martha Avery (London: Secker & Warburg, 1994; Boston, Massachusetts: Godine, 1995. 247p.) is a memoir in which the author tries to come to grips with Cultural Revolution labour camp life, and is based on his actual diaries of the time.

1173 **The hurricane.**
Zhou Libo, translated by Xu Mengxiong. Peking: Foreign Languages Press, 1955; reprinted, 1981. 450p.

A documentary novel of class struggle during the 1946 land reform in a Manchurian village. The plot and characterization are sturdy and straightforward rather than sophisticated, but the description of the conflicts and class interests are serious and grounded in personal observation. Zhou (1908-79) evokes the problems of the outside work team of veteran party cadres and newly recruited intellectuals who deploy Chairman Mao's 'mass line' but who win over the poor peasants only with difficulty. Particularly vivid are the 'struggle meetings' with the landlords; they and their lackeys are shown as giving in grudgingly and temporarily as the revolutionary struggle continues. In the 1950s Zhou Libo and Ding Ling's writings were used as study material for land reform cadres.

History and criticism

1174 **The limits of realism: Chinese fiction in the revolutionary period.**
Marston Anderson. Berkeley, California; Los Angeles; Oxford: University of California Press, 1990. 225p.

The period 1915-42 was one of 'cultural emergency' when China's revolutionary literature took on unique aims and characteristics as seen in the debates over European concepts of literary 'realism'. Anderson begins by using recent literary and cultural theory to analyse 1920s theories of realism. He then describes the 1930s criticisms of the individualism and middle-class allegiances implicit in realism; he looks in detail at the writings of Lu Xun, Ye Shengtao, Mao Dun and Zhang Tianyi in order to consider the moral and social impediments to realism as a fictional technique. The final chapter, 'Beyond Realism: The Eruption of the Crowd', examines the collectivist vision which came to dominate literary sensibilities.

1175 **Modern Chinese women writers: critical appraisals.**
Edited with an introduction by Michael S. Duke. Armonk, New York; London: M. E. Sharpe, 1989. 272p.

Provides scholarly essays on fourteen Chinese women writers and an American woman writer of Chinese descent, with an introduction giving useful background and references. Topics include: Ding Ling's 'Mother'; Eileen Chang and Maxine Hong Kingston; Chen Ruoxi (Ch'en Jo-hsi); Li Ang; Zhang Jie; Zhang Kangkang; Zhu Lin; Shen Rong; Zhang Xinxin; three Hong Kong women writers; the image of young female intellectuals in post-Mao women's fiction; and feminist consciousness in Chinese male fiction since the 1920s.

1176 **Worlds apart: recent Chinese writing and its audiences.**
Edited by Howard Goldblatt. Armonk, New York; London:
M. E. Sharpe, 1990. 253p. (Studies on Contemporary China).

A compilation of thirteen scholarly essays. Part one includes five background essays. Part two comprises studies on: *The Bus-Stop*, a play by Gao Xingjian; the poets Yang Lian, Zheng Chouyu and Huang Guobin; and the fiction of Li Ang. Part three includes two remarkable critical essays: Michael S. Duke's 'The Problematic Nature of Modern and Contemporary Chinese Fiction in English Translation'; and W. J. F. Jenner's 'Insuperable Barriers? Some Thoughts on the Reception of Chinese Writing in English Translation'. Jenner proposes that we recognize the fact that Chinese literature in English translation is of little interest to general readers; most is of primarily documentary interest, is derivative or prolix (Chinese writers are paid by the word). In addition, it is often clumsily translated with 'unsayable dialogue, ineptly chosen vocabulary, and sentences and paragraphs strung together with little respect for the living idioms, the natural structures, the rhythms, and the ebb and flow of any of the varieties of English'.

1177 **Modern Chinese literature in the May Fourth era.**
Edited by Merle Goldman. Cambridge, Massachusetts: Harvard
University Press, 1977. 464p. (Harvard East Asian Series).

These seventeen essays from a 1974 conference and workshop discuss how the 'new' literature of the 1910-20s synthesized Chinese literary tradition with western literary romanticism, realism, naturalism and symbolism; many remain standard critical studies. Part one, 'Native and Foreign Impact', includes chapters on: the origins of modern literature; the impact of Japanese literary trends; the impact of Russian literature; and images of oppressed peoples. Part two, 'May Fourth Writers', covers: the social role of May Fourth writers; Lu Xun's education and writings; Mao Dun; Ding Ling; and Yu Dafu. Part three, 'Continuities and discontinuities', has chapters on: traditional style in urban popular fiction; Qu Qiubai's Chinese Marxist literary criticism; and change and continuity in Chinese fiction.

1178 **The unwelcome muse: Chinese literature in Shanghai and Peking, 1937-1945.**
Edward M. Gunn, Jr. New York; London: Columbia University
Press, 1980. 330p.

An historical and literary study of writing in Japanese occupied Shanghai and Beijing, during which period literature did not wither away, but adapted to a difficult situation. Many of the writers treated, such as Lu Xun's brother, Zhou Zuoren, were later reviled as collaborators, but Gunn explains the ambiguity of their position and the creativity of their work.

1179 **Rewriting Chinese: style and innovation in twentieth-century Chinese prose.**
Edward Gunn. Stanford, California: Stanford University Press,
1991. 361p. bibliog.

An historical and literary analysis of the conscious and unconscious changes in grammar, vocabulary and style of prose compositions over the last century. Gunn draws on information theory and Gestalt psychology, as well as Chinese and Western theories of rhetoric, to explain these changes as not merely technical, but as responses to larger political and cultural forces. An extensive appendix lists specific words and phrases, giving sources and commenting on their specific significance. Federico Masini, *The formation of modern Chinese lexicon and its evolution towards a national language: the period from 1840 to 1898* (Berkeley, California, 1993. 296p. [Journal of Chinese Linguistics Monograph Series, no. 6]) is a careful examination of the linguistic side of early Chinese assimilation of European and Japanese influence.

1180   **A history of modern Chinese fiction, 1917-1957.**
C. T. Hsia.   New Haven, Connecticut; London: Yale University Press, 1971. 2nd ed. 701p. bibliog.

Esteemed as the basic history of modern Chinese fiction from a humanistic and moral perspective of literary trends and concepts from the New Culture Movement through the anti-Rightist campaigns of 1957. Hsia presents biographical sketches of twenty authors, with clear summary and critical analysis of works he considers influential and skilful. Hsia favours the modernist aesthetic approach over political message or the 'obsession with China'. Part one (1917-27) covers the Literary Revolution, Lu Xun, the Literary Association (including Ye Shengtao and Bing Xin), and the Creation Society (Yu Dafu). Part two, 'A Decade of Growth (1928-1937)', deals with Mao Dun, Lao She, Shen Congwen, Ba Jin, Wu Zuxiang and Communist fiction. Part three, 'The War Period and After (1937-1957)', includes the later work of veteran writers already introduced and younger writers Eileen Chang, Qian Zhongshu, Shi To and other Communist writers. The bibliography of Chinese and English works lists surveys and histories, anthologies, bibliographies and works by the writers analysed. For a critical exchange on this book, see Prusek, *The lyrical and the epic* (q.v.).

1181   **Heroes and villains in Communist China: the contemporary Chinese novel as a reflection of life.**
Joe Huang.   London: C. Hurst, 1973; Hong Kong, Singapore, Kuala Lumpur: Heinemann Educational Books (Asia), 1977. 345p. bibliog.

Analyses the popular, all but official, novels of the 1940s-60s. Mostly based on fieldwork or research, they present a heroic, relentlessly optimistic, and sometimes readable panorama of the revolution. Huang provides detailed plot summaries, discussions of sources, and an evaluation of criticism and reception. Topics and novels (all published in Beijing by Foreign Languages Press) include: the formative years in the city and the village, such as Liang Bin's *Keep the red flag flying* (1963); the pre-1949 underground struggle, including Yang and Lo's *Red Crag* (q.v.) and Gao Yunlan's *Annals of a country town* (1959); guerrilla warfare, including Qu Bo's *Tracks in the snowy forest* (1962); the civil war, including *Red sun* (1961); land reform, including Zhou Libo's *The hurricane* (q.v.) and Ding Ling's *Sun over the Sanggan River* (q.v.); the role of the worker in the revolution; and agricultural collectivization, including Zhao Shuli's *Sanliwan village* (1964) and *Great changes in a mountain village* (1961), and Liu Qing's *The builders* (1964).

1182   **Reading the modern Chinese short story.**
Edited by Theodore Huters.   Armonk, New York; London: M. E. Sharpe, 1990. 212p.

A compilation of papers from a workshop which sought to explore the interaction of narrative theory and modern Chinese short fiction, together with translations of five stories. The editor's introduction sets the problem: how do we find the critical tools to understand why Chinese post-May Fourth fiction was appealing to its audience, but did not live up to the hopes of its originators? Essays illustrate critical approaches to stories by Lao She, Xiao Jun, Mao Dun, Shi Tuo, Ru Zhijuan and Zhu Xining.

1183 **Literary authority and the modern Chinese writer.**
Wendy Larson. Durham, North Carolina; London: Duke University Press, 1991. 209p.

Writers in the late 1920s and early 1930s lost Confucian self-confidence and came to look down upon the professional activity of writing. Larson reads autobiographies and novels, and finds that writers propose four positive alternatives to mere intellectual status: manual labour; physical revolutionary work; physical military work; and a redefinition of writing that puts it in the socio-material world; they do not see the peasant as an alternative role model. Writers studied include Shen Congwen, Ba Jin, Hu Shi, Lu Xun and Guo Moruo.

1184 **The romantic generation of Chinese modern writers.**
Leo Ou-fan Lee. Cambridge, Massachusetts: Harvard University Press, 1973. 365p. bibliog. (Harvard East Asian Series, no. 71).

A rich history and critical appreciation of the generation of writers who used European romantic life-styles and literature to rebel against tradition and change China. Part one, 'The Setting', discusses the emergence of the 'literary scene' and the *wenren*, or literati, such as Lin Shu (1852-1924) and Su Man-shu (1884-1918). In Part two, Lee then adapts insights from Eric Erickson's life-cycle psychology to present the lives of flamboyant romantic poets Yu Dafu (Yü Ta-fu; 1896-1945) and Xu Zhimo (Hsu Chih-mo; 1898-1931). Part three, 'The Romantic Left', looks more briefly at Guo Moruo (Kuo Mo-juo; 1892-1979), Jiang Kuangzu and Xiao Jun (Hsiao Chun). Part four, 'The Romantic Generation: Variations on a Theme', reflects on the modern *wenren* (literati), Chinese society and the Romantic heritage.

1185 **Voices from the iron house: a study of Lu Xun.**
Leo Ou-fan Lee. Bloomington, Indiana: Indiana University Press, 1987. 254p. (Studies in Chinese Literature and Society).

A vibrant psychological, intellectual and literary biography. Lee argues that Lu Xun (pseud. of Zhou Shuren; 1881-1936), was 'not a systematic or even a coherent thinker', but transcended revolutionary messages to transform his ideas into artistic structures of meaning and had a complex relation to politics. Lee examines Lu Xun's early years and his classical studies to show how they prepared him for the great works of the middle period, which are meticulously scrutinized in terms of influence, image, metaphor and archetype. Earlier or specialized studies include William Lyell, Jr., *Lu Hsün's vision of reality* (Berkeley, California; Los Angeles; London: University of California Press, 1976. 355p.). *Lu Xun and his legacy*, edited by Leo Ou-fan Lee (Berkeley, California; Los Angeles; Oxford: University of California Press, 1985. 324p.) is a symposium whose topics include: Lu Xun and patterns of literary sponsorship; the political use of Lu Xun in the Cultural Revolution; Hu Feng and the critical legacy of Lu Xun; the morality of the mind and the immorality of politics – reflections on Lu Xun the intellectual; Lu Xun in Japan; and Lu Xun as a scholar of traditional Chinese literature.

1186　**Mandarin ducks and butterflies: popular fiction in early twentieth century Chinese cities.**
E. Perry Link, Jr.　Berkeley, California; Los Angeles; London: University of California Press, 1981. 313p.

In order to understand the mindset of a new urban middle class of the 1910s and 1920s, Link studies the best-selling fiction which was disparaged by intellectuals as tawdry and lacking in social utility: love stories (known as 'mandarin duck and butterfly novels' for their use of this classical symbol of star-crossed lovers); martial arts tales; detective novels; and scandal fiction. Chapters cover: the love stories of the 1910s; the rise of the fiction press (the early growth of modern printing and newspapers in Shanghai); the passage from Liang Qichao's advocacy of modern fiction as nation-building to fiction for 'time killing' to fiction for profit; the life-styles, group organization and outlook of authors and readers; and an afterword on popular fiction in China in 1979.

1187　**Translingual practice: literature, national culture, and translated modernity – China, 1900-1937.**
Lydia H. Liu.　Stanford, California: Stanford University Press, 1995. 474p. bibliog.

Language and literature are analysed as discourses which both reflected and shaped the struggle between Western domination and Chinese anti-imperialism as the nature of 'culture' was being contested. Liu focuses on Liang Qichao, Lu Xun, Lao She, Ding Ling and Xiao Hong. The introduction surveys the problem of language in cross-cultural studies. Chapters discuss: the introduction into China, translation and shaping of foreign words and practices; Lu Xun and the concept of 'national character' in Arthur Smith's *Chinese characteristics* (1894); the discourse of 'individualism'; novelistic realism and writing in the first person; nation building and culture building; and the 1930s formation of the 'modern' canon in literature. Appendices list and classify over 1,800 loanwords and neologisms taken from English, Russian and Japanese.

1188　**Marxist literary thought in China: the influence of Ch'ü Ch'iu-pai.**
Paul G. Pickowicz.　Berkeley, California; Los Angeles; London: University of California Press, 1981. 259p.

The author shows how Marxist literary theory replaced romanticism, realism and other liberal Western schools in China. Qu Qiubai (1899-1935) was China's most significant Marxist literary critic and was briefly head of the Chinese Communist Party. Pickowicz focuses on Qu's life and literary thought, recounting: his youth; his journey to revolutionary Russia in the early 1920s; the introduction of Marxist literary thought; the Leftist literary scene; and romanticism, realism and proletarianism. Chapters also cover Qu's activity as Commissioner of Education in the Jiangxi Soviet before his capture and execution by Nationalist troops. The leftist literary scene is explored in: Wang-chi Wong, *Politics and literature in Shanghai: the Chinese League of Left-wing Writers, 1930-1936* (Manchester, England; New York: Manchester University Press, distributed by St. Martin's Press, 1991. 254p.); and Ng Mao-san, *The Russian hero in modern Chinese fiction* (Hong Kong: Chinese University Press; Albany, New York: State University of New York Press, 1988. 332p.).

1189   **The lyrical and the epic: studies of modern Chinese literature.**
Jaroslav Prusek, edited by Leo Ou-fan Lee.   Bloomington, Indiana:
Indiana University Press, 1980. 268p.

Provides nine essays on the social history and analysis of Chinese prose writings by the
leading Czech scholar of Chinese literature. Prusek sensitively deploys a scientific
approach to literature inspired by socialist humanism, a position he debated with C. T.
Hsia in an exchange reprinted here from *T'oung Pao*, no. 49 (1961-62) and no. 50 (1963).

1190   **Inside a service trade: studies in contemporary Chinese prose.**
Rudolf G. Wagner.   Cambridge, Massachusetts: Council on East
Asian Studies, Harvard University Press, 1992. 558p. bibliog.
(Harvard-Yenching Monographs, no. 34).

A pace-setting, multifaceted exploration of the role of professional writers in the
People's Republic and their literary products. Wagner contrasts the Western ideal of
the independent creative artist with that of the Chinese writer who is supported by the
state and expected to 'serve the people' with 'politics in command'. Individual post-
1949 works are then studied in both political and literary contexts.

1191   **Fictional realism in twentieth century China: Mao Dun, Lao She,
Shen Congwen.**
David Wang.   New York: Columbia University Press, 1992. 567p.

In the May Fourth period, Lu Xun and his cohort established realism as the literary
mode most favoured by fiction writers. After Lu Xun, writers developed their own
voices within this realist discourse. Wang here examines the historical and political
fiction of Mao Dun (such as *Rainbow*), the farce and melodrama of Lao She (such as
Cat Country and *Rickshaw*) and the 'critical lyricism' of Shen Congwen. Each body of
writing is examined both for political content and in formal literary terms, using
contemporary critical theory.

1192   **From May Fourth to June Fourth: fiction and film in twentieth
century China.**
Edited by Ellen Widmer, David Der-wei Wang.   Cambridge,
Massachusetts; London: Harvard University Press, 1993. 435p.
(Harvard Contemporary China Series).

These twelve essays from a conference held in 1990 consider whether and how post-
Cultural Revolution literature shows continuity with the 1920s; both periods sought to
liberate literature from orthodoxies, looked abroad for inspiration, and sought to free the
'self' from (Confucian or Maoist) social conformity. In part one, 'Country and City',
essays address: Han Shaogong's fiction; Mo Yan's fiction of the 1980s; Shen
Congwen's legacy in the 1980s; 'imaginary nostalgia' in Shen Congwen, Song Zelai,
Mo Yan and Li Yongping; and urban exoticism in modern and contemporary literature.
Essays in part two, 'Subjectivity and Gender', treat: the representation of the 'writing
self' in Lu Xun, Yu Dafu and Wang Meng; the making of a female tradition; and living
in sin from May Fourth to the present. Part three, 'Narrative Voice and Cinematic
Vision', includes essays on: the use of myths of creation by Lu Xun, Zhang Xinxin and
Han Shaogong; the authorial voice in modern and contemporary literature;
melodramatic representation and the 'May Fourth tradition' of Chinese cinema; and
male narcissism and national culture in Chen Kaige's film *King of the Children* (1987).

1193 **Village echoes: the fiction of Wu Zuxiang.**
Philip F. Williams. Boulder, Colorado; San Francisco; Oxford:
Westview Press, 1993. 303p.

Wu Zuxiang (1908-), although not a Marxist, was among the most widely read writers of the 1920s and 1930s who helped to fix an image of the helpless and exploited village. Williams' life and detailed literary explications put Wu into context; the gap between the city and the countryside was at first a geographical one, then in the later writings becomes a chronological gap between the modern, desolate city and the golden age of the village past. Wu depicted Anhui village life and conflict, but emerges as a 'meliorist' whose stance was more cultural than political; he stopped writing fiction in 1942, and lived to be interviewed for this book. Wu Zuxiang, *Green bamboo heritage* (Beijing: Panda Books, 1989. 259p.) contains ten stories from the 1930s and 1940s, including 'Eighteen hundred piculs', his famous depiction of rural exploitation.

The gate of heavenly peace: the Chinese and their revolution, 1895-1980.
See item no. 120.

A bibliography of studies and translations of Modern Chinese literature (1918-1942).
See item no. 1489.

Bibliography of English translations and critiques of contemporary Chinese fiction, 1945-1992.
See item no. 1495.

Contemporary Chinese novels and short stories, 1949-1974: an annotated bibliography.
See item no. 1500.

Modern Chinese fiction: a guide to its study and appreciation: essays and bibliographies.
See item no. 1502.

Classical poetry

1194 **Popular songs and ballads of Han China.**
Anne Birrell. London: Unwin Hyman, 1988. Reprinted, Honolulu:
University of Hawaii Press, 1993. paperback ed. 226p. maps.

Presents seventy-seven *yuefu* songs and ballads from the Han dynasty. *Yuefu*, one of the longest lasting poetic forms, were developed from the 'folk' songs and ballads supposedly gathered by the official Bureau of Music (*yue* = music, *fu* = bureau). Birrell's introduction, which is aimed at the general reader of poetry, provides a sketch of Han dynasty culture, explains the origins and activities of the Bureau of Music, and discusses the genre's later growth. She also considers the oral nature of these songs, their singers, and the musical aspects of their art. Joseph R. Allen, *In the voice of others: Chinese Music Bureau poetry* (Ann Arbor, Michigan: Center for

Chinese Studies, University of Michigan, 1990. 292p. [Michigan Monographs in Chinese Studies]) shows how this convention was created by poets writing in older forms *as if* they were folk forms and studies the development of the tradition dynasty by dynasty, with many translations and commentaries on individual poems.

1195   **The evolution of Chinese tz'u poetry from late T'ang to Northern Sung.**
Kang-i Sun Chang.   Princeton, New Jersey: Princeton University Press, 1980. 251p.

The *ci* poetic genre – 'song-words' – developed in the Tang dynasty from the practice of setting new words to tunes from Central Asia. Chang considers the theories of its origins, explains the technical aspects, and assesses the poets who were important in its evolution, including Wen Tingyun (813?-70), Wei Zhuang (836-910), Li Yu (937-78), Liu Yong (fl. 1034) and Su Shi (1037-1101). Marsha Wagner, *The lotus boat: origins of Chinese tz'u poetry in T'ang popular culture* (New York: Columbia University Press, 1984. 199p.) focuses on the role of the performers. The standard earlier study is James J. Y. Liu, *Major lyricists of the Northern Sung* (Princeton, New Jersey: Princeton University Press, 1974. 215p.), which examines the *ci* form in the work of six major poets, including Ouyang Xiu (1007-72), Liu Yong, Su Shi and Zhou Bangyan (1056-1121).

1196   **The late-Ming poet Ch'en Tzu-lung: crisis of love and loyalism.**
Kang-yi Sun Chang.   New Haven, Connecticut; London: Yale University Press, 1991. 183p.

Chen Zilong (1608-47) was loyal to (and died for) the Ming dynasty in the time of the Manchu invasions and became a hero of Confucian patriotism. Chang's study contends that his literary contribution is also considerable; she finds that Chen used poetry to frame impending defeat in terms of both patriotism and romantic love. His romance with the poet and courtesan Liu Shi, long concealed by historians, demonstrates the belief that emotional purity sustains and redeems the full meaning of life. Part one discusses loyalism and changing ideals of romantic love, late Ming images of women, and the history of the relation between Chen and Liu. Parts two and three examine love and loyalty in *ci* (song lyric) and *shi* (lyric) poetic forms.

1197   **Six dynasties poetry.**
Kang-yi Sun Chang.   Princeton, New Jersey: Princeton University Press, 1986. 216p.

Contains chapter length studies of six poets, including Tao Qian, Xie Lingyun and Bao Zhao. Chang places the poets and their work into historical perspective, then presents aesthetic and critical analysis and appreciation. *Poetry and politics: the life and works of Juan Chi (210-263)*, by Donald Holzman (Cambridge, England: Cambridge University Press, 1976. 316p.) presents an engaging sinological study of Ruan Ji, one of the Seven Sages of the Bamboo Grove (*zhulin qixian*). The Seven Sages were educated literati aristocrats who took refuge in the Yangzi valley from the invasions in the north and the fall of the Han dynasty; their learned decadence opened philosophy to new influences, especially Buddhism and Daoism. Holzman sketches the historical age, examines Ruan's life, and translates eighty-two of his poems.

1198   The Columbia book of later Chinese poetry: Yüan, Ming, and
Ch'ing dynasties (1279-1911).
Translated, edited by Jonathan Chaves.   New York; London:
Columbia University Press, 1986. 483p.

Chaves' introduction observes that later Chinese poetry and painting were both neglected, each victims of a 'golden age syndrome'. This anthology redresses that situation with selections from forty-two poets, each represented by a substantial group of poems, a short biography and annotations. Another anthology presentation is Yoshikawa Kōjirō, *Five hundred years of Chinese poetry, 1150-1650: the Chin, Yuan, and Ming dynasties* (Princeton, New Jersey: Princeton University Press, 1989. 215p. [Princeton Library of Translations]). Yüan Hung-tao, translated by Jonathan Chaves, *Pilgrim of the clouds* (New York; Tokyo: Weatherhill, 1978. 143p.) includes poems and essays, together with a graceful introduction on the iconoclastic stance and Buddhism of Yuan Hongdao (1568-1610). The Qing dynasty is extensively represented in *Waiting for the unicorn: poems and lyrics of China's last dynasty, 1644-1911*, edited by Irving Yucheng Lo, William Schultz (Bloomington, Indiana; Indianapolis, Indiana: Indiana University Press, 1986. 423p.).

1199   T'ao Yuan-ming (A.D. 365-427), his works and their meaning.
A. R. Davis.   Cambridge, England: Cambridge University Press,
1983. 2 vols. bibliog. (Cambridge Studies in Chinese History,
Literature, and Institutions).

Tao Yuanming (a. k. a. Tao Qian; 365-427), was a poet and stylist of the first rank whose image helped to fix the tradition of the literary recluse. His classic 'Peach Blossom Spring' (*Taohua yuan*) tells of a fisherman who wandered into a hidden utopia where the people avoided the rigours of Qin dynasty unification. James R. Hightower, *The poetry of T'ao Ch'ien* (Oxford: Clarendon Press, 1970. 270p. [Oxford Library of East Asian Literatures]) perceptively translates and explains Tao's poetry. *Tao Qian and the Chinese poetic tradition: the quest for cultural identity*, by Charles Yim-tze Kwong (Ann Arbor, Michigan: Center for Chinese Studies, University of Michigan, 1994. 281p. [Michigan Monographs in Chinese Studies, no. 66]) places Tao between classical tradition and later influence.

1200   Poems of the late T'ang.
Translated, with an introduction by A. C. Graham.   Harmondsworth,
England: Penguin Books, 1965. Reprinted with an additional preface,
1977. 176p.

Graham introduces poems by seven of China's greatest poets who lived in the late 8th and early 9th century (omitting Bo Juyi and Han Shan, two favourites who are translated widely elsewhere). In 'The Translation of Chinese Poetry', Graham sympathetically critiques Ezra Pound and Amy Lowell, who worked from translators' drafts; he goes on to explain the process of translation by giving word by word, image by image, examples. He argues that the selected poets – Du Fu (Tu Fu), Meng Jiao (Meng Chiao), Han Yu, Lu Tong (Lu T'ung), Li He (Li Ho), Du Mu (Tu Mu) and Li Shangyin (Li Shang-yin) – show a decisive turn towards ambiguity and allusiveness.

1201 **The poetry of Han-shan: a complete, annotated translation of Cold Mountain.**
Han-shan, translated by Robert G. Henricks. Albany, New York: State University of New York, 1990. 486p. bibliog. (SUNY Series in Buddhist Studies).

'Han Shan' – 'Cold Mountain' – was the place of refuge and name taken by a Tang dynasty Buddhist recluse, often depicted with his broom-wielding companion, Shide (Shih-te). His family name and dates are not known, but his three-hundred or so poems are recognized for their Zen sensibility which fused spirituality and nature. Henricks translates all surviving poems with notes explaining literary allusions and Buddhist references. Translations which emphasize the playful insights of the poetry include: *Cold Mountain: 100 poems by the T'ang poet Han Shan*, translated by Burton Watson (New York; London: Columbia University Press, 1970. 118p.); and *Riprap and Cold Mountain poems*, translated by Gary Snyder (San Francisco: Four Seasons Foundation, 1965. 61p.).

1202 **A little primer of Tu Fu.**
David Hawkes. Oxford: Oxford University Press, 1967. Reprinted, Hong Kong: Chinese University Press, 1990. 243p.

Demonstrates 'what Chinese poetry is really like and how it works to people who either know no Chinese at all or know only a little'. Du Fu (712-770) is considered, together with his friend Li Bo, China's pre-eminent poet. Hawkes translates all of Du's thirty-five poems contained in the standard 18th-century anthology, *Three hundred Tang poems*; other translations of these poems appear in standard anthologies. Each poem is printed in Chinese characters, with interlinear phonetic transliterations, commentaries, identification of allusions, a word by word exegesis and translations into English prose 'intended as cribs'. A classic and enduring life and times, with many translations, is William Hung, *Tu Fu: China's greatest poet* (Cambridge, Massachusetts: Harvard University Press, 1952. 300p.).

1203 **The songs of the south: an anthology of ancient Chinese poems by Qu Yuan and other poets.**
Translated by David Hawkes. Harmondsworth, England: Penguin Books, 1985. rev. ed. 352p. maps.

One of the two basic ancient anthologies of poetry: the other, the *Shijing*, or Book of Poetry, represented the Northern style, while the *Chuci*, 'Songs of Chu' or 'Songs of the South', represented the romantic style of the State of Chu in the lush Central Yangzi valley. Hawkes first presents background for the general reader, explaining, for instance, the role of shamanism in Chu religion, then elegantly translates and annotates the poems. About half of them are attributed to Qu Yuan (403-221 BCE), the loyal minister who drowned himself in moral protest to his ruler. Famous poems include 'Li sao' (On encountering trouble), 'Tian wen' (Heavenly questions) and 'Zhao hun' (Summons of the soul).

1204 **The art of Chinese poetry.**
James J. Y. Liu. Chicago: University of Chicago Press, 1962. 165p.

An elegant introduction to Chinese poetry, aimed at the general reader of literature. The volume opens with 'The Chinese Language as a Medium of Poetic Expression', then explores traditional views of Chinese poetry, with many examples, finishing with a concise, thoughtful consideration of how to synthesize various approaches. Liu's

The interlingual critic: interpreting Chinese poetry (Bloomington, Indiana: Indiana University Press, 1982. 132p.) treats these themes and the theory of translation in a work intended for a more scholarly audience. Taken with Liu's *Chinese theories of literature* (q.v.), these form an excellent introduction for the serious reader.

1205 **Sunflower splendor: three thousand years of Chinese poetry.**
Edited by Liu Wu-chi, Irving Yucheng Lo. New York: Doubleday, Anchor Books, 1975. Reprinted, Bloomington, Indiana: Indiana University Press, 1990. 634p. bibliog.

Contains about a thousand poems in translations commissioned from over fifty contributors. All major genres and periods are featured, and within each, the chief exponents of major schools of Chinese poetry are included, with preference to poems not previously translated. Sections include: 'In the Beginning: the Legacy of *Shi* and *Sao*' (12th-3rd centuries BCE); 'A World Fragmented: Multiple Voices in a Period of Intellectual Foment' (3rd century BCE-6th century CE); 'Expanding Horizons and the Full Flowering of the *Shi*' (Tang dynasty); 'Cross Pollination of the *Ci* or Lyric Meters' (10th-13th centuries); 'The Rise of the *Sanqu* or Song-poems' (Mongol-ruled society, 1234-1368); and 'In the Long Tradition: Accommodation and Challenge' (Ming and Qing dynasties and the Republic). The last poet translated is Mao Zedong. There is an extensive listing of English-language translations, general works and studies of individual poets. Burton Watson, *The Columbia book of Chinese poetry: from early times to the thirteenth century* (New York: Columbia University Press, 1984. 385p.) is an anthology which features Watson's earlier translations.

1206 **Remembrances: the experience of the past in classical Chinese poetry.**
Stephen Owen. Cambridge, Massachusetts: Harvard University Press, 1986. 147p.

A thematic anthology of poetry and prose, with commentaries and accompanying essays by the author, which provides the history and highlights of the literary form called *huaigu* ('remembrance of the past'). Owen gracefully sketches the framework for the pieces, discusses the literary issues in comparative perspective, and sensitively evokes shifting Chinese senses of the past – contemplation, evocation, reminiscence and longing. Writers treated include the essayist Ouyang Xiu, and the poets Tao Qian, Meng Haoran, Du Mu and Li Qingzhao. See also Han Frankel, 'The Contemplation of the Past in T'ang Poetry' in *Perspectives on the T'ang* (q.v.).

1207 **The great age of Chinese poetry: the high T'ang.**
Stephen Owen. New Haven, Connecticut; London: Yale University Press, 1981. 440p. bibliog.

The standard study for the serious general reader or student. Owen provides the historical background of the age, literary developments, critical perspectives, lives of the leading poets (especially Li Bo and Du Fu) and extensive references to secondary literature. This work forms a series with Owen's two other volumes: *The poetry of the early T'ang* (New Haven, Connecticut: Yale University Press, 1977. 455p.), which comprehensively presents the poetry, largely written at the court, which prepared the way for the following Golden Age; and *The poetry of Meng Chiao and Han Yü* (New Haven, Connecticut; London: Yale University Press, 1975. 294p.), which deals with two poets of the middle period.

1208   **Traditional Chinese poetry and poetics: omen of the world.**
Stephen Owen.   Madison, Wisconsin: University of Wisconsin
Press, 1985. 303p.

An imaginative and learned introduction for the serious but not specialist reader to the art of Chinese poetry. Owen presents an excursion into the experience of reading classical Chinese poems of the 8th to 11th centuries, particularly the *shi*, or lyric, paying particular attention to Chinese and western use of metaphor, allegory and analogy. Owen does not invoke historical reading rules, but experiments with recreating how Chinese readers experienced particular poems, with digressions into personal commentaries. Literary theory and insights are drawn both from traditional Chinese critics and from the contemporary West, with the aim of forging new frameworks. Poets examined include Bo Juyi, Du Fu, Li He, Li Bo, Meng Jiao, Qu Yuan, Su Shi, Tao Qian, Wang Anshi and Wang Wei.

1209   **The Confucian odes: the classic anthology defined by Confucius.**
Ezra Pound.   Cambridge, Massachusetts: Harvard University Press,
1954. Reprinted, New York: New Directions, 1959. 306p.

A classic translation. The *Odes*, or 'Classic of poetry' (*Shijing*), was an anthology of some three hundred Zhou dynasty poems, one of the Classics. From the publication of his first translations from the Chinese in *Cathay* (1915), Ezra Pound was inspired by the misconception that Chinese characters were pictures – false theory, true poetry. Other estimable translations include: Arthur Waley, *The book of songs* (London: Allen & Unwin, 1937; New York: Grove, 1960. 349p.); and James Legge, in *The Chinese classics*, vol. 4 (q.v), which contains a Chinese text.

1210   **The orchid boat: women poets of China.**
Edited by Kenneth Rexroth, Ling Chung.   New York; London:
McGraw-Hill, 1972. 150p.

Contains 120 poems by women from all periods, together with a brief essay on Chinese women and literature. Included are: early anonymous poets; Cai Yan (162?-239?), considered to be the first great woman poet; Empress Wu; and Li Qingzhao (1084?-1151), the most highly regarded woman poet. The translations are lively and generally reliable, though often more sexual than the original Chinese. Rexroth and Chung also collaborated on *Li Ch'ing-chao: complete poems* (New York: New Directions, 1979. 118p.). *Brocade river poems: selected works of the Tang dynasty courtesan Xue Tao* (Princeton, New Jersey: Princeton University Press, 1987. 110p.), translated and introduced by Jeanne Larsen, presents the work of Xue Tao (Hsueh T'ao; 768-832).

1211   **One hundred poems from the Chinese.**
Translated by Kenneth Rexroth.   New York: New Directions, 1959.
160p.

Rexroth is an American poet whose translations are widely appreciated for their poetic vitality. However, they are often criticized for not understanding the literal meanings of the poet and for introducing more overt eroticism than is present in the original, where sensuality is indirect. This volume contains thirty-five poems by Du Fu and eighty-five by Song dynasty poets. *Love and the turning year: one hundred more poems from the Chinese* (New York: New Directions, 1970. 140p.) includes poems from earlier and later dynasties.

1212   **Translations from the Chinese.**
Arthur Waley.   New York: Knopf, 1941. 325p.

Gathers poems from Waley's *170 Chinese poems* (1918) and *More translations from the Chinese* (1937). Waley was *the* translator of Chinese and Japanese literature for English-language readers of his time; he translated poems with which he felt an affinity, mostly those of a 'gentle and reflective attitude' which he thought would go well into English. The translations here range from poems from the earliest times down to the Tang, with a few later essays and short stories. Also included is a brief biography of and extensive translations from Bo Juyi (Po Chu-yi; 772-846). Waley's life, writings and influence are memorably treated in essays by various hands in *Madly singing in the mountains: an appreciation of Arthur Waley*, edited by Ivan Morris (London: Allen & Unwin; New York: Walker, 1970. 403p.), which includes a good selection from Waley's translations.

1213   **Chinese rhyme-prose: poems in the *fu* form from the Han and Six Dynasties periods.**
Burton Watson.   New York; London: Columbia University Press, 1971. 128p. bibliog. (UNESCO Collection of Representative Works, Chinese Series).

A dependable and enjoyable introduction. The *fu* (rhyme-prose) poetic form flourished in the Han dynasty and for a few centuries after its fall; the form was characteristic of the court and aristocracy, emphasizing florid rhetoric and fantastic subjects. Watson provides the general reader with historical background and a sketch of the origins, and translates a representative selection. Poets include Jia I (Chia Yi), Sima Xiangru (Ssu-ma Hsiang-ju), Cao Zhi (Ts'ao Chih) and Bao Zhao (Pao Chao). *Wen xuan, or Selections of Refined Literature*, by Xiao Tong (Hsiao T'ung; 501-531), translated with annotations and introduction by David R. Knechtges (Princeton, New Jersey: Princeton University Press, 1982, 1987. 2 vols.) contains the first two volumes, covering the *fu* (future volumes will cover other genres), from the Six Dynasties anthology which collected and defined early literature. The extensive introductions and annotations make this a basic reference.

1214   **Chinese lyricism: *shih* poetry from the second to the twelfth century.**
Burton Watson.   New York; London: Columbia University Press, 1971. 232p. (Companions to Asia Series).

The *shi*, or lyric poem, is the most popular and enduring of the three basic forms of Chinese poetry (along with the *fu* and the *ci*). Watson traces its development and historical background from the late Han revival of ancient forms to its height in the Song. Chapters topics include: the nineteen 'old poems' of the Han; *yuefu* (pseudo-folk songs); the poetry of reclusion (Tao Qian, Ruan Ji, Xie Lingyun) and friendship; the poetry of love; Li Bo and Du Fu; Buddhist quietism (Wang Wei, Han Shan); the middle Tang (Han Yu, Bo Juyi); the Tang twilight (Li He, Li Shangyin); and poetry of the Song. *The vitality of the lyric voice: shih poetry from the late Han to the T'ang*, edited by Shuen-fu Lin, Stephen Owen (Princeton, New Jersey: Princeton University Press, 1986. 405p.) is a productive scholarly symposium.

1215 **Washing silk: the life and selected poetry of Wei Chuang (834?-910).**
Robin D. S. Yates. Cambridge, Massachusetts; London: Council on East Asian Studies, Harvard University, distributed by Harvard University Press, 1988. 289p. bibliog. (Harvard-Yenching Institute Monograph Series, no. 26).

An appealing life, work and times. Wei Zhuang was a poet during the late Tang dynasty, and helped to shape the *ci* poetic form which developed from the practice of setting new words to melodies from Central Asia. Part one provides a study of Wei's life as an official in tumultuous times; the Huang Chao rebellion drove the court to exile and debauchery in Sichuan. Part two illuminates Wei's use of the *ci* form and the way in which its conventions differed from those of *shi*, or 'regular poems'. Part three, 'Selected Translations', translates into attractive English all of the *ci* considered genuine and 110 of Wei's *shi* poems, with helpful annotations. An appendix, list of poems' locations, bibliography and glossary offer help to scholars.

1216 **An introduction to Sung poetry.**
Yoshikawa Kōjirō, translated by Burton Watson. Cambridge, Massachusetts: Harvard University Press, 1967. 191p.

An eminent Japanese scholar introduces the poetry of the Song dynasty to a general readership. Yoshikawa sketches the background of society and politics, then introduces the major figures and the forms in which they worked. He compares Tang poetry to wine, Song poetry to tea. A charming biography and sophisticated literary history is presented by Jonathan Chaves, *Mei Yao-ch'en and the development of early Sung poetry* (New York; London: Columbia University Press, 1976. 254p.). *Heaven my blanket, earth my pillow*, by Yang Wan-li (1127-1206), translated, with an introduction by Jonathan Chaves (New York; Tokyo: Weatherhill, 1975. 118p.) offers a biography and poems. *Song-poems From Xanadu* by James Crump (Ann Arbor, Michigan: Center for Chinese Studies, 1993. 138p. bibliog. [Michigan Monographs in Chinese Studies, no. 64]) presents and deftly translates 120 of the short lyric poems which swept China in the late Song and early Yuan dynasties, with a brief introduction which sets the stage.

1217 **Voices of the song lyric in China.**
Edited by Pauline Yu. Berkeley, California; Los Angeles; Oxford: University of California Press, 1994. 410p. (Studies on China, no. 18).

A symposium from a 1990 conference on the *ci* (*tz'u*), or 'song lyric', from its origins in a popular tradition of performance songs from Central Asia, through the formation of a tradition of literary authors using those forms for their own compositions, to the 19th century. Part one comprises three essays defining the song lyric voice in the early centuries. Three essays in part two, 'Man's Voice/Woman's Voice: Questions of Gender', take up the implications of the fact that the original performers were women, the voice of the song was female, but later authors were men. Part three, 'From Voice to Text: Questions of Genealogy', contains four essays, which discuss: the problem of the reputation of the *ci*; the context of the *ci* (communications technology, social change, morality); the *ci* of Wang Guowei (1827-1927); and the problems involved in textual transmission. Anthologies of *ci* include: *Among the flowers: a translation of the tenth-century anthology of tz'u lyrics, The Hua-chien chi*, edited and translated by Lois Fusek (New York; London: Columbia University Press, 1982. 232p.); and

Beyond spring: tz'u *poems of the Sung dynasty,* translated by Julie Landau (New York; London: Columbia University Press, 1994. 267p. [Translations from the Asian Classics]).

1218 **The poetry of Wang Wei: new translations and commentary.**
Pauline Yu. Bloomington, Indiana: Indiana University Press, 1980. 274p.

Presents the poems and life of Wang Wei (699-759), a physician, court official, landscape painter, and one of the Tang dynasty's most treasured poets, known for his mystic evocations and Buddhism. Yu first tells what is known of the poet's life and the background of his age, then gives her own gifted translations, with poem by poem commentaries. *Hiding the universe: poems by Wang Wei* (New York: Grossman, 1972. 131p.) provides translations by Wai-lim Yip, a noted poet and critic. *Poems by Wang Wei,* translated by Chang Yin-nan, Lewis C. Walmsley (Rutland, Vermont; Tokyo: Charles E. Tuttle, 1958. 159p.) is impressionistic and less successful.

1219 **The reading of imagery in the Chinese poetic tradition.**
Pauline Yu. Princeton, New Jersey: Princeton University Press, 1987. 239p.

An important theoretical study of ideas and techniques of poetic meaning, principally concerned with the Tang period. Yu first surveys Western literary criticism, with an emphasis on recent literary-critical studies. She then defines the ways in which Western concepts, especially metaphor and allegory, do not help to understand Chinese poetry and criticism. Subsequent chapters show how Chinese critical readers approach the *Shijing, Lisao* and early poets as direct responses to reality cast in literary convention, looking for 'categorical correspondence', as in the *Ijing,* not metaphor. Chapters deal with the highlights of poetry and poetic thought in the Han, Six dynasties, and Tang. Many of the works discussed are translated.

Word, image, and deed in the life of Su Shih.
See item no. 346.

The road to East Slope: the development of Su Shi's poetic voice.
See annotation to item no. 346.

Su Tung-p'o: selections from a Sung dynasty poet.
See annotation to item no. 346.

The poet Kao Ch'i (1336-1374).
See item no. 351.

The life and times of Po Chu-yi, 772-846.
See item no. 357.

The poetry and career of Li Po, 701-762 A.D.
See item no. 358.

Yuan Mei: eighteenth century Chinese poet.
See item no. 359.

Guide to Chinese poetry and drama.
See item no. 1467.

Modern poetry

1220 Selected poems of Ai Qing.

Ai Qing, edited by Eugene Eoyang. Bloomington, Indiana: Indiana
University Press, 1982. 457p.

Ai Qing (pseud. of Jiang Haicheng; 1910-96) studied painting in Hangzhou, spent
time in France, returned to Shanghai in 1932, joined the Left-wing Writers League,
was jailed, and went to Yan'an before joining the Party in 1945. He was among those
who introduced European style symbolism and modernism. Eoyang introduces Ai and
his poetry, with an emphasis on literary issues, and presents extensive translations.

1221 Old snow.

Bei Dao, translated by Bonnie S. McDougall, Chen Maiping. New
York: New Directions, 1991. 81p.

Bei Dao (pseud. of Zhao Zhenkai; 1949-) is a leading member of the *Jintian* (Today)
group of writers which emerged in the 1970s atmosphere of experiment and
modernism. Other volumes of his poetry include: *The August sleepwalker*, translated
by Bonnie S. McDougall (London: Anvil, 1988. 140p.); and *Notes from the city of the
sun: poems by Bei Dao*, edited, translated by Bonnie S. McDougall (Ithaca, New
York: China-Japan Program, Cornell University, 1984. rev. ed. 118p. [Cornell East
Asia Papers]). Seven of his short stories appear in Zhao Zhenkai, *Waves*, translated by
Bonnie S. McDougall, Susette Ternent Cooke (Hong Kong: Chinese University Press,
1985. 234p.). Stephen Owen, 'The Anxiety of Global Influence: What is World
Poetry?' (*New Republic*, vol. 203, no. 21 [19 November 1990], p. 28-32) contends that
Bei Dao's poetry appeals directly to non-Chinese audiences across translation with its
active language and powerful images rather than working within Chinese traditions;
this assertion is controverted in Chow, *Writing diaspora* (q.v.).

1222 A splintered mirror: Chinese poetry from the Democracy Movement.

Translated by Donald Finkel, with additional translations by Carolyn
Kizer. San Francisco: North Star Press, 1991. 117p.

An anthology, accompanied by a brief preface and biographical notes, of poets who
emerged in the 1980s and often wrote in the 'misty' (*menglong*) or, as the translators
suggest, 'imagist' vein. Prominent are: Bei Dao, Duoduo (pseud. of Li Shizheng;
1951-), Gu Cheng, Jiang He, Mang Ke, Shu Ting and Yang Lian. Their rise to
political prominence is presented in *Beijing street voices: the poetry and politics of
China's democracy movement*, edited by David S. G. Goodman (London; Boston,
Masachusetts: Marion Boyars, 1981. 202p. bibliog.), which describes the April 1976
Tiananmen demonstrations commemorating Zhou Enlai, and collects and introduces
wall posters and verse from 1978-79, including much material from *Jintian* (Today)
magazine. In addition to entries in this section under individual authors, translations
include: *Looking out from death: from the Cultural Revolution to Tiananmen Square*,
by Duoduo, translated by Gregory Lee, John Cayley (London: Bloomsbury, 1989.
125p.); and *The red azalea: Chinese poetry since the Cultural Revolution*, edited by
Edward Morin, translated by Fang Dai, Dennis Ding, Edward Morin, introduction by
Leo Oufan Lee (Honolulu: University of Hawaii Press, 1991. 235p. bibliog.). *Under-
sky underground: Chinese writing today*, edited by Henry Y. H. Zhao, John Cayley

(London: Wellsweep, 1994. 247p.) selects fiction, essays and poems from the first six issues of *Jintian* (Today) after it recommenced publication in Sweden in 1990.

1223 Selected poems.
Gu Cheng, edited by Seán Golden, Chu Chiyu. Hong Kong: Chinese University Press, 1990. 181p. (A Renditions Paperback).

Gu Cheng (1956-93) was another leading member of the *Jintian* (Today) group which emerged in the 1970s Democracy Wall Movement; he committed suicide in New Zealand. His poetry is wide-ranging in inspiration, form and content, often called 'misty' (*menglong*). This authorized translation includes: a·specially written preface by the author; 'An Autobiographical Montage'; early lyrics; 'The Bulin File', poems about a character Gu created as a boy in the mode of the Monkey King and Don Quixote; 'A Eulogy World: A Poem Cycle'; 'Quicksilver: A Poem Cycle'; 'Misty Mondō', a series of questions and answers about 'misty' poetry; and a brief biographical 'Afterword' by the translators.

1224 Paths in dreams: selected prose and poetry of Ho Ch'i-fang.
Ho Ch'i-fang, translated by Bonnie S. McDougall. St. Lucia: University of Queensland Press, distributed by Prentice-Hall International, 1976. 244p. (Asian and Pacific Writing).

He Qifang (1911-77) joined the revolution in Yan'an in 1937 after trying many different political approaches and literary stances. McDougall's biography and anthology focuses on the period 1931-42, the years of He's greatest productivity, with poems, prose poems and essays. The introduction describes He's early life and times in Sichuan, new literary movements 1917-37, and his move from literature into politics during the war of resistance against Japan. He's poems and descriptions of life in the countryside are especially vivid and thoughtful.

1225 Dai Wangshu: the life and poetry of a Chinese modernist.
Gregory Lee. Hong Kong: Chinese University Press, 1989. 362p.

A full critical study and biography of a major modernist poet. Dai Wangshu (1905-50) was of a generation which used both Chinese and Western poetic traditions. His youthful dissatisfaction with Chinese tradition led him to appropriate from French Romanticism, Spanish Surrealism and Neo-Symbolism, but he integrated them with Chinese poetic forms and references. Lee argues, contrary to many People's Republic scholars, that Dai's radical political sympathies date from the 1920s but that he maintained independence of the CCP and the Shanghai League of Left-Wing Writers. Modernist poets who followed after Dai include Ai Qing, He Qifang and Bian Zhilin, for whom see Lloyd Haft's well-regarded study, *Pien Chih-lin: a study in modern Chinese poetry* (Dordrecht, the Netherlands; Cinnaminson, New Jersey: Foris, 1983. 210p.).

1226 Red candle: selected poems.
Wen I-to, translated by Tao Tao Sanders. London: Kape, 1972. 84p.

Wen Yiduo (1899-1946) was a leading poet and literary intellectual who made his reputation in the 1920s as a modernist with a firm command of tradition and became a literary elder statesman. He was assassinated in 1946 by right-wingers. For an insightful brief literary and personal biography, see Hsu Kai-yu, *Wen I-to* (Boston, Massachusetts: Twayne, 1980. 247p. [Twayne World Authors Series, no. 580]).

1227 **Masks and Crocodile: a contemporary Chinese poet and his poetry.**
Yang Lian, translations and introduction by Mabel Lee. Sydney: Wild Peony, 1990. 146p. (University of Sydney East Asian Series).

Lee's introduction, 'The Philosophy of the Self and Yang Lian', places Yang (1955-) in the context of the 1970-80s move to 'modernism' in Chinese poetry, and briefly describes his association with the magazine *Jintian* (Today) along with Gu Cheng, Bei Dao, Shu Ting and Jiang He. This group took part in the 1979 Democracy Wall Movement, and fused their art with their politics. In the 1980s, Yang travelled widely in China and abroad, absorbing many influences and creating bold poetic experiments, some of which Lee translates here. The body of the book provides English translations and Chinese texts of two series of poems, *Masks* and *Crocodile*.

1228 **Anthology of modern Chinese poetry.**
Edited, translated by Michelle Yeh. New Haven, Connecticut; London: Yale University Press, 1992. 245p. bibliog.

A standard anthology for both general reader and student, presenting more than 300 20th-century poems by sixty-five poets, accompanied by a substantial introduction. The selection is not meant to be comprehensive, but rather represent major trends and characteristics. There are biographical notes for each poet. The select bibliography lists books of translations and critical studies of individual poets, as well as anthologies and journal publications of further translations. An appealing and balanced earlier anthology is *Twentieth century Chinese poetry: an anthology*, translated and edited by Hsü Kai-yu (Garden City, New York: Doubleday, 1963. 434p.).

1229 **Modern Chinese poetry: theory and practice since 1917.**
Michelle Yeh. New Haven, Connecticut; London: Yale University Press, 1991. 252p. bibliog.

Discusses theoretical and artistic aspects of modern poetry, focusing on 'representative efforts and conspicuous results'. The May Fourth Movement of the 1920s saw a transition from traditional to modern; the 1930s and early 1940s brought experiments with form, imagery, metaphor and the poetics of discontinuity; in the 1960s and 1970s modern poetry was practiced largely in Taiwan; poets in both the PRC and Taiwan then entered a stage in the 1980s of 'pluralistic creative experiments and theoretical discourse'. Yeh notes that this poetry has been predominately lyric, continuing an ancient tradition; that there has been substantial continuity between developmental stages; that an 'aesthetic consciousness' valued poetry independent of all ulterior motives, insisting on the creative freedom of the poet; and that there has been a dialectical use of both foreign modernity and historical models, producing a 'self-renewing' tradition and 'innovative continuities'. Chinese texts are supplied. The select bibliography lists useful works by category, in Chinese and English. An earlier standard analysis is Julia C. Lin, *Modern Chinese poetry: an introduction* (Seattle, Washington: University of Washington Press, 1972. 264p.).

Seeds of fire: Chinese voices of conscience.
See item no. 301.

The romantic generation of Chinese modern writers.
See item no. 1184.

A bibliography of studies and translations of Modern Chinese literature.
See item no. 1489.

Drama

1230   **Master Tung's** *Western Chamber Romance*: **a Chinese** *chantefable*.
Translated, with an introduction by Li-li Ch'en.   Cambridge,
England: Cambridge University Press, 1976; New York: Columbia
University Press, Morningside Edition, 1994. 238p. bibliog.
This charming 13th-century love story by Dong Jieyuan (Tung Chieh-yan; fl. 1190-
1208) elaborates on the Tang dynasty tale, 'The Story of Ying-ying' (translated in
Mair, *Columbia anthology of traditional Chinese literature,* (q.v.), which is again used
in Wang, *The moon and the zither: the story of the western wing* (q.v.). Its form, the
zhugongdiao ('various modes'), developed in the entertainment quarters of the Song
dynasty capital in the 12th and 13th centuries, and became important in Yuan dynasty
drama. As in the European *chantefable*, prose and verse passages alternate in a
performance mode halfway between narrative and drama. Ch'en's introduction
explains the form and the comments on the plot.

1231   **A history of Chinese drama.**
William Dolby.   London: P. Elek, 1976. 327p. bibliog.
An authoritative history which devotes most attention to the period since the 13th
century. Chapters cover: Tang, Song and Jin dynasty plays; Yuan *zaju*; Ming theatre
world and new forms – *nanxi* (Southern drama), *chuanqi* (dramatic romance) and early
kunqu (Southern style); early Qing varieties; the emergence of Beijing opera in the
19th century; Western and traditional drama in the 20th century; and drama in the
People's Republic. Colin Mackerras, *Chinese drama: a historical survey* (Beijing:
New World Press, 1990. 274p.) is an expert but more summary history of these
dramatic forms and practices, including both traditional operas and modern spoken
drama, and giving more coverage to the post-1949 period. Dolby's *Eight Chinese
plays from the thirteenth century to the present* (London: P. Elek; New York:
Columbia University Press, 1978. 164p.) complements these surveys with a selection
of eight traditional plays, six from before the 20th century. Included is *Hegemon King
says Farewell to his Queen (Bawang biejie),* which is featured in Chen Kaige's film
Farewell my concubine.

1232   **Selected plays of Guan Hanqing.**
Guan Hanqing, translated by Yang Hsien-yi, Gladys Yang.   Beijing:
Foreign Languages Press, 1958. 237p.
Presents readable translations of eight plays by the best known Yuan playwright. The
play known here as *Snow in midsummer,* concerning false conviction in court and
cosmic vindication in (and by) heaven, appears in an annotated scholarly translation
by Chung-wen Shih, *Injustice to Tou O (Tou O Yüan)* (Cambridge, England:
Cambridge University Press, 1972. 390p.).

1233 **Twentieth century Chinese drama: an anthology.**
Edward M. Gunn.   Bloomington, Indiana: Indiana University Press,
1983. 517p.

Presents the texts of sixteen representative plays, including Hu Shi's *The greatest event in life* (1919), Sha Yexin's *If I were real* (1979), and Yang Mu's *Wu Feng* (1979). Also included are Tian Han's *Guan Hanqing* (1958-61) and Wu Han's *Hai Rui dismissed from office* (1961). Translations of individual plays include: Ts'ao Yü (Cao Yu; pseud. of Wan Jiabao, 1910-96), *Thunderstorm* (Beijing: Foreign Languages Press, 1958. 182p.), a realistic drama of the 1930s; and Lao She, translated by John Howard-Gibbon, *Teahouse* (Beijing: Foreign Languages Press, 1980. 86p.), a popular play of the 1950s, *Chaguan*, which depicts several generations of neighbourhood life through the action in a teahouse.

1234 **The peach-blossom fan (*T'ao-hua shan*).**
K'ung Shan-jen, translated by Chen Shih-hsiang, Harold Acton, Cyril
Birch.   Berkeley, California; Los Angeles; Oxford: University of
California Press, 1976. 312p.

Kong Shanren (1648-1718) was a descendent of Confucius and high official in the early Qing; his 1699 play concerns treachery, intrigue and romantic love in Nanjing during the Manchu takeover in 1644-45, dealing with virtually contemporary (by Chinese standards) people and events. It was a sensation on stage and considered a literary masterpiece in the *kunqu* or 'southern' style, but led to Kong's being cashiered. Kong's life and times is well-told in *The world of K'ung Shan-jen: a man of letters in early Ch'ing China,* by Richard E. Strassberg (New York: Columbia University Press, 1983. 456p.). Another great love drama is *The peony pavilion (Mudanting)*, by Tang Xianzu, translated by Cyril Birch (Bloomington, Indiana: Indiana University Press, 1980. 343p.).

1235 **The golden age of Chinese drama: Yüan tsa-chü.**
Chung-wen Shih.   Princeton, New Jersey: Princeton University
Press, 1976. 312p. bibliog.

A comprehensive, largely non-technical presentation of the *zaju*, or 'variety play', which combined dance, song, monologue, ballads and comic turns into a serious vaudeville; modern Beijing opera is an eventual descendent. Shih describes: its origins in the 12th century; the social milieu; conventions and structure; characterization; love themes; Confucian, Buddhist and Daoist themes; social justice themes; versification and figurative language; musical modes and song sequences; and Yüan period performance, dramatists and audience. *Double jeopardy: a critique of seven Yüan courtroom dramas*, by Perng Ching-hsi (Ann Arbor, Michigan: Center for Chinese Studies, University of Michigan 1978. 178p.) is a helpful literary analysis, with historical background, including a chapter introducing Yuan drama.

1236 **Drama in the People's Republic of China.**
Edited by Constantine Tung, Colin Mackerras.   Albany, New York:
State University of New York, 1987. 353p. bibliog.

A symposium from a 1984 conference, with a summary introduction and conclusion by the editors. Thirteen chapters are divided in four parts: dramas on historical themes, including material on social background and political implications; drama, ideal and theory, including studies of Bertolt Brecht and an analysis of one of the model plays of the Cultural Revolution; post-1976 theatre and drama (the longest section); and foreign theatre in China, including studies of translated and foreign drama.

1237 **The contemporary Chinese historical drama: four studies.**
Rudolph G. Wagner. Berkeley, California: University of California Press, 1990. 378p.

A hermeneutic study of the authors, plots and cultural milieu of plays on historical themes written between 1956 and the beginning of the Cultural Revolution, when intellectuals duelled in historical code. Chapter one enumerates twenty-three hermeneutic rules, chapter four returns to general principles and other chapters discuss particular plays. Wagner demonstrates: how Tian Han's *Guan Hanqing*, translated by Yang Hsien-yi, Gladys Yang (Peking: Foreign Languages Press, 1958. 237p.), supposedly set in Khubilai Khan's court, actually concerned Mao's; and how Guo Moruo's *Cai Wenji* (1959), set in the Three Kingdoms period, defends the Machiavellian ruler Cao Cao as a stand-in for Mao. Guo Moruo's *Wu Zetian* (1960) and Tian Han's *Xie Yaohuan* (1961) continue the Aesopian debate over the nature of imperial leadership; *The Monkey King subdues the white-boned demon* illustrates the demonological political rhetoric of the Cultural Revolution.

1238 **The moon and the zither:** *The story of the western wing.*
Wang Shih-fu, edited, translated, with an introduction by Stephen H. West, Wilt Idema, with a study of its woodblock illustrations by Yao Dajuin, preface by Cyril Birch. Berkeley, California; Los Angeles; Oxford: University of California Press, 1991. 503p.

A meticulous full translation, with extensive annotations and reproductions of woodblock illustrations, of the 13th-century drama, *Xixiang ji* or *The story of the western wing*, China's most important early love comedy. The story features the winsome young lovers Oriole and Student Zhang and their amorous adventures. The introduction portrays the world of the play, its author, its place in Chinese literature, and problems of textual pedigree. The paperback edition, entitled *The story of the western wing* (Berkeley, California; Los Angeles; Oxford: University of California Press, 1995. 328p.) reprints the complete translation and introduction and makes some corrections but omits the essay on woodblock illustration. The translation supersedes the serviceable but bowdlerized *The romance of the western chamber*, translated by S. I. Hsiung, with a critical introduction by C. T. Hsia (New York; London: Columbia University Press, 1968. 280p.).

A selective guide to Chinese literature, 1900-1949. vol. 4: the drama.
See item no. 1107.

Deathsong of the River: a reader's guide to the Chinese TV series *Heshang*.
See item no. 1372.

Guide to Chinese poetry and drama.
See item no. 1467.

Folklore and popular culture

1239 Chinese mythology: an introduction.
Anne Birrell, with a foreword by Yuan K'o. Baltimore, Maryland:
Johns Hopkins University Press, 1993. 322p. bibliog.

A broad selection of over three hundred texts, with commentaries on sources, variations and significance. Birrell's introduction discusses: definitions of myth; theoretical approaches to Chinese myth (*shenhua*); the comparative method in earlier studies of Chinese myth; Chinese and Japanese studies since the 1920s; the nature of Chinese mythic narratives; and possibilities for future research. Fifteen chapters of myth narratives are organized around such standard themes and motifs as: culture bearers; saviours; destroyers; miraculous birth; the Yellow Emperor; Yi the archer; Yu the great; goddesses; immortality; metamorphoses; love; heroes; fabled flora and fauna; strange land and peoples; and founding myths, including the founding of the Shang and Zhou dynasties. The bibliographies list classical Chinese texts, research works, and works on comparative mythology. Indexes list concepts and Chinese names and terms.

1240 Folktales of China.
Wolfram Eberhard. London: Routledge & Kegan Paul; Chicago:
University of Chicago Press, 1965. rev. ed. 267p. bibliog. (Folktales of the World).

A survey introduction by one of the pioneer masters of the field; revised and expanded from his *Chinese fairy tales and folk tales* (London: Kegan Paul; New York: Dutton, 1937). The introduction provides a brief history of the study of folklore in China. Succeeding chapters illustrate various types and motifs: the origins of human, animal and plant characteristics; luck and good fortune; love, including Meng Jiangnu (Faithful Lady Meng), who mourned her husband who was conscripted to build the Great Wall; supernatural marriages; magic, spirits and gods; kindness rewarded and evil punished; and cleverness and stupidity, including tales of the Kitchen God. A section of notes discusses sources and comparative motifs.

1241 Festivals and songs of ancient China.
Marcel Granet, translated by Eve Edwards. London: George
Routledge, 1932. 281p.

A classic of French sinology, useful for its rich selection of illustrative texts and stimulating insight into individual myths, translated from *Danses et légendes de la Chine ancienne* (*Annales du Musée Guimet*, Bibliothèque d'Etudes, volume 64 [1926]; 2 volumes. Reprinted, Paris: Presses Universitaires de France, 1959). The work is characterized by its sociological approach, based on the work of Emile Durkheim, which requires that a relation be found to social formations. See Maurice Freedman's introduction in Granet, *The religion of the Chinese people* (q.v.).

1242 Art and ideology in revolutionary China.
David Holm. Oxford: Oxford University Press, 1991. 405p.

A detailed political and literary study of the development of new 'folk' forms in the Communist base areas during the period 1937-47. Holm focuses on the *yangge* – the dances, songs and plays originally performed in North China villages after New Year.

The party and local activists took up indigenous forms and transformed them into a patriotic expression of mass participation in the New China. The first section of the book describes Communist Party cultural policies and the role of the 1942 Rectification Campaign. The second section covers particular cases, such as the *yangge*, the development of peasant symbols such as the sickle and hatchet, the role and activities of the Propaganda Troupe of the Lu Xun Academy of Art, and the role of this politicized popular culture in land reform campaigns.

1243 **Going to the people: Chinese intellectuals and folk literature. 1918-1937.**
Chang-tai Hung.   Cambridge, Massachusetts: John King Fairbank Research Center, Harvard University Press, 1985. 275p. (Harvard East Asian Monographs, no. 121).

The movement to study folklore emerged in the New Culture Movement of the 1920s as part of the romantic attempt to find and shape popular culture. Particularly important figures were Hu Shi, his student Gu Jiegang, and Zhou Zuoren, who established the study of folklore as a professional academic field and patriotic concern. Hung describes first the history of folklore, then the efforts in China to collect and edit folk songs, legends (e.g. Meng Jiangnu, Zhu Yingtai), children's literature and proverbs.

1244 **Popular culture in late imperial China.**
Edited by David Johnson, Andrew J. Nathan, Evelyn S. Rawski. Berkeley, California; Los Angeles; London: University of California Press, 1985. 449p. (Studies on China, no. 4).

A key volume in which scholars of history, politics, literature and religion probe the interaction of official culture with non-élite culture, including women. Part one contains theme-setting essays on 'economic and social foundations' and 'communication, class, and consciousness'. Part two comprises eleven essays, covering: literacy specialists and written materials in the village; the levels of audience for Ming-Qing vernacular literature; the social and historical contexts of Ming-Qing local drama; Hong Kong regional opera; religious syncretism; values in popular Buddhist texts; the transmission of White Lotus Sectarianism; official and local promotion of Tian Hou ('Empress of Heaven') as 'standardizing the gods'; written popularizations of the Qing emperors' *Sacred Edicts*; and the beginnings of mass culture in late Qing journalism and fiction.

1245 **Mythology and folklore of the Hui, a Muslim Chinese people.**
Li Shujiang, Karl W. Luckert, translations by Yu Fenglan, Hou Zhilin, Wang Ganhui, Chinese editorial assistance by Yu Zongqi; assistance with Arabic, Mahmoud Abu Saud.   Albany, New York: State University of New York Press, 1994. 459p.

These stories, collected at the University of Ningxia and the Research Center for Hui Nationality Literature, were arranged and translated with help from Karl W. Luckert. The introduction sketches the history and current position of the Hui (Muslim) communities, explaining that their minority status is not a fixed condition, but has been politically and culturally negotiated. The stories, gathered in recent decades, are arranged into fourteen chapters, with topics ranging from: origins and first ancestors

(Adan and Haowa – Adam and Eve); the quests of culture heroes and saviours; Muslims in history (origins of the Hui nationality, under the Emperor, etc); family, love and courtship; social satire; tricksters and wise guys; and stories about animals.

1246   **Unofficial China: popular culture and thought in the People's Republic.**
Edited by Perry Link, Richard Madsen, Paul G. Pickowicz.   Boulder, Colorado: Westview Press, 1989. 238p.

Brings together conference papers which explore the conflicts, exchanges and diversities in official and unofficial culture, accompanied by a substantial introduction. Sections are devoted to: 'Literature, Cinema, and Authority'; 'Marriage and the Family'; 'Religion, Ethnicity, and Propriety'; and 'Social Currents'. Topics include a study of romantic love and free (not arranged) marriage in village operas of the 1930s, but also recent studies of villages in which family, hierarchy and traditions rule. Other essays look at small-scale private business (*getihu*), Catholicism, critical films and the underground circulation of hand-copied fiction.

Mandarin ducks and butterflies: popular fiction in early twentieth century Chinese cities.
See item no. 1186.

Popular Chinese literature and performing arts in the People's Republic of China, 1949-1979.
See item no. 1326.

Fine Arts

General

1247 **Chinese folk art: the small skills of carving insects.**
Nancy Zeng Berliner. Boston, Massachusetts: Little,
Brown/Graphic Society, 1986. 254p. map. bibliog.

An affectionate, systematic presentation of the household arts long dismissed by literati as 'the small skills of carving insects'. Berliner collected examples in China from the Qing dynasty to the present day, and she explains the uses and types of papercuts, shadow puppets, embroidery, dye-resistant printed fabrics and woodblock prints. Many colour illustrations are included. Po Sung-nien, David Johnson, *Domesticated deities and auspicious emblems: the iconography of everyday life in village China* (Berkeley, California: The Chinese Popular Culture Project, distributed by Institute of East Asian Studies, University of California, Berkeley, 1992. 208p.) catalogues an exhibition of woodblock prints including the Stove God and New Year's door gods, with a meaty introduction.

1248 **Theories of the arts in China.**
Edited by Susan Bush, Christian Murck. Princeton, New Jersey:
Princeton University Press, 1983. 447p.

Provides influential essays on literary and artistic theory and their applications. Essay topics include: periodization and patterns of change in literary history; 'The Human Body as a Microcosmic Source of Macrocosmic Values in Calligraphy'; images of nature; music theory and poetics in the Six Dynasties period; Song dynasty views of the arts; and issues in Ming criticism.

1249 **The Chinese art of writing.**
Jean François Billeter. Geneva: Skira; New York: Rizzoli
International, 1990. 319p. bibliog.

Sets brush writing in the context of Chinese word culture and the meaning of Chinese writing. Billeter provides many historical examples, with sensitive commentary,

431

which show in detail the artistic development of the form. His theory that calligraphy reflects 'body sense' – the active body and records of its activity – is disputed. In *Chinese calligraphy: an introduction to its aesthetic and technique* by Chiang Yee (Cambridge, Massachusetts: Harvard University Press, 1973. 3rd ed. 250p.), originally published in 1938, a genial master introduces the Western reader to the basic principles and an appreciation of brush writing, with many drawings and diagrams. *Four thousand years of Chinese calligraphy* (Chicago; London: University of Chicago Press, 1990. 442p. bibliog.), by Léon Long-yien Chang, Peter Miller, is a well produced survey.

1250　**The Silk Road and the Shosō-in.**
　　Ryōichi Hayashi, translated by Robert Ricketts.　New York: Weatherhill; Tokyo: Heibonsha, 1975. 181p. maps. (Heibonsha Survey of Japanese Art, no. 6).

A profusely illustrated general history of the artistic and cultural interchange along the Silk Road, the Central Asian passageway between China and the Eastern Mediterranean. Japanese 8th-century emperors collected Buddhist treasures from Tang China in the Shosō-in, the repository of the Tōdai-ji temple in Nara, Japan. Hayashi first recounts the background of the Shosō-in, then surveys Tang dynasty cosmopolitan culture and its Persian vogue through works from Persia, India and China, especially glassware, ceramics, clothing, musical instruments and motifs in textiles and mirrors.

1251　**Chinese art and design: art objects in ritual and daily life.**
　　Edited by Rose Kerr, texts by Rose Kerr, Verity Wilson, Craig Clunas.　London: Victoria and Albert Museum; Woodstock, New York: Overlook Press, 1991. 255p. map.

A guide to thinking about Chinese art written in the form of a guide to the comprehensive collections in the T. T. Tsui galleries of London's Victoria and Albert Museum. Instead of a catalogue by chronology or form, curators present seven illuminating essays on art objects in Chinese ritual and daily life, covering not only 'fine arts' but also crafts and religious objects. An opening essay, 'Four Questions Answered', explains: what Chinese art objects are made of; where they were made and who made them; what their decoration is about – the stories, symbols and historical figures; and how these objects came to the museum. Following chapters site art objects in history, sociology and anthropology: 'Burial in China', 'Temple and Worship', 'Living', 'Eating and Drinking', 'Ruling' and 'Collecting'.

1252　**History of far eastern art.**
　　Sherman Lee, edited by Naomi Noble Richard.　New York: Harry N. Abrams, 1994. 5th ed. 576p. maps. bibliog.

A standard text which covers all periods of time and all countries of Asia with magisterial concision and lucidity, containing excellent chapter bibliographies of works in English. A profusely illustrated overview of Buddhist art in Asia is David Snellgrove, *The image of the Buddha* (Tokyo; New York: Kodansha International, 1978. 482p.), which includes chapters on early Chinese paintings of the Buddha, cave carvings at Yungang and Longmen, and later statuary and paintings.

1253   **Chinese art under the Mongols: the Yüan dynasty (1279-1368).**
Sherman Lee, Wai-kam Ho.   Cleveland, Ohio: Cleveland Museum of
Art, 1968. 403p.

A balanced and comprehensive symposium occasioned by an exhibition at the
Cleveland Museum in 1968. The editors provide introductory essays, 'The Arts of the
Yan Dynasty' and 'Chinese Under the Mongols', and then descriptively catalogue the
exhibition's sculpture, silver, ceramics, paintings, calligraphy, woodblock prints,
lacquer, jade and ivory, and textiles. Each item exhibited is photographed.

1254   **The path of beauty: a study of Chinese aesthetics.**
Li Zehou, translated by Gong Lizheng.   Hong Kong: Oxford
University Press, 1994. 244p.

An 'impressionistic overview' of Chinese beauty in successive ages by a leading
philosopher and aesthetician. Published in China as *Mei di licheng* (1981), the book
was widely read as a breakthrough in interdisciplinary, East-West aesthetics. Starting
with prehistory – 'the era of dragons and phoenixes' – Li highlights an evolving
tension between emotion and rationality; chapters explore the 'rational spirit of pre-
Qin', the 'romanticism of Chu and Han', and 'the Buddha's worldly countenance'.
Two chapters look at vying tendencies in poetry, prose and painting of the Tang, a key
transitional age. 'Landscape painting of Song and Yuan' relates aesthetics to social
and intellectual changes. 'Main Trends in Art and Literature of the Ming and Qing'
looks at new fiction, a resurgence of romanticism and sentimentality, and painting.
Throughout the volume there are well-chosen illustrations.

1255   **Handbook of Chinese art.**
Margaret Medley.   London: Bell & Sons, 1973; New York, Harper
& Row, 1974. 3rd ed. 140p.

A handy and reliable dictionary reference, which defines important terms, concepts,
historic periods and types of art, with numerous line drawings. The earlier editions are
still useful.

1256   **Sacred mountains in Chinese art.**
Kiyohiko Munakata.   Urbana, Illinois; Chicago: Krannert Art
Museum, University of Illinois Press, 1991. 200p. maps. bibliog.

An exhibition catalogue of paintings and other representations of sacred mountains.
Munakata's substantial introduction explores the significance of mountains in early
Chinese thought and religion, and traces the development of the sacred mountain in
paintings.

1257   **Artists and traditions: uses of the past in Chinese culture.**
Edited by Christian Murck.   Princeton, New Jersey: Princeton
University Press, 1976. 230p.

Provides important theoretical and descriptive essays on purposeful cultural
traditionalism, archaism and orthodoxy, in the Yuan, Ming and Qing dynasties. Part
one, 'The Past in Chinese Cultural History', includes general thematic essays: 'The
Arts and the "Theorizing Mode" of the Civilization'; 'Inner Experience: The Basis of
Creativity in Neo-Confucian Thinking'; 'Tradition and Creativity in Early Ch'ing
Poetics'; and 'The Relationship of Early Chinese Painting to its Own Past'. Essays in

part two explore modes of archaism by Li Gonglin and in Yuan landscape, and discuss 'Archaism as a "Primitive" Style'. Part three, 'Orthodoxy and Individualism', has essays on Dong Qichang's new orthodoxy, convention and creativity, fragmentation and reintegration, in painting, politics, and poetry of the Ming and Qing. The two essays of part four look at the volume's themes in 20th-century art.

1258 **Ancient China: art and archeology.**
Jessica Rawson. London: British Museum; New York: Harper & Row, 1980. 240p. maps.

A companion to the British Museum collection of early Chinese art and archaeological material which forms a concise survey from the Neolithic period (roughly 5,000 BCE) to the fall of the Han (220 CE). Rawson considers both technical and aesthetic factors in order to examine the relations of art, technology and social organization. There are 200 black-and-white illustrations and twelve colour plates.

1259 **The art and architecture of China.**
Laurence Sickman, Alexander Soper. Harmondsworth, England; Baltimore, Maryland: Penguin Books, 1971. 3rd ed. 527p. Reprinted, New Haven, Connecticut: Yale University Press, 1989. (Pelican History of Art).

A richly illustrated standard survey for the student and general reader, which incorporates a great deal of cultural history. In part one, 'Painting and Sculpture', Professor Sickman describes the development of the pictorial arts; in part two Professor Soper surveys architecture. The work was researched before recent archaeological finds and the multi-disciplinary international scholarship of the last generation, but is still valuable for its breadth, insight and detail.

1260 **Chinese painting style: media, methods, and principles of form.**
Jerome Silbergeld. Seattle, Washington; London: University of Washington Press, 1982. 68p. bibliog.

An introduction to Chinese painting style as a visual language. Chapters first cover materials (brush, ink and pigments; ground, such as walls, silk, paper, ceramics, lacquer). They then describe: formats (wall paintings, screens, hand and hanging scrolls, albums, fans); elements of paintings (line, wash, colour, texture); composition, or the art of illusion (plasticity and organic form, linear and atmospheric perspective); and composition (abstract shapes, pattern, voids, design, and dynamics of tension, balance and rhythm). There are profuse illustrations, many in colour, of paintings chosen for their availability to readers in other studies of Chinese art. Chiang Yee, *The Chinese eye: an interpretation of Chinese painting* (London, 1936; New York: Norton, 1960; Bloomington, Indiana: Indiana University Press, 1964. 239p.) offers a personal but systematic presentation.

1261 **The arts of China.**
Michael Sullivan. Berkeley, California; Los Angeles; Oxford: University of California Press, 1984. 3rd ed. 320p. bibliog.

A compact, detailed survey, which was originally written for undergraduate courses. Sullivan provides balanced coverage of the visual high arts and incorporates political and cultural background. The work is arranged largely chronologically, from the early pottery of prehistory, through the bronzes of the Shang and Zhou, the painting and calligraphy of the empire, and ceramics to more recent centuries, and the influence of Western art and revolutionary politics. The bibliography presents selected references for further reading.

1262   **The meeting of Eastern and Western art: from the sixteenth century to the present day.**
Michael Sullivan.   Berkeley, California; Los Angeles; Oxford: University of California Press, 1989. rev. ed. 306p.

Examines the dialogue of European with Chinese and Japanese art, focusing on the creative levels, not merely the exchange of motifs and techniques (chinoiserie is excluded), in order to assess how awareness of diverse aims and ideals altered and enlarged the vision of artists. Chinese themes treated are: the influence of the Jesuits, such as Matteo Ricci and Giuseppe Castiglioni, at the Qing court and their use of perspective and realism; Europe and Chinese art, 1600-1800; the revolution in Chinese art and the ingestion of Western technique in the 20th century; and the use of Asian influences by American Abstract Expressionists such as Jackson Pollack, Mark Tobey and Morris Graves.

1263   **Caves of the thousand Buddhas: Chinese art from the Silk Route.**
Roderick Whitfield, Anne Farrer, edited by Anne Farrer.   London: British Museum, 1990. 208p. maps. bibliog.

An exhibition catalogue, with plates, descriptions and essays, which forms a key general introduction to mediaeval Buddhist art. The Museum's paintings, prints and relics – brought back in the 1910s by Sir Aurel Stein – were part of a collection accumulated in Dunhuang, a Central Asian oasis in Gansu province through which Buddhism travelled and left its mark. Valuable items were sealed in the Mogao caves against invaders over a thousand years ago, rediscovered by a Daoist monk, and parcelled out in the 1910s and 1920s to British, French and Japanese buyers. The senior scholar of Dunhuang studies in China is Duan Wenjie, whose oeuvre is splendidly presented, with many well reproduced photographs, in *Dunhuang art through the eyes of Duan Wenjie*, edited and introduced by Tan Chung (New Delhi: Indira Gandhi National Centre for the Arts, 1994. 456p. maps. bibliog.); substantial chapters analyse the style and artistry of the works (especially the wall paintings), the local history of Gansu from the 4th-12th centuries, Buddhist themes and allusions, and modern Dunhuang studies.

1264   **Foundations of Chinese art: from neolithic pottery to modern architecture.**
William Willetts.   London: Thames & Hudson, 1965. 456p. bibliog.

A 'completely new and revised' version of *Chinese art* (Harmondsworth, England: Penguin Books, 1958. 2 vols.), with 322 illustrations in colour and black-and-white, as well as 91 maps and line drawings. Archaeological discoveries and scholarly advancement have outdated aspects of this survey, but it is still valuable for its artistic perceptiveness on how epochs and genres connect and develop from each other.

1265 **Encyclopedia of Chinese symbolism and art motives; an alphabetic compendium of legends and beliefs as reflected in the manners and customs of the Chinese throughout history.**
C. A. S. Williams, introduction by Kazumitsu Kato. New York: Julian Press, 1961. 468p.

A reissue of *Outlines of Chinese symbolism and art motives* (Shanghai, China: Kelly and Walsh, 1932). Uncritical and historically undifferentiated articles explain symbols and symbolic objects, emphasizing the exotic 'superstitions' of Daoism and Buddhism, compiled largely from Western-language sources. The coverage is idiosyncratic – the first article is 'agriculture', followed by 'alarm-staff', 'amber', 'Amitabha' and 'amusements'. There are many line illustrations.

The history of cartography.
See item no. 26.

The Han dynasty.
See item no. 140.

East Asian art and American culture: a study in international relations.
See item no. 824.

Dictionary of Chinese and Japanese art.
See item no. 1446.

Pictorial art to the Tang dynasty

1266 **Stories from China's past: Han dynasty pictorial tomb reliefs and archeological objects from Sichuan province, People's Republic of China.**
Edited by Lucy Lim. San Francisco: Chinese Culture Foundation, 1987. 209p. bibliog.

Pre-Han art was dominated by religious symbolism or aristocratic ostentation, whereas later art was limited by the fastidious taste of the gentleman-scholar. The art of the Han, often commissioned from artisans by the *nouveau riche*, encompassed an earthy delight in everyday humanity; tomb reliefs, statues and murals of the period, here represented in an exhibition catalogue, show lively craftsmen's enjoyment of life, love and the economy. There are over one hundred plates and figures, with a select bibliography of works in Chinese and English. Accompanying essays include 'Social Values and Aesthetic Choices in Han Dynasty Sichuan', 'Music and Voices from the Han Tombs' and 'Myths and Legends in Han Funerary Art'.

1267   **Art and political expression in early China.**
Martin J. Powers.   London; New Haven, Connecticut: Yale
University Press, 1991. 438p. bibliog.

Relates changes and conflicts in artistic style to political and social struggles during
the last century of the Han dynasty. Like Wu Hong in *The Wu Liang shrine* (q.v.),
Powers believes that the decay of imperial family control and political scruples went
along with a cultural move towards ornate and extravagant styles. The restraint and
elegance of the Wu family shrine, discussed by both Powers and Wu, was a moral
rebuke which took the form of stylistic antiquarian revival. Powers richly explicates
the political struggles and court background of other shrines, and ranges widely in
providing comparisons and context.

1268   **Contemplating the ancients: aesthetic and social issues in early
Chinese portraiture.**
Audrey Spiro.   Berkeley, California: University of California Press,
1990. 259p. bibliog.

Discusses a tomb relief dated to the late 4th or early 5th century CE which depicts the
famous Seven Sages of the Bamboo Grove (*zhulin qixian*) (see item no. 1197). Spiro
examines a range of issues in early Chinese portraiture: physical 'likeness' was not the
prime quality of portraits, but rather the representation of the moral and doctrinal
qualities which the individual was thought to possess, as shown in pose, clothing and
gestures. In works of later periods, the individual sages were portrayed quite
differently as succeeding eras came to value new concepts.

1269   **The Wu Liang shrine: the ideology of early Chinese pictorial art.**
Wu Hung.   Stanford, California: Stanford University Press, 1989.
412p. bibliog.

Explores the general social and symbolic theories of Han dynasty art by focusing on
the shrine of a Confucian, Wu Liang, who died in 151 CE, and placing its decorations
and pictorial stones in the context of both intellectual and art history. Wu begins with
a review of earlier scholarship and theories, then presents and explicates the
iconography in the shrine. A final section provides translations and the full exegesis of
the historical and mythical stories depicted (many also found in Sima Qian's *Shiji*),
including the early sage kings, the Queen Mother of the West (Xi Wang Mu), and
filial sons and wives. Particular care is taken on a ceremonial scene of homage, which
Wu reads as an allegorical comment on political sovereignty and a critique of Han
emperorship.

Painting and calligraphy to 1911

1270 **Li Kung-lin's *Classic of Filial Piety*.**
Richard M. Barnhart, with essays by Robert E. Harrist, Jr., Hui-liang
J. Chu.   New York: Metropolitan Museum of Art, 1993. 176p. bibliog.

A specialized study. Li Gonglin (c. 1041-1106) was vital in transforming Song
dynasty painting from an outward and imperial art which glorified the emperor and
aristocratic families, into a private and moral mode, which, like poetry, expressed the
consciousness of the scholar-official artist. One of Li's three surviving works is a
handscroll illustrating the text of the *Classic of Filial Piety*, attributed to Confucius,
which expounds family values. Barnhart's richly illustrated book contains an essay on
'Li Kung-lin and the art of painting', Li's biography, his calligraphy, and 'The *Classic
of Filial Piety* in Chinese art history', which includes scene-by-scene explication of
the scroll and translations of the text. Appendices cover the colophons and
documentation and the conservation and remounting of the scroll.

1271 **Transcending turmoil: painting at the end of China's empire,
1796-1911.**
Claudia Brown, Chou Ju-hsi.   Phoenix, Arizona: Phoenix Art
Museum, distributed by University of Washington Press, 1992. 369p.
bibliog.

A catalogue with substantial introductory material which argues that scholars have
unjustly stereotyped and neglected the painting of the Qing dynasty. *The elegant
brush: Chinese painting under the Qianlong Emperor, 1735-1795*, edited by Ju-hsi
Chou, Claudia Brown (Phoenix, Arizona: Phoenix Art Museum, 1985. 376p. bibliog.)
catalogues ninety-one works and contains excellent interpretive essays on the history
of the period, the rule of the Qianlong Emperor, and court painting. *In pursuit of
antiquity*, by Roderick Whitfield (Princeton, New Jersey: Princeton University Press,
1969. 240p. map. bibliog.) is a well introduced catalogue of a collection which is
strong on Qing painting, especially orthodox painters of the 17th century.

1272 **Early Chinese texts on painting.**
Compiled and edited by Susan Bush, Hsio-yen Shih.   Cambridge,
Massachusetts; London: Harvard University Press for the
Harvard-Yenching Institute, 1985. 391p. bibliog.

An anthology for non-specialists and students of Chinese culture which translates essays
on the theory of painting up to the 14th century. Chapters cover: pre-Tang and Tang
interpretation and criticism (problems of representation, optical illusion, landscape,
genre classification, social status and creative activity); Song art history (figure painting,
brushwork, Buddhist and Daoist subjects, landscape, animals, flowers and the role of the
emperor); landscape texts; Song literati theory and connoisseurship; Yuan criticism; and
writing on special subjects. Selections are lightly annotated. An appendix contains brief
biographies and an annotated bibliography. Susan Bush, *The Chinese literati on
painting: Su Shih (1037-1101) to Tung Ch'i-ch'ang (1555-1636)* (Cambridge,
Massachusetts: Harvard University Press, 1978. 2nd ed. 227p.) presents the later
development of *wenren* (literati) painting theories through annotated translations. Lin
Yutang, *The Chinese theory of art: translations from the masters of Chinese art* (New
York: Putnam's, 1967. 244p.) constitutes an urbane, well-informed personal anthology.

438

1273   **Chinese painting.**
James Cahill.   Geneva: Skira; New York: Rizzoli, 1977. 214p.
bibliog. (Treasures of Asia Series).

A standard interpretive introduction, with 100 colour reproductions. Sherman E. Lee, *Chinese landscape painting* (Cleveland, Ohio: Cleveland Museum of Art, distributed by Abrams, [1968?]. 2nd ed. 159p.) is another well-illustrated overview. Max Loehr, *The great painters of China* (London: Phaidon Press, 1980. 336p. bibliog.) discusses high points in the history of painting, focusing on the most significant works of master painters, rather than on the cultural context. James Cahill, *An index of early Chinese painters and paintings: T'ang, Sung, and Yüan* (Berkeley, California: University of California Press, 1980. 391p.) is an indispensable reference catalogue, with biographical sketches of painters, known works, their location, reproductions, and publications concerning them. This work incorporates and expands Oswald Siren, *Chinese painting: leading masters and principles* (London: Lund Humphries; New York: Ronald Press, 1956-58. 7 vols.), which will remain the basic work until Cahill's volumes for Ming and Qing appear.

1274   **Hills beyond a river: Chinese painting of the Yuan dynasty, 1279-1368.**
James Cahill.   New York: Weatherhill; Tokyo: Heibonsha, 1976.
198p. maps. bibliog.

The first of a series which synthesizes postwar scholarship on Chinese painting. Each volume surveys a period in a rigorous but approachable way, lays out historical background and trends, and carefully explores individual painters, schools and works. The Yuan volume discusses the 'revolution' in painting, scholar-amateur painting, and landscape. Following volumes are *Parting at the shore: Chinese painting of the early and middle Ming dynasty, 1368-1580* (New York: Weatherhill, 1978. 281p. bibliog.), which discusses academy painting, the emerging Zhe and Wu landscape traditions, and the Suzhou professional masters, Shen Zhou and Wen Zhengming. *The distant mountains: Chinese painting of the late Ming dynasty, 1570-1644* (New York: Weatherhill, 1982. 302p. maps. bibliog.) devotes chapters to: later Suzhou masters; Songjiang painters; Dong Qichang; the scholar-amateurs; professional masters; and figure painting, portraits, birds and flowers, including Wu Bin and Chen Hongshou.

1275   **The compelling image: nature and style in seventeenth century Chinese painting.**
James Cahill.   Cambridge, Massachusetts; London: Belknap Press of Harvard University Press, 1982. 250p. bibliog. (Charles Eliot Norton Lectures, 1978-79).

These masterly lectures, accompanied by more than 200 illustrations and maps, explore what painting reveals about mid-Qing China, its intellectual tensions, and its adjustments to the introduction of Western ideas by the Jesuits and to the Manchu conquest. Artists variously dealt with these challenges to Confucian culture by re-working 'traditional' techniques and styles. Cahill advances a strong argument that Western influences were critical. Six chapters deal with major painters: Zhang Hong and the limits of representation; Dong Qichang and the sanction of the past; Wu Bin, influences from Europe, and the Northern Song revival; Chen Hongshou and portraits of real people and others; Hongren and Gong Xian and nature transfigured; and Wang Yuanqi and Daoji (Shitao).

1276 **The painter's practice: how artists lived and worked in traditional China.**
James Cahill. New York; London: Columbia University Press, 1994. 187p. maps. bibliog. (Bampton Lectures in America).

Presents key lectures on aesthetics and social and economic history. Chapter one, 'Adjusting Our Image of the Chinese Artist', shows how the Chinese literati 'myth' of the elegant 'amateur ideal' was a cultural achievement comparable to the myth of romantic love in mediaeval Europe or the myth of rational man in the Enlightenment. Chapters two, 'The Painter's Livelihood', and three, 'The Painter's Studio', examine daily life, the patronage network and material surroundings, showing that painters were indeed professionals and cultural politicians. Chapter four, 'The Painter's Hand', shows the fundamental change from viewing paintings as representing a subject to viewing paintings as objects for aesthetic contemplation created by particular masters. Cahill's *Three alternative histories of Chinese painting* (Lawrence, Kansas: Spencer Museum of Art, University of Kansas, 1988. 112p. [Franklin D. Murphy Lectures, no. 9]) is an important treatment of political themes and aims in the history of painting, focusing on content and style.

1277 **The painting of T'ang Yin.**
Anne de Coursey Clapp. Chicago; London: University of Chicago Press, 1991. 300p.

A sophisticated life and works study of the mid-Ming professional painter Tang Yin (1470-1523), his affiliations and patrons, literati artistic circles in Suzhou, and particularly his innovative manipulation of earlier Song and Ming styles. Tang's contemporary Wen Zhengming is the subject of a catalogue and pioneering symposium: Richard Edwards, with an essay by Anne de Coursey Clapp, *The art of Wen Cheng-ming (1470-1559)* (Ann Arbor, Michigan: University of Michigan Museum of Art, 1976. 244p. map. bibliog.).

1278 **Eight dynasties of Chinese painting: the collections of the Nelson Gallery – Atkins Museum, Kansas City, and the Cleveland Museum of Art.**
Compiled by Cleveland Museum of Art. Cleveland, Ohio: Cleveland Museum of Art, in cooperation with Indiana University Press, 1980. 408p. bibliog.

Catalogues two of the richest collections of Chinese paintings in North America. The detailed descriptions of the works and the background essays form a sweeping and approachable survey for the general reader, with detailed annotations for the serious student.

1279 **Beyond representation: Chinese painting and calligraphy 8th-14th century.**
Wen C. Fong. New York: Metropolitan Museum of Art; New Haven, Connecticut: Yale University Press, 1992. 549p. bibliog. (Princeton Monographs in Art and Archeology).

A history of painting and calligraphy from the Tang through the Yuan dynasties based on the collections at the Metropolitan Museum. Fong describes the literati (*wenren*) as a rising intellectual élite based on Neo-Confucian learning and bureaucratic status; the arts of the brush – painting and calligraphy – became the characteristic way in which these literati expressed and justified themselves. Fong chooses 118 works, each shown in colour, to show the stylistic evolution from formal representation to self-expression, a change, for instance, from the monumental objective landscapes of the Song to the passionately individualist but almost abstract paintings of the 13th century which express moral cultivation and cultural responsibility.

1280   **Zen painting and calligraphy.**
Jan Fontein, Money Hickman.   Boston, Massachusetts: Museum of Fine Arts, distributed by New York Graphic Society, Greenwich Connecticut, 1970. 173p. bibliog.

A catalogue, with a substantial introduction, of an exhibition which surveyed the Chan (Zen) arts in China and Japan. The introduction provides a brief history of Chan Buddhism, with sections on the birth of Chan art in Tang dynasty China and its development in the Northern Song. It also discusses: Chan monks and literati; the repertoire of Chan themes; the Chan eccentrics in art (e.g. Han Shan, Shi De); Chan monks and literati in the Southern Song and Yuan; the end of Chan art in China; and Zen in Japan. There are over seventy plates, some in colour, which are described and their inscriptions translated.

1281   **Traces of the brush: studies in Chinese calligraphy.**
Shen C. Y. Fu in collaboration with Marilyn W. Fu, Mary G. Neil, Mary Jane Clark.   New Haven, Connecticut; London: Yale University Press, 1977. 314p. bibliog.

An exhibition catalogue, with six essays surveying the field and introducing problems for research. The first essay, 'Reproduction and Forgery in Chinese Calligraphy', distinguishes the tradition of copying and imitation from the practice of forgery. Three essays then introduce calligraphic masterpieces, with many illustrative figures and plates, and explain the major script types (seal and clerical script traditions, the cursive script tradition, and the running and standard script traditions). 'Format and the Integration of Painting and Calligraphy' discusses calligraphy and colophons on paintings. The catalogue then describes and annotates the ninety works of the exhibition. Wen Fong, with essays by Alfreda Murck, Shou-chien Shih, *Images of the mind: selections from the Edward L. Elliott family and John B. Elliott collections of Chinese calligraphy and painting at the Art Museum, Princeton University* (Princeton, New Jersey: Princeton University Press, 1984. 504p.) is a catalogue, accompanied by substantial and sophisticated essays on the relation between calligraphy and painting.

1282   **Studies in connoisseurship: Chinese paintings from the Arthur M. Sackler collection in New York and Princeton.**
Shen C. Y. Fu, Marilyn Fu.   Princeton, New Jersey: Princeton University Press, 1976. 375p. maps. bibliog.

The catalogue of a collection which includes many works from the lower Yangzi valley in the early Qing. Introductory essays sketch the historical setting and focus on issues in connoisseurship, such as style and quality, and the problems of forgery and identification. Another essay describes the life, paintings and calligraphy of Daoji (known in China more often as Shitao), an early Qing Buddhist monk who, like Bada Shanren, retreated from politics into artistic innovation. *The painting of Tao-chi, 1641- ca. 1720* (Ann Arbor, Michigan: Museum of Art, University of Michigan, 1967. 200p. maps) presents an extensive catalogue and symposium with critical essays.

1283   **The century of Tung Ch'i-ch'ang, 1555-1636.**
Edited by Wai-kam Ho, Judith G. Smith, Coordinating Editor.
Kansas City, Kansas: Nelson-Atkins Museum of Art, in association
with the University of Washington Press, Seattle, Washington;
London: University of Washington Press, 1992. 2 vols. maps. bibliog.
A full-scale examination of Dong Qichang, one of the four great Ming painters. His
synthesis of Song and Yuan traditions ensconced landscape as the genre of the
cultured 'scholar-amateur', while his aesthetic theory of 'Northern' and 'Southern'
schools authorized a new canon of painting. This volume, published for a
comprehensive exhibition, catalogues fifty-five of Dong's paintings (mostly
landscapes), nineteen pieces of calligraphy, and thirty-four ink rubbings of his writing
(*fatie*), with ninety-seven works by contemporaries. Five major, sometimes technical,
essays in volume one explore Dong's life, artistry, manipulation of tradition, and
moral stance. Volume two comprises catalogue entries which document and describe
the exhibition items, and a masterly biography of Dong.

1284   **Mi Fu and the classical tradition of Chinese calligraphy.**
Lothar Ledderose.   Princeton, New Jersey: Princeton University
Press, 1979. 131p. bibliog.
The Song dynasty calligrapher and critic Mi Fu (1052-1107) was a pivotal figure. He
helped to fix the canon of calligraphy by sorting out and discussing earlier works,
virtually none of which now survive and copies (or copies of copies) of which differ
wildly. Ledderose examines how Mi studied and transmitted the calligraphy of the
Eastern Jin dynasty (CE 317-420) as models through his criticism and copies. Chapter
one deals with Mi's treatment of Wang Xizhi (307-365) and Wang Xianzhi (344-388)
and the development of the classical tradition. Chapter two discusses Mi Fu's
historical and aesthetic criticism, with several analyses of the problem of copying and
forgery. Chapter three deals with the particular works Mi knew and described, and
also traces their subsequent history. Appendices offer translations of Mi's critical
essays.

1285   **The scholar's studio: artistic life in the late Ming period.**
Chu-tsing Li, James C. Y. Watt.   London; New York: Thames &
Hudson, published in association with the Asia Society Galleries,
1987. 218p. map. bibliog.
The catalogue of an exhibition from the Shanghai Museum, with well-informed
general essays on the theme of literati life-style and art. Essays include 'The Literati
Environment', which describes the studio of the scholar as revealing literati culture
through its accoutrements such as ink and brush, ceramics, decorative arts, books and
rubbings, and collected objects. Other chapters include: 'The Artistic Theories of the
Literati'; 'The Late Ming Literati: Their Social and Cultural Ambience'; 'The Literati
Life'; 'The Songjiang School of Painting and the Period Style of the Late Ming'; and
'The Arts of Ming Woodblock-printed Images and Decorated Paper Albums'.

1286   **Learning from Mt. Hua: a Chinese physician's illustrated travel record and painting theory.**
Kathlyn Maurean Liscomb.   Cambridge, England: Cambridge University Press, 1993. 229p. bibliog. (RES Monographs on Anthropology and Aesthetics).

A specialized study. Wang Lü was a 14th-century literatus who practiced the arts of medicine and the painter's brush. This scholarly monograph brings a multifaceted analysis to Wang's album of forty paintings, which record his experience of climbing Mt. Hua, one of the prominent sacred mountains. Liscomb explores the paintings and accompanying texts, including a travel diary and two essays on painting, translated here, and 150 poems. She shows the tension between what the painter could learn with his own eyes (which Wang compared to a physician's symptomology) and the importance of pictorial convention, largely inspired by Song painter theory.

1287   **Words and images: Chinese poetry, calligraphy, and painting.**
Edited by Alfreda Murck, Wen C. Fong.   New York: Metropolitan Museum of Art; Princeton, New Jersey: Princeton University Press, 1991. 589p. bibliog.

A symposium volume in honour of the collector John M. Crawford, which provides twenty-three diverse essays by scholars from the People's Republic, Taiwan, Japan and North America. The general theme is the interaction between writing (either textual content or calligraphic style) and pictures; some pieces examine particular works of art and others general problems and history. Essays cover: a general survey of relations among poetry, calligraphy and painting; the changing cultural perceptions of words and images in Chinese culture; Qing painters' poems on painting; compositional practices; and the relationship between poetry, surface and space in Song and Yuan landscapes.

1288   **Ma Hezhi and the illustration of the *Book of Odes*.**
Julia K. Murray.   Cambridge, England: Cambridge University Press, 1993. 256p.

A technical study which combines literary, political and art history to interpret a set of scrolls illustrating the *Shijing*, 'Book of Odes' or 'Book of Poetry'. The illustrations were painted in the Southern Song dynasty by the otherwise obscure painter Ma Hezhi, with calligraphy by the Gaozong Emperor (r. 1127-62). Murray explains: the significance of the Confucian Odes in the Southern Song revival in the face of 'barbarian' invasion; the themes, styles and structures of the illustrations, which showed expert awareness of earlier styles; problems of connoisseurship; and the transmission of the scrolls – they were selected for enshrinement by the Qianlong Emperor in the 18th century but eventually given away by the deposed emperor in the 1920s and dispersed, only to be (photographically) reunited in this book.

1289   **Boundaries of the self: Chinese portraits, 1600-1900.**
Richard Vinograd.   Cambridge, England; New York; Victoria: Cambridge University Press, 1992. 191p.

An analytical essay which examines personal portraits from the 17th to the 19th centuries in order to understand the artists' evolving 'construction of self'. Vinograd first describes the tradition of portraiture, then devotes a chapter to each of the three centuries. He makes a distinction between the portrait as 'effigy', such as ancestor portraits or official icons which realistically depict the subject, and the portrait as 'emblem', informal portraits (particularly self-portraits and portraits of fellow painters) which reveal the sitter's own character. By the 19th century, artists emerge as professionals who are insecure and anxious in their use of tradition, but inventive in their attempts to replace it. Thomas Lawton, *Chinese figure painting* (Washington, DC: Smithsonian Institution, 1973. 236p. bibliog.) catalogues paintings in a 1972 exhibition at the Freer Gallery, with a general survey.

1290 **Master of the lotus garden: the life and art of Bada Shanren (1626-1705).**
Wang Fang-yu, Richard M. Barnhart, edited by Judith G. Smith.
New Haven, Connecticut: Yale University Art Gallery, Yale University Press, 1990. 300p. bibliog.
Bada was a descendent of the Ming royal family who lived on into the Qing dynasty. He created a deeply individualistic, even quirky, body of painting, unprecedented in its almost romantic washes and splashing exercise of colour. Because of his Ming loyalty and eccentric nature, he sought refuge in obscurity as a Buddhist monk and eccentric. Even his name is unfixed: known also in Western writings as Zhu Da, he had at least eight others. This comprehensive volume includes essays on his life and art, interpretations of the paintings and calligraphy, translations of his poems and letters, scholarly apparatus, and an extensive catalogue which individually describes more than 300 works.

1291 **Views from jade terrace: Chinese women artists, 1300-1912.**
Edited by Marsha Weidner. New York: Rizzoli, 1988. 231p. bibliog.
An exhibition catalogue, with a scholarly introduction, which forms a useful preliminary survey of a long neglected topic. The symposium *Flowering in the shadows: women and the history of Chinese and Japanese painting*, also edited by Marsha Weidner (Honolulu: University of Hawaii Press, 1991. 315p.) includes five essays on Chinese women painters and painting for women.

Art in the 20th century

1292 **Painters and politics in the People's Republic of China, 1949-1979.**
Julia F. Andrews. Berkeley, California; Los Angeles; Oxford: University of California Press, 1994. 480p. bibliog.
Mao's revolution established a politically shifting orthodoxy in painting style, technique, medium and genre. Landscape painting, for instance, was taken in directions which differed both from tradition and from developments in other parts of the Chinese culture world. Andrews follows the political and artistic careers of individual artists, balancing consideration of revolutionary politics, Chinese cultural

reference and genuine aesthetic development. Joan Lebold Cohen, *The new Chinese painting, 1949-1986* (New York: Abrams, 1987. 167p.) describes the emergence of younger independent artists in the 1980s based on her own talks with Chinese artists, observations in their studios, and collection of their paintings. Ellen Johnston Laing, *The winking owl: art in the People's Republic of China* (Berkeley, California; Los Angeles; Oxford: University of California Press, 1988. 194p. bibliog.) is a survey which pays particular attention to the political messages encoded in paintings.

1293 **Art and revolution in modern China: the Lingnan (Cantonese) school of painting, 1906-1951.**
Ralph Croizier. Berkeley, California; Los Angeles; London: University of California Press, 1988. 224p. bibliog.

The history of a style of painting and a cultural biography of its founders – 'about art, but not just about art'. Croizier develops concepts from his mentor Joseph Levenson to probe the regional origins of a national movement; *Xin Guohua*, or New National Painting, aimed to produce art which was 'modern and still distinctively Chinese'. Chen Shuren (1883-1949) and the brothers Gao Jianfu (1879-1951) and Gao Qifeng (1889-1935) studied with a Canton master, then went to Japan; on their return, they joined revolutionary art and political movements in Canton and Shanghai over the period 1912-27. Chapters analyse the history, Buddhist influences, style, and content of the paintings, with many illustrations, then explain the demise of the school 1937-49, and its contrasting legacies in Hong Kong, the People's Republic and Taiwan.

1294 **The cartoonist Feng Zikai: social realism with a Buddhist face.**
Christopher Harbsmeier. Oslo: Universitetsforlaget; New York: Columbia University Press, 1984. 215p. bibliog.

A well-rounded study of the life, thought and art of a pivotal painter and writer, with illustrations. Feng (1898-), trained in classical art and calligraphy, was a prominent Buddhist layman in the New Culture era when religion of any sort was intellectually unfashionable. He developed an informal, realistic style, sometimes in cartoons, sometimes in illustrations for books (many on Buddhist themes), which often portrayed children and everyday life; his illustrations of the writings of Lu Xun were especially noted.

1295 **Brushes with power: modern politics and the Chinese art of calligraphy.**
Richard Kurt Kraus. Berkeley, California; Los Angeles; Oxford: University of California Press, 1991. 208p. bibliog.

A lively examination of the changing meanings of calligraphy in modern social and cultural politics. The first section introduces the art of brush writing and summarizes its role in imperial China, especially as a key skill of the Confucian gentleman. In the second section, 'Calligraphy and Revolution', Kraus, a political scientist, focuses on power but also includes aesthetics. He shows how revolutionaries such as Mao Zedong used the traditional prestige of calligraphy to empower their movement and how many organizations were created to practice this 'traditional' art. The debates over the role of élitist aesthetics and revolution are also presented.

1296 **Contradictions: artistic life, the socialist state, and the Chinese painter Li Huasheng.**
Jerome Silbergeld, with Gong Jisui. Seattle, Washington; London: University of Washington Press, 1993. 264p. (Jackson School Publications in International Studies).

Explores the 'contradictions' between the artistic ambitions of the Sichuan landscape painter Li Huasheng (1944-) and the politicized bureaucracies and personal relations which continue to dominate culture in ways that are different from the West. A rich sub-plot discusses Li's painting master, who was a local bully, a martial arts bodyguard of a warlord (who was a connoisseur of the Qing dynasty painters Daoji and Bada Shanren), and ended up as a ward of the *wenshiguan* (Hall of Learning and History), which pensioned off cultural figures who survived the revolution into the 1950s. Young Li defied politics on his singleminded path to landscape painting. He became a victim of the Cultural Revolution, but was politically adept enough to accept the secure patronage of the state painters' federation, which included all who made a living at painting.

1297 **The paintings of Xugu and Qi Baishi.**
Jung Ying Tsao. San Francisco: Far East Fine Arts; Seattle, Washington: University of Washington Press, 1993. 447p. maps. bibliog.

A sumptuously illustrated presentation and analysis of the lives and paintings of two artists who used traditional brush and ink techniques in strikingly modern ways, Xugu (1823-96) and Qi Baishi (1864-1957). Tsao carefully traces their artistic developments and lines of influence from earlier painting, and shows how Qi became a cultural emblem in the People's Republic.

Bronzes, pottery and ceramics

1298 **Ancient Chinese bronzes from the Arthur M. Sackler Collections.**
Washington, DC: Arthur M. Sackler Foundation; Cambridge, Massachusetts: Arthur M. Sackler Museum, distributed by the Harvard University Press, 1987- . 3 vols. bibliog.

These sumptuous volumes, a comprehensive catalogue of the Arthur M. Sackler collections, constitute a detailed history and survey: volume one, *Shang ritual bronzes in the Arthur M. Sackler collections*, edited by Robert W. Bagley; volume two, *Western Zhou ritual bronzes from the Arthur M. Sackler collections*, edited by Jessica Rawson; and volume three, *Eastern Zhou ritual bronzes from the Arthur M. Sackler collections*, edited by Jenny F. So. A team of scholars based at Harvard prepared detailed descriptions of the hundreds of pieces, each photographed (often in colour), together with introductory essays, appendices, bibliographies, character glossaries and notes.

1299   **Ming pottery and porcelain.**
R. Soames Jenyns, introduction by William Watson.   London: Faber,
1988. rev. ed. 237p.

A slightly revised and updated re-issue of a 1953 classic. It attractively synthesizes the
pioneering 1910s-1940s scholarship which established the study of Ming ceramics in
the West. Watson's introduction presents an appreciation of the author; Jenyns was a
British government officer in Hong Kong, where he acquired fluent Cantonese, a
pioneer's enthusiasm for collecting, and practical connoisseurship. His book surveys
the Ming dynasty (1368-1644) and its culture, then describes the forms, styles,
technical aspects, and the distribution of its pottery and ceramics.

1300   **The Chinese potter: a practical history of Chinese ceramics.**
Margaret Medley.   Oxford: Phaidon Press, 1989. 3rd ed. 288p. maps.

Describes techniques of manufacture and conditions under which earthenware,
stoneware and porcelain were produced. Medley first introduces 'The Potter and his
Materials'. Part one, 'The Basic Technology', then covers the pre-Han unglazed
earthenware of neolithic North China, moves on to the glazed wares of Shang, Zhou
and Han dynasties, and finishes with 'technical consolidation' following the fall of
Han. Part two, 'The Period of Discovery and Innovation', describes: new inspiration
in the Tang; classic and popular wares; and regional production, including Longquan
(Wade-Giles: Lung-ch'üan), Guan (Kuan) ware, Jizhou (Chi-chou), Jian (Chien), and
the rise of Jingdezhen (Ching-te Chen), in Fujian. Part three, 'Development and
Variations', covers: Ming imperial styles; popular tastes and new markets (e.g. blue
and white and export); and the technical virtuosity of the Qing.

1301   **T'ang pottery and porcelain.**
Margaret Medley.   London; Boston, Massachusetts: Faber, 1981.
151p. map. (Faber Monographs on Pottery and Porcelain).

A detailed but accessible survey, accompanied by numerous plates. Medley begins with
a presentation of Tang history, then examines the origin and development of the major
pottery sites and their distinctive products. There are many colour and black-and-white
illustrations. Medley's *Yuan porcelain and stoneware* (London: Faber & Faber, 1974.
139p. [Faber Monographs on Pottery and Porcelain]) treats the Mongol Yuan period.

1302   **Song ceramics.**
Mary Tregear.   New York: Rizzoli, 1982. 262p. maps.

A comprehensive, handsomely illustrated overview of the Song dynasty (960-1278)
when a developing and sophisticated society demanded a new variety of forms and
styles of decoration in ceramics. The introduction discusses the history of the period,
potters and ceramics in earlier society, the role of the imperial court, new social
classes, styles of stoneware and porcelain (shapes, decoration, techniques), kilns and
workshops. Chapters then survey: Ding (Ting) ware; Cizhou (Tz'u-chou) type wares
(the most popular stoneware); Yaozhou (Yao-chou) greenware from the Linru kilns;
Jun, Ru and Guan ware, with their new styles of glazing; Jingdezhen, the beginning of
the great tradition; Longquan ware; dark-glazed wares; and tea bowls from Fujian.
The final chapter is 'Trade and the Influence of Song Ceramics on the Ceramic
Cultures of Foreign Lands'. Each chapter contains a map of the kiln sites involved and
a catalogue of its ware.

1303   **Handbook of Chinese ceramics.**
Suzanne Valenstein.   New York: Metropolitan Museum of Art,
1989. rev. and enlarged ed. 331p. maps. bibliog.

A survey of ceramics from the early Neolithic to the present, with many useful notes
for collectors or specialists. Thirteen chapters, divided chronologically, present a
history of ceramics through the more than 335 objects illustrated (more than half new
from the first edition). There is a thirty-two-page section of colour plates. The first
edition (1975) was based on the collection of the Metropolitan Museum; since that
time, new scholarship based on excavations in China has given a far more detailed and
comprehensive picture. There are extensive notes, a glossary and a list of selected
readings.

1304   **Tang and Liao ceramics.**
William Watson.   New York: Rizzoli, 1984. 283p. maps. bibliog.

The Tang dynasty (618-907) saw territorial expansion, economic growth and multi-
cultural influences, all of which were reflected in its ceramics. Watson uses excavation
and fieldwork to make a detailed artistic survey of pottery – earthenware, stoneware
and porcelain – as well as its manufacture and sale. Part one covers: Tang history;
style in painting and Buddhist art; pre-Tang ceramic history; and uses for ceramics
(tea-drinking, decorative, ceremonial). Part two, 'Techniques', describes high-fired
ware and glazes, kilns and areas of production. Part three, 'Ceramic Types: Their
Ornament and Dating', catalogues shapes and functions (e.g. gourd-shaped bottle,
cuspidor, pillow). Part four, 'Figurines', includes all types, including soldiers, ladies,
musicians and dancers, and animals. Part five discusses the ceramics of the Liao (947-
1125) dynasty, and part six covers ceramics as export ware outside China. There are
notes, a glossary, and a select bibliography.

**The great bronze age of China: an exhibition from the People's Republic
of China.**
See item no. 85.

Sculpture

1305   **Chinese Buddhist sculpture under the Liao (free standing works
in situ and selected examples from public collections).**
Marilyn Leidig Gridley.   New Delhi: International Academy of
Indian Culture and Aditya Prakashan, 1993. 204p. maps.

Argues that the neglected sculpture of the Liao dynasty (947-1125) is actually in the
mainstream of Chinese art even though its rulers were not Han Chinese but Qidan
(also spelled Khitan). Earlier scholars interpreted the period as the inconsequential
prelude to the Song and Yuan. However, Gridley shows that the Chinese artisans who
produced the Buddhist sculpture continued the traditions of the Tang; the successor
foreign dynasties of Jin and Yuan broke this tradition to produce innovative Lamaist
Buddhist art. The book provides detailed technical analysis of surviving sculptures,
comparisons with other documented works, and much background material.

1306 **Chinese tomb figures.**
Ann Paludan. Hong Kong: Oxford University Press, 1994. 66p.
bibliog. (Images of Asia).

An introduction for the general reader. Paludan first explains the origins of the Chinese custom of enclosing figurines in tombs to replace expensive luxury items (or human sacrifices). She then devotes chapters to 'The Han World of Figurines', 'The Northern Dynasties: A Period of Transition' and 'Sui and Tang: The Second Flowering', and finishes with an epilogue which brings the story to the present day. There is a chronological table and a selected bibliography of works in English.

1307 **The Chinese spirit road: the classical tradition of stone tomb statuary.**
Ann Paludan. New Haven, Connecticut: Yale University Press, 1991. 290p.

Surveys, with many photographs, the statuary which lines the roads leading to major tombs, the most famous of which are those at the Ming imperial tombs outside Nanjing and the Qing tombs outside Beijing.

1308 **Chinese sculptures from the fifth to the fourteenth century.**
Osvald Siren. London: Benn, 1925. Reprinted, New York: Hacker Art Books, 1989. 4 vols.

A catalogue and description of surviving or recorded sculpture.

The art and architecture of China.
See item no. 1259.

Architecture, building and gardens

1309 **Chinese architecture and town planning: 1500 B.C.-A.D. 1911.**
Andrew Boyd. London: Alec Tiranti; Chicago: University of Chicago Press, 1962. 166p. map. bibliog.

A concise survey of the main theories of classic architecture and town planning, with some reference to the reality behind them. Chapters include: 'Structural Principles, Evolution, and Style'; 'Planning Principles and the Chinese City', with sections on Chang'an, Song cities, Suzhou (Soochow), Hangzhou, Beijing and comparisons with Europe; 'The House, The Garden, and the Artificial Landscape'; 'Religious and Funerary Buildings'; and 'Engineering Works: Some Examples'. *Chinese traditional architecture*, by Nancy Shatzman Steinhardt (New York: China Institute in America, 1984. 168p. map.) is an exhibition catalogue with an imaginative and lucid introduction. Michele Pirazzoli-t'Serstevens, *Living architecture: Chinese* (London: Macdonald; New York: Grosset & Dunlop, 1971. 191p.) provides a concise overview for the general interested reader, with many photographs and plans. Following a general discussion of the cultural context, Pirazzoli-t'Serstevens devotes chapters to: town planning; imperial palaces and temples; religious and funerary architecture; and houses and gardens.

1310   **Chinese earth-sheltered dwellings: indigenous lessons for modern urban design.**
Gideon S. Golany.   Honolulu: University of Hawaii Press, 1992. 179p. bibliog.

China has 4,000 years of experience with *yaodong*, the 'earth-sheltered vernacular habitats' known as cave dwellings. These hitherto disdained structures have recently been recognized for their energy efficiency, affordability and positive impact on the modern city sprawl. This comprehensive book offers lessons in regard to: design and thermal principles for energy savings and comfort; deficiencies and applicable solutions; and relevant lessons for modern urban design. Golany's information comes from one and a half years of fieldwork, interviews and translations which he commissioned of recent Chinese publications. Chapters cover: regional environmental determinants; distribution; design; and structural and environmental restraints (including thermal performance and health considerations). Copious figures, technical drawings and statistical tables are included. The bibliography lists Chinese and English-language works concerning earth-sheltered dwellings worldwide.

1311   **Scholar gardens of China: a study and analysis of the spatial design of the Chinese private garden.**
R. Stewart Johnston.   Cambridge, England; New York; Port Chester, New York; Melbourne; Sydney: Cambridge University Press, 1992. 331p.

Draws together secondary work in English, the author's own tours of classic gardens in China, and translations of Chinese scholarship by the author's Chinese colleagues. The garden was one of the acceptable interests for the cultivated gentleman, but the affluent merchant was more likely to have the money to build one; much work remains to be done to reveal how Confucian theory, social snobbery, and commercial practicality interacted in garden aesthetics. This book meanwhile provides a rich selection of photographs, plots, line drawings, translated texts and personal observation.

1312   **The Chinese garden: history, art, and architecture.**
Maggie Keswick, contributions and conclusion by Charles Jencks.
London: Academy Editions; New York: Rizzoli, 1978. 216p. maps. bibliog.

Profusely illustrated general history and appreciation. Chapters cover: Western reactions; origins; imperial gardens; the gardens of the literati; the painter's eye, with an informal précis of landscape painting; architecture in gardens; rocks and water as aesthetic elements; flowers, trees and herbs; and a speculative conclusion, 'Meanings of Chinese Gardens'. Edwin Morris, *The gardens of China: history, art, and meaning* (New York: Scribners, 1983. 273p.) provides a well-illustrated reflection on the garden as a gateway to Chinese culture. Rolf A. Stein, *The world in miniature: container gardens and dwellings in Far Eastern religious thought*, translated by Phyllis Brooks, with a new foreword by Edward H. Schafer (Stanford, California: Stanford University Press, 1990. 393p.) presents Daoist and Buddhist ideal conceptions and some actual buildings and miniature gardens which represented spiritual architecture and ideal universes.

1313   **Chinese bridges.**
Ronald G. Knapp.   Hong Kong; Oxford; New York: Oxford
University Press, 1993. 78p. bibliog. (Images of Asia).
A compact, colourfully-illustrated introduction. The Chinese have a 'rich history of
bridge building that, while similar in evolutionary pattern to that of the West,
generally developed independently and with innovations that predate those in the
West'. Knapp provides a precise but non-technical survey of Chinese bridge-building
traditions, stone bridges, the world's first segmental span, garden bridges, bridge
ornamentation and a brief chapter on modern bridges. A glossary covers bridge-
building terms in English and Chinese. A selected bibliography lists works in Western
languages.

1314   **China's vernacular architecture: house form and culture.**
Ronald G. Knapp.   Honolulu: University of Hawaii Press, 1989.
195p. bibliog.
A sympathetic, detailed description of how village houses express and affect daily life,
based on recent field observation undertaken in Zhejiang province. Knapp first
describes the process of settling a village (landscapes, sites, transitions), then the
organization of space in the house – climate and form; *jian*, or rooms; *jia*, or
home/family; courtyards and sky wells; verandas; floor plans; living space; kitchens;
toilets; storages; and productive space. Two chapters then describe structure and
details of construction and decoration, from foundation to roof. A final chapter
discusses 'tradition', the conscious or unconscious preservation of customs and styles.
There are copious photographs and plans, as well as a glossary of Chinese terms.

1315   **China's traditional rural architecture: a cultural geography of
the common house.**
Ronald G. Knapp.   Honolulu: University of Hawaii Press, 1986.
177p. bibliog.
Knapp provides a lively history of the village house, arguing that the folk tradition,
while mainly utilitarian, echoes classic architectural patterns and is guided by
cosmological sentiments and patterns of social relationships. Chapter one reviews the
evolution of the Chinese dwelling from neolithic times to the Ming, demonstrating a
remarkable continuity of form, layout and materials. Chapter two expounds the
regional variety created by farmer pioneers – Northern houses, loessial earth sheltered
dwellings (caves) and Southern houses. Chapter three describes the construction of
foundations, framework and roofs, and chapter four the Taiwan frontier. Chapter five
outlines the folk tradition – geomancy (*fengshui* or 'mystical ecology'); almanacs,
instruments and charms. There are many illustrations, plans and photographs, and a
glossary of Chinese terms. Knapp's *The Chinese house: craft, symbol, and the folk
tradition* (Hong Kong; New York: Oxford University Press, 1990. 87p. bibliog.
[Images of Asia]) presents a well-illustrated overview.

1316   **A pictorial history of Chinese architecture.**
Liang Sicheng, edited by Wilma Fairbank.   Cambridge,
Massachusetts: M. I. T. Press, 1984. 200p.
Liang, the son of the reform intellectual Liang Qichao, undertook the task of recording
China's architectural tradition in the 1930s, a time of wars, pessimism and world
depression. The manuscript of this book was rescued by the editor, and translated and

published first in English; it is both a document of cultural history and a seminal study. Liang travelled widely, taking photographs of historic structures and conducting research in obscure archives; many of the copious pictures and diagrams are the only surviving records of lost buildings.

1317 The imperial Ming tombs.
Text and photographs by Ann Paludan. New Haven, Connecticut; London: Yale University Press; Hong Kong: Hong Kong University Press, 1981. 251p.

When Paludan lived in Beijing from 1972-76, one of the few outings allowed to foreign residents was to the Ming tombs; she and her family picnicked and explored the area which she describes and analyses in this well-illustrated volume. Paludan, an amateur in the best sense, culls the Western-language literature and offers detailed plans of the thirteen tombs (*shisan ling*) near Beijing and two near Nanjing. She also describes their history, construction, decoration and condition in the early 1970s.

1318 Carpentry and building in late imperial China: a study of the fifteenth century carpenter's manual, *Lu Ban Jing*.
Klaas Ruitenbeek. Leiden, the Netherlands; New York; Köln: E. J. Brill, 1993. 520p. (Sinica Leidensia, no. 23).

Translates and explicates a traditional carpentry handbook to illuminate both house building technology and its social meanings. Ruitenbeek uses wide reading and anthropological observation of contemporary builders to provide a multifaceted introduction, drawings of tools, and annotations which bring the text to life. Sections describe materials, tools, the status and organization of labourers, and the stages of construction. But the family house was a spiritual, almost ritual object as well as being a dwelling and an investment. The manual explains siting done by geomancers (*fengshui*), the calculation of favourable days, ritually correct measurement, rites to be observed at various points of construction, and the social meaning of the house. The original Chinese text and illustrations are photo-reproduced.

Chinese imperial city planning.
See item no. 437.

Decorative and applied arts

1319 Chinese furniture.
Michel Beurdley, translated by Katherine Watson. Tokyo; New York; San Francisco: Kodansha International, 1979. 199p. bibliog.

A general but well-grounded description, covering all types and periods of Chinese furniture and its influence in Europe. Chapters concern: Chinese furniture before the Ming; the art of living in China (the scholar's retreat; the example of the 17th-century scholar Li Yü; a house in 18th-century Canton); and from the Ming to the 20th century (hardwood, lacquer, cloisonné, Canton enamel, porcelain sets and furnishing, metal hinges, locks and handles). There is a Chinese-English glossary. *Chinese furniture: Ming and early Qing dynasties*, by Wang Shixiang, translated by Sarah Handler and the author (San Francisco: China Book & Periodicals, 1986. 327p.) provides more scholarly coverage, with numerous illustrations.

1320 Chinese lacquer.
Sir Harry Garner. London; Boston, Massachusetts: Faber, 1979. 285p. bibliog.

Discusses the development of Chinese lacquerwares from the Yuan dynasty onwards, categorizing by technique rather than chronologically. Chapters consider: the nature of lacquer and the distribution of lacquer trees in East Asia; early lacquerwares of China, before the technique had travelled abroad; traditional Chinese scholarship and modern studies; the origins of carved and marbled lacquer; and carved, *qiangjin*, filled-in, surface gold-decorated, mother-of-pearl, painted, coromandel and Southeast Asian lacquers. There are over 200 plates and a bibliography which annotates Chinese-language sources and lists European scholarship.

1321 Imperial wardrobe.
Gary Dickinson, Linda Wrigglesworth. London: Bamboo, 1990. 203p.

An examination of the ceremonial garments and accessories of the Qing dynasty court. The copious illustrations include photographs as well as illustrations and imperial portraits from a manuscript treatise probably commissioned in 1759 by the Qianlong Emperor and looted by the British from the Summer Palace in 1860. Chapters follow the order of this imperial treatise, and describe both the court dress (hats, coats and robes) and their prescribed ritual uses. Valerie Garrett, *The mandarin square* (Oxford: Oxford University Press, 1990. 66p. [Images of Asia]) concisely describes the origins, types and history, with a list of selected readings, of the 'mandarin square', the name given by foreigners to the embroidered cloth worn as sign of rank by Qing high officials. They are now collected for their historical association and colourful patterns.

1322 Chinese clothing: an illustrated guide.
Valerie M. Garrett. Hong Kong; Oxford; New York: Oxford University Press, 1994. 224p. bibliog.

A copiously illustrated historical survey, based on English-language sources, of clothes and their social uses. Garrett begins with the claim that 'throughout most of China's long history there has been a common style of dress within each social stratum of the Han people, unlike other countries where traditional dress often varied greatly from region to region'. Individual chapters cover the Ming, Qing and 20th century. They picture and describe clothing for men, women and officials (Manchu and Han), as well as urban and rural styles. Further chapters show military uniforms, children's wear, minority dress (north and south), and materials (fibres and fabrics, dyes and embroidery). A select bibliography lists works in English.

1323 Chinese carved jades.
S. Howard Hansford. London: Faber, 1968. 131p. bibliog.

A magisterial, amply illustrated history of artistic jade by a leading British collector and Orientalist connoisseur. After an introduction and explanation of the material and its sources, Hansford concisely surveys the history of the craft. Chapters then describe design, purpose and usage, first in the classic period (Neolithic, Shang, Zhou) and then what Chinese collectors consider 'new' jade (Han to Qing). A final chapter is devoted to archaeology. James Watt, *Chinese jade from Han to Ch'ing* (New York: Weatherhill, Asia Society, 1980. 235p. bibliog.) is an illustrated catalogue of an imaginative exhibition of 'new' jade, with a well-informed introduction which incorporates recent findings on technical and aesthetic aspects. Joan Hartman-Goldman, *Chinese jade* (Hong Kong; New York: Oxford University Press, 1986. 81p. bibliog. [Images of Asia]) provides a concise introduction.

1324   **Chinese art: gold, silver, later bronzes, cloisonne, Cantonese enamel, lacquer, furniture, wood.**
Soame Jenyns, William Watson.   Oxford: Phaidon, 1981. 2nd ed. prefaced and rev. by William Watson. 277p.

A sumptuously illustrated scholarly history and connoisseur's appreciation of the 'minor arts' as a sophisticated craftsman tradition. Individual chapters are devoted to each of the areas mentioned in the title. *Chinese art: textiles, glass and painting on glass, carvings in ivory and rhinoceros horn, carvings in hardstones, snuff bottles, inkcakes and inkstones*, by Soame Jenyns, with the editorial assistance of William Watson (Oxford: Phaidon, 1981. 2nd rev. ed. 243p.) continues the coverage. The chapter on textiles is organized chronologically from the Zhou to the Qing, with further sections on export textiles, velvets, embroidery and woollen rugs. Robert Kleiner, *Chinese snuff bottles* (Hong Kong: Oxford University Press, 1994. 74p. bibliog. [Images of Asia]) is an introductory guide; this practical genre arose after tobacco became available in the Qing and was invested with artistic ingenuity (much like netsuke in Japan). Lee Allane, *Chinese rugs: a buyer's guide* (London; New York: Thames & Hudson, 1993. 144p. maps) is a well-illustrated brief handbook, with practical descriptions of history, symbols, types, techniques of manufacture and buying tips.

Performing Arts

General

1325 The performing arts in contemporary China.
Colin Mackerras.   London; Boston, Massachusetts: Routledge &
Kegan Paul, 1981. 243p. bibliog.

Surveys performing arts policy and practice since 1976 and helpfully explains how
political aims, traditional forms and present performers interact. Chapter one
summarizes historical background. Mackerras then devotes chapters to: official
policies; traditional forms of performing arts; modern theatre; cinema; and music. A
chapter, 'Bringing Performances to Fruition', describes practical problems and
techniques. The conclusion assesses the balance between respect for tradition, political
exigencies, and commercial pressure to appeal to new audiences.

**1326 Popular Chinese literature and performing arts in the People's
Republic of China, 1949-1979.**
Edited by Bonnie S. McDougall.   Berkeley, California; Los Angeles;
London: University of California Press, 1984. 341p. bibliog.

These essays, taken from a 1979 conference, apply literary and political analysis to the
popular arts. Part one, 'The Ground Prepared, 1937-1941', examines the *yangge* (rice-
sprout song) movement in Yan'an, the development of modern *huaju* (spoken drama)
in occupied Shanghai, and transformation of May Fourth cultural theories. Part two,
'The Push to Popularize, 1949-1979', contains eight essays which deal with:
xiangsheng (comedic patter songs); *geming gequ* (revolutionary anthems); the 1961
musical film, *Liu Sanjie*, about the folk musician 'Third Sister Liu', in which romantic
love vies with class struggle; Cultural Revolution 'model operas'; the film industry
during the 1970s; Mao's dictum 'make the past serve the present' in fiction and
drama; the fiction of Hao Ran; and contemporary poetry. Part three is the editor's
essay, 'Three Decades in Historical Perspective'. A selected bibliography list
materials in Western languages for further reading and reference.

Handbook of Chinese popular culture.
See item no. 1451.

Music

1327 **Suspended music: chime-bells in the culture of bronze age China.**
Lothar von Falkenhausen.   Berkeley, California; Los Angeles;
Oxford: University of California Press, 1993. 481p.

Ancient Chinese philosophers agreed that both government and social order were regulated by music. Surviving flutes, mouth-organs, ocarinas, zithers, bell-chimes, lithophones (stone bells) and drums already made it possible to reconstruct ritual orchestras from the Neolithic down to Imperial times and to infer much about some ancient music. However, in 1978 an extraordinary 5th-century BCE tomb belonging to the Marquis of Yi was excavated. His set of still playable bronze bells provided exact pitch values for notes and was inscribed with full and systematic texts of music theory. Falkenhausen combines analysis of this musical 'Rosetta stone' with technical bronze studies, classic poetry, economics and social theory to present a 'new panorama' of music and society which is quite different from (but ancestral to) that of later times. Although technical data is presented, the exposition is clear and there are numerous helpful pictures and diagrams.

1328 **Like a knife: ideology and genre in contemporary Chinese popular music.**
Andrew F. Jones.   Ithaca, New York: East Asia Program, Cornell University, 1992. 180p. (Cornell East Asia Series).

Surveys popular music in China from the late 1980s, places it in the context of a developing youth culture, and interviews leading Chinese musicians. Jones distinguishes virtually official *tongsu* (popularized) music, based on Chinese melodies, from *liuxing* (popular) music, based on Western harmonies and targeted at the young. Rock (*yaogun*) music, which is different from both, first came from the West, then from Canton or Hong Kong; musicians like Cui Jian developed a distinctive domestic style emphasizing autonomy and individuality, but within a Chinese collective context.

1329 **Pianos and politics in China: middle-class ambitions and the struggle over Western music.**
Richard Kurt Kraus.   New York: Oxford University Press, 1989. 288p.

Piano music was considered by liberal modernizers to be a international scientific language, by radical nationalists to be imperialist, and by populists to be élitist and alien to the masses. Kraus, a political scientist, first sketches the rise of bourgeois music in Europe and its very different significance for the middle class in China. Chapters then cover the lives and cultural politics of four musicians: Xian Xinghai, who first introduced European classical music; Fou Ceng (Fou Ts'eng), who defected in 1959 but returned to China just in time for the Cultural Revolution; Yin Chengzong, 'court pianist to the Cultural Revolution' which detested cosmopolitan culture but played Maoist hymns on the piano in Western harmony; and Liu Shikun. They emerge as men ambitious to internationalize China's culture, as victims of xenophobia, but also as socially ambitious snobs in regard to China's native arts.

1330   **The new Grove dictionary of music and musicians.**
Edited by Stanley Sadie.   London: Macmillan; New York: Grove's Dictionaries of Music, 1980. 20 vols.

The set of articles under 'China' in volume four, with cross-references to other articles, form a comprehensive survey of theory, forms, instruments and history. *Jade flute: the story of Chinese music*, by T. C. Lai, Robert Mok (Hong Kong: Swindon Book Company; New York: Schocken Books, 1985. 196p.) provides an essay on Chinese music, with illustrations and anecdotes. The chapter, 'The People's Republic of China', in *New music in the Orient: essays on composition in Asia since World War II*, edited with an introduction by Harrison Ryker (Buren, the Netherlands: Frits Knuf, 1991, p. 189-215. [Source Materials In Ethnomusicology]), describes both political and art music, with lists of composers and compositions.

1331   **Music of the billion: an introduction to Chinese musical culture.**
Liang Mingyue.   New York: Heinrichschofen Edition; Wilhelmshaven, West Germany; Locarno, Switzerland; Amsterdam: Heinrichschofen's Verlag, 1985. 310p. (Paperbacks on Musicology, no. 8).

An attractive general treatment for the Western music lover or student. Part one is an historical survey, opening with a chapter, 'Musical and Cultural Traits of Chinese Music', which deals with: the predominance of programme music; the association with social and political values; gentry versus professional musician; the predominance of regional music; the performer as composer; and polychronomicism; and multiplicity of temperaments. Liang then examines the growth of forms, instruments and genres dynasty by dynasty. Part two, 'Content and Context of Chinese Music', contains chapters on: psycho-aesthetic approaches to interpretation; oral and written transmission; the art of the *qin* (seven-stringed zither, or 'lute'); regional instrumental music; traditional opera, including *kun* and Beijing; and general characteristics. Throughout the work there are many musical examples. There is also a section entitled 'Selected Bibliography and References Cited' and a 'Selected Discography'.

1332   **The lore of the Chinese lute: an essay in the ideology of the ch'in.**
Robert H. van Gulik.   Tokyo: Charles Tuttle, 1969. 271p.

The *qin*, a seven-stringed zither translated here as 'lute' because of its similarly cultured associations, was the instrument *par excellence* of the Confucian literary gentleman. Van Gulik gathers and translates essays on its origins and associations, and accompanies his commentaries with paintings and calligraphy which show the connections between music, literature and the cult of the gentleman.

1333   **A song for one or two: music and the concept of art in early China.**
Kenneth J. DeWoskin.   Ann Arbor, Michigan: Center for Chinese Studies, University of Michigan, 1982. 202p. (Michigan Papers in Chinese Studies, no. 42).

A lucid, scholarly study which describes and evokes the diversity of musical activities and ideas in Chinese culture from the classical period to roughly the 3rd century CE. Since ancient Chinese viewed music as continuous with acoustics, politics, cosmology and art, DeWoskin considers all these topics. Chapters include: 'The Study of Music'; 'Music, Hearing, and the Mind'; 'Classical and Han Theory'; 'Mythology and Cosmology'; 'The *Ch'in* [*qin*] and its Way'; 'Critical Terminology, Notation, and Ideology'; and 'The Concept of Art', which considers the role of music in the formation of Chinese aesthetics.

Chinese music: an annotated bibliography.
See item no. 1466.

Theatre and Chinese opera

1334   **Chinese theater in the days of Kublai Khan.**
J. I. Crump.   Tucson, Arizona: University of Arizona Press, 1980. 429p.

A vivid, genial portrait of classical theatre in the Mongol or Yuan dynasty for the curious general reader and theatre student. In part one, 'Behind the Scenes', Crump sketches the wars and social disruption of Mongol conquest, outlines the earlier history of Chinese entertainments, then provides a lively and detailed picture of: stages and theatres; the actor's art (pantomime, horses and other 'critters', performance modes, make-up, costuming and pageantry); and the background of the plays. Part two consists of lively translations of three plays: 'Li Kui Carries Thorns', concerning an incident which also appears in the novel, *Shuihu zhuan*; 'Rain on the Xiaoxiang'; and 'The Molohe Doll'.

1335   **The Chinese conception of the theatre.**
Tao-ching Hsü.   Seattle, Washington; London: University of Washington Press, 1985. 622p.

Provides a compendium of information and lore on the traditional theatre and its heritage, including Beijing opera, from the point of view of a scholarly enthusiast. Part one, 'The Chinese Theatre of To-day' (actually before 1949) has chapters on: the theatre building, audience and programme; the Chinese stage; stage conventions, including indications of scene and character; types of characters and costumes; music; style of singing; scripts; and the actors' training and professional life. Part two, 'The Artistry of the Chinese Theatre', covers: conventions and dramatic illusion; the mood of the unadorned stage; the world of the Chinese drama; the function of the story; the psychology of the mask; and the aria as vocal acting par excellence. Parts three and four are a history of the Chinese theatre from early times and a discussion of its heritage. Part six compares Chinese with Greek, Elizabethan and modern European theatre.

1336 **Ritual opera, operatic ritual: 'Mu-lien rescues his mother' in Chinese popular culture.**
Edited by David Johnson.   Berkeley, California: IEAS Publications, University of California, 2223 Fulton St. Sixth Floor, Berkeley CA 94720, 1989. 324p. bibliog. (Publications of the Chinese Popular Culture Project, no. 1).

In this ritual traditional opera, *Mulian rescues his mother*, which lasts for many days, the Buddhist monk Mulian descends into hell to rescue his sinful mother; skits and playlets of the story were often performed at funerals, illustrating the characteristic blending of ritual and drama in Chinese local religion. This symposium volume contains essays on the Mulian operas and on: the cultural significance of Chinese ritual opera; the theatrical and funerary traditions of Fujian; Taiwanese funeral rituals; the Daoist liturgical context; and relations to the Ghost Festival, 400-1900 CE.

1337 **The Chinese theater from its origins to the present day.**
Edited by Colin Mackerras.   Honolulu: University of Hawaii Press, 1983. 220p. bibliog.

Specialists introduce and describe individual eras and topics in the development of Chinese plays and theatre, with useful chapter bibliographies. Topics include: early Chinese plays and theatre; Yüan drama; the drama of the Qing dynasty; the performance of classical theatre; theatre and the masses; and traditional theatre in contemporary China. Colin Mackerras, *The rise of the Peking opera 1770-1870: social aspects of the theater in Manchu China* (Oxford: Oxford University Press, 1972. 316p.) is a multifaceted social and institutional history which discusses the off-stage social and sexual roles of actors. Mackerras traces this distinctive form to its origins in 16th to 18th-century popular and literati drama, and also covers the sponsorship of wealthy salt merchants in Yangzhou, and the adoption of the troupes by the imperial court in the 19th century.

1338 **Salesman in Beijing.**
Arthur Miller.   New York: Viking, 1984. 254p.

A thoughtful journal of directing *Death of a salesman* in Beijing in Spring 1983, with many observations on the situation in China. Miller perceptively describes the portrayal of Willy Loman by the classical Chinese actor Ying Ruocheng, the changes in the play developed in rehearsals, the reactions of the actors, and the audience reception. He also provides insights into both cultures in the process.

1339 **China on stage: an American actress in the People's Republic.**
Lois Wheeler Snow.   New York: Random House, 1972. 328p.

A sympathetic presentation of Jiang Qing's cultural programme during the Cultural Revolution, with texts of four 'model operas': *Taking Tiger Mountain by strategy*, *Shajiabang*, *Red detachment of women*, and *The red lantern*. Ms Snow, herself an accomplished actress, was warmly received on a visit to the People's Republic with her husband, Edgar. She saw enthusiasm and innovation where subsequently Chinese and foreign critics have seen repression and stultification.

1340 **Listening to theater: the aural dimension of Beijing opera.**
Elizabeth Wichman. Honolulu: University of Hawaii Press, 1991. 342p.

A technical, clearly organized study of the musical aspects of *jingju* – Beijing (Peking) opera. Wichman herself trained and performed in these operas, and gathered technical lore and information from her teachers. The opening chapter sketches the background, such as character types, plots and aesthetic principles. Chapters then describe: the language of the operas; the melodic, metrical and modal structures; the collaborative process of composition, which involves tradition, text and performance; voice production, pronunciation and speech; and the orchestra.

1341 **Cantonese opera: performance as a creative process.**
Bell Yung. Cambridge, England: Cambridge University Press, 1989. 205p. (Cambridge Studies in Ethnomusicology).

A technical presentation and description of Cantonese opera (*Yueju*), still widely performed in Guangdong and Hong Kong. Yung develops a taxonomy of sixteen 'oral delivery types' (such as patter speech and poetic speech, types of arias); it is only necessary for the performer to know the texts, as the quite strict forms and tones of the words dictate the melodies.

Chinese village plays from the Ting Hsien region. . .
See item no. 609.

The Cambridge guide to Asian theatre.
See item no. 1434.

Cinema

1342 **Perspectives on Chinese cinema.**
Chris Berry. London: British Film Institute; Bloomington, Indiana: Indiana University Press, 1991. 234p.

An expanded edition of *Perspectives on the Chinese cinema* (Ithaca, New York: Cornell University East Asian Papers, 1985). Twelve essays, some reprinted, introduce and discuss film in the People's Republic, Taiwan and Hong Kong. Subjects covered include: the tradition of modern Chinese cinema; the Chinese montage, from poetry and painting to the silver screen; sexual differences and the viewing subject in the Shanghai made rural comedy, *Li Shuangshuang* (1962); political pressure and cinematic responses in the 1950s and 1970s; Chen Kaige's *Yellow earth* (1984); Zhang Yimou's *Red sorghum* (1989); the origins of the 'Fifth Generation' of directors in the 1970s; the market pressures of the 1980s; perceiving women cross-culturally in recent film; popular cinema in the PRC and Hong Kong; and animated film. There are filmographies, brief biographies of major directors, a chronology and a character glossary. *King of the Children and the new Chinese cinema* by Chen Kaige, Tony Rayns (London; Boston, Massachusetts: Faber & Faber, 1989. 121p.) includes both a substantial essay on 1980s film and the shooting script of Chen Kaige's film.

1343   **New Chinese cinemas: forms, identities, politics.**
Edited by Nick Browne, Paul G. Pickowicz, Vivian Sobchack, Esther
Yau.   Cambridge, England: Cambridge University Press, 1994.
255p. bibliog.

Nine essays by film scholars examine film and its theory in the People's Republic,
Taiwan and Hong Kong in the 1980s. A substantial introduction provides background
on the interaction of film, theory, politics and social change. Part one, 'Film in the
People's Republic', includes articles on Xie Jin's *The Herdsman* (1982), *Hibiscus
Town* (1986), which embodies an official reformist view of the Cultural Revolution,
and *Wreaths at the foot of the mountain* (1984), an heroic story of the war with
Vietnam. It also covers: the political economy of Chinese melodrama; Huang Jianxin
and the notion of postsocialism in such films as *The black cannon incident* (1986),
Dislocation (1987), *Transmigration* (1989) and *A good woman* (1985); and 'Toward a
study of the viewing subject and Chinese cinema in the 1980s'. Part two deals with
film in Taiwan and Hong Kong. There are detailed chronologies, a glossary, and a
bibliography of scholarly works on Chinese film-making in the 1980s.

1344   **Primitive passions: visuality, sexuality, ethnography, and
contemporary Chinese cinema.**
Rey Chow.   New York: Columbia University Press, 1995. 252p.
bibliog. (Film and Culture Series).

This series of essays presents both an interpretive close reading of recent Chinese
films and an attempt to produce a cultural history and anthropology of modern China.
Part one, 'Visuality, Modernity, and Primitive Passions', argues that photographic
technology changed the way in which Chinese 'saw' themselves, and taking
'modernity' as a reference point led to the invention of the 'primitive' (including
rural, aboriginal and female). Part two examines the interplay of ideas of culture and
modernity in the films *Old well*, *Yellow earth*, *King of the children*, *Red sorghum*,
Judou and *Raise the red lantern*. A concluding section, 'Film as Ethnography; Or,
Translation Between Cultures in the Postcolonial World', discusses translation in
language, anthropology and ethnography.

1345   **Chinese cinema: culture and politics since 1949.**
Paul Clark.   New York: Cambridge University Press, 1987. 243p.

Surveys and assesses Leftist and political film from the 1930s down to *Yellow earth*
(1984). In the pre-1949 section, Clark analyses the rivalry between cosmopolitan
Shanghai films and politically conscious films in Yen'an, a tension which he sees as
continuing after 1949. Copious notes, an extensive multi-language bibliography, and a
1926-84 filmography are also included. Jay Leyda, *Dianying* (Cambridge,
Massachusetts: Massachusetts Institute of Technology Press, 1972. 515p.), by an
American who studied in the 1930s with the Soviet film-maker Sergei Eisenstein, is a
pioneering effort which provides much insight into Chinese films from the 1910s to
the 1960s, but does not use Chinese documentation or film scholarship.

1346 **Cinematic landscapes: observations on the visual arts and cinema of China and Japan.**
Edited by Linda C. Erlich, David Desser. Austin, Texas: University of Texas Press, 1994. 345p.

Film and art scholars ask 'what makes film from different cultures *look* so different?' and explore how spatial consciousness, compositional techniques and construction of images are shared between traditional and modern art forms, and between film and art. Sherman Lee leads off with an essay contrasting Chinese and Japanese art. Part one, 'Film and the Visual Arts in China: An Introduction', contains five essays: 'Chinese Visual Representation: Painting and Cinema' and 'Chinese Classical Painting and Cinematographic Signification', both by Beijing based film scholars; an analysis of post-socialist strategies in *Yellow earth* and *Black cannon incident*; Daoist principles and Chinese landscapes in Chen Kaige's *King of the children* (1987); and experiments in colour and portraiture in Zhang Yimou's *Judou* (1989). Part two has essays on Japanese film. A filmography and list of selected books and articles are appended.

1347 **Film in contemporary China: critical debates, 1979-1989.**
Edited by George S. Semsel, Chen Xihe, Xia Hong, foreword by John Lent. Westport, Connecticut; London: Praeger Publishers, 1993. 204p. bibliog.

Contains articles from Chinese journals and interviews. In the 1980s the work of such veteran directors as Xie Jin was criticized as melodramatic and sentimental in classic Hollywood style; new styles arose as 'Fifth Generation' films emerged after 1976 and 'entertainment films' came to dominate by the late 1980s. Part one, 'The Call for New Social Concepts', contains 'Innovation in Social and Cinematic Ideas' and 'The Modern Consciousness of the Filmmaker'. Part two, 'The Issue of Culture', has four essays which debate Fifth Generation films such as Chen Kaige's *Yellow earth* (1984), Tian Zhuangzhuang's *Horse thief* (1986), Huang Jianxin's *Black cannon incident* (1986), and Zhang Yimou's *Red sorghum* (1989). Parts three and four represent the debates on screenplay writing, the entertainment film and film theory. The bibliography is virtually useless as it does not indicate whether items are in Chinese or English. *Chinese film theory: a guide to the new era*, edited by George S. Semsel, Hou Jianping, Xia Hong (New York: Praeger, 1990. 222p.) and *Chinese film: the state of the art in the People's Republic*, edited by George Stephen Semsel (New York: Praeger, 1987. 191p.) contain edited translations of articles from Chinese film journals and interviews with film-makers representing contending views. Unfortunately, the effort is marred by errors in translation, a lack of identification of references for the non-specialist reader, and a patchy knowledge of the Chinese background.

From May Fourth to June Fourth: fiction and film in twentieth century China.
See item no. 1192.

Food and Cooking

History and food culture

1348 **The food of China.**
E. N. [Eugene] Anderson. New Haven, Connecticut; London: Yale
University Press, 1988. 313p. bibliog.

A description of the history of food, food production and agriculture, cooking
strategies, and the role of food in present-day China. An opening chapter sketches the
natural environment and the stages of development of agriculture and the food system,
arguing that China's history of sustainable agriculture offers a model to a crowded
world. Following chapters outline food history: the food system took shape in the
Zhou through Han period, absorbed influences from Central Asia, underwent
definitive shaping in the Song, and then suffered 'involution' and the 'climax of
traditional agriculture'. Further chapters explore: foodstuffs today; basic cooking
strategies; regional variation; traditional medical values of food; and food in society.
The bibliography lists books and articles in English.

1349 **Food in Chinese culture: anthropological and historical**
perspectives.
Edited by K. C. Chang. New Haven, Connecticut; London: Yale
University Press, 1977. 429p. bibliog.

Eight lucid, sometimes charming essays by various hands interpret the foods and
cooking of successive dynasties from earliest times to the 20th century. The editor's
introduction argues that the essential features of Chinese food and meal construction
were set early on: natural resources and breadth of ingredients; interacting and
opposite categories of *fan* (grain) and *cai* (vegetable or meat dishes), which require
preparing food into morsels; flexibility and adaptability; cultural emphasis on health,
dietetics and links with the moral order; and the centrality of food in culture.
Individual chapters by historians, however, analyse patterns of change, often quite
basic, for the Han, Tang, Song, Yuan, Ming and Qing periods, and modern China

(North and South, including Guangdong). The bibliography lists Chinese and English books and articles, including those on food anthropology.

1350 Cannibalism in China.
Key Rey Chong.   Wakefield, New Hampshire: Longwood Academic, 1990. 200p. bibliog.

Collects references to cannibalism from traditional Chinese sources and begins to classify and analyse them. The preface and introduction set the problem in a context of world cannibalism and anthropological study, distinguishing 'survival cannibalism' from 'learned cannibalism' (publicly and culturally sanctioned practices). Part one devotes chapters to learned cannibalism in the various time periods of China's history. Chong finds that motives included hatred, punishment, taste, love, loyalty and filial piety (preparing one's own flesh to nourish parents). Part two contains chapters on 'Cannibalism in Chinese Literature', 'Methods of Cooking Human Flesh in China' and 'A Statistical Analysis of Cannibalism in Imperial China'. The bibliography includes references in Chinese and Western languages.

1351 All the tea in China.
Chow Kit, Ione Kramer.   San Francisco: China Books, 1990. 187p.

The authors argue that tea is at least as worthy of studious appreciation as wine; they bolster the claim with a well illustrated history of tea and descriptions of fifty famous Chinese teas. They also evaluate the health claims for the drink, describe the role of teahouses in China today, and tell where and how to buy unusual varieties they describe, such as 'Lushan Cloud and Mist' or 'Green Snail Spring' (they include Chinese characters to show to the tea shop clerks). They explain how to brew a 'nice cup of tea', and even describe how to get the most out of a teabag. A more historical account is *Tea in China: the history of China's national drink,* by John C. Evans (New York; Westport, Connecticut: London: Greenwood Press, 1992. 169p. [Contributions to the Study of World History, no. 33]).

1352 The taste of China.
Ken Hom, photographs by Leong Ka Tai.   New York; London: Simon & Schuster, 1990. 192p.

An exploration of food and cooking in China today, as found on a 'personal odyssey' by a leading cooking teacher and author returning to his family homeland. Chapters, each with rich photographs, cover: the taste and flavours of China; influences from the past and from abroad; the imperial legacy; the glorious cuisine of Canton; family traditions, which explains the foods of the yearly cycle of holidays and those used for family rituals; city and country fare; restaurant cooking; and snacks and street foods. Each chapter includes many recipes. Hom's closing 'Reflections' concludes that after so many years in the 'desert of proletarian functionalism', Chinese cuisine is 'slowly but demonstrably on the mend'.

1353 Chinese gastronomy.
Lin Hsiang-ju, Lin Tsuifeng, with an introduction by Lin Yutang. London: Thomas Nelson & Sons; New York: Hastings House, 1969. 211p.

A learned and graceful essay on Chinese aesthetics in food and eating, beautifully illustrated, with more than one hundred recipes (many of more historic than practical interest). Especially interesting are the essays by the 17th-century literatus Yuan Mei and the recipes from this gourmet.

1354   Food in China: a cultural and historical inquiry.
Frederick J. Simoons.   Boca Raton, Florida: CRC Press, 1991. 501p. bibliog.

Emphasizes the history and origins of plants, animals and food nutrition in traditional China. Simoons, a leading food anthropologist, uses secondary works to broadly survey all types of food, food production, and food beliefs from a comparative point of view, with an emphasis on Guangdong (Canton) and south China.

1355   Swallowing clouds.
A. Zee.   New York; London: Simon & Schuster, 1990. 378p. map. bibliog.

A series of playful essays on the lore of Chinese food, culture and the relation of the Chinese writing system to them. Zee lightly explains many heavy linguistic questions, for instance, why 'swallowing clouds' is the literal meaning of one set of characters used to write 'wonton'. Many historical incidents and anecdotes are introduced as well as dozens of Chinese characters. Much of the information is accurate.

Cookery books

1356   Joyce Chen cookbook.
Joyce Chen.   Philadelphia, Pennsylvania; New York: J. B. Lippincott, 1962. 223p.

One of the first cookbooks to introduce the American public to relatively authentic cooking techniques for beginners not shopping in Chinatown. The recipes are not great in number, but are thoughtfully chosen to show basic techniques. Directions are clear and practical, with illustrations and step by step instructions to produce a recognizably Chinese meal. Eileen Yin-Fei Lo, *New Cantonese cooking* (New York; London: Viking Penguin, 1988. 258p.) provides a selection of simple but authentic recipes for the home cook. More advanced technique descriptions include: Nina Simonds, *Classic Chinese cuisine* (Boston, Massachusetts: Houghton, Mifflin, 1982. 353p. map); and Ken Hom, *Chinese technique: an illustrated guide to the fundamental techniques of Chinese cooking* (New York: Simon & Schuster, 1981. 345p.).

1357   Everything you want to know about Chinese cooking.
Pearl Kong Chen, Tien Chi Chen, Rose Y. L. Tseng.   Woodbury, New York; Toronto; London; Sydney: Barron's, 1983. 504p.

This volume represents a virtual encyclopaedia, a 'self-learning text on Chinese cookery, a handy reference manual on Chinese cuisine and nutrition, and also a source of entertaining information about the Chinese and their food', with many illustrations and helpful comments. Part one, 'Background Information', describes the history of Chinese cooking and regional cuisines, including Chinese food in America, ingredients, tools and equipment, and techniques (with detailed photographs). Part two, 'Major Cuisines', provides hundreds of recipes, some familiar, some which deserve to become so. Part three, 'Food in the Chinese Context', discusses planning a Chinese meal, tea, wine, liquor, food as a Chinese tradition and Chinese food and health.

1358 **Pei Mei's Chinese cook book.**
Fu Pei Mei.   Taipei: Chinese Cooking Class, 1969, 1974. 2 vols.
These two volumes, each usable independently, present recipes developed at Ms Fu's cooking school for foreign and Chinese audiences in Taipei. They carefully explain a range of dishes and styles which a serious but not professional Chinese home kitchen could produce. In volume one the chapters are divided according to regional cuisine: Eastern (e.g. Shanghai); Southern (e.g. Canton); Western (e.g. Sichuan); Northern; and snacks and desserts. The chapters in volume two are arranged by ingredient – chicken, duck, pork, beef, fish, eggs and beancurd, vegetables, soups, etc. Chinese and English texts are on facing pages. The directions are clear enough for those already familiar with the techniques, but some ingredients will be hard to find outside Chinese markets.

1359 **Mrs. Chiang's Szechwan cookbook.**
Ellen Schrecker, with John Schrecker.   New York; London; Toronto: Harper & Row, 1976. 359p.
Chiang Jung-feng grew up on a farm outside Chengdu, the fertile heart of Sichuan province; the Schreckers were American graduate students. This cookbook emerged from their coming together on Taiwan and their exploration of highly spiced but subtle Sichuan cooking. The recipes, mostly within the capability of reasonably experienced cooks, are limited in number, but include a representative sampling of dishes and tastes. The basic principles are clearly explained and illustrated, and the ingredients commonly available. Interspersed are Mrs Chiang's observations on the food and memories of her Sichuan upbringing.

China's food: a traveller's guide to the best restaurants, dumpling stalls, teahouses and markets in China.
See item no. 50.

Sports and Recreation

1360 **Training the body for China: sports in the moral order of the People's Republic.**
Susan Brownell. Chicago: University of Chicago Press, 1995. 393p. bibliog.

Brownell combines experience in China as a competitive athlete with anthropological theory of body culture and ritual to explore the political and social roles of competitive athletics over the last century. Particular sections cover: the Qing dynasty Grand Sacrifice; the 1987 National Games; sex; gender and the body; body building and old people's disco; sports and morality in the economic reforms; and the bid for the 2000 Olympic Games. Brownell's article 'Sports', in *Handbook of Chinese popular culture* (q.v.), p. 113-35, describes the history and bibliography of sport in traditional China, the top-down modern introduction of Western sports, the establishment of the Communist sports system, developments after 1949, and the position of the athlete in Chinese society.

1361 **Sport in China.**
Edited by Howard G. Knuttgen, Ma Qiwei, Wu Zhongyuan.
Champaign, Illinois: Human Kinetics Books, 1990. 222p.

A collection of articles translated from Chinese publications. Topics include: ancient games and sports; the introduction of Western sports; martial arts exercises *taijiquan* and *qigong*; and modern Chinese physical education and athletic competitions, including the structure and operations of the government sports commission. *Sports and games in ancient China* (Beijing: New World Press, 1986. 135p. [China Spotlight Series]) also provides a useful overview.

1362 **Sports, politics, and ideology in China.**
Jonathan Kolatch. Middle Village, New York: Jonathan David Publishers, 1972. 254p.

Covers the introduction of Western sports into China and the role of sports in modern history. Kolatch also discusses: the introduction of Western sports by missionary schools; the YMCA; the political promotion of athletic competition by the Nationalist government in the 1930s; and the first decades of the People's Republic. James T. C. Liu, 'Polo and cultural change: from T'ang to Sung' (*Harvard Journal of Asiatic Studies*, vol. 45, no. 1 [1985], p. 203-24) argues that the Central Asian sport of polo disappeared as the horse-riding Tang aristocrats gave way to gentlemanly Song civil servants.

Libraries and Museums

1363 Les bibliothèques en Chine au temps des manuscrits (jusqu'au Xe siècle). (Libraries in China at the time of manuscripts [up to the 10th century]).
Jean-Pierre Drège. Paris: Ecole Française Orient, 1991. 322p.
(Publications de L'Ecole Française d'Extrême Orient, clxi).

Describes the early development – before the advent of printed books – of libraries, paper and other materials used in book and manuscript production, and changes in the form of books. Chapters in chronological order cover: the imperial and official libraries from Han to Tang; bibliographical classification schemes; private libraries; and Buddhist and Daoist libraries. Coverage is most detailed for the mediaeval period, and special attention is paid to the collections found at Dunhuang. There are many translations of sources, bibliographical references and indexes for people, places and books. See also *Les bibliothèques en Chine pendant la première moitié de XXe siècle* (Libraries in China during the first half of the 20th century) by Roger Pelissier (Paris: Mouton, 1971. 366p. bibliog.).

Books and Printing

1364   Written on silk and bamboo: the beginnings of Chinese books and inscriptions.
Tsuen-hsuin Tsien.   Chicago: University of Chicago Press, 1962. 233p.

Uses archaeological evidence then available and abundant literary records to show how words were written and how early records, inscriptions, engravings and documents were physically produced. The author also discusses: writing on bamboo; the emergence of silk as writing material; quasi-paper and paper manuscripts; and tools of writing, such as the writing brush and ink. The conclusion looks forward to the development of the Chinese book, the evolution of script, and the order of Chinese writing.

1365   Printing and publishing in medieval China.
Denis Twitchett.   London: Lund Humphries; New York: Frederic C. Bell, for the Wynken de Worde Society, 1983. 94p. bibliog.

Based on a 1977 talk. Twitchett discusses: the invention of paper and the origins of Chinese printing; early publishing and bookselling; large-scale printing under the Song dynasty; the economics of printing; printing in Korea; and the technology and advantages of woodblock printing. Numerous illustrations are included.

1366   The invention of printing in China and its spread Westward.
Thomas Francis Carter, revised, edited by Luther Carrington Goodrich.   New York: Ronald Press, 1955. 2nd ed. 293p.

A standard older study, originally published in 1925, which still has some material on the spread of printing not covered in the now standard work, Tsien's *Chemistry and chemical technology: part 1: paper and printing* (q.v.).

1367   **Calligraphy and the East Asian book.**
Frederick W. Mote, Hung-lam Chu, with the collaboration of Ch'en
Pao-chen, W. E. Anita Siu, Richard Kent.   Boston, Massachusetts;
Shaftesbury, England: Shambala Publications, 1988. 248p.
A catalogue accompanied by substantial background essays, from a 1989 exhibition at
Princeton University which gathered Chinese books and calligraphy, including ink
rubbings as a form of printing. Mote's introductory essay, 'Calligraphy and Books –
Their Evolving Relationship Through Chinese History,' contrasts calligraphy in China
and the West. The body of the book reproduces examples of calligraphy from many
periods which illustrate the different styles of writing.

Chemistry and chemical technology: part 1: paper and printing.
See item no. 1079.

**Domesticated deities and auspicious emblems: the iconography of
everyday life in village China.**
See item no. 1247.

Mass Media and Communications

1368 **The great wall in ruins: communication and cultural change in China.**
Edited by Godwin C. Chu, Ju Yanan. Albany, New York: State University of New York Press, 1993. 366p. (SUNY Series in Human Communication Processes).

Basing their work on an extensive survey which they conducted in the People's Republic, the authors chart changes in cultural values and expectations which came with the economic growth and social transformation under reforms. Chu and Ju discuss how the electronic media and new social patterns interacted to produce unprecedented cultural change. These themes are addressed in the earlier symposium, *Popular media in China: shaping new cultural patterns*, edited by Godwin Chu (Honolulu: University of Hawaii Press, 1978. 263p.). *Media and the Chinese public: a survey of the Beijing media audience*, edited by Brantly Womack (Armonk, New York: M. E. Sharpe, 1986. 200p.) presents articles from Chinese publications, originally published as *Chinese Sociology and Anthropology*, vol. 18, nos. 3-4 (1986).

1369 **Voices of China: the interplay of politics and journalism.**
Edited by Chin-chuan Lee, foreword by John K. Fairbank. New York; London: Guilford, 1990. 353p.

Provides seventeen stimulating articles by practising Chinese journalists, foreign journalists covering China, political scientists, and historians which consider and debate the gains and setbacks for mass media in the 1980s economic reforms. Fairbank's foreword argues that the autocracy of late imperial China was limited and passé, not an enduring cultural given. Part one, 'Overview', reviews the history of relations between journalists and the government in modern China, discusses democracy as an 'elusive goal' of journalists, and introduces the 'epistemology of reporting China', that is, how the 'culture of journalism' affects the nature of reporting on and in China. Footnotes furnish references, unfortunately not always distinguishing whether they are in Chinese or in English. Part two, 'Media Reform in China: An Uncertain Experiment', focuses on the 1980s, while part three, 'American Media Coverage of China: Romanticism vs. Cynicism', covers the period from 1900 to the events of Tiananmen.

1370   **China's media, media's China.**
Edited by Chin-chuan Lee.   Boulder, Colorado; San Francisco;
Oxford: Westview Press, 1994. 340p.

Scholars and journalists explore politics and communication in the contemporary People's Republic, Taiwan and Hong Kong. Part one, the editor's 'Overview', discusses institutionalized censorship, journalistic professionalism, technology, opposition and media reform in the 1980s. Nine essays in part two, 'Control, Change, and Opposition', discuss the role of the press and government use of media in 1980s People's Republic, press control in pre- and post-1949 China, and the role of the press in democratic change in Taiwan. Part three, 'Ideology, Knowledge, and Professionalism', contains essays on: the American correspondent in China; the historical fate of 'objective' reporting in China; Hong Kong journalists; the Voice of America as a model of professionalism and its tremendous impact in China; and US media coverage of the Cultural Revolution.

1371   **China turned on: television, reform, and resistance.**
James Lull.   London; New York: Routledge, 1991. 230p.

Lull, a San Francisco based writer on world television and mass culture, describes his sophisticated and vibrant study as an 'ethnography of culture and communication in contemporary urban China'. It is based on his interviews with Chinese TV executives and more than 100 urban families, and reading of English-language scholarship and theory. He describes the growing professionalization of TV workers, the disagreement among different sectors of the government, and the home audience's increasing experience and media sophistication. These developments produced 'polysemy', a situation in which viewers can decipher information not sanctioned by official sponsors; instead of spawning public compliance, TV families imagine new lives and politics outside government control, or even simply the 'freedom to have fun'. John Howkins, *Mass communication in China* (New York: Longman, 1982. 160p. bibliog. [Annenberg Communications Series]) is a survey by an authority in international mass media who sketches the relationship of politics to television and radio, film and advertising.

1372   **Deathsong of the River: a reader's guide to the Chinese TV series** *Heshang*.
Su Xiaokang, Wang Luxiang, introduced, translated, annotated by Richard W. Bodman, Pin P. Wan.   Ithaca, New York: East Asia Program, Cornell University, 1991. 349p. maps. bibliog. (Cornell East Asia Series, no. 54).

In June 1988, a six-part historical series, *Heshang* – 'Deathsong of the River' or 'River Dirge' – was shown on Chinese national television. Viewers were stunned and excited to see traditional culture presented as repressive and authoritarian; the Yellow River, symbol of an exhausted past, was shown flowing into the blue ocean of the democratic and rational outside world. Bodman and Wan present: a complete translation of the best-selling published script; interpretive background essays by themselves, Tu Wei-ming and Su Xiaokang; and a cross section of criticisms from orthodox historians. An extensive bibliography lists hundreds of items in Chinese, Japanese, German and English.

1373 **Government control of the press in modern China, 1900-1949.**
Lee-hsia Hsu Ting.   Cambridge, Massachusetts: East Asian Research
Center, Harvard University, distributed by Harvard University Press,
1974. 318p. bibliog. (Harvard East Asian Monographs, no. 57).

A scholarly history of cases, incidents and policies in Chinese publishing from 1900-49. Ting focuses cn the efforts of journalists and publishers to develop freedom of the press but finds governmental success in manipulating the media. After an introductory summary, chapters describe: the 'twilight' of the Qing Dynasty (reformist and revolutionary newspapers in China and abroad); the 'growing pains' of the new Republic, 1912-27 (the press under Yuan Shikai, corrupt journalists, arguments for freedom of the press); the Nationalist régime before the war, 1927-37; the war of resistance, 1937-45; and the aftermath of the war, 1945-49. Patricia Stranahan, *Molding the medium: the Chinese Communist Party and the* Liberation Daily (Armonk, New York; London: M. E. Sharpe, 1991. 204p.) shows how the Party developed its news organs in Yen'an, 1937-45.

1374 **History of the press and public opinion in China.**
Lin Yutang.   London: Oxford University Press, for the Institute of
Pacific Relations; Chicago: University of Chicago Press, 1936. 179p.
Reprinted, New York: Greenwood, 1968.

An anecdotal, well written history which interprets the topic broadly to include both publications for a public readership and the activities of students and literati; 'public opinion' is thus defined as the political ideas of the educated. Early sections cover the Han and Song dynasties, while later chapters deal with the 20th century.

1375 **China pop: how soap operas, tabloids, and bestsellers are
transforming a culture.**
Jianying Zha.   New York: New Press, 1995. 210p.

These sharply written, spirited essays were based on interviews and first-hand experience. After Tiananmen, young Chinese novelists, film-makers and artists left politics to pursue economic and cultural innovation. Zha first recounts the story behind the massively popular 1990 TV series 'Yearnings' (*Kewang*), the young intellectuals who made it, and the political machinations surrounding it. 'City Without Walls' describes Beijing's loss of architectural and cultural roots. Zha then explores the dilemma of film director Chen Kaige, whose *Farewell my concubine* was an international hit but did not connect with a domestic audience. Other chapters tellingly describe pop journalism, food hedonism, raunchy novels and Hong Kong chic.

**Mandate of Heaven: a new generation of entrepreneurs, dissidents,
bohemians, and technocrats lays claim to China's future.**
See item no. 788.

**Like a knife: ideology and genre in contemporary Chinese popular
music.**
See item no. 1328.

Periodicals, Newspapers and Yearbooks

Periodicals

1376 **Arts of Asia.**
Hong Kong: Arts of Asia Publications (1309 Kowloon Centre, 29-39 Ashley Road, Kowloon, Hong Kong), 1971- . bimonthly.

The richly illustrated articles, gallery reviews and news which appear in this journal are aimed at the collector and general audience. They deal with art and art history from all parts of Asia.

1377 **Asian Survey: A Monthly Review of Contemporary Asian Affairs.**
Berkeley, California: University of California Press, 1961- . monthly.

Contains scholarly articles on all regions of present-day Asia, with an emphasis on politics. Annual survey issues include an overview analysis of Chinese politics during that year.

1378 **Asian Theatre Journal.**
Honolulu: University of Hawaii Press, 1984- . semi-annual.

Carries articles, reviews, reports, performance reviews (often with photographs), and translations of plays and documents, written for theatre students and practioners on all aspects of contemporary and historical theatre in Asia from Japan to India, paying substantial attention to China.

1379 **Asiaweek.**
Hong Kong, Asiaweek (30/F Vicwood Plaza, 199 Des Voeux Road, Central, Hong Kong), 1975- . weekly.

This journal provides wide journalistic coverage of politics, current events and cultural developments in all countries of Asia, with regular feature articles, book reviews and editorial columns.

1380 **Beijing Review.**
Beijing: Foreign Languages Press, 1979- . weekly.
The all but official voice of the People's Republic, with official documents, feature articles on many subjects, and analysis of current developments. The publication is available in many major languages, including Esperanto. It was entitled *People's China* during the period 1950-57, then *Peking Review* until January 1979.

1381 **Bulletin of Concerned Asian Scholars.**
Boulder, Colorado: Bulletin of Concerned Asian Scholars (3239 9th Street, Boulder, Colorado 80302-2112, USA), 1968- . quarterly.
Established by the Committee of Concerned Asian Scholars during the Vietnam War as an outlet for critical scholarship, the *Bulletin* is now a free-standing journal of radical opinion and scholarship on the entire region, with conscientious representation of dissenting voices from Asian countries. Special topical issues are frequent, some of which are then separately published.

1382 **Bulletin of the School of Oriental and African Studies.**
London: School of Oriental and African Studies, London University, 1917- . 3 times a year.
A wide-ranging scholarly journal which covers all of Asia, the Middle East and Africa, emphasizing traditional scholarship in the pre-modern period, with articles, books reviews and notes.

1383 **China Briefing.**
Boulder, Colorado; San Francisco; Oxford: Westview Press, published in cooperation with the Asia Society, 1980- . annual.
These annual volumes are aimed at general readers and policy-makers, analysing all areas of politics, foreign relations (including relations with Taiwan and Hong Kong), economy, culture and society. There is an annual chronology and suggestions for further reading, sometimes with biographical sketches, charts or appendices. The 1992 volume, for instance, includes articles on public health, cinema, and China and the New World Order. Articles in the 1994 volume likewise treat rural China in transition, the Three Gorges Dam Project and environment, and ethnic identity.

1384 **China Business Review.**
Washington, DC: National Council for US-China Trade (1818 N Street NW, Suite 500, 20036), 1974- . bi-monthly.
Provides the China business community with up-to-date reporting, statistics and commentary on topics affecting trade, investment, living in China and general background. The 'Book Shelf' reviews items of interest in many area. It was formerly entitled *U.S.-China Business Review*.

1385 **China Economic Review.**
Greenwich, Connecticut: JAI Press (55 Old Post Road, No. 2 PO Box 1678, Greenwich, Connecticut 06836-1678), 1989- . twice yearly.
Provides scholarly analyses of the economy of the People's Republic and Taiwan, often with international comparisons. Special issues have included 'China's Transition to the Market' (Fall 1993) and 'Chinese Agricultural Policy' (Spring 1994).

1386   China Information.

Leiden, the Netherlands: Documentation and Research Center for
Contemporary China, 1986- . quarterly.

The detailed and well-informed articles and documents of this journal cover all
aspects of contemporary China, primarily by scholars in European countries writing in
English, paying special attention to documentation. The publication generally includes
articles on current politics and literature, and some scholarly reviews of books.

1387   The China Journal.

Canberra: Contemporary China Centre, Research School of Pacific
and Asian Studies, Australian National University, 1979- . twice
yearly.

A basic scholarly journal which focuses on modern and contemporary China, with
well-regarded and often innovative articles, book reviews and discussions. Until 1995
it was published as *Australian Journal of Chinese Affairs.*

1388   China News Analysis.

Hong Kong: China News Analysis, 1953-82, edited by Fr. Laszlo
Ladany; 1984- . fortnightly.

Each issue features a lead article based on publications in the People's Republic,
interviews with refugees, and other documents. Father Ladany was an early and
trenchant critic of Communism; his articles from the 1950s-1980s are still of use for
their detailed analysis. Current coverage continues under new editors in the same
format.

1389   China Now.

Cheltenham, England: Society for Anglo-Chinese Understanding (109
Promenade, Cheltenham, Gloustershire, GL50 1NW). quarterly.

A general interest magazine which reports sympathetically on all aspects of Chinese
life and culture today, with features on history and language.

1390   China Quarterly.

London: Congress for Cultural Freedom (Paris), 1960-68;
Contemporary China Institute, School of Oriental and African
Studies, 1968- . quarterly.

A standard outlet for scholarship on the People's Republic, Taiwan and Hong Kong,
and historical events related to the Communist revolution. There are extensive book
reviews, review articles and research notes. 'Quarterly Chronicle and Documentation'
gives a detailed and classified chronology, including texts of major policies, speeches
of government leaders, state visits, meetings, official appointments, treaties and
agreements, and substantial excerpts from other major documents.

1391   **China Report: A Journal of East Asian Studies.**
New Delhi: Centre for the Study of Developing Societies; Delhi;
London: Thousand Oaks, California: Sage Publications, 1964- .
quarterly.
Contains reports, discussions and analysis on China and its neighbours, primarily
written by Indian scholars, journalists and diplomats.

1392   **China Review.**
Hong Kong: Chinese University Press, 1991- . annual.
Journalists and scholars, most based in Hong Kong, provide clear-headed interpretive
articles on recent politics, economics, trade and foreign investment, military, social
change and culture. Essays put the events of the year in longer perspective and go
beyond current events. Recent topics included official and unofficial culture in
tension, the 'greying' of Chinese culture as young rebels grow older, and sex among
youth. A chronology and index are included.

1393   **China Review International.**
Honolulu: University of Hawaii Press, 1994- . twice yearly.
Devoted to substantial reviews of books in both Asian and European languages in all
fields and periods of Chinese studies, with an emphasis on the pre-current events
period. Each issue also contains lengthier review articles which focus on a particular
book, question or field.

1394   **Chinese Education and Society.**
Armonk, New York; London: M. E. Sharpe, 1968- . quarterly.
Carries articles (and occasionally full books) from the Chinese media, usually on
contemporary issues (especially during the Cultural Revolution) but sometimes on
historical themes. Topics of issues have included: the essays of Tao Xingzhi (1891-
1946) in vol. 7, no. 4 (Winter 1974-75); and the debate on Chinese characters in vol.
18, no. 2 (Summer 1985). This journal was formerly entitled *Chinese Education: A
Journal of Translations*.

1395   **Chinese Law and Government: A Journal of Translations.**
Armonk, New York; London: M. E. Sharpe, 1968- . quarterly.
A journal of articles (occasionally books) translated from the Chinese media, usually
centred around a particular theme or topic, sometimes a single Chinese book. An
example is Zhao Ziyang's 'Sichuan experience: blueprint for a nation', vol. 15, no. 1
(1982).

1396   **Chinese Literature.**
Beijing: Foreign Languages Press, 1951- . quarterly.
Presents fiction, poetry, essays and commentary translated by the Foreign Language
Press group of translation specialists. Works from all periods are treated, with an
emphasis on the 20th century and contemporary official literature. It was originally
entitled *People's Literature*, and is indexed in *Subject and author index to Chinese
Literature Monthly (1951-1976)*, compiled by Donald A. Gibbs (New Haven,
Connecticut: Far Eastern Publications, Yale University, 1978. 173p.).

478

1397   **Chinese Literature: Essays, Articles, Reviews.**
Bloomington, Indiana; Department of Comparative Literature,
University of Indiana, 1978- . twice a year.

Usually referred to as 'CLEAR', this journal publishes scholarly articles and reviews in all fields of literature, primarily before the modern period. It was published as *Chinese Literature* until 1980.

1398   **Chinese Science.**
International Society for the History of East Asian Science,
Technology, and Medicine.   Los Angeles: Center for Chinese
Studies, University of California at Los Angeles, 1975- . irregular.
From 1975-94, published at University of Pennsylvania.

An 'informal and irregular journal dedicated to the study of traditional and modern East Asian science, technology, and medicine in the Chinese tradition', which publishes scholarly articles, notes, reports on conferences and book reviews.

1399   **Chinese Sociology and Anthropology: A Journal of Translations.**
Armonk, New York; London: M. E. Sharpe, 1968- . quarterly.

Each issue selects and translates Chinese articles (and sometimes a whole book) on a topic of concern, usually with an introduction by a guest editor. Typical recent topics have included: 'The Debate on Neo-authoritarianism', vol. 23, no. 2 (Winter 1990-91); the origins and formation of the *danwei* (work unit); the boom in *qigong*, the neo-traditional exercise and breath control; and the impact of the television series *Kewang* ('Expectations' or 'Yearnings') and *Heshang* ('River elegy').

1400   **Chinese Studies in History: A Journal of Translations.**
Armonk, New York; London: M. E. Sharpe, 1967- . quarterly.

Provides translations from academic journals in the People's Republic and Taiwan, often with brief commentary, and sometimes original articles, showing recent developments in scholarship. Issues are often devoted to particular topics, such as: Shanghai Social Movements, 1919-49 (1994); Chinese Communist source materials (1991); intellectual figures such as Hu Shi and Liang Qichao; and the 1936 Xi'an incident. It was formerly known as *Chinese Studies in History and Philosophy*.

1401   **Early China.**
Berkeley, California: Society for the Study of Early China, 1976- .
annual.

A wide-ranging scholarly journal concerning pre-Han China, which includes articles, substantial book reviews, research notes and news of the field. As with the following newsletters or journals, the audience primarily consists of scholars in the field, but the subject matter, especially the airing of controversies and recent worldwide events in the field, is often of wider interest. Other scholarly newsletters or journals include: *T'ang Studies* (T'ang Studies Society, 1982-); *Journal of Sung-Yüan Studies* (1970-); *Ming Studies* (1975- . semi-annual); *Late Imperial China* (q.v.); *Chinese Republican Studies* (formerly *Chinese Republican Studies Newsletter*); and *CCP Research Newsletter* (Colorado Springs, Colorado: Chinese Communism Research Group, twice yearly).

1402   **Far Eastern Economic Review.**
Hong Kong: Review Publishing Company (GPO Box 160, Hong Kong), 1946- . weekly.
Specializes in current events, with reports from correspondents in all parts of Asia. The focus is on economics and politics, but useful sections on current cultural and social trends, columns of commentary, book reviews and cartoons are also included. Annual issues are devoted to summarizing developments in each major country; the China issue is particularly detailed and analytical.

1403   **Harvard Journal of Asiatic Studies.**
Cambridge, Massachusetts: Harvard-Yenching Institute (2 Divinity Avenue, Cambridge Massachusetts, 02138, USA), 1936- . semi-annual.
Provides substantial scholarly articles and full-length reviews, with an emphasis on pre-1850 East Asian history, literature, archaeology, art and related fields.

1404   **Inside China Mainland.**
Taipei: Institute of Communist Chinese Studies, 1979- . monthly.
A journal of translations of current documents from the People's Republic and original articles on politics, economics and foreign relations, usually emphasizing analysis over polemic.

1405   **Issues and Studies.**
Taipei: Institute of International Relations, 1964- . monthly.
A scholarly journal of analysis which focuses on the history of the Chinese Communist Party, politics, economy and social policies of the People's Republic.

1406   **Journal of Asian Studies.**
Ann Arbor, Michigan: Association for Asian Studies (1 Lane Hall, University of Michigan, Ann Arbor Michigan 48109, USA), 1941- . quarterly.
The most prominent general academic journal in the field of Asian studies in the United States, which carries articles, book reviews, review articles and correspondence on all aspects of Asian history, social science, culture and literature. It was formerly entitled *Far Eastern Quarterly*. The Association also publishes *Asian Studies Newsletter*, which carries news and notices of interest to academic professionals, and *Education About Asia* (Ann Arbor, Michigan: Association for Asian Studies, 1996- . twice yearly), aimed at school teachers and college and university instructors teaching about Asia. It contains articles, photographs and maps, reviews of books and electronic media, and notes on resources.

1407   **Journal of Chinese Linguistics.**
Berkeley, California: Project on Linguistic Analysis, 1973- . twice a year.
Contains technical articles on phonology, syntax, dialects and history. A wide range of topics in linguistics, language teaching and literature is covered in professional but less

specialized style in *Journal of Chinese Language Teachers Association* (Kalamazoo, Michigan: Chinese Language Teachers Association, Kalamazoo College, 1966-).

1408   **Journal of Chinese Philosophy.**
Honolulu: University of Hawaii Press, 1973- . quarterly.
This journal carries scholarly articles and reviews on all aspects of Chinese philosophy, primarily in the pre-modern period.

1409   **Journal of Chinese Religions.**
Society for the Study of Chinese Religions, 1972- . annual.
A multidisciplinary scholarly journal which concerns the history of religion in China, and includes book reviews.

1410   **Journal of Contemporary China.**
Oxford: Carfax, Center for Modern China, 1992- . 3 times a year.
Contains articles, research notes and commentary in the social sciences and humanities on current political, social and economic events, many written by young scholars from the People's Republic trained abroad. It consistently reviews books in Chinese printed in the PRC, Taiwan, Hong Kong and other parts of the world.

1411   **Late Imperial China.**
Baltimore, Maryland: Johns Hopkins University Press, 1975- . twice a year.
The scholarly articles of social science and historical interest which appear in this journal deal primarily with the Ming and Qing periods. There are occasionally special issues, for instance: 'Poetry and Women's Culture in Late Imperial China' (vol. 13, no. 1, June 1992). It was formerly known as *Ch'ing-shih wen-t'i*.

1412   **Modern China: An International Quarterly of History and Social Science.**
Thousand Oaks, California: Sage Periodical Press (Sage Publications, 2455 Teller Rd., Thousand Oaks, CA 91320, USA), 1976- . quarterly.
Provides scholarly articles on all aspects of China from the Qing to the present, with an emphasis on history and social sciences. There are frequent state-of-the-field articles, and an occasional book review. Important recent topical symposia include: 'The Paradigmatic Crisis in Chinese Studies' (July 1991); 'Ideology and Theory in the Study of Modern Chinese Literature' (January 1993); 'Public Sphere/Civil Society in China?' (April 1993); and 'Rethinking the Chinese Revolution' (January 1995).

1413   **Modern Chinese Literature.**
Boulder, Colorado: Department of Oriental Languages, University of Colorado, 1984- . twice a year.
Carries translations, articles, notes and books reviews on modern and contemporary literature in the People's Republic, Taiwan and Hong Kong. There is occasional coverage of films; for example, an extensive bibliography of cinema books, articles and documents in English and Chinese appear in vol. 7 (1993), p. 117-53.

1414   Orientations: the Monthly Magazine for Collectors and Connoisseurs of Oriental Art.
Hong Kong: Orientations Magazine (14th Floor, 200 Lockhart Road, Hong Kong), 1971- . monthly.

A magazine of sumptuously illustrated and well informed articles and gallery reviews on the visual arts of East, South and Southeast Asia, with reports on exhibitions, auctions, museum acquisitions and academic events in all parts of the world.

1415   Pacific Affairs: An International Review of Asia and the Pacific.
Vancouver, Canada: University of British Columbia Press (2029 West Mall, University of British Columbia, Vancouver B. C. V6T 1 W5, Canada), 1928- . quarterly. Volumes 1-33 published by the Institute of Pacific Relations. Volumes 34- published by University of British Columbia Press.

A standard academic journal with articles, research notes and books reviews on all parts of Asia and the Pacific, with an emphasis on current and modern topics.

1416   Philosophy East and West: A Journal of Comparative Philosophy.
Honolulu: University of Hawaii Press, 1951-69; 1984- . semi-annual.

Contains articles and book reviews, and stands as one of the major organs in the movement to make the study of philosophy genuinely comparative and worldwide. Early editors included Charles Moore and Wing-tsit Chan.

1417   Problems of Post-Communism.
Washington, DC: United States Information Agency, Government Printing Office, 1952- . bimonthly.

As *Problems of Communism*, as it was entitled until 1992, this publication provided critical articles, books reviews and state-of-the-field summaries about all Communist countries and Marxist theory. The coverage of China was especially rich from the mid-1970s to the events of Tiananmen. From 1994, *Problems of Post-Communism* promises to continue the tradition.

1418   Renditions: A Chinese-English Translation Magazine.
Hong Kong: Chinese University of Hong Kong Press, 1973- . semi-annual.

Provides translations and occasional articles, with handsome drawings and Chinese texts. The translations cover all genres and periods, paying special attention to contemporary writing, and there are frequent thematic issues.

1419   Social Sciences in China.
Beijing: Social Science Publishing House, Academy of Social Sciences, 1980- . quarterly.

The English edition of *Zhongguo Shehui Kexue*. It includes translations of current articles from Chinese academic journals in all aspects of social science, including economics (especially the current reform efforts), history, education, sociology, law, philosophy and aesthetics. Also included are English-language abstracts, reviews, lists of publications in Chinese and reports of meetings and conferences.

1420 **T'oung Pao: International Review of Sinology.**
Leiden, the Netherlands: E. J. Brill, 1890- . bi-annual.
The pre-eminent journal of continental sinology, featuring articles on China's history, literature, art, history of science and related fields, primarily in English (with some in French or German).

1421 **Universities Field Staff International Reports. Asia.**
Universities Field Staff. Indianapolis, Indiana: Universities Field Staff (620 Union Drive, Indianapolis, Indiana 46202, USA), 1947- .
These serially issued, substantive articles are aimed at the interested general public and students and written by the Field Staff's regional correspondents. These correspondents included A. Doak Barnett, starting in 1947, Albert Ravenholt, 1948-56, Loren Fessler and Suzanne Pepper.

Newspapers

1422 **Asian Wall Street Journal.**
Hong Kong: Dow Jones Asia (North American subscriptions: 200 Burnett Rd., Chicopee, Massachusetts 01020), 1976- . daily on weekdays.
Emphasizes in-depth journalistic coverage of business and economic developments, with interpretive coverage of politics, culture and society. Although the Hong Kong publication is a separate operation, the New York *Wall Street Journal* runs a number of the feature articles and draws on the Hong Kong staff.

1423 **China Daily.**
Beijing: China Daily (15 Huixindongjie, Chaoyang District, Beijing China 10029), 1981- . daily.
A virtually official daily, distributed in China for readers of English, and also printed via satellite in Hong Kong, New York and elsewhere. During the 1980s, the journal was an outlet for the official reform viewpoint, but in 1989 became much less outspoken. It covers economic, cultural and current social issues as well as politics, with frequent feature articles on a wide range of topics. The *China Daily Index*, a joint project of *China Daily* and Griffith University, Australia, is published six times a year, with the last issue being a cumulation.

1424 **China News Digest (Global news).**
Internet Electronic Edition: CND-INFO. LIBRARY.UTA.EDU. daily.
An Internet site for articles and user material.

1425 Foreign Broadcast Information Service.

Washington, DC: US Department of Commerce, 1941- . daily.

The *Daily Report*, often referred to by scholars as 'FBIS', presents a massive compilation and translation of radio broadcasts from around the world. China has appeared under changing and unpredictable headings. A discussion of the FBIS history and contents appears in *The People's Republic, Part 1* (q.v.), p. 557-58.

1426 Joint Publications Research Service.

Washington, DC: US Government.

Often cited as 'JPRS', this series constitutes various services presenting translations from Chinese-language newspapers and periodicals, especially such official organs as *Renmin ribao* (People's Daily), *Hongqi* (Red Flag) and *Xinhua* (Hsinhua; New China News Agency). The most prominent series were *Survey of the China Mainland Press* (SCMP), and *Survey of China Mainland Magazines* (SCMM), which provided so-called 'Pekingologists' with ample grist. For a description and evaluation of these series, see Peter Berton and Eugene Wu, *Contemporary China: a research guide* (q.v.), p. 409-30 and *The People's Republic, Part 1* (q.v.), p. 557-58.

1427 South China Morning Post.

Hong Kong: South China Morning Post, 1903- . daily.

Although published in Hong Kong, this newspaper includes full daily coverage of events in China by its own respected correspondents, as well as opinion columns, features and book reviews which often concern China and Taiwan.

1428 Summary of World Broadcasts. Part 3: Asia-Pacific (daily).

British Broadcasting Corporation.   Reading, England: British Broadcasting Corporation, 1939- . daily.

Transcribes and translates broadcasts from Chinese government media both in the capital and in the provinces, providing a quick but extensive view of current policy and local events.

Yearbooks and non-governmental statistical works

1429 China Facts And Figures Annual.

Gulf Breeze, Florida: Academic International Press, 1978- . annual. Cumulative Volume 1978-89.

An annual review of developments in the People's Republic which provides recent basic data in major areas and on varying historical topics. Data is drawn from the CIA, US Congress, departments of the US government, United Nations and publications of the Chinese government. Topics generally include: government (structure and institutions, major events, administrative divisions, constitution and national anthem); the Communist party (membership of major organs and constitution); the armed forces; demography; the economy (national and sectoral production); agriculture; trade and aid; transport; communications; institutions (universities, research institutes, libraries, culture and religion); and health, education and welfare. A section of special topics changes each year, but will typically cover major events of the year and useful reference material, for example, a list of holidays, the twelve hororary characters, a key to pinyin romanization, and a list of Chinese immigrants to the US, 1820-1975.

1430 China handbook, 1937-1945.
Chinese Ministry of Information.   Chungking, China: Chinese
Ministry of Information; New York: Macmillan, 1947. 862p. various
reprints.

A comprehensive survey of major developments in the Republic of China during eight years of war. Topics covered include: general information; brief histories of political parties; government structure; foreign affairs and relations with various countries; public finance; transport and communication; law; the military and the war with Japan; education and research; mineral resources; money and banking; foreign trade; agriculture; health and medicine; the press; the Christian movement; government directory; associations and societies; and a who's who guide.

1431 China directory.
Tokyo: Radiopress, 1988- . annual.

A reference work on the organization and personnel of the Chinese Communist Party, government, and mass organizations. Names, addresses, and telephone and fax numbers are listed in *China Phone Book and Business Directory* (Hong Kong: China Business and Phone Book Address Company Ltd [181 Gloucester Road, Hong Kong], 1988- . bi-annual).

1432 The China Yearbook.
Shanghai, China: North China Daily News, 1912-39. Reprinted, New
York: Gordon Press, 1977. 20 vols.

Although edited by the very British H. G. E. Woodhead from the foreign concession in Shanghai, this was the fullest, though not entirely reliable, year-by-year reference for the period from the fall of the Qing dynasty to the early years of the war. Coverage varied, and a volume was not published every year, but topics generally included: the Chinese government (Republic of China) organization; important events; communications and media; who's who; economic, banking and professional developments; and chronologies.

Encyclopaedias, Directories and Subject Dictionaries

1433 **Cultural atlas of China.**
Carolyn Blunden, Mark Elvin. Oxford: Equinox; New York: Facts
on File, 1983. 237p. bibliog.

With fifty-eight maps and hundreds of pictures, drawings, charts and diagrams, as well
as a bibliographic essay, gazetteer and index, this atlas stands as a multifaceted and
innovative introduction to Chinese culture and history. 'Space' (part one) presents the
land and its people. 'Time' (part two) offers a series of historical essays on 'the
archaic world', 'the imperial age', and the 'modern age', all of which go beyond
political summary to include economic factors (such as canals) and art (such as the
Qin underground army). 'Symbols and Society' (part three) provides a series of brief
entries on culture, including: the writing system and poetry; music; theatre; medicine;
and family life. Perhaps better suited for browsing than reference, these readable
essays are full of original thought and insights.

1434 **The Cambridge guide to Asian theatre.**
Edited by James R. Brandon, advisory editor Martin Banham.
Cambridge, England: Cambridge University Press, 1993. 253p.
bibliog.

Provides nineteen country chapters, including China, Hong Kong and Taiwan, with
Tibet included as a part of China. The articles are rewritten and expanded from the

Cambridge guide to world theatre (Cambridge, England: Cambridge University Press, 1988). The article on China (p. 26-59) begins from prehistoric times and covers the development of the various genres of opera and theatre, including *zaju* (*tsa-chü*), *kunqu* (*k'un-ch'ü*), Peking opera (*jingxi* [*ching-hsi*]), various regional styles, the Western style spoken play (*huaju*) and post-1949 styles. Each article is accompanied by a select bibliography of English-language works.

1435 A chronology of the People's Republic of China from October 1, 1949.

Peter Cheng.   Totowa, New Jersey; Rowman & Littlefield, 1972. 347p.

Covers the period 1949-70 day-by-day, with a brief introduction to the events of each year. A name and subject index is also included. Cheng's *A chronology of the People's Republic of China, 1970-1979* (Metuchen, New Jersey: Scarecrow, 1986. 629p.) continues the coverage.

1436 A dictionary of Chinese symbols.

Wolfram Eberhard, translated by G. L. Campbell.   London; New York: Routledge & Kegan Paul, 1986. 332p.

A mini-encyclopaedia of some four hundred Chinese objects, animals, plants, numbers, customs, gods, historic and mythic figures, foods and events, each briefly defined and symbolic associations given. The work was first published in German as *Lexikon chinesischer symbole* (Köln, Germany: Eugen Diederichs, 1983). Subjects are drawn from novels, plays and erotica, but are intended to represent what Chinese used, or at least recognized, in the 20th century; there are few specifically Buddhist or Daoist symbols. Eberhard's introduction, 'The Symbolic Language of the Chinese', discusses the social symbols in Chinese life, for which they 'regard the use of words as too "primitive"'. Illustrations accompany many of the entries.

1437 The encyclopedia of religion.

Mircea Eliade, editor in chief.   New York: Macmillan, 1987. 15 vols. maps. bibliog.

A rich compendium of recent scholarship in the history of religions on all aspects and areas, including much on philosophy. Substantial articles are devoted to people, ideas, practices and writings, with extensive bibliographies, often usefully annotated. In addition to groups of articles on 'Chinese Religion' and 'Confucian Thought', for instance, there is a group of articles on Daoism – listed under 'Taoism' – which contains material not available elsewhere. Most major individuals in the history of Chinese thought are accorded individual articles.

1438 Encyclopedia of Asian history.

Ainslee T. Embree, editor in Chief.   New York: Charles Scribner's Sons, 1988. 4 vols. maps.

A basic reference. The four volumes contain 3,000 entries, including 1,213 biographies, 63 maps, and more than 100 illustrations covering all of Asia. The period since 1600 is most detailed, but all periods are covered. 'History' in the title includes biographies, places, books, religion, ideas (e.g. Marxism, shamanism), music and historical phenomena (e.g. slavery, famine and writing systems) as well as historical events. The maps are clear and adequate in number, and the index is thorough. Many entries have unannotated bibliographical references in English.

1439 **The Cambridge encyclopedia of China.**
Edited by Brian Hook, Denis Twitchett, consultant editor.
Cambridge, England; New York; Port Chester, New York;
Melbourne; Sydney: Cambridge University Press, 1991. new ed.
502p. maps. bibliog.

A comprehensive, generously illustrated handbook with several hundred articles arranged in topical chapters. A key thematic and historical introduction by Wang Gungwu probes 'The Chineseness of China'. Chapters cover: land and resources; peoples; society (e. g. social order, law, education, health and medicine, games and sports); the 'continuity of China' (archaeology, the dynasties, historical cities, emperors, government structure and events); 'mind and senses' (beliefs, cuisine, writing systems and literature); art and architecture; and science and technology. Appendices include: a guide for tourists and visitors; information sources in America, Europe, Australia and Asia; Wade-Giles/pinyin conversions; place-name transcriptions; tables of government, military, foreign trade and party organizations; a glossary of Chinese characters; and topical lists of books in English. There are numerous maps and illustrations.

1440 **A dictionary of official titles in imperial China.**
Charles O. Hucker.   Stanford, California: Stanford University Press,
1985. 676p.

A virtually exhaustive listing of official bureaucratic titles from all dynasties, with standard translations and capsule descriptions. Hucker's taxonomy illustrates the imperial bureaucratic system and its evolution and gives an idea of its functions.

1441 **Information China: the comprehensive and authoritative reference of New China.**
Edited by C. V. James, compiled, translated by the Chinese Academy of Social Sciences.   New York: Pergamon Press, 1989. 3 vols.

An encyclopaedic compilation, largely selected from official almanacs, yearbooks and statistical publications, which is usefully organized, cross-referenced and indexed by subject, name and place-name. The work is divided into twenty major subject areas, with copious cross-references. The first volume covers general information, the second business and economics, and the third information on history and culture. Appendices provide abundant statistics. The official Chinese view (as of 1989) is clearly presented, providing a balance to Western interpretations; for instance, the historical sections are divided into Marx's five stages of human development. A 'Further Reading' section lists English-language studies, mostly those published in China.

1442 **Dictionary of Asian American history.**
Edited by Hyung-chan Kim.   Westport, Connecticut; London:
Greenwood Press, 1986. 627p. bibliog.

A one-volume reference encyclopaedia on the historical experience in the United States of emigrants and their descendants from China, Japan, Korea, the Philippines and South Asia. Some 800 entries, ranging in length from one paragraph to several pages cover a wide range of topics, including events, people, places and concepts. The bibliography lists relevant books.

1443   **Directory of officials and organizations in China: a quarter century guide.**
Malcolm Lamb.   Armonk, New York; London: M. E. Sharpe, 1994.
1,355p. (Contemporary China Papers, Australian National University).

Follows organizational and personnel changes starting from October 1968, when the Cultural Revolution purges and upheavals had stopped, through the various stages of reform to June 1993. The directory thus provides clear information on career paths and affiliations of individuals, and on the restructuring, divisions and mergers of bureaucracies. Lamb tabulated primary sources for more than 10,000 decision-making officials, not just the very highest, in 793 governmental, semi-official, military and educational organs and organizations, including much provincial and municipal data. The index of names runs to more than 200 pages, giving: Chinese characters; gender (six per cent are female); birth and death dates when known; province of origin; and reference to organizations.

1444   **Historical dictionary of revolutionary China, 1839-1976.**
Edited by Edwin Pak-wai Leung.   New York; Westport, Connecticut; London: Greenwood Press, 1992. 566p. bibliog.

A basic reference work. Over seventy scholars from North America, China and Europe, but not Japan, contribute concise but substantial articles, most with bibliographical references. Entries include foreign and Chinese men and women, events, doctrines and organizations. The end matter consists of a select glossary, chronology, index and a list of books and some articles, chiefly in English and Chinese.

1445   **Modern China: a chronology from 1842 to the present.**
Colin Mackerras, with the assistance of Robert Chan.   San Francisco: W. H. Freeman; London: Thames & Hudson, 1982. 703p.

A detailed, classified chronology. Political or general incidents, whether military or civilian, foreign or domestic, are placed on left-hand pages. Right-hand pages are devoted to: economics; government (including Taiping and the pre-1949 CCP) appointments, dismissals and resignations; cultural and social events; the publication of books, major articles and fiction; the performance of plays; demonstrations, mass meetings and strikes; natural disasters; and births and deaths. Events in post-1949 Taiwan are omitted. The introduction includes an appraisal and listing of specialized and general chronologies and other sources on modern China. The index and geographical index, which also provide Chinese characters, provide access to many topics.

1446   **Dictionary of Chinese and Japanese art.**
Hugo Munsterberg.   New York: Hacker Art Books, 1981. 354p. bibliog.

Contains approximately 2,000 entries, aimed at the beginning student or collector of Chinese and Japanese art, and covering artists and historical figures, places, religions (including Buddhist and Daoist terms) and events. There is a brief list of reference works in English.

1447 **The Indiana companion to traditional Chinese literature.**
Edited, compiled by William Nienhauser, Jr., Charles Hartman,
associate editor for poetry, Y. W. Ma, associate editor for fiction,
Stephen H. West, associate editor for drama. Bloomington, Indiana:
Indiana University Press, 1986. 1,050p. bibliog.

Like the Oxford Companions to Literature, this magisterial volume provides both the
serious general reader and the specialist student with a reference of first resort for
background and framework, encyclopaedia information, and extensive references to
scholarship, criticism and translations. Part one is comprised of ten general essays:
Buddhist literature, drama, fiction, literary criticism, poetry, popular literature, prose,
rhetoric, Daoist literature and women's literature. Many of the surveys also deal with
theoretical considerations, such as how the categories 'poetry' or 'fiction' are construed
in China differently from Western expectations. Part two contains entries on particular
works, authors, genres and literary phenomena, each with references. There are name,
title and subject indices, and a general bibliography. Still insightful is James Robert
Hightower, *Topics in Chinese literature: outlines and bibliographies* (Cambridge,
Massachusetts: Harvard-Yenching Institute Studies, 1962. rev. ed. 141p.). *An
encyclopedia of translation*, by Chan Sin-wai, David E. Pollard (Hong Kong: Chinese
University Press, 1995. 1,150p.) provides authoritative articles on key concepts and
terms in the history and practice of Chinese-English translation.

1448 **The Asian-American encyclopedia.**
Edited by Franklin Ng. New York: Marshall Cavendish, 1995.
6 vols.

Deals with the history, culture, economics and politics of Asian immigrants and their
descendants, as well as relevant events, people and ideas from their countries of
origin. The entries on China and Chinese-Americans, for instance, include:
biographies of Hong Xiuquan (the Taiping rebel leader), Bruce Lee, the kung fu film
star, and Maxine Hong Kingston, the author; sketches of the Chinese Hand Laundry
Association, San Francisco Earthquake, the coolie trade, the Chinese in Mississippi,
and Triads; and longer articles on Chinese politics in the Chinese community, the
Chinese diaspora and Chinese students in the US.

1449 **Companion to Chinese history.**
Hugh B. O'Neill. New York: Facts on File, 1987. 397p. bibliog.

A compact dictionary-encyclopaedia of men and women, dynasties, places, events and
phenomena; many entries include references to basic scholarly works. Michael Dillon,
Dictionary of Chinese history (London: Frank Cass, 1979. 239p.) is briefer, without
references, but includes some material not covered in O'Neill.

1450 **Contemporary atlas of China.**
Nathan Sivin, consulting editor. London: Marshall; Boston,
Massachusetts: Houghton Mifflin, 1988. 200p. maps.

This general description and introduction to China begins with a dozen regional maps
(with a detailed index of geographical names), then provides topical overview essays
on major topics in history, culture, economy and society. It includes more than 200
smaller maps, charts, photographs and diagrams.

1451   **Handbook of Chinese popular culture.**
Edited by Wu Dingbo, Patrick D. Murphy.   New York; Westport,
Connecticut; London: Greenwood Press, 1994. 409p. bibliog.

A compilation of eighteen survey essays. 'Popular culture' is taken to include folk or traditional arts and customs but also topics which deal with individual choice, leisure activities and distinctive Chinese social values. Chinese and American authors, mostly academics, describe the history of the field and inventory research materials, interpret theories, summarize basic findings, and provide extensive but selective topical bibliographies of English and Chinese books and articles. An overall bibliography appears at the end of the volume, and an index covers names and some titles. Articles include: 'Lifestyles: Commercialization and Concepts of Choice'; 'Food'; 'Tea'; 'Religion'; 'Herbal Medicine', 'Sports' and martial arts (*taijiquan, qigong* and*wushu*); 'Mass Media'; 'Film'; 'Traditional Chinese Drama'; 'Gallant Fiction' (the *wuxia* novels, featuring knights and heroes); 'Science Fiction'; 'Comic Art'; 'Calligraphy'; 'Popular Rural Architecture'; and 'Transportation'.

The new Grove dictionary of music and musicians.
See item no. 1330.

China handbook, 1937-1945.
See item no. 1430.

Bibliographies and Research Guides

General and to 1911

1452　**Bibliographic Guide to East Asian Studies.**
　　　Boston, Massachusetts: G. K. Hall, 1990- . annual.
Presents information on publication, call numbers and subject headings for titles in all languages covering China, Japan, North and South Korea, Hong Kong and Taiwan. Data is taken from the Library of Congress MARC tapes and from the Oriental Division of the New York Public Library for items catalogued in the year covered. The initial volume covers 1989 and contains approximately 3,500 listings.

1453　**Revue Bibliographique de Sinologie.** (Bibliographical Sinology
　　　Review).
　　　Paris: Éditions de l'École des Hautes Études en Sciences Sociales,
　　　1961-70; Nouvelle Série, 1983- . annual.
Provides comprehensive brief reviews of current scholarly books and articles in European languages, Chinese, Russian and Japanese, encompassing all aspects of Chinese history and culture before 1949. The notices, running up to several hundred words, generally in French by French and European scholars, but frequently in English, describe the contents and main findings of the item, without lingering on controversial or alternative interpretations. The reviews are generally timely, but may run several years behind (with a hiatus of more than a decade in the 1970s). The publication is particularly valuable for Chinese and Japanese scholarship which would otherwise be virtually absent from Western-language reviews.

1454　**Bibliography of Asian Studies.**
　　　Association for Asian Studies.　Ann Arbor, Michigan: Association
　　　for Asian Studies, 1956- . annual.
A comprehensive listing for East, South and Southeast Asia, covering newly published Western-language books, monographs, articles in journals and joint volumes, and

government documents. The arrangement is first by geographic area, then by classified subject headings. The publication is preceded by *Far Eastern Bibliography* (Ithaca, New York: Far Eastern Association, 1941-). Both sets of volumes are brought together in *Cumulative bibliography of Asian studies, 1941-1965* (Boston, Massachusetts: G. K. Hall, 1969-70. 8 vols.) and *Cumulative bibliography of Asian studies, 1966-1970* (Boston, Massachusetts: G. K. Hall, 1972. 6 vols.). Technical problems, caused by the mass of data and the challenges of computerized information technology, slowed the compilation beginning in the mid-1980s.

1455 **Premodern China: a bibliographical introduction.**
Chun-shu Chang.   Ann Arbor, Michigan: Center for Chinese Studies, University of Michigan, 1971. 183p. (Michigan Papers in Chinese Studies, no. 11).

An introduction to sinology for beginning graduate students which describes basic research tools and the state of Western-language research. The lightly annotated bibliography sections are arranged by topic, and include selected books, articles and dissertations on all major fields of China from earliest times to roughly 1800. The items are carefully chosen and the brief annotations are useful, though many items are now superseded. An excellent 'Selected List of Western Reference Works' is included.

1456 **Current books on China, 1983-1988: an annotated bibliography.**
Peter P. Cheng.   New York; London: Garland, 1990. 268p. (Garland Reference Library of Social Sciences).

Continues Cheng's *China* (Oxford; Santa Barbara, California: Clio Press, 1983. 390p. [World Bibliographical Series, no. 35]). Cheng lists and lightly annotates recent books in all fields and periods.

1457 **Women in China: bibliography of available English language materials.**
Compiled by Lucie Cheng, Charlotte Furth, Hon-ming Yip.
Berkeley, California: University of California, Institute of East Asian Studies, 1985. 109p.

A bibliography of more than 4,000 entries of secondary and primary materials, some lightly annotated, classified by subject and period. The topics comprise major areas of social science interest in all periods, with the largest number of items referring to female emancipation under the socialist revolution. Western-language research and reporting, extensive translations from Chinese newspapers and magazines, Chinese fiction and documents available in translation are all listed and analysed, including chapters or sections in larger works.

1458 **Bibliotheca Sinica.**
Henri Cordier.   Paris: E. Guilmoto, 1904-08, 1924. Reprinted, New York: Burt Franklin, 1968; Taipei: Ch'eng-wen, 1965-66. 5 vols.

A comprehensive listing, arranged by topic, of approximately 18,000 European-language books and articles published before 1922. The last volume of the reprint includes an author index, compiled by the East Asia Library, Columbia University (1953). Yüan T'ung-li, *China in Western literature: a continuation of Cordier's Biblioteca Sinica* (New Haven, Connecticut: Far Eastern Publications, Yale

University, 1958. 802p.) covers books up to 1957, while articles are listed in *Index Sinicus: a catalogue of articles relating to China in periodicals and other collective publications, 1920-1955*, compiled by John Lust (Cambridge, England: Heffer, 1964. 663p.). Lust also compiled *Western books on China published up to 1850: in the library of the School of Oriental and African Studies, University of London: a descriptive catalogue* (London: Bamboo, 1987. 331p.); entries are topically arranged, and indexes of titles, names and subject are included.

1459 **A guide to the Oriental classics.**
Edited by William Theodore de Bary, Ainslee Embree.   New York; London: Columbia University Press, 1989. 3rd ed. 324p.
(Companions to Asia).

Provides introductions, for the student or general reader, to the 'Great Books' of China, Japan and India. The section on China includes Confucian classics, with descriptions of: the Four Books; Zhu Xi; Wang Yangming; the basic Buddhist texts; major novels; and poetry. For each topic there is a brief essay and lists of useful translations, secondary readings and discussion questions. A companion is Wm. Theodore de Bary, Irene Bloom, editors, *Eastern canons: approaches to the Asian classics* (New York; London: Columbia University Press, 1990. 395p.), which introduces and describes the Asian 'Great Books' for study in an ordered sequence.

1460 **Japanese studies on the history of water control in China: a selected bibliography.**
Mark Elvin, Hiroaki Nishioka, Keiko Tamura, Joan Kwek.
Canberra: Institute of Advanced Studies, Australian National University, 1994. 240p.

A selective, analytical bibliography, with a substantial introduction by Mark Elvin, which covers man-made systems for drainage, irrigation, urban water supply, inland water transport, and defence against floods and tidal incursions. It also deals with the related technology and hydrological and hydraulic theories; the social and administrative aspects; and themes such as the debate on 'communities', the shaping of settlement patterns, and water power. China after 1950 is not covered. Japanese scholarship has been at the centre of debate about the nature of Chinese traditional society.

1461 **Guide to Chinese philosophy.**
Fu Wei-hsun, Wing-tsit Chan.   Boston, Massachusetts: G. K. Hall, 1978. 262p. (Asian Philosophies and Religions Resource Guide).

One of a set of guides which uses the topics and scope agreed upon by the Asian Philosophies and Religions Project. The series also includes Yu's *Guide to Chinese religion* (q.v.) and the volumes on Buddhism listed in that entry. Fu and Chan authoritatively discuss scholarship and translations in books, articles and sections of books in English on a range of philosophical topics from 'Ethics' and 'Theories of Human Nature' to authenticity of texts; the coverage extends to the mid-1970s. The categories are arranged by topic (see the entry on Yu's volume); annotated references direct the reader to relevant sections of the major surveys and comparisons with other important traditions of thought.

1462 **China: a bibliography of doctoral dissertations in western languages, 1945-1970.**
Leonard H. D. Gordon, Frank J. Shulman. Seattle, Washington; London: University of Washington Press, published for the Association for Asian Studies, 1972. 317p.

A bibliography of approximately 2,000 doctoral dissertations from North America, Europe, Australia and India, which are classified by subject, and indexed by author, institution and subject. Coverage is continued on the same basis in Frank Joseph Shulman, *Doctoral dissertations on China, 1971-1975* (Seattle, Washington; London: University of Washington Press, 1978. 329p.), which includes a section on where to buy or consult the dissertations listed. A continuation volume, edited by Frank Shulman, is promised for late 1996, with 9,500 entries, annotated, classified and indexed (Westport, Connecticut: Greenwood Press).

1463 **China: a critical bibliography.**
Charles O. Hucker. Tucson, Arizona: University of Arizona Press, 1962. 125p.

An annotated, selective bibliography of some 2,000 scholarly books and articles in history, social science and the humanities, mostly in English. Hucker's annotations of one to two sentences are models of clarity and balance. The foundations of continental sinology are indicated, but are fully listed only in the bibliographies of Cordier and Yuan (q.v.).

1464 **Islam in China: a critical bibliography.**
Raphael Israeli, with the assistance of Lyn Gorman. Westport, Connecticut; London: Greenwood Press, 1994. 172p. (Bibliographies and Indexes in Religious Studies).

Over 9,000 annotated entries of books, articles and parts of books offer a 'critical guide to the essential literature on Islam in China in Western languages'. The author's introduction and the opening chapter, 'Islam in China', present an overview of the field. The entries are divided by topic: bibliographies and inscriptions; general works; historical periods; culture, religion and theology; social discontent and upheaval; geographical area; Jews of China; and missionary reports. There are author, title and subject indexes, and an appendix which lists the journals consulted.

1465 **A history reclaimed: an annotated bibliography of Chinese language materials on the Chinese of America.**
Written and compiled by Him Mark Lai. Los Angeles: Asian American Study Center, University of California, Los Angeles, 1986. 152p.

Based primarily on collections in the San Francisco area, this bibliography of primary sources offers in its brief section headings and annotations many useful facts and comments on the history of the Chinese in North America.

1466 **Chinese music: an annotated bibliography.**
Frederic Lieberman.   New York; London: Garland Publishing
Company, 1979. 2nd ed. rev. and enlarged. 257p. (Garland Reference
Library of the Humanities, no. 75).

A comprehensive listing of 2,441 Western-language books, articles, unpublished
theses and essays in edited volumes, which provide critical annotations or descriptions
for some items.

1467 **Guide to Chinese poetry and drama.**
Richard John Lynn.   Boston, Massachusetts: G. K. Hall, 1984. 200p.
(Asian Literature Bibliography Series).

Provides helpful introductory essays on major topics of poetry and drama, each
outlining important questions, with a selected list of major scholarship in Western
languages and Chinese sources. Part one groups important bodies of poetry
chronologically and annotates 138 books and articles on them. Part two, 'Drama',
annotates some thirty books and articles. Part three covers twenty topics in 20th-
century poetry and drama. This work supercedes Roger B. Bailey's 1973 volume of
the same title and publisher.

1468 **The American Historical Association's guide to historical
literature.**
Mary Beth Norton, general editor.   New York: Oxford University
Press, 1995. 3rd ed. 2 vols.

An exemplary bibliography, indispensable for the student of history, which comprises
the starting point for finding historical scholarship on any field, period or nation.
Sections ten, 'China to 1644' (380 titles), edited by Patricia Ebrey, and eleven, 'China
since 1644' (764 titles), edited by James Cole, provide excellent and extensive
coverage of China from prehistory to 1976, including Taiwan, Hong Kong and Macao;
coverage is primarily of academic works in English published after 1960 and up to
1992. Each section opens with a succinct historiographical review of the field, then
lists books and some articles, with authoritative annotations in one or two sentences.
Important state-of-the-field articles are included. Works of history predominate, but
relevant items in related fields are also included. The volume is indexed by author and
subject.

1469 **Asia: a selected and annotated guide to reference works.**
Raymond G. Nunn.   Cambridge, Massachusetts: M. I. T. Press,
1971. 223p.

An ample but selective listing of reference works in all languages, with valuable, brief
annotations. The section on China (p. 106-43) cites English- and Chinese-language
encyclopaedias, handbooks, yearbooks, dictionaries, geographical works, chronologies
and bibliographies, including those from imperial times. However, Chinese-language
works are more fully covered in Wilkinson (q.v.).

1470 **Guide to Chinese prose.**
Jordan Paper. Boston, Massachusetts: G. K. Hall, 1973. 137p.
(Asian Literature Bibliography Series).
Contains entries on 142 works, including the philosophical classics, history, philosophy, belles-lettres, short stories and novels, with a shorter section on 20th-century literature. Paper briefly describes each work and its significance, lists translations, and provides basic references to useful scholarship.

1471 **The Jews of dynastic China: a critical bibliography.**
Michael Pollack. Cincinnati, Ohio: Hebrew Union College Press, in association with the Sino-Judaic Institute, Menlo Park, California, 1991. 236p. (Bibliographica Judaica, no. 13).
Supplements and continues Rudolph Loewenthal, *The Sino-Judaic bibliographies of Rudolph Loewenthal* (Cincinnati, Ohio: Hebrew Union College Press, in association with the Sino-Judaic Institute, Menlo Park, California, 1988. 2 vols.). Professor Loewenthal taught at Yenching University in Beijing during the 1930s, and had a wide interest in world culture and Asian history. Pollack follows Loewenthal's work with mostly English-language material published or discovered after its compilation. Both define their scope broadly, including background on Chinese culture and thought, and most items refer to the pre-20th-century period.

1472 **Modern Chinese society: an analytical bibliography.**
G. William Skinner. Stanford, California: Stanford University Press, 1973. 3 vols.
Provides the social science researcher or historian with bibliographical access to published secondary sources, whether articles, books, sections of books or pamphlets, in all disciplines, on Qing, Republican and Communist periods, on the Communist movement prior to 1949, and on Taiwan under the Republic of China. Topical coverage includes most aspects of the domestic social structure, economy, polity, culture, and personality of the Han Chinese; excluded are non-Han peoples, international relations, sciences, élite arts and letters, and technical linguistics. The topical arrangement is by Skinner's own analytical categories. There are extensive indexes by historical period, geographical region, local systems, author and general topic. Each entry is annotated by these categories. Coverage is by language: volume one, *Publications in Western languages, 1644-1972*; volume two, *Publications in Chinese, 1644-1969*; and volume three, *Publications in Japanese, 1644-1971*.

1473 **Protest and crime in China.**
Teng Ssu-yü. New York; London: Garland Publishing, 1981. 455p.
(Garland Reference Library of Social Science).
Covers secret associations, organized crime, popular uprisings, rebellions, and other such topics. The compiler lists nearly 4,000 scholarly and journalistic articles (including historical reporting), books, reviews and dissertations, divided into sections on Occidental and Oriental languages. A subject index is included.

1474   **Chinese religion in Western languages: a comprehensive and classified bibliography of publications in English, French, and German through 1980.**
Compiled by Laurence G. Thompson.   Ann Arbor, Michigan: Association for Asian Studies, 1985. 302p. (Association for Asian Studies Monograph, no. 41).

A broadly conceived and carefully executed bibliography, which lists books, articles and sections of books on all aspects of religious thought and practice. The coverage is extended in *Chinese religion: publications in Western languages, 1981-1990,* compiled by Laurence G. Thompson, edited by Gary Seaman (Ann Arbor, Michigan: Association for Asian Studies, 1993. 288p. [Association for Asian Studies Monographs]).

1475   **China: an annotated bibliography of bibliographies.**
Compiled by Tsien Tsuen-hsuin in collaboration with James K. M. Cheng.   Boston, Massachusetts: G. K. Hall, 1978. 604p.

A basic reference tool which meticulously describes and annotates roughly 2,500 bibliographies in English, Chinese, Japanese, French, German and Russian, with preference given to those in Western languages. Included are separate works published as books up till the end of 1977, substantial bibliographies included in periodical and serial articles, essays and comprehensive bibliographies in monographs. Indexes are by author, title and subject.

1476   **The T. L. Yuan bibliography of western writing on Chinese art and archeology.**
Edited by Harrie A. Vanderstappen.   London: Mansell Information/Publishing, 1975. 606p.

An exhaustive listing of over 15,000 items in Western languages, published between 1920 and the mid-1960s, and arranged by detailed subject divisions, with an author index. T. L. Yuan initiated the project to continue the work of Cordier, *Biblioteca Sinica* (q.v.); Vanderstappen and his staff provided the listings for 1956-65, approximately half the material.

1477   **Women in China.**
Karen T. Wei.   New York; Westport, Connecticut; London: Greenwood Press, 1984. 250p. (Bibliographies and Indexes in Women's Studies).

Includes more than 1,100 annotated entries on books, articles, dissertations and sections of books, mostly in English, but with some important titles in other European languages. All aspects of women's history, roles and activities are covered, from earliest times to the early 1980s.

1478   **The history of imperial China: a research guide.**
Endymion Wilkinson.   Cambridge, Massachusetts: East Asian Council, Harvard University, 1973. 213p.

Annotates and explains how to use basic works of reference, dictionaries, biographical dictionaries, compilations of documents, guides to research and bibliographies in

Japanese, Chinese, and Western languages. Wilkinson also explains basic technical problems, such as the conversion of dates from the Chinese system into the Western calendar, and discusses how to find out what sources are available for a given period. Although aimed at beginning graduate students and researchers, it will be useful to others in some situations. Coverage is extended in James H. Cole, *Updating Wilkinson: an annotated bibliography of reference works on imperial China published since 1973* (New York: James H. Cole [7 East 85th St., #4C, New York 10028], 1991. 111p.).

1479 **Classical Chinese fiction: a guide to its study and appreciation: essays and bibliographies.**
Winston L. Y. Yang, Peter Li, Nathan K. Mao. Boston, Massachusetts: G. K. Hall; London: George Prior Publishers, 1978. 302p. (Asian Literature Bibliography Series).
A critical and bibliographical guide to the study and appreciation of Chinese fiction before the 20th century, with an emphasis on English-language publications over the period 1950-76. The first section comprises introductory essays on the major periods, types of fiction and major novels. These essays briefly describe the background of the author, if known, the circumstances of the publication and history of the texts, a summary of the work's plot, and critical approaches. The second section consists of a series of bibliographies; included are studies and translations in all languages found in books, sections of books and articles, with preference given to Western languages.

1480 **Religion in postwar China: a critical analysis and annotated bibliography.**
Compiled by David C. Yu. Westport, Connecticut: Greenwood Press, 1994. 365p. (Bibliographies and Indexes in Religious Studies Series).
These entries on 1,005 books, journal articles and book chapters cover more than the title implies, as religion is quite broadly defined. Yu covers: all periods (from archaeology to the cult of Mao); mainland China, Taiwan and Hong Kong; and religious facets of politics, philosophy and social organization. Each item is summarized and analysed. Part one comprises two methodological chapters on scholarship in China and Western views of traditional Chinese religion, with extensive references. Part two (302 entries) covers works by Chinese scholars, including many in Chinese, on a wide-ranging list of topics in religious history. Part three (703 entries) is entitled 'Postwar Western Views of Traditional Chinese Religion'. There are author, title and subject indexes, as well as occasional cross-references, but judicious browsing is still necessary to find items on a particular topic. Yu excludes works covered in the next item.

1481 **Guide to Chinese religion.**
David C. Yu, with contributions by Laurence G. Thompson. Boston, Massachusetts: G. K. Hall, 1985. 200p. (Asian Philosophies and Religion Resource Guide).
An annotated bibliographical guide to all aspects and manifestations of religion, and a series companion to Fu, *Guide to Chinese philosophy* (q.v.). Yu gives his opinion on English-language books, articles and sections of books up to 1977. The eleven categories are modified from those of the series, including 'Religious Thought', 'Authoritative Texts', 'Popular Literature', 'Arts, Architecture, and Music', 'Social,

Economic, and Political Developments', 'Practices', 'Ideal Beings, Biography, and Hagiography', 'Mythology, Cosmology, and Basic Symbols', 'Sacred Places' and 'Soteriological Experiences and Processes'. Buddhism is largely excluded, as there are two volumes on world Buddhism in this series which devote sections to China: *Guide to Buddhist philosophy*, by Kenneth Inada (Boston, Massachusetts: G. K. Hall, 1985. 226p.); and *Guide to Buddhist religion*, by Frank Reynolds (Boston, Massachusetts: G. K. Hall, 1981. 415p.). *A select bibliography on Taoism*, edited by Julian F. Pas (Stony Brook, New York: Institute for Advanced Study of World Religions, 1988. 52p.) lists books, parts of books and articles by topic.

1482 **China bibliography: a research guide to reference works about China past and present.**
Harriet T. Zurndorfer. Leiden, the Netherlands; New York; Köln, Germany: E. J. Brill, 1995. 348p. (Handbuch der Orientalstik, no. 4).

An essential handbook which explains where and how to gain access to information in both Asian and European languages on sinology and a wide range of topics for all periods of time. The introduction includes a forty-page 'Brief History of Chinese Studies and Sinology'. Zurndorfer then lists and comments on: bibliographies; journals and newspapers; biography; geography, including historical and modern sources; dictionaries, including Chinese, Chinese-foreign language, and specialist dictionaries; encyclopaedias, yearbooks and statistical references, both traditional and contemporary; literary and historical collectanea; indexes and concordances; and guides and indexes to translations.

Soviet studies of premodern China: assessments of recent scholarship.
See item no. 98.

An outline and an annotated bibliography of Chinese philosophy.
See item no. 497.

Chinese patterns of behaviour: a sourcebook of psychological and psychiatric studies.
See item no. 663.

20th century

1483 **Sino-Soviet conflict: a historical bibliography.**
Santa Barbara, California: ABC-CLIO, 1985. 190p.

Provides brief abstracts of 842 articles from European, American and Russian English-language journals published from 1965-82 on relations between the two countries (rather than merely 'conflict') since 1914.

1484   **The United States in East Asia: a historical bibliography.**
Compiled by ABC-CLIO Information Services, introduction by
Jessica S. Brown.   Santa Barbara, California: ABC-CLIO
Information Services; Oxford: Clio Press, 1985. 298p. (ABC-CLIO
Research Guides, no. 14).

A bibliography of 1,176 annotated periodical articles published between 1973 and
1984 in English, compiled from the ABC-CLIO computerized database of American,
European and Asian journals. Chapter one covers general and multilateral relations
between Asian nations and the United States. Further coverage includes articles on
diplomatic, political, economic and cultural relations between the United States and
China.

1485   **Contemporary China: a research guide.**
Peter Berton, Eugene Wu, edited by Howard Koch, Jr.   Stanford,
California: Hoover Institution on War, Revolution, and Peace,
Stanford University, 1967. 695p. (Hoover Institution Bibliographical
Series, no. 31).

Sources for the People's Republic and Taiwan in Chinese, Japanese and English, for
the period 1949-64, are listed and described in exemplary detail. Part one is devoted to
bibliographies, newspapers, periodicals and indexes to them. Part two covers general
reference works of all sorts, including statistics. Part three deals with selected
documentary sources and collections, including Chinese government publications. Part
four covers newspapers and news releases, as well as the major translation and
monitoring services (including Hong Kong Consulate General Service and Joint
Publications Research Service [JPRS]), and lists of publications in major scholarly
series in the field. Appendix A lists important research libraries and institutions in all
parts of the world. Indexes are by subject and author-title.

1486   **Historiography of the Chinese labor movement, 1895-1949:**
a critical survey and bibliography of selected Chinese source
materials at the Hoover Institution.
Ming K. Chan.   Stanford, California: Hoover Institution Press, 1981.
232p.

A series of critical essays which evaluate published sources and a selected
bibliography of Chinese and foreign-language sources found in the extensive
collection at the Hoover Institution. Part one, 'Chinese Labor Conditions', describes
pre- and post-1949 publications on labour problems and labour legislation. Part two,
'History of the Chinese Labor Movement', analyses the issues and sources, period by
period, from the late Qing dynasty to 1949.

1487   **Nietzsche in China, 1904-1992: an annotated bibliography.**
Compiled, with introduction by Cheung Chiu-yee.   Canberra:
Australian National University. 145p. (Faculty of Asian Studies
Monographs, New Series).

Lists books and articles, principally in Chinese. The substantial introduction describes
the influence of Nietzsche in China, with references to the literature listed in the
bibliography. Section one lists 100 translations, and section two lists 385 works about

Nietzsche. Appendix I gives 'Parodies' and Appendix II lists works published outside China. An index of authors is also included.

1488 **Science and technology in the development of modern China: an annotated bibliography.**
Genevieve C. Dean.   London: Mansell, 1979. 265p.
Lists and briefly describes books and articles.

1489 **A bibliography of studies and translations of Modern Chinese literature (1918-1942).**
Compiled by Donald A. Gibbs, Yun-chen Li.   Cambridge, Massachusetts: Harvard University Press, 1975. 239p. (Harvard East Asian Monographs, no. 61).
Lists studies and translations of Chinese-language works written in the period starting with the May Fourth New Culture Movement, down to Mao's 'Talks at the Yan'an Forum'. Chu Pao-liang, *Twentieth century Chinese writers and their pen names* (Taipei: Center for Chinese Studies, 1989. new enlarged ed. 2 vols.) is the standard index for more than 18,000 pen names, pseudonyms, allonyms, *noms de guerre*, and other nominative obfuscations for roughly 6,784 writers.

1490 **Japanese studies of modern China since 1953: a bibliographical guide to historical and social science research on the nineteenth and twentieth centuries.**
Noriko Kamachi, John K. Fairbank, Chūzō Ichiko.   Cambridge, Massachusetts: East Asian Research Center, Harvard University, distributed by Harvard University Press, 1975. 603p. (Harvard East Asian Monographs, no. 60).
This bibliography lists and annotates major books and articles in Japanese, with a substantial and insightful introduction on the organization and patterns of Japanese scholarship. The annotation and summaries are useful even for those who will not read the originals. Japanese scholarship before 1953 is covered in John King Fairbank, Masataka Banno, Sumiko Yamamoto, *Japanese studies of modern China: a bibliographical guide to historical and social science research on the 19th and 20th centuries* (Cambridge, Massachusetts: Harvard University Press, 1953. 331p.).

1491 **Understanding Communist China: Communist China studies in the United States and the Republic of China, 1949-1978.**
Tai-chün Kuo, Ramon Myers.   Stanford, California: Hoover Institution, 1986. 172p.
A methodological and intellectual critique of political, economic and cultural studies produced in the United States and on Taiwan. Kuo and Myers conclude that American scholarship has defined the People's Republic in four different models: 'communist totalitarian', aimed at preserving monolithic Party rule; 'modernizing communist', with economic development as the goal; 'revolutionary socialist', with the egalitarian Cultural Revolution being the model and the American New Left the audience; and a Chinese Communist régime with leadership divided in rivalry. Scholarship in Taiwan

follows a fifth, totalitarian, model, with an emphasis on personal power struggles among the élite. The authors provide many examples of each view, and call for cooperation between North American and Taiwan scholars.

1492 **Mao Zedong: a bibliography.**
Alan Lawrence. New York; Westport, Connecticut; London: Greenwood Press, 1991. 197p. (Bibliographies of World Leaders).
Includes English-language books and articles, together with brief descriptions and annotations, a short life of the late Chairman, a chronology, and a table, 'Mao's Zedong's Wives and Children, 1893-1976'. Chapters cover: the life of Mao, listing collateral works which touch on Mao; sources in English; published works (collections published in English in China, edited collections published outside China, and works published during the Cultural Revolution); individual works in chronological order; the successive periods of Mao's activity, again including many collateral works; and topical chapters on military strategy, poetry and historiography. The work is indexed by author and by subject.

1493 **A research guide to central party and governmental meetings in China, 1949-1986.**
Kenneth G. Lieberthal, Bruce J. Dickson. Armonk, New York; London: M. E. Sharpe, 1989. rev. ed. 339p.
Lists the date, type, location, attendance, major items of agenda, speeches, reports, decisions and major secondary sources for more than 500 meetings. A name-subject index is also provided.

1494 **Research guide to education in China after Mao, 1977-1981.**
Billie L. C. Lo. Hong Kong: Centre of Asian Studies, Hong Kong University, 1983. 221p. (Centre of Asian Studies Bibliographies and Research Guides, no. 21).
Lo lists articles, books, speeches and broadcasts classified by level or type of education. Included are items written or translated into English.

1495 **Bibliography of English translations and critiques of contemporary Chinese fiction, 1945-1992.**
Kam Louie, Louise Edwards. Taipei: Center for Chinese Studies, 1993. 171p.
Lists translations into English and literary criticism of fiction written during the period 1945-92 in the People's Republic, Taiwan and Hong Kong. PRC authors are listed in pinyin, and Taiwan and Hong Kong authors in Wade-Giles, with Chinese characters given for the names and titles of most entries. Sections include: general anthologies of translated fiction; translations of mainland fiction; criticisms of mainland fiction; translations of fiction from Taiwan and Hong Kong; and criticism of fiction from Taiwan and Hong Kong.

1496   **Modern China, 1840-1972: an introduction to sources and research aids.**
Andrew James Nathan.   Ann Arbor, Michigan: Center for Chinese Studies, University of Michigan, 1973. 95p. (Michigan Papers in Chinese Studies, no. 14).

Nathan provides basic information on research aids and documentary sources for beginning graduate students. Although the archival and published sources of the last twenty years are not included, the coverage is still of some use for earlier material. Part one covers research aids and libraries: bibliographies, major collections, chronologies and biography. Part two describes major types of primary sources and evaluates their usefulness: English and Chinese newspaper and radio; Chinese periodicals; Chinese government publications; collections of documents, published and microfilmed; Japanese-language sources; diplomatic archives; Russian-language material; and material on Taiwan.

1497   **Education in the People's Republic of China.**
Franklin Parker, Betty June Parker.   New York; London: Garland, 1986. 845p. (Garland Reference Library of Social Science; Reference Books in International Education).

Lists and briefly describes more than 3,000 books, articles, chapters in books, pamphlets and selected newspaper accounts, primarily in English. Much of the material dates from before 1949, and the arrangement is by topic and period.

1498   **The People's Republic of China: a bibliography of selected English language legal materials.**
Jeanette L. Pinard.   Washington, DC: Library of Congress Law Library, 1983. 72p.

A bibliography of secondary and English-language primary sources in the field of law for the period after the 1976 end of the Cultural Revolution. For earlier materials, see *Chinese law past and present: a bibliography of enactments and commentaries in English text*, edited by Lin Fu-shu (New York: East Asian Institute, Columbia University, 1966. 419p.).

1499   **The modernization of Manchuria: an annotated bibliography.**
Edited by Ronald Suleski.   Hong Kong: Chinese University Press, 1994. 228p.

Lists and briefly annotates both scholarly works and primary sources, including books, articles, government documents and publications, memoirs and travellers' reports, in English, Chinese and Japanese. Chapter topics include: general works; basic collections of data; civil affairs; military affairs, such as Zhang Zuolin and his assassination; and diplomatic events. A name index is provided.

1500   **Contemporary Chinese novels and short stories, 1949-1974: an annotated bibliography.**
Meishi Tsai.   Cambridge, Massachusetts: Fairbank East Asian Research Center, Harvard University Press, 1978. 408p.

Tsai lists and briefly describes, with plot summaries, post-1949 fiction, and indicates translations where appropriate.

1501   **The Cultural Revolution in China.**
James C. F. Wang.   New York; London: Garland, 1976. 246p.
(Garland Reference Library of Social Science).

An annotated bibliography, with introductory and background essays on Mao's Great Proletarian Cultural Revolution. Wang includes books, monographs and journal articles in English which are commonly available to students and researchers. Material in Chinese or translated from Chinese is not included.

1502   **Modern Chinese fiction: a guide to its study and appreciation: essays and bibliographies.**
Edited by Winston L. Y. Yang, Nathan K. Mao.   Boston,
Massachusetts: G. K. Hall, 1981. 288p.

Provides critical, brief essays on fiction in the 20th century, together with extensive, annotated bibliographies of books and articles. Essays include 'Modern Chinese fiction, 1917-1949' and 'Chinese Communist fiction since 1949'.

Bibliography of Sun Yat-sen in China's Republican Revolution, 1885-1925.
See item no. 697.

Indexes

There follow three separate indexes: authors (personal and corporate); titles; and subjects. Title entries are italicized and refer either to the main titles, or to many of the other works cited in the annotations. The numbers refer to bibliographical entry rather than page numbers. Individual index entries are arranged in alphabetical sequence.

Index of Authors

508

K

K'ung Shan-jen 1234
Kahn, Harold L. 350
Kallgren, Joyce 114, 731, 1058
Kaltenmark, Maxime 564
Kamachi, Noriko 1490
Kamm, John 774
Kane, Penny 416-17, 421
Kaplan, Edward H. 938
Kaplan, Fredric M. 48
Kaple, Deborah A. 968
Kapp, Robert 272
Kaptchuk, Ted J. 670
Kates, George N. 323
Kau, Michael Y. M. 715, 749, 762
Kauffer, Rémi 728
Keenan, Barry C. 1032, 1042
Keene, Donald 1102
Keightley, David N. 86-87, 470
Keith, Ronald C. 887
Kelliher, Daniel 994
Kelly, Jeanne 1143
Kelly, David 757
Kennedy, Thomas L. 853
Kent, Ann 884
Kenworthy, James L. 957
Kerr, Rose 1251
Kessler, Adam 170
Keswick, Maggie 1312
Kidd, David 323
Kierman, Frank A. Jr. 90, 569, 851
Killingley, Siew-Yue 487
Kim Hyung-chan 1442
Kim, Samuel S. 5, 840
Kimura, Hisao 320
King, F. H. 977
King, Frank H. H. 936
Kingston, Maxine Hong 461
Kinkley, Jeffrey C. 343, 1108, 1165
Kinney, Anne Behnke 621
Kirby, William 807
Kirkby, Richard J. 440
Kizer, Carolyn 1222
Klein, Donald W. 260, 340
Kleinberg, Robert 962

Kleiner, Robert 1324
Kleinman, Arthur 664-65
Knapp, Ronald G. 27, 1313-15
Knechtges, David R. 1213
Knowblock, John 524
Knuttgen, Howard G. 1361
Ko, Dorothy 636
Koch, Howard Jr. 1485
Kohn, Livia 565-67
Kolatch, Jonathan 1362
Kong Demao 373
Kong Jiesheng 1104
Korzec, Michael 1012
Kracke, Jr., E[dward] A. 159
Kramer, Ione 1351
Kranzler, David 325
Kraus, Richard Kurt 600, 647, 1295, 1329
Kraus, Willy 941
Kretschmer, F. A. 1061
Kuan Yuchien 46
Kueh, Y. Y. 923
Kuhn, Dieter 1086
Kuhn, Philip A. 195, 206, 218
Kuo Tai-chün 1491
Kwok, Danny 1065
Kwok, R. Yin-wang 442
Kwong, Charles Yim-tze 1199
Kwong, Luke S. K. 229

L

La Fargue, Michael 520
Laaksonen, Oiva 946
Lach, Donald 332
Ladany, Laszlo 691
Lagerwey, John 568
Lai, David Chuenyan 457
Lai, Him Mark 1465
Lai, T. C. 1330
Laidler, Keith 76
Laidler, Liz 76
Laing, Ellen Johnston 1292
Laitinen, Kauko 384
Lall, Rajiv 929
Lam, Willy Wo-lap 784
Lamb, Malcolm 1443

Lampton, David M. 679, 763, 765, 1059
Landau, Julie 1217
Landes, David 1077
Lane, Kevin P. 841
Lang, Olga 1164
Langlois, John D., Jr. 168
Lao She 1154-55
Lao-tzu 520
Lardy, Nicholas R. 902, 955
Larson, Wendy 1183
Lary, Diana 250, 273
Latham, Ronald 65
Lattimore, Owen 59, 169
Lau, D. C. 518, 520, 522
Lau, Joseph S. M. 1128, 1156
Lawrence, Alan 1492
Lawton, Thomas 125, 1289
Lawyers Committee for Human Rights 885
Le Blanc, Charles 495, 526
Ledderose, Lothar 1284
Lee Chae-jin 374, 847
Lee Chin-chuan 1369-70
Lee Chong-sik 709
Lee, Franklin Ching-han 609
Lee, Gregory 1222, 1225
Lee, Gus 461
Lee Hong Yung 750, 764
Lee, James 896
Lee Keun 942
Lee, Leo Ou-fan 54, 1156, 1184-85, 1189
Lee, Mabel 1227
Lee Ngok 859
Lee, Peter N. S. 969
Lee, Robert 811
Lee, Sherman E. 1252-53, 1273
Lee, Sky 457
Lee Ta-ling 389
Lee, Thomas H. C. 1033
Leeming, Frank 28
Legge, James 518
Leibniz, Gottfried Wilhelm 333
Leibo, Steven 232
Leng Shao-chuan 876
Lenk, Hans 532
Leonard, Jane Kate 808, 894

514

Index of Titles

524

543

Index of Subjects

570

Macartney, George
  mission to China (1793)
    805, 810
Macroregions 436, 978
Madness *see* Psychology
Magistrates
  history and function 686
  legal roles 354, 672,
    869, 1132
  memoir 1130
  role in local government
    604
Management 160, 653,
    660, 958
  factory 735, 942,
    968-69, 972
  post-Mao reforms 919,
    940-42, 946, 991
  psychology 943
  training 946, 962,
    1025
Manchukuo 363, 818
Manchuria 71, 253, 320,
    791, 798-99, 819,
    1153, 1173
  1911-28 272
  bibliography 1499
  revolution pre-1949
    709, 817
Manchurian crisis (1931)
    820, 823
Manchus 97, 167, 206,
    209-10, 339, 363,
    383, 428, 1322
  anti-Manchu attacks
    209, 267, 384, 552,
    700
  education 1031
  ethnic identity 226
  see also Qing dynasty
Mandarin duck and
    butterfly novels 1112,
    1186
Mandarin squares 1321
Mandate of Heaven 124,
    687, 788
Mao Dun 1174, 1180,
    1182, 1191
  biography 1108
  criticism 1111
  writings 2, 1160
Mao Zedong 9, 494,
    716-17

and Chinese political
    culture 722, 741
  and education 1024,
    1027, 1046, 1056
  'autobiography' 300
  bibliographies 1480,
    1492
  biographies 341, 723
  calligraphy 1295
  death rituals 605
  emergence of Maoism
    (1935-45) 720
  foreign relations 796,
    819, 833, 838, 846
  Gang of Four 756
  Jiang Qing 394
  Memorial Hall 543
  on class 647, 650
  on state power 695
  poetry 718, 1205
  'Report on the Hunan
    Peasant Movement'
    275
  studies of thought 241,
    719-20, 752, 757, 909
  thought 752, 757
  women and suicide 638
  writings 715, 717-18,
    721
Marco Polo *see* Polo,
    Marco
Markets and marketing
    256, 604, 940
  and macroregions 436,
    897, 978, 999
  imperial China 629, 865
  market economy 112,
    115, 160, 193, 880,
    887, 891, 896, 898,
    901-02, 915-16, 976
  market towns 191, 193,
    251, 433, 436, 599
  People's Republic 421
  post-1976 reforms 769,
    773
Marriage 371, 416, 419,
    422-23, 606, 617,
    619, 622, 624, 634,
    638-39
  and divorce 619, 626,
    865
  dowry and bride price
    14, 619

imperial China 131,
    153-54, 610, 617, 620
  law 255, 626, 863, 865
  supernatural 1240
  see also Family and
    kinship
Marshall, General George
    829
Martial arts 68, 214, 600,
    1186, 1451
Martini, Martino 97, 590
Marxism 584, 662, 691,
    724, 752, 972
  analysis of Chinese
    science 1073, 1101
  and historiography 95,
    100, 115, 185, 190,
    249
  Christianity's
    confrontation with
    591
  critique 100, 719, 883,
    885, 911, 948, 978,
    983-84, 1417
  critique of ultra-Leftism
    747
  Cultural Revolution
    747-48, 750, 752
  development pre-49
    703, 720-21
  literary theory 1115,
    1177, 1188
  origins in China 243,
    248, 268, 295, 374,
    705, 713
  post-Mao 755, 757, 762,
    883
Mass Education
    Movement 254, 275
Mass line 297, 993, 1173
Masturbation 641
Mateer, Calvin Wilson 403
Mathematics 199, 1031,
    1070, 1075-76, 1089,
    1095
Mawangdui tombs 89, 520
May 30 1925 incident 260,
    315
May Fourth Movement
    240, 246, 260, 401
  and intellectual
    revolution in modern
    China 236

Nanjing 177
  guidebooks 51
  history 436-37
Nanyang Brothers
  Tobacco Company
  890
National identity 5, 17-18,
  430, 780
National People's
  Congress 768
Nationalism 245, 266,
  270, 384, 811
  and foreign relations
  811, 814-15, 819-20,
  823, 827, 837
  and language reform
  473
  and national identity 5,
  780
  and science 677, 1066
  and xenophobia 213,
  267, 317, 796
  Boxers 214
  Coxinga as symbol 345
  Great Wall as symbol
  186
  Li Dazhao 243
  Lin Zexu as symbol 215
  Mongol 169
  peasant 222, 708
  popular 430
  Song dynasty 342, 558
  Sun Yat-sen 697-98
  Zhang Binglin 384
Nationalist China 278,
  286, 288, 290
  and bourgeoisie 249,
  276, 281
  control of press 1373
  education 1041, 1045
  German influence 807
  government 277-79,
  685, 695-96
  in literature 1143,
  1154-55, 1160, 1163,
  1168, 1226
  opposition parties 284
  political traditionalism
  233
  revolution (1923-27)
  252
  rural reform 254, 278
  Soviet advisers 289

sports and politics 1362
  yearbooks 1430, 1432
Native place association
  (*huiguan*) 430
Navy
  history 181, 207, 224,
  230, 851, 855
  modernization 861
  Qing dynasty 853
  see also Pirates; Zheng
  He
Needham, Joseph 1090-91
Negotiating style 842,
  954, 960-61
Neo-Confucianism 155,
  157, 497, 548, 551,
  556-57
  Changzhou school 199
  education 1030
  in East Asia 3
  medicine 669
  Ming 501
  Ming-Qing 198-99
  painting 1279
  Taizhou school 198
  Tang dynasty 550
  see also Chen Liang;
  Cheng Hao; Cheng I;
  Dai Zhen; Fang Izhi;
  Gu Yanwu; Huang
  Zongxi; Jiao Hong;
  Liu Zongyuan;
  Ouyang Xiu; Shao
  Yong; Sima Guang;
  Su Shi; Tang Chunyi;
  Wang Anshi; Wang
  Fuzhi; Wang
  Yangming; Zhang
  Xuecheng; Zhu Xi
New Culture Movement
  1174
  and Hu Shi 240
  in fiction 1161, 1164,
  1171
  intellectuals and study
  of folk literature
  1243
  literature 1174, 1177,
  1180, 1183-85,
  1187-88, 1191-92
  science 1065
  traditional vs. Western
  medicine debate 677

see also May Fourth
  Movement
New Life Movement 807
New Year's door gods
  1079, 1247
Newspapers *see*
  Journalism
Ni Yuxian 396
Nian rebellion 222
Ningbo 43, 152, 173, 445,
  899
Nixon, Richard M. 832,
  839, 845
Nomenklatura system 758,
  918
Northern Expedition 275,
  285, 294, 334, 714
Novels 1137, 1140, 1181
  about China 16
  guides 1107
  Qing dynasty 1244
  literary theory 1141
  traditional
  commentaries 1141
  see also Fiction
Nuclear weapons 833,
  860-61
Numerology 568

O

Odes see Shijing
Oil 23, 847, 949, 957
  in foreign trade 956
  see also Energy
Old well (1987 film) 1151,
  1344
One Hundred Days
  Reforms 228-29, 372
One Hundred Flowers
  campaign 305, 310,
  392, 740, 1109, 1167
One-child policy
  see Population
Open Door Policy 825-26,
  829
Opera 7, 61, 1434
  Buddhist ritual 1336
  Cantonese 1244, 1341
  Cultural Revolution
  748, 1103, 1236,
  1326, 1339

587

596

Violence *contd.*
  Ming dynasty 185
  village revolution 770,
    990, 992-93, 1162
Voice of America 1370

W

Waley, Arthur 16, 1114,
    1169, 1212
Waln, Robert 328
Wang Anshi 155, 158, 548
  reforms 161
Wang Anyi 1108, 1111
Wang Fuzhi 197
Wang Gen 552
Wang Guowei 234, 1217
Wang Hongwen 756
Wang Jingwei 277, 815
Wang Juntao 775
Wang Lü 1286
Wang Mang 136, 341
Wang Meng 1108-09
Wang Ruoshui 757
Wang Ruowang 788,
    1108-09
Wang Shiwei 305, 704
Wang Tao 237
Wang Wei 1121, 1208,
    1214, 1218
Wang Xianzhi 1284
Wang Xishan 1068
Wang Xizhi 1284
Wang Yangming 341, 501,
    552, 560-61, 1459
Wang Yuanqi 1275
Wanli emperor 180
War and warfare 852-55,
    1078, 1084-85, 1127
  early China 123, 126,
    128, 523
  imperial China 167,
    179, 232, 851
  modern China 250, 258,
    270, 274, 278, 282,
    286, 709
  see also Army;
    Military; individual
    wars by names, e.g.
    Korean War
Ward, Frederick
  Townsend 232, 410

Warlordism 258, 272-75
  origins of term
  'warlord' 270
Washington Conference
  (1922) 814, 820
Water control 24, 1460
  history of hydraulic
    engineering 1078
  People's Republic 616,
    763, 1016, 1018
  Yellow River 1016
  see also Dujiangyan;
    Three Gorges Dam
*Water margin see Shuihu
  zhuan*
Waterways
  Ming dynasty 1006
  traditional engineering
    1078
  traditional river and
    canal transport 1004
  see also Canals; Grand
    Canal
Weapons
  arms trade 274, 857-58
  arsenals 853
  atomic bomb 833, 860
  seapower 861
  traditional 854, 857,
    1069, 1084-85
Weber, Max 123, 513
  critique 551, 553, 556,
    652, 943, 974
Wei Yuan 808
Wei Zheng 149
Weihaiwei, Shandong 604,
    811
Wen Yiduo 120, 1226
Wen Zhengming 1274,
    1277
Wenzhou 445, 925
West China Union
  Medical College 676,
    716
White Lotus 544, 648, 1244
White Lotus Rebellion
    207, 218, 220
White Wolf 250, 262
White, Theodore 324
Wilson, E. H. 'Chinese'
    74, 79
Wittfogel, Karl August
    100, 713

Women 2, 14, 627, 630,
    632-33, 635, 637,
    639, 1112
  autobiography 364, 371,
    378, 397
  Ban Zhao's
    Admonitions 637
  bibliographies 1457,
    1477
  death of Woman Wang
    354
  feminism and socialism
    628
  Gold Flower's story
    (1948) 290
  Han dynasty 131, 637
  history 636
  in fiction 1123-25,
    1130, 1142, 1150,
    1153, 1159, 1161-62,
    1164
  in late imperial popular
    culture 1244
  invention of the
    category 'funü' 22,
    641
  literature 1447
  marriage resistance 638
  painters 1291
  poets 1210
  Qiu Jin 255, 266
  Queen Mother of the
    West 562
  revolution 255, 627-28,
    630, 632-35, 638-39
  sexual practices 644
  Song dynasty 152, 153,
    629
  suicide 638, 1164
  violence against 648
  widows 367, 620, 629,
    631
  see also Family and
    kinship; Female
    infanticide;
    Feminism;
    Patriarchy
Woodblock prints 1247,
    1285, 1365
Wool 966, 1324
Work-Study Movement in
  France 254, 295, 374,
    1038

598

Map of China

This map shows the more important towns and other features.

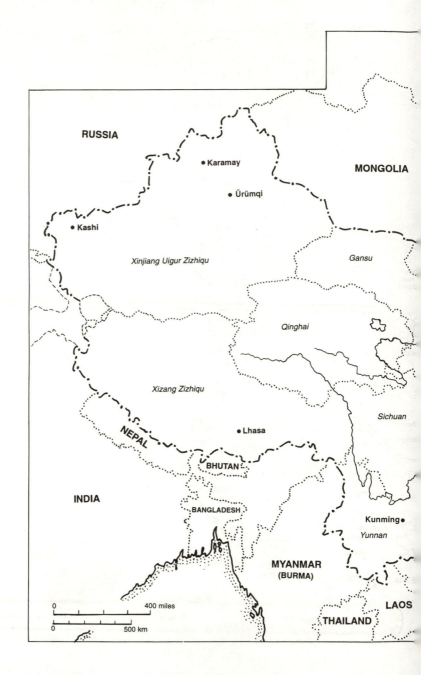

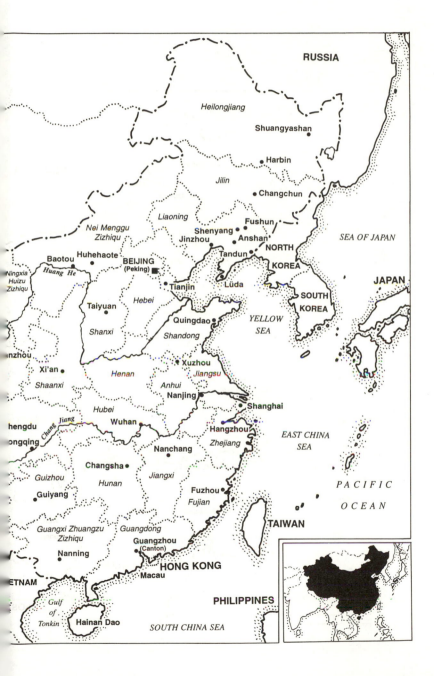

ALSO FROM CLIO PRESS

INTERNATIONAL ORGANIZATIONS SERIES

Each volume in the International Organizations Series is either devoted to one specific organization, or to a number of different organizations operating in a particular region, or engaged in a specific field of activity. The scope of the series is wide-ranging and includes intergovernmental organizations, international non-governmental organizations, and national bodies dealing with international issues. The series is aimed mainly at the English-speaker and each volume provides a selective, annotated, critical bibliography of the organization, or organizations, concerned. The bibliographies cover books, articles, pamphlets, directories, databases and theses and, wherever possible, attention is focused on material about the organizations rather than on the organizations' own publications. Notwithstanding this, the most important official publications, and guides to those publications, will be included. The views expressed in individual volumes, however, are not necessarily those of the publishers.

VOLUMES IN THE SERIES